Just an E

An autobiography

My journey from school and choir, to St. Peter's Aldborough Hatch, the Ordnance Survey, National Service, the City of London, The Scout Association, Editor of SCOUTING magazine, Magistrate and Chairman of the Bench, Editor of MILK INDUSTRY, Green Belt campaigner and into an active retirement as a non-executive director in the NHS and volunteer at the Redbridge Night Shelter – amongst other things

Ron Jeffries

Tom and Mary

With thanks for your

friendship.

13.3.2008.

Published by the author

First published in Great Britain in 2009
Some sections of the text were first published in the BROADSHEET, the monthly newsletter of St. Peter's Aldborough Hatch, Essex

A CIP catalogue record for this title is available from the British Library.

Paperback ISBN 978-0-9561877-0-3

Printed and bound in England by SPS Communications

Published at
37 Spearpoint Gardens,
Aldborough Road North,
Newbury Park,
ILFORD,
Essex IG2 7SX
United Kingdom
Email: ronjeffries@hotmail.com

To Yvonne
without whose support, encouragement and love
little – if any – of this would have been possible.

I acknowledge with gratitude the help and guidance I have received
from Simon and Nicholas Smith of SPS Communications
in the preparation of the manuscript,
the design of the cover and the printing of this book.

Contents

Introduction

"I did what I could, where I was, with what I had"
Theodore Roosevelt

"Comedy expresses the whole contrast between the seriousness with which we take ourselves and the actual truth"
Sir John Mortimer

I come from a long line of chimney sweeps (on my father's side) and of painters and decorators (on my mother's). More surprising was the discovery that there was a skeleton in my family's cupboard (on my mother's side, I should add, for I believe it only fair that if any fingers are to be pointed, they should go in the right direction). I knew about the chimney sweeps and the painters, but the skeleton was never hinted at, not even in hushed tones or behind closed doors.

And who would have guessed that at the tender age of three there is the probability that I played in a garden in South London with Petula Clark (who was five months older than me at the time – and still is, for that matter), sat across a desk from a Peer of the Realm or two, shared a platform with a couple of MPs, stayed overnight on the Scottish estate of a Knight of the Realm at his invitation and did some ghost writing for another, remanded Charlie Kray – that well-known character from London's East End – into custody and was responsible for the making and cooking of what was at that time the world's longest sausage (all 9.89 miles of it). Although, for the record, apart from the playing in the garden with Petula, all the other events took place in later life and not when I was three-years-old.

But it was not all beer and skittles. I was part of the team in the late 1960s and 1970s that edged the Boy Scouts Association into The Scout Association, out of the Boar War, big hats and shorts, and into long trousers, mixed units with girls and contemporary life.

I led the team that launched the Redbridge Magistrates' Court Drug Initiative in the late 1990s when illicit drugs took a vice-like grip of British society.

I played a very small part in the team at the turn of the Century that recognised that the growing number of the homeless in the London Borough of Redbridge needed support to get back on their feet.

Be all that as it may, my story starts between the two world wars of the twentieth century in the 1930s. What follows is a canter through the first seventy-five years of my life – a life that started before there was a television in every room and when few folk had a telephone in their home (I was thirty-five when we had our first telephone installed), let alone mobiles (which had probably not been invented, but if they had, they had kept quiet about it). The FAX machine, the personal computer, Walkmans and Ipods, all these were to burst forth during my lifetime, but when I first toddled around in my Persil white Turkish towelling nappies such luxuries were the stuff of dreams and dreamers.

The next three-quarter century would see massive – and at times dramatic – change, some of which impinged upon me (as I grew from a skinny, stammering boy to a scrawny senior citizen) and some of which simply passed me by (for I could be oblivious to what was going on around me if I really tried hard enough).

Throughout my life I have taken a philosophical view of things and looked for the good in others, whilst seeking out the more hilarious side of the experiences that came my way.

And in the pages that follow, I have concentrated on the light-hearted and more amusing aspects of the journey that took me to some interesting and even exotic places – from Walthamstow Market to Atlanta, and you cannot get much more exotic than the former, whilst the latter had some unforgettable moments. But thankfully, for I have a fondness for the place, my travels kept bringing me back to within a stone's throw of the spot in the London Borough where I was born.

Part One
Where it all started – my early life

Sweeps, weavers and such like

My father, Leslie Thomas Jeffries, was the youngest of six children. The family home was in Almorah Road, Islington in North London, and his father, Charles, was a chimney sweep. And not only his father, but both his father, also Charles, and his son were of that profession, too, and Charles' wife took over the business on his death. A husband and wife, both chimney sweeps, must have been somewhat unique even in the 19th Century. My father recalled that his father would bring home the coins he was paid for sweeping chimneys and tip them into the sink where they had to be washed to remove the soot before counting.

My father had told me that his side of the family was descended from the Huguenots who came over from the Continent to escape persecution in the 1680s and that our ancestors were weavers. Textile manufacturing, in particular silk weaving, formed the largest single occupation for the refugees, with the work concentrated in Spitalfields in London's East End – making their owners extremely wealthy.

If this is so (and the wealth bit is an historical fact), I can only conclude that by the time my great grandfather came onto the scene, all the money had disappeared or been squandered – for he was a chimney sweep and there is no record of any weaving taking place in his family (although I am aware that a few of the ladies were adept with knitting and darning needles. The click of the former, as woolly hats and bed socks, were produced is a sound that I recall from when I was young, and darning was an ongoing occupation for my mother as we boys wore holes in our socks. Knitting appears to have all but disappeared as a pastime in our family and we no longer darn socks, but discard them before holes appear in the heels. All part of today's throw-away society – sad, but true.)

My grandfather died in 1905 at the age of fifty-five when my father was just seven years old. My father's mother – Annie Jeffries neè Bonsor – was a short, bustling, busy, but somewhat severe lady in black who wore a bonnet at all times, indoors and out – although she appears to have removed the bonnet when photographers were about. A domestic servant before her marriage, she would have had to return to work when left a widow with a young family.

On visits in the 1930s, the terraced house in Almorah Road seemed many storeys high. White-washed steps ran up to the front door, but we were never permitted to climb them, always entering the house via a flight of stone stairs with iron railings at the top, leading down into the gloom of the basement. From here we passed through a large kitchen with a scullery and wash-house at the back opening into an enclosed yard with high brick walls and an outside toilet, which had an all pervading smell of carbolic. Toilet paper consisted of squares of newspaper with a hole at one corner through which a circle of string was threaded – the whole being hung on a nail on the wall. We had proper toilet rolls at home, although from time to time during the war we reverted to the newspaper-on-a-string – either due to financial necessity or because toilet rolls were in short supply.

My father's sister, Tall Auntie Rose, lived in the house in Almorah Road with Uncle Ernest and daughter Lily. Ernest Stanley had a clipped moustache and smarmed down hair, and at home he lived in a waistcoat with a shirt devoid of a collar with the collar stud showing at his scraggy neck. He was a civil servant – which marked him out as a cut above most – but he gave the appearance of being ever frightened of something. His family name was Seberg – his Jewish father, Charles, had fled Germany to Portsmouth prior to the First World War and had changed his surname to Stanley (his mother's maiden surname) to avoid internment.

Fat Uncle Ernie, another of my father's brothers, was also married to a Rose – Pavitt was her surname, but we called her Auntie Jeff to distinguish her from Tall Auntie Rose. Auntie Jeff was a waif of a lady, small, emaciated and with a look of fear about her. Fat Uncle Ernie was a mumbler and on the outbreak of the Second World War and for months afterwards would sit with his head in his hands saying: *"We don't know what we're going to do, and they don't know what they're going to do, and no-one knows what anyone's going to do."* All of which I found confusing – especially as he repeated the words whenever and wherever I was present. Uncle Ernie and Auntie Jeff had two children – another Rose (often called Rosie) and Edward (Eddie). Perhaps they, too, were confused. They all lived elsewhere in the tall house in Almorah Road.

My father had another elder brother, Charles, who wore dark suits and long johns – although I am mystified as to how I knew that he sported the latter. He had a lot of facial hair and smelt of stale beer and tobacco. I guessed that he lived at the very top of the house – but I never asked, nor was I told. I avoided him.

There were two older sisters. Edith was generally considered to be the snob of the family – at least, that is what I overheard my father and mother saying. Edith had married, my father confided, above her station – a headmaster, no less. They lived in Arnos Grove in a semi-detached house, which my father vowed was very posh. I recall visiting once and meeting their son, Peter, who later qualified as a doctor and emigrated to Canada.

I was frightened of Annie, the other sister, who wore long, dark dresses, had a vacant stare and would give me the most horrendous cuddles a young boy has ever had to endure. By the outbreak of war in 1939, my grandmother had died and Annie moved to Guildford, where she lived in a large detached house on the by-pass with a maiden lady who seemed very, very old and two other ladies who looked a bit like Auntie Annie. We visited the house in Guildford two or three times until Auntie Annie died, travelling by train into and then out of London. No-one explained to me at the time that Auntie Annie suffered severe mental illness throughout her life. These things were not talked about and if they were, not within the hearing of a child. I felt intensely sad after every visit to Auntie Annie, so much so that I cried myself to sleep for a night or two just thinking about her. I sensed that something was badly wrong, but I did not know what or why. I did not ask and was not told.

Visits to the house in Almorah Road were few. A pre-war Christmas pantomime matinee at the Lyceum (then a theatre and later a dance hall before reverting to a theatre) in London's West End was followed by a ride on the tram up through Holborn Viaduct to Essex Road, Islington, to visit my grandmother. I had new slippers for Christmas – soft and pink with rabbits' heads and floppy ears at the front. My mother had not wanted me to take them, but I insisted. Inevitably they became caked in dark dirt and grime through playing in the yard at the back of the house. They never looked their best again – although why I was given pink slippers for Christmas is a mystery.

Across from Almorah Road, on the corner of Downham Road and Sherborne Street, was the sweet shop where you chose your sweets from jars on shelves high up behind the counter. The lady would take a torn sheet of newspaper and twirl it into a cone-like shape into which the sweets were poured from the brass tray of the weighing scales. Dolly Mixtures and Liquorice Sticks were my choice.

War looms and the bully boys

The house at 19 Church Road was built in the early 1930s. My parents were the first occupants, marking this fact by having the words '*St. Boniface*' inscribed in the coloured glass window beside the front door – a reminder that they had spent holidays on the Isle of Wight where they had walked over St. Boniface Downs, behind Ventnor. When I was born in 1933 my parents had already moved there from 13 Tyson Road, Hackney, Stoke Newington, where they lived when they first married and where my brother, Leonard, was born.

The nearby Newbury Park Station was on a loop line off the main London North Eastern Railway (LNER) running from Liverpool Street out into Essex and beyond.

The loop started at Ilford and ran through Newbury Park onwards to Chigwell and Woodford, then back to Leytonstone and Stratford where it joined up with the main line from Liverpool Street.

What is now the A12 dual carriageway was a roadway that petered out beyond Newbury Park Station into a rough track leading up to Little Heath. A few houses – built in the late 1800s and occupied by railways workers – stood near the station, but north and east from here there were farms, fields and market gardens running up to Hainault and Epping Forests, and South Weald. South from the station the new houses of the 1930s were joining up with the late 19th Century estates of Seven Kings. Built by the Rowallan family (Lord Rowallan was Chief Scout during part of my time as a Scout Leader locally), who were strictly teetotal, there were no public houses or off licence premises permitted between the A12 and

Seven Kings High Road at the behest of the Rowallan's. And there are no public houses to this day.

War loomed in the late 1930s. My father gave serious thought to buying a second house a mile or so away from our Church Road home – in Bawdsey Avenue, Aldborough Hatch – and renting this to his sister, Tall Auntie Rose, Uncle Ernest and Cousin Lily. Taking out a second mortgage was considered too risky a project with war over the horizon and, in any case, those houses were selling for all of £600 whereas 19 Church Road had cost a mere £550 a few years earlier. No house could possibly be worth all that money, my father assured us.

When the bombing started in London's East End, Tall Auntie Rose, Uncle Ernest and Cousin Lily moved into a house in the next road to us – Newbury Road – which they rented from a local schoolmaster. Much later the house was purchased by Lily.

Uncle Ernest had retired by this time, but Lily travelled into London to work as a civil servant. All three attended the Congregational Church in Meads Lane and voted Conservative – two factors that made my father scoff and snort, which I found a bit odd but I kept such thoughts to myself.

Later Fat Uncle Ernie and Auntie Jeff moved into the front downstairs room of the same house in Newbury Road, sharing the kitchen. I sensed that Tall Auntie Rose was unhappy about sharing the kitchen with her sister-in-law. Not that she ever said so, but there were little signs that I picked up that made me feel uneasy when both were in the kitchen at the same time.

Tall Auntie Rose had a sad, dusty look about her and smoked heavily so that her grey hair had ginger nicotine stains at the front, whilst Auntie Jeff always appeared to be cold whatever the weather.

Uncle Ernie and Auntie Jeff lived there until Eddie returned from war service, when they all moved into a flat in Ilford Town Centre. Rosie married a soldier and they bought a workmen's café in Brighton. My father thought him a bit of a lad – an expression which puzzled me at the time, but he often had a cigarette hanging from the side of his mouth and his smile was somewhat lascivious now I come to think of it.

My brother and I would visit the house in Newbury Road, asking Tall Auntie Rose for stale cakes. Uncle Ernest insisted on silence when the news came on the radio as he sat drawing intricate ground plans on graph paper of buildings that would never be constructed.

Auntie Jeff would peer from the depths of the single room she and Fat Uncle Ernie occupied – rather like a scalded rabbit. If there were no stale cakes on offer, my brother and I would play knock-down-ginger on the way home – tying a length of stout string to two door knockers on opposite sides of the road. We pulled on the string and as the two door knockers banged away, we ran off to hide behind a hedge – watching the irate neighbours open their front doors to find no-one there!

On the opposite side of Newbury Road to where my relatives lived was the home of the local bullyboys – one or two a couple of years older than me and others in their teens. I never worked out how many there were. If I went alone to visit in Newbury Road, they would set about me and give me a duffing over. Once my brother got to know what had happened, he would go hot foot into Newbury Road to return the compliment. All this made sure that when next I ventured alone into the bullyboys' territory, I would receive an even harder beating. I could not win.

South of the river

My mother's family hailed from south of the River. Her father – my grandfather – was William Raine, a plumber by profession. Born in 1875, he died in 1954 aged seventy-nine and was, therefore, the one grandparent I came to know reasonably well. He was married to Florence Mary Ann Labdon, who was born in 1876. Florence was alive in 1926 for she features in the photograph of my father and mother's wedding on Boxing Day, 26th December in that year. I assume she died in the 1930s.

And it is here I lay bare the skeleton in the family cupboard. William (residing at the time at 22 Lockington Road, Battersea) and Florence (28 Gladstone Street, Battersea) were wed in the Church of All Saints, Battersea, on Sunday 16th October 1898. Both of their fathers – Henry Raine and Charles Labdon – were painters. The marriage certificate shows the witnesses as Henry Marmaduke Raine and Sarah Ann Labdon. It's good to have a Marmaduke in the family, but why was Sarah a witness and not Charles? Was Charles away painting? We will never know. But – and here's the rub – for my mother, Florence Violet Raine (later Jeffries), was born five months later!

My mother told we children that when she was born, the newspaper sellers outside the maternity hospital were calling out that Mafeking had been relieved. This cannot have been so, because news of the relief of Mafeking reached London on 18th May 1900 – and my mother was born on 14th March 1899 according to her marriage certificate. My mother told us that she was as old as the year, but in fact she was one year older than the year. Why did she tell us this? Did she realise that revealing the year of her birth would have made clear that there had been goings on before her parents married and she had been conceived out of wedlock? But moving her birth on a year to 1900 did not add credibility to the story of the newspaper boys and the relief of Mafeking, which clearly happened two months after my mother said she was born.

Early in her life my mother lived with her family at 50 Grant Road, Battersea – which runs alongside the station and railway lines at Clapham Junction (which today is said to be the busiest station in the country and might well have been when my mother lived nearby). On one side of Grant Road the brick built embankment rises up from the roadway – blackened and forbidding – towards the railway line. Today – on the other side of the road and facing the embankment – are flats built after the 1939-45 World War on the land where my mother's home once stood. The outlook must have been depressing for my mother's family with the constant chugging and clattering of steam trains and the sooty-grey smoke from the engines pouring over the embankment onto the terraced houses below.

My mother's family moved at some time to 68 Undine Street, Tooting – the address from which she was married. Now there is something of a mystery here. The marriage certificate shows that the wedding took place in Tooting Parish Church – so far, so good. Not unexpectedly my mother's *'residence at the time of marriage'* is given as 68 Undine Street, but – and here comes the intriguing bit – my father's *'residence at the time of . . .'* is also 68 Undine Street. Was he living there or did he give that address so that the banns of marriage had only to be read in one church (and, presumably, only one fee paid)? Was he snuggling down on the sofa or – no, no, no – were they living in sin? Again, we shall never know, but of one thing we may be certain and that is that my mother was not pregnant on her wedding day. My older brother, Leonard Richard Jeffries, was born well after the wedding – a year and a month later, in fact, on 16th January 1928.

Florence Violet, but always known as Vi – was a dressmaker. She had two brothers – Richard (known as Dick) and Charles. Both were married and had families, but we saw them rarely and probably never again after the war. I cannot fathom why this should have been so. My mother never spoke of them to me, but I sensed that there had been some kind of disagreement between them.

My grandfather was employed until his retirement as a plumber at the museums in South Kensington. He was proud of the fact that he had worked on the building of London's Tower Bridge, which opened to the public in 1894 when my grandfather was barely nineteen. Granddad could tell a tale and was prone to exaggeration – so my mother would say, when Granddad regaled us with stories of how men had *"dropped like flies"* from the top of the structure of Tower Bridge to their death in the waters of the Thames below. There were no safety harnesses or heath and safety regulations in those days – or, if there were, no-one worried about implementing them.

When I knew Granddad – before, during and after the war until his death in 1954 – he was still living in Undine Street, but he was now a lodger in a bed-sitting room with another family in the rest of the house. Undine Street is a stone's throw from Tooting Broadway. When I visited my grandfather at his home he kept canaries in an avery at the bottom of the garden – which looked as though it had seen better days and would collapse in a cloud of dust in a high wind.

Tell us about the time the canaries escaped, I would implore my Granddad when he came to stay with us at Church Road. And Granddad would launch into his story of how the birds flew the nest and avery, and roosted in a nearby very, very tall tree (which got taller and taller with the telling). My mother would smile as Granddad told us that he climbed the tree single-handed and *"picked the birds orf one by one wiv me bare 'ands"!*

I have a clear memory of visiting Granddad in his lodgings in Tooting on one occasion when I went to a matinee at the big cinema near Tooting Station to see Paul Robson in a film in which he sang '*Old man river*'. I believe Granddad was unwell and in bed at the time, so I was probably sent off to the cinema to get me out of the way. Did I go to the cinema alone or was I accompanied? I am unsure.

My memory is that the house in Undine Street was the last in the street, but when I visited in 2008, number 70 stood between number 68 and the end of the road. But the construction of number 70 was different to all the other houses in the street and may well have been added post-war. So perhaps my memory of number 68 being last in the street was correct.

I wanted to stand in the rear garden, but there was no-one at home when I called there in 2008. My mother and father's wedding photograph taken in 1926 shows the family assembled in their finery at the back of a house – with the felt roof of the outside toilet held down with bricks and the net curtains in the house all askew. Was this 68 Undine Street?

Myths and winkles

But whether or not I ever met – let alone played with – Petula Clarke, the international songstress, in a back garden in Tooting is a matter of either truth or myth . . . and I know not which. For many years my mother would tell the story of how I played with Petula until I believed it must have been a fact. Indeed, in my mind's eye I can see myself being lifted over the back garden fence near the avery housing the canaries to play in the garden with Petula when we were both about three. Petula shot to fame as a child star when she sang on the radio to her father who was serving in the forces overseas during the war. I became a fan – something I took into adult life (and I have the gramophone records and tapes to prove it).

When writing this in January 2008, I decided that the myth about Petula Clark had to be either proved or laid to rest. So I went into Google on the internet and found that Terry Young was President of the International Petula Clark Society and, in case you are interested, lives in Ramsgate in Kent. Petula, I learned from her website, was born in November 1932 – which makes her some five months older than me – and was brought up in Ewell in Surrey, which is not too far from Tooting. So I wrote to Mr Young setting out my problem and asking for his help. That was on Friday 18th. A week later – on Friday 25th – I was sitting quietly at my desk at around 1pm when the telephone rang.

"Is that Ron Jeffries?" a lady's voice enquired.

I said it was.

"Hello," said the voice. *"This is Petula Clark."*

Well, you could have knocked me down with a feather!

As I sat all of a blubber, Petula – for it was her – explained that rather than write in reply she thought it might be easier for us to talk on the telephone. But you live in France, said I. Oh, no, said Petula, you are out of date. I live in Switzerland now and also in America.

Petula admitted to being intrigued by my story, but could not recall the incident – which is hardly surprising as it is alleged to have happened some seventy-two years ago. Petula confirmed that she lived in Ewell and her parents may well have had friends in Tooting. Use the story, said Petula, but please mention that I have been unable to confirm or deny its authenticity.

After a few pleasantries about music and the weather, Petula rang off – and I was left to ponder what had happened. There were so many things I would have liked to ask Petula – but when you receive a telephone call right out of the blue on a Friday afternoon when you least expect it, the mind tends to go a bit blank.

This was not the only brush with celebrity by my family. In her teens my mother had been escorted on Saturday nights over some months by none other than Henry Hall – of *'Henry Hall's Guest Night'* fame. These were the days of the big dance bands and orchestras made famous on the wireless, and Henry Hall was a band leader with his own programme. Henry had a stammer and would announce: *"This is Hhhhenry Hhhhhall and tonight is my gggguest nnnnnight".* My mother would smile and say little about Hhhhhenry when asked, except that he was a good dancer.

My father and Fat Uncle Ernie were employed by a cigarette manufacturer in Commercial Road, Shoreditch. My father was a journeyman – someone who had completed an apprenticeship – and he worked in a small engineering maintenance department tasked with keeping the cigarette machines going at all costs. His was a 'reserved occupation' which meant that he was not conscripted for armed service during the 1939-45 World War – making cigarettes for the Troops was too important. Fat Uncle Ernie, too, was also in a 'reserved occupation'.

On Friday evenings my father – and all employees of the firm – would bring home a long, white cardboard box containing 200 cigarettes marked *'not for sale'*. When my grandfather came to stay for the weekend, my father would also bring home a packet of shag tobacco with which my granddad would roll his own cigarettes. When my father handed the packet to granddad, he would turn to my mother and say: *"Put it there, Vi"*, pointing to the mantelpiece, where the package would remain until he left us on Sunday evening. Granddad had grey hair and a full moustache over his upper lip. The moustache was, probably, grey too – but it had a yellow tinge as did his eyebrows caused, no doubt, by the nicotine fumes from the shag.

Granddad – in company with many Londoners – enjoyed winkles and brown shrimps, but they had to be purchased fresh and consumed the same day. So when granddad came to stay, I would be sent off to the stall outside the Cauliflower public house in Seven Kings before lunch on Sunday. With lunch out of the way, granddad would set about winkling the winkles from their shells with a pin, removing the black cap on the top and setting the winkle down into a plate of vinegar.

With the winkles winkled, granddad would work through the brown shrimps, pulling off their heads and tails, and removing the light shell covering from the body. All this was, of course, carried out whilst rolling a few cigarettes and smoking the roll-ups between his yellowing fingers. Hand-made cigarettes, lacking the burning quality of the machine-made variety, had to be re-lit and re-lit before the stubs were finally abandoned. I found the whole business totally and utterly distasteful and disgusting. My Sunday tea on these occasions consisted of bread and butter as the jam of other days was replaced on Sundays by winkles and shrimps. And I would have none of that.

We rarely accompanied any visitors to or from the station in those days – and I went all over the place unaccompanied as a very young child. Granddad would travel across London and walk from Newbury Park Station to our home and back again at the end of his visit – alone in both the dusk of summer and the dark of winter.

From the age of eight or nine, I would walk the mile or so to Seven Kings to buy the winkles and shrimps – alone. I was often sent on errands to the shops in nearby Brook Road or to the Co-op at the Green Gate. There was little traffic – and during the war years almost none whatsoever with petrol rationed or unavailable for most of the time. Mugging was a word we had yet to invent and child abuse a phrase that was not in our vocabulary.

Suburban pioneer

My father was something of a pioneer in moving from the East End of London out to the new suburbs on the fringes of Essex into a newly-built house complete with garden (rather than yard) and bathroom and toilet (rather than an outside loo). It was said that some East End families moving out to the new homes were confused by having a bath of their own – and used this to store the coal, but not us.

We were the centre of a block of five terrace houses in Church Road, but opposite were the semi-detached villas of the super rich. Their houses had the same three bedrooms, two reception and one kitchenette, with bathroom and toilet, but they also had a garage, which made their frontage wider and more imposing. We did not speak, but smiled and doffed our caps when they passed by. A number of those on the other side had live-in maids – young girls who came from the Village Homes of Dr Barnardo in nearby Barkingside. The maids wore frilly hats and aprons over long cotton dresses that went down to their ankles. If they had legs, we did not see them. When they were sent on errands to the shops, they would smile at my friends and me – and giggle – but we never spoke. Many of those folk sold up just before the war, moving to the country, and maids were not around after that.

Each house in Church Road had a tree outside on the pavement. Those buying the houses when first built had to pay a sum to the Council for the privilege of having their own tree. Ours was a huge flowering cherry with masses of pink and white blossoms in the spring that dropped as summer approached to make a carpet covering the pavement.

The new homeowners took great pride in their houses and the homes they created inside. Saturday was often a full work day – for the overtime helped to pay the mortgage. Sunday was the day of the week for gardening in the summer and decorating in the winter – although my father worked some Sunday mornings, especially during the war years. The whir of manual lawn mowers, the clip of sheers on trimmed hedges, the smell of freshly cut grass, the pungent aroma of creosote on wooden palings, the calling out of neighbours over garden fences – these were the sounds of sunny Sundays.

No-one on our side of the road gave a thought to the possibility of employing someone to tend the garden or do the decorating. It wasn't just a matter of not being able to afford to pay out, but simply that folk like my parents saw it as their responsibility to do this work themselves and if they did not have the skills, to acquire them by doing the job rather than attending classes to be taught.

Decorating the indoors was a serious business. My father had a work colleague, Wally, living in Newbury Road, whose wife dressed expensively and emulated a Hollywood starlet. They had a son, but he never came out to play and he might as well have lived on the other side of the world. We all felt sorry for Wally for hardly had he completed decorating one room, when his wife would set him to work on another. His house was like the Forth Bridge – when he had painted from top to bottom, it was time for him to start all over again. I only ever saw Wally in overalls, except at Christmas, and his face was pallid with what appeared to be a permanent dusting of dried whitewash or flour and water wallpaper paste.

My father was a skilled self-taught carpenter. He brought pieces of timber home from work – the longest plank at the bottom of a barrel containing tobacco leaves was the preferred option. He built a bookcase for me which he stained and polished. It smelt strongly of tobacco for many years – until I married and painted it with grey gloss. It stands on the landing outside my home office to this day, with the same knobs that open the double doors.

He spotted a three-piece wooden light fitting in a furniture store and made a replica for our dining room. He built the second shed – for our cycles – in the garden. Some wood was purchased from Gray's wood yard at the Green Gate – a mile or so away from our home – but the rest was timber from tobacco barrels. When I passed the Eleven-Plus for grammar school in 1944, leather satchels were either unobtainable or too expensive. My father made me a suitcase in tobacco barrel timber with gunmetal fittings. It was extremely heavy when empty and almost impossible to lift when filled with books. I am said to have long arms for my body and I blame that wooden suitcase.

The back room leading through French doors into the garden was where we lived for most of the time. The whole family would assemble there in the evenings – my father, mother, brother Len (five years older than me) and sister Lorna (born three years after me). Bedrooms were cold, inhospitable places for sleeping and nothing else, but the dining room was where the coal fire blazed on winter evenings or where the doors opened into the garden on warm summer days. And the summer days were always warm, whilst the winter was invariably cold and frosty. The water pipes in the roof froze every winter and had to be defrosted with hot water bottles and, occasionally, with a blow-lamp. Water in the cold tank in the loft froze, trapping the ballcock and denying water to the toilet for days – we carried buckets upstairs, drawing the water in the kitchen from the cold tap that ran into the house from the main.

The dining room contained a three piece suite, which was re-covered shortly before the war in brown Rexene – a sort of forerunner of plastic and much sort after, so my father told us. Two men spent three days or so at the task, working on the lawn to re-stuff the chairs and settee. Both drank bottled beer profusely and did not smell very pleasant. They travelled each day by train from inner London and made fun of the fact that we lived 'in the country'.

The dining room table (with its pull out leaves) and four chairs were dark mahogany, while pride of place was taken by a tall piece of furniture – described as the cabinet – which was topped by a gramophone and whose cupboard contained the collection of gramophone records purchased over the years at Saville's at the top end of Cranbrook Road near Ilford Station. Here you asked the shop assistant for a particular record which was handed to you to carry into one of a number of booths, where you played both sides, listening through headphones. Most of the records were of dance music played by the well-known dance bands – Mantovani, Henry Hall, Billy Cotton and Victor Sylvester to name but four. But later some classical music was bought by my parents – often following visits to the cinema where the classics were used as themes to the films, including Grieg's *'Piano Concerto'* and the *'Warsaw Concerto'*.

I bought my first gramophone records at Saville's shortly after the war – a George Formby classic and Betty Driver singing '*Mustn't miss the last bus home*'. Many years later in the 1970s I visited Linett Clough, the Manchester County Scout camp site in Cheshire, in my role as Editor of SCOUTING. On the Saturday evening, the County Commissioner and his team took me to the Devonshire Arms, a pub in a nearby Cheshire village, where Betty Driver – barmaid Betty Turpin in ITV's *Coronation Street* – was joint landlord with her sister and father. On being introduced to Betty, I told her that one of the first records I bought as a boy in the 1940s was of her singing *'Mustn't miss the last bus home'*. Betty denied ever recording the song or that she was a recording artist in the 1940s, vowing that she had not been born then. I sang a few lines of the song to her – but she still denied it (albeit with a wide and infectious grin!).

Special place

The front room was a very special place. Here was a three-piece suite of settee and two armchairs covered in a blue material that was of thicker stuff than velvet and which my parents called mouquette (which was in pristine condition and itchy to the legs of a boy in short trousers). Unlike the dining room where the floor covering was linoleum with thin hand-made and home-made rugs, there was a large square of blue patterned carpet with a much thicker and heavier home-made and hand-made black woollen rug in front of the gas fire (which was lit with a match when the black knob on the gas pipe was turned on and which always made a frighteningly loud sound of a minor explosion).

The fireplace had two mantelpiece shelves – one at eye level with a mahogany chiming clock in the centre and two blue china vases at either end. The top shelf carried the only books possessed by my parents – a set of encyclopaedias (which we were not permitted to touch unsupervised as they had been bought at the door over a period of weeks and were, therefore, very expensive) and a fat dark blue book entitled *The World Pictorial Gazetteer and Atlas*. I have the latter still. Its publication date is unknown, but the publishers were Fleetway. My guess is that it was printed in the early 30s – for the population of Ilford is shown in 1931 as 131,046.

A highly polished mahogany sideboard stood against one wall, with a cupboard at each end and three drawers in the centre with black metal fittings. On top in the centre stood a blue glass bowl with life-size glass coloured tulips and green leaves. This was mounted on a black base (which I painted white and now have in my porch as a plant stand). Ornaments included a glass ash tray with two horse heads in relief. When my brother died in December 2007 we found this ash tray in a box of old family photographs and this – together with the *'Gazetteer'* – are both with me now and, with the plant stand, are the only items I have from the family home.

In the window stood the Boy – a pale yellow plaster model copy of what we were led to believe was a famous sculpture. The boy wore baggy trousers, an equally baggy jacket and a floppy hat.

The front room was used at Christmas and sometimes, but rarely, on a Sunday. The door was kept closed, so it had a distinctive smell of its own – of polish and stale tobacco – and seemed icy cold until the gas fire was lit.

The kitchen – or kitchenette as we called it – housed a large wooden table, whose top was white wood and much scrubbed, and two kitchen chairs. The gas cooker took pride of place next to the table. High above both rode the airer, a slatted wooden structure lifted to its position on pulleys when it was loaded with wet clothes which need to be aired with the gas burners turned full on.

On the other side of the kitchenette was the dresser – or worktop in today's parlance except that this was fitted by the builders and had drawers and cupboards below and a glass fronted cupboard above. Next to this was the wooden draining board which led to the large Butler sink – the term '*Butler Sink*' being a generic term used to describe any traditional ceramic sink – typically with a good 3 to 4cm wall thickness. Ours was certainly that. Not only did my mother do her washing within it voluminous walls, but she placed her scrubbing board in there, rubbing the soaped clothes up and down its wooden ribbing, and bathed her three children there when we were small enough.

The mangle was housed in the large shed in the garden and brought out on Monday which was washday – the one and only day of the week when clothes and household linen were washed. If it was raining or cold, the mangle was man-handled (or woman-handled in our case) into the kitchen. The mangle was of wrought iron construction and very heavy, with two wooden rollers which were rotated by a large wheel at the side. The clothes were squeezed between the rollers, so that the water ran down and into a galvanised bath tub below, which had a handle at either end for lifting and tipping the water down the outside drain. Clothes were put through the mangle whilst still soapy and then again when they had been rinsed in clean – and often bitterly cold – water. If we were at home on washday, turning the wheel of the mangle was a task for young boys.

A cupboard for storing boxed, tinned and dry foods extended from the kitchen under the staircase. Bread was stored in a white enamelled bin. Beside the back door and built out into the garden with a sloping, tiled roof and small window was a larder – just big enough for one person to stand inside. The window opened about six inches before it hit the large garden shed. On the inside of the window was a wooden frame with light wire mesh – so that the window might be left open for cooling air to come in whilst the mesh kept insects and other predators at bay. I climbed through this window once when my mother had left the house keys indoors. Squeezing through the gap – just and bruising my tummy at the same time – I sat on the shelf amongst the eggs, bacon and butter, and pushed on the door which burst open and let me into the kitchenette.

On the shelf stood a muslin covered frame with a handle on top – this went over cold meats or cheese and kept off any stray flies that had circumvented the wire mesh frame. The floor had thick red tiles and was, therefore, cold so milk was stored here – in buckets of cold water in summer. There was an all-pervading aroma of butter, cheese and bacon, together with a feeling of chilly damp. This was our refrigerator and freezer.

The floorboards in the hall, the upstairs landing and rooms were covered with linoleum, probably the floor covering of choice in the 1930s as it was comparatively cheap. At some stage a light fawn runner of carpet was installed in the hall – extending from the front door to the kitchenette. It was made very clear to us by my father that this was a luxury of which we could all be justly proud. On wet days the carpet was covered by a stiff grey waterproof runner which we called the drugget (a word, I subsequently discovered, which describes a coarse cloth used as floor covering – so my father was right in instructing us to call it thus).

In the bedrooms carpet squares and handmade rugs meant that we did not have to pad about on lino in winter, but it was cold lino in the bathroom and toilet which made both rooms uninviting and not places for lingering. I dreaded early winter mornings in the bathroom and would lie in bed for as long as possible – anything to avoid standing barefoot on the freezing lino and washing in lukewarm – and often freezing – water.

The only heating came from the coal fire in the dining room and a gas fire in the front room. A portable electric fire with two bars was purchased at some time – and was used to boost the heat in the depths of winter, but as my father explained, painstakingly and in great detail, this was yet another luxury to be used sparingly.

Upstairs there were two bedrooms, a box room, a bathroom and separate toilet. My parents had the front bedroom. When I was very young, my brother and I inherited their bedroom suite (a double bed with high mahogany top and bottom boards, and metal springs with a feather bed rather than a spring mattress, two very large wardrobes, a dressing table with mirror and a chest of drawers) whilst they had a new suite of light walnut and more modern design. My brother and I slept in the double bed. When granddad came for the weekend, he joined us – which was a bit of a squash and not much fun for granddad had a late night and early morning roll-up cigarette in bed, and slept in the long johns and socks he had been wearing during the day, and probably for the past week or two. I never remember granddad taking a bath and there was a pungent smell of canaries, shag, winkles and shrimps about his person.

My sister had the box room with a single bed, chest of drawers and chintzy curtains as befitted a girl.

The toilet was housed in a small room of its own with the cistern high up on a wooden shelf on the wall with a chain and rubber handle. The whole contraption cranked a bit even when working at full capacity.

The bathroom was always cold – even in summer for it was at the back of the house which faced north. Friday night was bath night for the whole family. During the war we were exhorted to have no more than five inches of water in our bath tub – but we had always had that amount for taking more water would have meant that those who followed later in the evening would have had a lukewarm or even cold bath as the water was heated by the coal fire in the dining room. Sometimes we would half fill the bath and all three children would use the same water.

Bars of carbolic smelling red Lifebuoy soap were used with flannels and scrubbing brushes for our knees, which were often caked in mud and grime from a week of playing in shorts with a few grazes and cuts where the blood had dried. Our hair, too, was washed in the bath with Lifebuoy.

Heating was by a back boiler behind the coal fire in the dining room – it was much later that we had an immersion heater to warm the water in the hot tank so that more than one bath might be taken in an evening. Yet another luxury, my father informed us at considerable length – for he was a great one for making sure that we all understood how kind and generous he was to his family. I would guess he must have wondered where it would all end?

Every house had coal fires and some burned wood logs, too, if the price was right. A man selling logs would come in winter on a horse drawn cart. Smoke-free zones had yet to be invented and as a result a pall of smoke hung over the area from the first cold snap in autumn until the sun broke through to herald the spring. Fogs – really thick pea souper fogs where you could not see beyond the end of an outstretched arm – were the norm. Coughs and colds were something we lived with. Journeys by bus would often be laborious for the vehicle would crawl and go through a series of stops and starts – with the occasional burst of speed as the wind whipped the fog up and away, only to return a few minutes later to reduce visibility to a matter of feet.

Home entertainment

The gramophone, housed in the dining room at home, worked on a spring coil which was wound up by a handle on the side. A complete wind of the coiled spring would last for two sides of a record, but if the record ran for a bit longer than usual, the sound would run down – until the handle was wound up again.

Behind the settee, on top of a slim, tall table (made by my father from plywood and not the usual tobacco barrels) which fitted into the corner, stood the wireless. This was operated by an accumulator, which was housed in a glass container and which had to be taken most Saturday mornings to a shop in nearby Brook Road. A fresh accumulator was collected and taken home, whilst the other was left to be recharged. I was warned that the accumulator contained acid which would burn me if I dropped it or spilt the contents on my way to the shop. The accumulator was heavy and I had to rest a number of times as I walked to and from Brook Road for the wire handle cut into my fingers

I loved the radio. I would lie spread out on top of the back of the settee with my ear as close as possible to the loudspeaker behind a piece of brown Hessian stretched across the bakelite front, twiddling the knobs to find Luxembourg, which my father said was abroad and therefore not to be taken seriously.

Saturday was the evening for the radio – with '*In Town Tonight*', when the roar of London's traffic was brought to a standstill by a voice bellowing *"Stop"* to allow interviews to take place with celebrities who were in town tonight, followed by '*Music Hall*', with stars who toured the country's theatres. Many had catchphrases, repeated over and over again to raucous laughter from the studio audience – Rob Wilton's *"Can you hear me mother?"* and *"The day war broke out"* were among my favourites.

Double and comedy acts abounded – Gert and Daisy and their brother, comedian Jack Warner (later to star as Dixon of Dock Green on TV), Bennett and Williams (who played one string fiddles), Two Ton Tessie O'Shea (who thumped around the stage, singing and telling jokes), Old Mother Riley and her daughter Kitty (played by husband and wife team Arthur Lucan and Kitty McShane). Tommy Handley in '*ITMA*' *(It's That Man Again)* was a family favourite – we all waited in eager anticipation for Mrs Mop to declare: *"Can I do you now, Sir?"*, and for Colonel Chinstrap to say: *"I don't mind if I do"*.

Sunday radio was more solemn – until the evening when we had '*Hi Gang*', with Ben Lyon and Bebe Daniels (both American) and Vic Oliver (who had a thick guttural Jewish voice and played the violin) followed by '*Happidrome*' (with Mr Lovejoy, Ramsbottom and Enoch).

Tall Auntie Rose and Uncle Ernie took me to the Prince of Wales Theatre in London to see '*Happidrome*' live on stage as a birthday treat during the latter years of the war. We had dinner at the Strand Corner House – the upmarket version of the Lyons Tea Rooms that vied for our pennies in every high street with the other tea emporia rejoicing under the name ABC (Associated Bread Company). The soup was followed by fish and I expected the pudding next, but we had the main meat course, then the pudding followed by a cup of tea. My expression of surprise at a fish *and* a meat dish in the same meal amused the waitress in her uniform of black and white with matching bonnet. I felt very grown up – for this was the first time I had eaten in a restaurant.

On occasional pre-war and wartime Friday evenings we would go by train from Newbury Park to Ilford and take seats in the gallery at the Ilford Hippodrome, where we saw many of my music hall favourites from the radio, including Two Ton Tessie O'Shea and Old Mother Riley.

The return journey from Ilford Station in the late evening had an ethereal feel about it. It was dark, cold and smokey from the steam engines. As we stood on the down platform waiting for the train to Newbury Park, we would see the girls from the chorus running down the stairs to catch the up train to London – at least, that is what my father told me they were doing.

I found it all very exciting, but I clung to my mother's skirt when a fast train roared through the station without stopping, spewing smoke, steam and coal dust in its wake.

The Ilford Hippodrome took a direct hit from a landmine in 1944 when there was a capacity audience for the Christmas pantomime starring Renee Houston and Donald Stewart. Both were injured – Donald retiring soon afterwards, whilst Renee took her career in a different direction as a radio quiz show participant.

My ambition from an early age was to go on the stage as a singer and actor. I did a passable impersonation of crooner Vera Lynn, the Forces Sweetheart, and of Hutch (Leslie A. Hutchinson), a well-built black man who appeared in photographs in evening dress and sang '*When they begin the begin*' at the piano in a deep resonant bass. Years later I learned that Hutch had a liaison over some thirty years with Lady Mountbatton. Had my father and mother been aware of this, I doubt if I would have been permitted to entertain the family with my impersonation of Hutch – they would have had to make do with Vera Lynn (who, incidentally, was born not far from where I lived – in Barking). But from the age of five or so I developed a stutter and stammer, enabling me to sing but to speak only with great difficulty, and any ambition I might have had to be an actor was clearly out of the question.

My father built me a stage from timber – some two feet square with a brightly painted proscenium arch, cardboard wings, velvet curtains (stitched by my mother) that swished across the front, a safety curtain and lights run from batteries. I bought cut-out story books with money given to me at birthdays and Christmas, colouring the figures and mounting them on cardboard, to be operated by thin sticks from the sides. I made my own puppets – again cutting out the figures and colouring them. I wrote stories which I played to the family on Sundays.

Perhaps my most treasured Christmas present was a microphone which my father mounted onto a wooden base with an 'on' and 'off' switch, which ran on batteries. This was wired into the radio, the wire tacked to the skirting boards from the front room into the dining room.

I devised radio programmes, setting them out in my own hand-written version of the *Radio Times*, for broadcasting on Sundays. I would make the sounds of the individual instruments of the orchestra. There were but two crooners – Vera Lynn and Hutch, naturally. My broadcasts of the news featured local gossip and stories drawn from my imagination.

I did my broadcasting from the front room – cool in summer and bitterly cold in winter, for the gas fire was not turned on for only one person. My parents and sister had great patience, but my big brother spent much of his time in our bedroom with his chemistry set and bunsun burner, where the stinks from his experiments remained until bedtime and the occasional 'bang' or series of 'pops' sent my father rushing upstairs to see what damage had been done.

Father's influence

Working in Commercial Road in Shoreditch meant that my father saw and heard much of the pre-1939-45 World War politics of the East End of London. Oswald Moseley's Black Shirts were on the march and the Jews were being hounded across Europe. We listened to the news on the wireless, and the *Daily Mirror, Sunday Express* and the weekly magazine *John Bull* were in the house, but I just looked at the pictures.

I picked up snatches of conversation between my parents, but neither my father nor my mother made any attempt to engage me or my brother and sister in what was happening as Europe rushed headlong towards the Second World War. My parents talked, but always in hushed whispers.

What I did know was that my father had a deep dislike – almost akin to hatred – for the Jews of East London. He would talk of the *"Jew boys"* in such a derogatory manner that I had to believe that they were about to take over the world and we would all be massacred and die horrible deaths in our beds. When my father took the family to Petticoat Lane one Sunday, I feared for my life for I knew that there would be *"Jew boys"* there.

My father was an out and out racist. Whilst I recognised this from an early age, nevertheless his views on the Jewish race became deeply ingrained in me. It was something that happened almost unconsciously, but it took many, many years for me to completely eradicate my fear of the Jews. Even when I matured as a young adult and had many good friends who were Jewish, I still had this distrust at the back of my mind and it took a long time for me to clear my head of such unacceptable racist concepts.

What were my father's views? I do not know – and that is a fact. He just hated Jews – but I will never know why. Perhaps he feared for his job? If my father hated the Jews, he felt much the same about the Nazis and Oswald Moseley's black shirts. But I heard him say on more than one occasion that the one good thing about the black shirts was that they might rid us of the Jews he so hated. It was racism at its most intolerant and very worst.

Over the years that I knew my father – for he died when I was eighteen – he expressed opinions ranging from the extreme to the plain stupid – opinions that I found repugnant and offensive. Civilisation, he told me, ends at the tip of Dover pier. Do not trust the French, he said. They buy water in bottles in shops rather than drink it from the tap, and they eat snails and frogs.

Oddly, it seems now – although at the time I thought little of it – my father was a staunch Labour supporter. Tall Auntie Rose and Uncle Ernest Stanley were known to support the Conservative Party and were therefore – as far as my Dad was concerned – beyond all hope as a result. He derided them in our house and when we called to see them at their home in the next road. Tall Auntie Rose just smiled, but Uncle Ernest glowered, although neither challenged my father.

My father was a vain man. Over six feet tall, he dressed well. He would stand in front of the mirror in the bathroom, preening himself and admiring what he saw.

My mother took responsibility for the family's financial affairs. On Friday evenings my father handed his pay packet to my mother and after the evening meal, the mottled blue holdall with two handles and a zip fastener was carried downstairs from my parent's bedroom where it was stored under their bed throughout the week. Inside were a dozen or so tin boxes each with a hinged lid; these held dress-making pins when they were bought and were in plentiful supply because my mother – being a dressmaker by trade – continued to make her own clothes and some for the family. A sticky label on the top of each tin stated what the contents were for – mortgage, gas, electricity, housekeeping, children's bus fares, school dinner money, insurance premiums, holidays, clothes, Christmas, birthdays. A set amount was placed inside each tin every week (as shown on the label) and as my father's salary was paid in pound notes and a small amount of change, there was much moving of coins from one tin to another to ensure that the exact amount was put away each Friday evening. When everything was sorted, my mother handed my father his train fare and pocket money for the week.

My parents cannot have had money to spare. When my father died in 1951, he was earning £600 a year and so I would guess that in the 1930s his annual salary was less. My mother fed us well – by checking prices at different shops before making purchases and during the war our food was supplemented by the rabbits we kept and the vegetables we grew on the allotments and in the garden.

We had family holidays in the 1930s, went to the theatre and the cinema, and had adequate clothing (with a lot of home-made or home-knitted clothes, and hand-me-downs from within the family and amongst neighbours). I never heard my mother grumble about money or the lack of it.

School and the rabbit costume that did not arrive

I was five on 18th March 1938 and within a matter of days I was enrolled at the brand new William Torbitt School – which had opened its doors a mere six months or so earlier. My big brother, Len, had transferred from Downshall School when the new school opened.

Built on what we called the Eastern Avenue or the Arterial Road, which had trees down the middle separating the two tracks, it is now the A12 trunk road out of London to the East Coast. The local council must have foreseen this development for outside the school they dug what was one of the first subways in the Borough so that those of us who lived south of the Eastern Avenue might cross in safety. Houses were built on both sides of the Eastern Avenue – ribbon development – which meant that when the traffic increased, the road could be widened to two lanes each way, but no more. And the houses suffered the blight that comes from being sited on the edge of a main trunk road. How little foresight existed amongst governments, councils and planners in the 1930s. Few houses were built with garages, which meant that by the Millennium much of London's outer suburbia resembled a giant car park, with front gardens concreted over to provide parking for the family's one, two, three, four or even five cars. But in the 1930s none of this was foreseen.

I would walk to school with my brother and I was supposed to come home with him. He usually ran off to be with his friends on the way to school and rarely waited for me afterwards. That in itself is remarkable. Seventy years later no child under the age of ten or eleven walks to school unaccompanied. Indeed, few walk for most are taken by car and no parent allows a child to walk alone. The newly-opened subway ensured that I did not have to cross the dual carriageway, but there were a number of side roads. And I walked this half-mile alone at the age of five.

Mr Train was head teacher. My class teacher was Miss Billington. Beryl Faulkner, my first girl friend, lived in Aldborough Road South. The parents of Maureen Henderson, a ginger-haired girl in my class, ran the sweet shop opposite King George Hospital on the other side of the Eastern Avenue near Newbury Park station. Maureen gave us all Christmas cards from the shop and I considered her to be very rich as a consequence. A boy called Dan drank from the inkwells and had a mouth that was permanently black. The mother of another boy ran the fresh fish shop opposite the school – in the small single storey premises next door to the post office. He sat next to me in class and his clothes stank of fish.

The school corridors were so very long that they seemed to stretch to eternity. The main hall was massive. There was a lingering smell of warm milk throughout the building. The sports' field seemed just huge and went on for ever and ever.

On my first day I sat near to a boy who I learned was Jewish. How I found this out I do not know – but I did. So frightened was I that he would eat me, that on returning home for the first time I told my mother than I would have to go to another school. I had heard my father complain so often about the *"Jew Boys"* – and for a reason which defies logic, I assumed that *"Jew Boys",* in particular, would eat boys like me. I took some persuading to return to school next day, but I went – and avoided that boy from then onwards.

We were warned that gypsies had camped on some grassland opposite the school – where Aldborough Court now stands on the corner of Aldborough Road North and the A12. During an assembly in the main hall, a male teacher demonstrated how gypsies would snatch small children and take them off in their caravans. I was petrified and ran all the way home that night. For years afterwards I had an intrinsic fear of gypsies.

I was to take part in the end of term Christmas entertainment which would be attended by parents. This might have been a nativity play, but I was not told. I was to be a rabbit (and because I was not told, I remain unclear as to how a rabbit had a role in a nativity play). On the day of the show disaster struck for the costume had not arrived. I sat out the play. It was the first major disappointment in my life and it lingered for a long time. I do not think the damage was long-lasting or had a permanent effect on me in later life, but I cannot be sure.

Warm haze and growing tension

The summer days of my childhood passed in a warm haze, but in the late 1930s I sensed a growing tension in the air that cut into what seemed to be an idyllic time of my life.

Five years older than me, my brother, Len, was something of a control freak. His best friend was Norman, who lived in Merton Road, off Meads Lane, near Seven Kings Park. I would tag along with them, but I was clearly something of a nuisance and I was, to say the least, naïve.

On a fishing trip to Wanstead Park, Len had a fine rod, with sections that linked together, and reel, line and bait. He would give me a small section of the rod, fix a piece of line to one end and some bait on a hook – and allow me to fish from the bank (with no hope of catching anything except weed) whilst he strode into the lake in his wellies to reel in fish after fish. I carried the sandwiches and lemonade in my new haversack. When it was empty, Len called me over to some wet grey stuff on the ground. Dad would like some of that, he said, so I scooped it up with my hands and filled the haversack, paying specially attention to the pockets to make sure that they were filled to the brim. It was heavy to carry onto the bus, but spurred on by my now grinning brother's assertion that my Dad would be pleased, I staggered onto the bus with this weight on my back. On arriving home, I discovered that the grey stuff had gone rock solid – for it was quick drying cement. And my brand new haversack was ruined.

The fishing lake in Hainault Forest and the River Roding at Passingford Bridge were favourite spots for my brother and Norman to fish. They had big boy bikes, but I had one with small wheels – and my legs seemed to go round many more times than theirs. The pond at Hainault was two miles of so from home, but Passingford Bridge was twice that – and I would spend most of the time resting in preparation for the long and arduous pedal home. Fishing at Passingford required a permit which had to be purchased from the village post office. On occasion my brother would buy a permit but at other times he did not – and I would have the task of keeping an eye out for the gamekeeper. I was given a whistle and had to blow if I spotted anyone who might be a gamekeeper – when we would all run to hide in the bushes. These were always false alarms and I do not recall us ever being caught.

Every boy dreamed of having his own cart – a wooden box-like affair with wheels and axles taken from a perambulator. The superior carts had a proper wooden box in top, often with a seat inside (with a cushion in the very best carts).

Most had four wheels, two fixed at the rear and two at the front, with the axle mounted on a board that pivoted, and ropes were attached to each end of the board so that the wheels could be steered to take corners. A few carts had one wheel at the front. The cart had to be pushed from the rear on the flat – and, naturally, the job of pushing fell to me. There were a few slopes around – mainly on bridges over railway lines – but before you could relax as the cart sailed away down the slope you had to push it to the top. I spent my time pushing or belting after the runaway cart.

My mother bought one woman's magazine each month and Norman's mother another, and they would swap when they had finished reading. Len and Norman would sit astride the cart, reading the magazines on the way to and from Norman's mother's house – with me pushing, of course. I could not understand why Len and Norman found these magazines so absorbing until much later in life when I discovered that women's magazines have problem pages.

My brother had a fascination for white mice – something not shared by my mother. From time to time Len would buy a white mouse and keep it in a cardboard box at the bottom of the garden, feeding it with bread and milk which he took from the house when my mother was not looking.

Amongst other pets we had a tortoise who wandered around the garden for many years. In the winter months he had a bed of hay in a cardboard box in the cycle shed. We polished his shell with linseed oil from time to time.

Len joined the Wolf Cubs and I followed – but more of that later. My brother, sister and me were sent to Sunday School at the Meads Lane Congregational Church – not because my parents were Congregationalists (like Tall Auntie Rose, Uncle Ernest and Cousin Lily who were dutiful attendees) but rather because Sunday School was from three on a Sunday afternoon for an hour – and that suited my father who enjoyed a late Sunday lunch after overtime at work, decorating, toiling in the garden or on the allotment, followed by a nap, undisturbed by chattering children.

Miss Putney, an attractive lady of indeterminate age, wore black, silky dresses and had her dark hair in a bun at the back of her head, presided over the class in an upper room which had a stale smell of dusty hymn books and chalk. Miss Putney accompanied our singing on a piano, but I remember little else. Except that sometimes after Sunday School my brother and I would leave our sister with her friends and scuttle off to the sand and gravel pits.

These were open pits that had long since ceased to be worked, sited on the corner of Oaks Lane, north from Whites Farm (today this area is a recreation ground and playing fields for Oaks Park High School). The area was a small boy's paradise with sandy slopes to slide down on your bottom and deep pools of brackish water in which you could fish out newts or frogs with your hands if you were lucky.

Today such an area would be surrounded by high fences and patrolled by security guards – but in the late 30s and early 40s they were our playground, until one Sunday afternoon when I slid down a sandy bank and into the water. My brother pulled me out and took me home – dripping all the way. My father was not best pleased for I was in my Sunday clothes.

Street games

Lorna, my sister, was three years younger than me. There were few boys of my age in the road where we lived, but Lorna seemed to have many girl friends. Her closest friend was Angela – who lived up the road with her mother, father and two older sisters, Edna and Thelma. At one time I was madly in love with Edna, but it passed. Thelma was a very big girl and a bit frightening to a small scraggy boy. Angela and Lorna were tomboys, according to my father, and would spend much of the daylight hours upside down with their frocks tucked into their knickers doing handstands against any convenient fence or garden wall. I called Angela "Ugly" and my sister "Frumpy" which did not appear to worry them but was most unkind for they were neither ugly nor frumps, but they would give me the occasional good natured thumping for my trouble.

Denis lived two doors away from us in the corner house and we were friends from time to time. I thought his father was tough looking and I avoided his house when he was there. The street was our playground, rather than our gardens or houses. There were few cars on the roads and I do not recall anyone in Church Road having their own car – even those who had a garage attached to the house. Milk was delivered from a horse-drawn float. The oilman dispensed paraffin from the rear of a horse-drawn cart. Groceries and fruit and vegetables came to the door on horse-drawn vehicles. The insides of these emporia were dark, musty and a little mysterious, and when business was complete in our road, the cart would set off at a gallop, with goods rolling about in the back and pots and pans jingling against each other. I longed to climb aboard and explore the innermost parts of these vans, but I never dared to do so. How I envied the boys who had Saturday jobs, riding on the tailgate of these carts with their legs dangling over the edge.

Colin lived further down the road and I avoided him whenever I could. He had ginger hair and freckles, and puffed a lot for he was on the tubby side. His mother and father ran the tobacconists and sweet shop on the bridge at Newbury Park Station. This was one of two wooden structures, built on stilts adjoining the station building. The other was the coal merchant's office where you went to order your coal deliveries. The coal yard was at the back, running parallel with the station platforms. At night the coal trains arrived and were shunted into the sidings from where the coal would be unloaded into three-sided wooden structures without a roof – the sound of coal trucks would drift through the night air, sometimes muffled in a thick pea souper fog, into my bedroom at the back of the house.

Crammed into the small space beside the counter in Colin's father's shop were two or three American cloth covered tables with chairs where lorry drivers and coalmen sat supping tea and eating wads (whatever they were).

Colin was generally considered by both boys and girls to be something of a wimp. He would come out to play in the street but cry at the least thing and run home to Mummy. And Mummy would tell our parents that we had been unkind to Colin and we would get a tanning for our trouble.

But all this had to be put aside and out of mind when it came to being invited to Colin's home for tea. The occasion might be Colin's birthday or some other excuse for a party, for his mother and father owned the sweet shop and sweeties there would be in abundance. Even during the war when sweets were on ration, there was no shortage in Colin's household. And we boys and girls knew this.

At the bottom of Colin's garden was a shed. It was Colin's very own bolthole, furnished with table and chairs. Colin would invite three or four of us in for tea and Colin's mother – who was a lady of ample proportions – would plod up and down the garden carrying plate after plate of sandwiches and cakes, which we would work through steadily. But I was not over keen to stay after tea, for Colin would insist we played 'doctors and nurses' – and I was always the patient who needed things done to him. I would find an excuse to leave before any of those things were done. I never stayed to find out what might have been done, but I did not like the look on Colin's face as he prepared to do them – whatever they were.

A number of us were taken to the Super Cinema, opposite Ilford railway station, to see the new Walt Disney film '*Snow White and the Seven Dwarfs*'. As Colin's mother was paying, we had the very best seats in the house – the front row of the circle – and, of course, lots and lots of sweets. All went well until the Wicked Witch appeared – when Colin started to scream the place down. Such was his screaming that his mother had to take him outside where he refused to calm down. We were told that Colin and his mother had gone home, but we all stayed to see the film out – and to eat Colin's bag of sweeties which he had left behind!

My mother kept a wooden cane to punish us if we were naughty – with a bent handle and somewhat frayed at its extremities. My brother was often given a hiding with this cane, I was threatened with it but always apologised (and was invariably let off) whilst my sister was given the occasional cut across the top of her legs. Memories of the fear with which I viewed this cane meant that I never lifted a hand to chastise my children physically.

Holidays and Christmas

Family photograph albums show that my father took us all away for a two week holiday every summer in the 1930s and each year we went back to Ryde on the Isle of Wight. Some years my mother's parents appear in the photographs.

Looking through the photographs it is amazing how formally the holidaymakers were dressed. The men paddled in the sea with trousers rolled above the knees, jacket, shirt and tie – and often a trilby hat or cap. The ladies had large floppy hats and dresses that covered their knees and very nearly obscured their ankles, too. The children were in warm woollies irrespective of the weather. Buckets and spades, but no sun glasses or sun cream.

We stayed at a boarding house for the two weeks where we were served a hearty breakfast and a substantial evening meal. We travelled by train and ferry, whilst on the island we used the local buses or went on coach outings. At Alum Bay we purchased glass tubes and filled these with the coloured sands found along the cliffs, bringing them home to be displayed in the best room of the house.

One year after the war we went on a coach outing every other day over a fortnight in the summer holidays – to Southend, Clacton, Brighton, Folkestone, Margate, Ramsgate and Worthing. We looked out of the windows as the countryside zoomed past on the outward journey and slept on the return, playing on the sand in the middle of the day and eating sandwiches brought from home. Ice creams were again on sale – the first cornet I had after the war was bought at an Italian café at the Green Man, Leytonstone, in 1946.

The one post-war family holiday we took before my father's death in 1951 was to Babbacombe in Devon. My mother, sister, father and I stayed in a boarding house, spending the days on the sandy beaches and in the sea. We went to the concert party show at the hall on the cliffs and saw comedian Cyril Fletcher and his singer wife Betty Astell in their summer show in Torquay. I was in seventh heaven, seeing in the flesh the great man I had listened to on the radio with his *"Odd Odes".* Coach trips took us across Dartmoor and to Dartmouth.

Christmas was a secular affair for whilst I knew the story of the nativity, it had little relevance in my family where we went to church for weddings, christenings and funerals. Christmas was about Father Christmas coming down the chimney, bringing nuts, some sweets and an orange and putting them into one of my father's socks which was hung over the bottom of the bed.

There were presents from the family – books and sweets, and bigger gifts which were often very special and more often than not homemade. My sister had a dolls' pram, but my mother made all the blankets, sheets, pillows and pillow cases by hand, with an eiderdown made up from knitted squares in different colours. My brother had a farmyard, with farmhouse, barns, fences and yards. The animals and people were hand-painted and made of lead, and added to at subsequent birthdays and at Christmas. My father made a large board on which he painted roads and fields.

The stage and microphone mentioned earlier were my Christmas presents, together with books when I started to read. I enjoyed Enid Blyton's *Sunny Stories,* entering an essay competition when I was ten, and winning a copy of a book of my favourite Enid Blyton stories about Shadow the sheepdog.

We made paper chains – strips of coloured paper bought in packs, made into circles and interlinked, the joins being secured with flour and water paste – the same paste that was used when wall papering. Some years we had a Christmas tree which we decorated with glass baubles and tinsel – there were no Christmas lights or candles.

Christmases in the war years found us having somewhat frugal fare. My mother cried one Christmas Eve because we would have so little different from the normal food we had all year round. We did not send or receive Christmas cards. One Christmas I decided to spend my pocket money on cards for the family, but the Christmas cards in Woolworths in Seven Kings were too expensive, so I bought picture postcards. In my innocence I had purchased the Bamforth seaside postcards with scantily dressed fat ladies and red faced men – saucy and near the knuckle. My mother was not amused and at first I was upset that my generosity with my pocket money was not appreciated, but Mum explained the problem and I felt better.

The evenings of Christmas Day and Boxing Day were for partying. Our aunts and uncles from Newbury Road joined us. The furniture in the dining room was moved back to give space for dancing in the centre. The wind-up gramophone played Victor Sylvester, Mantovani and Henry Hall. Some years my father's friend Wally and his wife from Newbury Road would join us for the evening. My father spent much of the time dancing with Wally's slim and attractive wife, to my mother's clear annoyance.

Later in the evening games of cards would be played – for matchsticks. I wanted the music to continue, but the gramophone was turned off and cards took over. I disliked card games then and refused to learn how to play poker or whist or anything else. Staying up late was part of the fun of Christmas, but when the cards came out I went to bed. I dislike card games to this day.

The Christmas holiday was two days only – Christmas Day and Boxing Day. Offices and factories closed on Christmas Eve and re-opened the day following Boxing Day, unless it happened to be a Sunday. New Year's Eve and New Year's Day were normal working days – we did not sit up to see the New Year in for my father would be off to work early next morning.

War breaks out

The realisation that something momentous was about to happen dawned on a six-and-a-half-year-old as August 1939 faded into September.

My mother, brother, sister and I were evacuated from Ilford to Ipswich a day or so before hostilities were announced on Sunday 3rd September. My memory of that Sunday is sharp and clear. From early morning we knew that something was afoot. We took our time to wash, dress and have our breakfast. We were in our bedroom just after ten when a fellow lodger in his pyjamas and dressing gown walked past and told us that war was about to break out. There would, he said, be an announcement over the wireless. As he was the only person in the house who had a wireless, we had to wait for him to tell us what was happening.

The Prime Minister made the broadcast to the nation at eleven-fifteen. A few minutes later, the lodger told us that we were at war with Germany. I do not know what I expected to happen and I waited in eager anticipation, but it didn't and I was very disappointed.

Evacuation had taken place from the William Torbitt School. There were coaches. We had suitcases and sandwiches. Our gas masks in brown boxes and name labels were hung with string around our necks. It was very warm and the sun blazed down.

In Ipswich we were taken to a large school where we stood around in family groups for what seemed like an eternity. The single children were selected by local residents first, then brothers and sisters, but as a family unit we were left until late evening before we were told that we had a home to go to.

To me it was very exciting and there was little to worry about, for I was with my mother, my brother and my sister. The fact that in the home where we were billeted we drank our tea from glass tumblers and sat on packing cases did not concern me – in fact, I was rather intrigued by the change from cups, saucers and chairs. The children of the house seemed to be scantily dressed and grubby, but why should I worry?

When the lady of the house told us on the Monday morning that we should go out for the day and not return until six in the evening, I thought this was just great as Rushmere Common was nearby with gorse and yellow broom in which to play hide and seek.

I knew that my mother had little money, but she took us all to the shops and spent what she had on us – and not on herself. I felt very, very sad for I sensed that my mother was petrified as to what the day would bring. But the sun beat down relentlessly and by the end of the week the strain was beginning to show on my mother's face, and I realised that things were far worse. By Sunday when my father came to spend the day with us we were all suffering from severe sunstroke and later than evening we were back home in Church Road. Our war had begun.

Phoney war

The period from September 1939 to the following September will be remembered as the time of the 'phoney war' – when we expected everything to happen and little did. It was the calm before the storm. On 7th September 1940 – a year later – the Blitz of London began and ran until 11th May 1941, but those months in late 1939 and early 1940 had a sharp impact on our family.

Initially on our return from evacuation to Ipswich, all was quiet on the home front. The schools were closed – as teachers and children were evacuated – but gradually many of the evacuees returned home and classes were set up in our homes. A teacher visited our house for an hour or so each week with children from the road joining us, when we were set tasks to complete for the following week.

The house had to be prepared for the expected air raids by Germany – which we thought would commence at any moment, so there was some urgency about this. Sandbags were delivered to our front door and carried into the front room – yes, the *front room* which had only been used on high days and holidays – and piled up from floor to ceiling on the inside of the bay window. Green sticky backed mesh was supplied in sheets and this was stuck to the inside of the windows. The theory was that if a bomb dropped nearby, the window glass would shatter but remain in place and not send shards of glass through the air to cause injury or death.

In fact, that worked when the bomb was some distance away but when a bomb fell near my friend's house in nearby Brook Road, the glass and mesh in the houses around just disappeared in a cloud of dust and rubble. My friend's house was totally destroyed but he and his family escaped. He had leg wounds which healed with dark scars which he would show to us if we asked and sometimes if we didn't. We all stared wide-eyed and open-mouthed.

The arrival of the Anderson shelter meant that we had to make some major alterations to the garden which my father had so lovingly designed from the thick London clay left by the builders. Named after Sir John Anderson, Home Secretary at the time, the shelter consisted of six corrugated curved steel sheets which formed the sides and roof, and two end pieces for the front and back. When erected it was six feet high, four-and-a-half feet wide and six-and-a-half feet long. The shelters were free to those earning less that £250 a year with a charge of £7 to those on higher income. I guess my Dad had to pay. They were designed to hold up to six people.

I cannot be sure when our Anderson shelter arrived. The first models were delivered as early as February 1939 – well before the outbreak of war. My father dug out the trench – three feet deep by ten feet by four feet. The six corrugated steel sides were bolted together. There was a doorway, but no door. My father hung a piece of Hessian over the entrance and there was a covered area outside so that the rain did not pour in – my father constructed this from timber and tarpaulins. He built bunks – two on each side – and a set of steps which had to be lifted from the outside covered area and fixed into position before we could go down into the shelter. On occasion we would be in such a hurry to get into the shelter as the bombs rained down that we would forget to put the steps in place – and tumble down on top of each other. There was a small light bulb – from a torch, as I recall – in the ceiling powered from a battery which did not last very long – so we economised by turning the light out and going to sleep as the German planes droned overhead and the bombs dropped with dull thuds, sometimes making the earth shake if they were nearby.

When the blitz started in September 1940 we slept every night in the Anderson shelter. The air raid warnings would sound in the early evening and we would trudge down the garden with our dinner on our plates ready to eat in the shelter. It was damp, dank and cold in the shelter that winter so we wore woolly underwear with thick hand-knitted sweaters pulled over the tops of our pyjamas, and went to bed early.

My father was an Air Raid Warden, which meant that he patrolled the streets for part of every night, watching for incendiary bombs which caught light on impact with the ground and could cause spreading fires. The Air Raid Wardens' post was a brick built building with a flat concrete roof on the corner of Brancaster Road and Brook Road, down the side of Mr Biggs' corn chandler's shop.

Come the dawn and the sounding of the all clear, and we boys would run round the streets looking for shrapnel – bits of bombs or pieces of metal from shot-down aircraft. A piece of shrapnel was a much prized possession to be displayed to all and sundry. My forays for shrapnel were more often than not abortive – on one occasion I arrived home with an armful of the stuff only to be told by my brother that I had collected pieces of coke that had dropped off the back of the coal lorry.

Cousin Lily had a friend, Dorothy, who would stay from time to time with Lily in Newbury Road. Dorothy took something of a shine to me and I found her very attractive and somewhat alluring, for as she came near there wafted some quite pungent scent. I can only have been nine or ten, but I wanted to hug and cuddle her.

At some time during the war I travelled with Cousin Lily to Turkey Street in Enfield to stay with Dorothy and her family for a week or so until Lily came to take me home. I enjoyed the few days there, playing with Dorothy's brothers by a stream which ran the length of Turkey Street. And I saw Dorothy every morning and evening. Bliss! If this was love, bring it on!

Air raids during the daytime were rare, but if they occurred we children would be sent to sit in the cupboard under the stairs – for bombed buildings were often found to have their staircases intact. Once when my parents went out for the day, Cousin Lily and her friend Dorothy were left to look after my sister and me. The siren sounded mid-morning heralding an air raid and we spent until early evening cramped in the cupboard whilst our minders sat outside in the garden in deckchairs soaking up the sunshine!

Hospital, allotments and rabbits

There is some uncertainty in my memory as to the chronology of certain events during the war. I know that my brother, sister and I caught the highly infectious diphtheria, spending some six months at Chadwell Heath Isolation Hospital. That could have been in the early months of 1940 and the disease may have spread through having school classes in our home.

The doctor diagnosed diphtheria and whilst we waited for the ambulance to arrive to take us away, my parents wore masks as they decided which clothing and toys we should take with us. When we had left, officials from the local council arrived to fumigate the bedrooms by spraying with a white liquid which stained the furniture. Our bedding, remaining clothing and toys were taken away to be burned.

We spent the first few weeks at Chadwell Heath in a large ward just inside the gates leading from Grove Road. Some years later I went back to the hospital which was then a geriatric unit. The ward was still there, with small brick piers outside each window. My parents stood on these when they came to visit and shouted to us through closed windows for diphtheria was not only contagious but deadly. (It was in this same ward where my mother died many years later.) I was moved – leaving my brother and sister behind – to a single storey ward with individual rooms that opened onto a balcony. Fresh air was a vital part of recovery – and the doors and windows would be left open on the coldest of days and nights.

The six months we spent in hospital left few memories. For a reason I could not fathom we missed breakfast one morning and the nurse in charge walked over the road to the sweet shop, buying lollipops for us all. Odd, but my recollection is clear. Enemas were feared and syrup of figs was consumed in great quantities when the threat of an enema loomed.

On return home, my brother caught scarlet fever – which was just as contagious and deadly as diphtheria. Off he went to hospital again and the men in brown overalls swooped down to fumigate the furniture and cart the bedding, clothing and many toys off for burning. My parents were not wealthy and I would guess that replacing the essentials was costly. Did they receive help? I hope they did.

My older brother, Len, had passed the eleven plus for Beal High School, which had been evacuated from Ilford to a hutted encampment outside Reading in Berkshire. Len went there but when we visited on two or three occasions he made clear that he was unhappy and wanted to return home. He probably stayed at the school for six months or so. There were hushed conversations between my parents as to the reason for my brother's return. I gathered it was not just homesickness that was the root cause, but I never discovered anything more. On return home, Len went to Downshall Secondary School – a dark, hulk of a place on the corner of Meads Lane and Aldborough Road, built when Victoria was on the throne from black bricks with yellow stonework, and demolished in the latter part of the 20th Century to be replaced by a low level junior school.

At some point during the war my sister and I were sent away to Great Missenden to stay on a farm. Why this happened was never explained to us and we did not ask; rather we accepted the inevitability of it all. My mother appeared to me to be unwell. She cried a lot and when my father was home he spent much of his time comforting her. Was it the stress of the Blitz that had made her tired? Was this the first sign of depression and the mental illness from which she was to suffer in later life?

In my teens with my brother and sister married and living away from home, and following the death of my father, my mother suffered bouts of deep depression, necessitating regular periods in Goodmayes Mental Hospital where the treatment was electric shock therapy (ECT). My mother dreaded this above all else and watching her suffer had a profound and lasting effect on me.

The farmhouse at Great Missenden was in a gulley at the far end of a huge grass field on which cattle grazed. The house was surrounded on three sides by dense woodland, dark and eerie. I was frightened beyond words the whole time we were there. The farmer was rarely to be seen. The farmer's wife was large and overbearing. I cried myself to sleep most nights. Perhaps it was in the summer holidays for I do not recall going to school. My father visited on one or two weekends. I do not know how long we were there, but I was relieved to be taken home at last.

In the years following the war my father arranged for my mother to go to a boarding house in Worthing for two weeks – probably every year in the summer up to his death in 1951. Little was ever said as to why mother went to Worthing, but we would spend the day with her on the middle Sunday. Mum would be crying most of the time and I wondered why she stayed – but I never dared ask and was not told.

I do not recall ever having a meal out in a restaurant with my father and mother. A new tea room opened after the war in the parade of shops opposite Ilford Maternity Hospital on the A12. Called Nan's Pantry, it offered simple fare and was a cut above the workman's café with chintzy tablecloths and flowers on the tables. My father and mother had one or two evening meals there. Later the single shop front expanded until the entire parade of shops was Nan's Pantry – with a banqueting suite on the first floor running the length of the building.

Early in the war my father responded to the Government's demands that we should 'dig for victory'. The grass area between the tennis courts and the bowling green in Seven Kings Park was ploughed up and offered as allotments to local residents.

Having had some success with growing vegetables on what was previously the lawn in our rear garden, my father decided to take an allotment in the park. In fact, he took two – the second being at the end of a row adjacent to the footpath and, therefore, of an odd shape and smaller than the rest.

Here we cultivated potatoes (which had to be planted in trenches and earthed-up each time the greenery poked through the soil), cabbages, cauliflowers, Brussel sprouts, curly kale, everlasting spinach (so called because as fast as you cut it, it grew again – and how I loathed its bitter taste, but oddly I enjoy it as an adult), carrots and beetroot. In the garden we grew tomatoes, lettuces and radishes.

We also bred rabbits. At first we had three – Bebe Daniels, Ben Lyon and Vic Oliver – but Vic Oliver turned out to be a Victoria, so we ate her and kept Bebe and Ben as pets until the end of their natural lives. Ben was a Belgian Giant, who fathered many, many, many rabbits – and seemed to enjoy life to the full. Understandably, perhaps!

My father built a battery of wooden rabbit hutches, two-storeys high, each with an outer run with a door covered in chicken wire and a partition providing a warm nesting place with a small solid wood door. The floors sloped forwards so that the rabbits' water ran to the front where it was collected in a galvanised iron channel that ran into a pipe which stood in a large jam jar. The deep brown liquid collected in the jam jars was used to fertilise the tomatoes grown in the garden. The hay and the solids collected with it was bagged up weekly and taken by wheelbarrow to the allotments – where it either rotted on the compost heap or was dug into the ground in trenches.

At one stage we had sixty rabbits of various ages in our back garden. Every other Friday evening we would sit with my mother in the dining room with the radio turned up to full volume, whilst my father killed a rabbit for Sunday lunch. He would skin the rabbit, rubbing salt into the inside of the pelt before pegging it out on a board to dry in the sun. My mother would make rabbit fur jackets and hats for my sister and gloves to us boys.

Feeding the rabbits was a full-time task and this fell to me. I spent my weekdays on the allotments and with the rabbits, for my mother had declared that, after suffering diphtheria, I was too delicate to go to school and would need to be in the open air. There was talk of my being enrolled at the Open Air School in Benton Road, Seven Kings, but nothing ever came of that. I was fed with cod liver oil and malt morning and night. My mother took it upon herself to continue my education where the William Torbitt School left off. I learned to read and to print. I did sums – addition, subtraction, multiplication and division, but could not master long division. I got on well with fractions, but decimals were a foreign language to my mother and hence to me, too. I am unsure if my mother was able to recite her alphabet and I certainly could not, but I learned my times tables by rote. (I have now mastered the alphabet and can still recite my times tables.)

I revelled in my freedom as I watched the other boys in my road dashing off to school each day. I knew the shopkeepers in Brook Road, who would wave as I trotted off to the allotments in Seven Kings Park. No-one asked why I was not at school. At the weekend when the men were working on their plots, I walked round with a sack asking if I might take the outside cabbage leaves for my rabbits.

Highlight of the week was the visit to Mr Biggs, the corn chandler, in Brook Road. Inside the shop stood open sacks with loose products inside. My favourites were the sacks of dog biscuits – some various shades of brown and the best a dull reddish colour.

Whilst Mr Biggs took my sack out the back to fill with hay or straw, I would dip my hands into the sacks and fill my pockets with dog biscuits. These I stored in the bicycle shed where we kept the rabbit food. It was, of course, shoplifting, but I was never caught and if I had been, no doubt a clip around the ear would have sufficed.

Bringing out the best

Wartime food rationing brought out the very best in my mother. Registering my sister as a vegetarian meant that whilst we lost one meat allowance, we had extra cheese, eggs and butter. We did not need the meat – for the rabbits provided us with two or three meals every fortnight. Roast rabbit and rabbit stew were the popular dishes, the latter with big – and very filling – dumplings.

Shopping required all my mother's innate skills and cunning. My mother, sister and I would set out on Saturday morning for the main shop of the week, travelling to Ilford by train or trolley bus (the latter meant a walk to the Green Gate and a journey down Ley Street). Starting at one end of the high road, my mother made a mental note of the prices and availability of food stuffs. Placing my sister and me in queues meant that my mother could flit from one shop or queue to another.

With the shopping done, I would be left in Ilford to buy the horsemeat for Roy, our Welsh Border Collie, at a shop on the corner of Ilford Lane with Roden Street. There was always a queue at the horsemeat shop – my father being firmly convinced that some of those who bought the meat would eat it themselves, like the French for whom he had so little time. The stench was vile as you moved up the queue and approached nearer and nearer to the shop, and I was pleased to be going home at last clutching Roy's dinner for the week.

My mother boiled the horsemeat (again the smell was unpleasant) and mixed this with scraps from the table for Roy's meals. Mother also baked bread for the rabbits – it kept their teeth sharp. I loved the crustiness of baked bread and would often join the rabbits in a feast of the stuff, dry and without butter or margarine which were on ration and could not be spared.

Roy was a beautiful dog who would have been far better off on a farm rather than in a terrace house in suburbia. He was untrained, so that he pulled on the lead when we took him out for walks. He had to stay on a leash even in the forest or over the fields at Hainault or Chigwell – otherwise he would run off and chase whatever there was to chase. He was expert – in our eyes – at rounding up sheep but after a few run-ins with farmers, we kept Roy under control. He was good natured and never bit us or our friends however much we had rough and tumbles with him.

If we needed the Vet, we went to a lady Vet in Ley Street who did not charge set fees but asked you to pay what you could afford. In the fifteen or so years that Roy lived we bathed him on only two or three occasions – when the summer was very hot. Roy would be taken out for a walk whilst the galvanised bath – the one used on washdays – was prepared in the back garden; as Roy ran through the garden gate we would grab and carry him to the bath where he would splash around as he was soaped before being rinsed off with buckets of warm water.

Routine shopping for foodstuffs that would not keep in hot weather required either a walk to the Co-op at the Green Gate (where I had to remember my mother's dividend number in order for there to be a bonus at the end of so many months of loyal shopping) or a run *'round the corner'* as we called a visit to the shops in Brook Road – which was indeed *'round the corner'*. Here, next door to Mr Biggs was Mr Jones, the chemist. A small, slim, quiet Welshman with a soft lilting voice, he ran the shop alone and would glide – not walk – from the pharmacy at the rear to stand behind the counter, from where he would smile and invite your custom. I never saw him ruffled, nor did he ever raise his voice. He wore a starched and immaculate white overall with two big pockets on either side and one over his heart. The shop had a unique aroma of disinfectant.

Next door was Balls, the sweet shop – clean and almost pristine in its cleanliness, the counter and fittings were in stainless steel. Here we spent our pennies and, once war was declared, used our sweet ration coupons. Further down the parade of shops stood Billies, another sweet shop, but rather cluttered for they sold a variety of goods, newspapers and magazines from here. It was not the place to buy sweets, my mother declared. One more sweet shop at the far end of the parade, and beyond Downshall Junior School, was where we had our weekday and Sunday newspapers delivered. As a special treat, we would buy *Picture Post,* whilst my mother's *Woman's Own* came from here.

Dr Monroe, our family doctor, lived almost opposite the chemist. He was dark skinned, not black but a dusky colour, and may well have been Indian. Until the NHS came into being in 1948, we had to pay if we were taken to the doctor. If we were all ill, my mother would take one of us to see the doctor – and we would share the medication. Less serious ailments were diagnosed by Mr Jones, the chemist, who would then sell us his patent cure-all medicines.

Sainbury's was a mile or so away at Gants Hill, reached on the 66 bus. In the 1930s and 40s it was a small shop, perhaps 50 feet in depth and 20 feet wide. Inside was tiled from floor to ceiling, with a counter down each side and one across the bottom. Here we bought bacon, eggs, fresh butter (cut from a block and patted up between wooden platters), cream and other dairy products – all at different counters. It was cleanliness itself and had an aroma that reflected the products sold. The shop is there today, but now occupied by a computer technician or some such. However, the brown tiling at each side on the exterior remains as a reminder of what once was.

Occasional visits to Romford on market day were unpleasant and to be avoided at all costs. Here pigs and cattle would be unloaded into pens that took up half the area of the market-place. Mean-looking men with heavy sticks drove the animals around, whilst the pigs squealed when their ears were pierced for tagging. I found the noise terrifying and longed to climb aboard the bus for home.

School – again – and at last!

One day my seemingly idyllic lifestyle was shattered. The School Board Man spotted me working happily on the allotments and asked me why I was not at school. I am too delicate, I replied in my halting stammer – for that it what I had heard my mother say often enough to neighbours and it seemed to satisfy them so why not this nasty man with a scowling face? Grabbing me by the arm, he marched me home to confront my mother. Next day he called to take me to Downshall Junior School in Aldborough Road South and my schoolboy career was resumed after a break of two years or so.

I was a bit over nine and school was a frightening place. Miss Stenning, the head teacher, had grey hair swept back into a bun at the nape of her neck. Standing before her desk, I was told that I was way behind everyone else of my age and would have to work very hard if I was to pass the eleven plus entrance examination. To fail was unthinkable for if I did not go to a grammar school, I would be consigned to the dark hulk of the secondary school over the road where all the failures went. I would be finished before I had started. Fear gripped me like a vice.

My teacher expressed surprise at my first piece of written work for I had printed the text and not written this in what she termed 'real writing'. I was shown a copperplate book in which the letters of the alphabet and later words and sentences were set out in 'real writing' with space below for the pupil to copy the sleek, curving letters that were all joined together. I was dumbfounded to discover that my neat printing was unacceptable and that I would be required to do 'real writing' from now onwards. There was no time for me to complete the copying exercises in the books of copperplate. I was told to *"join your printing together"* – and that is what I did. Later in my school life my joined-up printing started to take a backwards lean and I wrote my School Certificate examination papers in that style. In adult life I reverted to printing and I lost the skill of joining the print up into *'real writing'.* The ability to use a typewriter saved me much later.

By this time in my young life I had developed a stammer and I stuttered and spluttered my way through each day, fearful that I would be finished before I had begun and unable to make myself understood for much of the time. Perhaps the worst thing that adults do to a child who stammers is to try to finish the word or sentence – for often adults get it wrong and the stammering child fails dismally to correct what the adult thinks you wanted to say. Speech therapy was not offered and so I spluttered through my schoolboy life until I was over sixteen – but more of that later. My first proper school report in the summer of 1943 made clear that considerable improvement in my scholastic performance was required. At the age of ten I was not doing very well and my father made clear his displeasure. I would have to pull my socks up or I would end up like my brother.

Len, meanwhile, left Downshall Secondary School – that dark hulk over the road where all the failures went – at the age of fourteen to work in the pathology laboratory at nearby King George V Hospital. Leaving without any qualifications, he set out to put this right. Night after night, summer and winter alike, he would cycle the four miles or so to the South East Essex Technical College in Barking where he studied at evening classes and matriculated. This was no mean feat for the war was droning on, incendiary bombs, flying bombs and landmines were falling all around.

My brother and I shared a bedroom, and it was here where he discovered a hobby that led to his eventual career. A Christmas present of a chemistry set – Bunsen burner, test tubes, litmus paper, bottles of acids and boxes of chemicals – sparked off an interest that became a passion. At the same time he shared my father's interest in fish, first with those in the pond in our garden and later with tropical fish.

My father built two aquaria, soldering the metal structure and fitting the glass sides with putty – which never seemed to set hard and was the cause of many a slow dripping leak. One aquarium was in the dining room, the second in our bedroom. Both aquaria were heated and had lights at the top which were switched on night and day.

Minor explosions and terrible stinks pervaded our bedroom. Worst of all was the monthly cooking of the hair cream. Made from a mixture which included beeswax, my brother concocted his own version of the highly popular – but virtually unobtainable during wartime – Brylcream, a patented hair gel which men, young and old, craved after. Poured into jam jars, my bother had regular customers who paid up for the chance to smother their hair in the greasy mixture. Some months things did not go quite right and the men of the area would sport greasy hair with small white lumps. Not a pretty sight.

Later my brother moved to Oldchurch Hospital in Romford. Here he would take his turn on the out of hours-on-call rota. We did not have a telephone at home – few people did – so when he was needed a taxi would arrive at our home out of the blue to take him to the Hospital. Often this would be in the middle of the night, but if it happened during the evening or at a weekend, I would be allowed to go with my brother. Riding in a taxi was a great excitement, although I did not enjoy sitting in the path lab as my brother carried out tests on blood samples and bits of bodies – at least I think they were bits of bodies, but I did not ask and closed my eyes. Later still my brother worked for May and Baker in Dagenham before moving to the pathology department of University College Hospital, London. Finally, his consuming interest in antibiotics and bacteria influenced his decision to join the research staff of Beecham in Surrey, where he remained until his retirement in the late 1980s when he was able to expand his interest in growing succulent plants – cacti to most of us.

In 1944 we installed a Morrison Shelter in the front room at home. This was a metal table like construction with wire grills on four sides. A mattress covered the floor and we all slept side-by-side whilst the doodlebugs (unmanned aircraft loaded with bombs) and landmines dropped all around. My father painted the top with white paint. When this dried, he painted it in sky blue and whilst the paint was still wet produced an effect of clouds by lifting the wet blue paint with a cloth. He and my brother played table tennis on the top whilst my sister and I tried to sleep below.

Eleven Plus terror

A year before the war ended the Eleven Plus Examination loomed on the horizon. Held at Danes School – another dark, dank, smoky black-brick building, but this time in the centre of Ilford – I was terrified at the prospect of failure. When I sat the day-long exam in March 1944, my brother was sixteen and doing well at evening classes, and my sister was a girl and therefore, in my father's eyes, not in the same academic league as his two boys. Girls, my father vowed, did not do examinations and, if they did, they were of no consequence. (I fear that not only was my father a racist, but a bigot and a misogynist, too.)

The reputation of the family and our standing in the local community rested on my puny shoulders. The *1944 Education Act* had yet to be enacted and my father explained that he would be required to pay £60 in school fees for the first year if I passed for the grammar school. After that the Act would provide free secondary education for all. Had my brother passed for a grammar school, my father told me, he would not have been able to afford to pay for me too – so I had better pass or else.

It was fortunate that I did not have to speak, but I found the examination papers confusing and at times almost impossible to comprehend. I returned home in deep and abject misery. Then the long wait started – for the results would not be known for some weeks. When the much-feared letter arrived it told me that I had not passed, but was a borderline case. My name was placed in a 'pool' and I would be referred to other nearby boroughs and if they had spare places at their grammar schools, I would be invited for interview. That came as a hammer blow to me and my family for we all knew that a stuttering skinny boy was hardly likely to shine in an interview where I would be expected to make some attempt at speech.

Invited for interview at Leyton County High School for Boys, my mother and I caught the 66 bus to the Green Man at Leytonstone and the trolley bus towards the Bakers' Arms at Leyton, alighting at Essex Road. Perhaps those conducting the interview felt sorry for me, for I doubt if they made much of what I said, but a few days later we received a letter confirming that I had a place.

My father was ecstatic. Off we went the next Saturday to Henry Taylor, school outfitters in Walthamstow, where we purchased the works. Black blazer and grey shorts (long trousers were worn from the second year upwards, but first year boys wore shorts); black and red blazer badge (two shields – one with the three swords of Essex and the other with three inverted chevrons topped by the Lion Rampant for Leyton); black and red alternate stripes in the tie; white shirts; black knee-length socks with turnovers at the top with red stripes; black shoes; black raincoat. It must have cost a mint of money, but nothing was spared.

On the next Sunday afternoon I dressed in my new school uniform. My legs were as thin as bean poles and the long socks would not hold up unaided. Elastic bands did the trick, although they restricted the circulation and made walking a hazardous process when one leg 'went to sleep'. Subsequently my mother made garters from thick strips of black elastic.

My father assembled my mother, sister and me – and off we went, up the road at a slow and measured pace so that all might see that Ronald had passed the Eleven Plus Examination and would be going to Leyton County High School in September. The fact that it was only June and I was boiling hot inside the heavy uniform did not deter my father, who was veritably glowing with pride at the family achievement.

Off to the Big Boys' School

Leyton County High School for Boys was founded in 1921, a red brick building with cream stone pillars. Oblong in shape on two floors, the classrooms were on the outside and corridors on the inside. The assembly hall was in the centre – with its lofty roof stretching the height of the building. On either side of the hall were quadrangles – starved of much light with grass that desperately needed bright sunshine and smelling stale at all times of the year. A pond was created in one of the quadrangles during my time at the school.

Fronting onto Essex Road, inside the low brick walls topped with railings were neat rose beds, shrubberies and lawns leading up to the main doors, reached via a flight of steps. I went up these steps once on my first day, but never again. At either side of the school were playgrounds with entrances – the one on the left for the lower year groups and the one on the right for the fourth, fifth and sixth forms. They joined at the rear behind the gymnasium in a sort of no-man's-land. Blast walls had been built at ground level outside the ground floor classrooms and cloakrooms on the two sides of the building but not at the front or rear. Standing about a foot from the windows and built of brick, they were to catch the blast from any bombs and, hopefully, to save the windows from being blown inwards and shards of glass causing injury to the pupils and staff who would be sheltering inside the building. One such shelter was in a cloakroom with its metal coat rails and hooks – I often wondered what would happen to us boys if a bomb dropped and all that metal fell upon us.

The school was surrounded by houses, mostly built at about the same time as the school. The sports' field at the rear of the school sloped downwards to the East where the ground rose up again to Whipps Cross Hospital, whose brick built towers loomed in the distance – much as they do today.

I travelled by the same route to and from school that my mother and I had used on the day of my interview. On two buses and two trolley buses I had to ask the bus conductor for a *"twopenny-half",* but I found it almost impossible to say those two words, so my mother – bless her – would ensure that I had eight pennies every day to hold up, two at a time, for my fare. At mid-morning break a local baker would cycle into the playground to sell freshly baked cakes from the box on the front of his machine. I sometimes bought a quarter of a round, flat current-less bun for a penny. To this day I can smell the warmth that came as I bit into the soft, still warm bun. Lunch was served in the assembly hall – watery cabbage, tasteless meat with yellow fat, and custard or semolina pudding.

Dr Leonard Couch, nephew of Quiller-Couch (Q) the author, was headmaster when I joined the school in September 1944. He wore a scarlet gown which flew out behind him as he raced around the school for ever in a hurry. I do not recall speaking either to him or to Mr John Cummings who succeeded him a year or two later, for headmasters kept their distance. The area outside the head's room at the front of the school on the ground floor at the top of those steps I only ever climbed once was a total no-go – if we needed to reach a classroom on the other side, rather than cross it we would walk round to the back and up the far side.

Almost all the masters and mistresses wore black gowns with hoods. Teachers had their own rooms from which they taught their subject and these doubled up as our form rooms. So we pupils were constantly on the move from one room to another, carrying everything with us in our bags. The wooden suitcase made for me by my father weighed mighty heavily by the end of the day.

English was taught by Mr Fitzpatrick – who had ginger hair and freckles – and Miss Duff – who had long blond hair and was very attractive. I looked forward to seeing Miss Duff smile, but one day I made a terrible mistake. She told me off for something or other and I wrote on my blotter *"Miss Duff is a silly old fool".* Sadly, Miss Duff spotted this over my shoulder and I was given a detention for my trouble – staying behind after school for three-quarters-of-an-hour to write out lines.

George Ryle – George to the boys, but not within his hearing – who taught Maths, was tall and angular, and his long hooked nose and voluminous black gown gave him the appearance of a vulture as he homed down the classroom towards some unfortunate boy who had incurred his displeasure. His gown was a dirty grey rather than black – from the chalk dust, for he was a great blackboard man, writing and then rubbing out with a duster that merely spread the particles of chalk hither and thither in the air and about his person.

French was taught by Mr Muswell, who chewed sweets throughout lessons, masticating and chomping noisily with the bones in his cheeks. Unlike Mr Ryle who was always standing or moving stealthily around the classroom, Mr Muswell sat almost motionless at his desk at the front, resembling a bloated frog, peering through his thick glasses and apparently relishing the discomfort of any boy who had trouble with his translation. Reading around the class was Mr Muswell's favourite wheeze – either in the original French or in translation. My classmates would vie to sit immediately behind me, for they knew that once it was my turn to read or translate, I would stutter and splutter until the bell sounded the end of the lesson. Mr Muswell gave the appearance of enjoying watching me squirm as I wrestled with the words that would not form in my mouth – as his lips curled around yet another peppermint in an evil smile. In the intervening days before the next French lesson those who sat immediately behind me knew exactly where they would be required to start reading or translating – and could prepare at their leisure and with the help of dictionaries. Mr Muswell would heap praise upon them all, whilst leering at me for my failure during the previous lesson.

In the second year I opted for Latin rather than German. The latter was taught by a teacher whose shouts and jeering in guttural German could be heard all over the school. Mr Muswell was enough for me to contend with without a bellowing bucolic whose hair stood up as if he were in a constant state of fright. In any case, a few months ago a war in which we had been fighting the Germans came to an end, so what was the point in learning to speak to them in their own language? We beat them, so let them learn English was the view of my father and I – for once – agreed.

Percy taught Latin. He had a surname, but we all called him Percy to his face. At lunchtime, Percy would take himself off to the Bakers' Arms, the local public house next door to Leyton Swimming Baths. He reeked of stale beer throughout many a sunny afternoon, sitting at his high desk and fixing me with a bloodshot eye as he intoned *"O me miserum, O woe is me"*. I failed Latin at School Certificate. Caesar, his Roman hordes and Pliny the Elder (let alone Pliny the Younger) were quite beyond me.

I am unsure what The Bear taught. It could well have been French, but I doubt if it was German for Mr Cohen was Jewish. Short, rotund and very swarthy, he fitted his nickname perfectly. He did not teach me.

Mr Buckley taught history. I wrote up a field trip to Salisbury, Old Sarum and Stonehenge in a notebook. Travelling by coach we left the school at nine in the morning and reached Salisbury three-and-a-half hours later – a journey that would take less than half that time by road today. We left Stonehenge at six in the evening. I did not record the time we arrived home, but I would guess it was dark.

Music was taught in – yes, you have guessed – the music room by Mr Rushton, a genial fellow who cycled to school in all weathers. His lessons were what I would call unstructured, for sometimes nothing happened throughout the period. Mr Rushton would sit in a corner behind his desk, whilst a gramophone played a piece of classical music. I assume we were supposed to listen and perhaps we did. Occasionally he would teach us about staves and the values of notes, but it was somewhat hit and miss. Not that we minded. It was a pleasant change from the skirmishes in the maths class or the intoning of French or Latin.

At some stage I took up the recorder and even made the ranks of the school orchestra. However, I did not receive any lessons and was largely self-taught – and not very well self-taught at that. In fact, I was pretty useless as a musician, but managed to cover up the fact by pretending to play the recorder, but not making any sound because I was not actually blowing any wind into the thing.

My earlier ambition of going on the stage as an entertainer found me joining the school dramatic society. I auditioned for every part possible, but as I stammered and stuttered I was only ever given the role of an understudy for largely non-speaking roles. I was encouraged to work backstage, which I did with considerable enthusiasm in the vain hope that one day this wretched affliction would go away and I would be able to speak like other boys. Remarkably in retrospect no-one ever suggested that I needed speech therapy. Perhaps it was not available in East London in the 1940s.

The dramatic society was in its infancy in my time at Leyton County High. One of my classmates, Michael McStay, was a member and moved into a career in films and TV – appearing in *No hiding place, The Inspector Lynley Mysteries* and *Dr Who.* Frank Muir, who wrote comedy for radio and TV, and excelled as a participant in radio quiz shows, preceded me by some years at Leyton. Derek Jacobi followed me in the 1950s, became a famous actor and was later knighted. Bobby Crush, the popular pianist, was another famous old boy and Jonathan Ross followed me – but much, much later.

Sex and cold showers

Three sciences were taught – chemistry, biology and physics. Each subject had its own laboratory, with dark brown benches and high stools. The physics lab housed brass scales in wooden cases with glass sliding doors, spring balances and the like. In the chemistry lab were Bunsen burners, test tubes and bottles containing chemicals and acids.

Biology was taught by Dr Rice who – like Dr Couch – wore a red gown. There was some attempt at sex education within the biology classes. However, Dr Rice tended to mumble and often appeared to be speaking to himself rather than addressing the class. The bit about sex was taken at speed, for clearly Dr Rice was embarrassed and would have much preferred a repeat of the lesson where we had to dissect a dead frog. I must have been day-dreaming when sex was discussed, for I only realised what had happened when my fellow class mates made lewd jokes as we ran off to the next lesson. I listened intently to their conversation over the next few days, but ended up little the wiser.

Mr Whitehead – we called him Pip – who taught physics and was Deputy Headmaster, was short and rotund. He would busy himself around the assembly hall each morning and appeared to have some role in ordering examinations. I had my first orgasm one afternoon in the physics lab at around the age of fourteen, but since I had missed out on Dr Rice's sex lessons and my parents had avoided the subject, I was overwhelmed with the mystery of it all. It was some months before I worked out for myself what had happened and why.

Art was taught by a short, scruffy fellow who wore a white paint splattered overall which billowed out behind him as he ran around the corridors. His name was Mr Young, but we called him Arty Young. He encouraged us to draw self-portraits in charcoal and later to splash watercolour paints around. We learned nothing of art appreciation or the history of art – it was all hands-on drawing and painting. I learned how to draw a tree in winter, but did not progress to a tree with leaves and foliage. If you showed promise, you were encouraged, but for the rest of us the teacher took a cursory glance at our daubs, sighed and moved on.

Mr Dan taught woodwork and like the art teacher, he did not wear a gown, but an overall – in brown as befitted a man who worked in wood. Mr Dan was a gentle, tall, thin man who was kindness itself to a boy who struggled to make himself understood. In the two years of woodwork I made various joints and a photo frame holder. The latter consisted of a base into which two upright were dropped, which had grooves cut into them into which slid a piece of glass, a photograph and a wooden backing piece. I wrestled with chiselling the holes in the base into which the uprights would slide. Generous doses of wood glue failed to make the uprights secure, but I succeeded finally by mixing in some sawdust with the glue. That picture frame stayed with me for some years.

My PE teacher was much feared until he disappeared and was replaced by a genial fellow – who seemed very old and had the same surname as me. This created some sort of affinity between us and no longer was I held in ridicule because of my skinny frame. The gymnasium ran across the rear of the school building, behind the stage of the assembly hall. The dreaded wall bars were fixed to all four walls where we would hang to perform – or not – many and varied contortions. The only enjoyable time I spent in the gym was at end of term when we played a game called *'Pirates'*. The vaulting horses and boxes, wooden benches, mats and the like were scattered around the gym. The class was divided into two teams who chased each other around the gym, leaping from one piece of equipment to another in mad abandon. If you touched the floor you were *'out'* and had to stand at the end of the room to watch the others. Later these end of term sessions were stopped – health and safety had started to rear its head.

At the end of a gym period we were herded into the communal showers where the water was cold or freezing – generally the latter. Perhaps that was intentional for no-one lingered longer than necessary.

The school had a fine sports field at the rear but its football pitches, tennis courts and cricket squares were reserved for the top teams, whilst the riff-raff had to walk once a week a mile or so to the Eton Manor Sports Ground on Hackney Marshes for football (in winter) or the Essex County Cricket Ground in Leyton High Road for cricket (in summer).

I shivered on Hackney Marshes for I was no footballer. It was invariably cold with a drizzle of rain, and when the wind blew from the west it brought with it the sweet-smelling stench of the soap-making factories of Stratford, mixed in with the stomach-retching aroma of boiled animal bones which were used in the manufacture of toilet soap. The changing rooms were open to the driving rain and chilling winds. Things were little better at the cricket ground, but at least it was summer and even when fielding I could find a shady spot from which to ignore the cries of my fellow players to run – pointlessly, I considered – this way and that for the ball. I was rarely – if ever – given the bat to play with.

The 1948 London Olympics came and went. With commentary on the radio, the games lacked excitement and largely passed my family by. Little did I know that sixty-four years later the UK would be hosting the Olympics on land close by the ground where I had shivered on muddy, slimy football pitches.

Swimming was another nightmare. Swimming baths were largely closed during wartime and as a result I did not learn to swim as a child. My mother would take a group of children from the road to the open air swimming pool in Valentines' Park, but even in high summer the water was bitterly cold and I tended to sit on the side, dangling my feet in the water.

Swimming lessons took place in the summer months at Leyton County. Many of my classmates could swim and dive, and revelled in showing their prowess. The non-swimmers – generally regarded as the wimps of the class – gathered shivering at the shallow end to be cajoled into learning to swim. There were no floats to aid us, but there was a long wooden pole with a harness dangling from the end into which some hapless boy would be strapped only to be dropped into the deeper water and dragged unceremoniously from one end of the pool to the other by an instructor who clearly revelled in the discomfort and embarrassment he was causing the luckless lad.

To make matters worse, my mother knitted a pair of swimming trunks for me, which were fine until they got wet, when they had a tendency to be drawn towards my ankles by the combined weight of wool and water. Here again there were freezing cold showers and equally cold changing rooms. Not surprisingly I did not learn to swim whilst I was at school.

My favourite teacher was Mrs Cathell-Jones whose subject was Geography. Short in stature, with grey bobbed hair, twinkling eyes and a lilting Welsh accent, Mrs Cathell-Jones was probably the one teacher at Leyton – apart from the kindly Mr Dan – who had the patience to cope with a skinny stammerer. She would commend me for my homework, for I had some skill at drawing maps and annotating them in an attractive manner, which seemed to please Mrs Cathell-Jones.

Interestingly enough, Geography was the subject in which I excelled – achieving a Distinction in the School Certificate examination (the equivalent of an "A" in today's GCSEs). It was fortuitous that one question in the Geography paper required an intimate knowledge of Lancashire – for I had memorised the map of the county and could draw it with my eyes shut, well almost. And it was Mrs Cathell-Jones who encouraged me to apply for training with the Ordnance Survey when I was about to leave school at the end of the fifth year.

Belsen Bill of the 'B' stream

It was around the time of my moving to Leyton County High that the first photographs appeared in newspapers of the inmates of Belsen, the notorious concentration camp in Germany. Starved and starving, the inmates' ribs stood out on their emaciated bodies – as did mine. My father would tell visitors to our home that he could play a tune on my ribs. My classmates called me Belsen Bill – not in a spiteful way but simply because I resembled those poor wretches, despite the cod liver oil and malt which my mother continued to spoon into me twice a day.

I guess I must have been something of a sight to behold as an eleven-year-old schoolboy, thin to the point where folk felt sorry for me, carting a wooden box filled with books that dragged my puny arms to the ground and almost totally unable to take part in any meaningful conversation due to the stammer that continued to haunt me. And yet, I made a number of good friends at school. Some were in my form and year, but one or two others were older. One in particular, who was probably in the fourth year when I was in the first and who I knew only by his surname – Clough – became a sort of protector. From time to time a few of us would be set upon by a group of boys a year or two above us, their favourite game being to wedge us up together at the far end behind one of the blast walls – and then run full pelt into the last boy and push us against the far brick wall. If Clough happened to be passing, he would wade into the fray, cuff one or two of the bullies, and lift me out and dust me down – before wandering off into the distance. He was tall, angular and blond, and was always around to rescue me in my first few terms. Then he disappeared and I did not see him again.

In our first year there was a half-hearted attempt to copy the public school practice where the younger boys act as fags for the older brethren, but being a day school with no boarders meant that it did not work. From time to time bully boys in the third or fourth years would descend on the first year boys – and rough us up a bit or make us run errands for them.

I started my life at Leyton County in the 'B' stream. We were told that the boys from each East London Borough who passed the Eleven Plus and went to a grammar school each year were the cream of the crop. But if you were in the 'C' stream at the grammar school you were made to feel like the dregs and tended to be treated so. The 'C' stream looked dejected and as though they were finished before they had even started. My first term was, therefore, a time of great fear for I dreaded the possibility of being sent down to the 'C' stream. I came third in class for each of the three terms in my first year and, as a result, was sent up to the 'A' stream for my second year. This was a big, big mistake for I had been amongst the high achievers in the 'B' stream and now I was down amongst those who had just scraped through into the elite and aspiring 'A' stream.

At the end of the first year I received a prize in recognition of my progress. I was bitterly disappointed that when the Prize Giving Day arrived I could not go to collect the prize – I had a nasty carbuncle, a sort of boil, but much, much bigger, just below my knee on my left leg. Visits to the doctor every other day were painful as I hobbled along, but relief came when the carbuncle burst and half filled a cup with dark red and yellow puss.

Everyone in the 'A' stream was brilliant – except me and a few others who wallowed around at the bottom of the pile. I would be placed twentieth or twenty-fifth in class and even coming first in geography with the heavenly Mrs Cathell-Jones did not make up for the ignominy of coming so near the bottom overall. And to make matters worse, my father was completely unable to comprehend how a son of his who came a consistent third in the first year now dropped to below twenty in the second year. No amount of explanation about 'A', 'B' and 'C' streams made any sense to him. I was a complete and abject failure, whilst my elder brother – who had passed the Eleven-Plus but missed out on its benefits due to the war and was taking his matriculation by cycling to evening classes through rain, hail, fog, snow and every type of weather that was being thrown at us – was doing brilliantly and would save the family name from everlasting damnation. It was fortunate that the *1944 Education Act* had come into force by this time, for I doubt if my father would have continued to pay the £60 that he told me he had to dosh out for my first year at Leyton County for a son who was so clearly a total academic failure.

My experience of being deemed a failure at grammar school convinced me that I would never push my children into selection or grammar schools.

I looked up to the high achievers. Tony Morgan was tall with dark hair and bronzed, a good athlete and brilliant at every subject. Brian Timms – blond and somewhat washed out to the eye – was a bit like me, although brighter and not so far down the list at the end of term. Morgan was in the Boys' Brigade and Timms was a Scout. I envied both their friends and the things they did at weekends and during the holidays. Morgan went on to qualify as a doctor; Timms became a librarian, but sadly died in his twenties from Leukaemia. I met Timms' father many years later when he was actively involved and revered in Scouting in Leyton.

The Pownall twins were athletic. Derek was in the 'A' stream, but his brother David languished in the 'C' stream – and did not take too kindly to the constant comparison being made by teachers with his high-flying academic brother. Excelling in all sports, they were a match for each other only on the sports' field.

Other friends included Jack Groom. Tall and lanky as a boy, we caught up in our sixties when we were both magistrates – Jack in North London and me at Redbridge. He was a retired bank manager, pillar of his local church in Woodford and member of an Old Tyme Music Hall group that performed for charity. Colin Pryke lived in Goodmayes. I once went to his home for tea where his mother asked me if I liked cheese rolls. Unsure what a cheese roll was, I said yes – and found that it was a bread roll with cheese inside. He was the only school friend whose home I visited – with the exception of Michael McStay, of whom more later. A boy called Downes travelled on the trolley bus with me to the Green Man where he caught the 148 home for he lived in Dagenham – a place I considered to be a very, very long way away.

Trolley buses on the route from the Bakers' Arms in Leyton to the Green Man in Leytonstone picked up my school friends and me at Essex Road and as we approached the Green Man the young ladies from Leyton County High School for Girls joined us at James Lane. But we ignored them totally. Were we warned not to talk to them? Was it just that we did not like girls? I cannot recall. All I know if that we took no notice of them – although I did take the occasional sneaky look and liked it when a girl sat in the seat in front or beside me who was wearing scent.

My journeys on the 66 bus to the Green Man and thence by trolley bus to Essex Road were largely uneventful – with the exception of the winter of 1947. From late January to the middle of March of that year, the country experienced record low temperatures and persistent snow cover. The snow was piled high on the pavements where householders had shovelled it to clear a pathway – and remained there, hard and frosted, for weeks. The 66 bus failed to make it to the top of the incline from the River Roding at Redbridge leading up to the George at Wanstead. I walked the remaining two miles or so, but there were days when the buses did not run at all – and I stayed in the warmth of home.

One autumn Monday morning when I was about thirteen a car pulled up at the bus stop outside Newbury Park Station. The driver, a well-spoken and smartly dressed man in his thirties, asked me if I would like a lift. He recognised my school uniform and said he would drive me to the school gates. I declined politely, having been brought up to refuse sweets from strangers or lifts from men in cars. The man did not press me, but suggested I might ask my parents if I could accept a lift. He wrote down his name and explained that he had homes in London and Essex – and drove into London on Monday mornings – and was public relations officer for a large chemical company in Stratford in East London.

The next Monday the man stopped again – and this time I accepted the lift for my father had agreed that I should do so. By a remarkable co-incidence my father had mentioned my encounter to a lady from the company that cleaned his telephone in his office. She also cleaned the telephones for the chemical company in Stratford and knew the man who had offered me a lift. And so over the following weeks I was given a lift to school on Monday mornings. In a way I suppose I was flattered that someone who owned a very fine car and had an important job would want to drive me to school. We talked about the subjects I was studying and it made a pleasant change from the cold and draughty bus stops and buses. At some time during the winter the man asked me if I would like to go ice skating. My parents agreed that I could do so and one Saturday I found myself at an ice rink in West London with the man and another boy about my age. A few weeks passed and then one Monday morning the car did not arrive and I had to catch the bus. I never saw the man again.

Next summer I was cycling through the Essex countryside on a day outing from home. I was nearing the coast around Burnham-on-Crouch when I noticed four or five boys playing in a cottage garden. They called to me as I cycled by and asked me if I would like a cold drink. Leading me into the garden, they showed me a shed extension to the cottage which contained a number of bunk beds. The boys explained that they lived in East London and came to the cottage at weekends and during school holidays. The cottage was owned by the man who drove me to school that winter. He was at work that day in Stratford.

I thought nothing more of this incident until some years later when a friend went to work at the same chemical factory. I told him about my encounters with the public relations officer and learned that he was serving a prison sentence for abusing young boys. I had had a lucky escape.

War end

The end of the war in 1945 came as something of an anticlimax. Living in an air raid shelter in the garden, spending time under the staircase during daytime air raids and sleeping as a family in the Morrison in the front room – all these things were exciting. Growing food on the allotments and keeping rabbits in the back garden for food was different. And suddenly all this came to an end. No longer could we use the war as an excuse for not doing something – like going to school.

On VE Day (Victory in Europe) my father took the family to London where we walked amongst the vast crowds through Trafalgar Square, up the Mall to Buckingham Palace. The Royal Family and Prime Minister Winston Churchill waved from the balcony and then went inside for what seemed an interminable time before they came out and did it all over again. We waited patiently for this to happen a number of times.

VJ Day (Victory in Japan) came and went uneventfully. I knew that atom bombs had been dropped on Japan and that these had hastened the ending of the war, but this was hardly discussed at home or in the street where I lived. Nor was this raised at school, where academic achievement was totally divorced from the events that were going on around us. History centred on the Samarians and the Egyptians, whilst current affairs was not considered an appropriate subject for grammar school boys. The magnitude of what happened and the horror of the carnage was totally lost on me at that time.

There were street parties to celebrate VE Day. Church Road was bisected halfway down by Buxton Road and it was at this junction where we had the bonfire – and a mighty fine bonfire it was too. Almost as high as the houses, it swayed about in the wind for days before it was finally lit. I wonder how we got away without setting fences and houses on fire but we did. Tables were laid out in the centre of the road and, despite rationing and food shortages, they overflowed with food – jellies being the main stay of any party.

Homemade ginger beer had intermittent periods of popularity – until an accident occurred when it ceased to be made for a few months whilst the furore died down. A ginger beer plant – a grey squishy lump – was divided up and placed in the bottom of a bottle which was then filled with water. The bottle required a screw cap or some device for making it air tight. Left for a few days, the ginger beer plant would ferment and make something that could be passed off as fizzy ginger beer. The knack was knowing when the fermentation had reached the point where the stuff should be drunk – for, if left too long, the bottle would explode with disastrous results. Many a bathroom had glass embedded in the walls as the result of a ginger beer plant eruption.

Men came back from the war and resumed their old jobs. My father was especially bitter when a man who had ranked below him at the outbreak of war returned as an ex-soldier to a hero's welcome – and was promoted above my father, who had worked throughout the war in the factory in a reserved occupation. Much swearing and cussing went on after I had gone to bed as my father poured out his anger by verbally haranguing my mother, who took it all without a murmour.

The General Election in 1945 was my introduction to national politics. My father made clear that he was Labour through and through, but insisted that I should accompany him to meetings of all three candidates standing in our constituency of Ilford North so that I might learn what idiots – in my father's view – the other two candidates were. The sitting Conservative MP was Geoffrey Hutchinson and everyone expected him to be returned. He appeared at his meeting in a local school wearing a black jacket, pin striped trousers and wing collar with black tie – looking for all the world like an undertaker. He was well and truly heckled by a gang of men at the back of the hall, led by Mr Biggs, the corn chandler whose dog biscuits I had filched. Geoffrey Hutchinson had the pinched look of a Dickensian character and did not appear to me to be someone who would represent my interests in the Mother of Parliaments. Mention the fact that Uncle Ernest Stanley and Tall Auntie Rose would be casting their votes for him and my father's face would turn bright purple.

Lady Rhys Williams stood for the Liberals and, in my father's view, had about as much chance of being elected as one of our rabbits. An elegant lady in a floral dress and matching hat, Lady Rhys Williams had the support of a man my father often talked with on the allotments in Seven Kings Park. My father expressed surprise that this man should put his cross for a Liberal and even though the poor fellow explained that he was supporting the Liberals to keep the Tories out, my father refused to speak with him ever again.

Mabel Ridealgh was the Labour and Co-operative Candidate and to everyone's surprise was elected as our MP. A homely but determined lady, Mabel served the constituency well for one term before being ousted at the 1951 election by none other than Geoffrey Hutchinson, who later moved to the House of Lords as Lord Ilford.

In the early 1980s I sat at Redbridge Magistrates' Court with Mabel's son, Dr John Ridealgh, who was a GP in Goodmayes. By this time Mabel was living with her son's family and died shortly afterwards following a long illness.

Freewheeling

In summer in the war years my father and mother cycled, with my sister sitting astride a seat fixed to the back of my father's saddle. I had my own cycle – at first one with small wheels and latter a big boy's Raleigh Lenton with green paintwork which cost all of three pounds ten shillings, which I saved with birthday and Christmas money before the cycle was purchased. My brother had his own cycle.

On summer weekends my father, mother, sister and I would set out together into the Essex countryside. Between Chigwell Row and Abridge lived a lady – who we called the 'Old Girl' – who sold fresh eggs and fruit from a table in the back yard of her cottage which fronted onto the roadway. Food rationing meant that fresh eggs, apples, pears and plums were real luxuries. The 'Old Girl' did not have scales – but sold her goods by number or the bowl full.

After the war when I cycled alone, I would come home to report to my father on the products for sale by the 'Old Girl' – and Mum and Dad would set out on their bicycles to make the purchases.

During the war all road signs and signposts were removed and no road maps were on sale. This was to confuse the enemy spies who, we assumed, were hiding behind every hay stack. Should there be an invasion of our shores, the lack of road signs would further confound the invader. At least, that is what we were told. For some odd reason, however, the public houses – of which there were many in the Essex countryside – retained their name signs. Perhaps it was thought that Germans would not be able to understand our pub names or were teetotal. Thus when I returned from a cycle ride I could tell my family and friends that I went via the Dick Turpin, the Maypole, the Beehive, the Rabbits and the White Bear to Ongar, and returned via the Mole Catcher and the Robin Hood.

I started to venture forth alone on my bicycle at around the age of twelve. Southend-on-Sea was twenty-nine miles from home and I would cycle there and back in a day during the school holidays. If the wind was behind me, I could cover the twenty-nine miles in less than two hours; with a head wind it would take twice as long. By now the A12 running past Newbury Park Station had two carriageways separated by a grass verge in the centre. A cycle track ran from my home right to Southend town centre, which meant that I was not in danger from lorries and cars, although there were few enough of these until petrol again became available.

Cycling into the Essex lanes was great fun. I was alone. I could go where I wanted and do as I pleased. The round trip of sixty miles or so from home to Dunmow and Bishops Stortford took a day. Later I crossed the River Thames by the Woolwich Ferry and cycled to Maidstone and back also in a day.

At the age of fourteen I joined the Youth Hostels Association, which opened up totally new opportunities for a lone cyclist. One summer holiday I toured for fourteen days through Surrey, Kent, Sussex and Hampshire. During an afternoon nap outside Arundel, my light cycling jacket was stolen, but my money was safe inside a pocket stitched into my vest by my mother and, therefore, on my person at all times. But I was cold in the mornings and evenings.

Another cycle tour took me through Hertfordshire to Norfolk and Suffolk. This was the only Youth Hostel tour when I was not alone for Geoff, a fellow choirboy at St. Peter's, joined me. That summer was scorching hot and Geoff had sunburn on his blond arms and legs. Yvonne – one of two girls in the church choir and later to be my wife – was at home for the holidays with her parents in Suffolk. Knowing that we would be cycling through Saxmundham on a certain day, Yvonne waited in the main street in the vain hope of seeing me cycle by – but we had passed through the previous afternoon.

My big Youth Hostel fourteen day tour took place when I was sixteen and waiting for my School Certificate results. I caught a train to Winchester, cycling from there to Land's End along the South coast, and back along the North coast of Cornwall and Devon, through Somerset to Salisbury – for the train home.

I was content to be alone. The only time I was frightened was when I crossed Dartmoor in driving rain alternating with a heavy mist. As I approached Dartmoor Prison, a lorry stopped and it was with considerable relief that I accepted a very welcome lift. In the daytime people would invite me to join them in their gardens for a cold drink and cakes. In the evenings there were always folk to talk with at the hostels. I was never lonely. Being almost incapable of stringing three or four words together due to the stammer did not hinder my making friends – in some ways it probably helped.

Perhaps the most intriguing encounter occurred when I cycled to Maldon Youth Hostel in Essex over a bank holiday weekend. The previous night I had stayed at High Roding Youth Hostel – a converted tithe barn. I slept on a top bunk which was immediately by an open window and awoke in the middle of the night to find myself flat on my back amongst stinging nettles in a wire enclosure and surrounded by squawking chickens. With no obvious way out, it was shear willpower that sent me climbing up the exterior timbers of the barn to return to my sleeping bag.

Later that day as I neared Maldon, I spotted an elderly man wearing a smoking jacket and matching headgear, standing at the entrance to what I later discovered was Beeleigh Abbey. He called over to ask if I would like a cold drink. Taking me into the house, he led me through to the library where I was enthralled to be shown books the like to which I had never seen before – books with padlocks, books with hidden compartments amongst the pages used by smugglers, and paintings of great size and beauty. After an hour or so I was sent on my way with some fruit and cakes in my saddlebag.

It was much later that I discovered that I had been entertained by a member of the Foyle family of the world famous Foyle's Bookshop in Charing Cross Road.

Beeleigh Abbey was founded in 1180 for the White Canons and in 1587 a farmhouse was added as an extension. The Abbey was not at that time open to the public nor has it been since – which means that I had a somewhat unique opportunity to view things that few others have seen.

A later youth hostel tour took me to Chester by train and round North Wales – again alone. On Anglesey I found a beach that was totally deserted. I walked to the top of Snowdon and back again in a day wearing cycle shoes – I could not afford to take the train, nor did I appreciate that cycle shoes were hardly suitable footwear for the mountains, but it was in the summer.

The dreaded examinations

Fifth year examinations loomed ahead. It did not occur to me at any time that I might remain at school after the fifth year and my sixteenth birthday, and move into the sixth form. Of the ninety boys in my year, perhaps a dozen or so became sixth formers and went on to university or other further education. It was almost as if school was nothing more than preparation for work and for an East London grammar schoolboy in 1949 that meant something in the City of London – a bank or insurance company.

My father had instilled into me that he did not want me to become what he termed a "pen-pusher" and my prowess at geography under the watchful eye of Mrs Cathell-Jones led me to the belief that I should consider map-making as a career. After all, I could draw splendid maps of Lancashire and Cheshire, placing all the main towns in the correct spots and writing the main business of each place in brackets – thus Nantwich (salt), Liverpool (docks) and Eccles (cakes), St. Helen's (glass).

I was unaware of any structured career advice within the school, but with the encouragement of Mrs Cathell-Jones, I wrote to the Ordnance Survey offices in Southampton, was interviewed and accepted for training as a surveyor – leaving school at the end of July and starting my new career in September.

But first the examinations for the School Certificate had to be faced. If certain grades were achieved, not only did you attain a School Certificate, but Matriculation, too, which enabled you to enter university. The months and weeks before the dreaded examinations were filled with terror for me. I feared failure and yet it seemed to me that there was little I could do to ensure success.

The set texts for English Literature were *Silas Marner* and *Macbeth*. I found the former dreary and uninteresting, whilst the latter was almost totally incomprehensible. Early in our final year *Macbeth* was to be shown one Sunday evening on television. Only one boy in my year had TV at home – he was Michael McStay who lived in Walthamstow and went on to a distinguished career in films and TV. The whole class trekked over to Michael's home that Sunday evening and filled the lounge to watch Macbeth on what must have been a very small screen, but which to me seemed almost magical. Michael was the class extravert and I realised why when we went to his home, for he seemed to possess everything that I did not – and a mother who was both charming and the perfect hostess to a gaggle of teenage boys, and a father who said little that evening but was always there in the background (and who would blame him?). We had lots and lots of cakes and soft drinks – it was bliss.

The examinations were taken in the main school hall in June 1949. I recall little of the exam days, except that it was oppressively hot and I had a sinking feeling in the pit of my stomach for most of the time. The weeks that followed were spent on the playing field at the back of the school. There was little for us to do but attend morning assembly and then relax. It was a somewhat eerie time of my life. I took to wearing white shirts and shorts, and caught the sun, but little else.

In late August I learned that I had gained my School Certificate with a distinction in Geography and passes in English Language, English Literature, Mathematics, History, General Science and Art. I failed Latin and French. Failure in the former came as no surprise and I guess it was inevitable that I would stumble in the latter, for the oral examination had found me stuttering and spluttering as I attempted to describe a picture of a farmyard scene to an examiner who must have wondered what on earth she was doing hearing this stammerer. No matriculation for me which, again, disappointed my father but did not bother me, for I had my sights firmly set on a career as a surveyor with the Ordnance Survey and had no wish to go to university.

I returned to Leyton County just once after the summer of 1949 – in the late autumn to collect my School Certificate. I had bought some new clothes with my first wage packet – a brown stripped double-breasted jacket with dark brown trousers, check shirt and brown tie. These were the very latest fashion for young men about town, but the double-breasted jacket hung about my skinny frame as if it was uncertain whether or not it should be there. I thought I would look the cat's whisker, but came away with the distinct feeling that I had been over-dressed for the occasion.

I drove past the school once some thirty years later. More recently I looked up the school on the internet to discover that it is now a Sixth Form College with a splattering of new buildings all around. I do not think I will go back to have another look.

Part Two
A choirboy I would be

Too young at seven – too old at eleven

St. Peter's Church has played a major part in my life since 1944 – the year when I moved from Downshall Junior School (a few streets away from my home) to Leyton County High School for Boys (one bus and a trolley bus ride towards London).

I wanted desperately to join a church choir for, although I could hardly string three words together due to my stammer, I could sing. And so for six months at the age of eleven I sat in the congregation at morning service at St. John's Church, Seven Kings – the nearest church to where I lived – waiting to pluck up the courage to ask if I might join the choir.

I found the hymns – for these were numbered – but locating the words of the service in the prayer book was beyond me. And no-one – in all that time – offered to help. Just one elderly lady spoke to me – to reprimand me for biting my finger nails.

After the service on most Sundays I walked home via the Cauliflower Public House in Seven Kings, where I bought the winkles and shrimps for tea.

Mr Jones, the Organist and Choirmaster, had some twenty or so boys and a dozen men under his eagle eye. Finally, having mustered all the courage at my command, I approached him with fear and in awe – and posed the question.

"I want to join the choir," I stammered.

"How old are you, boy?" asked Mr Jones.

"Eleven, Sir," I replied.

"Too old," said Mr Jones dismissively and curtly, turning on his heels, his surplice flying out behind him. *"You have to be eight to join my choir."*

Cut to the quick that I was too old at eleven, my mother consoled me with the suggestion that I might try my luck at St. Peter's in Aldborough Hatch where my sister, Lorna, was baptised – a mile or so away and on the edge of the countryside. The next Sunday I made my way to St. Peter's, ready for a rebuff but still determined to try. The church was bitterly cold, for the three electric fires that served as heaters battled against the fact that there was a yawning gap between the top of the north wall and the roof – the result of a landmine which fell up the road from the church and opposite the Dick Turpin hostelry, to which my parents would take us from time to time for a lemonade, a packet of crisps or a Wall's Ice Cream on a sunny Sunday summer's evening – of which there were many.

The Vicar, the Rev. Joseph Palanque Byng, walked in solemn procession behind three choirboys. There were perhaps a dozen or so in the congregation, whilst the organist peered over his glasses from his stall behind a railed curtain to see who this lad was who was trilling away at the top of his high soprano and sitting near the front so that I would be noticed. For whilst I had failed dismally to find my way around the prayer book at St. John's, I had learned some hymns and knew how to give them a bit of welly.

With the service over, the Rev. Byng was at my side like a shot out of a gun.

"Boy," he said, peering over his rimless spectacles, *"where do you live?"*

I spluttered out my answer, but before I could ask the question, the Rev. Byng told me to be at the church the next Thursday at 7pm for choir practice. I did so. And I am here today, but I no longer have to go to the Cauliflower to buy the winkles for tea. Thus it was that I was too old at eleven, but earlier I had been too young at seven to join the Wolf Cubs – but more of that later.

Goings on at the Dick Turpin

I mentioned the landmine that dropped at the Dick Turpin, causing damage to the roof and windows of St. Peter's. I was oblivious to the whole affair, but my friend Keith was a part-time air raid warden during the 1939-45 war, based at a post in the Banjo of Bawdsey Avenue. Keith recounts the following tale of goings on at the Dick:

"There was no air raid in progress on the Saturday morning of the day of the incident. I responded from home going straight to the scene. I was a bit delayed because I was in the bath at the time. It was a V2 rocket which had impacted on the forecourt of the Dick Turpin public house.

"On the way to the scene I saw Mrs Dipper, who lived in Applegarth Drive and was a cleaner at the Dick Turpin. She was in a distressed state, her face and arms cut from flying glass. She was the first war widow in our locality in 1939 when her husband, a regular sailor in the Royal Navy, went down with the 'Royal Oak' in Scapa Flow. I stopped to help her, but she wanted to get home to her daughter who was left on her own.

"When I arrived at the scene I saw the crater and nearby three bodies – two of them were RAF Officers and the third was the landlord at the Dick Turpin, Phil Perkins. A badly damaged RAF staff car was nearby. The whole of the area – the bodies and the staff car – was showered with cigarettes – suggesting that an exchange was going on when the rocket landed – drinks for cigarettes?

The RAF Officers came from their quarters at Painters Hall, where the Aldborough Hall Equestrian Centre is sited today. The National Fire Service and the Police were already on the scene.

Some were in the building and down the cellar – from where a fireman emerged with a large vase full of banknotes. I left shortly afterwards as there was nothing I could do."

An early example of recycling

And what of the church itself which was to become so much a part of my life? The beginnings of St. Peter's are to be found some twelve miles away in Westminster. St. Peter's was built from the stone of the first Westminster Bridge over the River Thames, which was opened in 1750. It was on this bridge that on 3rd September 1802 Wordsworth wrote his poem – *Upon Westminster Bridge ("Earth has not anything to show more fair: Dull would he be of soul who could pass by a sight so touching in its majesty").*

The bridge – 1,038 feet long and 44 feet wide – tended to sway on its foundations and was never fully trusted. When the old London Bridge was removed in 1831 the scour of the river upstream undermined the foundations of Westminster Bridge and it became dangerous. Work began on a new bridge in 1854, but the old bridge was in use until the new one was nearing completion in 1862.

The new seven-arch wrought-iron bridge – 827 feet long and 84 feet wide – opened in May 1862. At the time the contractor for the new bridge also had the order from the Crown for the new Church at Aldborough Hatch. Portland stone from the old bridge was brought from Westminster to Aldborough Hatch to build the new St. Peter's Church, the remainder of the stone was used for other building purposes in London – an early example of recycling. Built at a cost of some £2,000 and consecrated in 1863, St. Peter's stood then and stands today on the edge of the countryside.

Until the first half of the 19th Century, Hainault Forest came down to Aldborough Hatch – the word 'Hatch' itself denoted a hatch or gate into the forestland. In 1851, an Act of Parliament 'disafforested' Hainault and 100,000 trees on Crown land were felled within two years.

Large farms were laid out on the Plain with housing for labourers and the straight roads – Hainault Road, Forest Road and New North Road – were cut through.

St. Peter's was born of the need for a church to serve the expected increase in the local population as farms replaced forest.

The Crown gave the land and the Government gave £1,000 – said to be some sort of recompense for the destruction of the forest – towards the cost of the church's erection. No doubt in the 1860s the population of Aldborough Hatch was sparse – by 1901 it had grown to some 500.

And so that was the church I joined in 1944 – little changed over the eighty-one years and much the same today.

When the choirboys went on strike

Three boys made up St. Peter's church choir in 1944 – the men being away at the War with some boys still evacuated. The choir swelled after the War to ten or so boys (of varying vocal ability) and six men (who were not averse to twisting the ear of a recalcitrant choirboy).

The choir vestry was an area behind heavy-duty green curtains inside the church building at the north-west corner. Boys being boys, we would talk in loud and penetrating whispers, and clomp around on the uncarpeted wooden floor – with much huffing and puffing in the congregation, and a few clipped ears inflicted by the men of the choir.

Mr Butler, the Organist and Choirmaster, rode his bicycle from Clifton Road at the Green Gate to choir practice on Thursday evenings and two services on Sunday. His wife and daughter, Ann (her of the ginger hair and freckles with whom I was madly in love), would walk to morning service.

The choirboys were paid quarterly by Rev. Byng, the Vicar, who would doll out the five shillings (twenty-five pence in today's money) with an air of some reluctance and a pained expression upon his face as though it were his hard-earned money and not that of the church.

However, it was the weddings which made us rich, for Mr Byng would drop half-a-crown into our sticky paws, and we could have two or even three of these on a good summer Saturday.

All went swimmingly but the balloon went up when we discovered that the boys in St. John's Choir in Seven Kings were paid ten shillings a quarter and five bob a wedding.

A deputation – the two sons of one of the churchwardens were chosen as possessing the greatest political clout – put our case to Rev. Byng, who was unyielding and crossly adamant.

And so the majority of the choirboys decided to go on strike. Over the next few weeks, the men of the choir would process down and up the aisles in their robes singing robustly, whilst the boys of the choir sat in the front rows below the pulpit. Throughout the strike the boys attended two services each Sunday – but with sealed lips from which not a single note emanated. This was, of course, highly embarrassing for the churchwarden whose two sons were seen as the strike leaders.

I guess there were behind closed doors negotiations for after three or so weeks parity was struck with St. John's and the pay of St. Peter's choirboys doubled overnight.

To keep the record straight, I should admit – with hand on heart – that there was one blackleg amongst the choirboys who refused to go on strike. He was the Head Chorister and Sole Soloist, whose repertoire at weddings consisted of *'I'll walk beside you'* and *'Count your blessings one by one'* for which he was paid ten shillings a wedding. No way was he going to forego such a lucrative income. Sunday by Sunday the blackleg sat alone in the boys' stalls under the glare of the strikers.

And who, you may ask, was the blackleg? Now that would be telling, wouldn't it?

Choirboy perks

There were some perks to being a choirboy in the 1940s. A red, rosy apple at the end of Evensong at the Harvest Festival was one. Another was the annual choir outing to Southend-on-Sea, re-started after the 1939-45 War when the barbed wire was removed from the beaches.

The outings were led by the Vicar, the Rev. Joseph Palanque Byng (whose wife called him Joey, much to the amusement of the choirboys, who would mimic a parrot behind their backs). We travelled by steam train from Ilford Station, where the trick was to get in the carriage with Mrs Byng and not with the Rev. Joey – for Mrs Byng was something of a sport on these occasions, whilst the Rev. Joey carried a care-worn look of resigned resignation throughout the day and was not averse to flicking the odd ear if a boy stepped out of line – and sometimes if he didn't.

Armed with pea shooters, those of us lucky enough to be in Mrs Byng's carriage would lean out of the window, firing split peas at our fellow passengers on station platforms and into the carriage occupied by Rev. Byng and the unfortunates who had to behave themselves for the entire journey. Mrs Byng – whose false teeth rattled when she became excited and who wore thick glasses that made her eyes stand out like organ stops – would join in, hanging out of the window with the smoke from the steam engine streaming through her greying hair. I do not recall any other passengers daring to enter our two carriages on either the outward or the return journeys.

The walk from Southend Station to the sea seemed interminable, but finally we caught sight of the pier stretching into the far, far distance. I guess there were amusement arcades in Southend in those days, but if there were, we did not go into them. It was all sharp healthy walks along the seafront with the command that we should take deep breaths.

Paddling was permitted. Rev. Byng would roll up his trousers whilst Mrs Byng tucked her skirt into what appeared to be voluminous underwear. Peering into the muddy water, we would fish with our hands for any tiny crabs unlucky enough to be in that part of the beach at that time.

We had no bathing trunks and certainly there were no towels. Our feet, legs and the bottoms of our short trousers got wet – and dried off as we walked along, carrying socks and shoes.

Once when we were walking on the pavement at high tide, a newly-joined skinny boy slid down the rocky slope into the sea. Mrs Byng soon fished the lad out, landing him on the paving stones with a flourish, but his clothing was soaking wet.

I was instructed to remove my underpants so that the wretched boy could spend the rest of the day wearing them. I considered it to be highly undignified and, furthermore, I do not recall that those underpants were returned to me.

We took a packed lunch (most of which had been consumed by the time we reached Southend) and the day would end with high tea in a café on the seafront – definitely the highlight of the outing. I cannot remember what we had to eat (although in my mind's eye I can see tier upon tier of cream cakes), but whatever it was, it was a change from post-war rationing.

I realise in retrospect that, strangely, the men of the choir did not attend these outings. I wonder why?

The night the fire alarm went off!

Choir practice had its lighter moments in the late 1940s. The Rev. Byng would appear most Thursday evenings halfway through practice, taking his place in his stall, from where he would conduct the speed of singing by banging with his right hand on the side of his reading desk – much to the annoyance of Mr Butler, the

Organist and Choirmaster, who would make his displeasure known by tutting aloud and going beetroot red in the face.

On one such balmy summer's evening young-son-of-the-churchwarden-Ken was sent outside by the Rev. Byng for some misdemeanour. A few minutes later we choirboys spotted Ken creeping up the aisle with a goodly armful of fresh grass cuttings. We could hardly contain ourselves as Ken crept nearer and nearer to the unsuspecting Rev. Byng who, by now, was banging the side of his stall with more than usual gusto. We boys collapsed in gales of laughter as Ken threw the grass cuttings over a startled Rev. Byng! The last we saw of Ken that evening was the Vicar leading him by the ear down the aisle and out the church door – no doubt taking him home for suitable admonishment by his churchwarden father.

On another balmy summer's evening (for the evenings were always thus) we choirboys stood on the pavement on Aldborough Road North outside the churchyard, waiting for Mr Butler to cycle along. Choirboy Brian – whose long blond hair and husky voice set all the maidens of the parish ajitter (especially, it has to be recorded, Pat and Val) – was explaining to newly-joined Jimmy the purpose of the tall red post with a glass box on top which stood on the pavement edge. Jimmy was barely seven, a slip of a lad and skinny with it – and as innocent as a newborn rabbit, who he somewhat resembled in facial features.

That, said Brian, pointing to the post, is a sweet machine and if the glass is broken and the handle inside the box is pulled, sweets will pour out like it was Christmas. Jimmy's eyes stood out on bean stalks at the very idea – for sweets were still on ration in post-War Aldborough Hatch.

Ever helpful, Brian found a stone and picked Jimmy off the ground until his face was in front of the glass box. Smashing the glass, the by now wide-eyed Jimmy tugged the handle – at which a piercing alarm bell rang out and not a single sweet appeared!

Fortuitously at that moment Mr Butler pulled up on his bicycle. Summing up the situation in less time than it took to remove his cycle clips, Mr Butler told us to run like the wind into the church. Seated at the organ, Mr Butler played hymn after hymn after hymn, whilst we choirboys stood in the stalls, singing our hearts out. We heard a fire engine arrive, with bells clanging. A fireman appeared at the door of the church, noted that we were fully engaged in our choral activities and looking cherubic with it, and quietly withdrew.

Some twenty or more hymns, and an hour or so later, Mr Butler swung his legs over the organ stool and moved towards the choir stalls. Not a word of what had happened was spoken as he told us to open our Psalters to go through the pointing for Sunday's appointed psalm.

Keeping the bellows filled with air

The organ at St. Peter's was – and is – a mighty and imposing instrument. Built by Gray and Davison Limited (established 1750) for the 1862 London Exhibition, the organ was later installed in a public house in London's East End, before being acquired by Charles and Bessie Painter of Aldborough Hall, who presented the organ to St. Peter's in 1893 in memory of their son, Charles Alec, who died on 11th February of that year aged six months.

We choirboys of the 1940s knew about the Painters – for a brass plaque told us so – but the other historical facts were unearthed by a later incumbent – the Rev. Lawrence Pickles – who also discovered that Sir Frank Dicksee, PRA (1853 to 1928), used this organ as the model for his painting *Harmony (1877).* Not only that, but the Rev. Pickles placed a reproduction of the painting on one side of the organ which is there to this day.

The organ was hand pumped until 1951 and a rum old business this was. The bellows may still be seen if you peer through the cracks in the timbers at the side of the organ, but the handle that did the pumping (aided by the arms of the pumper, of course) is, sadly, no longer there. The task of pumping the organ fell to the Verger at Sunday services, weddings and funerals. Now it should be obvious to the most casual observer that certain musical renderings – with crashing crescendos and roaring reeds, requiring all the pipes to be used at once – would need more air in the bellows than a soft smoochy piece. But Mr Young, the Verger in the 40s, would have none of it. He pumped with the same rhythm irrespective of the music being played. As a consequence, the bellows would run out of air throughout the playing of *'Onward Christian soldiers'* and *'Fight the good fight'*, whilst there was always a surfeit of air when we trilled *'Blest are the pure in heart'*.

When the air did run out, the bellows would drop with a loud thud as the sound from the organ wound down with a sort of whine. Indeed, it was rumoured that it was Mr Young who removed the plumb line that indicated when the bellows were about to empty.

When the hymn before the sermon came to an end at morning and evening Sunday services, the white haired and whiskered Mr Young would remove himself from the organ and depart through the Vicar's vestry door – returning exactly twenty minutes later to resume his pumping duties.

We choirboys were never certain where he went, but the Dick Turpin, our local hostelry, was a sure bet in our eyes, for a tell-tale aroma of stale beer and an unwashed body pervaded Mr Young's grubby black cassock. If the sermon under-ran the statutory twenty minutes, a choirboy would be summoned to pump the organ until a puffing and ruddy faced Mr Young returned. Should the sermon over-run, Mr Young would snooze the time away until his snoring alerted the preacher to the fact that his time was up.

The task of pumping the organ at Thursday choir practice fell to a choirboy – often a boy whose voice had broken and who was clinging on to pocket his quarterly pay. At other times, Mr Butler would pick a boy who was singing well and did not, in Mr Butler's view, need the practice. But it was hard work and four or five boys would be given the task during a two hour practice. Any boy who allowed the bellows to empty would find Mr Butler leaping from the organ stool to inflict a sharp cuffing to the ear (in fact, so much ear-cuffing went on in the choir that I wonder I have any ears left).

The men of the choir

The men of the choir appeared to mere boys to be a strange breed in the 1940s. They attended all Sunday services and the second half of Thursday night choir practice – but were let off weddings and funerals.

Mr Vernon had two sisters – maiden ladies – a superior-looking wife and two pasty-faced sons. They lived on the Eastern Avenue and appeared at festival services only, although one of the sons had a spell in the choir.

We liked Mr Webb, who lived in Ramsgill Drive. He had a round, cherubic, well-scrubbed face and would occasionally share a cough sweet. Married with a bustling jolly wife, they appeared to have many young children.

We avoided Mr Couzens, who would walk at the trot to and from his home which was some distance away off towards Gants Hill. He was forever in a foul mood, taking perverse pleasure in twisting the ear of any choirboy within reach. His wife was a bit of a looker, turning a head or three on the infrequent occasions when she graced the pews with her presence.

Mr Fairey brought with him his wife, Mrs Fairey, and her sister, Mrs Wilson. If there was a Mr Wilson, we did not see him and as the subject was never raised, we remained in ignorance on this score. All three had tired, worn, heavily lined, pinched faces and cold hands.

The ladies sat near the front of the church in their black or dark navy blue coats and frocks, all topped with hats of some severity and wearing black or navy gloves that were so tight that they could have been born with them on their hands. As a trio they were inseparable, attending services and church functions together. The only time George – for that was Mr Fairey's name – was allowed out unaccompanied was for choir practice, and weddings and funerals when he was organist.

The Faireys and Mrs Wilson lived at the far end of Colenso Road in Seven Kings and walked to and from St. Peter's twice each Sunday – a distance of almost two miles each way.

They trudged to and fro in all weathers – sunshine and rain, hail, sleet, snow and blustery winds. Nothing – but nothing – seemed to deter them. When the bitter winter set in, George would wrap newspapers around his spindly legs, pulling his socks over the newspapers and up above his knees, there to be clipped into suspenders. He would then tie string around the bottoms of his trousers to stop the wind blowing where he did not want it.

We choirboys had a soft spot for George and never played him up. His hands had a permanent shake and when he had to perform as organist, his fingers would sometimes go where they ought not to have gone.

The hymns and psalms were played at a pace that might be described as dead slow and full stop. The Rev. Byng would reach new and dizzy heights of exasperation as he beat time on his reading desk in a vain attempt to get the choir to lead the organ. And we boys sang even slower – just for George.

Three men joined the choir in the late forties. We held Mr Cornish in some awe for he was a mounted policeman and very tall with it, who rode his bike to and from church.

Mr Smith was something of a mystery man who walked to St. Peter's from the depths of Seven Kings. He had a permanent beatific grin on his face.

Mr Bretton was an architect, choirmaster and an organist, too. He would play the organ from time to time if Mr Fairey was unwell or away. He designed the extended church halls at St. Peter's – about which more later.

'Count your blessings one by one'

I seemed to fall effortlessly into the role of Head Chorister and Sole Soloist – or perhaps it was just that the other choirboys preferred playing conkers, fishing for sticklebacks in Happy Valley, or being chased by Pat and Val down the rhubarb fields next to the church.

They nicknamed me D'Arcy, one of three schoolboys in comedian Will Hay's fictitious school that had us laughing in the cinema. I felt rather flattered, for D'Arcy was the brightest boy of the three and, in any case, I picked up all the soloist's fees at weddings (ten bob a time – ten shillings or fifty pence in today's parlance).

I sang the first verse of *'Once in Royal David's city'* at the Service in Nine Lessons and Carols at Christmas in a darkened church, with the lights flicked on for the second verse as the choir and congregation joined in. The choir did not carry candles, nor were candles placed artistically amongst the poinsettia and red-berried holly in the windows – candles were a luxury that could not be afforded in cash-strapped austerity Britain of the 1940s and poinsettia were nowhere to be seen in those far off days. Just lots of holly picked in the churchyard for free – sometimes with berries, sometimes not, depending on whether or not the birds got there first.

My wedding solo repertoire consisted of one song only – *'I'll walk beside you',* made famous by such well-known artistes as Josef Locke, Anne Zeigler and Webster Booth (of blessed memory). But this changed when the Rev. Byng informed Mr Butler that the bride had requested that *'Count your blessings one by one'* should be sung as a solo at her forthcoming wedding.

Now that ballad should not be confused with the other *'Count your blessings',* first published in 1897 in *'Songs for Young People'* in Chicago, Illinois (words by Johnson Oatman Junior, music by Edwin O. Excell, no less) which ran: *'Count your blessings, name them one by one, Count your blessings, see what God hath done! Count your blessings, name them one by one, and it will surprise you what the Lord hath done.'* No indeed!

The version requested by the bride was secular and not religious with words that ran thus: *'Count your blessings one by one, when dawn appears and day has just begun. They will light your hearts with happiness, make each hour bright and bring your gladness.'* Quite different. Quite.

And you will not be surprised to learn (if you did not know this already) that the words and music of that version were written in 1946 by none other than Reginald Morgan and Edith Temple.

I knew that Mr Butler was not amused on hearing that Reginald and Edith's version of *'Count your blessings'* was to be sung as a solo, for his neck went bright red and his glasses steamed up. That, said Mr Butler, is sentimental trash, slush and twaddle, and I will not have one of my choirboys singing such rubbish.

But the Rev. Byng was insistent, as Mr Butler dug his heels in and went a darker shade of purple.

There was much glowering and mumbling between Vicar and Organist for a week or two – until Mr Butler told me to stay behind after Sunday morning service to practice the now infamous – and, in my mind, somewhat naughty – *'Count your blessings'.*

Not wishing to be entirely beaten, Mr Butler made clear to me in no uncertain terms that the piece was totally unsuited to a religious ceremony and that he would even have preferred to play any song by Vera Lynn, the Forces Sweetheart (who he viewed as a crooner and, therefore, beyond the pale) if he had any choice in the matter, which he did not.

The day of the wedding where *'Count your blessings'* was to be sung arrived, but the Rev Byng was nowhere to be seen. In his place was a Vicar we did not know.

We choirboys stood as Mr Butler struck up the well-known *'Here comes the bride, all fat and wide'.* But we spotted something before Mr Butler – for the bride was leaning on the arm of the Rev. Byng as they processed up the aisle.

It was the Vicar's daughter, Favil, who was marrying David Greer, an airman serving on Fairlop Airfield. They had decided that a song that was sentimental trash, slush and twaddle should be sung at their wedding.

I got my ten shillings and Mr Butler went an even darker shade of purple.

The day the girls arrived!

On Trinity Sunday in 1951 a second girl joined Brenda, who had been in the choir for a few weeks. We choirboys believed firmly that church choirs were the prerogative of boys and men, and that there was no place for one girl, let alone two. But we faced the situation with stoicism, whilst doing our best to frighten them off our male-only territory.

The girls wore a cassock with a small, round skull cap with a tassel – which asked to be pulled. We brought grasshoppers into the choir stalls in matchboxes, letting them loose during the sermon, but Yvonne was a country lass hailing from the Suffolk coast – grasshoppers held no fears for her.

But some of our voices broke at that time and we decided to stop running down the rhubarb field whenever a girl gave us the eye and set off in hot pursuit. And there are a number of ladies living in Aldborough Hatch – who today flash their Freedom Passes at bus drivers – who used to leg it down the rhubarb field after us boys, but it would be ungentlemanly to reveal their names.

My earlier love for Ann Butler, the daughter of the Organist and Choirmaster (her of the ginger hair and freckles) took a tear-drenched tumble when she appeared at church on the arm of a rugby player as wide as he was tall. And so it was that we boys of the choir started to go out with girls. Soon the back row of the Savoy Cinema at Gants Hill on Saturdays evenings and hand-in-hand walks in the cornfields on Sunday afternoons became the norm.

It was at this point when the Rev. Byng told the Head Chorister and Sole Soloist with a broken voice that he would start to read lessons in church. Nothing remarkable in that, perhaps, except for the fact that the boy – as you will recall – had the most appalling stammer and could not string more than two words together without spluttering and stuttering.

In recent years Gareth Gates of TV's *Pop Idol* fame brought to the fore the fact that those who cannot speak through a stammer are able to sing – and such was the case with the broken voiced Head Chorister. Today, of course, as Gareth Gates has demonstrated, there are clinics where a stammer can be almost completely obliterated, but it was not so in post-War Aldborough Hatch where sweets were still on ration and the water pipes froze in the loft every winter, it always snowed at Christmas and the sun shone from dawn till dusk throughout the long, hot summer days.

And so Thursday after Thursday the Rev. Byng gave speech practice and Sunday by Sunday the lad stammered and spluttered through four or five verses of the New Testament. The Vicar must have briefed the congregation out of earshot for they sat through ten minutes of stammers without a murmour, a tut or a titter. Six weeks or so passed and – suddenly and without warning – the stammer had gone. And it has not come back to this day.

From church school to church halls

Stand with your back to the porch at St. Peter's and look over to the church halls, where you will see a cross etched in cement high up in the brickwork below the roof eves. Until the church halls were extended in the 1950s, the school bell hung there. Where is it now, I ask myself?

In 1867 – four years after St. Peter's was consecrated – Aldborough Hatch Church School was built in the church grounds. The site was given by the Crown and the school was said to have been built to accommodate one-hundred-and-thirty boys and girls. They must have been very slim boys and girls for that number to get inside. The original school building can be traced – it comprised two rooms beneath the pitched roofs which stand today. Both rooms were heated with open coal fires – the boarded up chimney of one can be seen to this day in the larger of the two rooms. The smaller room was also used as a kitchen, whilst the larger room was the main hall. The school was closed in 1912 when the building was adapted for use as St. Peter's church halls.

To the South of the larger room stood a two storey cottage with a garden – this is now the grassed area on the corner of Aldborough Road North and Oaks Lane. The cottage was used in living memory as accommodation for the St. Peter's Verger and his family. A door at the rear of the cottage led into the larger of the two schoolrooms. The Verger would appear through the door with a grim look on his face if an event in the church halls was running over time.

The church halls were extended in the mid-1950s when the two flat roofed structures were added – the large hall fronting onto Aldborough Road North and the vestry room on the north-west corner. The smaller of the two schoolrooms was divided up into an entrance hall, a kitchen, and ladies and gentlemen's toilets – very much as they are today, although the kitchen went through a major refit and refurbishment more recently. The new toilets were a welcome improvement on the two outdoor toilets that had served church school and halls since the days of Queen Victoria. Cool in summer, they were draughty on a winter's night when the stars could be seen through the gaps at the top of the doors and the wind whistled down below.

The new halls – as they became known – were opened by the Bishop but disaster struck in the ladies' toilets a few hours before the Bishop was to descend on Aldborough Hatch. Delivery of the toilet pans was delayed, but they arrived in the nick of time on the Friday before the Saturday opening. The Vicar and

Churchwardens carried out a final ceremonial tour of inspection on the Friday evening – to find that the doors of the cubicles in the ladies' toilets had been in the open position when the pans were fitted. As the doors opened inwards, the doors were wedged behind the pans and would not close. Curtains were hung in haste and the ladies' toilets were removed from the Bishop's tour itinerary (if they were ever on it).

A day or so later the pans were removed, the doors closed and the pans put back in position. But now a further problem arose, for the doors were too wide and ladies of the narrowest girth could not squeeze inside the cubicles. A carpenter was brought in to cut the doors down to a size that allowed access – and hence you will find that the doors in the ladies' toilets are not as wide as the standard doors you will encounter elsewhere in the United Kingdom.

This former school appears in the local list of buildings of special architectural or historic interest in the London Borough of Redbridge. But I guess this listing has nothing to do with the size of the doors in the ladies' toilets.

A few rum characters

St Peter's has had its share of characters, most of whom seemed for ever involved in raising funds for some worthy cause or other.

Once a year in the 1940s we were urged to give our pennies to the Windward Islands – and we did so, without having a clue as to where these Islands were or why we had to give them pennies and, when we did so, what happened to them. We also collected for the waifs and strays. It was many years later when I appreciated who the waifs and strays were – as a child I firmly believed them to be dogs and cats.

When money was needed and the congregation was asked for ideas, the suggestion from Mrs Cooper, wife of one of the Churchwardens, was always the same – that we might *"run a little whist drive".* Weekday whist drives were held weekly, but the *"little whist drives"* to which Mrs Cooper was so attached would take place on Saturday evenings. And these were grand affairs, the whist being played in total and complete silence, with tea and cakes during the interval. And woe betides anyone who dared to speak, titter or cough whilst the games were in progress. The games were played on wooden folding card tables covered on top with green baize. Again, woe betides anyone who used one of these tables for anything but the playing of whist.

Whist drives – little or otherwise – appear to have played an important part in the life of St. Peter's in the days of yore. There is mention of the gatherings in the parish magazine for November 1936 – I was three at the time and had first visited St. Peter's in April of that year for my sister's baptism. There it is recorded that *"short whist drives"* would take place *'during the evenings'* of the two-day All-Seasons Bazaar.

A bit like the raffles of more recent years, for it is said these days that *'whenever two or three are gathered together at St. Peter's, there shall be a raffle'.* (It has been whispered that this is stated in the *'Book of Common Prayer',* but in spite of intensive searching amongst its pages, I have been unable to locate it to date. But I am still looking.) I guess it was very similar with the whist drives.

Mr Young, the Verger in the late 1940s (him of the grubby black cassock that reeked of stale beer) fell foul of the Vicar and Churchwardens at some point in time. We did not know why, nor did we dare ask (for in those days one did not ask questions of your betters), but the first we knew that something was amiss was when Mr Young and family were evicted from the cottage adjoining the church halls. Not to be outdone, Mr Young camped out in the Vicar's vestry – off the chancel below the tower – as the nation's tabloids descended on Aldborough Hatch. One of my fellow choirboys invested in a copy of a tabloid – the name of which I was not allowed to say aloud in the choir vestry, let alone read, on pain of having my ears twisted yet again. Oh, the excitement of it all, but then it blew over and was referred to in hushed tones whenever we boys hove within spitting or ear twisting distance.

A later Verger ran what appeared to be a lucrative sideline by catering for wedding receptions. There was a rumour that other caterers were warned off should they attempt to step into his fiefdom. I know what happened to him after he moved on from St. Peter's, but the least said about that the better.

I hesitate to refer to those who I would describe as today's characters at St. Peter's – with one exception for she is a lady with a big heart and a great sense of humour, who is happy enough for me to tell stories of some of her escapades. Linda is very short – barely three feet eight inches in height. Fiercely independent, Linda was shopping in Sainsbury's in Barkingside when she leaned over into a freezer cabinet to reach a frozen dessert that caught her eye. Reaching even further forward, Linda toppled over into the cabinet. Standing amongst the frozen puddings, Linda attracted the attention of the manager who took one look at her rising above the black forest gateaux and said: *"What have we here amongst the desserts today!"* as he lifted her out and back onto the store floor.

On another occasion, Linda was told to park at the rear of a shop in Romford and to make herself known by ringing the bell at the back door at the top of a flight of stairs. Unfortunately, the bell was out of Linda's reach, so she went back down the stairs, spotted a milk crate, removed the milk bottles and carried the crate back up the stairs. Standing triumphantly on the milk crate, Linda rang the bell. The door was solid wood, which meant that whoever was inside did not see Linda perched on the crate. As the door was opened outwards, it caught the crate and toppled Linda to the ground. It says much for Linda's courage and tenacity that she is able to laugh about this – and many other similar incidents.

Bazaars I have known and not known

My earliest recollection of a Bazaar-type event at St. Peter's was in the 1940s when these gatherings were called the Sale of Work – for that was largely what they were, sales of things that folk had made. The stalls were arranged round the walls of what is now the back hall, whilst in the middle the Rev. and Mrs Byng reigned supreme over a stall filled with all manner of delights. Towards the end of the event, the Rev. Byng would reduce the prices down to a penny or twopence – I went home once with what he assured me was a teapot stand, but which turned out to be an old (and cracked) tile.

St. Peter's parish magazine for November 1934 informs us that the Bazaar was a two day event, starting at 3.15pm, with Brig-General Colvin and Lady

Gwendoline opening the proceedings on the Friday and the Mayor and Mayoress of Ilford (Councillor and Mrs Griggs, who had been in office for one day) officiating on the Saturday. Readers were promised *'all kinds of stalls and you needn't go home to tea or even supper, both will be obtainable at reasonable prices, and it is common knowledge that for those who are in time, fried fish and crisps'* (yes, *crisps!*) *'will be procurable.*

'Everything must buzz,' the writer proclaimed, adding: *'there mustn't be a dull moment. For two days re-arrange your home duties and your shopping expeditions so as to be present – nay, do your shopping as far as possible in the Parish Hall . . . A welcome awaits you, even if you cannot spend much; because if you are there, everyone will think you are spending and will catch the craze, and do likewise.'*

The following year the event was named – appropriately enough – the Jubilee Year Bazaar. Lady Bethell did the opening honours on Saturday, whilst the stalls and stallholders were as follows: Fruit and Flowers (Mrs Shipton), Confectionery and Toys (Mrs Bennett and Mrs Webbe), Needlework (Ladies' Working Party – Mrs Ferris), Fancy (St. Peter's Guild – Mrs Byng, Vicar's wife), Grocery (Mr and Miss Phypers and Mr Jenvey), Household Good (Girl Guides – Miss Singleton), Men's Stall (Mr and Mrs Goddard), Young People's Stall (Mr and Mrs Walters and Mr Reedman), Treasure Hunt (Young People) and Meccano Working Model (Master P Allies). Mrs Allies and Miss Cranston took charge of Refreshments, whilst *'Madame Foresee will tell you your Past, Present and Future'.* And, of course, there were *'Short Whist Drives at intervals'.* The proceeds were to go to the Forward Movement (whatever that was), Parish Hall Drainage and Church Maintenance Funds.

A year later – 1936 – the event was re-named the All-Season Bazaar and the Friday opener was – you've guessed! – Lady Wise. The stalls and stallholders were much the same – although Mrs Ferris had handed the Needlework to the Misses Jennings and Phypers, Fancy has disappeared and Mrs Byng has moved over to the Grocery Stall with Mr Jenvey, the Organist, and Master P Allies now needs J. Goddard to help him with the Meccano Model – had it grown in size over the year? The Parish Hall Drains appear to have been sorted for the proceeds were going to the Churchyard Extension.

Church and Chapel – built within a year

I wrote the booklet *'From Westminster to Aldborough Hatch – A history of St. Peter's Church'* and this was published by the Parochial Church Council in November 2007. This refers briefly to the Chapel – not a church – of St James which stood on the North-West corner of the junction of the A12 with Hainault Road at Little Heath in the London Borough of Havering, a mile or so from St. Peter's.

Major G. E. Ibbetson built the chapel in 1862 – whilst St. Peter's was also being built – behind his residence at Heath House, Little Heath. It was originally intended for the use of his family and friends, but it attracted a considerable congregation from outside. Major Ibbetson maintained it and employed a succession of curates until his death in 1908, when the Heath House estate was bought by the County Borough of West Ham for the extension of Goodmayes

Mental Hospital. The chapel was leased by West Ham to the congregation, and the last curate, the Rev. Horace R. Landon, remained until 1918.

My good friend and neighbour John knew the Rev Landon in later years – he went on to become the curate at St. Alban's in South Ilford, where John was a choirboy and where he continued to serve as curate until his death at eighty-two in 1940. Rev. Landon was a Tractarian (a supporter of the Anglo-Catholic Revival, which began in 1833). He lived a very disciplined life and would not use public transport on a Sunday, but would walk from his bachelor lodgings in Douglas Road, Goodmayes, to and from St. Alban's Church. A couple of families in the parish would take it in turns to give him Sunday lunch to save him a double journey; and when either was not available to do so, John's Mum would do it.

John recalls that the Rev. Landon was a delightful old man to have at the meal table. He always wore his cassock in the street with a black cloak and a top hat. When listening to John and his fellow young servers talking about bicycles one day, he announced that he used to ride one when he was up at Oxford University. When John asked him the 'make' he said it was a 'penny-farthing'. He would have been an undergraduate in about 1876.

Financial difficulties then caused the congregation at St. James to appeal to the Bishop in 1918, who executed a new lease and placed the chapel under the administration of the Vicar of Aldborough Hatch, in whose parish it lay. Services were continued until about 1930. In 1933 the building was demolished.

The chapel of St. James was never consecrated. It was built of brick, with stone dressings, and consisted of nave, chancel, aisles, transepts and a west tower with five bells. The panelling from the chapel was moved to St. Peter's, where it was installed in the sanctuary and remains there to this day. The brass processional cross was also taken to St. Peter's and these days is used only at festivals, for it has developed something of a wobble, which can be a bit scary when the cross is carried in procession if you are of a nervous disposition and sitting near the aisle at the time. The baptismal registers have been preserved in St. Peter's.

Bernard, who sings lustily these days at St. Peter's, was born and brought up in Little Heath. His father went to the Aldborough Hatch Church School in the grounds of St. Peter's – now part of the church halls. Bernard, who was baptised at St James' Chapel, has numerous relatives buried in the churchyard at St. Peter's, whose graves he tends with regularity. Not only that, but Bernard has reserved a burial space for himself in the churchyard. I would guess there will be a jolly reunion when he is finally laid to rest, although I trust this will not be too soon as characters like Bernard are hard to find these days and we enjoy his attempts to sing '*The Twelve Days of Christmas*', albeit against the better judgement of Jean, his dear and ever patient wife.

And he assures me that he has stopped climbing trees since he fell out of one a year or two ago whilst engaged in some pruning.

The boys in blue

Towards the end of the 1940s, the voices of some of the young choristers at St. Peter's began to break. Their fathers watched as these young tearaways showed a preference for the new-fangled safety razors over the cut-throat variety which they used – as had their fathers before them and, in all probability, their fathers before that.

Clearly, thought the Rev. Byng, something needs to be done if we are to retain the interest in Sunday services of these young fellows who are starting to shave and going out with girls, and probably doing other things of which the Rev. Byng knew little (and of which he might – or might not – have approved). And so it was that the first servers came into being – young men who assisted the Vicar at the altar and in a variety of other ways before, during and after services.

The first thing that had to happen was that a series of whist drives (now there's a surprise!) were scheduled, the profits from which would purchase the light blue cassocks, the white cottas (surplices, but shorter in the body and arms than those worn by the choir, and with square necks,) and the blue belts. In those days – as will be appreciated if you have been paying attention up to now – whist drives were the major fund raising activity at St. Peter's. The potential servers were involved in these events – putting out the tables and chairs, making the tea, plating up (and eating) the cakes and biscuits, and clearing away afterwards. But when the whist was being played complete and absolute silence had to be maintained – or the wrath of some of the more formidable players would come down upon the miscreants like a mighty ear-splitting roar of thunder (but no lightening).

To kit out a server cost around seven pounds, give or take a shilling or two. But the whist players of the 1940s were rather like today's adherents of '*Coronation Street*' or '*Eastenders*' – given the opportunity, they would have played every night of the week with a omnibus meeting on Sunday afternoons. And so it was that within a month or two the whist players were nearing exhaustion point as the cash piled up in the Vicarage and the Rev. Byng set forth with Mrs Byng carrying the coinage (for she was the stronger of the two) to the House of Vanheems, suppliers of all things clerical and religious, in London Town.

The servers sat in the sanctuary, behind the communion rail and on either side of the altar. The two large bishop's chairs, which came from the chapel of St. James at Little Heath, were used with two wooden chairs placed behind so that four servers might be seated at any one time. Later two antique chairs replaced the wooden ones. Dated 1693, the chairs were presented to St. Peter's by Len and Joyce Chapman, who lived throughout their married life in Bawdsey Avenue and worshipped at St. Peter's.

The church had two wooden kneeling desks and two more were made by Mr Dearlove in his workshop in the garden of the bungalow opposite the Vicarage on the corner of Oaks Lane. The desks carry brass plaques in memory of David Michael Greer (but known to everyone as Tuppy – short for Twopence for he was very little), the son of Favil and David Greer, and the grandson of the Rev. and Mrs Byng, who drowned tragically in the Vicarage lake in 1949 when he was two-years-old.

The first four servers were Brian, Geoff, Tony and me. Others joined us as the years went by so that we had eight or more servers at any one time with new members joining the ranks from the choir as their voices broke. Some went off to national service, others moved away, whilst David Ford and Hugh Wybrew entered the ordained ministry. David was at one time a Canon at a Cathedral in the North, whilst Hugh served in London, Jerusalem and Oxford, retiring as a Canon to live in Oxford.

There were servers at every Sunday service – two at Holy Communion at 8am, and four at Morning Prayer at 11am and Evensong at 6.30pm. On Festivals one server got up in time for the 7am Service of Holy Communion – but no-one rushed for that honour.

At morning and evening services, one server rang the bell (two sessions of five minutes each, fifteen and five minutes before the service commenced), another put the hymn numbers on the boards (and took them down afterwards, wearing just cassock with cottas removed as is the correct mode of dress before and after service), another lit the candles before the service and put them out at the end of the prayer book service and before the sermon, another was crucifer carrying the processional cross, one took the choir collection bag round and another accepted the congregation's offerings on the big brass plate. There were jobs for everyone, with a monthly rota so that the tasks were shared around fairly. Those who aspired to do so were encouraged to read lessons.

One problem with being a server was that you could not guarantee that you would be off duty on Sunday evening to sit with your girl friend in the back rows of the church. As the Vicar ascended into the pulpit at evening service, the lights in the body of the church were switched off – need I say more? There are some who regret the passing of this practice of Sunday evening sermonising being carried out in the dark but, sadly, there is no longer a rush for the pews at the back of the church.

Simple pleasures

Much of the social life in these parts in the 1940s and early 1950s revolved around St. Peter's and our pleasures were simple ones. The highlight of the social calendar was the monthly St. Peter's Birthday Party held in what is now the back hall.

These events were a cunning ruse – invented by the Vicar, the Rev. Byng, I'll wager – to have the refreshments paid for by those luckless ones whose birthdays happened to fall in that month. In this way, the church coffers were filled with the entrance fees (all of one-shilling-and-sixpence in real money) with no deductions for expenses. And not only did the birthday lads and lasses have to pay for the tea, milk, sugar and a delicious selection of austerity cakes, but also for the spot prizes.

An important, nay vital, part of the evening was the spot waltz. Here the dancers pranced around the floor until the music stopped, when the Master of Ceremonies (often, but not always, the Vicar) would blindfold some hapless soul (occasionally one of the Churchwardens, but others could be press-ganged into this role if you happened to be standing about looking a bit vacant). The latter would move amongst the dancers as instructed by the MC: *"Two paces to the left, four paces to the right, two paces backwards – touch the nearest couple on your right".* The pair who were touched received one of the spot prizes. Simple enough, but the excitement was intense, I can tell you.

The music was provided by the redoubtable Nora Wilkinson who was a dab hand on the pianoforte. One-time Captain of the Girl Guide Company and, I am sure, a force to be reckoned with in the company's forerunner, the Girls' Friendly Society, Nora had entertained the troops during the war by tinkling the ivories when tea and buns were served in the church halls to the lads and lasses stationed far from home on Fairlop Airfield. Now that the dark days of wartime were behind us, Nora brightened many a Saturday evening at the piano in the grey post-war era.

Later Harry Harmer joined Nora with his piano accordion – and a mighty machine it was too. The trio was complete when Nora's husband, John, joined in with his drum set – and they called themselves the Harmonics. It has to be said that John was the unlikeliest of folk to beat the drums and tinkle with the cymbals, for whilst Nora would smile away with enjoyment and Harry squeezed for all he was worth with a look of contented determination, John had a dour, fixed expression on his face with not a movement of a muscle. But he made a jolly sound with the drums and was adept at clashing the cymbals when the need arose – as it often did.

The dancing was interspersed with games, which would be the excuse for the more daring amongst us to slip outside for a kiss and a cuddle in the churchyard. If only the gravestones could talk, what a story they would tell!

The last dance of the evening was crucial for any lad who was tilting his cap (as the saying went) at a particular young maiden, for whoever you tripped around the floor with in the last waltz of the evening was the girl you would be duty bound to walk home afterwards. There would be much posturing and positioning as the last dance hove into view. Those lads who were not quick enough were left to meander home alone, although it has to be said that occasionally a lass would spurn the boy with whom she had waltzed and walk home arm in arm with a girl friend who had missed out and had sobbed throughout the first verse of the National Anthem, the singing of which brought all social events to an end in those days, with us all standing with backs like ramrods, fists clenched with hands at our sides and thumbs down the seam of our trousers, and with heads held high.

Vicars I have known

I have sat through the sermons of some eight vicars of St. Peter's Aldborough Hatch. I have listened to many of them, but would admit that as a choirboy I would often revert to counting the stars painted on the ceiling in the chancel – I made it ninety-nine or one-hundred-and-one, depending on how wide awake I was at the time.

The Rev. Byng clasped his hands firmly behind his back when preaching from the pulpit, fiddling with his fingers, chomping on his jaws and licking his lips. The Rev. Lawrence Pickles spoke through one side of his mouth, whilst staring out through the window adjacent to the pulpit as though seeking inspiration from the fields beyond. It was he who erected the sounding board above the pulpit to assist the voice of the preacher to reach the distant parts of the church building. Later – much, much later – we installed a sound system with static and roving microphones, something never even dreamt about in the days of the Rev. Pickles.

The Rev. and Mrs Byng retired to a house in Southbourne, left to Mrs Byng by a relative. Yvonne and I spent one Easter there early in our married life. The house was so cold that we longed for bedtime so that we might cuddle-up under the blankets. I would guess that money was tight for a Vicar in retirement, for as we moved into a room they would switch on one bar of an electric fire and turn it off as soon as we left.

The Rev. Pickles lived with his mother in the Victorian vicarage at St. Peter's with its huge garden, lake and meadow – all where St.Peter's Close now stands. A former journalist on the *Yorkshire Post* (a fact of which he was very proud and rightly so, for it was – and is – a prestigious newspaper), Rev. Pickles was a keen gardener, but preferred to work with fork and hoe in the nude. Callers at the Vicarage when the Vicar happened to be gardening were advised by Mrs Pickles to shout out as they searched for the Vicar amongst the geraniums and lavender to give him time to pull on a pair of corduroy shorts which were all the rage at the time.

The Rev. Jack Hesketh came to St. Peter's following a stint as chaplain to the deaf. It was the Rev. Jack who sold off the Vicarage meadow in the early 1960s – as was his right under church law at the time – to a developer who erected the homes that now stand in St. Peter's Close. There was sufficient cash to build what was then a state-of-the-art vicarage and to give the Vicar a salary that exceeded that of the Bishop. But within a year or so, ecclesiastical laws changed and the money was scooped up by the diocese, leaving subsequent vicars with the same salary as their counterparts elsewhere. So in the end the Vicars who followed did not benefit from the sale of the land and the parish lost a valued amenity, a fine garden and meadow where members of the Scouts and Guides camped.

The Rev. Hesketh's daughter continues to love locally and smiles when I remind her of the day I returned to my home to find a somewhat distraught Yvonne standing on the doorstep where she greeted me with the news that *"the Vicar is in our bedroom with a bird!"* Fearing the worst, I dashed upstairs to find the Rev. Hesketh on his hands and knees under our dressing table, trying to catch a sparrow that had flown in through an open window.

Sadly, the Rev. Hesketh died whilst in post shortly before Christmas, to be succeeded by Rev. Bill Barnes, whose wife died within a year or two of them moving into the brand new vicarage, leaving Bill to bring up his two sons alone. Two tragic deaths within a matter of a few years.

But enough about Vicars – for those who followed are hale and hearty. If they had any idiosyncrasies (and I am not saying if they did or did not), I am too much of a coward to divulge them.

Part Three
The world of work

A workman's ticket

In 1949 the aim was to catch a train at Newbury Park Station just before seven-thirty each morning when the return fare into London was half the price charged after that time. These were known as workmen's tickets. As seven-thirty approached, the sounds of fast running feet could be heard on the pavements leading to the station – only to die away as the half-hour passed.

Even if it meant arriving at your destination well before work started, it was worth catching a workman's train for the massive cash saving this entailed.

My father always caught the workman's. He walked at a leisurely pace. I ran. He never missed the workman's. I often did.

The career advice at Leyton County High School for Boys was non-existent. The elite in the 'A' stream – a dozen at the most – were earmarked for two years in the Sixth Form followed by University. The remainder of the A-formers were steered towards a job in the City of London – in the bank or the insurance industry. The B-streamers were sent to look for apprenticeships, whilst the C-streamers were ignored as being worthless. That may appear to be a harsh judgement, but it is how it seemed to me at the time.

My first employment on leaving school at the age of sixteen was with the Ordnance Survey, a Government Department tasked with keeping the maps of the United Kingdom up to date. In fact, shortly after the 1939-45 war, a complete resurvey of the entire country was started and, although I was unaware of this at the time (because no-one had told me and I had not thought to ask), was about to come to an end within a matter of a year or so. Hundreds of men – many ex-service – had been taken on after the war to carry out this task. Few would be required to keep the survey updated once the major work was completed. In my blissful ignorance, I joined something that had almost no career prospects. Few would be made redundant; rather individuals were posted to remote parts of the country and decided to resign rather than risk having to come to terms with living far from civilisation. But at least my father was happy – for I would not become a pen pusher in an office.

Thoughts of going on the stage as an actor had faded as an impossible dream. A perceived ability to write reasonably interesting – and sometimes humourous – reportage was dismissed by my father as unworthy of pursuit. The Civil Service seemed a safe bet and the first thing I had to do was sign the *Official Secrets Act* – something I believe lasts for life.

A year or two after the war the steam trains that puffed their way from Ilford to Newbury Park and on to Barkingside, Fairlop, Hainault, Chigwell and beyond were no more. The railway line into Ilford was filled in; some of the land became allotments whilst flats were built on other parts. Before the war tunnelling had been completed for an extension of the Central Line from Leytonstone through to Newbury Park. The tunnels had been used during the war by Plessey in the manufacture of munitions. It was on the Central Line that we now travelled into London, rather than the LNER into Ilford and on to Liverpool Street Station.

My journey ended at Gloucester Road Station on the Metropolitan and Circle Lines followed by a short walk to the offices of the Ordnance Survey in Cromwell Road, South Kensington. Part of a converted house was occupied by a team of surveyors working in the area with one floor given over to the trainees who spent nine months learning the craft of map-making. Our mentor was a Mr Kelloway, who wore dark suits and ties with white shirts, and appeared to be constantly worried whether or not the twenty or so young men in his care would reach a high enough standard at the end of their time to move out into 'the field' – the term given to which ever part of town or country you would spend your time mapping. When Mr Kelloway was unwell or on leave, a risqué cove of a man took over, spending a lot of his time sitting rather too close for comfort to a few of the young men who seemed to attract his attention. Thankfully I was not one of them.

We young men – there were no girls anywhere to be seen and I can only assume that the civil service of the day considered that map-making was not an appropriate occupation for young ladies – sat on high stools at drawing boards inking over maps drawn on plates. Some map symbol transfers were available, but most of the work was hand-drawn.

I enjoyed the work and the company of my colleagues. We would have fights with chalk and blackboard dusters when Mr Kelloway left the room. Half-way through the morning we would take turns to go to the toilet, where the windows overlooked the Circle Line as it came above ground between Gloucester Road and High Street Kensington.

On the far side of the railway line were houses with flat roofs. In the winter of 1949 a young lady of very fine proportions would take her bath at around eleven, standing at the window of the bathroom for all to see as she dried herself. In the following spring she moved out onto the flat roof to sunbathe in the nude and once this started there was no holding us as we took two or three trips to the toilet each morning if the weather was warm and the sun full out.

Lunch was at a subsidised restaurant for civil servants in another converted house a few roads away. It cost all of ninepence a day, but I had by now found another – and, in my view, more rewarding – use for my pocket money. I had discovered the world of books. The famous red Penguin fiction paperbacks and blue non-fiction Pelicans sold for one shilling and six pence or two shillings and sixpence, depending on the number of pages. Ilford Town Centre had but two bookshops, but South Kensington was alive with them.

At the beginning of the month, I divided my wage packet much as my mother did with my father's pay on Friday evenings. I gave my mother money for my keep, put aside sums for train fares and clothes, and an amount for my ninepenny lunches, but the latter was not all spent on lunch. I divided the lunch money into two – half was for lunch every other day and what was left was spent on books. With ten shillings or so to lash out on books, I could buy a couple of paperbacks and keep some money aside for the big purchase – of a hardback every two or three months. At the beginning of the month I would spend my lunch hours browsing the bookshop shelves or visit the world-famous Foyle's bookshop in Tottenham Court Road on Saturdays to wander through its dusty floors.

J B Priestley's *Angel Pavement* had a sadness that appealed, whilst P G Wodehouse and James Thurber introduced me to humourous writing – I sat on the Central Line laughing aloud the first time I read Thurber's short story *The night the bed fell*. My cycling tours had given me a love of the countryside and my hardback purchases were books that put into perspective much of what I had seen from the saddle and taught me something of the history of the England that I had missed out at school.

The real world

My first – and only – posting after training with the Ordnance Survey was to the Stratford Office in East London. As most of our time as surveyors would be spent outdoors, the offices were sparsely furnished – bare boards on the floor, desks and chairs that had seen better days, a very basic toilet and kitchen. The offices were above a gents' outfitters on the high street – the Fifty-shilling Tailor or some such.

I spent some eighteen months based here, going out for the first six months with experienced surveyors and working as their chainman or theodolyte carrier. This was my first experience of the world of men at work. Many were ex-servicemen; almost all had families to feed and mortgages to pay; one or two had only themselves to worry about. A number swore incessantly and I found this embarrassing when it happened in public, for it was not something you heard in the 1950s. One surveyor was an avowed communist and took every opportunity to attempt to spread his philosophy to anyone who would listen. After a day with him I felt totally brain-washed and somewhat brain-dead.

When it came out that I went to church, sang in the choir and read lessons, there was some good natured ribbing, but one man took it upon himself to put me under pressure to stand up for my beliefs. I found this difficult enough, but the fact that I was just emerging from a life of stuttering made it worse – for I lived under constant fear that the stammer would return and stress was one of the sparks that set me off. Theologically I held my own but when he could see that I was being pressed too far, my interrogator would pull back.

Most of the surveyors used public transport, for only two or three had cars and these were brought to work when there was a dire necessity. This meant lugging heavy bags of equipment on and off buses and trains – chains and measuring tapes, theodolyte, poles, large club hammers and thick nails for banging into the space between paving stones. There was a lot of physical work, far more than I was used to.

The summer of 1950 was boiling hot and working outdoors in the heat of the day was exhausting. We did not carry water with us, for bottled water had yet to appear on the shelves of shops on this side of the English Channel (and if it had, I doubt I would have bought it for fear of what my father might say). We stopped at cafés for mid-morning and lunchtime mugs of hot tea. One day I was so thirsty that I drank water from the canal that ran behind Mansion House Station. Finding toilets was another problem and in an emergency many a bush came to my rescue.

The time arrived when I would be let loose to carry out a survey of my own. I was allocated the area of Wanstead Golf Course – which was fine with me for there were houses around the edges but a vast area of grass in the middle which clearly did not need a lot of mapping. The chief surveyor told me that, as an experiment, I would be required to include the bunkers and tees on my map – something that had not been done before.

And so in January 1951 I set forth with my own chainman to map a golf course and a few houses at fifty inches to the mile. Often the days were bitterly cold and having started work just after eight in the morning, I would find that by three in the afternoon I was physically exhausted and nearly frozen through and through. Early afternoons were often taken.

The chainmen that were sent out with me taught me a lot about surveying (in particular) and life (in general). Again, many were ex-servicemen. Some could have been surveyors, but preferred to take a job where there was little or no responsibility attached.

Growing up

Spending my weekdays with a group of men from a range of backgrounds ensured that I grew up rather fast. School and home had been protective environments, and I found the rawness and harshness of working life hard to take at first. But there were compensations in my social life.

The church played a big part in this. A youth club was started, meeting in the church halls on Thursday evenings. A number of us from the choir would go to the club after choir practice, including Yvonne – one of the two girls in the choir. Yvonne became club secretary and I was elected to the committee. Yvonne lived with her uncle and aunt in a bungalow in Oaks Lane, not far from the church. I would walk her home after youth club and church, and we started to go to the cinema on Saturday evenings.

My father died in the summer of 1951. He left home to catch the workman's train, which I missed that morning. Arriving at his desk, he had a heart attack and died before he could reach hospital. My elder brother had returned from honeymoon a few days prior to my father's death. He and my mother took command of what had to be done. The funeral was at St. Peter's with the burial plot a few yards from the hedge behind which Fairlop Plain stretches towards Hainault Forest. I doubt he had been in a church more than a dozen times in his life until his funeral, but I took comfort in the fact that his body was laid to rest near where I would spend much of my spare time.

There was no company pension for my mother. My brother accompanied my mother to an interview with a director of the firm for whom my father had worked all his life – who handed my mother a cheque for a couple of hundred pounds. Some years later I shared a platform with that director who was a big noise in The Scout Association in London. I decided not to challenge him with the fact that my mother was left virtually penniless after just twenty-three years of married life to a man who had spent his entire working life helping to make cigarettes that would send many to an early death and provide profits for others to enjoy.

My sister married a year or so later and I left home at the end of that year for national service, returning after two years to live at home for four years before marrying. My mother took in a lodger to augment her widow's pension. My mother managed her income and I never ever recall her saying that she needed money for anything. I guess that she had learned throughout her life to live within her means – however meagre.

National Service

Yvonne and I spent the evening of Tuesday 4th December 1951 together – I started my National Service next day. Later that evening I took her home to her Uncle's bungalow in Oaks Lane. We stood in the alley way leading off Aldborough Road North, outside the garages that served the first two houses – as we had done for the past year or so after evenings together. One of the garages was occupied by the Minister at the Oaks Lane Methodist Church. As he came home, he would drive down the alleyway with his headlights full on. I would open the garage door, he would drive in and I would close the door behind him as he called a cheery *"Goodnight".* But that evening something happened for the first time in my relationship with Yvonne. I kissed her – and Yvonne burst into tears!

It may seem bizarre as I write this at the beginning of the 21st Century, but the fact is that that Yvonne and I had been 'going out' for some months and it took my leaving for National Service for me to pluck up the courage to give her a kiss. I guess I was probably more bashful than most in the kissing department and few – in any – of my contemporaries would not have kissed their girl friends before this. But for almost everyone in my circle of friends things would not have gone further and sex before marriage or, heaven forbid, living together, were not only not done but not even contemplated. The very occasional mishap would be hushed up and not spoken about in public. If a neighbour's daughter was married on a Monday, you could guess that there was a 'bun in the oven' (as my mother put it when talking to friends and assuming that I did not know to what she was referring).

Next morning I left home for Brentwood and the Essex Regiment. It had been suggested to all trainees in the Ordnance Survey that we should apply to join the Royal Engineers for our National Service where our map-making skills would be used. When my call-up papers arrived for the infantry, I was more than surprised – and a little hurt – that my request had been ignored.

It was cold and blustery as I climbed the stairs from the platform at Brentwood Railway Station. An army pick-up was waiting on the roadway and two or three other youngsters were soon spotted by the driver, and told to climb abroad as the tailgate was slammed shut. For the next two years my life was not my own.

Warley Barracks stood stark and bleak on that Wednesday morning in December. Surrounded by woodland, it felt cut off from the world I had known since childhood. The next three weeks seemed endless in time and hopeless in purpose. Non-commissioned Officers (NCOs) shouted and swore at the miserable huddle of East London boys who would be transformed into fighting machines – if the NCOs had their way. For most it worked. For some it did not.

Of the dozen of so boys in my billet, at least two disappeared after lights out on that first night and were never seen again. The rest of us struggled to make sense of the orders that were screamed at us in a seemingly never-ending tirade. The rough cloth of the khaki battledress and shirts felt harsh against my skin, but the fleecy white long-johns meant that we kept warm and the irritation was lessened.

Up at six in the morning, we were rarely in bed before midnight. The hours in between were spent marching on the icy parade ground, polishing our boots, spreading Blanco on our webbing, out on the shooting range, in the gymnasium or attending lectures to learn the parts of the rifle and bren gun. Standing outside the quartermaster's stores, our rifles were thrown for us to catch. I missed and slid on the icy tarmac.

I was still a scrawny, skinny lad weighing just eight stone three pounds, and the gym, route marches and cross country runs were pure hell to me. If I was the lightest in my squad, I was not alone in finding the physical side of army life difficult to cope with. The icy cold and harsh winds on the parade ground meant that the skin on my hands and face was red raw.

Many foods remained on ration and few of the boys in my squad had any spare fat – obesity just did not exist. But muscle, too, was in short supply. Spending much of the day in the open air meant that we slept at night and rested whenever the opportunity occurred. For the first time in my life I found myself spending the few off duty minutes stretched out on my bed – not something I had ever done during the daytime at home.

Most of the boys and the NCOs smoked, and throughout the day there would be fag breaks. I did not smoke and had no wish to do so, but I was clearly in a minority of one or two. I sucked Zubes – a popular throat lozenge sold in small round tins – during fag breaks.

Our barrack room was heated with a coal stove which had a circular metal chimney running up to the roof. We were provided with coal, but no kindling to get the fire going. I learned to fold sheets of newspaper into tight balls and to light the fire with these.

Some boys crept off in the dark to find bits of fencing to use as firewood, but as some of this came from the gardens of the married quarters where the NCOs and Officers lived, our betters were not best pleased. We were never caught taking the fencing, but were warned what would happen if we were. Evenings were spent preparing for the morning inspection or for an extra inspection during the evening – imposed because the morning inspection had not been up to standard in the view of the NCOs or the Officers who came round with them.

Apart from during inspections, Officers were rarely seen – except in the cookhouse where we ate our meals. An Officer would appear with an NCO at his side, asking if we had any complaints. The NCO had that look on his face that implied that if we did, we would wish we have never spoken, such would be the wrath that would be unleashed when the Officer had disappeared back to the warm cosiness of his Mess.

I learned how to polish the toes of my boots until they shone so that you could see the reflection of your face in them. Using the bone handle of a toothbrush which had been heated in a fire, the leather was rubbed until the bumps had been smoothed down. Layer upon layer of boot polish was then applied, using a duster and working the polish in through a circular movement of the polishing finger – all the while adding a liberal dressing of spit (water did not work). We learned the skill from the NCO in charge of our barrack room. Too much spit and the polish sloshed around. Too little and the polish went hard. Just enough and a magnificent shine emerged. When we had mastered the toes, the heels were next for the glossy treatment. It was a skill once learned that was never forgotten, but the learning was filled with heartache. The NCOs on inspection were not averse to grinding the heels of their boots into the perfect polished toe-cap – so that you had to start over again.

Making your bed cover to square off your mattress and folding your blankets into a box were other mind-bending skills to be learned. Strips of cardboard – culled from cereal boxes left by the cookhouse dustbins – were used to make the mattress appear to be a box honed to perfection. Your fellow young soldiers were not averse to filching your cardboard whilst you were at the NAAFI canteen or taking a bath – and that meant you had to search around for used boxes to start all over again.

There would be no home leave for at least a month, but as we were approaching Christmas there was the half-promise that there would be leave over the holiday – if only to give the Officers and NCOs some time off with their families.

The twenty or so boys in my barrack room came from a variety of backgrounds, but I was one of only half-a-dozen who could read and write. The fact that so many could not read, let alone write, shocked me. I found myself reading letters aloud to some boys and writing letters in reply for a number whose girl friends or parents had managed to scrawl a few words. Waiting for a letter from home was often painful – and no letter would occasionally produce an outburst of manic behaviour or horseplay. The contents of food parcels were devoured within minutes – and sharing with those whose beds were nearest was not uncommon. There were no public telephones for us to use within the barracks, but we were permitted to go up the road to a 'phone box. As few people I knew had telephones at home, this privilege had little point.

But my time in the infantry was short-lived. My weight was against me for you had to be at least eight stone nine pounds to be an infantryman and I was six pounds short of the requirement.

I was put through a series of army aptitude tests which, so I was told, gave a clear indication that I had a leaning towards matters electrical and for this reason I would be transferred to the Royal Electrical and Mechanical Engineers (REME). I found this faintly amusing, for a matter of days prior to my call-up I had changed a fuse at home – and succeeded in blowing up the fuse box under the stairs in a burst of flash and flame!

But my protestations that I should be off hot foot to the Royal Engineers to engage in some map-making were met with blank stares. Instead I was handed a travel warrant and told to make my way – smartish – from Brentwood in Essex to Blandford Forum in Dorset on Friday 21st December, when most army folk were off home on Christmas leave for turkey, plum pudding and a few kisses and cuddles.

From the infantry to a corps

At Brentwood Station I made a telephone call to Yvonne who was working as a shorthand typist in the Ministry of Works in London. Would Yvonne please meet me at Liverpool Street Station during her lunch hour to assist me to reach Waterloo Station? Of course she would. On meeting Yvonne, I was able to offload some of the stuff I had on or about my person. Dressed in what was known as full service marching order, including full battledress and greatcoat, I had a large pack on my back with a smaller pack hanging below, two pouches at the front, a side pack, a kitbag and a shovel. Yvonne carried the kitbag and the shovel, whilst I just about managed to walk under the weight of the rest.

My arrival at Blandford Forum late on the Friday afternoon before Christmas coincided with a mass exodus of trainees and staff for the holiday break. A skeleton staff manned the bleak and inhospitable forest of huts that stretched as far as the eye could see in the dusk. No-one knew that I would be coming and no-one wanted to know that I had arrived. In fact, had I gone home instead of trekking halfway across Southern England, it is doubtful if anyone would have bothered to find me – but I was not to know that at the time and dutifully reported.

I was given three blankets and a pillow, and told to find a bed for the night somewhere – and preferably out of sight. Adding these to the already impossibly heavy load I had carried with me from Warley Barracks very nearly broke my back, but a kindly squaddie on his way to the cookhouse for his evening meal took pity on me. Settled into a barrack room next door to the place where I would eat seemed to make sense.

After a near sleepless night worrying that I might have to spend the next week or so in this near deserted hell-hole, I carried my blankets back from whence they came, where an orderly took pity on me and produced a travel warrant that would take me home for ten days. I was advised to buy some green Blanco at the NAAFI before departing so that I might spend part of the holiday washing all my webbing to remove the khaki ready for replacing with the correct colour for the REME.

Yvonne had returned home to Suffolk to spend Christmas Day and Boxing Day with her parents, returning to work the next day, which meant that I was able to see her for much of my leave. Indeed, Yvonne was a great help with the Blanco at which she proved to be something of an expert and she was a dab hand, too, at pressing my army greatcoat and trousers.

Back at Blandford Forum for basic training in the New Year, I discovered that many – if not all – my fellow national servicemen could both read and write, which came as a relief after my experience in the Essex Regiment. However, the drill, the cross-country runs, the time spent in the gymnasium hanging on the wall bars in a desperate attempt to pull myself upwards by my puny arms was much the same as at Warley Barracks. The wind howled across the parade ground during the daytime and round – and often through – the huts at night. The groups of barrack huts were called spiders in view of the fact that there were six dormitories – three on each of two sides – surrounding one central ablution block which housed washbasins, toilets, urinals, bath tubs and showers where the water varied from cold to freezing and what-the-hell-is-going-on-here-for it-could-not-get-any-colder-if-it-tried!

Everything during basic training was geared towards the Passing-out Parade at the end of six weeks of intensive preparation. Spit and polish was the order of the day and I learned that if it moved it was best to salute it, but if it stood still it should either be polished or treated to a liberal coating of Blanco or whitewash. Further, if one walked purposefully carrying a bucket of water, no-one questioned what you were up to. I learned never to volunteer for anything or to claim proficiency in any particular skill. Asked to step forward if we could play the piano, one lad did so – and was given the task of pushing an upright instrument from one end of the camp to the other, the purpose of which was never explained to him.

We were threatened with being put back to start training all over again with the next set of raw recruits if we did not meet certain basic standards. We had to complete the cross-country run, although no time limit was given within which this had to be achieved but it was assumed that you needed to return to base before lights out if the run started after breakfast. We also had to take part in a set of drill moves, without falling over, bumping into anyone or disgracing yourself by moving off in the wrong direction.

A further requirement was being able to pull yourself up by your arms when hanging from a wooden beam lowered from the ceiling so that your chest was level with the said beam. It was the latter that I most feared, but I had not reckoned with the fact that the corporal in charge of my billet – who was a regular and not a National Serviceman like the rest of us – would take it as a personal insult if any of his lads failed part of the final test. And so it was that as we hung from the beam before the officer-in-charge of this purgatory, that the corporal would slip along behind the line of heaving bodies to 'assist' the one or two who were in danger of failing to move upwards. And so I passed – but it was a close run thing.

However, as the day of the Passing-out Parade drew depressingly nearer and nearer, God – in His infinite wisdom – intervened. During the night of 6th February 1952 His Majesty King George VI – King of the United Kingdom and the British Dominions, the last Emperor of India (until 1947) and the last King of Ireland (until 1949) – died. When the news came on the radio on Thursday 7th February this threw everything and everyone from the Prime Minister down to the corporal in charge of our billet into a state of abject misery and deep, deep depression. Military and other sad music was played on the radio and every possible opportunity for fun, games or frivolity of any kind whatsoever was totally forbidden.

And thus it was that the Passing-out Parade at Blandford Forum of the Royal Electrical and Mechanical Engineers batch of latest National Service recruits in late February 1952 was cancelled, to be replaced by an informal shuffling about inside a drill shed – hidden from view by passers-by on land or in the air (the sea being some distance away). His Majesty's funeral took place in London on Friday 15th February and, again, we spent the day peacefully and without any larking about. God smiled on me – and of that there was no doubt.

Typing to the *'Post Horn Gallop'*

My father's fear that I would end up as a pen pushing clerk were very nearly realised at the conclusion of my basic training when I was directed to travel to Gosport. With the Passing-out-Parade-That-Never-Was behind us, we were now sent to destinations in the United Kingdom to be taught a trade – for no longer would I be a Private but henceforth I would be known as Craftsman Jeffries. And my trade would be that of Clerk – for which I would need to be trained to touch-type.

And so it was that I journeyed from Blandford Forum to St George Barracks, Gosport in Hampshire. Here I spent the next three months learning to type on a manual machine that was painted black with a metal cover over the keys – for we would become touch-typists who, at the end of three months, would be able to type in time to the *'Post Horn Gallop'*, a piece composed in the 19th Century for piano by H Koenig and arranged with a post horn accompaniment. I guess that H Koenig would have been surprised to learn that his music had such a mundane use.

St George Barracks, built in 1859 of solid stone construction, were formidable to behold. Standing above the harbour overlooking the river to Portsmouth, the wind whistled through every nook and cranny, day and night. Here again I mastered the art of lighting coal or coke fires without wood, using folded newspapers.

And we were not permitted to forget that whilst we were learning to type, we were still soldiers, for every morning we did a bit of marching up and down the parade ground, with the occasional lecture on what to do with a bayonet if the occasion should ever arise whereby a clerk might find he had one on the end of his rifle and someone standing before him who needed to be despatched. Evenings were spent drinking tea in the NAAFI, writing home or polishing in preparation for the never ending round of inspections.

Inspections were held weekly with the threat hanging over our heads that should we not meet the standard of perfection demanded by our billet corporal, all weekend leave would be cancelled. Forty-eight hour passes were available every second weekend and just after five on Friday evenings when we had a pass we lads would run downhill to the ferry that would take us from Gosport to Portsmouth Station and thence to London Waterloo and home. Back on Sunday evening by eleven, we would find those who had spent the weekend in barracks fast asleep – having tasted the delights of the Gosport night life on Saturday evening, they were now exhausted and probably almost penniless for the rest of the week until payday on Friday.

Portsmouth Station late on a Sunday evening was an empty, desolate place where every sound bounced back from the dripping walls and wet platforms. Cold and eerie, damp from the sea that lapped nearby, the place was inhospitable and unwelcoming. A mere forty-eight hours earlier it had been the sparkling entrance to a weekend at home; now it spelt two weeks of drudgery. The walk up that hill down which we had run on the previous Friday evening was interminable.

On the weekends when I stayed in barracks, I walked around Gosport and parts of Portsmouth. On Sunday evenings – for I had laid in my bed until lunchtime to catch up on my sleep – I went to a number of different churches where no-one spoke to me beyond saying a welcoming *"good evening"* as they thrust a hymn book into my hand and looked around to make sure that any daughters were safely out of the way of this uncouth soldier boy.

Typing was taught by an instructor who played records on a gramophone. The recordings were made by a drill sergeant who appeared to be giving orders on a barrack square as he shouted: *"A, B, C space; A, B, C, space; A, B, C, space; A, B, C, space; A, B, C space; A, B, C, space; A, B, C, space; A, B, C, space; carriage . . . return"* – the last two words were screamed in staccato and demanded instant attention and the return of all typewriter carriages in unison – or at the same time. Any craftsman who lagged behind with his carriage returning could expect trouble. As the days wore on, the letters changed and the combinations became more complicated, but the carriages had to be returned in like manner.

I made the *'Post Horn Gallop'* – played by a full brass band on the self-same gramophone – but only just. In fact, we all made the *'Post Horn Gallop'* – but many others only just, too. And having become a reasonably proficient touch typist, I spent the next eighteen months as a Craftsman Clerk, in typical army fashion, without ever being given the opportunity to touch a typewriter. But it was a skill that was to change my life in later years.

Posting

With the *'Gallop'* behind us, we all received notice of our postings for the next eighteen months or so. My widowed mother was increasingly unwell, suffering bouts of depression very largely as the result of loneliness. Her family and, in particular, her husband, had been her life for the twenty-five years she had been married. With her husband dead, two children with families of their own and me away in the army, my mother found it impossible to make friends – something she had not needed to do in the past. Because of my mother's position, it was a relief to learn that I would be spending my time in the UK rather than in Korea where many of my colleagues would be going. I yearned to have the opportunity to travel abroad, but I accepted the fact that my mother was unwell and needed support.

Poperinghe Barracks in Arborfield was the centre for REME servicemen returning from overseas postings and I was drafted into the offices of the Quartermaster's Stores. Here we would receive all the army clothing and equipment being handed in by ex-overseas servicemen and dish out the stuff that they would require in the UK. Most were national servicemen who would be demobilised back to civilian life within a week or two. They would have to sign on to the Territorial Unit nearest to their home which meant they needed to take with them a uniform and some basic equipment.

Poperinghe Barracks, named after a small town in Belgium, was previously located in the south-west of Arborfield Garrison, having been built back in 1939 to accommodate two Heavy Anti-Aircraft Regiments of the Royal Artillery. These remained at Arborfield until just prior to D-Day in June 1944. Following their departure and up to July 1946, the barracks were then used as an Army depot for the assembly and dispatch of troops bound for service in north-west Europe. Now the barracks were for national servicemen in the main returning from service overseas.

The Barracks consisted of wooden huts mostly grouped in the now familiar 'spiders'. The huts for the permanent staff – of which I was one – had single beds, but the servicemen awaiting demob slept on bunk beds, making about forty to a hut instead of twenty.

With so many troops there, the queue for meals had to be seen to be believed. The dining room was about as big as two tennis courts and, as you were walking up to it, you could see the queue winding round the outside of the building. After standing for some time, you would eventually reach the door only to find that the queue went all the way round the inside of the building as well.

The QM's staff was headed up by the Captain Quartermaster, who was something of a lad in my eyes. He did not care much about his appearance, unlike the Adjutant who was all spit and polish. The Captain had a jaunty walk, often had his battledress jacket buttons undone (a major sin for a Craftsman) with his peaked cap at an angle and his leather covered stick in his leather gloved hands. Next down the line came a number of NCOs, sergeants and corporals who did not stay for long – most were marking time towards demob after a stint as regulars.

The one permanent NCO was a corporal who hailed from Scotland. He was, to put it bluntly, a bit thick, but he made up for what he lacked in brain by shouting and swearing at everyone and everything. He was something of a figure of fun because his legs were too short for his body and he tended to waddle about, swaying from side to side. He spoke in guttural bursts with a strong Glaswegian accent; few understood what he was on about and most responded to his orders by instinct, and we were usually right. He lived in the small room at the end of our billet – a privilege afforded to regulars as opposed to national servicemen.

Throughout the depot there were civilian staff members, most of whom lived in the nearby villages, some travelling in by bus and others on their bicycles. Mr Bennett – who cycled – was the civilian in the office of the QM stores, assisted at one time by a lady who was somewhat mannish in her ways. It was rumoured that she lived in the village with another lady of like appearance. She frightened me for she made it crystal clear that she disliked men – all men, and not just me. Mr Bennett was a kindly soul and someone in whom I could confide. Another lady who worked in the QM's offices was tall and very attractive. Her husband was a regular soldier, a company sergeant major, and Mr Bennett and the Captain clearly liked having this lady around – and so did we all!

The national servicemen passing through the depot on their way back into Civvy Street did most of the guard duties, so that the permanent staff were only called upon if we were waiting for a batch of demobs to arrive. This meant that we could take forty-eight hour passes almost every weekend. We would go off on Friday afternoon by coach from the guard room, laid on by a local coach company with an eye for business. Trains from Wokingham to London Waterloo were frequent. On Sunday evenings the coach would wait for the train that arrived at Wokingham just before midnight – if you missed that train it was an hour's walk to camp.

For a few weeks I hitched a lift on the back of a motorcycle owned and driven by a rotund national service colleague who lived in Muswell Hill. He was a rather unpleasant character who worked as a clerk in the general offices, but I persevered with the lifts as he charged me half the train fare and I could do with the money that I saved. He would drop me off on Friday evenings at a London Underground station in North London, where I would have to meet him at 9pm on Sunday. We did not wear helmets and I lived in dread of an accident. If it rained, he wore special gear. I just got soaked through. He spoke fluent Russian and when this became known he was whisked away to join the Intelligence Corps. I was not sorry to see him go, but I missed the money I had saved.

The weekend would be spent at home with my mother. On Saturday evenings there were social events at St. Peter's church halls or visits to one of four local cinemas – the Savoy at Gants Hill (later the Odeon, then demolished to be replaced by flats), the Super Cinema opposite Ilford Station (demolished to make way for The Exchange shopping centre), the Regal in Ilford High Road (later the ABC, now a club) or the State at Barkingside (where today the lads and lasses congregate to play bingo).

There were, in fact, two other cinemas – the Kinema (next door to the George at Wanstead) and the Astoria (opposite Seven Kings Station). Both were considered fleapits and not the sort of places where you took your girl friend. Both have now closed – the Astoria building remaining and occupied by a Club serving the Irish community. (When we were younger my brother took me to the Astoria from time to time. He would buy a ticket whilst I would wait outside one of the exit doors. When the usherettes were otherwise engaged he would open the exit doors and let me inside!)

On Sunday afternoons Yvonne and I would take Roy, our collie, to Hainault Forest by bus, or we would walk along Painter's Road to the haystacks at the junction with Hainault Road where we would sit and have a kiss and a cuddle. Often my mother would accompany us on these trips – which meant that the kissing and cuddling would have to wait for another day. Whether or not there was any kissing and cuddling, Roy would run around in circles chasing his tail and enjoying the fun.

By now I was a server at St. Peter's, sitting in the sanctuary and reading lessons. Yvonne was in the choir and as the Vicar climbed into the pulpit to give the sermon on Sunday evenings, the lights in the body of the church would be lowered and I would leave my place in the sanctuary – smiling to Yvonne as I went – and go through to the Vicar's vestry where I left my cassock and surplus. A brisk walk home and then I would be off to the station for the journey back to Arborfield. Leaving Yvonne behind in church was a low point of the weekend, for I knew that she would be drying a tear or two in the choir stalls in the darkened chancel as the Vicar droned on and on.

My late Sunday night journeys back to barracks were a revelation, for I had not realised how many people travelled at that time of the weekend when, in the past, I would have been safely tucked up in my bed in the warmth of home. Not only that, but I was completely unaware of the potential dangers that were lurking around a main line station late at night.

One Sunday evening a man came up to me as I walked off the escalator from the Underground into the main station at Waterloo. He asked me where I was travelling to and, noting that I had half an hour to spare before my train left, he invited me to go for a drink with him. I declined, but he followed me, suggesting that we might sit outside the station and talk until my train was due to leave. Again I refused, but he continued to pester me and I found it difficult to shake him off.

The following Sunday evening the same man was waiting for me at the top of the escalator, but this time my train was leaving in a matter of minutes and I ran off and onto the platform. The next Sunday the man was there again, but this time I spotted him before I got onto the escalator and went back to find another exit from the Underground onto the mainline station.

I mentioned this to Mr Bennett in the QM's office on Monday morning and nothing was said until I was about to go on weekend leave the following Friday afternoon. The Captain called me into his office, where the Adjutant was sitting, for Mr Bennett had told him about my encounters at Waterloo. The Adjutant would be travelling back from London on Sunday evening and would be at the escalator where the man had been waiting for me. It was suggested that I should go up the escalator this time and when the man approached me, I should walk with him. At that point the Adjutant would appear and I should leave – and not look back.

I did as I was told. I heard some scuffling and spotted some Military Police moving swiftly across the concourse, and I was not troubled again on Sunday evenings.

A lorry load of tin helmets

Life in the QM stores followed a defined routine, the one exception being when we were threatened with a General Officer Commanding's Inspection. Fear would be written on every face, the whitewash would be brought out, lines would be marked in white on roads and pathways as though we were all half blind and needed to see more clearly in the dark.

But worst of all was the stocktaking in the stores. I cannot ever recall that we were down on any item of clothing or equipment, but we were often up – and well up at that, and being up was just as bad, I gathered, as being down. On one inspection day, I was out of bed before five and left the depot in a large covered wagon the inside of which was filled from floor to ceiling with tin helmets that were surplus to requirements. Seated in the passenger seat, I was the map-reader as we drove around the countryside, pausing only to eat our sandwiches and drink tea from flasks. We returned after dark. How we managed to accumulate so many tin helmets was never discussed, but I noted that they disappeared rapidly after that day.

From time to time gentlemen who we were assured were *bone fide* businessmen, but who looked more than a bit dubious to me, would arrive at the stores in lorries.

We would load them up with battledresses, overcoats, shirts, woolly jumpers, long johns, socks, boots, mess tins, cleaning kits, housewives (not of the female variety, but the name given to a sewing kit issued to every soldier to darn his socks and sew on loose buttons) – and tin helmets, of course, for we had a lot of those. These, we were assured, were contractors approved by the War Office as purchasers of second-hand goods for sale in army surplus stores throughout the country. And I guess they were, however shady they may have appeared.

National servicemen were encouraged to undertake further education. A number of my friends learned to read and write, or studied for the School Certificate, in the education block within the depot, whilst I decided to take evening classes at nearby Reading University. Looking through the prospectus, I chose two courses – one to extend my knowledge of mapping and the second to study bricklaying. The first made sense in view of my earlier work with the Ordnance Survey, but the second choice remains a mystery. My bus fares into Reading were paid and I was allowed to leave the QM stores early on evening class days – all of which seemed eminently sensible and gave me the chance to wander around Reading before classes began. But after a few weeks, a move away from Arborfield meant that my studies were short-lived – and I learned only the rudiments of bricklaying. All I am able to recall is that a house brick is nine inches in length and half that in width.

After a few months a major reorganisation of the way in which ex-overseas REME servicemen were demobilised took place – and I was despatched to Aldershot to be part of a small team that would work out of a huge barn of a former drill shed. Here we set up a conveyor belt to relieve the ex-overseas lads of their gear and send them on their way with what they would require for the Territorials. We formed an outpost of Arborfield and all had the rank of Lance Corporal, which meant that we were able to use our exalted positions to tell the squaddies what to do, but – more importantly – we could occupy the single rooms at the end of each dormitory.

The lads from overseas spent about ten days with us. The atmosphere was generally cordial – until the night before they were due to be released. Many would go out on the town, get roaring drunk and return to barracks ready to pick a fight with anyone who crossed their path. We permanent staffer Lance Corporals would take to our rooms and bolt the doors – praying that morning would come and the lads would be off home.

Evenings were spent in the big NAAFI building in the centre of town. To reach this we had to pass a series of shady shop premises – including a tattooist whose business was always brisk. I learned from colleagues that there were a number of prostitutes plying their trade, but I was never told where they could be found or what you had to do if you found one. And I did not ask.

My one and only run-in with a prostitute occurred at about this time. I spent a Saturday in London, going from bookshop to bookshop, and somehow strayed off the Charing Cross Road and into Soho, which is not difficult. Walking on a pavement in a road that I realised – too late – was devoid of the kind of bookshops I frequented, a young lady smiled at me and, being a friendly fellow, I smiled back. She called out to me, but I did not catch what she was saying, so I turned round and smiled again. This time the lady started to run towards me. Noting that she was somewhat taller than me and was showing more flesh than seemed decent, the truth of my situation hit me like a bolt of lightening – and I kicked my heels and was away!

Aldershot boasted a live theatre, where I saw a number plays including one starring Claude Hulbert and his wife, Cecily Courtnedge. I read a lot, buying Penguin paperbacks and building up my collection. Thurber remained a favourite author and my laughter often rang out through the billet as I read into the night.

The Coronation of Queen Elisabeth took place in London on 2nd June 1953. One national serviceman from the platoon of which I was a member would be chosen to be part of the gaggle of soldiers who would line the route from Buckingham Palace to Westminster Abbey. There was very keen competition to be chosen for this and as one of the smarter young men about barracks, I spent a lot of time polishing my boots and ironing the creases in my battledress jacket and trousers.

The selection involved marching up and down, and performing various turns, together with a close inspection of our turnout. Two of us were finalists – but the other guy was selected on the basis that, smart as I might be, it was doubted if I would have the stamina to stand for hours and hours and hours in broiling heat.

As it happened, I ended up on guard duty at Aldershot on the night of the Coronation. As all the Officers were away I was appointed Guard Commander, which seemed like justice to me – for the chance to stand in line on a London roadside for my Queen had been torn from me by a colleague who had a bit of muscle.

A lieutenant quartermaster decided that the permanent staff at the demob centre deserved a clubhouse on campus and opened what we called the Green Room in one of the billets. Here we would gather in the evenings to listen to music or play card and board games. From time to time beer would be available. It was here that I experienced being drunk for the first and only time in my life. I passed out and was carried back to my room, where I came round to find myself being put to bed in my clothes. After a night I would long remember, I never ever allowed myself to be drunk again.

Into the City

The two years of national service eventually came to an end. It had been a life-changing experience in many ways. I had learned to type and how to cut grass with a penknife. I had met young men of my own age from all parts of the country and from varied backgrounds – most of whom could read and write and some of whom could not. I had travelled on numerous trains and coaches going to and from home leave. I had tasted brown ale and decided I did not like it. I wrote letters to Yvonne and read her letters which came almost every day. I found out that hundreds of people are travelling late on Sunday evenings when I would have been tucked up in bed. I began to appreciate home comforts, which I had taken for granted in the past.

But in many ways it was two years wasted. Much of what I did lacked purpose. Granted that I learned discipline, but it was more fear that gripped me. From time to time there is a call to bring back national service. I cannot subscribe to that view unless there is a radical change in the way in which national service was operated after the 1939-45 war up to the late 1950s. It needs to have a purpose and clearly defined aims and objectives – something that my two years did not. The one thing that national service gave me was the ability to type, but having trained me to touch-type, I was placed in an office where the only typewriter was used by a lady civilian – who made it clear that if anyone touched her typewriter it would be on pain of death. On demob I found that two fingers worked equally well and, in fact, I type today with just two fingers at considerable speed – beating anyone who has challenged me to date to type faster than they are able to write with pen or pencil.

Anxious as I was to return to civilian life, I remained uncertain as to my future career. I recognised that my prospects with the Ordnance Survey were limited, but I wanted to work outdoors and surveying seemed the route I should take. I discovered that surveyors were required in the insurance business and that there were many vacancies in the City of London for young men who wanted to be trained. And so it was that I joined Norman Frizzell and Partners Limited, Insurance Brokers, in December 1953 on my demob from the army.

With offices in New London Street, next door to Fenchurch Street Station, Norman Frizzell was a leading city insurance broker. I worked in the fire department, which handled insurances ranging from house buildings and contents to commercial premises. A director and a manager were in charge, but I had little contact with them, apart from saying *"Good morning"* when they arrived half-an-hour or so after we underlings.

Two young men and I handled the routine correspondence and the placing of insurances with Lloyd's syndicates by brokers – men who went into the Room at Lloyds each day who were either the sons of directors or friends of the sons of directors or sons of the sons of friends of directors. We each had a shorthand typist to take our dictation. At the age of nearly twenty-one, I was paid three pounds ten shillings a week, whilst my shorthand typist – who was barely seventeen – was receiving five pound notes every Friday.

My immediate boss was a balding man of fifty or so with a well-scrubbed pink-skinned face who lived with his elderly mother in Watford. He wore a black jacket and black striped trousers, white shirt with stiff collars and black tie, and a bowler hat, with a dark overcoat in the winter. He would call each of his three underlings to take any problem cases to his desk once a day. One of my colleagues was married – to a girl in the typing pool – and he was not troubled as were my other colleague and I by the straying hands of our boss which would wander along our trouser legs until we pulled them sharply away. Nothing was ever said about this outlandish behaviour – we just accepted it as something that happened but had to be dealt with.

Two men in their forties worked as surveyors, visiting commercial premises and writing reports. I was told that if I worked hard and passed the examinations of the Chartered Insurance Institute, I too might one day rise to such dizzy heights. One of these was married – happily we gathered – whilst the other was a bachelor who lived with his spinster sister. He seemed a very sad and almost unfulfilled man – but I was told that he had his dramatics which kept him sane. Not one to ask too many questions, I pondered what this could mean. Later I discovered that he belonged to an amateur dramatic society and used the stage to vent his pent up feelings.

The Institute's examinations were three fold – preliminary, associate and fellowship. My School Certificate gained me exemption from the preliminary entrance examination and so I started on the three year associate qualification. Evening classes were available, but I decided to opt for a correspondence course. For the first two years all went well – I passed all three subjects each year first time. But the third year was a problem. The three subjects were insurance law, fire extinguishment and electricity. Over three years I passed the first two each time – but failed electricity. After a further year with the correspondence course, I took electricity at evening classes, but this made little difference. I still failed. The final straw came when at the fifth attempt, I passed electricity and law – but failed fire extinguishment. At this point I decided I had had enough.

Dark suits, white shirts with detachable stiff collars and sober ties (an old school tie preferably) were the uniform for office workers in the City in the 1950s. A company – aptly trading as Collars Limited – called at the office. Those participating in the collar scheme (and we all did) were given two cardboard boxes and twenty stiff white collars (from a selection of designs) on joining. You handed in ten collars and received ten cleaned collars in return every fortnight. Each collar was marked with your name. It cost a shilling or two and saved taking the collars to a laundry for steam cleaning. You would never have to buy a stiff collar again for all you had to do was to mark a worn collar with a cross on the outside and it would be replaced – free of charge. Apart from the fact that the collars were – inevitably – stiff there was a problem in that the tips of the collars would rub against the collarbone, causing holes to appear in the shirt fabric. These could be darned – but there came a point where there was more darning that shirt. I did try wearing my shirt back to front – but this required the co-operation of my mother who would have to do up the buttons down my back. It was an unacceptable solution.

Once again I divided my lunch money between eating and purchasing books. A substantial and satisfying two courses could be purchased at Millers near Aldgate Pump for ninepence – steak and kidney pie, mashed potatoes and cabbage, followed by the best baked jam roll I have ever tasted (then or since) and piping hot custard, all served by a young and sprightly waitress, who gave as good as she got when the lads pulled her proverbial leg. The bench seats had high backs with a table shared by four.

But food could only be enjoyed every other day and on the no-lunch day I would eat a chocolate bar.

Within sight of the office windows stood St. Olave's Church, where repairs were being carried out to the roof. I happened to be standing by the window one day when a workman dropped a heavy spanner from the scaffolding, hitting and denting the roof of a parked car in the street below. I telephoned the *Evening News* to report this momentous event – and received a cheque for ten shillings in the post a week or so later. Thereafter I was ever watchful, waiting for that scoop that would make me more money than I dreamed possible, but it did not happen.

At the bottom of the steps leading from Fenchurch Street Station into New London Street was a barber's shop, where I had my hair cut when I could afford to do so.

I purchased a Dansette record player – the case was red and grey – on hire purchase from Keith Prowse nearby, paying one shilling and sixpence every Friday. It cost around five pounds in all.

Onwards but not upwards

Some three years after joining Frizzells I decided that my prospects for promotion were somewhat limited. Equally important was the fact that – with marriage looming – I would soon need to obtain a mortgage and insurance brokers were not able to help with these things. The big insurance companies were best placed to assist their employees in buying their own home. And so it was that I moved to the Cornhill Insurance Company Limited, whose City office was – not unnaturally – in Cornhill. Here I joined the fire department, training as an underwriter in one of two sections under the eagle eye of the Fire Manager. Here, too, there were surveyors – but not just one working alone and having his dramatics in the evenings. There were four or five – and some were only a year or two older than me, which meant that my chance of getting in there was again remote.

But by this time I had a very active and absorbing private life away from work and concerns for promotion had receded into the background. I saw work as a means of earning sufficient money to enable me to take part in a range of voluntary activities during the evenings and at weekends. I was a server in St. Peter's Church and an adult leader in the Scout Group attached to the church. My spiritual development encouraged me to look more widely as to how I might use my life. No longer did I see the way forward as merely work. I wanted opportunities to explore new dimensions and new experiences.

More than all this, of course, Yvonne and I were now engaged – with the wedding scheduled for the summer of 1957. I needed a career with prospects if my life with Yvonne and my voluntary work were to continue and grow. But a sense of uncertainty took over a year or so before we were to marry as I felt a calling to the ordained ministry. I discussed this with the now retired Rev. Byng and the Rev. Pickles, by now the Vicar at St. Peter's, who arranged for me to attend a three day selection conference at a retreat centre in Surrey. Within hours of arriving, it was clear that I did not possess the academic qualifications needed for the Church of England ministry. Most of the candidates had university degrees and those who did not had matriculated. I was not surprised to receive a letter shortly afterwards advising me that I could not go forward for training, but suggesting that I should marry and reconsider at a later date.

From time to time Yvonne and I would spend a Saturday in London, reserving a place in the gallery of a theatre by purchasing a stool on which you sat to queue. You could leave the stool for a few hours after purchase in the early afternoon, provided you were back in the queue before the theatre opened in the evening. A seat cost all of two shillings or so.

I also saw plays at the Theatre Royal Stratford East, sometimes with Yvonne and occasionally alone. In 1956 Brendan Behan, the Irish playwright and Republican appeared in the cast of his own play *The Quare Fellow* (originally called *The Twisting of Another Rope*) in a production by Joan Littlewood's Theatre Workshop. Brendan had a minor role and I watched him sitting in the orchestra pit, singing and giving every appearance of being drunk, which he almost certainly was. He died in 1964.

I worked for the Cornhill for eleven years until 1968. I played a full part during each day, working hard and with commitment and loyalty to the company, but when the time came to leave the office, I forgot it until the following morning. My real life was outside work.

I moved from underwriting in the fire department to burglary and goods in transit insurances. Here I developed an interest in burglary protection and set up a library of information, making contact with safe manufacturers and lock specialists. I became something of an expert and staff at branch offices around the country would seek my opinion on the kind of protection required to match the risk that the company would be taking.

My first visit to an overseas country and my first flight arose through the contact I had with a major supplier of safes in the City. The company was taking on the franchise for a French safe maker and flew a group of insurance underwriters and surveyors to Paris for three days. We visited the factory to see the safes being made. One evening we had front row seats at *Les Folies Bergère,* where I enjoyed my meal whilst watching the remarkably athletic and beautiful dancers gyrating a matter of a few feet from my plate – until the realisation hit me that they were nude when, I was told, I sat there transfixed. I bought nougat for Yvonne and Graham, and a pair of red hot pants – all the rage at that time – for my daughter, Heather.

Later I joined the claims department, helping to settle claims but also to put in place measures to prevent a recurrence.

My growing interest in Scouting was well known throughout the company and my skill as a leader and lecturer were put to use when I joined a team of instructors at the company's head office in Guildford. This work took me there once or twice a month to lecture to new members of staff on company policies and procedures, using flip charts which were new at that time in the field of education.

The Cornhill's offices were on eight floors. The main male toilet and washroom was in the basement, whilst on each floor there was a smaller toilet. Three of these were designated for ladies whilst the remainder were used by managers who had keys to let themselves in so that they could not be used by the rest of the staff – sort of promotion by toilets. Smoking was not permitted at our desks until 5.15pm – fifteen minutes before the offices closed – and those who wished to smoke could do so in the toilet appropriate to their sex and position within the company.

An elderly member of staff, who was also a Scout Leader, travelled each day by train from Sussex, alighting ten miles of so from the City, where he jumped on his bicycle to ride into work. He would arrive fifteen minutes before the office opened, strip off his cycle gear in the basement toilet, sit naked in a wash basin whilst he splashed water over his body and dress ready to take his place at his desk at nine. It was an awesome sight, but one that we all got used to and thought little about.

In those days first aiders were not designated in offices, but it was assumed that because I was a Scout Leader, I would know how to deal with emergencies. Half way through one morning a staff member on the floor below had leaned back on his chair, which slid on the polished wood floor, tipping him backwards so that his head hit the metal desk behind. A telephone call from reception sent me scurrying downstairs to apply first aid whilst we waited for the ambulance to arrive. There was blood everywhere so I dashed into the toilet on the landing, tore at the roller towel with my teeth, pulled yards of towel out, tore it off and returned to the poor fellow who was on the floor in a pool of blood. Fortunately the ambulance arrived quickly and he was whisked off to hospital. But things did not end there.

Picture the scene in the toilet on the landing – which was designated for use by females only. Five young ladies are having a smoke after coffee when suddenly and without warning that nice Mr Jeffries bursts through the door, attacks the roller towel with his teeth, pulls down a yard or so of towelling, rips it off and rushes out of the door. The ladies locked the door and took some persuading to come out.

On completion of my two years' national service, I was required to join the Territorial Army locally. The nearest drill hall was half-a-mile or so from my home in Horns Road. Two hours on one evening every two weeks – later reduced to once a month – were spent sitting about doing very little. On occasion someone would be very keen and march us up and down for a bit, or give us a lecture on something or other. The occasional Sunday was spent crawling around in damp woodland for there seemed to be a belief in the Territorials that all future battles would be fought in woodland and that it would be damp. This went on for two years after I was demobed, and then came to a grinding halt. The Territorials were no longer compulsory – you joined if you wanted to do so, but I did not.

Two summer camps were held during my time in the Territorials – both just outside Edinburgh. Employers were required to give their staff two weeks extra holiday for this purpose. The Unit Sergeant, a regular soldier, living at home in Billet Road, who cycled down the A12 most mornings on his way to work and therefore got to know me on arm waving terms, knew that I was involved in Scouting. For this reason I was selected to join three or four others at the summer camps to organise the evening entertainment – coach rides into Edinburgh where we joined in the dancing below the Castle to the music of Jimmy Shand and His Band. I bought Yvonne a red and green tartan scarf (made in Scotland by Harrisons) which she has to this day and Jimmy Shand's recordings remain in my gramophone record collection.

My colleagues at the Cornhill were an interesting bunch, all working and earning with one purpose in mind – to keep food on the table for their families, to pay the mortgage and, for some, to take holidays (although these were in the UK for holidays abroad had yet to burst forth as do-able for run-of-the-mill City workers in the 1950s). Three maiden ladies – two quite elderly in my view and one a bit younger – took a shine to me and were very supportive of my Scouting, buying tickets for the annual Scout Group *Gang Show* and even taking their seats at the performances.

One young colleague was married in the same year as Yvonne and me, and was posted to our Bristol office. He and his wife moved into a new house, where he started to design the garden, when he pricked his finger on a rose bush – and died a few hours later. Another colleague – a bit of a lad, tall and gangling, whose wife appeared to put up with his dilly-dallying – was posted to the Norwich branch office and regaled us on the telephone with tales of weekends on the Norfolk Broads. Others were keen gardeners and almost fanatical about their lawns.

Grass seed and lawnmowers were hot topics of conversation at coffee and tea breaks – especially on Monday mornings and Friday afternoons.

The typists worked in a pool, whose manager was a formidable lady who you crossed at your peril. A young lady in her twenties spent much of her time flirting with the men; I am unsure where she worked or what her role was, for she went about flashing her heavily-made-up eyes before disappearing into the depths of the basement where her squeals could be heard from behind the cabinets housing the "dead" files. I was never invited to join her, so I do not know for certain what went on – but the lipstick splatters on the faces of others told their story. She subsequently left to have a baby and marry (in that order) and to live in a village in the Hertfordshire countryside, returning to the office from time to time with the latest addition to her fast-growing family. I recall that she had the most delightful turned up nose. In some ways I was sad that I was not invited to join her in the basement, although had she made an approach I would probably have died with fright on the spot!

A section leader in the fire department belonged to a religious group that would not permit him to eat with anyone who was not a member of his sect. He therefore did not drink tea or coffee when this was brought round to our desks and would sit alone in all weathers in one of the small parks scattered through the city to eat his sandwiches at lunchtime.

The more interesting folk were members of the Corps of Messengers – mostly ex-servicemen with a tale or two to tell. One showed me how to walk from the Bank of England to Liverpool Street Station without getting wet – by making my way through shops and offices. There were no security guards on the doors and you could walk down corridors and through offices without being stopped or asked why you were there. One tall messenger with a limp had moved into the top floor of a brand new post-war built skyscraper block of flats in South London and told me excitedly how it swayed about in the wind, six inches either way, he assured me.

Luncheon vouchers were introduced in the City with the Cornhill being one of the first companies to offer this perk to their staff. Initially they were for one shilling but increased over the years to two shillings and sixpence. A string of sandwich bars under the name Jollys opened where you could buy a freshly made sandwich or exchange your vouchers for tinned and packaged groceries. As a recently married couple, Yvonne and I found it useful to be able to buy some groceries at the end of the week – not what the vouchers were intended for, but valued nevertheless. A well-known boxer opened a baked potato restaurant in the basement of an office block near St. Paul's Cathedral, offering a reasonably priced hot meal on a cold day.

It was said that if you were earning £1,000 a year in the City by the time you were thirty, you had made it and had arrived. I was earning £950 by the time I was thirty. In 1968 I was earning £1,600 a year, but then something happened that would change the course of the rest of my life. At that time a job in the City of London was a job for life and I could in all probability have stayed within the insurance industry in the City until retirement. I have a friend who was with me at Frizzells in the 1950s, who retired from insurance at the age of 65 and lives happily with his wife nearby. He stuck it out for nearly forty-five years.

But for me the City was merely a means of earning sufficient money to enable my family to have a reasonable standard of living and for me to pursue the things I really enjoyed doing.

I said goodbye to the City in July 1968. Perhaps someone was looking down on me with a benevolent eye? A number of things had come together at the right time and I happened to be in the right place so that that I was able to move from the City through a career change that would give me real job satisfaction and open doors that had previously been firmly closed against me.

Part Four
My family

This may well be the shortest part of my book, not because I do not value my family, but rather because I intend this section to be a factual account rather than a peep behind the scenes. There will be no revelations, no prying – for everyone is entitled to their privacy. Things happened within our family that will remain there. Things happen in every family and that is where they should remain. And they will if I have anything to do with it.

However, an account of my life would be incomplete without a section on my family – for they have been the most important part of my time here on earth. They have been my inspiration, my support, my reason for living and striving after the impossible and the improbable. That I have spent insufficient time with them is unquestionable, and I have to thank Yvonne for being there for them when I was not. Yvonne, Graham, Heather and Richard have been the wind beneath my wings, holding me up when I was down and helping me to reach for the heights. If I did not always make it, it was not for the want of trying nor due to any lack of support on the part of my family. Very far from it. And so if they had secrets, they will remain with them to reveal if and when they wish to do so.

Suffolk wedding

Yvonne and I were married on Saturday 21st September 1957 in St. Andrew's Church, Aldringham, Suffolk – in Yvonne's home village. We met some seven years earlier in the choir stalls when Yvonne was one of two girls breaking into an all-boys domain, but the resilience and determination Yvonne displayed at that time in overcoming the opposition (largely led by me, I would add!) was to be repeated over nearly sixty years – years when we were engaged and then married, brought forth children, watched as our grandchildren and step-grandchildren developed, and then settled into an active retirement.

Yvonne was born nine months after me in Suffolk. Her father, Ted Friend, was born in Wenhaston on 10th April 1869, and was a millwright and later the estate carpenter on the Ogilvie Estate just outside Aldeburgh. He had helped to move the windmill which now stands at Thorpeness from its original position in Aldringham.

When the sails refused to go round after the move, Ted was called in to hit just the right spot with his hammer. They moved after that!

Yvonne's mother, Ethel Hammond, was Ted's second wife. Born at Stowmarket on 16th January 1905, Ethel had been destined for Cambridge University, but illness (something that was to follow her throughout her life) meant that she found herself as Ted's housekeeper following the death of his first wife. Later they were married and Yvonne was their only daughter. Ted never retired, but lived in a tied cottage a couple of minutes' walk from his workshop. The same distance in the other direction found Ted on his allotment.

When I first visited Yvonne's parents in Suffolk in 1951, electricity had only recently been laid on to their cottage. There was no piped water, but water for drinking, washing and bathing had to be hand pumped from a well below the back yard. Across the yard from the cottage – one of a row of four – was the wash-house. This doubled up as the kitchen and contained a boiler where the washing was done. Baths were taken in a tin bath in the wash-house and every drop of water had to be emptied down the outside drain. Yvonne attended the village school, reached by walking down the common opposite through gorse bushes that bloomed in radiant yellow for much of the year.

The main line train from Liverpool Street on its way through Ipswich to Norwich stopped at Saxmundham, from where we caught a local train that ran to Aldeburgh on the coast. Thorpeness Halt was Yvonne's local station – consisting of two old railway carriages drawn up onto a short platform. (Sadly, this branch line closed some years later when Mr Beeching's axe fell.) From there you walked the half mile or so to Yvonne's cottage along a road where there were no other dwellings, no pavements and no street lights. On a cloudy night the black was pitch and I was frightened out of my wits at having to walk alone – although the only living things I ever saw were a few rabbits and the odd fox.

Visits to Yvonne's home were always a joy. Teetotal as a family, I gather I was the first person to take alcohol into the home – a bottle of sherry at Christmas. At holiday time Yvonne and I would cycle across the gorse commons and further afield to Wenhaston and beyond. One Easter we picked primroses by the roadside. Once, I recall, the Vicar came silently cycling by as we lay in the sunshine amongst the gorse bushes, but I doubt if he spotted us.

Yvonne's father did not have a day's illness in his life until he was taken ill with liver cancer in his 89th year. He was unwell for but a few days and died peacefully in August 1957 – three weeks before we were to be married. He is buried in St. Andrew's churchyard, but he did not wish for a stone to mark the spot, preferring that the grass should grow over the top. And that is as it is to this day, a grassy mound, unmarked – as he would have wanted.

In the weeks before our wedding we looked for a flat in which we would start our married life. Few of our contemporaries could afford to take out a mortgage to buy their own house at the time of their marriage. If you found an unfurnished or partly furnished flat some weeks before the wedding, there would be the problem of paying the rent whilst still living at home (in my case) or with relatives (as was the case with Yvonne). Leaving it too near to the date of the wedding was fraught with the danger that you would not find anywhere in time.

We answered one advertisement, visiting a large semi-detached house in Gants Hill, where the lady of the house expected us to live in one room at the back from where we would have to cross a yard to a shared kitchen and bathroom. A month or so before we were to be married, we found a flat overlooking Valentine's Park in Central Ilford. We had two rooms upstairs with a small kitchen; we shared the bathroom and toilet with the owners of the house who lived downstairs. It was not a happy arrangement but fortunately it only lasted for just over a year. The lady was overtly house-proud, insisting that Yvonne should wash down the paintwork on the stairs at least once a week – and then inspecting her work by running her finger along the ledges. Living in an upstairs flat had its problems, for example, when you needed to crack a coconut – I took our coconut at Christmas into the park to attack it with a hammer. Being newly married we wanted to invite friends and relatives for a meal, but when we did so we were conscious of the listening ears below stairs.

Six Ford Zephyrs

A number of our friends in Aldborough Hatch wanted to attend our wedding on 21st September 1957. To make this possible we hired six self-drive Ford Zephyrs from Miles Car Hire of Ilford – each with bench seats front and back taking five passengers and the driver. The cost of hiring six cars from Friday evening until Monday morning was a massive five pounds each – eating up almost the whole of one month's salary.

I stayed on Friday night in an hotel in Aldeburgh with Geoff, my Best Man, whilst Yvonne was at her home with Sheila, one of her Bridesmaids, the other being her Cousin Jill. We had three vicars at our wedding – although a fourth was spotted later in the day in a car following us to the train station at Saxmundham. This "vicar" was, in fact, Harry who had donned his clerical hat and collar to lean out of the window of the speeding car to wolf whistle at all the girls! It was harvest festival at St. Andrew's, Aldringham, with the windows decorated with flowers, and fruit and vegetables lining the floor of the narrow aisle.

The reception was held in the village hall which stood behind trees in the vicarage garden a stone's throw from Yvonne's cottage home. Some seventy or so guests sat at long tables and after the speeches Yvonne and I changed, and were whisked away to Saxmundham to catch the fast train to London Liverpool Street. Our friends from Aldborough Hatch – including the "vicar" – joined us on the platform to give us a send off that told everyone on the train that I was a Cub Scout Leader and that we were just married – in spite of our efforts to look like an old married couple.

We found a toilet on the train and removed most of the confetti from our clothes and hair. At Ipswich more just marrieds joined us.

We had booked in overnight at the Great Eastern Hotel at Liverpool Street Station. This was the first large hotel in which we had both stayed and it was overwhelming. The bed was high off the floor, whilst the toilet was at the far end of a corridor of its own. A telegram or two addressed to the newlyweds were pushed under the door – from our Aldborough Hatch friends. Fearing that we would not know how to cope with a meal in a public restaurant, we ordered breakfast in bed – brought to us by two very tall waiters who had clearly been tipped off that we were newlyweds. Sunday was spent travelling by train to Boscastle in Cornwall for our week-long honeymoon.

Married life and two mothers

Our two mothers were widows, my mother living alone but nearby and Yvonne's mother now living with her parents in Stowmarket. Both were often unwell, my mother with a recurring mental illness and Yvonne's mother almost waif-like and needing hospital admissions in Ipswich.

We decided to take both mothers away for a week's holiday after we had been married for a year. Money was tight, but we hired a beach chalet at Mudeford near Christchurch. To reach the beach we had to take a ferry from Christchurch Quay. When the two mothers saw that this was, in fact, a rowing boat with a man at the oars who appeared to be either drunk or severely under the influence, both dug their heels in and refused to budge. When they realised that the only way that they would be able to reach the chalet would be by being rowed across by the demented fellow at the oars, they gave in – but we only came off the sandbank twice, once to go into Bournemouth and the second time to go home. (I viewed Mudeford as a slightly bizarre place at that time, something that was confirmed many years later when visiting my eldest son who was living nearby. The ferry was now motorised, but the charges for the crossing were listed for adults and children, with a separate cost for parrots. I could understand had there been a charge for animals, but there was not – just for parrots. Odd that anyone would wish to take a parrot onto a beach, let alone to a beach chalet!)

We slept in bunks – with my mother insisting on climbing up to one of the top bunks every evening. Against the advice of our mothers, Yvonne and I went on a fishing trip off Hengistbury Head. The sea looked calm from the beach, but once round the headland we ran into mighty waves – well that was how they seemed to me as I hung over the side of the boat being violently ill. So ill was I that the other fishermen insisted that I be taken back to shore – for the fish refuse to bite with me hanging overboard.

A few days before Christmas 1958, Yvonne and I moved from our flat to one on the other side of Valentine's Park, the ground floor of a double fronted house in Cavendish Gardens, off the Drive, owned by Tommy and Stella, who lived upstairs with Marion, their teenage daughter (who was madly in love with Cliff Richard, so much so that his name was painted on the walls we were decorating before the wallpaper was applied). The removal man who took our furniture and few possessions the distance of a mile or so thought we were moving from the frying pan into the fire – for the flat we vacated was very well decorated and the ground floor flat we were moving into needed a lick of paint. But for us it was heaven – for no longer would we have the lady of the house huffing and puffing about the place. We would have our own bathroom and toilet – privacy we had not enjoyed.

In addition to being a server at church, I was now very much embroiled in Scouting as a leader. Our friends were similarly involved at St. Peter's and when anyone married or moved into a flat or house, we would all lend a hand with any decorating. Shortly after Christmas we started decorating, much to the amusement of Tommy and Stella, who were pleased to have us as their new tenants. They were somewhat dumbfounded when Scout Leaders and Rover Scouts arrived most evenings to slap whitewash on the ceilings and wallpaper on the walls.

The ground floor flat was more than adequate for our needs as newly-weds saving hard for the deposit so that we could take out a mortgage on our own house. The extensive lounge ran from front to back of the house, but we could not afford to carpet this expanse of flooring. Tommy placed great faith in the ability of creosote to ward off all manner of insects that would eat their way through his beloved floor boards. Once a year he would descend to the cellar to spray the ceiling above him – and the floor boards in our flat – with creosote. We decided to join in by treating the floor in our flat with a generous coat of creosote and then proceeded to use an army bumper with liberal helpings of floor polish to produce the kind of shine that you could have seen your face in to shave.

We had the barest of furniture – two chairs known in those days as TV chairs which did not have arms and were low at the back so that you could not rest your head – presumably they were designed to keep you awake whilst watching television. Refrigerators and freezers were luxuries we could only dream about, but we made do with a small white box with a blue door called an O-So-Cool. This was above a foot square, made of hardened polystyrene with a dip in the top into which we poured cold water once a day, which worked its way around the O-So-Cool, keeping the contents cool and fresh. We stored our milk and butter here.

My inability to understand electricity very nearly caused Yvonne's demise. Tommy happened to be coming down the stairs when Yvonne picked up an electric fire in each hand – and would have been electrocuted, but for Tommy's quick action. Tommy refused to allow me to touch electrical appliances after that.

Our bedroom was on the ground floor at the front of the house, where we had net curtains on the bottom half of the windows. Early one morning I was dressing in the window when I looked up to see the folk on the top deck of a bus peering down into the bedroom at me in the nude! A road closure had caused a traffic diversion down Cavendish Gardens.

The windows were operated by sash cords controlled by heavy lead weights. Tommy and I worked out that there were over a hundred such cords in the house – and we renewed most of these during our time there. One afternoon Yvonne was cleaning the windows, when a sash cord broke, dropping the frame onto her lower arms. Yvonne was stuck there for some time, as most passers-by smiled and waved, until one realised that she was in trouble and came to her rescue.

Tommy had been born in a house opposite Yvonne's grandparents' home in Stowmarket, Suffolk, and Yvonne had known Tommy as a child. Stella met Tommy when they were serving in the forces during the war. Both now worked in the City, but in their spare time they were avid cinema and theatre-goers. More than that, Stella was a singer of some repute, singing at functions around London and taking part in amateur theatrical productions, whilst Tommy specialised in staging and stage lighting.

We saw Stella play the lead in the *Merry Widow* at the Scala Theatre and over the years enjoyed other amateur productions in which she acted or, in later years, was the producer. Tommy was always at her side directing the lighting.

When we married Yvonne had left the Civil Service and worked for an insurance company in the City. Later she moved to the shipping company as a PA where Tommy was employed. Tommy and Stella became our great friends. One week a rail strike shut down the trains into London from Ilford, so Tommy decided to cycle to the City and I joined him. Dressed in our suits, with white shirts and separate stiff collars, with Tommy sporting a carnation which he purchased each morning from the florist outside Ilford Station, we cycled along the Mile End Road. The traffic was nose to tail and moving very slowly, so that Tommy considered the safest place to cycle was along the white line in the centre of the road. When a motorist objected, Tommy would round upon him with a few well chosen words, safe in the knowledge that the car driver stuck in traffic would not be able to catch us on our two wheels.

Yvonne's mother travelled from Suffolk to visit us one Saturday – and stayed for nine months! She fell ill and was whisked into hospital, spending the following months with us. When Yvonne's grandparents died, her mother took two rooms in my mother's house, but it was not a happy arrangement as my mother was very demanding and difficult to live with. Yvonne's mother moved into a warden supervised block of retirement flats in Woodford, where she lived very happily for a number of years until her death in 1980. My mother's last years were unhappy for she became housebound and died in 1975, a sad and broken woman. Yvonne's mother had a firm faith which sustained her; my mother had none. Yvonne visited both mothers regularly and faithfully, helping them around the home and doing their shopping, and often taking our young children with her. I visited my mother regularly. In her last years I would take her bars of chocolate which she told me she enjoyed. When she died I found bars of chocolate hidden in drawers around the house.

Throughout our time with Tommy and Stella we attended St. Peter's for Sunday morning and evening services, Yvonne singing in the choir and me leading the group of servers. On Church Parade Sundays – the third Sunday in the month – we would leave home at around 7am, attend Holy Communion at 8am with the confirmed members of the Scout Group, and have breakfast with Auntie Bess – who lived upstairs in a house in Bawdsey Avenue, otherwise occupied by Mrs Hall, the grandmother of Graham, a member of the Scout Group.

Bessie Banwell was the spinster aunt of Bob and Ken, both leaders in the Scout Group and former choirboys with me. When their mother died, Auntie Bess (as she was known to us all) stepped in to look after the two boys and their sister. The boys' father married later for a second time – and Auntie Bess moved out. The boys never took to their stepmother and had a yearning for the days when their mother and Auntie Bess looked after them. Auntie Bess had worked in a haberdasher's store in Barking and was always dressed in a prim and proper manner as befitted someone who served lengths of lace and reels of cotton from behind a counter to the ladies of the town.

A home of our own

Four years after moving into Tommy and Stella's flat we had saved a deposit and I had persuaded the personnel director at the Cornhill that he should allow me to take out a mortgage. In June 1962 we moved across Ilford into Aldborough Hatch – a matter of two hundred yards from St. Peter's Church, the centre of our social life.

We had decided that we would try to find a house locally rather than move to one of the new housing estates that were growing up in outer Essex. A number of our friends had moved away, but Yvonne and I were content with our life at St. Peter's and we were near to my mother as well. We looked at a house in Bawdsey Avenue, but it had a sunken bath which I found unnerving and faintly Continental (I fear my father's influence lived on).

On Monday evenings I changed into Scout uniform and cycled across town to St. Peter's, where I ate a sandwich before the Cub Scout Meeting started. One Monday in early 1962 I happened to spot a 'for sale' notice in the window of number 37 Spearpoint Gardens – a matter of a few yards from St. Peter's. After the meeting, I called at the house where Mrs Dawson – who attended St. Peter's and therefore knew both Yvonne and me – told me the selling price. I asked Mrs Dawson to put a reserve on the house until I could bring Yvonne over the next evening. I cycled home and told Yvonne what I had done, and a few weeks later we were on the move – for the second and last time.

Talking one morning to older friends with whom I travelled into London, I realised that I had taken on a massive commitment with a millstone mortgage hanging round my neck that was likely to take me down into the depths of penury. They had paid some £600 for houses nearby of similar size in the late-1930s and had a few years to go before their mortgages would be paid off and they would be debt free. But here was I taking out a mortgage on a house that was being sold at what they considered to be an inflated price. How, they asked, could I ever hope to pay off such a massive and crippling debt? The semi-detached house opposite was going for £500 more than we were paying – and I was unable to obtain a mortgage for that higher sum.

Mr and Mrs Dawson must have purchased a job lot of pink paint before they moved out for every ceiling was richly endowed with liberal coatings of the stuff. The internal doors were dark wood panelled and all the fireplaces had mantelshelves popular when the house was built in 1936. Recognising that there would be much work to be done in getting the house into a style where Yvonne and I would feel comfortable, I had asked if I might have two months' leave of absence from my role as Cub Scout Leader in the 1st Aldborough Hatch (St. Peter's) Scout Group. This was refused – on the grounds that no-one amongst the adult leaders wanted to take on running a Cub Scout Pack of some fifty boisterous eight to eleven-year-olds. They would far rather spend their evenings and weekends ripping out fireplaces, taking down doors and covering them in hardboard, filling in the staircase balustrade, scraping walls and wallpapering, washing off pink ceilings and painting them glorious white.

And so it was that every weekend and evening for some two months there were always at least three or four friends in and about our house working away. Some of our friends were trying out newly-learned skills before taking on homes of their own. It was fortunate that Den's father was a plasterer, for he took over when the fireplaces had been ripped from the walls and made good any damage – and there was some. Another leader understood how to install a ring main – which was just as well because the electrical wiring was primitive if not downright dangerous, with power being supplied to one room via a wire running from a wall socket in the next room through a hole in the adjoining wall.

Whilst Yvonne was immensely grateful for the help we were being given, she did find it somewhat overwhelming – especially when she was taking a bath and could feel the brushes slapping the paint onto the ceiling immediately below.

On the day we moved in, Una, wife of the Scout District Commissioner, who lived further up the road, appeared with bacon and egg sandwiches, and lent a hand with the unpacking. Yvonne and I had a growing collection of books and Una could not get over the number of Bibles and prayer books that she unpacked and placed on shelves. In subsequent weeks, Una would appear from time to time with egg and bacon sandwiches to feed the hungry hordes of decorators.

Our first son

Graham David was born some eighteen months after moving into our house – on Maundy Thursday, 26th March 1964. I called at Ilford Maternity Hospital, having dashed home from the office in the City and changed into Scout uniform – for later that evening I would be at Easter Camp at Brickendon in Hertfordshire with the 1st Aldborough Hatch (St. Peter's) Scout Group where I was now Scout Leader. After all, there was little I could do now that our son was born and Yvonne was in the safe hands of the staff at the hospital, for nappy changing and such things were not skills that I learned.

On arrival at the camp site, I was greeted with a version of the pop song recorded the previous year by the Dave Clark Five – *'Glad all over'* – but with the words changed to *'Dad all over!'*

Graham was underweight at birth at 4lbs 6ozs. These things were worrying to young parents and Yvonne stayed in hospital for two weeks until his weight was such that they could come home.

Graham followed his father into the William Torbitt School at the bottom of the road where we now lived. Later he moved to Wanstead High School, his choice of comprehensive. Graham had taken the Eleven-Plus examination – not because he wanted to go to the only boys' grammar school in the Borough, but rather because he was keen to have a choice of comprehensives. He achieved sufficiently high marks to fall into the category where he could choose which comprehensive he wished to attend and after visiting two or three, he opted for Wanstead.

On one of his last days at the Torbitt in mid-July, Yvonne received a telephone call from the local education authority offering Graham a place at the grammar school. Apparently, Graham had just missed selection by a whisker and as someone who had been selected had dropped out, he was being offered a place.

But we had to give an answer within 24 hours – or the place would be offered to another boy. Graham decided not to take the place – a wise decision, in my view, for he would have been at the bottom of an academic pile at the grammar school, whereas he would be on the top layer at the comprehensive. It was Graham's decision, but based on my experience at a grammar school, I considered he had made the right choice.

Graham joined the 1st Aldborough Hatch (St. Peter's) Scout Group and, as far as I could tell, enjoyed his time as a Cub Scout and Scout. He entered into all the outdoor activities with gusto and much of what he learned stood him in good stead when he had to fend for himself at university and in later life. Graham is a very good cook. He camped out in our garden for a year or so – and was the inspiration for the national competition run in SCOUTING magazine (of which I was then Editor) to see who could camp outdoors for the longest period of time (a feat which later found a place in *The Guinness Book of Records*, the first entrant being a Scout).

Graham was not interested in gaining badges with which to festoon his uniform and when I challenged him about this, he made clear that he looked upon Scouting as a form of relaxation from the hard work of school. It was very much the same with chess. He joined a chess club in Wanstead, playing in one or two weekend-long tournaments in London. One day the secretary of the chess club came to our home to tell us that Graham had a bright future as a chess player, but that he needed to take it more seriously for he appeared to treat it like a game. The secretary was not amused when I replied that I thought chess was a game!

Graham enjoyed his time at Wanstead. We attended all the open evenings and it was clear that Graham was doing well academically, but it was not until his GCSE results that we appreciated just how well. The head teacher asked to see us, suggesting that Graham should try for Oxbridge – which came as a surprise to Yvonne and me, for whilst we realised that he would go to university, we had not considered Oxbridge as a possibility.

Graham gained a place at Lady Margaret Hall, Oxford. He lived in hall and read PPE – but dropped politics after the first year. He travelled to and from Oxford by train. At the end of each term I would meet him at Paddington with a mini-cab to convey all his worldly goods home. On one occasion he left his CDs in the carriage in which he was travelling – when we returned they had been stolen, but we had insurance cover.

I stayed in the guest room in Graham's hall of residence on one or two occasions. Graham took me to a debate at the Oxford Union and we would eat out during my visits – generally accompanied by two or three of his starving friends. On one visit Graham took Yvonne, Richard and me on the river in a punt. On the last day of Graham's examinations, Yvonne, Heather, Michael (Heather's boy friend at the time), Richard and I spent the day in Oxford – and were there as he came out of the examination hall amidst the popping of Champagne corks. We walked back to his room and sat drinking tea, looking over the gardens in summer bloom.

Graham graduated from Lady Margaret Hall with a 2:1 in philosophy and economics, and after two years at Law School in London joined a City firm as a solicitor. Yvonne and I attended the Law Society when Graham had completed his finals – he was amongst the top six in his year, but we only found this out as he was called with the other five to the rostrum.

Today Graham is a partner with a national firm of solicitors, where he is a member of the team of banking and finance specialists. In 2008 Chambers and Partners, the law intelligence company, wrote this about the firm: *The Southampton banking and finance lawyers work closely with their colleagues in the Bristol office, bolstering the group's resources. Market competitors acknowledge the firm's pre-eminent client base as the lawyers handle acquisition finance matters on behalf of big names such as Barclays, Lloyds TSB and Bank of Scotland. The firm has developed a niche specialisation in project finance in the renewable sector and recently acted for developer H J Banks in connection with £30 million facilities for a 13-turbine onshore wind farm in West Durham. Clients highlight the group for "its impressive, cost-effective work," while rival practitioners commend its "constructive working environment." Graham Jeffries leads the banking department and focuses on structured and project finance and asset finance. "Punchy and pragmatic," his technical skill and straightforward approach is unanimously praised: "If I had a serious conflict, I would go to him first," admitted one rival practitioner. His highlight work has included leading the team that represented Chemring Group in its £180 million refinancing, which involved cross-jurisdictional proficiency, and acting for Bank of Ireland on the provision of £10 million funding to Complete Care for the purchase of shares of numerous specialist care home companies.* Not unnaturally, Yvonne and I are very proud of Graham's achievements.

Graham married Polly Prail on 4th August 1985 when he came down from Oxford. The wedding was in Leytonstone, with the ceremony conducted by Polly's father, who was Minister at the church. It was a very happy, family affair – with photographs taken in the garden of Polly's home on the edge of Epping Forest. My brother, never a good driver at the best of times, managed to drive his car into a ditch in the forest – but there were sufficient folk around to drag him out. (In the first six months of driving, my brother backed into a brick wall in a car park, drove over the two-brick-high front wall at his home and right through the rear wall of his garage and into his back garden. Perhaps his exploits helped to convince me that learning to drive was not a good idea.)

Graham and Polly's first home was in a block of flats in Wanstead built to assist young professionals whilst they saved for a deposit for a home of their own. They spent two years there whilst Graham was at Law School. Their first house was in a Victorian terrace in Wanstead. From here they moved to a similar house in Sevenoaks in Surrey, and then to Christchurch in Dorset. Later they bought a chalet bungalow in Bransgore on the edge of the New Forest.

Graham and Polly have a daughter, Annily Joy – who is, indeed, a joy to her grandfather and a young lady of whom Yvonne and I are immensely proud. Born on 2nd September 1994, Annily has achieved much in her short life and I was especially delighted to be invited to be present when Annily was invested as a Sea Scout on 29th February 2008 in Christchurch.

In addition to being highly thought of within the legal profession, Graham has developed considerable skill as a photographer. When Graham and his brother, Richard, were eighteen I gave them each Pentax cameras similar to the one I used. Both have moved on to more sophisticated cameras and into the world of digital photography. I like to think that I have an eye for a good photograph, but I am pleased – and much gratified – to see that my sons have surpassed me in their professionalism behind a camera lens.

Sadly, things did not work out for Graham and Polly who were divorced. Both were determined that things were handled amicably and I know that Graham was generous in the settlement he made with Polly. Polly has a cottage some two or three miles from where they set up home in Bransgore. Graham continued to live in their chalet bungalow, whilst Annily shared her time between them both. Graham met Danielle, herself recently divorced and the mother of three young boys – Fraser, Finlay and Fergus. Both were members of the Bransgore Community Church where they were married in July 2008. As I write they are living in Danielle's house in Bransgore. Planning permission has been granted to extend Graham's bungalow and work is due to commence shortly. After some years of personal sadness, Graham is once again enjoying life – for which we give thanks.

Our family came together once again for Graham's wedding – with Richard and Stine flying home from Norway. We all stayed in a Bournemouth Hotel for the weekend. It was a joyous occasion.

I said at the beginning of this part that there would be no revelations, no prying – for everyone is entitled to their privacy. There is much I could write about Graham, but that is something for him or others to do. I will now turn to my daughter, Heather, and my youngest son, Richard, but – again – I will respect their privacy. Before I pass on, however, I will place on record the fact that whilst all three are very different, they all possess superb qualities of character of which we are so very proud. Yvonne and I have been blessed with fine, loving and supportive children. We have tried to give them the freedom to live their own lives and have not lived their lives for them or our lives through them. We will always be here for them should we be needed.

Our daughter

Heather Lee was born on 18th February 1966 – almost two years after Graham. All of our children were born – financially fortuitously as it happens – in the two months prior to the end of the income tax year on 5th April. In those days a child born at that time meant that there would be a useful income tax rebate – enough to carpet a room or two. In Heather's case, the rebate purchased the timber, concrete posts and brass screws – the materials with which I could build the ranch fence at the front of our house and along one side of the rear garden. And that fence is there as I write, some forty-three years later.

Steve, the taxi driver who lived across the road, was my carpentry mentor in those days, lending me his saws and drills. I had my own screwdriver and a light hammer which my father had used when mending our shoes as kids. Steve had urged me to use brass screws. These were – and still are – expensive, but worth their weight in gold for that fence has withstood the ravages of time and is as good today as it was in 1966.

Only one length of timber has had to be replaced. One morning at the turn of the century I noticed that the top rail on one side of the front fence was smashed. I assumed it had been jumped upon by a young vandal and took myself off to B & Q to purchase a replacement length of timber (which, incidentally, cost almost as much as all the timber to build the front garden fence when I had purchased this all those years ago).

Later that day a lady of our acquaintance who lived up the road called to confess that she was the vandal. Walking along the pavement, the lady had slipped and fallen against the fence. As she was in her late 80s we decided not to report her to the police for anti-social behaviour.

The front gate had to go after forty or so years. Being low it was rarely opened for most folk lifted their legs to climb over the top, but those who found it difficult to lift one leg let alone two had to open the gate – and after a time, the hinges gave out. Two pots stand where the gate once hung – planted with small Christmas trees and crocuses in the spring and bedding plants in the summer.

Heather, too, attended the William Torbitt School, before moving to St. Edward's Church of England Comprehensive School in Romford. Heather was a Brownie Guide and later a Guide. In view of my involvement with the Scouts, Heather was well-known to many of my Scouting friends locally. When Heather decided that she wanted to take her Camper badge, George, the Warden of the local Scout camp site, suggested that she might like to spend the requisite ten nights or so there. When Heather presented herself to the Guide badge examiner and told her where she had camped, the examiner was flabbergasted.

"Do you know what might have happened to you on a camp site with all those boys?" asked the examiner.

"Yes, I do," replied Heather, *"and it didn't."*

Heather was not awarded the badge.

Mel was one of Heather's friends at the William Torbitt. They went to St. Edward's together and have remained good friends to this day. Mel is of mixed race and for most of her life almost all of Heather's friends have been either of mixed race or Afro-Caribbean. (Later Mel married and is now a magistrate at Redbridge – I was pleased to be one of her sponsors when she applied for appointment.)

Yvonne and I recognised that we were living in a country that was fast becoming one which people of many cultures would call their home. Our view was – and is – that provided people were law abiding and had respect for others, we would take them into our home and be friendly. Sadly, not all our friends and neighbours were of like mind; nor, it has to be said, are all those who have moved into this country, for some who have taken up residence as our neighbours in recent years clearly want little or nothing to do with the local community in which they now live – which is very sad for many have held out the hand in welcome.

Two elderly ladies – long time local residents hereabouts – were talking one day in our church halls, not realising that Yvonne was within earshot. One mentioned to the other that Yvonne and Ron's daughter was going out with a black man – *"And Yvonne and Ron go to church, you know!"* one confided to the other. I was baffled by this at the time and remain so.

One evening when Heather was fourteen, there came a mighty splintering of glass outside our home. My office at that time was in the dining room at the front of the house. Dashing to the front door, I was surprised to find a young man standing on the doormat, having walked through the glass panel in the outer porch door.

"Who are you?" I asked.

"I am James, Heather's boy friend!" he replied.

We took him in and bathed a cut on his knee – before sending him on his way. Heather vowed that he was not her boyfriend, but he was a pleasant enough lad. Much later he appeared at Redbridge Magistrates' Court on some minor traffic offence, spotted me on the Bench and pleaded with the Ushers to move his case into another court.

That was, of course, right and proper, but I remain sad to this day that I have not been able to say to him that I would not have come down on him like a ton of bricks in court, as he appeared to think I would, just because he had walked through the glass in my front door.

The smashing glass panel has a sequel. Having replaced the glass panel, a month or so later the same thing happened again – but this time it was the Man from the Prudential. I purchased yet another pane of glass and was about to hit the last tack with a hammer as I fixed the pane into place, when I slipped and the hammer shattered the glass yet again.

I despatched Yvonne to the hardware shop on the parade down the road to buy a replacement pane, whilst I hacked out the broken glass. Realising that Yvonne might have trouble carrying the sheet of glass measuring some six feet or so, I ran off down the road – to meet Yvonne coming up the subway, having negotiated the crash barriers without mishap. We completed the journey carrying the glass between us.

To avoid any other folk walking through our front door, I placed a piece of card in a strategic position. Not long afterwards, we had double glazing installed and a new porch with sliding doors. There has been no repetition of the walking through glass episodes.

On leaving school Heather took a hotel receptionists' course at Waltham Forest College. Her first job was as a live-in receptionist at Baden-Powell House Hostel in Central London. Although I was no longer Editor of SCOUTING, Heather was often perceived as the daughter of Ron Jeffries – which must have been both embarrassing and difficult for her.

Heather learned to drive whilst at Baden-Powell House. Heather and her boy friend at that time owned jointly a red Capri, of which Heather had sole use at times. It was one such occasion when I received a telephone call at my office. Heather had overslept and the Capri had been clamped in Queen's Gate. I dashed off to the underground car park at Hyde Park Corner to pay the fine – and then rushed over to Baden-Powell House with the receipt to prove that we had paid, for the clamps would be released on payment but there was every likelihood of another clamping gang arriving to repeat the process.

Shortly after this as my bank balance recovered, sometime after midnight on a Friday night the telephone woke me from my slumbers. It was Heather who explained that there was a man in the telephone kiosk with her who wanted my credit card details. Without these, Heather told me, she would not be able to have the Capri sorted out.

Heather's boy friend had agreed that she could have the Capri for her weekend off which she was to spend with a girl friend at Baden-Powell House. However, Heather had not told her boy friend that she intended to drive to her girl friend's home in Newcastle. Neither the water nor the oil had been checked, so it was hardly surprising that the engine had completely seized up as they passed through Durham. I gave the man my credit card details. The Capri came home on the back of a low loader with the engine on the rear seat. And my bank balance took another dive.

When Heather moved to main stream hotels in Central London, she shared a flat in Crystal Palace, South London. We visited her there on two or three occasions – once in an emergency when one of her flatmates had flooded the flat and I borrowed from Val-Across-The-Road one of those vacuum cleaners that cope with flood water. Somehow I managed to carry this across London on the Underground.

There may have been other boy friends that we did not know about, but Heather's two boy friends that we met were both Afro-Caribbean and their experiences in and around London in the 1980s and 90s made Yvonne and me very conscious of the fact that racism was a force to be reckoned with. As a child it had been the Jews who were the subject of racist taunts and attacks. That was still so in some part of London, but now those whose skin was black were the target of the racist bigots.

Heather suffered greatly at their hands with vicious verbal abuse as the girl friend and later the wife of a black man, but she had the courage and resilience to face it and not let it spoil her relationships.

A wedding to be remembered

Heather and Robert's wedding on Saturday 13th October 1990 was an event that will be long remembered and savoured by the 150 or so folk who were there – most of whom were invited but some of whom just arrived, which made it all the more exciting.

Heather and I drove the long way round to St. Peter's Church via Painters Road, and then had to go round again, and again, and again. Our good friend and Vicar at the time, Michael Trodden, stretched himself on the seat outside the church in the sunshine. Why? Well, at the time appointed for the wedding to start, the church was only half full – with family and guests from Heather's side. The pews stood empty on the other side of the aisle. Robert's family and guests – most of whom had driven from Croydon in South London – started to arrive when the service was finally underway almost an hour late and were still arriving when the marriage ceremony was over.

We had two organists. Young Tommy, who lived next door and is an accomplished pianist and organist, played the hymns – which was fortunate, because he hit all the right notes in their correct order. Mr Best, a friend of Robert's parents, played the Bridal March by Wagner and other incidental music – which was somewhat unfortunate, because he may well have played all the right notes, but most, if not all, were most certainly in the wrong order. Indeed, as I led Heather down the aisle to what should have been '*Here comes the bride',* I had the distinct impression that we were processing to a new age symphony that was having its first – and probably its last – public performance.

The reception was held in the church halls at St. Peter's with the catering in the hands of a group of young ladies known to us. Our goods friend Brian arranged for us to borrow cutlery, plates, glasses and so on from his emporium in the City, which required the Rev. Michael Trodden and me driving into town on

Friday evening to collect the stuff and driving very, very early on Monday morning to take it back in time for the City lads and lasses to have their lunch.

We had a seating plan, but we had not reckoned with the fact that certain aspects of Afro-Caribbean family weddings were slightly different from those we might have encountered before. Some folk arrived who we had expected, but they insisted that they would not wish to sit where the seating plan suggested they might. Others arrived who were not on the guest list and therefore not shown on the seating plan. They insisted on sitting where they wanted to sit. I tore up the seating plan after a few minutes and everyone sat wherever they wanted to sit or stood if they preferred to do so – and some had to for we ran out of chairs.

Robert's mother arrived from across London with the curried goat nestling in a large pot in her lap – whilst her daughter coped with the rice. Mother insisted that the curried goat and rice would not be needed until much later that evening, possibly around midnight. I had to point out that we were required to vacate the church halls by eleven that evening. In addition to the three tiered wedding cake, baked by Yvonne and iced and decorated by Shirley and Beryl, Yvonne's mother brought three cakes – one a stunning shade of blue (for Robert), one in pink and white (for Heather) and the other in yellow, blue and white (for the first child). All four cakes were given equal status in front of the top table. The three-tiered cake was cut and distributed – with the top tier being kept for the first christening. One of Robert's mother's cakes was cut – but the three cakes went from here to whence they came, never to be seen again. Perhaps they came out for every wedding. We will never know.

I had slightly over-ordered on the sherry (and I had been warned that I had done so by Shirley, who had accompanied me to the cash and carry to make the purchases), but this was put to good use when it was added to a fruit punch. Many guests remarked how good the fruit punch was and how it improved as the evening wore on. Little did they know that Roger, Martyn, Derek, Brian, Alan and others who were in charge of the drinks were adding surplus sherry – and anything else that came to hand – to the fruit punch so that by late evening it was probably capable of laying anyone out stone cold who downed a tablespoonful!

I had been warned that the speeches at Afro-Caribbean weddings tend to go on for ever, with everyone wading in to add their two pennyworth after the traditional speeches were over. The trick, I was told, was for the bride's father to stand and call upon the disco to start – so drowning out anyone who insisted on speaking.

A number of relatives and friends took the opportunity to speak, but the speech of the evening came from Auntie Thelma who started by leading the gathering in a few well-chosen hymns, all of which demanded much hand-clapping, foot-stamping and not a few *'Praise the Lords'* but – fortunately – no musical accompaniment from Mr Best. Auntie Thelma took a shine to Bob and Derek, two upstanding members of the Aldborough Hatch community, sitting on their laps in turn and inviting them to join her in Barbados whenever they felt so inclined.

The message behind Auntie Thelma's speech was simple and direct. Looking firmly at Heather and Robert, Auntie Thelma told them that if they had an argument, they should move into the dining room, and if the argument continued, they should move into the lounge, and if it still had not abated they should go to bed!

Rev. Michael Trodden believes that this is probably the most memorable wedding at which he has ever officiated – and I guess he is right. Indeed, many of our friends have commented since that it was without doubt the best wedding they have ever attended.

Heather and Robert's eldest son, Luke Jerome, was born on 27th November 1991, and Marlon Anthony on 25th July 2000. With Heather and Robert working full-time, both Luke and Marlon spent much of their early lives during the daytime on weekdays with Yvonne and me. Yvonne met Luke from Coppice Primary School in Hainault and brought him to our home until Heather collected him in the evening. The journey necessitated Yvonne riding on four buses each afternoon. When Luke moved to secondary school, he no longer needed Nana to meet him. By this time, Marlon was with us each day and he went to the William Torbitt School, just down the road from our home – like his grandfather and mother, and two uncles before him. Heather, Robert and their two boys are a fine family. Yvonne and I are proud of them all and we love them deeply.

Luke was a Cub Scout in the 1st Aldborough Hatch (St. Peter's) Scout Group and enjoyed his time – but did not make it into the Scouts. He was a good runner and enjoyed a few months at an athletics' club, but did not take it up seriously. At high school he excelled in sports and in spite of the fact that his school was in special measures when he moved there, he did well in his GCSEs, gaining a B, six Cs and two Ds – sufficient to allow him to follow his mother to Waltham Forest College where he is studying accountancy.

Like Graham, Heather and Richard before him, Luke was taken to swimming lessons by Yvonne – although he went to the baths at Ilford County High School in Barkingside, whilst our three took their lessons at the Swimming Pool in Seven Kings. And Marlon went to Seven Kings for his swimming, too, but his Mum took him in her car and he did not have to walk there and back as had the others. How times have changed.

Marlon joined the Beaver Scouts when he was six. Slightly reticent about doing anything new, he seemed to enjoy all the experiences that the Beavers gave him, including sleep-overs at Hargreaves Scout Camp Site up the road from here. Marlon moved to the Cub Scouts in September 2008 and was the first Beaver Scout in the Group to be awarded the new badge – the Bronze Chief Scout's Award.

Robert is rightly proud of his boys and works hard to support them. His main job is with a local supermarket, but in his spare time he indulges his love of music with his sound systems which are installed in clubs and used at charity events around the country – and at the Notting Hill Carnival, about which more later.

There is much more to tell – but not by me. I said I would respect privacy and I will do so.

And then there was Richard John

Born on 28th March 1973, Richard John is our second son. Graham was nine and Heather seven at the time he was born. Graham decked Richard's cot in Arsenal Football Club colours. Heather gave up dolls.

Richard was two or so when Yvonne was suddenly – and without warning – whipped off to hospital on a Monday morning with appendicitis. Yvonne remained in hospital for some ten days, during which I had sole care of the family. By Wednesday evening I had spent what remained of the housekeeping allowance. Yvonne told me I should be more selective in my shopping and stop buying luxury items just to appease the children. In those days we had two machines for the washing – one to wash and the other to spin dry. All went well until I set the spin dryer in motion – when I flooded the kitchen. Richard had a smug look on his face as he said: *"Mummy usually puts a bowl under there!"*

I burned the peas one evening, ruining a saucepan as I did so – something that was to haunt me at family gatherings when the children would tell the story of the peas to my intense embarrassment. A few days after Yvonne returned to take up the reins in the household, Richard confided to his mother that he was pleased she was home as he no longer found it necessary to go to the toilet so often. I had purchased a quantity of fruit in Romford Market and made a fresh fruit salad in the biggest glass bowl I could find. I placed this in the 'fridge, taking it out each evening to be served with ice cream as the family's pudding. By the end of a week, the fruit had become highly alcoholic . . .

Richard joined the Cub Scouts and, like his brother, gained so much from the experiences that Scouting gave him over the years. He moved into the Scouts and Venture Scouts. Rather like Graham, badges did not seem to interest him – it was the camps and the expeditions that he really enjoyed. He learned to love the open air, the mountains and the sea. He also became a very capable cook – all of which helped him when he moved away from home.

He also joined the choir at St. Peter's, but never seemed totally at ease in the cassock, surplus and frilly ruff. In fact, he positively loathed being a choirboy and must have breathed an almighty sigh of relief when he was allowed to hang up his cassock for the last time. Connie Webb, our elderly Welsh Organist, probably did not help, for she would fix him with her beady eyes and call out from the organ bench: *"Sit up straight, boy!"*

From the William Torbitt School, Richard followed his sister to St. Edward's where his skills were in art rather than academic subjects. After O Levels he moved to Havering College and then took a degree in Art and Design at the Kent Institute of Art and Design, Maidstone College. Yvonne and I attended his graduation – when we discovered that he had turned blond, but it was only temporary. Richard lived at home for a time after college as he tried to find work in the design field. The openings were limited and there was a glut of graduates chasing the few jobs that were around. But Richard never gave up and, to his eternal credit, never signed on for unemployment benefit, preferring to find work of any kind to support himself.

He worked at times side by side with friends he had made in the Scouts in a company that carried out traffic and transport surveys. Much of it was boring work, sitting on railway stations counting passengers or on the roadside counting vehicles as they drifted by. Richard passed the time listening to music on his Walkman.

For some time Richard shared a house in North London with friends from college. We gained the impression that Richard was the most organised and often held things together when the others would have allowed their affairs to drift. He was by now a vegetarian and completely self-sufficient in the kitchen. From time to time Richard would return to live with us for a few weeks – then he would be off again to live in London.

Perhaps the most worrying time for Yvonne and me was when Richard became a courier in London. At first he was a cycle courier, which was dangerous enough, but later he tried his hand with a white van and then with a motorcycle. It was the latter that caused Yvonne and me the most anguish, although it was on the bicycle where he had the accidents.

Late one evening during one of the periods when Richard was living at home, the telephone rang. Richard was clearly confused and when I asked him where he was he said that he did not know, but that there was a constable standing beside him. I suggested that he might ask the policeman who informed Richard that he was in the A & E Department of University College Hospital. Richard had slight concussion but was fit to come home. I urged him to flag down a taxi to bring him all the way home where I would be waiting to pay the fare. He arrived home a couple of hours later. At first no taxi driver would take Richard with his bicycle, but when one did so, he would only go as far as Liverpool Street Station. Richard travelled the rest of the way home by train, cycling from Seven Kings.

On another occasion Richard was cycling in the rain past a restaurant when a well-known celebrity ballet dancer jumped out into the road in front of Richard who skidded on the wet surface and fell to the ground. When Richard protested, the dancer asked if Richard knew who he was? Richard said he did and the dancer pirouetted off down the road, with his friends following, shouting and laughing as they went.

Taxi drivers and cycle couriers did not always see eye to eye. On more than one occasion Richard was thrown off his cycle by a car or taxi door being opened directly in his path. I have nothing but admiration for the way in which Richard stuck it out as a courier.

Throughout this time Richard was developing a number of interests. Concern for the environment and a passion for animals were just two. He was also becoming a skilled snowboarder, taking holidays with like-minded friends in France and Switzerland. He enjoyed the cinema, art galleries and eating out. Richard was highly skilled on the computer and was becoming an accomplished photographer. He had a wide circle of friends with whom he shared his very active life.

Richard had one or two cars – including a Skoda at a time when that make of vehicle was the subject of some ridicule. Richard's Skoda was parked outside our house one afternoon when a car came roaring down the road, shunting the Skoda up onto the pavement outside our neighbour's house. I heard the noise, ran downstairs from my office, but too late for the driver had made off. I spotted that a friend – a former police officer – was out walking his dog on the opposite side of the road and he agreed to be a witness if we needed one. My neighbour and his son had also run from their house to see the car speeding away.

Two young police officers responded to my call. One officer took the notes, asking me for my name. I said that I was Ron Jeffries, but the officer said he would use the initial rather than my full first name. When I told him that the owner of the car was my son, Richard, the officer wrote down both our first names. I explained that I had three witnesses. The first was the former police officer – Robert Jeffries. The officer did a double take at yet another Jeffries and one with the initial "R". I gave the name of the second witness as Tommy Goldsmith Senior, but the officer said the senior bit was unnecessary – until I told him that Tommy's son was also – Tommy! The officers left soon afterwards. I sensed that they did not feel they had had a good day.

Richard's opportunity to break away from the world of the courier came when a friend told him about a vacancy in the offices of the World Society for the Protection of Animals (WSPA). He joined the organisation as their receptionist in their Vauxhall offices and then moved on to become Visual Resources Officer, where he honed his skills as a photographer and as a video editor. One of the many tasks he undertook whilst at WSPA was to go undercover to Spain to make a video showing the cruelty of bullfighting.

Richard was never one to wear his heart on his sleeve. He lived his own life and we did not pry. He talked of his many friends, both boys and girls, but never about one special girl – until around the turn of the Century when Stine's name cropped up. Stine is Norwegian and had known Richard at college in Maidstone. They had been in the same group of friends over the next few years – but it was not until Richard was nearly thirty that they started a serious relationship.

Stine decided that she wanted to return to her home outside Oslo and Richard joined her a year or so later. At first they lived in Stine's parents' house, but following the sad death of her father, Stine's mother sold the house to Stine's sister and has now bought a flat. Richard and Stine are now buying a flat in Central Oslo. Both Stine and Richard love Norway – spending time ski-ing, cross country ski-ing and snow-boarding near their home in the winter and following the snow north when the weather warms up. Richard has made a number of attempts to learn Norwegian which is a difficult language to master. He is getting there and will succeed.

Stine works as a website designer, whilst Richard has had a number of short-term contracts working at museums in Oslo, using his skills as a photographer. More recently he has been working at the leading fine art auctioneers in Oslo. WSPA have used him on two assignments whilst Richard has lived in Norway – following whaling ships along the coast to the north. Richard took the still photographs whilst a cameraman made the videos. Both worked undercover on what were dangerous projects where if they were found out they would have been severely beaten up and had their material seized.

Richard has linked up with an animal protection charity in Norway and has carried out undercover photography at night on mink farms in Norway, exposing the horrific conditions in which mink are bred for their fur. His photographs have been published, most notably in the *Independent on Sunday.* Richard was apprehended by the Norwegian police on one occasion during these mink farm excursions, but not charged as he had not broken into premises. We are immensely proud of Richard's dedication to the welfare of animals.

There is just one more story to tell about a member of our family. It is best that he should remain anonymous, which rules out Heather. My son – and I leave you to guess which one – was around ten when I decided the time had arrived when I should explain to him the facts of life. It was a Sunday evening. Heather was asleep, Yvonne was at church. It took all of five minutes, for he was – and is – a bright lad.

"Do you have any questions," I asked?

"Not exactly a question," said the boy, *"but I had thought that when the bride and groom go into the Vicar's Vestry at a wedding that the Vicar did something to them that allowed them to have babies. Are you telling me that I could give a girl a baby when I am fourteen?"*

"Yes," I said, adding, *"but we do not do that sort of thing."*

Quick as a flash he came back with the riposte that: *"You might not, but I may wish to do so."*

Hastily moving to ask if he had any further questions, the boy said that he had.

"Mum will not be home from church for at least forty-five minutes – may I go to the park to play football as Mum does not let me do so on Sundays?"

Promising to be back before Mum returned from church, I waved him goodbye – and sighed with relief.

Part Five
Scouting – at home and away

Too young at seven

My big brother was nearly twelve and would be leaving the Wolf Cubs at any moment to join the Scouts. I was nearly seven and wanted desperately to be a Wolf Cub like my big brother, whose green peaked cap with yellow piping, red and black scarf, and green garter tabs I had long coveted – although the green jersey might be a problem for I could not bear the irritation of anything rough against my skin. It was 1940 and, being wartime, Wolf Cubs not longer met on a weekday evening because of the blackout and the threat of air raids. Instead they gathered in St. John's Church Hall in St. John's Road in nearby Seven Kings on Saturday mornings to enjoy the sort of fun and games for which I would have gladly died.

Big brother told me that I had best join the Wolf Cubs whilst he was still a Sixer, for once he was in the Scouts I would be all alone and have to stand up for myself in the face of any bullies who might set upon me for a good old punch-up. And so it was that my big brother took me to the Wolf Cub meeting.

Mr Collier, the Wolf Cub Leader, was a tubby, smiling, jovial man who we called Akela (which I gathered had something to do with Rudyard Kipling's *Jungle Book*, but I never really got the hang of that side of things). He was a bachelor, living with his sister. My big brother did all the necessary introductions for my stammer made it difficult for me to do much but grin.

My mother decided that as my brother would be going into the Scouts shortly, she would buy him a brand new Scout shirt and I would have his old and well-worn green jersey, albeit that it hung somewhat large upon my skinny frame. Mum lined the itchy sleeves on the inside with her old silk stockings, which was thoughtful.

A month or so went by. I had learned the Promise and Law, and passed the tests of my Tenderpad. The latter was completed on a Saturday morning walk in the countryside – up Aldborough Road, into Painters Road and onwards to Hainault Forest. It was all of three miles, but we caught the bus back, which was just as well because my little legs were aching and I might not have made it home unaided; indeed, the last few yards into the forest were covered with me sitting astride

Akela's wide and well-padded shoulders. I recall that I had to learn the National Anthem, but as I stammered incessantly, it really mattered little whether or not I got the words right. I could have sung it, but this was not allowed – we had to recite.

I was invested as a member of the 2nd Seven Kings (St. John's) Scout Group in a ceremony which almost took my breath away and I carried my badges home for my mother to sew onto the jersey. Big brother went up to the Scouts and a few happy Saturday mornings passed without me getting beaten up before the thunderbolt struck.

Mr Collier called at my home with a form for my mother to complete and sign. I guess that as it was wartime, things on the admin side were a little lax for normally the form-filling would have been completed much earlier and certainly before investiture. To his horror, Mr Collier realised that I was only seven – and you had to be eight to join the Wolf Cubs. There was, said Mr Collier gravely, nothing for it – but I would have to leave and join again when I was eight. I was, indeed, too young at the age of seven.

I watched the bulky frame of Mr Collier disappear down the road and vowed to myself that I would never, ever join the Wolf Cubs, the Scouts, the Boys' Brigade, the Church Lads' Brigade, the Girl Guides, the Army, the Air Force, the Navy, the Fire Brigade, Police or Ambulance Service – or any other gang that required a uniform or had a law or a promise or any of that stuff.

Shortly afterwards my brother moved to the Boys' Brigade, where he wore a rather snappy pill box hat, a blue jersey and a leather strap that went across one shoulder and down his middle. Much as I admired what he was doing, I made a conscious effort to avoid following in his footsteps.

Much later I met Mr Collier again. He was a member of the Scout District Warrants' Committee that interviewed me when I applied for an adult leader's warrant following national service. He did not recognise me and I decided not to remind him of my first brush with the Wolf Cubs at the age of seven. Even later I was invited to speak at the 2nd Seven Kings Scout Group's Dinner and Dance. The event was held in the church hall at St. John's where I had gambolled about as a seven-year-old Wolf Cub and next door to the church where I had sat in the congregation waiting to pluck up courage to ask if I might join the choir. I told the story of my being too young at seven for the St. John's Wolf Cubs and too old at eleven for the St. John's Church Choir. But those who had put a damper on my youthful enthusiasm to be a Wolf Cub or a choirboy were no longer around, so we all laughed merrily.

One night a week

Some fourteen years later, at the age of twenty-one, with national service behind me, a job in the City, studies for the insurance examinations, the youth club and choir at St. Peter's, my mother needing my support and with weekends and occasional evenings to spend with Yvonne, my life seemed set to follow a fairly normal routine in the post-war early 1950s.

One very strong influence on my life, especially since my father died, had been Mr T, as Archie Titmarsh was known. A man then in his early forties, he was a civil servant – the work he did was a reserved occupation during the war – who had lived in East London until sometime in the late 1930s when he bought a house in Applegarth Drive, the road that ran opposite St. Peter's. Next door lived Mr and Mrs Sewell, a lovely East End couple who were great friends with Mr T. They seemed to be in and out of each others houses all the time and as a bachelor, Mr T clearly enjoyed having some meals prepared for him by Mrs Sewell. Both the Sewells and Mr T were members of St. Peter's, Mr T serving as Lay Reader in church and in the 1st Aldborough Hatch (St. Peter's) Scout Group, Mr Sewell taking the role of churchwarden for a time and always a general factotum, whilst Mrs Sewell baked cakes, cleaned the brasses in church and did all the other things that church ladies did in those days – including, of course, taking part in the inevitable whist drives.

Mr T is not to be confused with Mr T, the actor, who appeared in the popular American TV series in the 1980s – *The A Team*. Our Mr T pre-dated the one in *The A Team* by about thirty years. When Mr T – our Mr T that is – died in the 1980s, the Diocese of Chelmsford refused to allow us to erect a brass plaque in the church naming him as Mr T, making the point that people would assume it was in memory of the actor. What rubbish! Everyone in Aldborough Hatch knew Mr T (although some spelt it like the beverage when writing notes to Mr T regarding their offspring). When the plaque was unveiled many folk wondered who this Archie Titmarsh was, but we got round this by installing a bench seat in the churchyard where the plaque bears the name Mr T – for at that time the Diocese did not need to approve the wording on a brass plaque adorning a bench outside the church.

Mr T had that uncanny knack of being able to relate to young people who put their trust in him and yet both were able to keep their distance. I was just eighteen when my father died and Mr T took on the role of father-figure in my eyes – probably without realising this. Over the years I called at his home on numerous occasions, but rarely went beyond the front door, unless a meeting was to be held in his house.

Mr T had recently taken over as Acting Group Scout Leader of the 1st Aldborough Hatch, but continued to run the Wolf Cub Pack of some thirty-six lively 8-to-11-year-olds and needed some help. With my map-making experience, Mr T decided to use this to encourage me to join him in running the Pack.

"Come along and give me a hand," he said. *"It will only be one night a week and you can help with the map and compass work."*

I agreed and, like many others before me and, no doubt, many others after me, I assumed that it would be only one night a week, but it turned out to be a commitment that virtually took over all my waking hours outside work.

For two years from 1954 I worked with Mr T as Assistant Cub Scout Leader, together with Tony and Brian (both former choirboys and now servers) and Ann (whose home was somewhere up north. Ann was a teacher, lodging in Aldborough Hatch).

I was appointed as Cub Scout Leader in 1956, relieving Mr T to take on the role of Group Scout Leader. Tony and Brian found reasons why they wished to retire, but Ann stayed to work with me.

The 1950s and 1960s were in many ways the heyday of the Scout Movement in suburban London. The 1st Aldborough Hatch numbered well over a hundred strong – a full Cub Pack of thirty-six (with a waiting list almost as long), a

Scout Troop of forty or so, a Senior Scout Troop of twenty, and ten or so Rover Scouts of whom some were amongst the dozen or so adult leaders.

We were one of the largest Groups in the District, with a very clearly defined link to St. Peter's Church. On the third Sunday each month, all leaders, Rover Scouts, Senior Scouts and Scouts who were confirmed attended the 8am Holy Communion Service. The church would be packed for Church Parade at eleven that morning. Any member of the Group missing was expected to have an explanation ready for the next meeting. There was no pressure – it was just expected.

The commitment was made clear when a boy or adult joined the Group. It was as simple as that.

Members of the Scout Group sat on the South side of the church, occupying almost every pew and often being squeezed up like peas in a pod. The Brownies and Girl Guides – fewer in number, but still a goodly crowd – sat on the North side. There seemed to be an unwritten rule that the older the Scout, the shorter the shorts, especially on Church Parade – and there was a rush to sit at the aisle end of a pew opposite the bigger – and, therefore, more attractive – Girl Guides

The Scouts' well-known Bob-A-Job Week took place during the Easter school holidays, when Wolf Cubs, Scouts, Senior Scouts and Rover Scouts would offer their services to carry out any jobs at a shilling a time – a shilling being known in those days as a bob and worth about five pence in today's currency. It has to be said that the Wolf Cubs and younger Scouts enjoyed Bob-A-Job Week, whilst the older members of the Scout Group did not.

If you were a small boy with an appealing face and a squeaky voice, householders would often give you a shilling just to see the back of you. And if you smiled especially sweetly, you could receive a drink, a bag of sweets or even an ice cream. If you were older, many a homeowner thought Christmas had arrived and gave you time-consuming, back-breaking tasks that were worth far, far more than the bob they handed you – somewhat grudgingly – at the end of the day.

It was at a Church Parade in the late 1950s when the Vicar announced that, following the success of the Scouts' Bob-A-Job Week, the Girls Guides were to have a similar fund raising event. But when the Vicar informed us that the event was not to be called Bob-A-Job, but that the Girl Guides would be Willing-For-A-Shilling, there was a deathly hush soon followed by peel upon peel of laughter – from the Scouts, of course!

The Vicar turned a deep purple as he speedily announced the next hymn, but even the mighty organ had difficulty in drowning out the laughter that now gripped the congregation.

Yes, it is a fact of history that the Girl Guides launched a fund raising event called Willing-For-A-Shilling – without realising that this might have a meaning that had never crossed their pure and innocent minds. I am uncertain whether or not this was a local or national enterprise.

Not surprisingly, it only ran for one year and – equally unsurprisingly – I have never heard or read of it elsewhere. But my memory is quite clear and I can hear the laughter now.

Vibrancy

There was a youthful vibrancy about the Scout Group, for all the adult leaders were in their late teens and early twenties – with the exception of Mr T, who had a youthful manner in spite of his advancing years. The only sign of age was the fact that he became progressively more bandy as the years went by, which was all the more obvious in his corduroy shorts. He must have known that occasionally a young Scout would mimic his bandiness from behind as he walked up Applegarth Drive, but if he did Mr T never let on.

Ken was Scout Leader – he had joined the Group as a Scout, gained his Queen's Scout Award, did national service in the RAF in Cyprus and followed his father as a salesman in the stationery trade. Bob came right through the Group, gaining his King's Scout Award and doing his national service in the army before returning to work in the chemical industry in East London – and taking on the role of Senior Scout Leader. Brian, son of a police officer, who worked in financial services in the City, was Rover Scout Leader. A number of Senior Scouts decided to stay on in the Group, either as Rover Scouts or as Assistant Leaders – or both. Throughout my time as a Section Leader in the Group I always had two or three Assistant Leaders to work with me.

Before I joined the Group there had been one or two leaders who were not home grown. One character had caused Mr T much consternation for he spoke in a rich cockney brogue, often spiced with a few choice expletives and phrases of which Mr T did not approve. This leader would exhort the Scouts to take their Group scarves and *"hiron 'em hup, and hiron 'em darn".*

Whilst Ken was away on national service, a former Rover Scout who had moved into the area was Scout Leader. He held a responsible post in the London Docks but, sadly, he brought home with him the kind of language that was perfectly normal amongst dockers, but unacceptable to the ears of Mr T, the Vicar and many parents. We had one summer camp with this Scout Leader, during which the Scouts were treated as if they were dockers, which caused Mr T much grief, but which the Scouts found hilarious in the extreme. A number of parents were shocked to realise that their sons had acquired a somewhat lurid vocabulary whilst at Scout camp. When Ken returned from Cyprus, the leader joined the Rover Scouts for a time until promotion at work made involvement on the Group difficult as he spent a number of evenings entertaining clients – and, perhaps, adding to his already extensive vocabulary.

Not having been a Scout as a boy, I had much to learn about the technical aspects of Scouting and how to lead camps and expeditions. I knew all the leaders and older members of the Group through the church and youth club, and a number had been choirboys with me. I camped with the Senior Scouts and some of the leaders to be taught a few of the basics. We travelled by train to Ingatestone and hiked to Bacons' farm, where the Group had camped for some years, pulling a lightweight trek cart with the tentage and camping gear a distance of three miles or so. There were a number of similar farms around Essex where the Group was welcome to camp for we had a good reputation as people who could be trusted to camp well and not cause any damage to land or animals, and to leave the field as we found it.

I learned how to use a hand axe to chop wood, how to light a fire, how to cook, pitch tents, cope with wind and rain – and how to clear up afterwards, leaving the camp site so clean that no-one would know you had ever been there.

Whilst my role was primarily with the 8 to 11-year-olds and my colleagues were concerned with the older age ranges, there were no barriers and we tended to work together as a team – with the Scout and Senior Scout Leaders joining me in running Cub Scout Camps, whilst I took on a role at Summer Camps with the Scout Troop.

Splashing in the town hall lake

After a trial run in the vicarage meadow at St. Peter's, the Cub Pack camped over Whitsun weekends at the Mallinson Camping Ground in Woodford Green. The first camp was held in 1955 when some twenty Wolf Cubs over the age of nine-and-a-half (the minimum age at that time when Wolf Cubs were permitted to camp under canvas) and the leaders walked from St. Peter's to the bus stop on Silverdale Parade, opposite the William Torbitt School, carrying our kit – on our backs if we were strong enough or dragging our kitbags if we were not. We boarded a 66 bus to Gants Hill and a 145 to Woodford Green, and then walked a-quarter-mile through the forest to the camp site – where some arrived before others who sat on their kit bags and wondered if they would ever make it to camp.

It was 1955 and the parents of only one Cub out of thirty-six possessed a car. The boy's father was a plumber so we piled the tentage and cooking equipment high in the trailer behind the car. Writing this in the first decade of the 21st Century, I wonder how many Cub Scouts today would be prepared to go to camp by bus and carry their own equipment? Most, if not all, travel to and from camps by car, often one boy in one car. In the late 50s cars became more common amongst families and we gave up on the buses, whilst borrowing a van from the local farmer for the tentage and other gear.

I learned a camp catering lesson the hard way at that first camp. The food supplies were ordered from shops local to the camp site for delivery during the afternoon prior to the Cubs' arrival. Rather than order tomatoes by the pound weight, I stated the number of individual tomatoes required – believing that this would ensure that I neither over nor under-ordered. The leaders travelled to the camp site on Friday evening to set up the tents in readiness for the arrival of the Cubs on Saturday morning. There on the camp site stood the food – groceries, meat and vegetables, with a stack of boxes containing not ninety tomatoes but ninety *pounds* of tomatoes. I contacted the greengrocer next morning, but he was loath to take them back. Fortunately we had a parents' afternoon on Sunday – and were able to sell off the tomatoes we did not require.

We prided ourselves on a high standard of cooking. Plum Duff (or Spotted Dick as it was colloquially known) was a speciality, sewn into a muslin bag and cooked in a large dixie over the wood fire. Gauging the correct cooking time was an art and it was only when the muslin was cut that we knew whether or not we had got it right. One wet Sunday morning the area around the altar fire (so called because the fire was raised up on logs and bricks to waist height to avoid having to crouch down to tend to the cooking) was muddy, soggy and slippery. Carrying the dixie of stewed fruit to the tables where the Cubs were eating was a hazardous process and the Rover Scout engaged in the task slipped, scattering the fruit onto the mud. We happened to have a slab of fruit cake that someone's mother had provided for additional sustenance. Some quick thinking produced a pudding comprising cold fruit cake covered in piping hot custard. We called it Mowgli's Pudding (after the young boy in Kipling's *Jungle Book*). Mowgli's Pudding was so well received that on our return home I had several requests from parents for the recipe.

Cub camps were exhausting for both boys and leaders. The first night – Saturday – of a Whitsun Weekend was horrendous for, tired as they were, the Cubs were so excited that sleep would not come. Talk of midnight feasts with sweets and cakes from home hidden in sleeping bags kept them awake until, having had their feast at what they thought was midnight but was nearer ten, they dropped off to sleep – only to wake as dawn broke next morning.

The result of this was that come Sunday evening and most of the Cubs were dropping off to sleep around the camp fire as dusk came down, and once in their tents, they slept the sleep of the just and had to be woken from their slumbers next morning.

One Sunday evening, Mr T suggested that he and one or two of the younger Senior Scouts would stay in camp to keep an eye on the Cubs who, by now, were away with the fairies, whilst the leaders and Rover Scouts drove to a hostelry in Epping Forest for a well-deserved drink. At this time two or three leaders had cars, so we piled into them – seat belts were yet to be introduced and we would happily sit on each other's laps to get as many people into each car as possible. On our way back to camp we drove down Forest Road in Walthamstow, passing the Town Hall and Technical College. It was warm as we approached midnight and spotting the cool water of the lake in front of the Town Hall, we drove off the road, stripping to our underwear for a paddle and a splash about.

I fear that if we were to do this today, some 40 or so years later, we would all be made the subject of ASBOs – and, probably, rightly so.

'Gut rot'

Scout Troop Summer Camps were the highlight of the year and every boy and leader would want to be there for the full fourteen days. It was almost unheard of for a boy to miss out on summer camp. Few families took holidays away from home; those who did stayed in this country; only one or two ventured abroad for the days of the package holiday had yet to arrive; and those who did go away avoided the first two weeks of the school summer holidays.

Early in the year there would be a site hunt when some of the leaders and the Patrol Leaders would set out in a hired mini-bus to find a suitable farm on which to camp. Norfolk, Herefordshire, Somerset, Devon were some of the counties of England where we camped, with one foray into North Wales. The weather was invariably appalling with rain, thunder, lightning, hail and even snow interspersed with boiling sunshine, but that is August in the UK.

Mr T was in charge of first aid – believing that a hot poultice sorted out most cuts and abrasions – and malingerers who were tired of carrying water or searching for dry firewood in a downpour and gale of frightening proportions. Those in the know tended to keep their cuts to themselves.

One year when camping near Castle Coombe in Gloucestershire, the Scouts started to fall ill with a tummy upset within hours of arrival at the camp site. After thirty-six hours over half the boys in camp were in the sick tent – or tents, for we had to move things around to accommodate those who were falling ill by the hour. The area medical officer for health was called in and was about to close the camp and send us all home, when he contacted his opposite number back home to learn that a particular virus had broken out in schools in the Borough as they were about to close for the summer holidays. A few days later the sunshine (and the wind, rain and hail) had helped everyone to recover and by the time the parents descended on the camp for their annual parents' day visit on the middle Sunday, all was well.

Except that, unfortunately, one Scout had sent his parents a postcard in which he informed them that he, together with the majority of the boys in camp, had contracted 'gut rot' from which he was not expected to recover for some weeks. Indeed, his postcard had hinted that he might not be alive when the parents disembarked from their coach on Sunday, but in case he was, would they please bring plenty of food as there was none in the camp and he was starving.

News of the 'gut rot' epidemic spread like wildfire throughout Aldborough Hatch when the fateful postcard arrived on Thursday morning. Mobile phones had not been invented, but we relied on telephone messages being left with the publican who ran the hostelry at the top of the hill from the camp site. One or two of the leaders wandered nonchalantly up the hill that Thursday evening for a pint, to be confronted by a distraught publican who had been answering the telephone for the past two or three hours. Every time he put the receiver down and prepared to run down the hill to tell us that this or that parent was being driven out of their wits with worry, the phone would ring again with yet another frantic parent on the line. We telephoned the Vicar to ask him to put it about that all was well and that no deaths had taken place, nor were any imminent.

Those of us in camp feared the approach of Sunday's parents' day almost as much as the parents were fearful that they would find the camp site littered with corpses or, at the very least, emaciated bodies. Mr T and I were sent up the hill to meet the coach and to reassure the parents that their little darlings were safe and well, but as the door of the coach swung open, we were almost crushed in the stampede of mummies and daddies storming downhill to find their precious offspring.

Our summer camp programmes were always filled to the brim with activity. On arrival each Scout Patrol would set up its own camp site. Logs would be cut from nearby woodland to form the base for the altar fires. Timber was collected to be shaped into a dresser on which we placed the cooking utensils, and a table and bench seats made, again using timber on hand. Rope was used to tie the timber together, although occasionally an enterprising Scout would hide a hammer and some nails in his kit. If a nail was discovered in one of the gadgets, this was considered a heinous crime for which there was no appropriate sanction – except excommunication (although this rarely happened!).

We took a couple of trestle tables and one or two stools – but these were for the QM stores and the food tent – and the camp office, of course, from which everything was organised.

My role was ordering and distributing the food to each of the Patrol sites, but where necessary I would double up to take part in first aid. Not, I would add, to administer any – for that was Mr T's prerogative – but to accompany Scouts to A & E at the local hospital. The occasional broken arm or leg, and axe wound, would find me off to the A & E, there to sit for hours as the Scouts received treatment. On one occasion I was driven to hospital by an adult leader in his car with a Scout who needed attention – and stayed there for nearly thirty-six hours as three other Scouts were brought in over the period of time. I wondered if I would ever see the green grass and smell the wood smoke of camp again.

We camped one summer on the edge of the cliffs above Watchett in Somerset. It was a glorious spot, only spoilt by the almost continuous rain and incessant wind.

The farmer appeared one evening with some rabbits, which the Scouts skinned and roasted on spits over an open fire. A few were left, so Mr T made a rabbit stew. That afternoon one of our older Scouts disappeared from the site. He had fallen out with his mates over something or other, and told them he was going off home. We called the police and the boy's parents.

Later that evening the leaders sat around a fire in the dark, eating rabbit stew, when flashing lights told us that police cars were racing across the farmer's fields towards our camp site. Two police cars careered around a field where the wheat crop was about to be cut, tearing swathes of corn up by the roots and leaving channels of flattened crop.

The police came to tell us that the missing Scout had arrived home in Aldborough Hatch. He had hitched a lift on the road outside the farm from a lorry driver who – by remarkable co-incidence – was driving to Harwich and dropped the Scout at the bottom of the road where he lived in Aldborough Hatch. The Scout's father brought him back to camp the next day and did not seem over worried over the incident – which is more than can be said for the farmer, who sued the police and received compensation for his loss of crop.

Travelling to and from summer camps involved a variety of means of transport. We had at least one car on site, often driven by one of the adult leaders ahead of the main party on the Friday evening, with two or three older Scouts who would prepare a meal to be ready for the arrival of the Troop. This car would be used to ferry leaders into town to make purchases when supplies ran low and to take a seemingly never ending procession of Scouts to the local A & E.

Large pantechnicons – the kind used for household removals – were popular. The tentage and other gear would be piled up at the front of the vehicle and the Scouts and leaders would sit on the floor.

On the journey to Watchett in Somerset all was well until we entered the farmyard. As the Scouts piled out from the back of the van, almost all of them were promptly sick!

Later coaches and even rail were the preferred method of travel, with the tentage and camping gear going in a smaller lorry or by rail-container.

Trek carts and *Gang Shows*

We were fortunate in that St. Peter's was on the edge of London's green belt. Adjacent to the Vicarage garden stood a meadow where we could hold outdoor meetings once the warmer weather started.

Church fetes and garden parties extended into the meadow where the Scouts would demonstrate their cooking ability or pioneering prowess by running up a tower constructed with poles and ropes or an aerial runway on which children and adults alike might risk their lives as they clung perilously to a small wooden seat precariously secured with rope, running down from a tower way, way up in the air. How we got away without death or injury amongst those who took part was something of a minor miracle.

A mile or so up Aldborough Road, along Painters Road and down Hainault Road was Hargreaves, the Scout District Camp Site. Opened in the mid-50s by Sir Rob Lockhart, Deputy Chief Scout, the area had been the haunt of gypsies before the Scouts bought the ground. Parts of the land were boggy and it took much hard work by dedicated Scout folk locally to drain and turn it into the camp site and activity centre that would provide open air fun for so many young people over half a century and beyond.

The driving forces behind the camp site in the early days were Norman, Scout District Commissioner, and Bill, a bachelor Scouter and bank manager, who sold the house where he lived with his mother to build a bungalow on the site when he became the first volunteer warden.

Norman lived in Aldborough Hatch with his wife, Una (she of the egg and bacon sandwiches), and son and daughter, Ken and Margaret. Ken was a Wolf Cub in the Pack I was running, seemingly taking fiendish pleasure in ensuring that if things went wrong, his father – the District Commissioner – would know all about it. One evening his father came to appraise my abilities as a leader – and Ken and his friend, Colin, roped all the doors and windows in the church halls firmly closed, so that we could neither get in nor out of the building.

Una ran the Scout Shop on the camp site from the first day it opened until her death in 2003. Initially, the 'shop' operated from a trestle table in the only hut on the site. Later business was conducted from a purpose-built shop, which was opened by Ralph Reader of *Gang Show* fame. Supplies were ordered from Scout Shops' head offices, firstly in London and later in Lancing, Sussex, but Una prided herself on being able to offer a service that could not wait for deliveries by courier or parcel post. To achieve this, I was sent scurrying off to the branch of Scout Shops in the City of London, opposite the Old Bailey, during my lunch hours to pick up whatever was required.

As summer camps approached, Scout Groups would realise that they were short of tent pegs or other heavy items and I would have to lug them home on the Central Line.

Hargreaves was within trek-cart pushing distance from St. Peter's. The Group possessed two sturdy trek carts with large wheels of the type usually found on horse drawn farm vehicles. When camping at Hargreaves, the tentage and cooking equipment was piled high on the trek carts and pushed there and back. The Senior Scouts had a lightweight trek cart which they took on overseas camps.

The young leaders in the Group were encouraged to share their skills with others in the District, with their particular forte being Patrol Leader Training Courses and training and testing for the Camper and Cook Proficiency Badges. These were all held at Hargreaves.

The Camper and Cook Badge Courses ran over two weekends – the first being training and the second testing. Bread and cakes were baked in biscuit tin ovens; three course meals were prepared and served at table; tents had to be pitched so that the pegs were in alignment to the accuracy of one inch either way. From time to time a Scout or two would pull a fast one on the examiners – one resourceful Scout even managing to smuggle in a cake baked by his mother in her home kitchen. Such things were frowned upon for everything was taken extremely seriously and to a very high standard.

The London *Gang Show* was staged by Ralph Reader at Golders Green throughout this time. Coaches would take members of the Group to see the show each year in late November, by which time we had started rehearsals for our Group Show which would take to the boards in late February.

The first shows were at the William Torbitt School. Later we moved to St. John's Church Halls in Seven Kings and then to the larger stage at Ilford County High School for Boys. At the Torbitt we used classrooms for dressing, but had to go outdoors and up the fire escape to reach the stage in the hall on the first floor. At St. John's our dressing room was a small hall adjoining the main hall. We rigged up a platform carrying a spotlight towards the back of the hall, suspended above the audience on the wooden poles we used for our pioneering projects. The platform creaked and groaned ominously, putting the members of the audience seated below in fear that the edifice might come tumbling down upon them. Our shows started as one night affairs but such was their popularity that we later gave four performances over two weekends.

The Cubs were often the hit of the shows, where we wrote our own scripts – starting with an extension of a rhyming pantomime written by Ralph Reader where the couplet *"I am the fairy of the wood, I go about a doing of good"* occurred at regular intervals, reducing the audience to fits of hysterics. Free seats were given to two or three ladies – my mother amongst them – who could be relied upon to laugh at the slightest provocation. Seated strategically amongst the audience, they ensured that every night was a rip-roaring success.

We wrote our own words to many popular songs and these were sung at camp and in the shows. We used the tune of Lonnie Donegan's *Putting on the style* as the Wolf Cubs sang: *"Mr T our GSM, comes to camp each year, as long as he has tea in bed, we Cubs have nought to fear"*, while camping at Watchet the Scouts sang: *"We're camping in the Quantocks and swimming in the sea, With all our cuts and grazes we go to Mr. T".*

In at the deep end

My time as Cub Scout Leader came to an end in 1963 when some of our young adult leaders moved away – either to marry or to further their careers. It was decided that I should take on the role of Scout Leader, but before Mr T would permit me to do so, he insisted that I learn to swim – a skill I had not acquired as a youngster but which I now needed to master as I would be expected to be in charge of swimming parties at Scout camps.

The mother of one of our Cub Scouts was a swimming instructor who agreed to give me a crash course in the art. We met at Ilford Swimming Baths when they opened at 7am on Sunday mornings. Mrs K came into the water with me – in the deep end – and within six weeks I swam a width, more out of fear of Mrs K who was, to put it mildly, a somewhat formidable lady as swimming instructors invariably are. A week or two later I managed a length – a distance I have not bettered.

On Monday evenings members of the Group joined others in the District at the Scout Swimming Club at Ilford Baths. Meeting at the church halls, some would cycle, others would walk whilst a few would be lucky enough to have a lift in a car. Again, we would pile into the car, sitting on each other and on the floor, until no more bodies could be squeezed for fear that the roof might give way under the strain. I was given some rudimentary coaching so that I could help Scouts to learn to swim, standing at the side of the baths to do so. With ten minutes remaining to the end of the session, I would enter the water to swim my length – generally followed and surrounded by a gaggle of Scouts who found my swimming style amusing and possibly unique, for my chin or hair remained dry.

On the Sunday afternoon following my appointment as Scout Leader, we held the first of many Patrol Leaders' Council Meetings in my home. On entering the house, the five Patrol Leaders and my Assistant Scout Leaders removed their shoes, which were neatly lined up inside the front door. Yvonne served soft drinks and homemade cakes, which were devoured almost as fast as Yvonne could bake them. Such meetings were at the very heart of the Scout Troop. Decisions were made not by the adult leaders but by the Scout Patrol Leaders, guided – but not controlled – by the adults. It was the Patrol System introduced by the Scout Movement's founder, Baden-Powell, and honed over the years.

I was not surprised when the Patrol Leaders arrived together for that first meeting, although it should have alerted me to the fact that things were not quite right as their homes were scattered around the Hatch. The meeting went well and after the Patrol Leaders left, my Assistants stayed to chat. Half-an-hour or so later the mother of one of the Patrol Leaders called at my home – we did not have a telephone at that time, indeed few people did. Her son had not returned home and her car, which she garaged near to where I lived, was missing.

Eric, one of my Assistants, had his car outside so we drove to the nearest Patrol Leader's home. He was there and it did not take long for the picture to become clear. The missing Scout, barely fourteen, had driven round the Hatch in his mother's car to pick up the other Patrol Leaders from their homes before the meeting and dropped them off at their homes afterwards. He had told his pals that he would be taking a drive down the A12 before returning the car to the garage. My Assistant and I set of with his mother, finding a frightened young man sitting in the car in a parking lot off the A12 some five miles away. He was grounded by his father.

What is interesting is that a number of the Scouts with whom I came in contact at this time got into trouble of sorts. Nothing terribly serious, more boyish pranks – in their eyes at least. Those who did so have almost invariably turned out the best in later life. The Scout who had hitch hiked home from the camp at Watchett, later at the age of fifteen drove his father's car the sixty of so miles from Ilford to Beachy Head on the Sussex coast, poured petrol over the inside of the vehicle, took the handbrake off and watched as it moved slowly towards the edge of the cliff and fell in a ball of flame into the sea. No action was taken (his father was a police officer, which could explain a lot). That young man subsequently had an exemplary career overseas returning to England to retire.

The first time I appeared in a magistrates' court was to act as a character witness for one of my older Scouts. The back rows of St. Peter's Church were full on Sunday evenings with youngsters and some of the older Scouts would walk to my home after the service – for Yvonne's homemade cakes rather than my company. One evening on leaving my home a Scout knocked on the door of the first house in Roy Gardens – and hid behind the front garden fence when the householder opened the door. The Scout was not prepared for the fact that the man dashed down the garden path, grabbed him by the collar and took him indoors to await the arrival of the police. He was taken to the police station and charged with causing a nuisance of some kind.

I became aware of what had happened when he was summoned to appear at Stratford Magistrates' Court. The Scout, his parents and I attended at the Juvenile Court, which was chaired by Laurence Stringer, who happened to be Group Scout Leader of the 5th Seven Kings and Headquarters Commissioner for Senior Scouts – a man I knew from a distance, but with whom I would work very closely in later years. The Scout pleaded guilty and I spoke up for him. The lad was fined ten shillings – and went on to marry, work hard and have a family of his own.

A skinny lad who joined the Scout Troop came from a large family of young sisters and one younger brother, but no father that we ever saw. Visiting the family one evening, the younger brother called out from an upstairs window that the *"b****y Scoutmaster"* was here. The Rover Scouts offered to do some decorating, but we agreed that we would always go in pairs and preferably not in shorts. Throughout the time we were slapping on the wallpaper, men would call, climb the stairs, stay for half an hour or so and then depart.

One evening the lad's mother sent one of her daughters to tell me that the boy had run away from home a day or two before. We were given some likely places where he might be and we found him dossed down with the local ladies of the night in the goods yard at Ilford Station. He was cold and hungry, so Yvonne cooked something warming whilst he had a hot bath in our house before we took him home. Years later that same lad was the mini-cab driver bringing me home from Redbridge Magistrates' Court. Married, he had a family of his own and was making good of his life.

Cup Final in camp

I was fortunate in taking over the leadership of a Scout Troop that had an established pattern of training, good parental and church support, and a reputation for high standards. Everything was geared around the highlight of the year – the fourteen day summer camp. Indoor Friday night troop meetings in the winter months were supplemented by hikes and pioneering days at weekends – during the latter we would build bridges, towers or aerial runways using rope, poles, blocks and tackle. Days on a lake in Epping Forest found us building rafts with pioneering spars and oil drums for buoyancy. The drums were obtained from garages, washed out and sealed at the cap – and stored in the loft at my house. Following a rafting day, the drums were dried out (for although they were sealed, they let some water in) on the grass in my back garden. Yvonne did not forgive me when a rafting Saturday preceded the Sunday of my eldest son's baptism, so that the guests had to circumvent oil drums as they drank their tea and ate their cakes in our garden following the service.

A winter camp held in January each year was for Scouts who had been in the Troop for at least a year. This took place at Gilwell Park, the Scout Association's Training Ground and Camp Site in nearby Chingford. We were one of a very few Troops allowed to use the timber built Gidney Cabin as our indoor base for such an event. A log fire burned throughout the weekend, some slept in hammocks strung between the wood beams, others snuggled up on the wooden floor, whilst at least one of the Assistant Leaders slept in a hollow log outside. It was invariably cold and often snowed.

The camping season proper started at Easter, when the older Scouts in the Troop pitched their tents for the first time in the year. Easter Camps were for the very hardy – Easter, being a variable feast as far as timing is concerned, can produce extremes of weather. We had them all at Easter Camps – snow, hail, frost, wind, gale and even flood, but the Scouts who pitched their tent in a dip in the ground would not do so ever again. We camped at Easter for some years on land owned and farmed in Hertfordshire by a remarkable man who was honorary surgeon to one of London's leading football clubs. He would arrange an egg hunt around his estate when the Scouts had to search for fresh eggs produced not just by chickens, but by a variety of exotic laying birds. When they found the eggs, they would cook them for their tea – and sometimes they would even eat them. He would invite the adult leaders to his home on one evening for a drink – and display his gruesome sterile trophies in bottles from his many operations. I avoided these evenings, claiming that someone had to stay in camp.

A weekend camp for younger Scouts who had joined the Troop since last year's Summer Camp was held on the farm outside Ingatestone where I had spent my first night in camp with the Group, with Patrol Camps taking place at Whitsun, when each Patrol would camp on a farm in Essex.

I committed a major blunder in my second year as Scout Leader by inadvertently scheduling the camp for younger Scouts over the weekend of the FA Cup Final. The younger Scouts were up in arms at the thought of missing the Cup Final on television, but it was the Patrol Leaders – who were a vital part of this camp as they would be training the younger Scouts in their Patrols – who put their feet down and said that the date had to be changed. With a variety of events booked to take place during the weeks immediately prior to Whitsun, it became clear that the weekend of the FA Cup Final was the only one when this camp could be held.

The Patrol Leaders came to see me to put their case, reminding me that West Ham would be playing, but I would not budge.

"I will arrange for you to see the FA Cup Final on TV if you will agree to the camp being held," I said. *"And that is a promise."*

Not unnaturally, the Patrol Leaders agreed and I was left with the problem of sorting out just how this might be achieved.

Here I learned a simple lesson that would stand me in good stead on many occasions in the years ahead when I found myself in a near impossible situation. If you have a problem, pick up the telephone and throw yourself at the mercy of those who have the wherewithal to make something happen. Alternatively, do not stick your neck out!

Next morning I telephoned Radio Rentals, a national company that had been formed in 1932 to rent out radio sets and had since moved into the TV rental market. I explained my problem to a somewhat startled – and clearly amused – public relations officer, who promised to make some enquiries and ring me back. A day or so later, Radio Rentals told me that if I could find a suitable hall in the locality, they would install a TV set for the weekend at no charge. All they would ask from me was that I would allow them to place a sign on top of the set to the effect that the Scouts were watching the FA Cup Final through the generosity of Radio Rentals.

The farmer on whose land we would be camping arranged for us to use the village hall. On Saturday afternoon we watched as West Ham beat Preston by three goals to two. It was the first – and last – FA Cup Final I have watched from start to finish. But I have to say that my standing as someone who could fix things went up in the eyes of the Patrol Leaders.

Top of the hill

My first Summer Camp as Scout Leader was on a farm high above the village of Torcross on the South Devon coast. The ride downhill to the village on the camp bicycle was exhilarating, pushing the bike uphill on the way back was not.

One bitingly cold weekend in March the Patrol Leaders and I set out by train and local bus to this small village at the southern end of Slapton Sands, a narrow strip of coastal road and shingle beach separating Slapton Ley from Start Bay. The beach was used for rehearsals for the D-Day landings in 1944. Shivering in a hike tent over that weekend, I appreciated some of the horrors to which our troops must have been subjected. We found a farmer who was willing to let us have his field in the summer. The nearby woodland would provide us with timber for building the camp sites and for fires.

Having suffered a number of Summer Camps with heavy and often continuous rain, I presented a strong case for the Group to purchase an ex-army marquee which would act as the base for the camp so that when the rain thrashed across the site – as it invariably did in late July – we could meet together as a Troop and enjoy an evening in the dry. There were strong objections from a number of adult leaders – especially those who worked with the Senior Scouts and Rover Scouts – who thought that I would be mollycoddling the Scouts who would soon move up into their domain, but I won the day, having worked on the parents who sat on the committee that did the fund raising and made the decisions about spending what they had raised.

It was also agreed that we would purchase a water container on wheels, so that if we were camping on a site where water had to be carried some distance, it might be wheeled in bulk rather than carried by hand in buckets. My experience of such a means of carrying water has always been that you may set out with two full buckets, but irrespective of the distance and the state of the terrain, you invariably arrive with them half-full.

The marquee was delivered in good time prior to the camp, but the water container was delayed, finally dropping off at Ilford Railway Station on the evening before the tentage and camping equipment were to be loaded into a container for transporting by road and rail to the camp site in Devon. There was no guarantee that the water container would be dropped off at St. Peter's in time for our departure, so I had no alternative but to travel home from my office in the City to Ilford Station – and to push the water container the three miles home along suburban streets.

The bush telegraph soon informed members of the Scout Troop that their Scout Leader was pushing a water cart on the roads, dressed in dark suit, white shirt, stiff collar and sober tie, and carrying his briefcase. Half-way home Scouts on cycles and on foot started to join me and by the time we reached Aldborough Hatch most if not all the Scouts in the Troop were cycling or running in procession behind the water container.

The Scouts and leaders travelled by coach to Torcross, but when we arrived at the camp site there was no sign of the container with our tentage and camping gear that had been sent ahead by British Rail. Enquiries revealed that the container had been returned to Kingsbridge goods yard as the lorry with the container on board had been unable to negotiate the hill from Torcross village up to the camp site. We suggested an alternative route – avoiding the village in the east and coming at the farm from the west. There was considerable relief when the container was spotted lurching past the farm and onto the camp site.

Yvonne, who was in the early stages of pregnancy with our first son, travelled with Cyril, the Group Treasurer, and Muriel, his wife who also played the piano for our *Gang Shows*, staying at the farmhouse for a few days. The standard of cooking was not very high at the beginning of the camp and the adult leaders envied Yvonne her cooked breakfast and hot evening meals, whilst Yvonne remembers with horror and little affection the Scotch egg swimming in a sea of cold congealed fat that she was offered on her arrival by a Patrol. This was followed by a trifle made with chocolate sponge which was a dubious shade of khaki.

Being near the sea we had regular swimming sessions from the beach. We had been warned by the local Scout community that the beach shelved steeply and deeply within a few feet of the shore. We operated the buddy system, whereby each Scout or adult in the water had a 'buddy'. On the whistle signal, the two Scouts who were 'buddies' would link arms high in the air – so that if a Scout was spotted alone, the alarm would be raised. As this was my first summer camp and the shore was known to be dangerous, I was over cautious, blowing the whistle ever two minutes or so, but I felt it better to be safe.

We hiked along the cliffs to the south of Torcross to the village of Hallsands, which had clung to the bottom of the cliffs before being destroyed by a storm in 1917. An elderly wizened lady in black moved around one of the few remaining ruined cottages, waving to us as we passed by.

At the end of the two weeks, the farmer dropped a bombshell when he handed me an invoice for some £200 camp fees. Up to that time the Group had never been charged for camping on farmers' land and a fee had not been mentioned in all our discussions with the farmer. We had little alternative but to pay.

On our return home, the Scout Troop took a couple of months to raise the money to pay back into the Group's funds – whist drives remained popular together with jumble sales. Some generous donations were also received. But we learned a lesson and always asked in future if there would be a fee. The Devon coast was starting to be popular for family camping and caravan holidays, and farmers saw this as a means of making up for the income they were losing as farming became less and less financially viable.

Prison escape

My second Summer Camp held in 1964 was memorable for a number of reasons, not least the fact that an escaped prisoner may have made his dash for freedom through our camp site, but also because this camp was the spark that led to my taking on a full-time professional role with The Scout Association four years later.

We camped at Fritton Lake on Lord Somerleyton's estate on the borders of Suffolk and Norfolk.

The site, which comprised a largish field bordered by extensive woodland running down to a massive lake, was used by the Scouts of nearby Lowestoft. The lake was ideal for rafting and the woods provided all the timber we needed for fires and to build the Patrol sites.

We played wide games in the woods and had night hikes in the surrounding countryside. The only problem was that the fields to the east were home to a few hundred pigs, which was fine – except when the wind blew from that direction on a steaming hot day.

Forty Scouts, eight adult leaders and Rover Scouts camped that year and this fact, together with the extensive typed and duplicated programme booklet (copies of which were given to every Patrol prior to the camp) somewhat amazed the local Scout folk – so much so that they arranged for a professional photographer to visit the camp.

Sitting, kneeling and standing in five rows, we had a photograph taken that would appear early the following year in THE SCOUTER, the national magazine of The Scout Association.

Our notoriety spread, for I learned much later that Lord Somerleyton had commented to John Sweet, the Scout Field Commissioner for the area, that the Scout Leader was a very odd character who spent all the day in his pyjamas with the trousers rolled up to his knees. It was, in part, the truth for I would rise early, wash and shave in the peace and quiet – and then arouse the Troop, walking from tent to tent in my pyjamas with the trousers rolled up to my knees, to save the bottoms getting wet in the morning dew, and with plimsolls without socks. I would remain like this until shortly before the 10am inspection, when I would change into my immaculate Scout uniform which I would wear for the rest of the day. The problem was that Lord Somerleyton always visited the camp site on horseback at around eight in the morning.

This camp was the first time that the fathers of two Patrol Leaders came to a Scout Summer Camp. Les had been warranted as a leader for some time, whilst Roger was a yellow-plumed auxiliary. Both were somewhat apprehensive of the privations that they might have to suffer and came well prepared. They shared a tent, sleeping on camp beds (up to that time only Mr T had been permitted such luxury), with a length of carpet between the two beds on top of the groundsheet. A small bedside table served as a place for their early morning tea and late night cocoa, together with a battery operated lantern rather than the paraffin jobs used elsewhere in the camp.

Both Les and Roger assisted in the morning inspections of the Patrol camp sites. One morning Les was deputed to inspect each Patrol's cooking utensils. On looking inside the teapot on his Patrol Leader son's site, he spotted that tea leaves remained at the bottom of the pot. Les called David over, but was slightly taken aback when his son remarked that he thought that was the thing to do as they always left the tea leaves in the pot at home – as his father well knew.

On returning home, the day by day diary of the camp was published in THE HATCH, the Group's monthly magazine. The magazine was produced on a duplicator and bound into pre-printed yellow and green covers, with copies being given to all members of the Group and sent on wide circulation outside. I never edited the magazine, for we always found a parent to do so, but I wrote for it and was often called upon to fill spaces at the bottoms of pages.

One copy went each month to Rex Hazlewood, The Scout Association's General Editor and Editor of THE SCOUTER magazine. A short letter from Rex requested permission to publish the camp dairy in THE SCOUTER. It appeared over four pages under the title *A Summer Camp*, accompanied by the photograph taken on site, in the January 1965 issue of THE SCOUTER. Little did I know at the time that this was to be the start of something that would change the direction of my life.

And what of the escaped prisoner? Here is the diary entry for Friday, 7th August, 1964:

"And now for the excitement! After Supper round the fire, the Patrols drifted back to camp and into bed. A few were late leaving the warm embers and on their way back thought they had seen a man running from the camp, and were certain they had heard someone crashing through the undergrowth. Nothing strange in that you say . . . but we knew that a housebreaker had escaped a few days before from Blundesdon High Security Prison barely two miles away! The police had called earlier in the week to warn us of this and the night before he was said to be in our area still! Those who were still up surrounded a patch of undergrowth and the search was on! Finding nothing we left the Rovers on guard and returned to the camp; but it was clear something had been seen by a number of boys . . . and the 'noises' continued from the patch of undergrowth. We decided to call the police and finished up with tracker dogs doing the rounds at 12.30am. Finding nothing but the scent of forty-two Boys Scouts, they called the search off at 1am . . . and we all went to bed. Quite a way to end a summer camp and in spite of

the police cars and flashing lights, four Patrols went to sleep at 10.15pm and heard nothing!" (I apologise for the surfeit of exclamation marks – but that was how we wrote in the 1960s before a certain Rex Hazlewood took me in hand.)

This was not the first time that there had been brushes with the criminal fraternity at Summer Camps. Some years earlier when Ken was Scout Leader and I looked after the food and the bandages, we were camping near Machynlleth in West Wales when a policeman was shot at close range on a bridge over the River Dovey. The man who was subsequently tried and sentenced for murder was on the run for some days and came through our camp site whilst we were out, taking food.

Back to the cliff top

Summer Camps always started in St. Peter's Church very early on the morning of the day of our departure. If we were travelling a long distance, this might mean that we assembled in church at 5am or thereabouts. Scouts, leaders and parents met together and, led by the Vicar or Mr T if the Vicar was away, we would join in prayer for the coming camp. It took perhaps five minutes, but it set the tone for the days that followed.

We would attend the nearest church to the camp site on the middle Sunday of our stay or if this was not possible, Mr T would take a Scouts' Own Service on the camp site, with the Scouts taking part in readings and prayers. It was at Machynlleth where Mr T committed a cardinal error in the choice of hymns. The Minister at the chapel nearest to the camp site was away on holiday when we were in camp and took advantage of the fact that Mr T was a Lay Reader to invite him to lead the morning service. It was when Mr T announced that the last hymn would be *Jerusalem* that the faces of the all-Welsh congregation turned on us in sour scorn as we sang Blake's famous words about *"England's green and pleasant land".*

Summer Camp in 1965 found us back at Watchett in Somerset, camping at Perry Farm high above the Bristol Channel on the very edge of the cliffs. The farmer welcomed us, bearing no grudge about our last visit when police cars had driven back and forth through his crops. Perhaps the compensation he received from the police was generous.

Andy, one of the Rover Scouts in camp, spent the first ten days or so building what can only be described as a death-defying aerial runway that started at the top of the cliff and ended up in the sea below. The anchorage at the top of the cliff was achieved with a series of stout wooden pickets driven into the ground well back from the edge, whilst huge rocks and boulders in the sea itself were used to secure the other end.

Andy spent all his daylight hours testing the tension and working out the mathematics of what he was doing. Andy would come up from the beach for his meals and to sleep, but otherwise he was lost in a world of his own. Andy took the first ride downwards at high tide, finishing in the crashing waves. One or two others also enjoyed a ride – or so they said, but their faces were white with terror as they sped ever downwards. Health and safety regulations would preclude anything remotely like this being built today. No doubt it was dangerous, but Scouts like Andy had the skills and training, knew what they were doing and spent time getting it right.

Andy had one further claim to fame. In the late evening I would call a staff meeting when the adult leaders would gather in the marquee as I outlined plans for the next day. Not unnaturally, the leaders would be tired and ready for bed as I droned on. One evening Andy closed his eyes whilst perched on a wooden stool, went to sleep, toppled off the stool onto the grass and remained asleep as he lay there and the droning went on around him.

One of the more amusing visits to the local A & E came about as the result of what one Scout wrote home to tell his Mum had occurred because *"Pat ran into a stationary tree".* Pat had a head of rich, blond hair that hung down the back of his neck, with a fringe in front that very nearly covered his eyes. It was something of which Pat was immensely proud and which he spent much of the day grooming. Sadly, Pat had left the camp fire one evening to run back to his tent in the dusk through the woods, but he failed to spot a rather large tree that loomed into his path. Running flat out into the tree, he caused a nasty gash at the top of his head – and his blond hair soon turned a stylish crimson. On arrival at A & E, it was clear that they were understaffed and over busy, to the extent that the nurse who first examined Pat said that I would have to cut his hair before the doctor could stitch him up.

Pat smiled the resigned grin of a young man who knows that he is about to lose the one thing which stood him out in the crowd – in front of the many admiring girls, at least – as I clipped away with the scissors.

Dinner at Rules

Following publication of *A Summer Camp* in the January 1965 issue of THE SCOUTER, Rex Hazlewood, the Editor, wrote to ask me to meet him at his office where we talked for half-an-hour or so, and he suggested that I might contribute some articles to THE SCOUTER on my experience as a Scout Leader.

Later that summer, Rex invited me to join him for dinner one evening at Rules, in Maiden Lane, off Covent Garden. I was more than a little overawed at being invited out to dinner by Rex. I had eaten out in London perhaps four or five times in my whole life up to that time – and certainly not at Rules. Established in 1798, Rules it one of the oldest restaurants in London, serving traditional British food. On Rex's recommendation I joined him in Rules' speciality – steak and kidney pudding.

Offering me a brandy after the meal, Rex said that he only ever drank Armagnac. Again, I followed him, but I did not admit that this was not only the first Armagnac to pass my lips, but also the first brandy.

We walked to Holborn Underground Station, Rex to travel the short distance to his flat in St. John's Wood and me to take the longer journey to Newbury Park wondering where all this would lead. Standing on the down escalator behind Rex, I noticed that he waved and called out a greeting to a young man travelling on the escalator going up – and I recognised him as one of the soloists in the *London Gang Show.*

I learned later that Rex had built up his team of young writers over the years in the way in which he was starting to encourage me. Again, much later, Rex told me that he (and the Association for that matter) did not pay contributors to its magazines, but it fed them well. It was a practice that worked for Rex – and, later, much later, for me, too.

(I returned to Rules a number of times to entertain contributors – once when Michael Foot was dining – and to be entertained many years later by the Milk Marketing Board and by Scotts, MILK INDUSTRY's advertisement managers. My most recent visit was in December 2008 with Yvonne when we were hosted by our good friend Stella, and Frank Carson – *"It's the way I tell 'em"* – was on the next table. Rex took me to one of his favourite restaurants, the Cumberland Hotel in Marble Arch. Hamlyn's – publishers for some years of the Scout annuals – gave me lunch at The Ivy, and Eden Fisher (Southend), printers of SCOUTING, took Yvonne and me to Sheekey's, the world-famous fish restaurant in St. Martin's Court near Leicester Square.)

During dinner with Rex I agreed to write a series of articles which appeared in THE SCOUTER over three months from January 1966 under the title *Programming Summer Camp*. The articles set out the detailed planning that went into producing the *Summer Camp Programme* booklets we published each year in the 1st Aldborough Hatch.

In the same issue of THE SCOUTER a certain Colin McKay wrote the first of a series called *The Real McKay*. A Scouter in Tynemouth, Northumberland, Colin and I would become firm friends, a friendship that lasted through into our retirement. His series of articles – *A Canny Crack* – ran for over three decades.

Another meeting with Rex and I agreed to write a series of six short articles under the title *This and That*, which ran from August 1966 through to January 1967. These, again, drew on my experience as a Scout Leader, covering rafting, working with patrol leaders and parents, camp site hunts and go-karting. At that time Green Shield Stamps were being given as an incentive in most grocery stores and these could be exchanged for a variety of goods. We encouraged local families to give their stamps to the Troop – and we obtained a 35mm camera and tape recorder. The articles outlined how these could be utilised in Troop and Patrol programmes.

Around this time Rex would write to ask me various questions in connection with the technical aspects of Scouting and I was happy to reply. Some time later I discovered that the content of my letters had been copied word for word into books that Rex was writing at the time. Only on one occasion that I recall was I ever acknowledged as someone who had supplied him with material.

Change in the air

In the summer of 1966 The Scout Association published its long-awaited Advance Party Report. Set up by Sir Charles Maclean, then Chief Scout, and comprising a number of young and not so young leaders from across the country, the Advance Party sought to bring the movement up to date and to point it forward for the future.

Looking back, it was revolutionary in some respects but clung to tradition in much else. It was the uniform changes that hit the headlines. Out went shorts, in came long trousers. Out went neckerchiefs for leaders, in came green ties. The Boy was dropped and we became The Scout Association. First and Second Class Scouts disappeared and we aimed now for Awards and Standards. The emphasis on the outdoors and adventurous activities merely mirrored what many of the more successful Scout Groups were already doing. Canoeing, sailing, caving, mountaineering, ski-ing – all received a boost.

Perhaps where the Advance Party was too cautious was in its approach to the hierarchy of the Movement. Headquarters Commissioners were retained, although Boards comprising leaders from every part of the country were formed to offer advice to those who led the Sections. In some ways things became even more bureaucratic as any changes in programme had to jump through a series of board and committee hoops.

The awards system of medals for good service was kept in its entirety – with its graded awards ranging from the Chief Scout's Commendation for Good Services (for the lowly Scouter or lay helper) to the Silver Wolf (awarded to the Great and the Good, but rarely if ever to those at the coalface of the Pack, Troop or Unit, without whom the Movement would have ground to a halt). And even forty years later the awards system remained very largely unchanged, with merely a little tinkering on the surface.

The unwillingness to contemplate opening the movement to girls was to dog both the Scouts and the Girl Guides for three decades. The Scouts accepted girls into joint Venture Scout Units in the late 60s, albeit against much virulent opposition from the Girl Guides, which at times became quite nasty. It took another twenty years or so before girls were welcomed into all Sections, whilst the Girl Guides went it alone as a single sex organisation.

The opportunity for both movements to break with much of the past was lost and has never been recovered. It continues to mystify me as to why the two Movements remain stoically and immovably separate. There must surely come a time very soon when they will be one?

There is a story that went the rounds at the time – and I cannot be sure of its provenance – that Sir Charles Maclean went to Buckingham Palace to meet with the Duke of Gloucester, the Association's President, shortly before the Advance Party Report was to be launched at an afternoon press conference. The Chief Scout outlined the main recommendations of the Report over five minutes or so, before asking the Duke if he had any questions.

"Yes," the Duke is said to have replied, *"who won the first race at Newmarket?"*

I queued outside the Scout Shop below the Headquarters offices of the Association at 25 Buckingham Palace Road to purchase a copy of the Report – only to learn that the few copies available from the shop had sold out. I read my copy from cover to cover when it came through the post a few days later.

World Cup

Summer Camp in 1966 was at Ross-on-Wye in Herefordshire. The camp site extended over a vast field that ran from a narrow country lane bordering the winding River Wye up hill to the farmhouse and village church, with one or two small copses of trees scattered across the grass. Down the road was the headquarters of a fledgling company, PGL Holidays. At this time Ken, former 1st Aldborough Hatch Scout Leader, had joined PGL, which meant that we were able to call on the company's expertise in providing training, and hire canoes and other equipment for activities.

There were canoe cruises down the River Wye, with the Scouts being brought back in a mini-bus and the canoes on a trailer to be taken upstream for the next group to use. The river was utilised fully for rafting and swimming.

Training in survival techniques had long been part of our Troop programme – building shelters from natural materials to be found in woodland, baking twists and dampers over an open fire, skinning and cooking rabbits. This camp gave us the ideal opportunity to put that training to the test for the older Scouts in the Troop as we were given permission to use an island in the River Wye for this purpose. From 4pm on one day to the same time the next, some twenty older Scouts were marooned on the small island – with the minimum of food and equipment. They thought they were alone, but unknown to them two Rover Scouts camped on the river bank but well out of sight.

It rained – heavily – in the night, but the Rover Scouts slept through until the morning (which was not what they were supposed to do). Taking a canoe over to the island, they found that the river had risen during the night, flooding half the shelters that the Scouts had built – so that many of the young survivors spent the night up trees. Reality survival indeed, but not something that we told the parents afterwards.

The five Patrols were spread across the field, out of earshot and, in some cases, out of sight of each other. It took a minimum of ten minutes to walk right round the site. Fresh water was available from a standpipe at the top of the field. Prior to camp we borrowed lengths of garden hose from parents, which were coupled together (the hose, that is, not the parents) to provide a number of water points nearer the Patrol sites.

By now we had developed a sophisticated central base camp system with three fourteen foot ex-army ridge tents pitched on three sides of the marquee with one end of each opening into the marquee – one as the food store, the second for the quartermaster's stores and the third as the office. The latter was the hub of the camp complete with trestle table, chair, typewriter and duplicator. Communication was achieved through a series of field telephones, one on every Patrol site, linked in such a way that we could talk to all five Patrols at the same time from the office tent. In that way, the five Patrol cooks could all be briefed at the same time by the QM Food.

Former members of the Troop, now Senior Scouts or Rover Scouts, were an asset at a camp of this nature. Two or three spent the first few days in camp sorting out the hose pipes for the water system and running telephone wires between trees and on telegraph poles onto the Patrol sites. Later, a contraption of poles, pulleys, ropes and a tank produced a cold water shower.

1966 will be remembered as the year when England won the World Football Cup. The final was played at Wembley on Saturday 30th July when England beat West Germany by four goals to two. Every Patrol site had at least one transistor radio – normally these were only turned on in the late evening as radios blaring throughout the day would have stifled conversation and activity. With ears to their transistor radios, each England goal was greeted with shouts of joy, whilst when West Germany scored there was a deadly silence. Geoff Hurst completed the only World Cup Final hat-trick to date right at the end of extra time by running onto a long ball by Bobby Moore and shooting past the German goalkeeper into the roof of the net. At this the camp site went wild! The fact that both Geoff Hurst and Bobby Moore played for West Ham – the team that the majority of the Troop supported – added special interest to the game. It was at the end of this broadcast where legendary football commentator Kenneth Wolstenholme uttered the immortal words: *"They think it's all over; it is now!"*

Nine months to publish

Returning from Summer Camp in early August 1966 my first article in the series *This and That* had appeared in that month's SCOUTER with another five to be written. A telephone call from Rex Hazlewood's office inviting me to join him and others at Baden-Powell House, the Association's hostel in Kensington, one evening came as something of a surprise.

I reported to the Reception Desk where Reg Flower, then Deputy Warden at Baden-Powell House, greeted me. Reg and I had met on two or three occasions when he and Scouters from his Group in Bedfordshire had taken part in activities with the 1st Aldborough Hatch. Ken, our former Scout Leader, had served with Reg in Cyprus during national service.

Reg was clearly surprised to see me, dressed in my City suit complete with stiff collar. When I explained that I had an appointment with Rex Hazlewood, Reg looked non-plussed, for Rex was in the Warden's flat on the top floor with the Ted Hayden, Secretary to the Advance Party and shortly to be appointed as Executive Commissioner (Programme and Training), and Laurence Stringer, recently appointed Headquarters Commissioner for Scouts. My assurances left Reg mystified, but rather than turn me away (as, understandably, he was inclined to do, thinking that I might be getting a bit above my station with one or two articles in THE SCOUTER under my belt) Reg telephoned the flat – and was told to bring me up without delay if not sooner.

Rex introduced me to Ted, Laurence and David Harwood. Ted was his ebullient self, someone with whom I would work very closely over many years – not that I knew this at the time. I had met Laurence before – once when he had led the Parade of Queen's Scouts at Windsor when Den Day and I – both leaders in the Cub Scout Section – had been selected as section leaders and locally when Laurence was with the 5th Seven Kings Scout Group. I knew of David Harwood as the author of articles in THE SCOUTER and of some recently published books in which he told the stories of Scouts who had received bravery awards or who had taken part in adventurous activities.

Ted came straight to the point. The Advance Party Report had been published in the summer. The Commissioners' Conference in Manchester in the autumn would see the launch of the new programmes and uniforms. Implementation date would be 1st October 1967 – just over a year away – and by that time a range of new Handbooks had to be written and published. David and I had been chosen to write two of the Handbooks – David would write *The Scout Handbook* and I would write *The Patrol Leader's Handbook*. Laurence would be responsible for compiling *The Scout Leader's Handbook*, commissioning a number of authors to write individual chapters.

Clearly David, as an established author, was at ease with the idea; indeed, I believe he had been briefed earlier. David was setting out on a career as a freelance author and was viewed as a professional, so he would be paid a higher fee than me. My fee was fixed at £4 per one thousand words and I was told to write *"about 55,000 words or so".* I was so taken aback by what I was being asked to do, that I agreed to whatever was being put before me. I am unsure if I was ever asked if I would be prepared to take on the task – it was assumed that I would.

I had some material that would give me a start. I had written a short training manual for Patrol Leaders and had been taking a leading role in running training courses for Patrol Leaders within the Scout District. This, I was assured by those present, together with my experience in operating the Patrol System with my own Scout Troop, would give me all the background I would need. Rex offered to send me some handbooks published by the Boy Scouts of America, which were lavishly illustrated in colour and far superior to anything produced in this country.

I was given a month to produce a detailed synopsis. The manuscript would be required six months later in April 1967. I would be required to work with the artist and printer to see the book through the press for publication in July 1967.

Dinner was in the restaurant in Baden-Powell House. On the journey home by Underground the magnitude of what I had taken on began to dawn on me. To say that I was afraid would be to underestimate the feeling of abject fear that overcame me and held me in its grip for days afterwards.

In addition to having a Scout Troop to run and a handbook to write (and, of course, a young family and full-time job), I had been persuaded by Bill, District Commissioner for Ilford East, to take on the new role of Assistant District Commissioner (Leader Training) with the view to my helping train and prepare adult leaders for the new programme to be introduced following the Advance Party Report. It was in that role that I travelled with the District Commissioner's Team to the National Commissioners' Conference at Manchester University in late September.

Again, this was an eye-opening experience for me. Not only did I see The Scout Association's full-time professionals and national voluntary leaders strutting their stuff and addressing the gathering, but a number of them recognised me and were kind enough to speak. Further, my name was now getting known from my writings in THE SCOUTER.

It was in Manchester that it began to dawn on me that I might have a larger role to play in the development of Scouting nationally – and I felt both exhilarated but, at the same time, humbled and a bit frightened. The responsibility of writing *The Patrol Leader's Handbook* weighed heavily.

On Tuesday 11th October, Eric, one of my Assistant Scout Leaders, and I drove to Scout Headquarters in Buckingham Palace Road in Eric's little red van. Rex Hazlewood had accepted our invitation to attend the Group's *After Summer Camp Parents' Evening,* on the understanding that we would drive him there and take him back to his flat in St. John's Wood afterwards. Rex wrote in his *Luck of the Month* column in the December 1966 issue of THE SCOUTER:

"To Ilford way, to enjoy Mrs Ron Jeffries' charming hospitality (and excellent cooking) at a small dinner party before going to Ron's Group's 'After Summer Camp Parents' Evening', where the Patrol Leaders and Assistant Patrol Leaders commented with youthful naturalness and humour on the coloured slides of their Summer Camp, and where a very good seventeen minute colour film of the same camp was shown – a camp, incidentally, which included (as I may have already told you, but it's worth repeating), Patrols camping well apart, a day of training in canoe techniques by experts, an 11-mile canoe cruise for the younger and an 18-mile cruise for the older Scouts, a day's pony trekking, a Patrol bread-making (and what lovely loaves they seemed!) and cake baking and icing competition in their own Patrol ovens, a night on an island with survival kit and their own shelters for the older Scouts, plenty of pioneering, a commando course, and a medieval day where, amongst much else, a lamb was roasted on a spit. This – make no mistake about it – is the kind of adventure-activity Scout camp that is the blue-print of the future."

The writing commences

The synopsis for *The Patrol Leader's Handbook* was accepted with hardly any changes. David Harwood suggested that we keep in close contact to ensure that our two handbooks complemented each other. David lived in a flat in North London and I would travel after work in the City to the nearest Underground station where David would meet me and I would ride pillion on his motorcycle. Laurence joined us for dinner at David's flat on one occasion, commissioning me to write three chapters for *The Scout Leader's Handbook,* which he would edit.

I sent carbon copies of drafts of chapters to both David and Laurence, whilst David did likewise with his handbook. Laurence took great pleasure in pointing out that potato did not have an 'e' on the end – being the director of the family wholesale potato business meant that he would know this, spelling not being my strongest point.

I typed the drafts on a portable manual typewriter at home. The insurance company for whom I worked was changing its dictating machines and gave me two for my personal use – large green metal boxes with brown plastic floppy twelve inch discs, hand-held microphones and headphones. The sisters of two of my Scouts offered to type drafts from the dictating machines. They and the typist who produced the final manuscript were all paid by me from the £200 or so that I received on delivery of the manuscript.

Up to that time I had worked at the light oak bureau Yvonne and I bought from Heals in London when we were first married. I was left with sufficient cash to purchase a brand new desk, swivel chair and filing cabinet – and passed the bureau to Yvonne who continues to use it to this day.

I received a brief letter from Rex, acknowledging receipt of the manuscript and confirming that he had read this whilst pointing out that *"The good writer uses exclamation marks sparingly and never two together".* It is something I have not forgotten and Red's words come back to me whenever I am tempted to type an exclamation mark and I have never, ever typed two together or allowed two together in any material I have edited.

Rex arranged a meeting with a director of Richard Clay (The Chaucer Press) Limited at their London offices near the Law Courts; they would print *The Patrol Leader's Handbook.* I made numerous visits to those offices during my lunch hour in the weeks prior to publication in July – collecting proofs and returning them when corrected. Later I was taken to Clay's factory in Bungay, Suffolk, to see the book coming off the presses.

The artist chosen to illustrate all three handbooks was John Smith, who had been a member of Laurence Stringer's Group, the 5th Seven Kings. John was earning his living as a freelance artist, living with his wife and family at Asheldam, near Burnham on the Essex coast. John walked past my house one evening a week on his way to take riding lessons at the Aldborough Hall Equestrian Centre, half-a-mile up the road from where I lived, the business owned and run then – and today some forty years later – by Bob and Mary (Mary had been a Cub Scouter in the 5th Seven Kings and therefore knew both John and Laurence). On his way to ride, John would call at my home with his latest batch of drawings. John was a highly practical outdoor type who understood the technicalities of Scouting and camping. He did not need detailed descriptions of what to draw, he just did what was needed and did it brilliantly.

We were at the final stages of production when major changes had to be made to the drawings in all three handbooks. The new Scout uniform replaced shorts with long trousers, and so every sketch of a Scout had the boy in long trousers. Clearly this would be impractical in camp and when taking part in certain adventurous activities – and the word came down from on high that long trousers were to be removed and replaced by shorts where appropriate. The 'where appropriate' was left to David, John and me to decide and was achieved with liberal use of Tip-Ex.

Tragically, John drowned while white water rafting in Canada a few months after the handbooks were published – a severe loss to his family and to The Scout Association for I am sure he would have illustrated many books had he lived.

All the Handbooks were written anonymously and published at the same time in July 1967. There was no public launch, just a few skirmishes in the Scout Shop in Buckingham Palace Road when supplies ran out – as they did, over and over and over again.

It was known locally that I had some involvement with the new handbooks and when leaders were unable to obtain copies, I came in for some of the flack. It was something I would experience in the future, although invariably – as in this case – it was not my fault, but something I learned to take on the chin.

Within days of publication of *The Patrol Leader's Handbook*, letters started to arrive on Rex Hazlewood's desk from angry parents and Scout Leaders. The book contained a recipe for making toffee apples, suggesting that this might be a good project for a Patrol to try in one of their parent's kitchen. But pans of hot toffee were boiling over throughout the land, causing mothers to sink into the sloughs of despair as the sticky stuff edged its way down the sides of their Belling cookers. In producing a series of recipes for inclusion in the book with Yvonne's help and not being a cook myself, I had failed to notice that one teaspoonful of bicarbonate of soda had mysteriously changed to one tablespoonful. The error was corrected at the next printing, but not before I had been summoned to a home in Goodmayes to see for myself the devastation that a tablespoonful of bicarbonate of soda can cause in a domestic kitchen.

Here I learned a valuable lesson about publishing. Get something right and no-one will let you know that you have done so or that they have enjoyed reading what you have written. Get it wrong – and the hounds of hell will descend upon you with glee and happiness at your discomfort.

The success of *The Patrol Leader's Handbook* – in spite of the toffee apple incident – encouraged Rex to invite me to write articles for the October and November 1967 issues of THE SCOUTER under the title *Programming Patrol and Troop Activities*. At this time Laurence Stringer was engaged in promoting the new programme for the Scout Section with members of the newly-formed National Scout Board. My Assistant Scout Leaders and I journeyed with our Patrol Leaders' Council to Baden-Powell House in Kensington where we staged the second part of a Council meeting in front of the Board. Some of our Patrol Leaders were part of a panel at a weekend conference for Scout Leaders at a university in the Midlands. It was a busy time and the Scout Troop was being exposed to a lot of publicity. Driving home from the conference in heavy rain with Laurence, the windscreen wipers failed; Laurence spent the entire journey with his left arm on the driving wheel, leaning through the window on the driver's side so that his right arm could clear the windscreen.

Adventure Camp

The Troop Summer Camp in 1967 was based in a field on the banks of the Thames at Clifton Hampden in Oxfordshire. The field was used by the local Girl Guides, who were grateful when we left behind the altar fires on which the Patrols had cooked for the Guides use in the future.

It was, without doubt, the most adventurous camp we had ever undertaken. Indeed, we changed the name, calling this *Adventure Camp 1967*. At any one time Scouts would be at one of three centres – on the base camp at Clifton Hampden, on the Dorchester Lagoon nearby or at the Llangorse Adventure Centre in South Wales (the latter being operated by PGL Holidays who had worked with us the previous year at Ross-on-Wye) – or somewhere on the River Thames.

Canoeing on the river was a daily activity. Four two or three day canoe cruises with overnight camps took place on the Thames. Rafting was at Dorchester Lagoon, a lake formed where sand and gravel extraction had taken place.

A night wide game on that same lake found Patrols in canoes and on rafts – all were kitted out with lifejackets, but the excitement engendered produced something approach unadulterated chaos and mayhem. The Rev. Bill Barnes, Vicar of St. Peter's at the time, spent a few days in camp with us – and the night wide game on the lake happened to take place during his stay. Clearly concerned at what was erupting around him and fearing that death was not far away, the Vicar offered to prepare the hot soup for afterwards in the kitchen of a hut on the side of the water rather than watch the Scouts pelting one another with harmless missiles as the rafts crashed at full pelt into each other – all in the pitch black at dead of night.

Health and safety? We had not heard of it – yet – but, remarkably, no-one was hurt or harmed physically. Perhaps a few small boys grew up just a little on that lake that night.

The older Scouts in the Troop travelled to South Wales for the middle weekend where they were introduced to sailing, caving, rock climbing and abseiling under expert instructors from PGL.

In addition all the usual activities of Summer Camp took place – cooking and baking competitions, pioneering, day and night hikes, camp fires and so on. None of this would have been possible without a team of Assistant Scout Leaders, Senior Scouts and Rover Scouts who were trained and experts in all the activities in which we were engaged. Where we were not experts, we had the good sense to utilise the skills of those outside the Movement who were.

Yvonne spent a day at the camp with Graham, our eldest son, then three. Greg, one of the Patrol Leaders, offered to take him on the Thames in a canoe. Greg kept close to the bank, aware of the responsibility of having our son in his canoe. Wearing a lifejacket, Graham was happy enough for the first few minutes, but then announced to Greg that he would walk back to the camp – and made to step over the side of the canoe. Greg pulled him back, but Graham protested that it was only a puddle and he often splashed through those in his Wellington boots!

Although I did not know this at the time, it was to be my last Summer Camp with the 1st Aldborough Hatch.

More articles and another book

I took a break from the role of Scout Leader on returning from Clifton Hampden to concentrate on working with the District Team in preparing the dozen or so Scout Troops in Ilford East for the transition to the new programme in the autumn of 1968 – twelve months away. Eric, one of my Assistants, took over as acting Scout Leader, but we kept in touch.

During an evening meal in one of his favourite restaurants in the late Autumn, Rex Hazlewood told me that he was due to retire as the Association's General Editor next Summer and over yet another brandy (Armagnac, of course), encouraged me to consider applying for the post when it was advertised early in the New Year. He convinced me that what I lacked in experience of editing and printing could be put right over the coming months.

The idea had an instant appeal for my full-time employment in the insurance industry in the City was merely a means of earning sufficient money to pay the mortgage and bring up a family. The role of General Editor would give me the opportunity to do what I had long wanted do – to write. More than that, I would have the chance to be part of the national team that would carry forward the recommendations of the Advance Party Report and have a role in shaping the Movement for the future.

Meanwhile, Rex wanted me to be involved in more writing for THE SCOUTER. One of the recommendations of the Advance Party Report was that there should be more practical training material published regularly for adult leaders of the three training sections. Rex Hazlewood and the Programme and Training Department – now led by Ted Hayden – decided that there would be three four-page pull-out training supplements in the centre of THE SCOUTER every month, printed on fawn coloured paper and hole punched for filing in a ring binder. I was invited by Rex to write and edit the four-page training Supplement for the Scout Section for twelve months, commencing with the January 1968 issue. In fact there were four Supplements rather than three because sections of the magazine were printed as sixteen or thirty-two pages. Three Supplements would have been printed either at one sixteen and one eight page section – or a thirty-two with eight pages cut to waste. So the Cub Scouts, Scouts and Venture Scouts each had a Supplement – plus what was titled the *Bonus Supplement,* written and edited by the Programme and Training Department and offering ideas for all Sections, for Groups and Districts.

In February 1968 I was again called in to meet with Rex, Laurence and Ted – this time to be commissioned to write a book as *'an aid to training and programme planning in the Scout Section'.* The book would be published in my name and I would be paid royalties on sales. *Programme Planning in the Scout Troop* was published eighteen months later in September 1969. Launched at a national camp for Scout Leaders at Gilwell Park in that month, the book ran to some 218 pages and sold at eleven shillings and sixpence (about 57p).

Harry, a long-time friend (the fourth 'vicar' at our wedding) and by this time a Scout Leader in Hutton, near Brentwood, helped me in devising the planning sheets and inscribed the details into the printed planners that we reproduced in the book. These were sold in packs to complement the book. Harry decided to invent a Scout Group – the 2nd Childerditch – on the basis that Childerditch is a small village in Essex without a Scout Group. Whilst there was always the possibility that there might be a 1st Childerditch at sometime in the future, the probability of a 2nd was more than remote.

Interviewed and appointed

Advertisements for a number of appointments at Scout Headquarters appeared in the February 1968 issue of THE SCOUTER. In addition to that of General Editor, the posts of International Secretary and Assistant Director of Leader Training would become vacant on retirement, whilst a new post of Deputy Director of Fund Raising needed to be filled. It was a time of major change. The role of Camp Chief at Gilwell Park had gone and in its place came the Director of Leader Training. The Chief Executive Commissioner would have a team of Executive Commissioners reporting to him. A number of other holders of senior posts were due to retire within a year or two – not least the Chief Executive Commissioner and the Publicity Manager.

I was short-listed for the post of General Editor and interviewed on 10th April. I recall very little of the interview nor of the days immediately before or afterwards for I was unwell for some three weeks with a severe bout of dysentery which left me weak and dehydrated. I was so unwell that I was physically incapable of travelling into London other than by car. The Rev. Bill Barnes offered to drive me to and from the interview. I lay on the back seat of the car and had to be assisted by Bill and Yvonne into the lift at 25 Buckingham Palace Road.

The interview panel was chaired by Henry Collis, Chairman of the Programme and Training Sub-committee, and included Rex Hazlewood, Don

Grisbrook (who would retire from the RAF as an Education Officer and take up the appointment of Executive Commissioner, Relationships, in a year or so) and a designer friend of Henry Collis.

Returning home, I remained on my sick bed for some days, unable to recall anything about the interview and dreading the worst. Rex wrote one of his charming – but, as ever, short – letters to me on 16th April, expressing his concern that I had been so unwell.

His comments that *"it was obvious when we saw you last week"* left me in little doubt that I had not impressed the panel. But a week or so later, Rex telephoned to tell me that I was to be offered the appointment. The delay was due to the fact that the appropriate committee had to endorse the panel's decision. The letter in confirmation was dated 29th April.

I learned later that Jack Cox, until recently Editor of *Boys' Own Paper*, was amongst those interviewed. Published at the end of its life by BPC Publishing Limited, *Boys' Own Paper* was closed down the previous year in 1967 at the same time as THE SCOUT ceased publication. Jack had edited *Boys' Own Paper* for twenty-one years and its closure must have come as a bitter blow to him for he was nearing retirement, but with a few years of working life left. Equally, I would guess, not being appointed as General Editor must have hurt. I came to know Jack well over the coming years when he contributed to both THE SCOUTER and SCOUTING and edited the Purnell Scout Annuals from his retirement in North Wales.

Jack had a wide knowledge of so many topics and wrote text that ebbed and flowed seemingly with ease, but I knew that he was a word craftsman who spent hours honing his articles and books.

A well-known Scout author had contacted me prior to the interviews. He, too, was considering applying, but said that he would withdraw his application if I would agree to offering him certain freelance assignments should I be appointed to the post. I made the point that I could not commit myself in that way, but he withdrew his application none-the-less.

The Cornhill Insurance Company were generous in their understanding. I would serve out my three months' notice, but I would be given a day each week to spend time at Scout Headquarters, and visit printers and other businesses with whom I would work in my new role as General Editor.

In at the deep end

In those three months I tried to absorb much of the technicalities of editing a monthly magazine together with a range of books. I travelled to Norwich to see THE SCOUTER on the press at Page Bros. Magazines and books were typeset using machinery that had not changed for many years, but the whole printing process was about to go through a major revolution. I saw paper being produced in mills along the Thames; again, all this would change.

Rex ran a tight ship, with just himself and Clare Wyatt – who had recently been appointed Assistant General Editor in recognition of the fact that Clare had been at Scout Headquarters for something over 30 years. When Clare first entered the offices at 25 Buckingham Palace Road in the late 1930s, Baden-Powell had his office down the corridor.

Clare and her husband, Len, lived in Bexley in Kent. They had no children, but enjoyed a very active social life, with Scottish dancing at the top of the list. Clare mothered bachelor Rex, who had rooms in St. John's Wood where he lived from Monday to Friday. I would guess, but I never dared ask if it were true, that Rex had a lady there who cooked his meals, did his laundry and cleaned for him. Although he had written countless books and compiled numerous recipes, Rex admitted to me that he could barely cook an egg.

At weekends he went home to Newmarket, where he had built a self-contained one bedroom flat over the garage of his brother's house. Rex's brother was Group Scout Leader of a lively Scout Group in the town. Rex's nephew – then around six or so, was his pride and joy. Rex would work his way through the newly-opened shops in Carnaby Street to buy the latest fashion garment for his young grandson.

It was agreed that I would join the staff at 25 Buckingham Palace Road at the beginning of August to work side by side with Rex, who would leave towards the end of that month.

The September 1968 issue of THE SCOUTER would be Rex's last and the October issue my first. In fact, Rex had completed his part of the work on the September issue by the time I arrived, leaving Clare to see it through proof and print stages. Rex spent but an hour or so each day in the office, wandering off to see friends around the building, having lunch with those with whom he had done business over the years – and getting off to Newmarket to spend time with his nephew as soon as he could each week. Not that I minded. He had given me all the help I needed. Now it was up to me. And Rex had served the Movement superbly well over many, many years.

On my first day as General Editor, Steve across the road brought his taxi to the front of our house, where we loaded in the back my four drawer filing cabinet filled to the brim with programme and activity material. It was my lifeblood and I wanted it ready at hand. We drove to the back door of the offices in Buckingham Palace Road, where we unloaded the cabinet, carrying it and the files to the lift, and up to the third floor back, which I would occupy for the next four years or so.

Clare was anxious to ensure that the changeover should be as seamless as possible, explaining that there were three things she did regularly for Rex and which, no doubt, I would wish her to do for me. Firstly, she placed his bets on the horses at the nearest betting shop. I explained that I did not bet on anything, let alone the horses of which I had scant knowledge. Clare sighed an acceptance of this.

Secondly, Clare would be pleased if I would hand over my medication and any tablets so that she might administer these at the appropriate time of day. Again, I explained that I was not on any medication nor did I have any tablets. Clare was not satisfied and pressed me to think hard. I doubt she believed me when I assured her that I was a tablet-free zone. Finally, Clare informed me that she would make an appointment once every month with the gentleman's hairdresser in the Army and Navy Stories in Victoria Street. I was not asked, but told that this would be so – and it was. The hairdresser was somewhat alarmed when I appeared on my first monthly visit, for I had a full head of hair whereas Rex was fast balding. An adjustment to the price previously charged had to be accepted, for I feared Clare more than the hairdresser.

I had been told by the young men in the Programme and Training Department that I would be well advised to order any furniture I might require before joining the staff. I had noted that some staff in the General Office were sitting on ammunition boxes rather than chairs. Rex's desk was falling to pieces and whilst he had a chair, it too had seen better days.

I broached Rex, who generously agreed that I should spend the Association's money (for it was not his!). Clare and I went off to Heal's in Tottenham Court Road to meet with Kerry Dix, who worked there, was a Scout Leader and contributed articles to THE SCOUTER. We arranged for a set of new curtains to be made for Rex's – now my – office. Using my contacts in the City, I ordered a new desk, a chair, a bookcase and telephone cabinet.

The first I knew that the furniture had arrived was when the man on reception telephoned to advise me that the desk was too big to go into the lift and would have to be returned from whence it came. I dashed downstairs to find a small group of staff gawping and, I sensed, more than a little amused at this new whippersnapper of an editor thinking he could have a brand spanking new desk when theirs – if they had desks at all – were well past their use-by date.

The lift was of the open-plan variety, with metal gates and metal grids all the way up alongside the staircase. The desk which, I would have to admit, was rather large had been upended in an attempt to get it into the lift, but to no avail. Some bright spark, knowing that I had written on the subject of pioneering projects, suggested that we might rig up a block and tackle outside the editor's window and haul it up to the second floor.

At that point a young man appeared from the General Office, suggesting that the answer might be to tip the upended desk slightly, whilst easing higher the metal struts immediately above the lift gates. It worked – and I had the distinct impression that one or two of those watching were disappointed that the desk was not returned. That young man was Jock Barr, who later rose to be Headquarters Commissioner for Venture Scouts and a senior professional with the Prince's Trust. I was more than grateful to Jock for saving my face that day – but more of Jock later.

Time-warp

The Headquarters offices of The Scout Association at 25 Buckingham Palace Road were in something of a time-warp in 1968. The Association had occupied the three floors above the Scout Shop for some 50 or so years. Baden-Powell had walked these corridors as had his successors, Lord Somers, Lord Rowallan and Sir Charles (later Lord) Maclean. There was an austerity about the set-up and a certain military exactitude with a lingering aroma of battledress and boiled potatoes.

The library was claustrophobic with its musty bookcases bearing down on the long, highly-polished table surrounded by chairs covered in green leather with the Association's crest on the seats. The table and chairs occupied almost the entire floor space, so that you had to shuffle between chairs and bookcases to get from one end to the other.

Once a week Fred Hurll, Chief Executive Commissioner, would hold what he called the Secretaries' Meetings, but which some of my newly-appointed colleagues and I rather disrespectfully referred to as the Sex Tea Parties, but not – I would hasten to add – in Mr Hurll's hearing. All heads of departments were expected to attend in the library at 3pm on Tuesdays to take tea with Mr Hurll. Many of these departmental heads retained the archaic title of Secretary (thus International Secretary, Relationships Secretary) in the manner of Government (Foreign Secretary).

It was a very gentlemanly affair, which was not surprising for all the heads of departments were male. One lady was appointed to such a role shortly after I came to Headquarters, but I regret to say that she did not last long. Here we would chatter about the latest gossip and be expected to report briefly on what we were doing.

Fred Hurll's son, Michael, was at that time a top BBC producer – responsible for shows such as *The Two Ronnies, Top Of The Pops, Blind Date, The Billy Cotton Band Show, Surprise Surprise.* It was said that Ralph Reader, who was a close friend of Fred Hurll, had steered the young Michael Hurll in the early stages of his career. A number of members of the senior staff at Scout Headquarters had been amongst the cast of the early *London Gang Shows*, including Fred, Rex and Geoff Birch, then Managing Director of Scout Shops Limited, the commercial arm of the Association. Laurence Stringer was on stage in the final two or three *London Gang Shows.*

There were certain precedents and protocols which had to be observed at 25 BP Road, especially in the restaurant on the top floor. This served both staff and members of the public, who could – if they were so minded and very few were – walk in off the street and partake of lunch. The cooks were all ladies of uncertain age and a kindly, motherly, friendly lot at that. The food they produced was substantial and filling, lots of pies and puddings and fresh vegetables – the latter being cooked until the very stuffing had been boiled or beaten out of them so that they were limp and watery. Afters, sweets or puddings were made on the premises with liberal helpings of custard with everything, served by a lady with a huge ladle. If you did not want custard, you had to be pretty nifty in moving your tray out of her reach, for the custard would come swooping down before you could wink an eyelid.

The tables were wooden topped and scrubbed every afternoon. One very large table stood in the centre of the room and there was an unwritten rule that only the professional heads of departments and Headquarters Commissioners or volunteers who were members of committees might sit at this table. The remaining staff and members of the public (if any dared venture here) sat at smaller tables around the outside of the room.

On my first day I went to sit at one of the smaller tables, but before my bottom touched the chair, I was told – in hushed tones, I would add – that I was about to commit a cardinal sin and it was best that few should know about it. I moved over to the large table in the middle – and you could hear the sighs of relief from those in the know.

The be-whiskered caretaker and his blonde wife lived in a small flat on the top floor. They were said to have a teenage daughter, but I never saw her if they did. The flat roof was their garden, with an array of flower pots and chairs for taking the sun. The caretaker was a man to be feared and someone best humoured. When I worked late in the evening, he would wander around the building, grunting his displeasure at seeing me still there. Others who worked late were the lads in the Programme and Training Department, who were often set impossible timescales in which tasks had to be completed by their effervescent and equally hard-working Executive Commissioner, Ted Hayden.

Don Grisbrook joined the staff at 25 Buckingham Palace Road as Executive Commissioner (Relationships) shortly after I took up my post. Don enjoyed working long hours and often Mike Sloane in the Programme and Training Department, Don and I would be the only ones there in the late evening. Don would suggest that those who were working late might join him in the late afternoon at Bumbles, a tea rooms on the other side of BP Road. This establishment had green curtains in the windows hanging from brass rods with furnishings that had been there for decades. (Wandering through Victoria in the autumn of 2008 – some forty years later – I was pleased to see that Bumbles is still there, although the green curtains and the brass rods had gone.)

Don made a number of contacts with politicians in his relationships role and would bring them to meet with me when he entertained them in his office. One such was David Ennals, Labour MP for Dover and then for Norwich North, later created a life peer as Baron Ennals of Norwich. David Ennals attended a national camp for leaders at Gilwell Park which, in itself, was hardly noteworthy, except for the fact that – remarkable as it may sound today – in the 1960s few members of the Scout establishment had ever met, let alone spoken to, a Member of Parliament, let alone a Labour MP.

Also in the 1970s the tradition of the British Youth Council (BYC) to appoint vibrant Chairmen started to make an impression on national youth policy. The BYC elected David Hunt as Chairman (later a member of the House of Lords), Janet Paraskeva (later First Civil Service Commissioner) and Peter Mandelson (later a Labour MP and now Lord Mandleson).

At the time when Don brought Peter Mandleson to meet me, Peter was a Venture Scout and about to lead the BYC contingent to the controversial 11th World Festival on Youth in Cuba where motions were passed on the human rights record in the USSR and USA.

This caused more than a few raised eyebrows along the corridors at 25 BP Road, especially amongst the more right wing Headquarters Commissioners and members of staff and committees, who feared that the Association was going to the dogs – and fast – now that we were allowing our young members to rub shoulders with Cubans, and communist Cubans at that.

The Scout Association moved ponderously from being The Boy Scouts Association, and throwing off the shackles of the past was painful and, for many, more than a little difficult. The offices at 25 Buckingham Palace Road – fondly referred to as 25 BP Road in honour of the Founder – held memories that were difficult to discard.

And none of this would change until the decision was made in the early 1970s to move from BP Road to purpose-built offices adjoining Baden-Powell House, the Scout hostel, a mile or so away in South Kensington.

Change, but not for the sake of it

There was an expectation that I would bring about change to THE SCOUTER and to the books. Rex commented that he would expect me to do so with my first issue of THE SCOUTER and that if he did not like what I had done, he would let me know and I should count that as sign that I had succeeded in doing what was necessary. In fact, Rex did write to me in early October. He did not like what I had done and, therefore, offered his sincere congratulations.

Rex had a very simple – and, in many ways, sensible – method of running THE SCOUTER. Towards the end of each year, he would decide how many regular series of monthly articles he wished to run in the magazine during the following year. There were a number that had appeared for some years, others had started more recently. Well over half the pages each month were filled with regular features – in this way, Rex had at least half the magazine filled before he looked around for fresh and current material. I decided to retain all the regular features for the remaining three issues of the year, which would give me time to make some decisions about the future.

With the demise of THE SCOUT magazine a few months earlier, no regular programme or training material was being published. The lack of this was being met partially by the 16 pages of pull-out training supplements in the middle of THE SCOUTER, but more was needed. I knew I would be walking something of a tightrope here, for there were those in high places who saw THE SCOUTER as a journal for adults and who believed there was no place within its pages for programme or training material.

They accepted – reluctantly – that the training supplements now had a firm place in the magazine, but were critical of me whenever they sensed that I was increasing the more practical material at the expense of the theoretical and the inspirational.

It has to be said that Rex was well-read and a brilliant writer – and I was neither of these things. Rex had written under the pseudonym of Delta for many years. These were warm pieces of considerable literary merit, which had been the inspiration of many – me included – over the years. There was no way that I could emulate this and I did not intend trying. I had to plough my own furrow.

There was some reportage within the pages of THE SCOUTER, but this tended to be of national events, such as the annual Windsor Parade of Queen's Scouts and Ralph Reader's *Gang Show*. From time to time someone would send in a few photographs and a description of an event that had taken place, and this would be pulled together by Clare into a readable article.

I decided that over the coming months I would retain some of the regular features, dispense with others, introduce some new regular articles, encourage a group of – yet to be found – young writers with practical day by day experience of being involved in the movement of the day and build a team of writers and photographers who would go out to report on some of the exciting and innovative things that were happening. In addition, I would get around the country to report on what was happening. I had no intention of being desk-bound in London.

I wanted to make an impact with my first issue and one way to do this would be to change the design. Without being unfair to Rex, his SCOUTER was not designed, it was put together almost by chance. Money was tight and so the photographs and artwork were turned into printing blocks en masse rather than individually – with the result that the photographs did not always fit the column width.

Within a few days of my joining the staff, I had a telephone call from the designer who had been a member of the panel that interviewed me for the post. Would I be interested in using his services to modernise the magazine? I met with him and whilst he was offering a good service, it was clear that the budget would not stretch to hiring him.

It so happened that at that time David Goodman, a member of the 1st Aldborough Hatch and one of my former Patrol Leaders, was in the final year of a degree course in graphic design. David lived 300 yards or so away from my home and I asked him if he would like to use his newly acquired skills to help me redesign the magazine. David readily agreed to do so and we fixed a small monthly fee that would help him – and provide me with a good service.

In 1968 publishers had to rely on their printers to come up with some novel designs for headings to feature articles or you could use sheets of Letraset. David and I opted for the latter. I would bring home paste-up sheets with the galley proofs cut up and stuck down, leaving space for the headings. David would make these up in Letraset and return the sheets to me a day or so later. And so this was how my first issue of THE SCOUTER was produced and subsequent issues for some months to follow.

I waited in my office when the October 1968 issue of THE SCOUTER arrived and copies were distributed to staff and volunteers around the building – hoping that someone would call by to say that they had noticed some changes. But I waited in vain – for that at least. A day or so later Cyril Goodhind, the Association's grim faced General Secretary, poked his head round my door. *"Sep-a-rat,"* he called as he withdrew. It was the first of many spelling lessons, culminating when Clare retired in her presenting me with *A Dictionary of Difficult Words* – which I have on my bookshelves today.

It all sounds terribly amateurish – and it was. If there were electric typewriters around, I did not see one. Computers had yet to be mass-produced for offices and publishing. There were no facsimile (FAX) machines, but we did have a photocopier. It was what might be termed a "wet" copier, in that it involved pulling damp sheets of paper with a brownish tint off the machine – sheets that had to be left to dry. However, if you made the mistake of leaving the sheet in direct sunlight, everything disappeared and you were left with a dry sheet of brown hardened paper that was prone to crack.

My first brush with the media came four months after taking up my appointment – on Boxing Day 1968 when I took a call from the BBC at around lunchtime. They sent a car and I found myself in a studio at Broadcasting House having to explain away the fact that the Scout Diary for 1969 included a piece about how to make a homemade bomb! The text had, of course, been written and approved prior to my appointment as General Editor, but I now had to take the rap – just at the time when the troubles were beginning to reach boiling point in Northern Ireland where the diary had gone on sale. The recipe for the bomb involved salt peter and was comparatively innocuous, the kind of thing that schoolboys (including my older brother) had played with for years.

I took the blame – as I had to – and apologised profusely. But I learned a hard lesson that day.

Eleven magical years

The next eleven years were truly magical for me – for I was doing what I enjoyed and getting paid to do it. What more could a man ask?

From those distinctly amateurish beginnings with me as editor, THE SCOUTER developed and grew – and it has to be said that had Rex still been at the helm it would, no doubt, have developed in a very similar way. Different, but similar. But develop it would have done.

The books, too, moved forward for as General Editor I had the responsibility for those published by the Association and also for books and training aids that were produced under licence by outside publishers.

From a staff of Clare and me, the editorial department grew to meet the needs of an organisation that was moving forward at a rapid pace. The movement was crying out for a magazine and publications that would enable its voluntary leaders to implement the recommendations of Advance Party Report – and that could not be achieved by two people in a back office. Not only did we need an army of dedicated and committed volunteer and professional writers, photographers and artists, but a trained staff to support them and one that would ensure that their work was presented in a professional manner.

THE SCOUTER changed its name to SCOUTING in 1970. Not exactly a dramatic thing to do, but one which galvanised the adult leaders throughout the country into those who saw this as a move forward (and recognition that we needed a magazine not just for Scouters, but for all leaders and supporters – including Patrol Leaders) and those who saw this as the beginning of the end of the movement as they had known it. Guessing that such a change would unleash the hounds of hell upon my shoulders, I hatched a cunning plan – encouraging one or two readers in different parts of the country to write to our *Letters* columns suggesting that a change of title was long overdue. Thus it was never my idea but a decision made to meet the groundswell of opinion amongst the readership. And it worked.

A Patrol Leader's Supplement replaced the Bonus Supplement of earlier days. With the aid of generous sponsorship from Webb Ivory (whose fundraising Christmas and everyday cards were – and still are – the lifeblood of many Scout Groups) we were able to take the front covers first into a second colour and later into full colour. We were also able to afford to introduce a second colour into one or two sections of the magazine. And if all that sounds a bit unexciting, I would remind my readers that this was the 1970s – when electric typewriters were just beginning to take off and word processors and personal computers were something akin to Dr

Who. Digital photography and computerised setting would revolutionise printing and publishing in a decade or two – but not just yet.

I made a number of errors of judgement from the editorial chair, but this was inevitable during eleven years. But I was accused of other errors and blunders which, in my view, I did not make. Bobby Brown wrote a series – *It occurred to me* – which ran for some years in which he recounted incidents that occurred in his life as a family man and as a Scout Leader in Edinburgh. In one article he recalled that one evening whilst his wife was out with the Girl Guides, his two-year-old son had asked for the *"bloody potty"* – and went on to make the point that we have to be very careful as parents and as leaders about the language we use in front of those to whom we should be setting an example.

I received a number of letters of complaint that I had allowed the word *"bloody"* to appear in the pages of the magazine, whilst a Headquarters Commissioner made it known that he would be calling to see me to register his disapproval. Imagine my surprise when he did so – and told me that he found the word *"potty"* offensive!

I was on leave when one of a regular series of articles on young men's fashions arrived in the office. Written by a PR consultant who was a member of the Association's PR Committee (and who, in his younger days, claimed to have shared a Thames Riverside apartment with Lord Snowdon when Anthony Armstrong-Jones – as he then was – courted Princess Margaret), we were publishing these in an attempt to attract Venture Scouts to our readership. Clare Wyatt proof read the article and thought nothing of the statement that a new range of male briefs would be *"the start of gay beginnings"* – for the word *"gay"* had changed its meaning in recent years without Clare seemingly being aware of this. Once more I took the flak.

In addition to my work in leading the editorial department, I was part of the senior team of professional staff and as such I was expected to become involved in a range of duties over and beyond those of editing. Speaking engagements as a member of the Headquarters team took up an increasing amount of my time as my reputation for being willing to undertake these grew. I took a role in helping to support the volunteers who were the lifeblood of the movement – and often in steering them, although few members of the professional staff would admit that they did so, but many did. Indeed, had they not done so the movement could well have remained moribund.

Editorial staff

It soon became apparent that I would generate correspondence and so we expanded the editorial department by taking on an audio typist and, of course, installing audio equipment which was unchartered territory at 25 BP Road. This young lady was a superb typist, but she caused some consternation with her mini-skirts – which were highly fashionable at the time. The Chairman of the Religious Advisory Board asked if he might see me to express his concern for he considered that my typist was not wearing a mini-skirt but a large belt – and what was I going to do about it?

An office junior was the next step in the expansion of the editorial empire – as some of my longer-in-the-tooth and longer serving colleagues started to refer to the gang at the second floor back. When it became known that there was a vacancy, Jock Barr – he who had facilitated my desk being moved into the lift – was first in the queue. Jock moved up from the General Office, staying for about six months. He was keen as mustard and a great asset in that he knew his way around 25 BP Road and the characters that inhabited it. At that time he had started to run a lively Venture Scout Unit in his home town of Southend. I knew that I would not be able to keep Jock for long and when a vacancy occurred in the Programme and Training Department I encouraged him to apply. But that was not the last I was to see of Jock.

Whilst Jock was still with me, we appointed the magazine's first graphic designer. David Goodman had continued to help me at home with designing the pages of THE SCOUTER week by week, but had now completed his graphic design course and was looking for full-time work. David spent some two years with me, making a considerable contribution in updating and modernising the magazine as we launched SCOUTING and the books. He moved on to design part-works before setting up his own design business.

David Saint, a young Scouter from South London, was next to join the staff. David was instrumental in persuading me that the editorial department could fill a need for training charts for the Cub Scout and Scout Sections. We had published a training chart on tracking over a double-page spread in the Cub Scout Supplement. Drawn by Doug Mountford, this had proved very popular. We produced a reprint – which sold out within days. The drawing lent itself to enlargement and reprinting as a wall chart. Within days of advertising the availability of the chart, we were being swamped with orders. Postal tubes and labels had to be ordered and a system set up for despatch. David handled this with considerable skill and we started to expand the list of charts – publishing them first in the Supplements and then producing enlarged reprints.

David wanted to write and had a regular monthly column which was fed with material from readers and through David's growing contacts around the country. David enjoyed trips away from the office when he would drive me in the staff car. This was referred to as the Chief Scout's car for it was used by the Chief from time to time when he was in London. A small purple flag could be flown from the front of the bonnet – passers by would often mistake this for an indication of royalty.

On one occasion David drove his girl friend, Graham and me to the Welsh Jamboree in North Wales. On the way we stopped over for an hour or two at a convent where one of David's aunts was a nun – talking to her through a small wicket gate in a massive wooden door. That night a violent storm hit the North Wales coast – blowing tents away and causing havoc throughout the jamboree site. Our tents survived, but only just.

As with a number of young men and women who worked for me during my eleven years as General Editor, there came a time when we could no longer provide the progression that David needed and, indeed, deserved. David left to work as a fund raiser for a medical charity, but continued as a Scout Leader. He set up a publishing company to produce Scout booklets, which he sold initially through mail order and later – when the company was established – through Scout Shops and Gilwell Park. David was a successful entrepreneur who worked hard to achieve a unique place in the annals of Scout publishing.

Much later – in 1990 in fact – David Saint established Action Planning after working for sixteen years in regional fundraising and fundraising director posts with Scope, Sense, SANE and Arthritis Care. He was recognised as one of the not-for-profit sector's leading authorities on strategy, management and fundraising. He advised the Boards and Senior Management Teams of some of the most significant organisations in the sector. Today David is a member of the Institute of Fundraising (where he was the founder chairman of the Consultants Group), former Chairman of EU Consult, a European network of consultants, a trustee of Andrews Charitable Trust, the Christian Initiative Trust and Advantage Africa, and a non-executive director of Andrews and Partners. I mention all this because I am very proud of what David has achieved – which had little to do with me but a great deal to do with David's enthusiasm, commitment and determination to succeed.

A string of young graphic designers came and went. The department provided a good starting point for a designer but we could not keep them for long. The move from 25 BP Road to purpose-built offices at Baden-Powell House would eventually resolve the problem of designers not staying for more than a few months. We created one design studio for both the editorial and publicity departments, and whilst this had problems from time to time, it did solve the difficulty of coping when one designer had left and another had yet to be appointed.

The book side of the department gathered momentum and to keep pace with the demands that were being made by the programme and training departments for more support material, we appointed a book editor and later an assistant.

The move from 25 BP Road to the new offices was in two stages. First, we decamped and set up shop on one floor of Baden-Powell House, the Association's hostel in South Kensington. Three floors of offices at 25 BP Road were to be crammed into three dormitories and a couple of single rooms. It was a tight squeeze for some nine months. Ken Stevens, who has succeeded Fred Hurll as Chief Executive Commissioner, occupied a single bedroom as his office. Next door was a toilet, but Ken considered that the sound of constant flushing was not conducive to his status and so a lock was fitted to the toilet door to which he had the only key.

The editorial and publicity departments occupied one dormitory. My desk was wedged into the far corner with barely room for me to move my chair in and out. Indeed, I was sitting there whilst working late one evening when an IRA bomber blew himself up in the mews on the opposite side of Cromwell Road. The blast was such that I was lifted from my chair and onto my desk. This was the second time I had been in the office in the late evening when the IRA had struck. The first time was at 25 BP Road – when a bomb had blown up the pillar box outside Victoria Station. Again the earth moved and me with it.

Shortly before the move, Eric Mawbey had joined the department, largely to manage the growing business with the training charts. At Baden-Powell House Eric had his own office – in a bathroom! Eric was Group Scout Leader of a thriving Scout Group in my home District – a Group with its own Headquarters on the side of a main road. Eric – who had worked all his life in the docks until he took early retirement and came to work for us – was an astute fundraiser for his Group. Huge bill boards shielded the Scout Headquarters and the grassed grounds from the road and passing traffic – and these were hired out to advertisers, the income from which paid most of the bills for heating and lighting.

The editorial gang expands

There were a number of members of the staff of the editorial department with whom I had particular affinity and we have kept in touch over the years.

With Clare Wyatt's retirement imminent soon after we moved from 25 BP Road, we appointed Geoff Platt as her replacement in the role of Deputy General Editor. Geoff, a Venture Scout Leader in Hitchin working in the London Offices of British Rail, and I had met at a national Venture Scout event in the late 60s, where I learned that he had ambitions to write.

I went to meet Geoff in his home town of Hitchin in Hertfordshire, where he introduced me to his mother, his father having died when Geoff was younger. Geoff took me for a meal in the town and later to his Venture Scout Unit. It was a thriving affair, with lively, articulate youngsters who rose to Geoff's leadership skills. Expeditions overseas and close links with the Scout County Team meant that the Unit had the kind of programme that the Advance Party intended.

Through Geoff I later met Judge James Kingham, who ran one of the first Joint Scout and Guide Units in the country, and Conrad Ascher, Assistant County Commissioner (International) for Hertfordshire. Conrad was a barrister involved with the Society of Socialist Lawyers who stood for parliament in a Norfolk seat. When the country turned to the Labour Party to form a government, Conrad's constituency was one of the few that voted the other way. Conrad gave my eldest son, Graham, the chance to shadow him one summer when Graham had decided that he wanted to be a lawyer.

Geoff agreed to become the voluntary sub-editor of the *Patrol Leader's Supplement* which I decided to launch as part of the move from THE SCOUTER to SCOUTING in January 1971. Geoff joined the professional staff in late 1974 during our last few days at 25 BP Road. Most of the furniture had to be disposed of and Geoff took my desk home – and used it for many years after that. I took my bookcase and telephone cabinet – and have them today. Terry Stringer, the book editor at the time, trudged home to Clapham each evening clutching everything and anything that no one else wanted from the building. Indeed, if the bricks or tiles had been loose, he would have taken them too.

The editorial secretary moved on and we advertised for a replacement. Charlotte, a young lady Assistant Cub Scout Leader in Hampstead, applied and arrived for interview wearing a fur coat which I considered had seen better days. (I have since learned that the fur was, in fact, racoon and belonged to Charlotte's grandmother. It is still in Charlotte's possession, although the moths have had a few meals and it is not in the best condition.)

Neither Clare nor Geoff were impressed with the young lady in the questionable fur. Indeed, Geoff went out of his way to tell me that if the decision was down to him, there way no way he would appoint the girl in the fur. However, I decided that Charlotte would make a superb secretary and offered her the post.

Charlotte joined us a few days later and moved with us to the dormitories at Baden-Powell House.

I noticed that whilst Clare remained somewhat frosty towards Charlotte, Geoff appeared to be warming to her. One afternoon Geoff asked me if I could recommend a good restaurant in South Kensington as he wished to entertain a friend. When I asked if this friend might be Charlotte, Geoff blushed and changed the subject somewhat rapidly. It was only a matter of a few months before Geoff and Charlotte were engaged.

My daughter Heather was a bridesmaid at their wedding in Hitchin in 1976 – riding for the first time in her life in a horse-drawn carriage. Yvonne and Heather – who was ten at the time – set out very early from our home on the day of the wedding to travel to Hitchin. I was left to herd twelve-year-old Graham and Richard, who was barely three, by bus, underground and train to Hitchin – with the very clear injunction from Yvonne that the two boys were to arrive in pristine condition and clean from head to toe. I succeeded – but only just and it was with considerable relief that I handed Graham, but more especially Richard, over to their mother. The wedding was a grand affair – but not without incident. A highwayman held up the newly weds in their horse-drawn carriage in the middle of Hitchin on a busy Saturday afternoon, but all was well for the fellow calling for their money or their life was one of the Venture Scouts.

Life in the editorial dormitory at Baden-Powell House was not without incident. Jack Olden, the Publicity Manager, and his gang shared with us – they were near the door whilst we were ensconced at the far end. Harold Wyld, the Press Officer, and Maureen Downing, Jack's Secretary, enjoyed a somewhat raucous relationship.

There was a feeling abroad that the editorial gang were a bit too fun-loving for their own good. In addition to Geoff and Charlotte, the team included Peter Brooks, a Scouter in Chingford, Richard Bonwick, the designer, and the irascible Terry.

When Eileen, the tea and coffee lady, arrived with her trolley, there would be a general stampede from the editorial end to ensure that all the Mint Yo-Yos and Wagon Wheels were snapped up by the time Harold and Maureen got there. For a reason which escaped me at the time, Eileen always served the editorial gang last but collected our cups first. I learned to gulp my coffee.

One day some Cub Scouts were staying at the House, sleeping in the dormitory immediately above the editorial stronghold. They started lowering various objects down on ropes from the windows above and the editorial team sent other objects back. I was away from the office at the time, let it be said.

Geoff, Charlotte, Heather and I went to Brands Hatch one Sunday for a jolly involving scout cars and *Radio One.* Mike Batt, the composer, famous for *Bright eyes* among many other pop songs, was there and recognised Charlotte from her previous life – although I did not know what that life was. Heather came away with Mike's autograph.

Both Geoff and Charlotte played a significant part in the development of SCOUTING. Geoff was enthusiastic about everything and nothing was ever too much trouble. He had a wicked sense of humour and was a popular speaker around the country. Geoff would drive the office car, taking me to and from events, writing and playing a full part in the life of the magazine. And Charlotte was supportive in every possible way to us both – but especially to Geoff because, after all, she married him. They have a son, Charles, whose ambition from an early age was to be a paramedic. He joined the St John Ambulance Association and after dogged and committed persistence achieved his ambition to be a paramedic in the NHS in his mid-twenties.

The Honourable Tim

After some nine months in the dormitories we were shifted into the new offices next door. Terry moved on and the time came to appoint two new editorial assistants – one to work on the books and the other on the magazine. Short-listing and interviews were arranged in the autumn of 1976 – in those days we did not have two or three days of assessments and complicated interview processes, with panels of the great and the good. Appointments were often made by gut-feeling, which appeared to work. Geoff and I spent half-an-hour with each of the half-dozen candidates and made the decision. But this time Geoff and I found ourselves in something of a quandary.

Three candidates stood out from the rest – Bill Bruce, Tim Lamb and Paul Moynihan. Bill had already proved himself to me as an aspiring artist, designer and writer. Tim had the bounce and self-assurance of an English county cricketer who was looking for work over the winter – and would only be with us for six months or so. Paul was also known to me and was keen as mustard to join the staff of SCOUTING.

Geoff and I decided that we would offer Bill one post and tossed a coin to decide who the second editorial assistant would be. Tim won and stayed until the following April, when Paul was invited to join SCOUTING.

The Honourable Timothy Michael Lamb was a right-arm fast-medium bowler playing professional cricket for Middlesex when he joined the staff of SCOUTING at the end of the season in 1976.

When he came down from Oxford the previous year he had worked over the winter as a journalist on *Lloyds List,* but relished the chance to join SCOUTING – not only because he would have the opportunity to do some writing but also because his flat was immediately across the road from the offices in Cromwell Road.

In his six months with us, Tim was never on time when arriving for work. Invariably late, Tim would explain that because he lived so close at hand, there was no way that he could make up the time over such a short journey.

"If you are late for work," Tim explained, *"you can walk faster to the station and run up the escalators to make up the time. I can't do that – so I will always be late."*

My suggestion that he might set out earlier was met with a look of total incredulity that I might even think such a thing would be possible for a young man who enjoyed a lively social life outside the office.

Tim was a sparky character who fitted in well with the rest of the team, who would pull his leg unmercifully over his constant need throughout the day to telephone Denise, his girl friend (and future wife), to check what they would be cooking for dinner that evening or where they would be going at the weekend.

Tim disliked the fact that he was an Honourable, a title for which he qualifies as the second son of the second Baron Rochester. His grandfather, the first Baron Rochester became Liberal MP for Rochester in Kent in 1906, was ennobled in 1931 and for nearly five years was Paymaster-General.

Tim's Father and Mother, Lord and Lady Rochester, dropped into the editorial offices late one afternoon on their way to have dinner with Tim. Lord Rochester subsequently became involved with the Scouting and the Unemployed Programme.

On leaving SCOUTING in April 1977, Tim went back to play for Middlesex before moving to Northamptonshire. He entered sports administration as Secretary and General Manager of Middlesex County Cricket Club in 1984, became Cricket Secretary of the Test and County Cricket Board in 1988 and Chief Executive in 1996. Under his leadership the sport of cricket witnessed a period of unprecedented reform and modernisation. Tim stepped down in 2004 amid mounting pressure over the proposed England tour to Zimbabwe and the rejection of plans he put forward to further reform the county game. Tim was appointed as Chief Executive of the Central Council for Physical Recreation in 2004.

Enter Prune

Sometime in the early 70s I received through the post a series of comic strip cartoons under the title *The Adventures of Prune*. I thought these had promise and wrote to suggest that the artist might like to meet with me at my office when he was next in London.

When Bill Bruce walked through my office door I was taken aback to find that the artist was, in fact, a young Venture Scout of barely sixteen who had travelled with his mother from his home in Wiltshire. I agreed a fee and the strip appeared in SCOUTING for four months from January 1975. Bill's artistic and writing talents had been encouraged by David Harwood, a Scouter in Wiltshire running the County Magazine, who had worked with me on the Association's handbooks following publication of the Advance Party Report in 1966.

Bill had started a degree course in design, but aborted this after a year or so. Bill told me later that he felt his talent was being directed rather than encouraged to develop. Bill was an accomplished musician, playing the piano, organ and guitar. In their spare time Bill and his older brother toured the clubs and pubs in the South West and South Wales – appearing on one occasion on the same stage as Bonnie Tyler (of *Lost in France* fame – the female Rod Stewart). By the Autumn of 1976 Bill was working for a pharmaceutical company in Cardiff designing labels for their products. The advertisement for the vacancy on SCOUTING was drawn to Bill's attention and this proved to be the break he was looking for.

Bill took the ground floor flat in the building – owned by the Association – next door to Baden-Powell House in Queen's Gate where he could often be seen in the evenings through the windows looking over the street playing the organ he had brought from home. Whenever I hear Procol Harem's *A lighter shade of pale*, I think of Bill – although he will tell you that he never played that song on the organ in his flat, but I know better. Nor that a young lady in red trousers visited him there but – again – I know better; a young lady who was to be the mother of his three sons.

Bill was – and still is – a workaholic. He was constantly on the lookout for an opportunity to write, take photographs or draw for SCOUTING – and jumped with both feet at every chance he was given. Bill was a diligent researcher, producing in-depth features on subjects as different as the history of Gilwell Park and the National Society for the Prevention of Cruelty to Children (NSPCC). Bill was commissioned by the NSPCC to design and illustrate a poster that would be a major part of their fundraising. He used my youngest son as the model for this – taking a photograph of Richard huddled into a corner with his hands up to protect his head and wearing a woollen jumper that was far too big for him (mine, in fact.). From this Bill drew the pen and ink illustration under the strap-line *'Children should be seen and not hurt'.*

That poster appeared in the press and on billboards throughout the country. Richard and I were in Romford Town Centre a year or two after the poster was first issued – Richard was convinced that people recognised him as the boy on the poster high up on the advertising hoarding above the market stalls and insisted we went straight home.

Bill perfected his writing and pen and ink drawing skills with illustrated features on a range of subjects from skateboarders to bag ladies. He shadowed a Scout Leader who worked down a coal mine for a day, going with him after work to the Scout Troop he ran near the colliery. From there Bill travelled to our home overnight, taking a bath before some well-earned sleep. It was the first – and last – time Yvonne had to remove coal dust from our bath tub.

In 1979 Bill went freelance, working from an office near Oxford Circus in Central London. When I moved to edit MILK INDUSTRY in 1980, Bill and I continued to work together on that magazine and on a number of freelance projects. Later Bill set up The Creative House, a design business in Saffron Walden. Today Bill is a director of a thriving magazine publishing company whose success owes much to Bill's energy and commitment.

Not only that, but Geoff Platt works with Bill as Editor of one of those journals – but more of that later.

In the three years Bill was with the magazine, he made a substantial contribution to its development. The front cover of the July 1979 Seventieth Anniversary issue of SCOUTING is just one example of Bill's skill. This reproduced the covers of twenty magazines, starting with the first issue of the *Headquarters Gazette.* Bill had to reconstruct that first cover – for, try as we might, we were unable to locate an original!

The rocking chair

The third young man to join the staff at this time first hove into my view through a problem I had with a rocking chair. Late in 1973, I purchased a rocking chair kit by mail order through the *Observer* newspaper. It was a somewhat reckless thing to do for whilst I have wrestled with – and beaten – most do-it-yourself tasks around the home over the years, woodwork was never a strong point – as kindly Mr Dan discovered some thirty years earlier.

Writing in my editorial in the January 1974 issue of SCOUTING about my attempts to make clear plastic castings and candles from kits sold through advertisements in the magazine where the manufacturers had sent me samples to try (during which I ruined the saucepan in which Yvonne boiled the baby's milk), I concluded the story with the following: *"A few days ago the postman arrived with a rocking chair kit I had ordered in a moment of sheer madness. I've looked at the bits twice and put it back in the box again. One day, perhaps . . ."*

A young Venture Scout from the 28th Croydon contacted me, offering the services of his Unit to build the rocking chair. The Venture Scout called in at my office to collect the kit and shortly before Christmas members of the Unit arrived at my home in their Group Scout Leader's mini-bus with the finished chair. Yvonne laid on some of her home-made cooking and a pleasant evening was passed, with each and everyone enjoying a rock or two in the chair. So fine a job did they make of it that the rocking chair stands to this day in my dining room – nearly four decades later.

Thanking the Unit in my March 1975 editorial I had this to say: *"I take my hat off to them all – in particular I would thank Paul Moynihan (he's the member of the Unit who can write) and his merry men for their kindness in making provision for my approaching old age. Magnificent!"*

And it was that self-same Paul Moynihan who joined the staff of SCOUTING in April 1977 when Tim went off to knock a few cricket balls around for Middlesex.

Paul was tall and thin with it, to the extent that if he was delayed in his journey from Croydon to South Kensington, the staff would – rather unkindly – wonder if he might have fallen through the grating over a drain somewhere en route. But Paul has a great sense of humour and was able to ride the rather ungenerous comments made from time to time about his sparse frame.

Paul was an assiduous deputy editor whose proof reading skills saved us from many a printing blunder. More than that, he had an almost photographic memory as far as SCOUTING magazine was concerned. Paul could tell you the second colour on the front cover and the colours used inside the magazine for issues going back over the years and if we wanted to know in which issue a particular article, cartoon or photograph had appeared, Paul was your man.

Paul moved to join a major magazine publisher in his home town of Croydon at the end of 1979 where his skills as a writer and editor were shared with a wider audience in the camping and caravanning leisure industries. After Paul and I moved from SCOUTING, we worked together on *The Scout Troop*, a book for the Association, and *Camping,* published by in the *Whizz Kids Series*, by Macdonald.

Later in the 1993 Paul returned to The Scout Association as Archivist, a post which suited his attention to detail and his remarkable memory.

In 2007 – the Scouts' Centenary Year – Paul had a major part in writing and editing Hamlyn's glossy hardback *An Official History of Scouting*. In a letter to me dated 19th October 2006, Paul wrote: *"As the person who gave me my first break into writing, I thought you might like this complimentary copy of my latest."* A number of events in which I was involved feature in the book, whilst I am mentioned twice by name. It is somewhat humbling, especially when I realise that there are probably only half-a-dozen people whose names appear in the book who were still alive in the Centenary Year – and I was one of them!

During the Centenary year Paul appeared in a BBC documentary on Scouting with Ian Hislop, editor of *Private Eye.* I understand that Ian had set out expecting to make a TV programme with a somewhat sceptical view of the influence of Scouting over the years – a view which changed dramatically as his research progressed. I would guess that Paul should take some credit to this, for he was always a superb salesman for the largest Movement for young people in the world.

A committed Christian, Paul had been Master of Ceremonies over many years at the Roman Catholic Church his family attended in Croydon. At the turn of the Century, Paul took up a similar post at Westminster Cathedral.

Like Geoff, Tim, Bill, David and others, Paul made a major contribution to the development of SCOUTING as a vibrant, entertaining and practical magazine.

As I write Paul is in limbo in that he was made redundant from his post as the Association's Archivist in the summer of 2008. A new structure to the professional staff meant that Paul's post disappeared, to be replaced by something similar but different. By now Paul was in his early fifties and married to Ann. He was devastated by redundancy, which came at the time of the credit crunch and as unemployment soared, making the chances of him finding a job more than remote. It is a sad reflection on a movement that has caring at its heart that it is able to toss loyal professional staff members to the wind with – seemingly – little if any thought for the effect on their lives.

There were others who made their mark on SCOUTING. Peter Brooks worked tirelessly on the book side of things over a number of years and accompanied me on many trips around the country. It was Peter who drove Yvonne and our children to Southend on that day in 1975 when my mother lay dying at Chadwell Heath Hospital. It was Peter who helped Graham fill his small boy Wellington boots with conkers from the trees at Woodford Green. It was Peter who kept his cool in SCOUTING's offices when all around him was turbulence and madness. Peter emigrated to Australia in the early 1980s – a few months after I moved from SCOUTING.

Nigel Baynes hailed from Northumberland and found himself at Gilwell Park one summer, staying there for a few months before moving to Baden-Powell House on the hostel staff and then to the General Editor's department in the late 70s. Here he took over from Guy Marshall to manage the highly successful SCOUTING charts and reprint sales. Guy, too, had come over to SCOUTING from Gilwell Park where he had been Secretary to the Venture Scout Board. Guy, who lived with his parents in Loughton, kindly invited Yvonne, Heather, Richard and me to Sunday tea at his home. Heather was in her early teens and was most put out to be sent to the nursery with Richard, who screamed and screamed when he was invited to ride a huge Victorian rocking horse. Guy married Glenis and now lives in St. Albans with his family, where he manages a Christian bookshop.

Nigel lived the life of a carefree bachelor whilst working for SCOUTING. He continued to reside in staff accommodation at B-P House, had a girl friend living nearby and became friendly with Julian Simmonds who, as a young Scout in Greater London North East Scout County won the Kodak Scout Photographer of the

Year Competition in SCOUTING in the mid-70s. Julian decided to make his career as a photographer and carried out a number of photographic assignments for SCOUTING whilst he continued his studies.

Nigel – sometimes accompanied by his girl friend – would join me on speaking engagements, selling the SCOUTING charts and reprints. We took a range of goods for sale to a number of events – staging the SCOUTING Magazine Roadshow, complete with disco music, when most of the team would serve behind the counters, act as disc jockeys, dancing and generally enjoy themselves. Here we would be joined by contributors to the magazine and, often, their wives, families, girl and boy friends. It was all great fun for the team and, hopefully, for those who stood agog and in awe at our antics!

In addition to the charts and reprints, we launched SCOUTING T-shirts (in brilliant red with black lettering), SCOUTING carrier bags, SCOUTING Pens (which hung around the neck on a cord) and SCOUTING Button Badges (with a range of slogans including *SCOUTING is the Greatest!* – which, of course, it was).

In 1979 Nigel returned to his home in the village of Allendale, near Hexham, to work with his mother and brother on the family smallholding and caravan site, where he married and had a family. Julian married an attractive American lady, living in a flat in a warehouse in the Docklands at Wapping. I was invited to the reception in the flat following the wedding, where we supped champagne sitting on the edge of the floor with our legs dangling over the River Thames that lapped at the walls beneath.

Julian and my paths crossed in 1987 at the St. John Ambulance Brigade Centenary Party in Hyde Park and again later in Docklands when I helped out on a water station for the London Marathon. On both occasions Julian was working for the *Telegraph* as a staff photographer, where he travelled the world. In 2005 Julian and his journalist colleague Toby Harnden hit the headlines when they were accused of spying in Zimbabwe. Toby and Julian were arrested but later acquitted of breaching immigration laws and reporting illegally on the country's parliamentary elections. They spent more than a week in a filthy overcrowded cell near Harare and were lucky it wasn't longer.

When I flick through the bound volumes of SCOUTING for the years from 1976 to 1979, I find that a great sense of passion for the Scout movement shines out from those pages – and Geoff, Bill, Tim, Paul, Peter, Nigel, Guy, Julian and many others had a substantial role in this. There is a freshness still – over thirty years on – in the articles, cartoons and photographs recording the fun, friendship and adventure of Scouting. There was an ability to laugh at ourselves and to enjoy people laughing with us, rather than at us. The correspondence pages and many of the articles were critical of much that was happening as Scouting moved forward, but critical in a constructive sense. Uniform, the cost of being a Scout, the programme – all were put under the spotlight in letters and articles, and often torn into shreds before being patched up and put together again.

Two writers, in particular, set out to be controversial. Lanius was the pen name of Harold Wyld, then the Association's Press Officer, whose post gave him a unique insight into the machinations of an international youth organisation struggling to keep its position in a fast-changing world. Lanius and I were taken to task by Jimmy Young when we both appeared on *Radio One* in the *Jimmy Young Show* – which was fun of sorts, but Jimmy's questioning was incisive and both Harold and I had to be on our toes not to be caught out by the sort of question that interviewers delight in posing.

Alan Black remembers, written by a Venture Scout Leader in the south who wished to remain anonymous, was another series that questioned and probed. Both sparked lively, stimulating – and, I believe, valuable – correspondence, without undermining the movement which both writers held in high regard.

When I retired as Editor of SCOUTING after eleven years, I vowed that I would not comment on the magazine under its new editors – and I will not do so now. As I write there is no longer an Editor – but an editorial team. I know of no successful magazine that does not have an Editor. Be that as it may, I have to make the point that controversy and debate are no longer to be found within the pages of SCOUTING. I fear that in subsequent years that willingness to criticise – and to offer constructive criticism – has disappeared from the magazine. Is this because the readership is unwilling to debate or is it that debate is no longer tolerated in print? Is the movement self-satisfied and do its members think they have all the answers? Or has the willingness to criticise been stifled by bureaucracy at the top? Either way, Scouting (the movement) and SCOUTING (the magazine) are both the poorer for it.

Of MPs, Mayors and the like

Part of my role as General Editor involved speaking at annual general meetings, St. George's Day Services, dinners and conferences up and down the land. These were Scout County or District events in the main, but from time to time I would have the chance to attend a Scout Group event or the opening of a headquarters, where I would meet leaders, boys and supporters at the coalface of the Movement.

Perhaps the most bizarre "openings" in which I took part involved ablution blocks on Scout camp sites. Not unnaturally, few – if any – of my colleagues on the professional staff, nor volunteer Headquarters Commissioners, wanted to have the somewhat doubtful pleasure of performing the opening ceremony for a toilet block. But – oddly, perhaps – these provided publicity for the magazine and there are those who say that all publicity is good publicity.

For example, people have commented that when visiting Great Tower Camp Site in the Lake District, they had noted a plaque stating that Ron Jeffries, Editor of SCOUTING, visited this building on such and such a date – when the toilet block was opened. I did not have to do anything other than visit. Unlike at Perry Wood Camp Site in Surrey where, before the assembled campers and my family, I was required to climb a tall ladder onto the roof of the new ablution block to turn on a tap which allowed water to pour through the system in a noisy cacophony of flushing urinals. I have two brown earthenware mugs emblazoned with Perry Wood in my summerhouse – as a daily reminder of the flushing.

On rare occasions Yvonne and my children would accompany me on a SCOUTING engagement. Most of the visits I carried out would have been intensely boring for the children, but there were times when they would be able to join in. One such was a national family camp at Gilwell Park, when Graham, Heather and – to a lesser extent in view of his age – Richard were able to try their hand at a range of activities. The day ended with a service with hymns, prayers and an address. We were all invited to sit on the platform, but it was the end of the day and Graham was very tired, so much so that in the midst of the address, he let out a few mighty yawns. Unfortunately, he was sitting close to a microphone and Graham's yawns were broadcast across the leafy lawns of Gilwell Park for all to hear.

Publicity Manager Jack Olden and his wife, Jo, drove my family and me to a County Cub Scout Camp where some anniversary or other was being celebrated. Jack took photographs whilst I chatted to leaders and boys, and Jo, Yvonne and our children wandered off into the woods. A huge and delicious iced cake was brought forth and cut with all due ceremony. Slices were handed round to the assembled Cubs and their leaders – but no-one thought to offer a slice to Jack, Jo, Yvonne and me – let alone to Graham, Heather and Richard, who looked on with those big eyes that starving children have when others are eating scrumptious iced cake. Perhaps the leaders thought that as we came from Scout Headquarters we did not have normal appetites.

The most memorable occasion when we were able to enjoy Scouting as a family came in July 1971 during the Greater London Scouts' Cruise to Scandinavia with some 600 Scouts, their leaders and families. I was invited on board the *SS Nevasa* for the ten day trip to work on the ship's daily newspaper and Yvonne, Graham and Heather were with me as guests – which was kind and generous of the organisers. I worked in the bowels of the ship, typing stencils and churning out the paper on a duplicator, whilst they enjoyed the sea air and the trips on land in Sweden, Norway and Denmark. Our first stop was Gothenburg where Graham and Heather were keen to try out the few words of Swedish they had learned. On entering a shop to buy some sweets, they were taken aback to be addressed in perfect English. Later Yvonne had to dissuade them from dropping their coins into slot machine dispensing condoms which they thought were for sweets; such things were common on the streets of Gothenburg, but not back home in Ilford.

It was in Oslo where I met the leader of Norway's professional Scout team. After five minutes of discussion in English, for I could not speak Norwegian, the young man held up his hand and said: *"Say, Ron, I have understood every word you have said, for I am American. Will you please stop waving your arms in the air, sit on your hands and speak normally rather than shouting."*

The St. George's Day Service in Rochdale was a combined Scout and Guide affair held in the magnificent town hall. Cyril Smith, the larger than life Liberal MP for the town, and I joined the minister who would be leading the service in a side room as the hall filled with row upon row of youngsters and their leaders. Take my advice, beamed Cyril, who was clearly delighted that he had spoken to the assembled gaggle the year before and was able to sit back to enjoy the fun this year.

Take my advice, he said, and do not – under any circumstances whatsoever – ask questions, because two thousand voices will try to answer at the same time. I had no intention of doing anything of the kind and told Cyril so, for I had learned many years before that there is only one way to survive when facing a St. George's Day audience of two thousand Scouts and Guides – or even a lesser number – and that is to go out with all guns blazing, to stand up, to speak up and then to sit down, and all in the space of no more than eight minutes flat.

Another MP with whom I shared a platform was Greville Janner, who became a Life Peer in 1997. In the 1970s, Greville Janner was MP for one of the Leicester constituencies and was active in the Jewish Scout community in London. I spoke at their annual meeting, sitting on the platform next to Greville. As I rose to speak, I noted that he had a clear plastic folder in front of him with a sheet of paper inside on which were typed a series of headings and short phrases.

With my speech over, Greville told me that when he chaired a meeting at which there was to be a speaker, he always took the plastic file so that if he found the speech boring, he could find a topic listed on the typed sheet on which he was currently working on which he would concentrate his mind whilst appearing to be listening to the speaker. He told me that on this occasion he had not glanced at the file, for he had found my speech absorbing from the moment I stood up.

I would guess that Greville must have suffered the speeches of many mayors for I have found that – with one or two notable exceptions – they are the most boring and pompous public speakers. There is the anecdotal story of the speaker who had prepared a thirty minute speech, but was preceded by the local mayor who was to say a few words before inviting the speaker to take the stand. The mayor droned on for over half-an-hour before finally asking the speaker to give his address. The speaker stood up and said: *"37 High Road, Such-and-Such-a-Town"* – and promptly sat down!

I learned very early on to avoid all fidgeting habits whilst addressing an audience. Speaking at the Essex Scout County Conference in the late 1960s, my notes were typed on a series of postcards, which were held together by a rubber band. Harry Ffitch, the same Harry who was the fourth 'vicar' at our wedding, was sitting in the front row. With the speech over, Harry dashed up to remove the rubber band from my hands. I had been playing with it throughout the speech – twisting, pulling, flicking – so that Harry had been mesmerised, fearing that the elastic band would suddenly ping from my fingers and score a direct hit in the eye of some unsuspecting member of the audience.

One evening in a North London Scout Headquarters I sat at a table perched perilously near the back of the platform. Those of us at the table were warned that the chairs on which we were to sit were but inches from the edge – beyond which was a dark void leading to I know not what.

The mayor, wisely, moved to the front of the table to address the awaiting hordes so that all I could see was the wide expanse of his excessively broad back as he ranted away. Placing his hands behind his back as he spoke, the mayor lifted the bottom of his jacket to grip his elasticised braces with both hands. He then proceeded to pull his braces down as far as they would stretch, before allowing the braces to gently pull his podgy hands upwards – before repeating the whole process over and over again.

Having spent much of my childhood and early teens as a serious stammerer who stuttered, it often seemed to me to be remarkable that I could speak from a platform with apparent ease and without a single stutter. One evening I addressed a County annual meeting in the North of England. As I came off the platform, the County Commissioner's wife took my hand and told me that she was a speech therapist.

"Did you have a speech impediment when you were young," she asked, and I confessed that I did.

"I knew it," she said, *"as soon as you started speaking and I can tell you the break sound you made which enabled you to utter a few words before the stutter started again. It was 'though'"* – and she was right.

Apart from having to explain away the homemade bomb recipe in the Scout Dairy 1969 and taking part in the *Jimmy Young Show* – both on radio – I had a number of appearances before TV cameras. Some were in connection with the 70th Anniversary of the Scout Movement – in 1977 – and the same anniversary for the magazine – but a year later. Janet Street Porter interviewed me live one Sunday lunchtime – and was pleasant and kindly, although I had feared that she might be somewhat abrasive. *Pebble Mill at One* was a popular lunchtime magazine programme broadcast live from Birmingham studios in the heart of that City. The Scouts of Birmingham set up a camp site in the grounds in mid-winter, watched by passers by and folk on the tops of buses who must have thought we were crazy for it was freezing cold. Whilst the Birmingham Scouts ran up and down to keep warm, the interviewer and I sat on hot radiators inside the building – dashing outside on cue to do a live walk about.

I took part in *Open Door*, a community programme broadcast live on BBC Two late on a Sunday evening. This was scripted by two Hampstead Scout Leaders who worked professionally as comedy writers for the BBC. It was here that I first met Charlotte, later to be my Secretary and Geoff Platt's wife. Yvonne tried to watch the programme at home – but was called away to the telephone by friends ringing from around the country to tell her that I was on TV!

Generous

Generally and almost invariably the Scout folk who were hosting me as their speaker were generous and kind in the extreme. I arrived at a Yorkshire town with but a few minutes to spare before I was due to speak to a Scout annual meeting. *"You must be starving,"* said the District Commissioner, as I alighted from a much delayed train from London. *"But do not worry for we are all going to mother's after the meeting for a slap up meal. You will love it,"* he assured me and I hoped I would for I was famished.

With the meeting over, a number of us piled into four or five cars and sped off out of town and into the Yorkshire countryside. At this point I began to feel sorry for mother, whoever she was, for by now it was nearly eleven and pitch black. Not only was it late, but I wondered if mother knew just how many of the Scout Leaders of that town and their partners would be descending upon her for what I had been promised would be a meal to be remembered. On and on and on we drove and as midnight approached all became clear as we pulled into the car park outside Mother Hubbard's world-renowned fish and chip emporium. I had overlooked that I was in the Harry Ramsden and Mother Hubbard fish and chip country. Never has fish and chips tasted like it, complete with liberal helpings of white bread and butter and pots of steaming hot tea.

Some colleagues at Scout Headquarters refused to stay with Scout folk when undertaking speaking engagements, preferring to use hotels. I respected and understood their reasoning for there was no doubt that if you accepted an invitation to stay with Scout Leaders or Commissioners, there would be the distinct possibility that they would keep you up half the night to bend your ear about a controversial aspect of the movement. Even worse, they might try to get you onto their side in a local Scouting dispute.

There was, too, the danger that you might find yourself in a compromising situation staying in someone's home. I was (and I hesitate to say this but it is necessary to prove my point) a young and – possibly – good-looking late thirty-year-old when I was given a bedroom on the top floor of a rambling baronial pile far from anywhere in wild and forbidding countryside in the North of England. The room was huge, with a massive more-than-double-bed in the centre. I had been warned that two Great Danes would be sleeping on the bed and that I should push them off before climbing under the covers myself. Easier said than done, but hardly had the dogs slunk away down the corridor when I heard the voice of the Commissioner's voluptuous seventeen-year-old daughter intoning poetry as she moved slinkily over the polished wooden floorboards immediately outside my bedroom door. The word erotic hardly describes the poetry and the voice became more and more sexy. I watched – terrified – as she moved effortlessly past my open bedroom door, wearing a skimpy see-through nightdress that left little to the imagination. Waiting until the voice told me that she had moved a few paces down the corridor, I leapt from the bed and closed the door silently – before making a dash for the covers. After a while my potential seducer was heard no more.

At least I slept that night, unlike the occasion when the District Commissioner explained that his hobby was breeding hamsters. In the room next door to my bedroom small hamster cages were arranged around all four walls, stacked one upon the other from floor to ceiling. Hamsters tend to be nocturnal when allowed to be and they also enjoy running around in those little wheels that hang inside hamsters' cages. The noise of the scampering and scratching, the creaking of wheels and other goings on of a salacious nature that I guess were happening kept me awake until the dawn broke and the little darlings decided it was time for them to take their rest.

I spent many happy times in Tynemouth with Colin and Shirley Mckay, whose *A Canny Crack* was voted the most popular article in SCOUTING – and rightly so – when we carried out a readership survey. One Friday evening we visited every Scout Group in the District, starting at just before six and finishing after ten, but in time to join a number of the Scout Leaders in the Dolphin, their favourite pub, before the landlord called time.

Colin – a Scout Leader, then District Commissioner, for many years District Chairman and a magistrate – was a personal friend of Ralph Reader who had visited the *Tynemouth Gang Show* produced by Colin. I watched the show one night and as I walked through the darkened theatre in the late evening I was transfixed as the figure of Ralph Reader in his familiar white suit walked onto the stage and started to sing. The voice, the walk – it was so real, but was, in fact, Colin doing his uncanny impression.

On Saturday 30th November 1974 I was privileged to perform the opening ceremony at the 12th Tynemouth (Baptist) Scout Group's new headquarters. I unveiled a plaque and was presented with a brass key – with the injunction that if I was ever passing that way, to use the key to drop in. Perhaps I will do so one day for the key has rested on the shelf inside my front door for over thirty years.

Late that afternoon I boarded a train at Newcastle bound for Edinburgh, where I was to address the Scottish Scout Conference next day. The train was packed solid with football supporters who sat on the tables, in the aisles and even lay in the luggage racks. And the beer flowed like Niagara Falls.

When travelling to speak at the other end of the country, I crossed over from Devon into Cornwall at Plymouth. Talking to a young Scout, he asked me if I had travelled from England that day.

From time to time I would be invited to speak at a Girl Guide event – usually because one of the Guiders was married to a Scouter who had heard me speak at a Scout gathering. I travelled from my home one Saturday to Christchurch, then in Hampshire, to address the County Girl Guides' Conference. On arrival at the school where the conference was to be held, I was told that all the toilets that day would be for ladies, irrespective of what the notices said outside, with the exception of one – a staff toilet with two cubicles – which would be for my personal use.

I found the appropriate toilet and was having a wash and brush up – as you do after a train journey – when a tall man dressed from head to toe in black motor-cycling leathers burst through the door.

"Hello," he cried from within his helmet, *"I am usually the only man at these events – what are you doing here?"* I told him.

"I see," he cried as he unzipped, *"I am the Roman Catholic Chaplain."*

The day ended with a service in Christchurch Priory. Little did I realise that some thirty years or so later my eldest son would settle to live near Christchurch, that I would attend the investiture of my granddaughter as a Sea Scout in the 10th Christchurch (Mudeford) Sea Scout Group and that I would tell the story of that Girl Guide Conference during a speech at the reception of my eldest son's second wedding.

Happy and noisy

Cub Scout Leaders' events were invariably happy, noisy, lively gatherings – largely, I would guess, because in the 1970s at least half the Leaders in the Cub Scout Section were women – who had yet to percolate into the Scout Troops of the land and had only just started to make their presence known in Venture Scout Units. I was the guest speaker at the Northern Ireland Cub Scout Leaders' Conference held in the seaside town of Portrush when the Troubles were at their height – but that did not cast a damper on the leaders who were determined to live every minute of the weekend as though it were their last.

On the Friday and Saturday night, the official conference events ended around ten-thirty or so, but it was then that everyone started to live it up – and how! Everyone, that is, except the Northern Ireland Headquarters Commissioner for Cub Scouts, who was a short, plump and dour fellow of advanced years. The Commissioner was of the opinion that all the conference participants should be in bed by eleven at the latest, but the leaders had other ideas. Clandestine parties took place in a number of hotel bedrooms, but if the Commissioner sensed that one was being held, he would burst through the door in a fit of near rage. However, if the speaker from Scout Headquarters in London was in the room, the Commissioner would be all sweetness and light as he made a smiling exit. And so, as I soon discovered, the secret was to keep moving the speaker from Scout Headquarters in London from one bedroom party to the one where it was anticipated that the Commissioner might raid next.

For two nights I was thus carted – literally – from one bedroom to another, but not through warm carpeted hotel corridors, but up and down fire escapes and through rain soaked shrubberies and half opened windows. And all the while the Cub Scout Leaders were enjoying the time of their lives and I was the most popular man in town.

I did not always feel wanted, however. One evening I travelled by train from London to a town on the North-East coast which had best remain nameless. I had been told which train to catch so that I would arrive about 20 minutes before the start of the annual general meeting at which I was to speak. It was clear that there would be no meal at the end of my three or so hour journey so I had a snack on the train.

I was met at the station by the District Commissioner who stuck the knife in from the moment I was seated in his car.

"I think you should know," he said, *"that you were not our first choice of speaker."*

He went on to explain that they had *"started to look for a speaker just over six months ago. We wrote first to Ralph Reader, but sadly he could not come, although he took a long time to reply. We then tried the Chief Scout but he, too, was busy. We asked a number of Headquarters Commissioners, but none of them could help us."*

By this time my heart was in my boots, if not actually rolling around the floorboards of the car as it bounced relentlessly towards the hall where, no doubt, a phalanx of leaders would be waiting – all of whom had hoped to hear Ralph Reader or the Chief Scout or anyone except me.

"We were desperate, for time was getting short" said the District Commissioner, *"and then one of our leaders suggested your name."*

And as if that were not enough, he rubbed the salt further into the wound by adding that he had never heard of me because he did not read SCOUTING.

We entered the hall where I was to speak, going straight onto the platform. I was feeling pretty desperate by this time, wishing that the ground would open up and swallow me into a deep dark chasm, but looking out into the hall I spotted Peter Drake, the local Scout Field Commissioner, and my good friend Colin McKay, both of whom – unbeknown to me – had travelled across the Tyne to give me support, without having a clue as to why I needed that support so desperately.

I vowed to give the audience my all. For forty-five minutes I used every trick in the book to get them rolling in the aisles. All my best stories got an airing that night as I reeled them off one after the other to what started as a titter, moved on to a roar of laughter and ended as a standing ovation. I wowed them – and how!

Half way through I spotted the District Commissioner in urgent conversation with the District Secretary, who left the platform hurriedly, returning as I was about to sit down to tumultuous applause. He was clutching something that had clearly been hastily gift wrapped. Thanking me profusely, whilst clearly embarrassed by what he had told me earlier, the District Commissioner handed me the package, asking me to accept this with the thanks of the District for making their annual meeting the best ever.

The package contained a piece of very fine Caithness glassware – a tall, green vase which stands to this day on the mantelpiece in our lounge. I would guess it had been purchased to be presented to Ralph Reader or the Chief Scout or whoever – and was only brought to the meeting when the District Commissioner realised that I was not such a bad speaker after all.

I spent a fascinating week in Northern Ireland in the mid-70s. The tragedy of the religious divide was self-evident in church and school, but there were one or two Scout Groups where catholic and protestant boys and leaders played side by side – albeit without making this widely known. One evening I attended a Scout Troop meeting in Londonderry. Towards the end of the evening badges were presented and an investiture was held, following which I was called forward. A young Patrol Leader presented me with a rubber bullet, one of the kind being used at the time in Northern Ireland by British Troops. The lad commented that I should think myself lucky to be given this, for it would fetch at least a fiver from an American tourist.

Later that week the hotel in which I was staying outside Derry was under attack as I slept. The British Troops who repelled the attack were still there next morning, but lips we sealed as to who the attackers were and I was hurried away.

The further I travelled from London to undertake speaking engagements, it seemed that the hospitality got better and better. London Scout Districts were almost notorious for assuming – almost certainly because it never occurred to them to think otherwise and not out of any maliciousness – that I would have eaten before an evening meeting and that I would enjoy late evening travel from some remote part of the capital on a night bus – or, on one occasion, walking.

I had spoken at a Scout District in North London and stayed to talk with members of the audience over tea and buns. It was approaching eleven and dark and cold as I stood on the pavement outside the hall, saying goodbye and watching folk climbing into their cars and driving away.

A small crowd was left and as I turned to walk away, the District Commissioner asked me where I was heading. I explained that I did not have a car and would need to take public transport to Liverpool Street Station, from where I could catch a train home. Looking into the dim distance, the District Commissioner pointed out the floodlit dome of St. Paul's Cathedral and suggested I should walk. *"Aim for that,"* he said, *"and turn left when you reach the City,"* with which he waved as he climbed into the warmth of his car. I flagged down the first taxi that passed.

Speaking in Surrey one evening, I arrived at the station just as the train for London was about to leave the platform. Running down the stairs, I made it as the doors closed. Unfortunately, the train was not going to London, but was speeding in the opposite direction towards Brighton. The guard was helpful, suggesting that I alighted at the next stop and took a taxi across country to a distant town to pick up the last train going into London that night.

Arriving early at a church hall in outer London where the Scout District Annual Meeting was to be held, I stood outside until a man in uniform arrived who, I learned later, was the District Secretary.

Running past me at a belting pace, he opened the door with a key and called out to me to follow him inside. There he told me how the chairs were to be laid out – so many to a row and so many rows – explaining that he would have to leave the task to me as he would be busy sorting out the papers for the meeting and he needed to be ready to greet the speaker who was a man of some importance from Scout Headquarters. I had almost completed the task when the District Commissioner arrived – and recognised me.

The Queen's heathers

As Yvonne and I strolled around the gardens of Buckingham Palace, I was struck by one thing – that the heather shrubs in my garden were far superior to those we came across around Her Majesty's lake. They were in dire need of some judicious pruning, but it was neither the time nor the occasion for me to help out with this.

In April 1979, my final year as Editor of SCOUTING, Sir William Gladstone, then Chief Scout, had presented me personally with the Silver Acorn for my services to the Association. Shortly afterwards, Ken Stevens, the Chief Executive Commissioner, told me that Yvonne and I would receive an invitation to one of The Queen's Garden Parties at Buckingham Palace in July.

The occasion demanded a new outfit for Yvonne and the hire of morning dress for me – complete with top hat. We changed into our garb at Baden-Powell House and were driven to Buck House by Deputy General Editor Geoff in the office car. Geoff drove into the courtyard at the Palace, dropped us off and went down the Mall to a reserved parking space. Here he watched as chauffeurs to the Great and the Good parked their Bentleys and Rolls Royce's, opened the boots of their cars and took our hampers of fine foods and wines – whilst Geoff searched in his pocket to find that Charlotte had given him a KitKat and a flask of coffee.

We walked through the palace to the garden at the rear, down steps and onto the lawns, where the crowds were gently (but firmly) marshalled into rows. In the centre of each gangway, selected guests were paraded to be introduced to whichever member of the Royal family would walk past.

We caught near glimpses of The Queen and the Queen Mother – the latter standing in the tea marquee where she removed her shoes which were clearly killing her! We did not make it to the tea tables, nor did we get close enough to a cucumber sandwich, but we had a pleasant walk around the lake and were surprised how quiet it seemed for the traffic that swirled around on the roads outside was just a gentle rumble in the distance.

My other brush with The Queen came a few months earlier when Her Majesty visited the offices at Baden-Powell House. I discovered that the stories about The Queen having a special toilet installed for the occasion of her visit were true. A white marquee was erected on the flat roof over the main hall at Baden-Powell House in which Her Majesty met yet more of the Great and the Good.

During the tour of the offices, the staff of the General Editor's Department were lined up to smile benignly and I had the task of showing The Queen how we put the magazine together. Here I learned that The Queen uses an interesting technique when meeting people – she asks a question by following up on what she has just been told. So, for example, when I said that we were working on the next issue of SCOUTING magazine, The Queen asked me what issue that would be? When I said it was for a certain month, The Queen asked me if it came out monthly? I replied that it did and (because I wanted to get a few points over to her and her accompanying throng) that it was read by leaders throughout the country, The Queen asked me how many leaders read the magazine? And so it went on. It was all very friendly and homely, rather like showing your mother around on parents' afternoon at school.

The guard of honour for The Queen was provided by Scouts from Kensington and we ran a full colour cover on SCOUTING the following month showing The Queen talking to some of the young Scout Patrol Leaders. All the Scouts were smart and well-turned out, but the Scout on the cover standing nearest to The Queen has his membership badge on the wrong breast pocket. In the rush of the afternoon, no-one noticed this and neither did we when the proof of the cover arrived. The lad's mother had decided that he should have a new Scout shirt if he was to meet The Queen and she (his Mum that is, not The Queen) had dashed out the day before the big event to buy the shirt, sewing on the badges after her son had gone to bed. He spotted the error next morning, but by that time it was too late and he hoped it would not be noticed.

I can say with my hand on my heart that I received more letters about the badge being on the wrong side of that Scout's shirt than on any other topic during my eleven years as Editor. The floodgates opened for Disgusted of Tonbridge Wells and his cohorts, so much so that I decided to publish one or two of the letters in the correspondence columns. This in itself produced a rash of letters complaining that it was a pity that people had nothing better to do with their time than write letters about badges being stitched on the wrong side of a shirt.

One reader who was so incensed that the young Scout's big day had been spoiled in this way invited him and his Patrol to spend a weekend on his ocean going yacht in the English Channel. The Scout and his Scouter came into the offices to meet with us and to hear the news about the weekend on a yacht. Not unnaturally, the Scout was grateful to his mother for making the mistake in the first place.

Sausages I have known

It was Norman Garnett, a Scouter in Bury, Lancashire, and a leading magistrate in that town, who first had the idea of doing something imaginative – but crazy – with sausages. Norman's brainwave for organising SCOUTING's Super Sausage Sizzling Spectacular came to him as he was riding on the top deck of a bus in Manchester.

Promoting the idea through his regular column in SCOUTING, it was not long before the idea caught on and Cub Scouts throughout the country were cooking sausages in the most unusual places – up towers, on beaches, in forests, in amusement parks, on piers – and it was this that inspired my involvement with sausages, very big ones.

I made the *Guinness Book of Records* twice – once in 1979 and again in 1987 – when I was responsible for organising the making, cooking and serving of the World's Longest Sausage. Others have taken over the world record, but only for making a longer sausage. No-one has cooked and served one that was longer than my nine-miler in 1987, but the *Guinness Book of Records* has its rules and they are concerned about the making and not the cooking. It does not bother me for I have a copy of the Certificate confirming that the 1987 sausage was 9.89 miles in length and that we cooked it and served it in nearly 100,000 portions. The original Certificate resides with the Scouts of Greater London North East County whose 300 Scouts, Venture Scouts and Leaders worked through an eleven hour day in searing heat. But we need to go back eight years to the start of this sausage saga.

1979 was International Year of the Child and the Great Children's Party was to be held in London's Hyde Park to mark the occasion. The Scouts were invited to become involved and Jack Olden, the Association's Publicity Manager, trotted off to a meeting to decide how best to employ the Scouts. So far, so good.

(Jack was born in Peabody Buildings in Holborn. Both parents were white, but Jack was black as black could be. He was one in a million – a pure black baby born to pure white parents, and a throwback to years gone by. His colour did not worry Jack, although he had suffered racist remarks and discrimination when abroad on Scout Association business – not being permitted to stay in a whites-only hotel for example. As a boy he lived a few flats away from the young Kenneth Williams, the actor and comedian, who Jack had to take to school, but the young Kenneth was something of a wimp, whingeing all the way there and back. When Robertson's Marmalade wanted to run an advertisement in SCOUTING, I refused to take it because it showed a gollywog, which I considered racist. Jack was furious, accusing me – with a whimsical smile on his face – of being a bigoted liberal. Jack – as a black man – saw nothing wrong with gollywogs. Interestingly, my black son-in-law tells me that he had a gollywog as a boy and saw nothing wrong with that either! Jack was a kind, friendly and generous colleague to whom I owe much.)

On his return from his meeting, Jack called me into his office. The Hyde Park Party would be organised by Major Michael Parker, who produced the Royal Tournament and other national events.

Jack explained to me that Major Parker wanted to cook the world's longest sausage and serve this to the assembled throng. The world record at that time was one-and-a-half-miles in length. *"We would need to cook a two miler,"* said Jack, *"or, rather, you will do so."* And to my amazement, I found myself agreeing with Jack that I would do just that.

Over the next few days I made a series of telephone calls to obtain one of the items we would need to make all this happen. First the sausage, then the frying pan, next the charcoal and so on. Having asked to be put through to the public relations department, the call to Dewhursts, the Master Butchers, went something like this.

"Hallo, my name is Ron Jeffries and I am editor of SCOUTING, the national magazine of The Scout Association. I am organising the cooking and

serving of the world's longest sausage at the Great Children's Party in London's Hyde Park as part of International Year of the Child and I wondered if your company would be prepared to make a two mile sausage and deliver this to Hyde Park in a refrigerated vehicle?"

As I paused there would be a stunned silence, followed by the person at the other end of the telephone asking me to hold on whilst the matter was referred to someone more senior or, if I had already reached the top man or woman, he or she would ask for my telephone number and promise to ring me back. The latter happened more often than not – simply because the person receiving this unlikely and somewhat preposterous call wanted to be sure that I was who I said I was – and as at that time few of us had direct lines, this meant going through a switchboard which would at least confirm that the lunatic making the request was who he said he was.

Dewhursts agreed to make the sausage at their Thamesmead factory in South London. Tony Bolton, the London Field Commissioner, arranged for some Scouts to join me whilst the sausage was being made – and this, and subsequent events, made the national press. British Steel and Dexion combined to make a frying pan 50 feet in length, we used half a tonne of charcoal and the bakers of Mighty White supplied the sliced bread.

Geoff, Bill, Peter, Paul and Nigel led the team of volunteers – drawn from my Scout friends in North East London and contributors to the magazine – and set things up on the designated spot in Hyde Park. And the man who dreamed up SCOUTING's Super Sizzling Sausage Spectacular – Norman Garnett JP – was there in the thick of it together with Joyce, his wife, and David, their eldest son. A group of soldiers were to roast an ox on a nearby spot, but had some difficulty in getting their fire to light. Geoff and Peter sorted them out in the time it took to open a box of firelighters.

The Party ran over two days. On the first Her Majesty The Queen and The Duke of Edinburgh visited the sausage. Yvonne had prepared a bed of fresh salad on a silver salver with a fork and just as The Queen arrived, a portion of well-cooked sausage was placed amongst the lettuce and cucumber. Young Jamie, a Scout from Chingford, stepped forward to proffer the sausage on a silver salver to Her Majesty, who took things in quick as a flash and said: *"I won't, but the Duke will!"* – with much emphasis on the *"but the Duke will"*. And the Duke did.

With half the sausage cooked and eaten, we were able to relax that evening. I had feared that we might not find sufficient takers for the sausage and had a contingency plan to dig a deep hole at Gilwell Park in which to bury any surplus sausage, but clearly this was not necessary. The team met at Baden-Powell House that evening, when I gave them a briefing for the next day – during which most fell sound asleep.

Next day Princess Anne visited the Party. The Princess was known to be somewhat curt when the mood took her and we were taken by surprise when she marched purposefully towards the fifty foot frying pan – almost as though her father had told he that she should do so – and asked for a piece of the sausage. Jamie stepped forward once again with the sausage-on-a-silver-salver. Taking a bite in her gloved hand, Princess Anne said that it tasted good – but did I mind if she did not eat it all? Of course I agreed, and the remainder of the sausage was placed back on the bed of salad. Yvonne took that piece of sausage home, put it in the fridge and showed friends and neighbours the imprint of Princess Anne's teeth for days afterwards.

Repeat performance

Eight years later and it happened all over again – except that this time the sausage was much, much longer. 1987 was the Centenary of the St. John Ambulance Brigade and there was to be a party in London's Hyde Park with Major Michael Parker once more at the helm. Recalling the 1979 event, Major Parker contacted me.

No longer Editor of SCOUTING, I was now editing MILK INDUSTRY and, in my spare time, Chairman of Greater London North East Scout County. Alan, then County Commissioner, worked with me and persuaded Brian to join us – a former Scouter and Commissioner in the County and then Managing Director of a catering business in the City of London. Brian worked miracles, persuading an Essex company to build four twenty-five foot frying pans which would stand astride decking produced once more by Dexion and encouraging young staff in his business to help with the cooking on the day.

By this time the world record for making a sausage stood at five miles so we agreed to make a six miler – or, rather, Dewhursts the Master Butchers said they would do so, but this time at their Nottingham factory. I happened to be speaking at a Scout annual meeting somewhere in North London a week or so prior to the party – and mentioned the forthcoming sausage sizzle – when a lady in the audience made herself known to me. She worked at the *Guinness Book of Records* – and knew that very recently the Australians had set a new world record having made a sausage of eight miles in length. So we made our sausage nine miles, or more precisely, 9.89 miles. That was a close run thing.

A sheep's intestine – from which sausages were made before the advent of man-made fibres – is roughly forty-four feet in length. Guinness insisted that every packet of forty-four foot of man-made sausage skin that was opened should be verified with the signature of a local Nottingham worthy.

Being a magistrate by this time meant that I had a direct line to Nottingham justices – who gamely agreed to do the verifying, which required one of their number to be present at all times over a period of thirty-six hours as the sausage meat was squeezed into the skins.

Overnight and two days before the party, the sausage travelled to London in a refrigerated vehicle (where it was stacked on a series of pallets, one above the other with a hole down the centre) escorted by a St. John Ambulance. Arriving at Kensington Palace just before 8am on the day prior to the party, the Duke of Gloucester, as President of The Scout Association, had breakfast of sausage cooked on his doorstep before the waiting photographers by four Patrol Leaders from the Scout County.

I had persuaded a London firm of scaffolders to build a covered way down two sides of the Scout site, under which were forty serving stations. Clear plastic sheets would keep off the rain and act like a magnifying glass should the sun shine

– which it did, so that the Scouts serving the sausage slowly (and sometimes not so slowly) cooked in the intense heat beneath.

A day or so prior to the great day itself, Major Parker confessed to me that the scaffolders who had promised to build the rostrum on which The Queen would stand to perform the opening ceremony before 100,000 members of St. John Ambulance and the assembled TV and press cameras – those scaffolders had disappeared from the face of London (and, for all, Major Parker knew, could have been swimming across the Channel to escape from their commitment). Would the company that had worked with the sausage be good enough to erect the rostrum, he asked me? I contacted the Managing Director who dashed hot-foot to Hyde Park. There were no plans or scale drawings for the rostrum, just an artist's impression on the front cover of the 100,000 souvenir programmes that had been printed and stood ready for distribution to the mighty throng in less than twenty-four hours' time. In the sketch the rostrum rose up on all sides from the platform on which the dignitaries would stand – and the scaffolders produced one that did just that. With barely twenty hours in which to do so, they worked throughout the night under arc lamps and were slapping on the final coat of paint as The Queen arrived on the steps below.

We lit the fires at 6.30am – or, rather, the fires were lit by representatives of an American company that had devised a spray-on ingredient that would make charcoal burst into flame. After a few abortive attempts, some firelighters were smuggled under one end of a frying pan and we were off. The Americans were thrilled! We used a tonne of charcoal and over eleven hours we served 100,000 portions of sausage using 5,000 loaves of Mighty White bread from the forty serving stations. A pantechnican of gargantuan proportions had rumbled down the A12 from Norwich to my home, where it ground to a halt in the roadway before dropping off twenty-four gallons of Coleman's Mustard in huge glass jars. An equal quantity of Heinz Tomato Sauce arrived in similar fashion at my home. Both had been devoured by midday.

Everything we used that day – and back in 1979, too – did not cost the Scouts a penny piece. Manufacturers and suppliers were generous and took little persuading to help. All we could promise was publicity on the day amongst those attending the parties and in the national and local press who would be present or to whom we would send photographs. As Editor of MILK INDUSTRY I was able to persuade dairy companies and carton manufacturers to supply milk and juices, and to make financial donations which we used to purchase three hundred aprons and T-shirts bearing the slogan *SCOUTING's Super Sausage Sizzling Spectacular,* and white chef's hats and to cover all incidental expenses.

Setting up on site took a week and I was helped by Scout Leaders, some of whom took annual leave to join me during the daytime and others who came across to Hyde Park after work each evening.

Some three hundred Scouts and Leaders travelled to Hyde Park in the early morning of the day itself. We experienced one problem when the heat from the charcoal became so intense that the metal buckles of the Scout's belts started to stick to the boys' tummies. Fortunately, the paramedics of St. John Ambulance sorted this out – and we removed all belts.

The Duke of Edinburgh visited the sausage site – and asked for a piece. Just after 5pm Phillip Schofield came on site with a TV crew and gave me a practice interview. A minute or two before the *BBC News at Six,* Phillip's interview with me went out live to the nation.

Shortly after six, Hyde Park suddenly fell quiet as the partygoers departed from whence they had come – and we were left with some two hundred feet of sausage and three hundred Scouts and leaders who vowed that, nice as the sausage tasted at the start of the day, they did not wish to see another sausage all their lives. We also had some fifty loaves of Mighty White sliced and a few cartons of milk and juice.

Suddenly men – and a few women – started to come from all directions across the now deserted park. Most were shuffling with the feet of the homeless and the destitute, drawn no doubt by the wafting aroma of burnt sausage. Within minutes the sausage site, too, was bereft of anything worth eating.

We made the *Guinness Book of Records.* Major Michael Walsh, Chief Scout, received an award from St. John Ambulance. We were both presented with silver cups inscribed by Dewhursts and the Chief Scout gave me his Personal Award, a badge which Yvonne sewed onto my uniform in its rightful place. Perversely, perhaps, one of my favourite home-cooked meals remains a tasty sausage with fried onions and lashings of Coleman's mustard.

Those whose paths crossed with mine

During my eleven years as The Scout Association's General Editor, my path crossed with a number of interesting men and women, some famous in their own right and others not so. Many of those with whom I brushed shoulders were generous, pleasant folk that I was pleased – and often privileged – to meet. But that could not be said for them all, and they are perhaps best forgotten.

Over the years during which I worked in the City of London and edited a range of different publications I received many letters. Most were a pleasure to receive, but there were a few – and a minority, let it be said – that were anything but pleasant. Those letters were sometimes abusive, but very often hurtful in the extreme. And it may come as a surprise when I say that the abusive and hurtful letters were not sent to me when I was handling insurance claims in the City or fretting about retaining the doorstep delivery service of milk, but were addressed to me as Editor of SCOUTING from members of the Scout movement. Sad, but true – and I developed a tough outer skin, but remained raw inside.

When I joined The Scout Association as General Editor, the Chief Scout's office was down the corridor from mine on the second floor back at 25 BP Road and it was only a matter of days before Sir Charles Maclean poked his head around my door to welcome me to the building. He insisted that his friends called him Chips and I soon discovered that he looked upon me as a friend.

Chips had inherited the tradition of writing monthly in THE SCOUTER under the title *The Outlook*, but whilst he was happy for his name to appear as the by-line, he made it very clear that he would not be doing the writing. It was for him a task too far. That would be down to me, although from time to time Fred Hurll, the Chief Executive Commissioner, might put pen to paper on behalf of the Chief. Chips would spend a few days each month in London, returning to his home at Duart Castle on the Isle of Mull or setting off on a trip abroad, for in addition to being Chief Scout of the United Kingdom, he was also Chief Scout of the Commonwealth. On those visits to London he would call into my office, stand at the window and suggest a topic on which he would wish to write. He would be back a day or so later, take away the script I had written, make two or perhaps three very minor changes in the language – just to prove that he had read it – and hand it back to me. Later I encouraged other members of the senior staff to ghost write, but Chips always dealt with me and was not concerned if others had a hand in things.

I never knew a time when Chips was anything but smiling and, apparently, happy. He always had a cheery word, shot his hand out and shook yours with such gusto and firmness that your arm ached for some time after the assault. He was well-known for the firmness of his handshake throughout the movement and for his phenomenal memory. And Yvonne had his memory to thank when she lost a brooch that had a sentimental value.

Chips was created a Life Peer on appointment as Lord Chamberlain in 1971, a post he held until 1984. Chips retired as Chief Scout of the UK in September 1971, but continued as Chief Scout of the Commonwealth until 1975. Shortly afterwards he invited the staff at 25 BP Road with their partners to his official residence at St. James' Palace. It was a pleasant, informal hour or so, with Chips and Lady Maclean greeting everyone at the door and taking their coats.

On arrival home late that evening, Yvonne realised that a marcasite brooch in the shape of a maple leaf was missing from the coat she had worn – I had given the brooch to Yvonne on our wedding day. First thing next morning a hand-written note from Chips was delivered to my office with the brooch. Chips remembered that he had seen it on Yvonne's coat when she arrived the previous evening and guessing that she would be sad to lose it, he made sure it was returned as soon as possible – without realising its sentimental value.

On an earlier occasion, Lady Maclean had been kind to Yvonne. Chips was holding a Queen's Scout Award Reception at the Mansion House in the City of London. As the event was within easy reach of our home, Yvonne was invited to join me for the evening. It was our first visit to the Mansion House and whilst I was arranging some photography, Lady Maclean took Yvonne on a tour of the building. Later Yvonne sat with her at the Reception.

Sins of Editorship

Early in 1971 I spent some fourteen hours with Ralph Reader in his home, drinking one gin and tonic after another, whilst he berated me one minute for the sins of my editorship, congratulated me the next for what he saw as my successes and spent the rest of the time telling me of the lost opportunities in his life – lost because, in his view, his professional show business colleagues had written him off as a West End producer and impresario because he insisted in continuing with the Scout *Gang Show*. But why was I there?

When I first went to 25 BP Road, Ralph Reader shared an office down the corridor from me with Ron Meyer, then the *Gang Show* Secretary; later, Ron took on the role of Secretary to the Chief Scout. Ron, who was an accomplished shorthand writer, lived with his mother and was involved in Scouting in Bermondsey, whose District *Gang Show* he produced brilliantly for many years.

Ralph would come into his office from time to time. Occasionally he would call out to Clare, who he had known for many years. I tried to make contact with him on these visits, but he was always in a hurry. He appeared almost dismissive of me, but I assumed that he was perhaps shy of making new friends and I did not push myself onto him.

Ralph was surrounded by what I would describe as sycophantic hangers-on. Some were current members of the *Gang Show* who appeared to be currying favour for they hung on his every word and gesture; others were older, former *Gang Show* members who probably found it difficult to break the ties. If the activities of the former were understandable, those of the latter seemed to me to be sad.

In my defence, for there are many who believed otherwise at the time and probably still do so, I was a great admirer of Ralph Reader and the *Gang Show*. My home Scout Group had used his material over many years with great success. On my appointment as General Editor I continued the tradition set by Rex Hazlewood of attending the opening night of the *London Gang Show* with a large party of contributors to the magazine, the printers, paper merchants and advertising agents. I believe that *Gang Shows* were great publicity for the movement, with TV specials at Christmas and a number of appearances at the *Royal Command Performance*. And as I write in the early part of the 21st Century it is a fact that *Gang Shows* continue to be staged in the UK and abroad – albeit now augmenting Ralph's material with other scripts and music.

It was a particular disappointment to me that I was unable to attend the last performance on Saturday 2nd November 1974 of the *Farewell London Gang Show*. There were those at the time who viewed this as a snub to Ralph and the Gang on my part, but it was never intended to be. I had taken the usual party from SCOUTING to the opening night, but I had been invited to open the Nottingham County Conference on Sunday 3rd November – which meant that I would have to travel to Nottingham on Saturday evening and stay overnight to be in time for the first conference session next morning.

I realised that this would mean that I would miss the final show, but I would be able to attend the matinee on that last day – with the added bonus of being able to take my son and daughter to see the *Farewell London Gang Show* – which would be their first and last chance to witness a *Gang Show* produced by Ralph Reader. Graham was ten and Heather eight – too young to have been taken to see an evening show – but well up for a matinee. Graham had a new suit and Heather a new dress. Both were photographed in the staircase at home. Auntie Una (Una Paul of Hargreaves Scout Shop and Heather's Godmother) accompanied us, whilst Yvonne stayed at home with one-year-old Richard. Una brought Graham and Heather home afterwards, whilst I journeyed on to Nottingham by train.

That same year Ralph's autobiography – *Ralph Reader Remembers* – was published. It was – not surprisingly – ghost-written by the ever faithful and loyal Ron Meyer, and I would doubt if he received more than a few pennies for all the time he gave so unstintingly. The book was offered for publication to The Scout Association and I read the drafts in my role as General Editor. I wanted the Association to publish, but there were some members of the professional staff who Ralph counted as his friends and buddies who – in the anonymity of the Association's Publications Board and General Purposes Sub-committee – were vehemently against doing so, claiming that it would not sell and would be a financial loss to the Association. I guessed Ralph would have been amazed had he known the names of those who black-balled his book, but as they are now dead things should rest there.

I found a publisher for Ralph – Bailey Brothers who had offices then on the South Coast. The book sold well in hardback and went into paperback the next year.

Searching the internet in 2008, I found that the paperback was selling at around £1.60, but the only hardback up for sale was listed at £208!

Over the years since that first *London Gang Show* at the Scala Theatre in 1932 the *Gang Show* had been an all-male preserve. Girls joined the cast for the first time in 1968 and soon became an established part of the Gang. But it was the review of the *Gang Show* published in the December 1970 issue of THE SCOUTER that upset Ralph and many of his friends and cronies.

I decided to invite one of our occasional contributors, Robert Langton, to write the review. Robert was a Scouter, had been at school with Don Grisbrook and was a journalist on the *London Evening Standard*. For the first time a review of the *London Gang Show* was openly critical. In my view the points made by Robert were fair comment and not in any sense destructive, but that was not how they were perceived by many readers who were clearly appalled that a voice of criticism should be raised against Ralph. Oddly, I did not receive any letters, nor did those who were critical of what had been written speak to me personally. I just heard second-hand.

So what did they object to? Robert wrote that *"the sketches were not very amusing this year"; "the senior citizens in the cast of 125 were not so much in evidence – but this is a good thing"; "some words were lost because of an over enthusiastic orchestra"; " it was essentially a boys and girls show, but still the old gang were front-lined, hiding the gay youngsters. The old comrades' figures are none too shapely these days and they would have been better somewhere at the back. Now that the show has young mixed talent – especially the lovely female talent – please Ralph, let it be seen".*

Putting to one side the use of the word "gay" which, in 1970, had yet to have the meaning with which we were to associate with it later in the decade, the criticism – such as it was – appeared to me, when I had my blue pencil poised, perfectly harmless and legitimate comment.

But not in the eyes of Ralph and his cohorts, who made sure that I was left in no doubt whatsoever of their views.

One of the more outlandish and ridiculous things that were said was that my son should not apply to be a member of the *London Gang Show* as he would not be welcome. Graham was six-years-old at the time.

It was as a result of this review that I found myself at Ralph's home one sunny morning early in 1971 around lunchtime – but lunch was never mentioned, nor was tea, nor supper for that matter. Ralph poured a succession of gins and tonics as he talked almost without pause.

I hardly got a word in edgeways. I supped the gin slowly, very slowly, and some potted plants were treated to almost neat gin with little tonic when Ralph's back was turned.

What did we talk about? Everything and everyone, I guess. He was in the Intelligence Corps during the 1939-45 war, but was he a spy? He staged shows all over the world for the Troops, but did he very nearly fall for Hitler's blandishments with the Hitler Youth in the mid-30s when he took some members of the *London Gang Show* to Germany?

Did he write some of the music for Lionel Bart's hit musical *Oliver* – particularly *Consider yourself?* Rumours abounded that all these things were true, but if they were Ralph did not tell me!

And at around two in the morning I made my excuses and walked into the cool night air. Hailing a taxi, I rode all the way home in a slight haze.

Not enamoured

Wife of the Founder, Lady B-P, and Chief Guide until her death in 1977, was not enamoured with The Scout Association at the time I was editor of SCOUTING. The Advance Party Report in 1966 was probably the final straw – consigning as it did the shorts and big hat to history (although the big hat had disappeared long before). I was told that Lady B-P no longer read the magazine once its name changed from THE SCOUTER to SCOUTING.

At one stage something clearly upset her, for I received a letter highly critical of the magazine in general and of me in particular. Typed personally by Lady B-P, sections were in all capital letters where she wished to add emphasis. At that time Lady B-P was living in a 'grace and favour' residence in Hampton Court and so I wrote to ask if I might meet with her at her home. I arrived at the appointed time for what I thought might be tea and cakes, but all I received was a sound verbal wigging for daring to make a single change to the magazine which her husband had launched. I left, saddened that such bitterness – for that is what it was – could sour someone who had given so much to the young people of the world.

I sensed staff at The Girl Guides Association were petrified of Lady B-P in her latter years. I was told – in the strictest confidence at the time – that Lady B-P's obituary and the detailed arrangements for her funeral were revised annually towards the end of her life.

One year in the 70s the revised and updated documents were printed off and circulated to the hierarchy at Guide Headquarters, via the post room where outgoing correspondence was placed in pigeon holes, each with the name of a Commissioner.

Not unnaturally, the Chief Guide also had a pigeon hole in the post room, but it was somewhat unfortunate that the member of staff placing the documents into the pigeon holes did not spot this fact. The first that staff knew that Lady B-P had received a copy of her own obituary and arrangements for her funeral was when she returned the papers with some corrections and suggestions as to how things might be improved. I believe a head or two may have rolled, but if they did the blood was quickly mopped up and did not seep along the pavements in Buckingham Palace Road.

Another lady from the past was also not enamoured with me and all that I had done. In the mid-70s I was invited to meet with Eileen Wade, B-P's Secretary, at her home.

At that time there was a resurgent interest in B-P – we had published some articles in SCOUTING and Eileen suggested we might meet. Eileen brushed aside some of the comment in those articles and elsewhere that questioned certain attitudes and beliefs held by B-P, which did not accord with current thinking.

Eileen made me a light lunch and we talked books. Her cottage was dark, cluttered and a little damp. If Eileen had any stories to tell, she was not going to reveal them to me.

Eileen gave me a number of green bound books, including her life of B-P – *The Piper of Pax*, first published in 1924. I have two copies – the other is a second edition dated 1931, with a signature on the flyleaf of Roy G. Shapley which is dated 1928. Odd!

Search for a successor

Following the retirement of Lord Maclean as Chief Scout of the UK, the search was on for a successor. The months from September 1971 through to the early summer of the next year were filled with speculation as to who the next Chief would be for it was the first time that a natural successor had not be waiting in the wings.

Ken Stevens, by then Chief Executive Commissioner, called Jack Olden, Harold Wyld and me to his office in the late Spring of 1972. We were to accompany Ken to meet the new Chief Scout, to take photographs and to prepare articles for SCOUTING and the press releases – all of which would follow the meeting of the Association's Council in July at St. James' Palace when the next Chief would be acclaimed (which was how things were done in those days). We were given the dates of departure and return, but were not told where we were going or where we would be staying overnight. Our families' point of contact would be Ken's Secretary in the event of an emergency. Furthermore, we were not to tell anyone why we would be away from our homes and the office. Real cloak and dagger stuff.

Ken drove us in his car and it was not until we reached Chester that he revealed over dinner at our hotel our destination and the name of the Chief Scout designate. Next morning we set out for Hawarden Castle in Flintshire to meet Sir William Gladstone and found him in the most unlikely of places, tending plants in the roadside garden centre attached to the castle! Next day on the way out I purchased two white heather plants which thrived in my front garden for many years. The four of us spent a couple of happy hours taking photographs of Sir William – alone, with Charles, his Cub Scout son, and with Lady Gladstone, his three children and a donkey.

After lunch it was back into Ken's car for the return journey to London – where we were sworn to secrecy until the afternoon of Wednesday 26th July at St. James' Palace.

The story broke in the September 1972 issue of SCOUTING with a front cover in full colour – the first – showing Sir William with his Cub Scout son. The following month's SCOUTING carried a *Face to Face* article with a series of photographs of the new Chief – and one of the back of my head as I interviewed the

Chief on tape. Both the Chief and I had hair down to and over our collars as was the fashion at the time.

Later Jack Olden and I journeyed to the Chief's Scottish estate where Venture Scouts were carrying out conservation work in the forests that swept across the hills and glens. Jack and I stayed in the main house, each having a cavernous bedroom with a freestanding bath in the centre of the room. A notice was hung over the taps warning visitors that the bath filled rather fast and was prone to overflow unless watched. The water had a brown earthy tinge to it.

Sir William wrote for the magazine from time to time, was kind and considerate to staff, but a little distant – the result of an inherent shyness rather than anything else. During his ten years as Chief Scout he steered the movement to look outwards through his SCOUTREACH project into areas of towns and cities where Scouting was failing to make an impact. It made considerable strides in taking Scouting into places where it had all but disappeared and amongst the growing ethnic communities in places such as Southall and Leicester, but in subsequent years things largely returned to how they were. I guess that Scouting will never attract one hundred per cent of the population of young people nor should we expect it to do so. Scouting appeals to some but not to others, and the huge gang-ridden estates which SCOUTREACH started to penetrate proved to be unlikely stamping grounds in which a Scout Group will survive.

Fighting back

Earlier I mentioned that it was Jock Barr who worked out how to get my new – and large – desk into the lift at 25 BP Road back in 1968. At that time Jock was just out of his teens and working in the General Office, living at home with his parents. His father was an invalid and his mother had poor health. Jock had been through the Movement as a youngster and was taking a warrant as a leader in the Venture Scout Section.

When a vacancy occurred in the General Editor's Department for a junior, Jock immediately applied and was appointed. His enthusiasm for Scouting shone through in everything he did. Nothing was too much trouble and if something needed doing – anything – Jock was there to do it. Jock became very friendly with David Goodman, then the Department's Designer. They were both about the same age and you might have expected their high spirits and pranks to upset Clare Wyatt, but she enjoyed the fun they brought into the office. But Jock was ambitious and wanted to get on, and the role of junior in the General Editor's Department was a dead end. When a vacancy occurred in the Programme and Training Department, I encouraged him to move to the floor above.

A matter of a few weeks later, we were all stunned to learn that Jock had been instantly dismissed and sent home. We were told that he had stolen a number of green outer garments from the Scout Shop on the ground floor. I knew that Jock purchased uniforms for his Venture Scouts from the shop and I questioned whether or not there might have been a misunderstanding. My enquiries were unwelcome and it was made very clear to me that as Jock was no longer working in my Department, any further questions would remain unanswered. This disturbed me greatly – and not just me but Clare and David too. But I protested in vain.

I contacted Jock at his home, to be told that he had suffered a breakdown. Later Jock spent a day at my home, where David and I met with him. Jock assured us that he had not stolen the outer garments and we believed him. He had an arrangement with the Shop Manager whereby he would take uniform items on sale or return for members of the Venture Scout Unit in Southend, and pay by cash when the items were sold. Jock had been seen taking garments from the shop up to his office, but his explanation as to why he was doing so was not believed. The Shop Manager was on holiday and the matter was referred to the senior member of staff responsible for personnel who refused to listen and dismissed him forthwith. I offered to take the matter up again, but by this time Jock was totally disillusioned with Scout Headquarters and asked me to leave things as they were. I never really got to the bottom of what had happened or why things had been dealt with in such a peremptory manner.

Jock talked about taking teacher training and David and I encouraged him to do so. He went to college in Oxford and became a teacher in Walthamstow, where he bought a flat. He invited Yvonne and me there for dinner one evening. I kept in touch with Jock over the years. Jock taught boys who were displaying difficult behaviour in mainstream schools and also in a remand home in North London. He became Venture Scout Leader of the Unit in Southend and took a leading role with Scouting for the handicapped in Essex. Jock invited my family and me to the opening of his Unit's Headquarters by Betty Clay, B-P's daughter, in July 1982. The Druid Venture Scout Unit had 170 members at one stage – both boys and girls – under Jock's leadership.

Jock led Extoree '83, an international camp for the handicapped at Gilwell Park, where I was responsible for co-ordinating the editorial team producing the *Daily Squirrel* newspaper. This brought together a number of colleagues with whom I had worked on SCOUTING – Don Grisbrook, Bill Bruce, Paul Moynihan, Nigel Baynes, Julian Simmonds and Norman Garnett amongst them. My daughter, Heather, was on the newspaper staff, spending most of her time – it has to be said – ogling Julian and Nigel, but she was a teenager at the time, so is forgiven. The newspaper was printed by SPS, a company in Loughton owned by my neighbour, Derek, who printed the St. Peter's BROADSHEET which I have edited since 1980.

To the amazement of his friends, for Jock had been an outspoken critic of The Scout Association's hierarchy, Major General Michael Walsh, then Chief Scout, appointed Jock as Headquarters Commissioner for Venture Scouts in the mid-80s. It was an inspired choice. Jock's target to raise the national profile of the Venture Scout Section with the slogan *"Venture Scouting Works"* included chartering a giant North Sea Ferry for a weekend cruise to Denmark and scaling the height of Everest for charity. In the short time that Jock was at the Section's helm his leadership was always at the practical level.

Professionally he moved to the Prince's Trust as Chief Executive, but his days were numbered as he contracted leukaemia. A mark of the esteem in which he was held was the fact that His Royal Highness, Charles, Prince of Wales, visited Jock in hospital on a number of occasions as his life drifted away.

I doubt if there are many alive today who remember the circumstances of Jock's instant dismissal from Scout Headquarters in the late 1960s – perhaps

David, one or two others, and me – for the man who would not listen and sent him out the door without giving him the chance to give his side of the story and others who were around at the time have long since passed away. It is right that Jock should be remembered for the immense contribution he made to Scouting in general and Venture Scouting in particular, to teaching and to the Prince's Trust. But I have wanted to tell Jock's story as it was for I believe it makes him an even bigger man – bigger than his many friends thought he was. For Jock rose above something that would have devastated a lesser man – something for which he was wrongly accused but which he was able to put behind him to fight back and overcome.

The man who called me Ronnie!

Laurence Stringer came from a farming family with its roots in Ilford and the markets of London. Laurence was one of four brothers who were brought up by their mother who was widowed when the boys were very young. Our paths first crossed when I had appeared at Stratford Magistrates' Court to support one of my Scouts and Laurence was on the Bench. Laurence was a director of the family wholesale potato merchants in Spitalfields market for almost all his life, rising in the middle of the night to be at his desk for 5am, leaving his office around lunchtime and then either sitting as a magistrate or going to Scout Headquarters where he held various appointments. Laurence was Group Scout Leader of the 5th Seven Kings in Ilford East. My Group and his had some joint activities.

Laurence came into Scouting almost by chance. Before the 1939-45 war Laurence's passion was cricket whilst his twin brother was immersed in Scouting. After the war, Laurence's brother asked him is he would accompany him to the Ilford East District Scout's Annual Meeting. Unbeknown to Laurence, the Scout District Commissioner had indicated to Laurence's brother that he was minded to appoint him as Assistant District Commissioner (Rover Scouts). Laurence and his brother were almost identical in looks and at the meeting the District Commissioner mistook Laurence for his brother – and offered the post to Laurence. Overwhelmed and not a little astounded, Laurence immediately accepted – and started on the long road that would lead to a CBE at the end, whilst his amused brother took Holy Orders (not immediately, but later in life).

The story was told that one evening Laurence was late for a Group Scouters' Meeting at the 5th Seven Kings. On arrival, he apologised profusely, explaining that he had had a bad day.

"The price of potatoes shot up overnight," boomed Laurence, *"my uncle has shot himself and the traffic was so bad that I have arrived late for this meeting. I apologise."* And with that he called the meeting to order and worked his way through the agenda.

Laurence's uncle, Farmer Edwards of Aldborough Hatch Farm, had indeed shot himself in the cellar of the farmhouse near to my home, down the rhubarb fields from St. Peter's. Farmer Edwards had lived all his life with his spinster sister until the mid-50s, when he married a much younger blonde bombshell who sat at the front of the congregation every Sunday morning in St. Peter's where I was in the choir. I had the impression that she was making eyes at our bachelor Vicar, but I doubt he would have been interested. It was rumoured that she went through Farmer Edwards' money in a matter of months and in desperation he shot himself.

I worked with Laurence on the handbooks following publication of the Advance Party Report in 1966 and we were colleagues when I joined the Association as General Editor, with Laurence in the role of Headquarters Commissioner for Scouts and Chairman of the General Purposes Sub-committee. When I retired from that post, Laurence and I were again colleagues – but this time on the Bench at Redbridge Magistrates' Court. Laurence was a great support to me in both roles.

Laurence Stringer was one of life's real gentlemen, a big man in many ways from his tall frame, his big heart, his concern for others to his deep and resounding voice. He was, in fact, the only person – apart from my mother – who called me Ronnie and got away with it simply because I was in such awe of the man that I could do nothing about it! Always immaculate in his appearance, Laurence excelled himself in his Scout uniform, where the pockets of his shirts and trousers were sewn up so that there would be no bagginess and his shorts were starched with knife-sharp creases. When Den Day and I joined Laurence at the Queen's Scouts Parade at Windsor in the late 50s as contingent leaders, we used the old army trick of putting soap behind the creases of our shorts. Fortunately it did not rain – had it done so, we would have had soapsuds running down our knees (not a pretty sight!). Yvonne, Den and his wife, Chris, and I travelled back from Windsor by train. Seated further down the carriage and seemingly completely in a world of his own was the Chief Scout, Lord Rowallan, who Yvonne vowed needed a good woman to do his ironing, for his shirt looked as though he had slept in it.

With representatives of The Scout Association and members of the 5th Seven Kings Rover Crew (whose annual reunions he continued to attend up to the year before his death), I attended the service celebrating Laurence's life at Christ Church, Chislehurst, in May 2008. I met his adopted son, Matthew, for the first time – now a grown man who had nursed his father over the last few months of illness.

My gardener!

Having sat on my interview panel, Don Grisbrook joined the Association's professional staff shortly after me – direct from the RAF where he had been an education officer.

Don had a great sense of humour and I guess he must have had a wry smile on his face as he read the GUARDIAN on Tuesday 18th November 2008 (for I am convinced that having read the GUARDIAN – like me – all his life, Don would be able to lay his hands on a copy, albeit an ethereal one, for how else will he be able to survive?). The GUARDIAN – ever famous for its literals – had even achieved one in Don's *Death Notice* on that day, referring to Scouting as Stouting.

Don and I travelled together around the UK, spending a particularly memorial time in Northern Ireland when the troubles were at their height. Don wrote with passion and it was always a joy to publish his articles, for he had a fine command of the English language which came through in his writing. He was also my unofficial article "titler" – if I was puzzling over the title for a feature article, Don would come up with something appropriate within minutes.

Don enjoyed eating out – and introduced many of our colleagues to 'Mother's', a bistro in a mews near Baden-Powell House, and so called (by Don and everyone who knew him) because Don assured us that the proprietor kept his mother chained to a hot stove out at the back where she did all the cooking. Don's love of a *"bowl of hot nourishing soup"* was well-known and I recall that he was partial to red cabbage, too. Don also vowed that if there was some uncertainty about the restaurant in which you were eating, you were safe in ordering a Crème Brule – advice I have followed.

Don was not over concerned about how he dressed. He was well laundered but often not so well pressed – which was understandable for Don was a bachelor and there were far more important things in his life than ironing (concerts, the theatre, books to name but a few). On one occasion, Don and I went by car to Norfolk to visit a Venture Scout conservation project. We had agreed not to travel in uniform but what I termed in the 1970s as my 'sports' wear' being a tweed jacket with slacks, a check shirt and tie. Don turned up in an old RAF shirt and trousers, with a nondescript pullover that had seen better days. On the way back, I asked Don to stop at a garden centre where I selected some shrubs. Don trotted off to find a wheelbarrow and took this to the car, where he started to unload the shrubs into the boot. The lady taking the money looked over towards Don and said to me: *"Do make sure that your gardener waters the shrubs in when he plants them, Sir!"*

Don once told me that he had never ever succeeded in walking the whole way from Chingford Station to Gilwell Park (a matter of a mile or so, although it seemed much longer on the few occasions when I had walked) for a car invariably stopped to offer him a lift. If, however, cars whizzed by without stopping, he would adopt an exaggerated limp – and that always did the trick. Late on a very dark and cold night, Don refused to allow me to use a taxi so we set off – both limping. We had hardly reached the golf course when a car stopped.

So many people, so little time

During my eleven years as General Editor I worked with some characters who brought colour and life to everyone who came into contact with them. Ted Hayden, Executive Commissioner (Programme and Training) and later the Association's Secretary, was larger than life. A man of immense organisational ability, he could have run a multi-million corporation with ease, but chose to work for far, far less doing something he enjoyed and believed in with passion.

At a national camp at Gilwell Park, Ted asked the 2,000 or so leaders on the training ground to sit on the grass when Chips Maclean was to address them standing on the back of a flatbed lorry – that way everyone would have a clear view. One leader stood up and in spite of repeated requests, remained standing when a panoramic photograph was shot. Ted asked me if I could paint the standing leader out of the photograph before publishing it in SCOUTING. We did so, replacing the leader with a carrot face. I often wonder how that leader explained to his wife that he had, indeed, been present at Gilwell – as the photograph would prove?

When John Sweet – of whom more shortly – promoted a wide game for Scout Troops in mid-winter which involved finding a hidden clue with the telephone number of SCOUTING magazine, Ted was one of the few members of the staff at

25 BP Road who agreed to stay in the office until 10pm on that Friday evening to answer the telephone and give the next clue.

I had many good friends amongst the dozen or so Field Commissioners who worked throughout England and Wales, but it was perhaps Tony Bolton with whom I spent more time than most. Tony, who lived in Thamesmead in his bachelor pad, covered Greater London. If he knew I was speaking on his patch and he was free to do so, he would invariably drive me. As London's Field Commissioner Tony was responsible for Scout participation in many Royal and national events – from the State Opening of Parliament to Royal Weddings and the annual Remembrance Day Service at the Cenotaph in Whitehall.

John Sweet retired as a Field Commissioner shortly after I joined SCOUTING to nurse his beloved wife, Nan, through a terminal illness. Later he was to marry Clare Schlund, one-time Housekeeper at Gilwell Park, living at Holton St. Peter in Suffolk until they both died in the late 1980s within a few months or each other. John wrote for both THE SCOUT and THE SCOUTER, transferring happily to SCOUTING; his articles also appeared in the CANADIAN LEADER magazine (by agreement) and were copied in Scout magazines throughout the world (not by agreement but John was happy enough for this to happen).

Without a shadow of a doubt, John's influence on the activity programmes of Scout Troops throughout the country and the world was immense. He was probably more influential that anyone else over the first 70 or so years of the movement, with the possible exception of the Founder, Lord Baden-Powell – although in truth John produced more games and activities than did B-P. A brilliant artist, John illustrated his ideas for projects involving pioneering ropes and spares, garden canes and rubber bands, and a host of other bits and pieces.

I enjoyed editing John's articles for he would never give the game away – always teasing and suggesting how something might be tackled, but leaving the reader to work out the 'how' and the 'why'. His book, *Scout Pioneering,* was – and remains – the definitive work on the subject. John and I enjoyed bouncing ideas off each other and I would intersperse his text with my 'editorial interjections' which were great fun to write. John launched the 'Lunatic Fringe' – a club for those who enjoyed trying out and foisting on others his madcap schemes. Readers had to apply for membership by writing to John, describing something they had done or tried out – and if John agreed that whatever it was had the right ingredients of fun and slight madness, the writer would be admitted to the 'Lunatic Fringe'. We kept stocks of signed certificates in SCOUTING offices, together with a register of members. By late 1979 something over a thousand souls had their names inscribed in the register and proudly displayed their certificates on appropriate – and sometimes inappropriate – occasions.

I spoke at the Caernarvonshire Scout County Annual Meeting, where the thirty or so members of the audience were at the upper end of the age range for adult leaders – with the exception of a dozen students from the Bangor University Scout and Guide Club, sitting quietly in the back row, waiting to make the tea and serve the cakes when the speechifying was at an end. I spotted that they seemed to enjoy my jokes and I was pleased to be invited to speak at one of their Club meetings. David Saint and I drove to Bangor in 1974, staying overnight in the guest rooms in the students' quarters. Early next morning Derek Twine, Club Chairman, and fellow Club member, Rhoda, served David and me with breakfast.

Derek's home was in Surrey; Rhoda came from Northern Ireland. I kept in contact with Derek, inviting him to meet with me in London when he was home for the holidays. Derek heard that I would be helping to judge the camping competition for Scout Patrols in his home District. Derek considered that, whilst these events had some purpose for those taking part, they excluded the very Scouts who would most benefit from a weekend in the open air under canvas. And so Derek ran what he termed "a camp for the deprived" in a field almost adjacent to that in which the elite would be showing off their skills in the camping competition. The District Commissioner made clear his annoyance at this and gave instructions that the Scouts in Derek's camp were to remain out of sight of all – but especially of me. Not unnaturally, Derek set his lads the task of appearing before me on every possible occasion. They succeeded!

I invited Derek to join the team of voluntary Sub-editors of the training supplements in SCOUTING. Derek worked on the Venture Scout Supplement for a year or two. On completing his degree at Bangor University, Derek applied for the post of Director of Venture Scout Training at Gilwell Park. He was appointed and spent the next thirty or so years working professionally for The Scout Association, moving to the top role of Chief Executive Commissioner. I take some pride in the fact that I may have given Derek the break which led to his taking a major role in the Scout Movement not only in the UK but throughout the world. Derek was at the helm when The Scout Association took some bold decisions in the first years of this Century, decisions that have had a far-reaching influence not only on Scouting but on young people in general. And Rhoda was at Derek's side throughout all this time for they married and lived near Gilwell Park with their son and daughter.

I mentioned Jack Olden, Publicity Manager, earlier. We travelled together to research photo-features for SCOUTING, Jack with his cameras, me with my notebook and pen. The journey from Cork to Dublin by car enabled us to tell the story of the Scouts in Eire in the 1970s – when money was tight, but nothing could dampen the enthusiasm of boys and adults. Jack held onto my ankles as I kissed the Blarney Stone outside Cork. A journey from Switzerland, through Germany, France, Belgium and Denmark showed me that Scouting in other countries differed as did chalk from cheese. In Copenhagen Jack took me to the red light district and to a night club where I was terrified as a lady of doubtful age sat upon my lap and left as soon as it was possible to do so. Jack was made of sterner stuff, I guess.

I enjoyed working with a number of artists and cartoonists. Doug Mountford was a school teacher and Scouter in my home town. I first spotted his talent for cartoons whilst sitting beside him as the monthly meetings of Scout Leaders in the District. Doug would take a sheet of paper at the beginning of the meeting and draw from the centre of the sheet to the outer edge; when the latter was reached and the sheet was filled with his doodles, he would get up and walk silently from the meeting. I encouraged Doug to illustrate books and articles on camping and a range of outdoor skills.

Brian Gough was a brilliant illustrator in black and white, but like many artists he was always short of ready cash. Brian would come into my office with a fist full of sketches and I would agree to pay him for these in the sure knowledge that I would be able to use them – and in the certainty that Brian and his family would eat for a few days. Brian invited me to a meal with a printer, who took us on to the Royal Albert Hall for an evening of wrestling. Seated in a box with liberal helpings of alcohol, I watched as old ladies in ringside seats beat the contestants with their umbrellas until restrained by minders – yes, it really happened and is not just a myth. The night took on something of an alcoholic haze and when I found myself on the pavement outside the Royal Albert Hall with an almost paralytic Brian, I waved down a taxi which took us to Liverpool Street Station, where I placed Brian on a train in the charge of the guard with the request that he be dropped off at his home station.

Bob Dewar worked as a freelance artist for D C Thompson of Dundee, living a few miles away with his wife and family. Talented and innovative, Bob enlivened many a feature article and continues to draw for SCOUTING to this day. *JAD's Christmas Quiz* took over from *Delta's Christmas Quiz* when Rex Hazlewood retired – and Bob has illustrated every one that John A Deft (JAD) has compiled over nearly four decades. Peter Harrison, who lived in Bristol and illustrated many of our books, including my *Programme Planning in the Scout Troop* and *The Scout Troop,* followed in the footsteps of his father whose illustrations appeared in publications in Rex's time. I visited both Bob and Peter, staying at their homes, meeting their families and enjoying their company.

Professional staff

I worked with some dedicated and talented people on the full-time staff of The Scout Association during my eleven years as General Editor. All were poorly paid, for at that time there was a belief amongst charities such as the Scouts that those who worked professionally for them should not receive the commercial rate for the job – for they were doing something they enjoyed. An odd credo, but one that was often repeated both in public and in private. Indeed, I am convinced that this was very nearly the demise of the Association's professional staff in the late 70s, for when mistakes were made by professionals or when things went wrong, the general cry amongst the volunteers was that *"if you pay peanuts, you get monkeys"*.

This was an insult that was hard to take, difficult to swallow and totally undeserved. In my experience the staff at Scout Headquarters worked long hours without any overtime ever being offered, expected or requested. Many of them were highly competent and could have doubled or trebled their salaries if they were minded to move into the public or private sectors. One or two – never more – were not very good at their jobs, but tended to be weeded out. Some were fortunate in having pensions from earlier employment – in the armed services or government. But most had to exist on a pittance.

I enjoyed my eleven years immensely, but with a growing family about to enter further education and university, I found that I could no longer provide the standard of living I believed they deserved on the salary I was being paid. Faced with a growing staff crisis in 1979, salaries were reviewed. In April that year I received a 20% increase – the biggest salary rise I had ever had up to that time – but this was not enough to avert what was a looming financial crisis in my family.

Ken Stevens, Chief Executive Commissioner, was sympathetic, offering to use a charitable fund which he administered to pay for my house to be painted when I could not afford either the time or the money to do so. A senior colleague with a family was having his salary topped up by the benefits system – something that I could not bring myself to contemplate.

Of course, I had the ability and the talent to earn additional income through writing as a freelance, but my role with The Scout Association demanded a seven day a week commitment – anything less would not have satisfied me nor, I would guess, the movement's volunteers who expected me to spend my weekends speaking around the country at Scout events. Had I taken time off during the week to compensate for the weekends I spent away from home (often three a month) I would not have been able to edit the magazine and books, run a department, keep in touch with a team of artists, photographers and writers spread throughout the country, and deal with the mountains of correspondence (at one stage I had one full-time audio typist and two part-timers working from their homes handling my output). In May and June 1979 – my last summer as General Editor – I spoke at some thirty-six District or County Annual Meetings up and down the country. On three consecutive nights I travelled by sleeper from Liverpool to London, worked in the office until mid-afternoon, returned by train to Liverpool to speak that evening – and then back by overnight sleeper to London.

Later that year I resigned to take up a post as Editor of MILK INDUSTRY, the dairy industry's national magazine – where my salary was increased by 50% overnight. Sad as I was to leave the Association, it was inevitable. A number of my young colleagues in the editorial department left at the same time for better paid jobs – not wanting to do so, but having it forced upon them by family responsibilities. I felt no bitterness when in later years salaries for professional staff at the Association were brought into line with commercial pay elsewhere. But it took the debacle of the late 70s for this to happen.

I departed from the professional staff of the Association on the evening of Friday 7th December 1979, having seen the January 1980 issue of SCOUTING arrive on my desk. Yvonne joined me as we walked to the conference room in the offices at Baden-Powell House where over a hundred and fifty folk were gathered – staff colleagues and those from the commercial world, volunteers and contributors. Some had travelled from distant parts of the country. I was delighted to see them all, for each had a special place in my life, but perhaps it was the presence of Lord Maclean, former Chief Scout and by that time Lord Chamberlain, that gave me particular pleasure. Amongst the gifts presented to me that evening were four loose leaf books, each with sheets of A4 written, photographed and drawn by my friends and colleagues. I have them to this day, but I find I can only read a page or two at a time.

Those eleven years had been a privilege and a delight. In the days leading to Christmas, I sat at home preparing for the new challenges as Editor of MILK INDUSTRY and looking back in gratitude for the experience of the past, at the memories, the fun, the friendships, the laughter and the tears, all of which would stay with me for ever and which no-one could take from me.

It took a very long time for me to come to terms with the fact that I was no longer Editor of SCOUTING. Those eleven years had given me so much artistic freedom and the opportunity to make an impact on the movement I admired and loved, and to play but a small part in its development and growth. For the next five years, at least, I felt inwardly sad and often bereft, but I tried not to show it and I believe I succeeded.

Part Six
Dallying in the dairy

Apart from the fact that milk had been delivered to my doorstep throughout my life – from Hitchman's horse drawn milk float in the 1930s through to the Co-op's electric vehicle in the 1970s – I knew little or nothing about the dairy industry, other than the fact that milk came from cows and was dropped off at my home in bottles. Until January 1980, that is, when I took up my appointment as Editor of MILK INDUSTRY, the magazine of the National Dairymen's Association (NDA).

I was forty-seven and I would remain as Editor of that journal until I retired eighteen and a bit years later at the age of sixty-five.

For an industry that had changed little over the previous forty-seven years since the Milk Marketing Board (MMB) was formed in 1933 – coincidently the year of my birth – and even the price of a pint of milk was regulated by the Government at Westminster, the next two decades were to see changes take place the like of which few milkmen – or politicians for that matter – could have imagined possible.

Indeed, it was said that when the MMB paid its farmers once a month in the 1970s for the milk that had been collected, it was the largest movement of money through British banks at any time that month. But all that would change. And how!

But I walked into the London office of MILK INDUSTRY on a raw January morning in 1980, worked there for a few years and then moved the office to the small bedroom at my home, from where I operated until retirement in March 1998.

Notes left out by housewives

I was soon to learn that the dairy industry has its own myths and culture. There is a wealth of folklore about milkmen – but especially about the notes that housewives leave out for their milkmen .

Gerard Hoffnung, the musician and raconteur who died at an early age in 1959, but left for posterity the recording of his speech to the Oxford Union in 1958, had a number of letters written to the benefits office where he had worked and a few notes left for milkmen. One of the latter read: *"Sorry not to have paid your bill before, but my wife had a baby and I have been carrying it around in my pocket for weeks".*

Once I had settled into the mysterious and politically sensitive world of milk, I asked my readers to send in notes that had been left out for the milkman. I built up quite a collection and from time to time I would be asked by a journalist to send some of these for publication. Not that I was paid a penny piece for them, but they made good starters for speeches over the years, going down especially well with meetings of ladies' groups in the leafy suburbs on Wednesday afternoons (and Mondays, too, for that matter). Here are just a few.

One note from a Surrey housewife read: *"Please leave an extra pint of paralysed milk".*

Another note in Dewsbury, West Yorkshire, read: *"Please cancel one pint after the day after today".* And that was written by a schoolteacher.

A note left out by a Wiltshire housewife read: *"Milkman. Please close the gate behind you because the birds keep pecking the tops off the milk".*

A note from King's Lynn read: *"No milk. Please do not leave milk at Number 14 as he is dead until further notice".*

And this note just had to come from Northern Ireland. It read: *"Please leave no milk today. When I say today, I mean tomorrow, for I wrote this note yesterday."*

But the classic came from Luton. It read: *"Leave one extra pint. If this note blows away, please knock."*

An elderly lady in Shrewsbury left this out for her milkman: *"Please knock. My TV has broken down and I missed last night's Coronation Street. If you saw it, will you tell me what happened?"*

Another note read: *"No milk thank you. We are away for the weekend – which is why I am hiding this note under the doormat so that nobody finds out".*

And another: *"From now on please leave two pints every other day and one pint on the days in between – except Wednesdays and Saturdays when I don't want any milk".*

A note dated 1964 written by a housewife in Lyme Regis read: *"Milkman. When you leave the milk will you please put coal on the fire, let the dog out and put the newspapers inside the door."* Great – but it's the postscript that is the clincher: *"Don't leave any milk."*

A note written in Elgin, Scotland read: *"Please cancel one pint of milk every day until further notice. Also please cancel one pint today and can we have an extra pint tomorrow?"*

And finally: *"My back door is open. Please put the milk in the 'fridge, get the money out of a cup in the drawer and leave the change on the kitchen table in pennies – because we want to play bingo tonight."*

Odd and even odder

But I am ahead of myself, for I need to start at the beginning.

Prior to my making the decision to move from editing SCOUTING to doing the same with MILK INDUSTRY, I discovered that a number of Scout folk were involved with the dairy industry. The Chief Executive of the National Dairy Council was a former Scout County Commissioner for London Central and at that time County Chairman for the Scouts of Greater London North East, whilst the Secretary of the NDA was District Commissioner for Kensington and Chelsea. From time to time – inevitably and not surprisingly – I would bump into people in the dairy industry who spent their spare time as leaders in Scouting, some of whom remembered me.

I had visited the offices of the NDA three or so times prior to my joining the staff, but I was ill-prepared for some of the oddities that awaited me. The NDA shared offices with the Dairy Trade Federation at 19 Cornwall Terrace. Cornwall Terrace was owned by the Crown Estates and consisted of a superb crescent of buildings designed by Nash, overlooking Regents Park, behind Baker Street Station and hard by Madam Tussauds and the Planetarium – the queues for which snaked round the back of Cornwall Terrace on most days of the year, but during school holidays would take over the roadway and make attempting to enter the office from the rear something of a marathon involving tourists from – seemingly – every country in the world, and all being entertained as often as not by Punch and Judy.

Bill Duxbury, who had edited the magazine for many years past, remained in post until the end of January. When I arrived – on Wednesday 2nd January 1980 – the January issue was going to press and would be published in the middle of that month. My first issue would be dated February – and would hit the doorsteps in mid-February. That was the first oddity, for I had been used to a world where the January issue came out in good time for 1st January and certainly not half way – or more – through the month. My last issue of SCOUTING was datelined January 1980, but copies had been delivered to the office on Friday 7th December. It took me a year or two and a printers' strike to bring MILK INDUSTRY's publication date back to the first day of the month.

Whilst Bill Duxbury was still a member of the staff, he appeared but rarely at the offices at Cornwall Terrace. He was said to work from home, but spent most of his time at the printers – Burts of Bedford, later to become Newnorth Burt. I gathered he had a room at the printing works which he occupied from time to time – much to the annoyance of the staff who had to print the magazine and to the embarrassment of the directors.

When I made my first visit to the printing works, it was made very clear to me that the facility of an office on their premises would not be extended to me. As I lived in Essex and Burts were in Bedfordshire, this was not a problem. Bill lived in nearby St. Albans He drove a massive motor cycle and wore full leathers, the combination of which made him an awesome sight to behold on a cold and frosty morning.

The second oddity was the typewriter that was bequeathed to me. This was a manual upright machine which printed at something like six point – minute and almost miniscule. The keys travelled a long way down when depressed and took an unacceptable time to return to their rightful place. I had the feeling that prior to my arrival there had been some swapping of typewriters and when it was discovered that there was no machine for me, someone remembered that a very, very old machine had been consigned to the basement. It was brought up, dusted down and left on my desk for me to wrestle with.

In SCOUTING's offices I had been using the very latest machine – an electric typewriter with correcting ribbon no less. Indeed, I had purchased a similar machine for home use with some of the cash I had been given as a parting gift by my friends and colleagues. On my first day at Cornwall Terrace I went hot foot to the nearest office machinery stockists in Marylebone High Street to order an Olympia electric typewriter – which arrived a day or so later to my intense relief.

My Assistant Editor, a young lady, appeared to be somewhat miffed at my appointment – although I never did discover if she had gone for the job herself. It was not the kind of question I would have dared to ask. We were to spend the next couple of years putting up with each other, which was not the happiest of arrangements. I was put in my place about many things – making it very clear that she would do what she wanted to do and nothing would shift her. I decided that I would let things ride and it seemed to work as well as could be expected.

My Assistant's boyfriend was at drama school nearby. He would work in the offices of the NDA from time to time during his holidays. On many afternoons he would call to accompany his lady friend home and tell her what he had been up to at drama school that day. He spent one term acting out as various animals and would come into the office crawling on all fours, growling like a lion or standing on tip-toe as a giraffe. I found it difficult to take any of this seriously and I know not whether he made it in the acting profession.

Both my predecessor and my Assistant had one thing in common – they were members of amateur dramatic societies. This seemed to create a bond between them. I knew that I would find it difficult to do other than bide my time. I think we were both relieved a year or two later when the young lady was appointed to a post with a company publishing our rival magazine.

Rugby reigns supreme

The professional staff of the NDA was headed up by a triumvirate of Chief Executive, Deputy Chief Executive and Accountant. David, the Chief Executive, had started his working life with one of the big oil companies before moving to the NDA. Roger, his Deputy, had taught at a grammar school on Tunbridge Wells – the Surrey town where he and David lived. Both were big noises in the world of rugby and it was not long before Roger gave up teaching for the high life at the NDA.

Tony, the Accountant, was one of those people who can turn their hand at anything. He kept the NDA's accounts in fine fettle and not only that, but if a shelf needed to be put up or taken down, Tony soon had his toolbox out and did the necessary.

Tony would be assisted in such endeavours by Mike, the Training Officer, who shared an office with me. Mike had been in the services and now spent his working days training milkmen to be salesmen.

Mike took his training courses around the country, staying in hotels when he did so. He would spend endless hours on the telephone, ringing all the hotels in the area of his next training course, before settling on which one he would give his custom. Mike had a series of questions he would ask when ringing an hotel – the most important of which required whoever was at the other end to give a detailed description of the Full English Breakfast they offered their guests. And the decision almost invariably depended on the breakfast.

It goes without saying that – like David and Roger – Tony and Mike were both rugby fanatics. I know that Tony continued to play, but I had my doubts about Mike, who seemed to go along with things but never committed himself one way or the other.

A succession of young graduates were employed as Product Managers and most of these had more than a passing interest in the game of rugby – with the possible exception of a young lady who left after a year or so to join the Metropolitan Police (although she may well have had a boy friend who played with that odd shaped ball and I would guess she probably had for how else could she have won through in an interview?).

One Product Manager looked after the interests of the milk processors (big dairy companies and smaller concerns, all buying their milk from the MMB) and a second was responsible for the bottled milk buyers. When I joined the NDA in 1980, there were around 7,000 BMBs – as they were affectionately called – but by the time I retired eighteen years later their numbers were down to 2,000 or so. These were the little men of the dairy industry – folk with one or perhaps two milk rounds which were operated by husband and wife teams with the children getting involved when they were big enough to carry a milk bottle without dropping it. Sometimes they would expand, buying up milk rounds until the man of the house could stay in bed in the mornings and spend the rest of the day on the golf course. Occasionally a BMB would cross the line to become a milk processor in a small way of business. More often than not he would be ostracised by his former BMB colleagues who looked upon him as a turncoat. But more of this latter – if I have the mind to go into detail (which is doubtful at this stage, but you never know).

Simon and Edmund were the survivors of a string of young Product Managers. There was David, who went off to do something with cars, and another young man who decided that being a police officer was preferable to worrying about keeping milk on the doorstep. Some stayed for a year or two, others for shorter periods of time.

Simon was – and still is – married to a delightful and very attractive lady, whilst Edmund, on the other hand, was – and probably still is, although I cannot be sure – a bachelor and keen on fast cars and nights in the pub. Simon delighted in calling me "Scoop" and if I had a nickname for him (which I did), you could put me on the rack and turn it as hard as you like, and I would never reveal what it was.

The rest of the team comprised a couple of lads in the accounts and PA-secretary-cum-typist types, some of whom considered themselves to be dolly birds and others who definitely were. I liked Anona, who was Irish and had an enormous appetite, especially for potatoes. An accomplished typist, Anona eventually succumbed to the blandishments of Tony, the Accountant, and married him. They made a charming couple – although I guess that Anona had a lot to put up with. Tony was always a keen rugby man and dabbled at one stage in local politics, finding himself elected to a parish council of some sort in darkest Berkshire, but it did not last long and he was soon back amongst the lads in his rugby shirt.

It took me some time – months, in fact – to even begin to understand what made the dairy industry tick. The professional staff at the NDA and those who owned or ran the processing and retailing dairy companies were so immersed in the business that they assumed that everyone else knew what was going on. For the first month I was completely at a loss to understand why people disappeared from time to time to visit someone call Maff. Was it Mr, Mrs or Miss Maff? And where did they live or hang out? And I dare not ask for it was very clear that everyone around me knew precisely who or what Maff was. Eventually the penny dropped – MAAF (not Maff) stood for the (now defunct) Ministry of Agriculture, Fisheries and Food.

Making changes

My task with MILK INDUSTRY was to bring it up to date, so the Chief Executive told me, but without alienating the readership who really liked things as they were. A very clear brief, but David was a kindly man and almost certainly knew what he had in mind, whilst I felt confused but happy to let things sort themselves.

My predecessor had been a newspaper man and the style of his magazine reflected this. He would start an article at the top of a page and run it until he reached the end of the text. If there was a small amount of space at the bottom of the page, he would insert a snippet of news or a juicy titbit of something or the other. If there was more space than he needed for his snippets and titbits, he would start the next article and run it until the text ran out – and repeat the process over and over again. The result was not what I had been used to.

My Assistant, not unnaturally, considered this perfectly acceptable practice and was somewhat annoyed when I said all this would change. There was a meagre budget for contributors, for the magazine had tended to rely on articles put out by suppliers to the industry, news releases from a variety of sources and technical material, where the authors of the latter were pleased to get into print and not worried about payment.

I decided to involve some of my colleagues from SCOUTING. Bill Bruce was freelancing from the office of a friendly print farmer off Oxford Circus and was pleased to give the magazine a new design. It was 1980 and we were still using Letratset and such like. I would drop off a few layouts to Bill during my lunch break and he would have the designed pages ready for collection a day or so later. It helped me and it helped Bill – me because I now had design expertise at my fingertips and Bill because it gave him a few extra pounds each month for freelancing was, and still is, a chancy business.

Leslie Cecil, my knife-grinding cartoonist from SCOUTING days, was very happy to illustrate what was a popular feature – *Around the NDA Regions*. I say 'popular', but I exaggerate for it was only enjoyed by some of those who contributed and the few dairymen who got a mention. But it would be a few years before I dared to ditch the regular monthly column. Written by the team of NDA Regional Secretaries who were scattered around England and Wales, it was a somewhat dreary collection of details of meetings and gatherings of dairymen. One contributor invariably had a death to report, so that one might have gained the impression after a few months avid reading of the pages that dairymen only died in his neck of the woods – and did so regularly amidst great mourning amongst their friends and colleagues.

Leslie – drawing under the name Cecil – did much to enliven these grim pages. Having spent years grinding knives for the very best hotels and restaurants in London and making the Scout movement smile in his spare time, he took to the dairy industry like a duck to water. It was a laugh a minute.

Later Geoff Platt, who had moved from SCOUTING to PR work with a national supermarket, went freelance and wrote feature articles for me most months – including the popular MILK INDUSTRY Interview, when leading dairymen would bare their souls in public. Geoff travelled around the country, interviewing, visiting dairies, covering exhibitions and conferences. Without Geoff, I would have been in trouble for he was highly adaptable and became a much respected figure in the industry. Later he would take over as Editor – but I am rushing ahead again.

From time to time I would write a feature article or interview a leading figure in the world of milk. The Rt Hon John Selwyn Gummer MP agreed that I might interview him when he was Minister of Agriculture, Fisheries and Food. I arrived at his Whitehall office just after 4pm, in good time for a 4.30pm appointment. I was called into the presence just before 6pm, when the Rt Hon told me that I could have three minutes of his valuable time as he was due to address MPs at 6.15pm down the road at the House of Commons. I taped his answer to my first question, when he rose and dismissed me, but I followed him out the door, explaining that I had reserved two pages in the magazine for his interview and unless he gave me more time, I would be forced use a full page photograph of him to fill the space and to tell my readers that the Minister of Ag, Fish and Food could spare only three minutes in his busy schedule for the dairy industry. Join me in my ministerial car, he called. I continued the interview walking down stairs, into Whitehall, in the car and sitting in the car park at the House. During my walk back down Whitehall I checked the tape recorder to make sure I had captured every precious word and nuance.

Directors and staff at the printers were helpful and appeared to welcome the steps I was taking to modernise the magazine. Keith, Mel and Bob – amongst others – kept me on the straight and narrow. Over the eighteen years we moved from galley proofs and paste-ups to computerised setting with material going over the FAX machine. My successors took things onto the Apple Mac and into the expanding world of emails and the rest. Things were on the verge of massive technological change when I retired in March 1998 and whilst I have since mastered the PC and emails, I think that my time to retire from professional journalism came at just the right moment. These days I am able to dabble with newsletters and the like for charities – and it suits me well. But – again – I am rushing onwards . . .

From time to time the Chief Executive would have a bright idea for increasing circulation – adding the word International to the title, inserting a quarterly four page Technical Supplement. But the magazine remained very much a publication that would be read by dairymen and the employees and staff of dairies in England and Wales. As such I tried to make it readable and, occasionally, controversial and campaigning.

Just how fresh?

Early in 1985 I caused something of a stir amongst the milk bottles by daring to asking the question: *Just how fresh is my British bottled Pinta?* I commented on the fact that milk bottles delivered to my doorstep had trundled along the A12 on the back of an open milk float, collecting diesel fumes on the way and washed with rain and the muddy spray of passing vehicles. I waxed lyrical about the state of dress of the average milkman when compared with the staff in our supermarkets. I lifted the lid on the manner in which dairy products were conveyed on the backs of open floats. I poured scorn on the state of dairy depots where stacks of empty and unwashed milk crates were home to the local vermin or to empty milk bottles with milk residue attracting disease ridden insects and pecking birds.

The reaction within the offices at Cornwall Terrace was interesting – there was a deathly, almost eerie, silence. For a few days after the magazine hit their desks, people went about their business as though nothing had happened. But after a week or so a thaw set in and it was made very clear to me – by implication rather than words – that I was in severe danger of being set upon with a blunt instrument if I happened to be around on a dark night. I seem to recall, but cannot be certain of this, that Simon threw out a few broad hints that he would happily wield any blunt instruments that were available. Although, in truth, he was a kindly sort of chap.

But my theme was taken up by the managing director of one of the top supermarket chains and the chairman of the NDA's Bottled Milk Buyers' Council at conferences later in the year – although, not unsurprisingly, I was given no credit for having raised the topic in the first place. And then, the floodgates were open!

First I faced a meeting of angry milkmen in Yorkshire, who had insisted that I go out on a milk round in Castleford earlier in the day. As I rose from my bed at 4.30am, I seriously wondered why I had started this campaign?

Next I was fed to the lions by my NDA colleagues who insisted that I face the flack at a London seminar in the autumn attended by directors and staff of the major dairies. Taking as my theme *The choice is mine!,* I showed some thirty or so coloured slides I had taken that summer of milk floats and their contents in and around London. After thirty minutes, the audience was stunned into silence. I had made my point and there was nothing they could say in their defence – although one PR man from a major dairy told me that he would be taking legal advice as to my right to take photographs of his company's dirty milk floats on the streets of London!

Warming to my theme, I decided that my next campaign would target milk crates – and their misuse. You know the kind of thing – milk crates on the pavement outside greengrocers' shops onto which are piled boxes of vegetables and fruit, milk crates being used by newspaper sellers outside railway stations to support piles of their wares. But first I needed to collect the evidence, which meant some early morning trips around London with my camera.

I had carried out similar reconnaissance when taking photographs of milk floats, but this time I would meet some resistance from an unexpected quarter. When taking photographs of grubby milk floats, the milkmen had been too busy to worry about a bloke with a camera and some, I would guess, were half asleep for I had wandered the streets of North London having caught the first Underground Central Line train out of Newbury Park at 5.20am.

When I set out to take photographs of the misuse of milk crates, some shopkeepers may have thought I was a spy from the local environmental health department for they scurried about with expressions of concern. But it was the newspaper seller outside Kings Cross Station who became vocal and abusive.

Leaving his milk crates and piles of the *London Evening Standard*, he ran towards me, shouting and waving his arms in the most menacing of manners. Fortunately, I was able to run faster than him – for I fear that had he caught me he might well have smashed my beloved Pentax. The series of photographs of misused milk crates ran and ran and ran.

Milk crates (and bread baskets for that matter) continue to be abused by shopkeepers and newspaper sellers. Although there are fewer households having their milk delivered to the doorstep, the milk floats in use have changed very little. Most are open-sided, with dairy products and other goods scattered around with but a few inside a cool box. But I tried.

The editorial ladies

During the early 1980s before I moved the editorial office to my home, I had two young lady Assistant Editors.

Liz came from farming stock – her parents had a beef farm in Leicestershire. One Sunday evening we travelled together to Paris for a dairy exhibition, but on arrival at Charles De Gaulle Airport, my bags were missing. All I had was what I stood up in – slacks, shirt and jumper.

First thing Monday morning Liz and I went to Galeries Lafayette to stock up. Having chosen a suit, shirts and, ties, Liz ambled off to sort out some socks whilst she sent me away to find underwear.

"Don't get anything dowdy," she called. *"Remember – you are in Paris."*

I wore my Parisian underwear for some years afterwards – and thought of Liz often over the years.

Liz was bright and sparky, a good writer and researcher, someone I was sure would carve out a career in the media, and because of this Liz was with me for a year or so before moving on to widen her experience.

Liz had her mind set on a career in television and it came as no surprise when I discovered that in the intervening years Liz has gone right to the very top. After working as a feature writer on newspapers and women's magazines, her TV career started at the BBC, in 1989, as a researcher and she worked thereafter for Diverse Productions and Granada. In 1993, at BBC youth programmes, she worked as deputy series producer on *The Living Soap,* the first contemporary docu-soap, about students living in a house in Manchester. In 1995 Liz was Editor of BBC2 Factual Programmes and later Deputy Head of BBC's Youth and Entertainment Department. Liz moved to Ginger TV then to Channel Four where she became Commissioning Editor for event pieces, which led to her commissioning the BAFTA award-winning *Big Brother*.

In 2001 Liz founded her own independent television production company which produces high-quality contemporary television, specialising in popular documentaries and factual entertainment relevant to modern Britain. Having watched for Liz's name in the TV credits over many years, I was delighted to see it appear as Executive Producer to the Channel Four series *Country House Rescue.*

Now married, Liz and her husband have adopted three children from the same family, live in Gloucestershire, alternating the days they work in London.

Liz visited our home on a number of occasions and became a firm friend of Yvonne and the children. I had the distinct feeling that the same could not be said of my second – and last – female assistant, Rachel.

Rachel's mother, who I met when she visited her daughter in London, called her daughter a Bimbo – a term in popular use to describe an often attractive, yet unintelligent woman, and derived from "bambino" meaning child. Whilst Rachel was most certainly attractive, she could not by any stretch of the imagination be considered unintelligent. After a year or two with MILK, Rachel moved to work on *The Builder* magazine. The last I heard she was dating an Army Officer.

There were two occasions involving Rachel which I recall with some amusement. The first occurred when Rachel, Geoff Platt and I stayed in an hotel in Buxton during an NDA Conference and Trade Fair. The hotel had all the trappings of *'Fawlty Towers'*. It was the mid-80s, but there were no telephones in any of the rooms, which meant that the hotel did not offer early morning calls for guests. Rachel was concerned that she might oversleep, so I offered to call her each morning. However, I had overlooked the fact that I had not packed a dressing gown, as I had not expected to leave my room each morning prior to getting dressed. There was nothing for it, but to wear my raincoat over my pyjamas. Rachel was a heavy sleeper and try as I might I could not rouse her by knocking on her bedroom door. It was only as I left her room, closing the door behind me and starting to walk back upstairs to my room that it began to dawn on me that others in the hotel might misunderstand what I had been up to. Fortunately, I did not meet anyone.

The second incident involving Rachel occurred on her 21st Birthday shortly before Christmas. I had been out to lunch with the agency handling the magazine's advertising, and on my return found Rachel out for the count and asleep on the floor behind her desk. Rachel had been for a celebratory drink with some of her office colleagues and was now paralytic. I knew that Rachel was due to meet friends for dinner in Covent Garden that evening, but clearly she was in no fit state to travel from the office later in the day. Indeed, she had been violently sick and she needed to change everything she stood up in.

I decided that I would take Rachel home by taxi and whilst I rang one of her flatmates to tell her my intention, other colleagues in the office took Rachel off to the ladies' room to clean her up. Imagine my surprise when they returned with Rachel – dressed in a milkman's smock, the only clothing they could find in the building!

We must have been an odd sight as the pair of us stood on the pavement in Cornwall Terrace, hailing a taxi – for I was clutching a bucket (in case Rachel threw up again) and Rachel was leaning on me as her legs would not support her weight. A number of taxi drivers drove past at speed, but finally one stopped and listened as I explained my sad or, rather, Rachel's sad story.

The journey to Golder's Green was uneventful, apart from the fact that Rachel went into a dead sleep whilst resting her head on my shoulder. I doubt if the taxi driver believed one word of my story and I spotted a wry smile on his face as I carried Rachel into her flat.

With Rachel safely inside – and stretched out on her bed – the first thing I did was ring Yvonne from the telephone in the flat (for this was before the days when everyone who was anyone carried a mobile phone). I learned long ago that when you are in a potentially embarrassing situation, it is best to come clean with your wife at the earliest possible moment. I am unsure what Yvonne made of my story initially, for she had more than enough to cope with at home with the children so did not question me too closely. My second call was to Rachel's flatmate, who told me that it would be a couple of hours before she would arrive home to help – and that meantime I should attempt to sober up Rachel. Make her walk up and down, her flatmate instructed, and feed her with dry toast.

All this was easier said that done. My first problem was rousing Rachel, now lying on her bed and – I would have to admit, although not within Yvonne's hearing – looking rather alluring albeit that she was dressed in a milkman's smock. I managed to arouse her, but getting her to stand upright was another matter. Slim, but nonetheless well-built, it took all my strength to move her into the kitchen, where I proceeded to make toast. In between bouts of stumbling along the hallway and eating dry toast, Rachel would regale me with moanings and apologies.

I sighed mightily with relief when her flatmate arrived home and insisted that Rachel take a bath. An hour or so later and dressed in their finery, both girls were ready to party. Gallant fellow that I am, I called a taxi and drove them both to Covent Garden. After handing them over to their friends, I took the London Underground to my home – there to explain to Yvonne what had happened. I have to say that she was very understanding, although I have found since that time that it is best not to mention Rachel's name when Yvonne is around and to avoid any reference to the incident involving the milkman's smock.

Meetings, b****y meetings!

As Editor of SCOUTING, I had spent an inordinate amount of time addressing gatherings around the country and I was determined not to repeat this in the dairy industry. But, inevitably, I found myself doing so from time to time, although more often than not I was an observer at conferences and seminars rather than a participant.

I mentioned earlier the NDA conference and trade fair. These were held in the autumn – alternating between the North and South of the England, but never ever stepping across the border into Wales. The nearest we ever got to the Principality was Cheltenham.

In my early days I shared a stand at the trade fair with the NDA, but later we branched out and had our own stand – from where we dispensed MILK INDUSTRY telephone pads or pens or carrier bags or model horse-drawn milk floats or other goodies.

Both Yvonne and Charlotte took turns joining Geoff and me, and Geoff would drive us there and back. Part of the fun of these events was seeing how many freebies we could amass between us. Some exhibitors were generous in the extreme, handing out dairy and drink products at the end of the event – yogurt, cheese, flavoured milks, fizzy drinks and chocolates, to name but a few. Geoff would wander the exhibition hall, taking notes for a feature article in the magazine whilst eyeing up the possibilities for freebies later. Geoff was meticulous in returning the empty bottles from the previous year – which always went down well with the suppliers and ensured that he would have a crate or three to take home this year. Other exhibitors were tough nuts to crack and as mean as mean when it came to freebie handouts.

With a stand of our own, Bill Bruce was called in to design posters and help with the giveaways. One year Bill designed a life-sized – but flat – milk float in timber with shelves on which we stood the dreaded milk cartons as sold in shops and supermarkets and much hated by milkmen who dropped – not literally, of course – those much revered (and recyclable) milk bottles onto doorsteps. Visitors to the stand had to throw bean bags (made by Yvonne – who else) and those who knocked a carton off received a MILK INDUSTRY telephone pad.

Blackpool was the most popular venue with bottled milk buyers for the event was held when the famous illuminations were at their peak and it made a day or two out for the family. Bournemouth, Brighton, Buxton (once and only once), Harrogate and Torquay were the other venues for the conferences and trade fairs. The hotel at Blackpool had a reputation as somewhere to avoid at all costs – but the NDA returned there time and again, and I never fathomed why. Tetra Pak's Bill Taylor was convinced that the pile of dust in the corner of one of the lifts had been there the previous year, but had just grown bigger. One night there was a fire at the far end of the rambling building, but those of us in the adjoining annexe heard nothing. We slept on whilst guests in the main building wandered aimlessly around the car park and on the sea front in the middle of the night dressed in their pyjamas, nighties and boxers. Newspapers stuffed in the sash windows to keep out the draughts were said – by those who removed them to have a look – to be dated a century before – but surely they were exaggerating?

One town where we held the event possessed conference facilities that had seen better days. I was prevailed upon to take part in a series of mock trials in which dairymen were arraigned for offences such as failing to deliver the milk before breakfast and carrying pots of cream on the back of their float unprotected from the sun instead of being placed in a cool box. Riveting stuff, I can tell you. Scripted by a dairyman who was something big in amateur dramatics back home, the costumes were hired from a theatrical costumier. No expense was spared and I played the judge in full bottomed wig and gown. The audience rocked with laughter as I sentenced one dairyman to a week at the conference hotel and another – for a lesser offence – to two weeks at the same hotel.

Dairymen were great guys for formal dinners and dances. One afternoon in the North East the men sat through a seminar on some red-hot topic around doorstep deliveries whilst their wives did some shopping and titivated themselves for the evening's fun and capers. Dinner took its usual course, but rather than have a speaker the decision was made to stage a grand raffle – to be drawn before the dancing. Suppliers to the industry were contacted and a very fine array of prizes was assembled – totalling one hundred and eighty in all. With a hundred or so sitting down to dinner, it requires little imagination to appreciate that a few of the guests would stumble home later that night with more than one prize. And what prizes!

Once the first few tickets had been drawn and the bottle of gin, the TV, radio and electric kettle had been won and collected by their delighted winning ticket holders, things went somewhat downhill until the final hundred or so prizes consisted of single bottles of Urn Brew or carbonated spring water and the like. But the NDA Regional Secretary and self-appointed Master of the Raffle was totally oblivious to the boredom that now hung like a death mask over the proceedings as he droned on and on and on, calling out the ticket numbers, as diners walked wearily from their seats to collect a bottle of Cherryade or a pack of yogurt. The dancing started sometime after eleven and as the licence ran only until midnight, there were a few disappointed ladies and a goodly number of dairymen whose ears would have been bent before they were tucked beneath the sheets that night.

Every industry has its quirks. In the dairy business it is milk bottle collecting. Yes, there are men (and women, I would guess) who are dead serious about collecting milk bottles – of all shapes and sizes, whilst those with printed advertisements are much prized. I have to admit that I have a small, but rather unique, collection of my own, housed in the shed-with-the-overhang at the bottom of my garden. Val-Across-The-Road heard about my collection in the days when decorated bottles were still being delivered on the doorstep (before it was discovered that the bottle scanners used to find foreign bodies in empty milk bottles could not detect creepy-crawlies and the like through the decoration) and decided to start a collection of her own. I am reliably informed that Val continues to treasure her bottle collection and is waiting for their value to go through the roof before selling.

Bonding

The NDA placed great faith in ensuring that staff bonded, for this was the 1980s when it became very popular amongst employers to arrange away days and suchlike jollies to encourage staff to get to know one another by playing games and taking part in way-out sporting activities – and the NDA was all for that, and how!

These events took two forms. There were the annual few days away for the Chief Executive and his management team, of which I was one. The other was a once a year gathering of staff from head office with the regional team. Great care was taken in finding venues in exotic spots within England and Wales where these events might be staged. Rarely if ever did the team return to the same place – partly because the lads liked to go to different areas of the country, but also because from time to time people's behaviour went somewhat over the top and a return visit was deemed inappropriate.

The management team meetings were attended by David, Roger, Tony and me. Later when Roger moved on to become a Chief Executive in his own right of another trade association, Simon joined us in his place – and was clearly delighted to do so. These meetings were held in the winter months over two or three days at hotels in the Home Counties. One hotel on the Thames was situated pleasantly enough on an island, connected to the shore by a strip of roadway. As we were staying there in January, it was not surprising that the river rose and flooded the roadway; by the time we left the waters had receded (which was a pity in a way because I am sure we would have enjoyed paddling in our bare feet to the shore – especially Simon who would have revelled in such goings-on).

I guess that these gatherings were necessary for the organisation, but I found that much of the discussion ranged over subjects that had little relevance to the magazine. An hour or so would be devoted toward the end of the time to MILK INDUSTRY, when I would be expected to justify what I was doing and listen to a number of brilliant ideas, few of which were feasible or practical let alone financially viable. But I believe everyone felt better when it was all over and as we were staying at the very best hotels, the food was of the highest quality. Being fitness fanatics, my colleagues took brisk walks from time to time, drinking the very finest ales and wines, and eating the good food.

The annual gatherings involving the regional staff were another matter altogether. These ran over three or four days, terminating on Friday evening with a dinner to which the NDA President would sometimes be invited. I say 'sometimes' because the invitation depended on a number of factors. One year the President – the managing director of a family dairy – had been chased around the hotel swimming pool by a senior member of staff whilst dressed only in his vest and underpants, which was not a pretty sight as he was of rotund build, to put it mildly, with a stomach that travelled before him. Presidents did not attend for a year or two after that.

There was little time to relax during these gatherings. We would be expected to be up with the larks to take breakfast. At the first conference I attended the Chief Executive was somewhat disturbed to discover that I read THE GUARDIAN.

"Had I known that when you were interviewed," he told me, *"you would not have been appointed."* And I think he might have meant it.

The Chief Executive had been told by one of the Presidents that he should insist that all male staff wore ties during the daytime conference sessions. Ties implied work rather than pleasure or leisure, apparently. Suits were optional, whilst those who wore an NDA jumper scored extra points and if the tie was of the NDA branded variety, you might even have a pint bought for you at lunchtime. Mike, the Training Officer, would be encouraged to arrange one or two sessions during which the very latest training techniques and gimmicks were tried out. But the highlight of the few days was the outdoor session where real bonding took place and the Chief Executive could see who were the men and who were the boys – and what the girls were made of, too, for that matter.

Paintballing in the North East stands out vividly in memory. Kitted out in camouflage denim and armed with a machine-gun-type weapon loaded with yellow paint balls, we were let loose in a dense forest, having first been divided into two teams. The Chief Executive had allocated staff to teams, making sure that all the young – and therefore most athletic – boys and girls were on his side. Sadly, he was called away at the last minute to a friend's funeral and missed the goings on deep in the woods. I recall little of the four hours or so that I stumbled around in the trees and bushes, except that Simon laughed and laughed whenever he spotted me as he fired off yet another volley in my direction. I know that when I finally made it to base my denims were no longer camouflaged but bright yellow. Later than evening I discovered that once the numbness went, I was covered from head to foot in dark, black bruises. Some of them took three months to disappear.

I came into my own when the conference was held in the Lake District and the outdoor activity took place – appropriately – on a lake. Pioneering spars, oil drums and ropes (of the sort I had been used to in the Scouts) had been acquired from somewhere. Divided into teams, we were to make rafts and sail these around an island a few yards offshore and back. My raft stayed intact and sailed out and back (for I had not forgotten my Scout knots and lashings), whilst the Chief Executive got away first but sank ignominiously a few yards from the shore (for he did not know a knot from a lashing) and watched his oil drums float away down the lake. He was not amused.

A treasure hunt was organised at another conference. This involved a lot of walking along country lanes in a heat wave. I agreed to do some research in a graveyard, looking for information that appeared very important at the time – and spent a couple of hours sleeping happily in the shade of a leafy tree.

In mid-Wales we were staying near an outdoor activity centre whose staff were engaged to put us through our paces. I coped with the canoeing, claimed age dispensation when it came to rock climbing and refused point blank to abseil down the side of the inside wall of a reservoir. The Chief Executive was not best pleased with me. The pony trekking another year was fun, except that my horse was clearly hungry and ate grass at every available opportunity – leaving me trailing behind the rest and in danger of rolling head first down the animal's neck.

Office parties

I know few people who can say with their hands on their hearts that they enjoy office Christmas parties, but my colleagues at the NDA were the exception. They revelled in them. In fact, I do believe they would have had one every week if it had been possible.

Some were held in London, others out of town necessitating a stay in an hotel or a very late journey home (by public transport in my case). Wives were invited to one or two – but never boy or girl friends, which upset the unattached, and so wives were dropped, too. Not that Yvonne minded. Watching grown men hurl bread rolls at each other was not her idea of fun.

A treasure hunt around Baker Street and Marylebone High Road was organised one Christmas and, inevitably, involved visiting every pub in the vicinity with a meal in a private room beneath a restaurant at the end. On two or three occasions, the Christmas celebration was held in an hotel in Tunbridge Wells, the home town of David and Roger. I stayed overnight and discovered that the hotel was yet another reincarnation of '*Fawlty Towers*'.

One year wives joined us for a Medieval Banquet near the Tower of London. Bad behaviour was positively encouraged for it was assumed that this was the done thing in medieval times. My colleagues needed little encouragement. We attended a similar Medieval Banquet in the Midlands on the final night of one of the annual gatherings involving regional staff. One member of the NDA head office team decided to take the rise out of the actor playing King Henry VIII, but the actor had met this kind of joker many times before and knew just how to put him down – and how! It was the only time I had ever seen this member of staff depart from a meal table and the chance to down a few pints to spend the rest of the evening sitting alone, outside and in the dark.

An anecdotal story did the rounds at one time which cannot be true, but I repeat it for it has a certain frisson. It is said that there was some skylarking after lights out at an hotel where the NDA staff were staying after a Christmas party. Two of the lads shared a room. One was what you might describe as sexually athletic, both enjoyed their beer, but the other – and older – guy was ready for some shut eye and not interested when two of the waitresses indicated that they would not be averse to spending the first half of the night under the duvet with the sexually athletic guy. The waitresses waited for a few minutes when they guessed that both lads would be in bed before knocking on their door.

One waitress sat in a chair whilst the other jumped into bed with sexually athletic, but was somewhat concerned to note that the second guy was in the adjacent single bed. Drawing the attention of sexually athletic to this fact, the waitress was told not to worry as he was fast asleep – but the waitress pointed out that this could not be the case as he was puffing away at a cigarette! The smoker was speedily despatched to spend the rest of the night wrapped in his duvet in the bath. Apparently having the second waitress sitting in a chair nearby whilst awaiting her turn was not a problem.

But, of course, this is just anecdotal. Nothing more.

Visits abroad

Following my appointment as editor of MILK INDUSTRY, the first dairy I visited was not in England – but in Rome. The invitation to join a group of journalists came from the major supplier of the pasteurisation plant at the newly commissioned Rome Dairy. On arrival we discovered that the plant was, in fact, not yet commissioned as there was a dispute with the unions which would take many months to resolve, and I walked around my first dairy miles from home and without any milk to be seen.

Rome was interesting for our hotel was near the amphitheatre. We had one day to ourselves for sightseeing, but as the recently-appointed editor I knew none of my fellow journalists and found myself alone. I decided to walk to the Vatican, but after a couple of hours I realised that it was in all probability like walking from Brighton to visit London's Westminster Abbey, and so I turned back. My grasp of Italian was such that I feared if I hailed a taxi, I might end up in a basement with the Mafia – and so I walked.

Over the years that followed I travelled widely in Europe and visited Iceland and America once – all courtesy of the two major carton manufacturers, Tetra Pak and Elopak. Both were most generous hosts and their PR men were kindly, considerate, helpful and great company. Would that my fellow journalists had been the same. To be fair, there were a few journalists who made good companions, but as a race those who wrote for or edited dairy and juice journals were a strange gang.

Invariably we would fly to the country we were visiting and from then onwards would be ferried around either by coach or car. If we were leaving early for a series of visits during one day, the Brits would be standing by the coach fifteen minutes early – alone and shivering if it was cold, for we invariably departed before the sun had risen – but anxious not to be late. Those journalists hailing from the warmer countries of the Mediterranean tended to be the last to arrive – often thirty minutes or so after we had taken our seats.

Pauline, who edited *Dairy Industries International*, our rival journal, joined me on many of these trips. Pauline understood the technical and scientific side of the industry, which I did not. A delightful companion, Pauline and I had great fun, although she could be a bit wearing after a few days. Arriving back at Heathrow from one overseas trip, Pauline was met by husband Brian. Not having met Brian before, he shook me warmly by the hand and asked if I had been with Pauline throughout the time we had been away? When I said that I had, he looked me in the eyes – and winked.

Pauline had the happy knack of causing embarrassment quite unintentionally. Travelling with a group of colleagues in a lift in an hotel late one evening, I was taken aback – as were those around me – when Pauline called over their heads, asking me for my room number as she might want to speak to me or visit me during the night!

Pauline loved to talk about anything with anyone and she would invariably have a string of questions to hurl at any unsuspecting speaker at a seminar, exhibitor at an exhibition or host during a visit to a dairy or juice plant. I could safely rely on Pauline to ask all the questions that I might have asked had I known what the hell we were looking at in the first place. Most comforting.

The 1980s were the heyday of massive trade exhibitions both in the UK and Europe. One year when PAKEX, the packaging exhibition, was held at the National Exhibition Centre, Birmingham, Tetra Pak took over virtually a complete exhibition hall where they had a number of working filling machines churning out cartons like there was no tomorrow and filling them with water.

Throughout the day a procession of trucks queued at the back of the hall, where water-filled cartons dropped onto their open backs; when full the trucks rumbled off to a recycling plant where the cartons were squashed and the water sent from whence it came – before dashing back to the hall for another load of water-filled cartons.

Two exhibitions on the Continent alternated every four years – SIEL in Paris and two years later the DLG, the German Agricultural Society's show in Frankfurt and later Cologne. Each year the suppliers to the dairy and juice industries appeared to vie with each other to put on bigger and better exhibition stands.

The carton manufacturers' stands were massive – with kitchens and restaurants to delight a gourmet. Every conceivable type of milk, juice, yogurt, soup, tea and coffee – to name but a few – were displayed in colourful and innovative packaging. Thirst could be assuaged throughout the day with a call at these stands.

Tetra Pak were brilliant hosts at these exhibitions. The night out on the town (and sometimes into the country) was awaited with keen and intense anticipation by the trade journalists. Dinner was invariably superb with the very best wines, and entertainment that was invariably amusing, if occasionally bizarre.

After dinner in the Frankfurt Opera House, we were entertained by Lisa Minnelli. I was entranced, but when she was followed after the interval by Marilyn

Monroe, I realised that there was something a bit odd. My colleagues were highly amused – for they had appreciated from the start that this was not *the* Lisa Minnelli, but a highly professional drag artiste.

On one occasion, having enjoyed dinner, the party of journalists was ushered down a flight of steps into a square at precisely the moment a tram came around the corner. Hired for the rest of the evening by Tetra Pak, we toured the city amidst an alcoholic haze and were returned to our hotels – fortunately – by taxi.

Memorable

Perhaps the most memorable overseas trip was when Tetra Pak took a group of journalists to Atlanta, Georgia, where we stayed at the Marriott Marquis Hotel. Some fifty storeys high, the hotel was built around a central atrium. Plant holders ran right round each floor with plants trailing over the edge.

It was said that a man started watering the plants on Monday on the fiftieth floor and finished on the ground floor on Friday – ready to start again the following Monday.

A young bellboy showed me to the elevator and carried my bags to my room. As I handed him a tip, he turned and said: *"Say, I love your accent. You sound just like Mrs Thatcher!"*

Open barely a month when I took up residence in my room on the 18th floor, I read with some care the fire instructions fixed (understandably, I would guess) to the inside of all 1,600 bedroom doors. After assuring me that *"your safely and security are of the utmost concern to us"* (which was kindly, pleasant and somehow comforting) the notice continued with a series of safety tips *("Never smoke in bed", "Count the number of doors to the nearest exit").* This was followed by some seventeen points as here (the capital letters and exclamation marks are as they appeared in the notice):

(1) DON'T PANIC; remain calm.
(2) Report fire to front desk or fire department as appropriate.
(3) If room is smoky, get on hands and knees (or stomach) and crawl to the door.
(4) Feel door knob; if HOT, do NOT open door; if cool, open slowly.
(5) If hallway is smoky, stay next to the wall and count the doors as you crawl to exit.
(6) Do NOT use any elevators. Elevators will not operate.
(7) Do NOT prop open doors to exit staircase.
(8) Hang onto the handrail and walk DOWN exist staircase.
(9) Pull fire alarm as you evacuate.

If you cannot leave this room

(10) Call front desk and let them know where you are.
(11) Wet sheets, towels or clothing and stuff them in all cracks around doors and vents.
(12) Check to see if there is smoke OUTSIDE window; if NO smoke or if any window can be opened, hang a sheet or light coloured material outside.
(13) Fill bathtub with cold water for fire fighting.
(14) Using the ice bucket or other container, keep doors and walls wet.

(15) If room is smoky, fold a wet towel in a triangle and tie over your mouth and nose. Stay low.
(16) Make yourself visible to rescue personnel through any window or balcony. DO NOT JUMP!
(17) Keep fire fighting until help arrives. DON'T GIVE UP!

One of my colleagues – a gentleman of a somewhat nervous disposition – decided that he would carry out his own recognisance of the escape route from his room as described in items (3) to (9) in the notice. Crawling on hands and knees, and staying next to the wall (being a stickler for doing as he was told), he made his way to the exit staircase. Once inside the door from the corridor to the staircase, he made the mistake of allowing the door to close behind him – which meant that he had to walk down the stairs from the 18th to the ground floor and then return to his room.

What made it all the more difficult for him was the fact that he had been about to go to bed when he made the decision to try out the fire escape. Fortunately, he had the foresight to put on his snowy white – and fluffy – dressing gown over his M & S pyjamas. The staff and guests in the hotel foyer accepted the sight of the elderly man wandering in his pyjamas and dressing gown from the fire escape as just one of the many eccentricities of the Englishman abroad.

On our first night in Atlanta, Tetra Pak took the party of journalists in a fleet of taxis to have dinner with an important US trade journalist and beverage expert. It had been arranged that we would meet this important person at the restaurant, somewhere in the suburbs of Atlanta.

Unfortunately, none of the taxi drivers knew the location of the restaurant and we finally arrived in time for the dessert, after asking directions at a number of filling stations. One of my colleagues who knew the geography of the place said it was rather like driving from London to Birmingham via Brighton. The taxi fares were impressive.

On our visit to Savannah the same colleague who wore the fluffy dressing gown over his M & S pyjamas was held up by the metal detector at the airport security check. Each time he tried to pass through it gave off an alarm, and each time he had to take off one more piece of clothing. He was down to his vest before he was allowed through, when the security men discovered his braces contained metal.

Bill, Tetra Pak's redoubtable PR man, recalls that he carried the case of the ever resourceful Pauline (of *Dairy Industries*) through US customs and was challenged as to why it wasn't his. Quick as a flash, Pauline called out from somewhere down the queue: *"It's OK! He's my carrier!"* The customs' official waved Bill through with a strange look.

I had a free day on Sunday whilst staying in Atlanta, so I decided to visit Martin Luther King's church. Fearing that I might lose myself if I set out by foot, I called a taxi and arrived an hour or so before the morning service was due to start. I spent a pleasant time walking in the nearby streets, enjoying the gardens and the houses, but I noticed that the area was totally deserted and I was alone. It was eerie and I was pleased when the bookshop adjacent to the Ebenezer Baptist Church opened its doors.

From about ten folk started to arrive for the morning service. They were almost without exception black, dressed in their Sunday best, happy and smiling as they greeted one another with calls and much laughter. Realising that the church would soon fill up, I approached the door, but was stopped in my tracks by a tall young man who told me – politely, but firmly – that until all the members of the church had been seated, I would not be permitted to enter – and then only if there was space, for whilst visitors were welcome, it was not my church and the folk who came Sunday by Sunday would have to be accommodated first.

A minute or so before the service was due to start, I was ushered into the foyer together with half-a-dozen other visitors, all German and white. My bag was taken from me and I was asked to empty my pockets. A body search followed whilst my property was locked in a small metal cabinet – the key was handed to me and I was told that I would not be permitted to leave the building until the service was at an end. That seemed fair enough, for at that point I did not appreciate that the service would, in fact, run for some three-and-a-half hours!

The church was packed, the singing led by the choir was magnificent, the music was varied – ranging from psalms and canticles to spirituals and hymns straight from *Ancient and Modern* with much hand-clapping and a good few *"Alleluias"* and *"Praise the Lords"* thrown in. It was uplifting, sincere and memorable.

I cannot recall how many sermons were delivered – for after two hours or so I was beginning to feel the heat. At one stage the Minister, announcing that local elections would take place during the following week, invited the candidates who were present to stand and show themselves. All were given a polite handclapping reception, but then the Minister took it upon himself to tell everyone who they should vote for – and why! His words were received with much shouting and calling, interspersed with laughter and lots of chattering in the pews and good humoured banter. It was all very jolly and even the candidates who did not receive the endorsement of the Minister seemed content and happy enough.

As the clock ticked towards two in the afternoon, we were let out into the open air – recovering our property on the way and waiting for fifteen minutes to buy a tape of the highlights of the morning's goings on.

Stepping into the warm sunshine, I started to walk back towards my hotel whose fifty storeys rose high into the sky in the near distance. But hardly had I taken a few steps along the footway, when a taxi pulled up beside me. The driver called for me to get in, but I assured him that I was content to walk. No way, he called, and urged me to climb aboard. I again assured him that I wished to walk, but this time he was taking none of this nonsense from me. Climbing from the cab, he grabbed me by both arms, lifting me into his cab, explaining that no-one walked in downtown Atlanta, especially white Englishmen, unless they wanted to be robbed or shot or both!

Later that day I ventured from the hotel over to the shopping mall where I wandered through departmental stores where all the shop assistants appeared to be leaning across the counters and talking on the telephone. None seemed in the least bit interested in serving me.

Bill and the other journalists were going elsewhere to visit fruit juice plants, leaving Pauline and me to spend two days together in Atlanta. We journeyed to a theme park, sitting in rocking chairs – I recall – for part of the day, but whatever else we did remains a blur in my memory.

Travelling home across the Atlantic from Atlanta, Pauline and I were booked into Club Class, but were transferred by the airline to First Class. After dinner and a drink or three, the air hostess made us comfortable for the night. Having tucked Pauline up, she told me that she would leave me to be tucked in by my mother. Pauline was not happy at this.

Tetra Pak were the hosts when I joined four or five journalists to fly around Europe, visiting seven countries in five days, to view school milk projects between dairies and governments. At Amsterdam we transferred to a light aircraft which made two abortive take-offs before finally rising into the air at the third attempt.

The stark contrast between poverty and affluence made me catch my breath in Portugal; we had eaten lunch at an exclusive – and expensive – beach-side fish restaurant and drove to our next school along a coast road where peasants lived in open-fronted hovels clinging to the sides of the cliffs and where everyone walked bare footed and was scantily clad. I shuddered to think what they had eaten that lunchtime.

The carton manufacturers were anxious to demonstrate to the world that they planted half-a-dozen trees to replace each one they felled to make into cartons.

A flying visit to Sweden to visit dairies included one day watching trees being cut down and another day at a tree nursery. We were kept at a safe distance whilst the trees crashed to the ground, but at the nursery it was hands-on as we worked our way along furrows planting six inch high fir trees into the rich soil. I smuggled one into my luggage – quite illegally of course – and planted it in my front garden.

Fifteen years or so later it was higher than my house and I cut it down with the help of Tom-next-door.

My final trip abroad as editor of MILK INDUSTRY was to Finland where Elopak were my hosts. We crossed the border into Russia for an evening meal – my one and only visit to that massive country.

Homeward bound

During the 1980s, whilst editor of MILK INDUSTRY, I did some freelance work for charities and commercial publishers – partly because I enjoy writing, but also because a growing family needed more financial support with university and college looming.

I wrote a couple of books for The Scout Association and some features for SCOUTING, and carried out a number of speaking engagements, but I sensed that there was a danger in trying to hang onto something for too long – and I pulled back from that.

Paul Moynihan was working for Link House, a magazine publisher in Croydon, and I wrote feature articles on the outdoors for them. Bill Bruce was freelancing for the NSPCC and I did some writing for them, including editing for a year or two a four page tabloid newspaper for their younger supporters. Bill and I tested the water with some publishing ideas – none of which came to anything. We put in a bid to edit the Weightwatchers magazine – which sounds slightly bizarre in retrospect for both of us were at that time as skinny as rakes.

Publishing a specialist magazine from an expensive office block in the West End of London began to make less sense in the late 1980s. The facsimile (FAX) machine had taken off, answerphones were becoming commonplace and office word processors were coming down in price to make them accessible for many small businesses.

Mike and Tony had the first Amstrads in the NDA, spending hours and hours playing with them whilst I got on with my – by now – electronic typewriter, which had a memory and a spell check.

I was something of a Luddite with the new technology. Told that there would be a demonstration of the new FAX machine, my response was that I had little or no use for such a contraption. I had managed without one for years so why should I change the habit of a lifetime now? Invited to try the Amstrad, I held out for as long as possible. In some ways I was shamed into agreeing to try an Amstrad when I learned that the editor of another trade journal – a man who was some years my senior and the chap who had wandered around in his M & S pyjamas in Atlanta – could not live without his word processor.

I recognised that there would be several advantages to be had if I moved the magazine's office to the spare room at home. There would be no train fares to be paid for daily travel into London. I would not need to buy two suits a year – one every two or three years would suffice. And the wear and tear on me personally would reduce dramatically. And so it was that after the Chief Executive saw the financial sense of such an arrangement, the March 1988 issue of MILK INDUSTRY was edited from 19 Cornwall Terrace and the April issue from my home at 37 Spearpoint Gardens, Aldborough Hatch.

My conversion to the Amstrad word processor was something of a baptism of fire. The machine travelled home with me in a mini-cab after a short, sharp lesson from Tony, the accountant, in how to turn the thing on and off – and then I was on my own. For three months I struggled. Elation followed despair as I discovered something new each day.

A FAX machine and photocopier were installed in the box room. Tommy helped me build an array of shelving on the walls, whilst Kip sorted out the electrics for we would need a veritable battery of sockets to cope with the technological nightmare that was now ensconced in the room measuring all of ten foot square.

A few months passed. The dot matrix printer ground and chugged away, but after a time the drum showed signs of wear and tear, and was replaced at a cost of some £300. Yvonne, trying to be helpful, knew that I needed some labels printed off and set things going in my absence once the new drum was installed. Sadly, the labels got stuck to the drum – and the magazine had to shell out another £300.

This was before the advent of the internet and the email. In my day the typed text of articles and galley proofs came and went over the FAX but I still produced a scissors and paste layout job. These could not be sent to the printer by FAX and had to be despatched by Special Delivery from the Post Office down the road.

When the final page proofs were cleared – usually over a weekend – I journeyed late on Sunday evening to King's Cross Station in London to send the package by Red Star. A day or so later, I travelled to Bedford by train to spend the day passing the pages for press.

I worked with a number of freelance contributors on MILK INDUSTRY. Following her retirement as Editor of *Dairy Industries*, Pauline was an assiduous writer for MILK. Her research would take her around the country on her telephone where she would engage in the deepest technical discussions, producing text that rambled across many, many pages. At times I could have cheerfully pulled my hair out in despair, but on reflection Pauline was a warm-hearted and genuinely helpful colleague. I owe her a great deal. She was – and is – a dear friend.

John Mountain was dairy manager with a family dairy in the Home Counties who wrote with considerable flair and good humour. He should have been a journalist, for he enjoyed poking fun at the hierarchy and the establishment within the dairy industry. Readers liked him or hated him – and I knew that my mentors in the NDA and Dairy Trade Federation (DTF) would have happily seen him banished from the pages of the magazine and hung from the nearest gibbet (or tree if no gibbet was available). The magazine needed his wit and his goading of the self-righteous and the pompous – and there were plenty of those, but they know who they are, so there is little point in naming them.

Michael Evanson had enjoyed a distinguished career stretching from a senior appointment with one of the major dairy companies to a post with the DTF. Shortly before he retired to his beloved Bath (where he was an eminent City Guide and supporter of the world-famous rugby team), Michael started writing a regular monthly column for me. In many ways Michael took over where John left off and although his style was different, he had all the brilliance and the wit that the magazine needed if it was to take the occasional independent stance.

Michael was meticulous in the language he employed. He would send his article to me in two or three drafts, each one an improvement on the last, but Michael would have second thoughts and a piece that had appeared to be a gem on first reading now moved on to have even greater sparkle and delightful thrust. How I enjoyed working with the man who was such a perfectionist in all that he did.

Michael's text often sailed very close to the political wind, for he knew how to prick the balloons of the pompous and the self-opinionated and milk was – and remains – highly political. I had to pull his article only once in all the time he wrote for me – and that was when a professional high up the dairy ladder somehow got wind of what Michael was writing. With tongue in cheek, Michael was poking fun, but with the threat of a libel action I had little alternative but to remove the page as we were going to press. The subject of the offending article had no sense of humour, but subsequently rose ever higher and higher in the world of dairying – to such dizzy heights, in fact, that I can barely think of him without getting down on my hands and knees. Although, on second thoughts, I do not think I will bother.

In his retirement Michael continued to be involved in the dairy industry, staging a highly successful international dairy conference in London in the mid-1990s. Michael was a man of great charm and generosity. Michael and his wife, Cynthia, invited Yvonne and me to dinner as a thank you for the help I had given him in promoting his dairy conference. We joined Michael and Cynthia at a new restaurant recently opened by the actor, Michael Caine, in a highly fashionable part of riverside Chelsea. Michael (Evanson) apologised that we did not have the table at the window overlooking the river, but we learned why after we had been seated for a few minutes – when Michael (Caine) swept in with a party of friends and occupied the best seats in the house (understandably, for he did own the place). Amongst his guests Michael (Caine) had Sean Connery and Joan Collins – and it was the latter who sent more than a shiver of excitement through Yvonne's spine. When Joan repaired to the Ladies' Powder Room, Yvonne – not unnaturally – followed. It is not recorded that they spoke, but just being there was probably enough for Yvonne.

Retirement

My retirement as Editor came in March 1998 when I was 65. Chief Executive David decided to call it a day at the same time, so there was cause for double celebrations as the pair of us ambled off into the sunset – well I ambled, but I guess that David ran all the way carrying that oval – and oddly shaped – ball as was his wont.

The NDA Executive Council threw a dinner at which I was required to make a short speech. I came away with a very fine bicycle, complete with a carrier on the back onto which I might strap my briefcase when cycling to the courthouse in Barkingside, together with a pair of cycle clips. My professional colleagues in the office gave me gardening vouchers – which I used to re-stock the front garden with shrubs – and a pair of superior cycle clips. Later, Michael Evanson, Bill Taylor and others good friends with whom I had worked arranged a most enjoyable luncheon party at a select dining club in London's West End at which I was showered with gifts, including glass bowls from Tetra Pak, wine glasses from Michael and some quite superb – yes, you have guessed – cycle clips.

The NDA allowed me to retain the computer, printer and photocopier, all of which proved invaluable as I moved from writing professionally to a range of publications for local charities.

I was succeeded as Editor of MILK INDUSTRY by Elizabeth, who came from a PR company. I had hoped that Geoff would take over, but those who carried out the interviews had other ideas. Their view – so I gathered – was that some new blood was needed. Geoff continued to freelance for the magazine, which was just as well because Elizabeth was away on maternity leave some months later, returning for but a few weeks afterwards, but then deciding – not unnaturally – that she would prefer to remain at home with her new baby. During this time Geoff stepped into the breach as acting editor and when Elizabeth departed, Geoff was appointed Editor of MILK INDUSTRY – at last.

As I was about to retire I was approached by Richard, a former dairy industry colleague, who invited me to edit a quarterly magazine he was about to launch for the water industry. After leaving the dairy industry, Richard had set up a consultancy based in Bath. Having spent the past forty-nine years in full-time employment, the prospect of having to meet publishing deadlines professionally again for the foreseeable future did not appeal for I wanted to do other things and – like many a politician – spend more time with my family.

It so happened that at that time Bill Bruce had fallen on hard times. After leaving SCOUTING, Bill had freelanced and worked with me on MILK INDUSTRY. He had moved to North Essex, setting up a design company which prospered for some years, until computers started to do some of the things Bill did – but at less cost. Bill diversified into a packaging venture involving making gift lines containing confectionary for companies such as the Docklands Light Railway. All went well until a salesman he employed was alleged to be engaged in dirty dealings which resulted in Bill's company going into administration.

I suggested to Richard that he would do well to consider Bill for his new quarterly. Richard took Bill and me to lunch at the Institute of Directors, met with Bill in Bath and soon afterwards Bill and Richard created a new publishing business. Over the next ten years or so a number of new magazines were added covering water and juice, and Bill became Group Editorial Director of the company.

Just when Geoff was enjoying having a magazine of his own and thought he was settled with MILK INDUSTRY, the publishers decided that they wanted to make a dramatic change. The NDA had merged with the Dairy Industry Association (formerly the Dairy Trade Federation) to form a new trade body rejoicing under the title Dairy UK. As part of the downsizing, the plush offices in Cornwall Terrace were vacated for an office suite round the corner in Baker Street. Geoff was given but a matter of weeks to come to terms with the fact that he would be made redundant as the magazine was moved to a publishing house. It was a brutal and callous thing to do, but that is the way of the world of business and Dairy UK was no different from many other bodies when the chips are down. I continue to read MILK INDUSTRY, but note that the advertising income is almost non-existent. It saddens me to see that it has completely lost its independence and become merely a mouthpiece for Dairy UK and little more than that.

Geoff was out on a limb, of course, but it so happened that at that time Richard and Bill were considering the launch of a dairy magazine. I heard about this, spoke to Geoff, suggesting that he might contact Bill. Now, a couple of years later, Geoff is editing the highly successful *dairy innovation* journal.

Both Bill and Geoff have come a long way since those days on SCOUTING. Geoff is one of a team of editors and Bill is Group Editorial Director for them all. The stable of magazines is successful and growing, with a number of the titles sponsoring international awards, conferences and exhibitions. Both Bill and Geoff travel to exotic places for these events and as I watch from afar, I am quietly content in the knowledge that I might have had a small part to play in their present well-deserved success.

Part Seven
The view from the Bench

I was appointed as a Justice of the Peace on 11th December 1980 and retired at the age of seventy on 18th March 2003. Those twenty-three years saw dramatic change in the criminal justice service and in the lay magistracy itself – so much so that anyone reading the following may well be surprised at how archaic certain of the practices prevalent in the early 1980s appear to the modern eye.

Whilst that may well be true, much of what we achieved at Redbridge Magistrates' Court in the 1990s and at the turn of the Century was innovative, bold and highly successful. The court was an integral part of the local community – and all the better for it – and those of us involved were not afraid to stick our necks over the parapet from time to time. And when we did so and were shot down, we were happy enough to try again.

I fear that in the years since I retired from the court on reaching the age of seventy, bureaucracy and the urge to centralise everything and everyone, has knocked the stuffing out of the magistrates' court service as I knew it. Be that as it may, here are some random recollections – one or two written from memory and others from notes made at the time. I will leave the reader to decide which is which.

One February morning in the snow

It snowed in Aldborough Hatch one Saturday morning in February 1980. I know, because I trudged through the chill to the post office on Silverdale Parade. Having done my business at the counter, I was about to work my way home again when Delia's mother took my arm and told me that she wished to ask me a question, but we would need to go outside, out of earshot of other customers. I had always been a little wary of Delia's mother for, like her daughter, she was not to be trifled with, and so I did as I was told.

I am going to ask you one question; I cannot tell you why I am doing so, but you must answer honestly, said Delia's mother – and as I was being frozen stiff stood standing outside the post office in the snow, I was happy enough to get it over with. Would I be right in saying that your politics are left of centre, she asked? More centre, I replied. But a bit to the left of centre rather than to the right, perhaps, she persisted? I agreed. That is all I need to know, she said. You may find that a lady will ring you on the next few days. More than that I cannot say. And with that we both went our separate ways through the blizzard which by now was roaring directly from the Arctic straight down Aldborough Road North.

A day or so later Nora telephoned and all became clear. Redbridge Magistrates' Court needs some younger justices with experience of young people, Nora explained. As you have a young family and have spent the past twenty-seven years or so involved with the Scout movement, said Nora, you would be ideal material for the juvenile court bench. I discovered later that Nora, who always drove a Skoda, was something big in the Co-operative Movement and even bigger in the Women's Co-operative Guild – and was Delia's Aunt Nora, no less. Nora was responsible for recruiting justices who were to the left of centre rather than to the right, hence the discussion in the snow with Delia's mother. All part of ensuring that the bench was balanced politically.

A week or so passed and I was summoned to appear at 8pm at an address in the posh part of Wanstead. Nora made clear that I was to arrive on time – neither early, nor late – and should walk directly from Wanstead Underground Station, not deviating nor peering from side to side. As if I would.

Nora introduced me to the Bench Chairman, whose house it was. The Chairman proceeded to complete an application form, reading each question and writing the answers, assuming, I would guess, that as someone who was more to the left of centre than to the right, I was probably incapable of reading let alone writing. Not only that, but the Chairman made clear that I was to tell the truth, the whole truth and nothing but the truth. I promised I would do so.

One question concerned my driving. Did I have any points on my licence, I was asked? I did not. Had I been charged by the police at anytime with a motoring offence? I had not. Had I ever been stopped by the police for some minor infringement of the law of motoring? Yet again, I said I had not. But at this point the Chairman's face went dark puce as he reminded me that I was expected to tell the truth.

"Are you telling me," he said, looking directly into both my eyes at the same time, *"are you telling me that you have reached the age of forty-seven and have never, ever been stopped by a policeman?"*

I said that it was indeed so. Warming to the fray, the Chairman posed another question: *"Am I to believe,"* he said, looking very angry indeed by this time, *"am I to believe that you have never, ever been stopped for speeding?"*

Again, I said I had not – adding: *"It may perhaps help if I tell you that I do not possess a driving licence, have never owned a car and do not drive".*

The Chairman moved swiftly on to the next question, but I fear he marked me down as something of a clever dick who would need to be watched should the Lord Chancellor be persuaded to go against his better judgment and appoint me as one of his justices of the peace.

With the form complete, the Chairman told me to go straight home. I was not to hang about outside his house as further candidates would be arriving later and under no circumstances were we to meet.

As it was a pitch black night with heavy squally March winds blowing up the A12, I was hardly likely to loiter.

Furthermore, the Chairman told me that I was sworn to secrecy about what had happened that evening and that I was to tell no one. Should it leak out that I had been interviewed as a prospective justice of the peace, my application form would be torn into shreds – and that would be the end of that. What's more, I might hear further from the Lord Chancellor and yet I might not. If I did not hear I would know that I had not passed muster, although how I would know this if I did not hear was not explained to me.

Finally, said the Chairman at his most menacing, if I meet you in the street in the future, I will deny having ever spoken to you. Nora sat silently throughout this tirade, looking down at her legs, which I later described to Yvonne as being like tree trunks (a result, I learned later, of being a near-Olympic swimming champion in her youth).

I scurried home as fast as my now frozen little legs would carry me. In hushed tones I revealed to Yvonne what had happened that evening – ensuring that no-one was listening at the keyhole and making Yvonne swear, on pain of instant death, not to tell a living soul. I know that Yvonne kept her word, for she did not even tell her mother, who died on 10th September 1980 – a matter of nineteen days before I heard that the Lord Chancellor would be appointing me as a justice of the peace. Sad, really, for Yvonne's mother would have been delighted at the news.

A year or so after I was sworn in as a justice, the Chairman took me on one side at the courthouse and asked me if I was a member of a Masonic lodge, but before I could catch my breath to answer, he assured me that had I been one such, it would have made not a jot of difference to his recommending me for appointment. He turned on his heel and did not wait for me to tell him whether or not I was a mason. In fact, I was – and am – not, but I guess the Chairman knew that already.

The day I joined two drinking clubs

I was informed by letter dated 29th September 1980 from Christopher Grundy, Barrister-at-Law, Secretary of the Lord Chancellor's Advisory Committee for North East London, that my appointment as a justice was imminent, but six weeks or so passed until a letter dated 11th November arrived from Sir Bryan Roberts, KCMG, Secretary of Commissions. The letter was – somewhat disappointingly – one of those printed missives where my details (name, commission area and date of appointment) were typed in and even the signature was a facsimile. It is not every day that you receive a letter from the House of Lords and when you do, it would be pleasant if the letter had a bit of class about it. But there we are.

Sir Bryan advised me that he had been *"directed by the Lord Chancellor to inform you that you have been appointed a Justice of the Peace and that your name was placed on the above Commission on 4th November 1980".* So that was that.

Shortly afterwards, Mr Grundy summoned me to attend at Snaresbrook Crown Court to take the Oaths of Qualification as a Justice of the Peace and to sign the Court Roll on Thursday 11th December 1980 at 10am. This was another of those printed letters with my details typed in.

I was invited to bring a member of my family or a friend, and to join the adjudicating justices for lunch (for which I could claim up to £3.66 subsistence – clearly some lunch!). Graham, my eldest son, then seventeen and in the Sixth Form at Wanstead County High School, joined me. Yvonne agreed that he should do so and willingly gave up her chance to attend, for Graham was planning to make his career in the law and this would be his first brush with it. What a typically generous gesture by Yvonne.

The new justices, members of families, friends, Clerks to the Justices and Bench Chairmen – and, I would guess, a few hangers-on who had slipped past security and were there for the chocolate biscuits – assembled in the judges' retiring room at ten in the morning of the swearing-in. The justices came from Redbridge and other courts in the local area.

I found one young man and asked him if he was being sworn-in.

"No, he is not," said the lady at his side, in a voice that appeared to come all the way up from her boots, *"but I am!"*

Perhaps it is not surprising that I have been terrified of the lady ever since.

The swearing-in was to be before His Honour Judge Peter, who – I gathered later – was a bit of a lad. He certainly turned a few ladies' heads in his rich red garb. I learned that he was affectionately known around the courts as Penal Pete. Chatting in the retiring room afterwards, His Honour Judge Peter advised Graham that he should buy his jeans from an expensive gentleman's emporium in London's West End – something of which I disabused Graham before he tossed down a further chocolate biscuit and hurried back to his studies at Wanstead High. Such extravagance would not go unnoticed whilst I was paying the bills.

The oath taking was a solemn affair, during which the Bench Chairman of Redbridge Magistrates' Court (he who had interviewed me back in March) sat beside His Honour Judge Peter. Most of my new justice colleagues spoke quietly or inaudibly, but having spent the previous twenty or so years engaged in public speaking, I boomed out the oaths as though I were standing on the platform of the Manchester Free Trade Hall – which made the Bench Chairman look up with a start and stare like a startled rabbit.

I have since wondered if the Bench Chairman had a premonition that in fifteen years time, I would don the mantle which he held that day with such pride and dignity – and, indeed, be sitting up there to observe the new justices going through the same process? If he did, I most certainly did not for such thoughts could not have been further from my mind that morning.

In the retiring room I was relieved of three pounds, which gave me life membership of the Snaresbrook Justices' Club, enabling me to purchase alcoholic drinks at lunchtime in the Judges' luncheon room. I assume this as this was membership for life, I continue to be entitled to slip into Snaresbrook Crown Court at anytime for a quick snifter. Not that I think I will bother.

Later, a further pound was extracted – and I found myself a member of the Redbridge Justices' Club, which not only allowed me to purchase alcoholic drinks in the Justices' Retiring Room at Redbridge Magistrates' Court, but also to participate in a social activities ranging from annual dinners to quiz evenings, concerts, garden parties, and other such goings-on.

As someone who had not attended a drinking club in the past, let alone belonged to one, I found that joining two in one day was the kind of experience you do not link with being sworn-in as a justice of the peace.

Early days

As a newly-appointed justice I was required to observe two court sittings at Redbridge and one at another court. I chose Newham and sat in the public gallery of one of their two courthouses – the one nearest to Stratford station. Number One Court at Newham had the dock in the centre, with defendants coming up from the cells and peering bleary eyed over the rails that surrounded it. As mentioned before, I had appeared at this court once some twenty or so years earlier, when I acted as a character witness for a member of the Scout Troop of which I was Leader.

After the Newham observation – where the building felt damp, cold and musty – I was glad to return to Redbridge, whose Courthouse had been open for just three years. From outside it resembled an incinerator in Siberia (not that I have been to Siberia, let alone seen an incinerator there, but you will get my drift), but inside was all soft carpeting and light furnishings.

(Much later when I was Bench Chairman, Michael Faraway, Clerk to the Justices, hatched a cunning plan to enhance the exterior of the Redbridge Courthouse. This involved planting out soil-filled troughs on the edges of the flat roof with trailing plants such as ivy. The idea received a lukewarm reception – somewhat unfairly, I considered – when members of the Magistrates' Courts' Committee were approached informally on the subject and the scheme was abandoned when it became clear that the ivy would cover not only the bleak concrete walls, but also all the windows. Light would be cut out and if the windows were opened to let in fresh air, creepy crawlies would take up residence inside. And so the building stands to this day, stark in its cold concrete and distinctly uninviting.)

Training took the form of a series of eight or so evening lectures, delivered in a quiet monotone by the then Clerk to the Justices, who rejoiced under the name of Kip Godfrey. One of my new colleagues, a retired bank manager, fell asleep after the first ten minutes or so every evening, but no-one seemed to mind. The poor fellow died about eighteen months later.

Sitting and adjudicating in court started once the three observations were completed. For the first few weeks I sat in Court One – the Remand Court as it was called – with the Bench Chairman and another justice. The role of the new justice was made very clear by the Bench Chairman. I would be required to complete the court register, writing in the decision of the bench and the sentence. I would, of course, be consulted on all matters, but as a new justice, I would not be expected to have any views one way or the other. In fact, it would be best if I just kept my head down and did the writing.

I fell out with the Bench Chairman within a matter of days. Unusually in Court One in those days we had to hear a trial in which the defendant was pleading not guilty. I recall nothing of the case apart from the fact that my other winger (as we two justices who sat either side of the chairman were called in polite society – or 'bookends' or 'woodentops' when folk wished to be rude) was a very experienced magistrate who wore her hair in a bun tied at the back and held a high position with a firm of legal publishers.

Having heard the evidence, we retired to the Chairman's Room to make our decision. The Chairman announced that *"of course, the fellow is guilty"*, at which my lady colleague made clear that she did not agree. I thought that the Chairman would explode, but he turned to me and asked me for my view. Clearly there would be no discussion or debate. I said that the evidence had not proved to me beyond reasonable doubt that the man had committed the crime and, therefore, I had to find him not guilty.

We marched – literally, for he was a former military man and a bank manager – into court where the Chairman announced that he found the defendant guilty. However, his two colleagues did not – so the defendant was free to leave the court, although the Chairman wished to make it clear that he totally disagreed with his colleagues and that he considered the defendant had committed the dastardly crime as charged. And woe betide him in he ever entered the courthouse again.

I was rather proud of my riposte some months later when sitting with that same Bench Chairman. As a defendant entered the dock from the cells below, I noted that he was wearing an earring – somewhat unusual in a male in the early 1980s. The Chairman spotted it, too, and whispered in my ear: *"He's a homosexual"* to which I replied: *"Is that the charge?"* Relations between the Chairman and me were never quite the same again.

(He was an interesting character – the Chairman, not the man with the earring. Sadly, his wife died shortly after his retirement from the Bench at the age of seventy. By this time he had moved from his house in Wanstead into a block of up-market flats on the leafy edge of the Borough. A widow of his acquaintance lived in the next door flat and they would share a meal together from time to time. Soon they had a door installed in the party wall between the two flats and later they were married. I learned of the impending marriage when a lady magistrate – daughter of the bride-to-be – told me with some amusement that the Chairman would shortly be her stepfather, although she would find it difficult to call him Daddy.)

Buggin's turn

Today there is a sophisticated – and ongoing – training programme for magistrates and a system of appraisal which should – and I say should – ensure that those who dispense justice to their peers do so without fear or favour and that they do so in a professional manner.

Those who chair courts undertake special training and appraisal before they are let loose on an unsuspecting public. In theory this should mean that things are considerably better than when I first joined the bench. Sadly, some slip through the net and there remain a few incompetent chairman and some equally incompetent magistrates. But in the main there has been a pronounced move to more professional chairing of courts, whilst the requirement to produce reasons for those decisions to be read out in open court means that decision-making has to be structured and based on evidence.

During my twenty-three years on the bench, chairmanship moved from Buggin's Turn through specialist training to appraisal. Buggin's Turn meant that he or she who had been around the longest sat in the middle and chaired the court. Well, that was the theory. In fact, it was often the Court Clerk who ran things from his or her seat below the bench. Without training or appraisal some of the worst examples of poor chairmanship went unchecked. The lay magistracy suffered a poor image both externally and internally.

I recall one magistrate – a general practitioner – who visited patients in their homes on his way to court. Depending on how many he was called to attend and the nature of their ailments, he would arrive at court with time to spare or dash in just as his two colleagues were about to go through the door and into the courtroom. No time for the pre-sitting briefing between magistrates and clerks introduced during my time as Bench Chairman at Redbridge Magistrates' Court – or for the equally valuable debriefing after the sitting, for the GP was always anxious to return to his surgery or the golf course. Debriefing – when we introduced it – proved its worth time and again for – apart from many other advantages – it gave the newly-appointed justice the opportunity to ask questions and to challenge some established practices.

Many magistrates who took the chair as the result of Buggin's Turn could not help the fact that they lacked the skills to be competent chairmen for they were not helped in any way. Moreover, this produced a sense of frustration amongst those who were capable at chairing a court and had experience in the chair in their business or voluntary occupations outside the courthouse.

Meeting in the car park

I had been on the Bench for a year or so when I was summoned to attend a meeting of the *Justitia Tenax* Editorial Board, comprising Deputy Chairman Peter (who chaired it, of course), a magistrate who had held a senior managerial post with one of the national tabloid newspapers and a widower justice who was retired and spent much of his time on ocean cruises where he pursued a string of ladies who were also of advancing years. *Justitia Texax* was the title of the court magazine, which came out twice a year and was due to have a new editor – me!

On arrival at the appointed time, I found the courthouse locked and barred. Unfortunately, Peter had forgotten to advise anyone at the courthouse that the Editorial Board would be meeting that evening and so the gathering was convened in the back of the car which had brought all three gentlemen to Barkingside.

There is, said Chairman Peter, only one item on the agenda and that is the election of a new editor. He proposed me, this was seconded by the man from the tabloid whilst the chap when spent his time chasing ladies on cruises indicated that he, too, was in favour. And with that I was told to get on with it and report back to Chairman Peter. The three drove off in a cloud of exhaust fumes, leaving me to catch two buses home.

The magazine was produced on a duplicator at that time. Stencils were handed out to any magistrate who was daft enough to admit that he or she could type or that he or she knew someone who could do so. Handwritten scripts were then passed out with the stencils. If the piece filled half a page, the rest would be blank. It was all somewhat hit and miss.

In the mid-1980s electronic typewriters with correcting ribbons were all the rage and I suggested that we might move from the duplicator to having the magazine printed professionally. I said that I would type the texts and produce a paste-up which would then be turned into a plate by the printer and off he would go. I suggested that we might have a separate cover, with a photograph of the outside of the courthouse.

Twice a year the magazine hit the decks. It had started as a magazine for magistrates only but I was determined that by widening the readership we would begin to get across to the wider public just what went on behind those stark, grey concrete walls. Members of staff started to write and we invited local solicitors, the probation service and judges at the Crown Court to contribute. I like to think that as the circulation widened it opened the windows and doors of the court onto the world beyond.

I stayed as Editor until 1995 when I was elected Bench Chairman. At that time I persuaded Shirley to take over as Editor – speaking to her in her lounge rather than in the back seat of a car in the justices' car park. Shirley made some much needed changes to the format and moved it forward as a lively and challenging publication. The front cover photograph disappeared – and rightly so in my view for it had been there for ten years or more. What Shirley may not have appreciated was the fact that I shot the black and white photograph of the outside of the Courthouse on a Saturday morning whilst Shirley was inside being interviewed by members of the advisory sub-committee with a view to her appointment as a justice.

Justitia Tenax has moved into other editorial hands since then and continues to be published as I write, although it has to be said not always with the twice-yearly regularity of past days.

Let the laughter ring out

A magistrates' court is more often than not a sad place, but from time to time laughter rings out in the court or retiring room.

In our early days on the bench, Martyn and I would often sit together on a Tuesday afternoon. The earlier part of the day would have been spent in one of the five courts running that morning, but after lunch there would be just one court – dealing with minor traffic offences or some other trivia with which the more experienced justices and clerks could not be bothered. As we were both sworn in around the same time, Martyn and I took turns to chair.

On one such afternoon the court clerk met with Martyn and me in the retiring room. Joseph, who had recently joined the court as a clerk, hailed from one of the African countries where he had studied before qualifying as a barrister in this country. Not unnaturally, his understanding of court procedure was somewhat limited, but he was a pleasant enough chap who we justices wanted to help settle down.

"Sir," said Joseph, addressing us both and looking at neither Martyn nor me, but with a worried expression on his face. *"Sir,"* he said, *"there has been a cock-up in the administration."*

Keeping straight faces with difficulty, Martyn and I asked Joseph to explain the problem? It soon became clear that something had gone badly wrong and that the case due to be heard that afternoon could not proceed. In view of this, we suggested to Joseph that we all go into court and that Joseph explain the reason why the case would have to be dealt with on another day.

"All rise," called the Usher as we entered the courtroom. Martyn asked us to be seated and invited the Learned Clerk (a delightful turn of phrase which we

used in those days when addressing the Court Clerk, so much more exciting than the Legal Adviser title of today) to address the court. Rising majestically to his feet (for he was an imposing fellow) and speaking (in a stentorian baritone), Joseph said: *"Sir, there has been a cock-up in the administration . . ."*

Poor Joseph, for he had no idea why the lawyers, defendants, members of the public – let alone the ushers and magistrates – were rolling around holding their sides in laughter. But composure was recovered and Martyn and I made Joseph a warming cup of tea in the retiring room, whilst explaining that some phrases he might hear around town were not necessarily suited to be aired in the rarefied atmosphere of the courtroom.

I have been called many things in court – apart from 'Sir' and 'Your Worship'. Some I would not dare repeat, but I was once called 'Your Majesty'.

A colleague was sitting in our court when an elderly lady went into the witness box. What I would call a good East End Mum, this lady was asked by the Usher what her religion was and she replied that she *"ain't got nun".*

The Usher asked her is she would affirm – but after it was done, the Chairman wanted to be certain that the elderly lady had fully understood what affirming meant.

"Do you know what affirm means?" he asked.

"Yes, of course, love," came the reply. *"My son works for one."*

I was chairing the court when we were considering whether or not two young men who were alleged to have broken into a house at two in the morning should go to the Crown Court for trial or remain in the magistrates' court. The Crown Prosecutor went to great pains to tell the bench that the house was occupied by a very elderly couple who woke in their bed and were very frightened. He laid it on about the very elderly couple and what a terrifying experience this was for them at their advanced age. The Bench decided that the offence was serious enough for committal to the Crown Court and after I had announced our decision, I asked the Prosecutor just how old this very elderly couple were.

"They were sixty-nine," he replied.

"Oh," I found myself saying, *"my age exactly."*

Some years earlier I was sitting in Court One when I had to announce a sentence in a case involving illicit drugs. Part of the sentencing required me to *"order the forfeiture and destruction of the drugs",* but I became tongue-tied and ordered the *"forfeiture and destruction of the judge".* Quick as a flash, a well-known defence lawyer called out from the back of the court: *"Which one, Sir!"*

At around the same time a Chairman of a Bench announced as a condition of bail that the defendant *"should sleep each and every night with his mother".* It is said that the defendant was somewhat startled at the prospect and implored the Bench to re-consider. I guess they did so.

Not something to laugh at was the time in 1981 when the following appeared in the *Ilford Recorder:* "*Guilty motorists faced with possible endorsements and fines for offences such as driving with excess alcohol were let off free due to a legal hitch. Cases at Redbridge Magistrates' Court, Cranbrook Road, Barkingside, were thrown out because a High Court test case has invalidated all summonses which had not been individually signed. In Redbridge summonses were rubber-*

stamped after being given bulk approval – leading to the let-offs. The court was then faced with the mammoth task of withdrawing and re-issuing thousands of summonses."

Many courts around the country – and not just Redbridge – used a rubber stamp of the Bench Chairman's signature on summonses. Following the High Court ruling, the Bench Chairman's rubber stamp was no longer acceptable. Each morning piles of summonses were sent up to the retiring room and justices sat at the long table signing away for days, weeks and months on end until we were up to date.

The bad, the mad and the sad

It has been said that there are three kinds of folk who appear in the dock at court – the bad, the mad and the sad. The bad are there because they deserve to be. Some are career criminals, who look upon prison as an inevitable, if unsavoury, part of life. Then there are the mad – who should not be there and would not if the community was prepared to insist that adequate provision be made for those with mental health and addiction issues. And, finally, there are the sad – you and me who would, but for the grace of God, be up before the courts. Whilst the mad gave me very real concern (and encouraged me to take up the role of non-executive director with the local mental health trust in my retirement), perhaps it is the sad who stand out in my memory.

One Christmas Eve a defendant pleaded with the Chairman in Court One to be remanded into custody because he had spent every Christmas for as long as he could remember in prison. He was before the court for some minor offence to which he had pleaded guilty and being a kindly soul with Christmas but hours away, the Chairman gave the defendant a conditional discharge, wishing him well for the festive season and asking him to kindly leave the dock. But the man would have none of it.

"Send me down," he cried, and when the Chairman refused, he pleaded again and again. But all to no avail and, finally, he was led – protesting vehemently – from the dock downstairs and out into the cold of a raw and bleak Christmas Eve in Barkingside High Street.

An hour or so later the man was back in the dock, for being Christmas Eve the police did not want him clogging up their nice clean cells. It appeared that the man had left the court, walked to the first jeweller's shop in the High Street, where he hurled a brick through the plate glass window. Not wishing to escape from his just rewards, the man wandered over the road to Barkingside Police Station where he gave himself up. On being brought back into court before the same Chairman, the man – who knew how to work the system – pleaded not guilty, which meant that he was remanded in custody over Christmas and that he would achieve his objective of spending yet another festive season in the clink. Turning to go down the stairs to the cells, he thanked the Chairman profusely, with a smile on his face that seemed to say that Christmas had arrived – at last!

I sat with Deputy Chairman Joan in Court One when a lady came before the bench charged with riding a bicycle whilst drunk – well, at least, that was the gist of the charge. It appeared that she had been seen by police on the A12 outside

King George V Hospital at Newbury Park, swerving from side to side and causing mayhem amongst the car drivers who were off to Southend for the day (with their families) and the lorry drivers bound for Harwich, the Continent and beyond (and delights of the kind most of us only dream about).

Appearing in court the following day, the lady had sobered up somewhat and was dealt with by Joan in her inimitable style – with a warning that further behaviour of like nature would bring down upon the lady's shoulders the hounds of hell (which Joan would personally assemble and release from their restraints but yards from the wretched woman who by now resembled Lot's wife who, you will recall, was turned into a pillar of salt).

A hour or three later found Joan driving to her sumptuous flat in Chigwell – by this time home to most of the East London's criminal fraternity and a splattering of footballers, the only folk who could afford to buy flats and houses in that neck of the woods. Negotiating the roundabout at the far end of Barkingside High Street and driving along Fencepiece Road, Joan was somewhat taken aback to see a cyclist ahead who was weaving and swerving from one side of the road to the other. Sure enough it was the lady who had been in court earlier that day. Reinforced with alcohol, she was back on her bike and causing mayhem to the wives of the criminals and footballers who were driving back to Chigwell, having purchased supplies in Sainsbury's and Tesco.

As this was in the days before mobile phones, Joan put her foot down, dashed into her flat and alerted the Barkingside Police to the fact that the lady was at it again. As far as I know, the lady was not arrested, nor was she seen again at Redbridge Magistrates' Court. She may well have taken her alcoholic cycling elsewhere.

I felt really sorry for another defendant who came into court time and again over a period of some 18 months, charged with stealing packs of razor blades from local supermarkets. Indeed, I believe it was as the result of this man's escapades that supermarkets in Ilford and hereabouts started to restrict the number of packs of razor blades on display at any one time and at one stage put them under lock and key.

The man, who lived with his wife and her sister, had recently retired after a lifetime working as a barber in a men's hairdressing salon at one of the London mainline railway stations. In that occupation his employer had sold him packs of razor blades at wholesale price, which the man then re-sold to his friends and acquaintances at a price below that which they would have paid in the shops – giving the man his beer money and providing a service to his friends.

On his retirement two things happened. Firstly, his employer stopped selling the man packs of razor blades. Secondly, his wife insisted that he did not sit around the house all day, getting under the feet of herself and her sister – and as both ladies were of ample proportions and somewhat fierce-looking, it was not surprising that the man wished to avoid any contact with their feet, let alone any other parts of their anatomy.

Turfed out onto the streets daily shortly after daybreak – summer and winter alike – the man was at his wits ends to know what to do. No longer could he socialise with his friends as he sold them cheap razor blades, nor could he buy himself – and them – the occasional pint of best bitter, for his wife refused to give him any pocket money.

Not unnaturally, the man sought a solution to his predicament – and decided to engage in some shoplifting. In that way he could continue to sell razor blades to his friends (and pocket some beer money) but he could also pretend that he was still working in the hairdressing salon in London, which would explain to the neighbours why he left home at daybreak and did not return until early evening.

At first the man appeared in court, pleaded guilty, was given a conditional discharge and walked from court – straight over the road to Sainsbury's where he filched some more razor blades. A week or two later he was back, this time to be fined. But when he came back again and again and again, it was clear that there was a problem – and a social inquiry report by the probation service revealed his sorry tale.

But nothing would deter him from his new-found life of crime. Eventually, custody loomed. I was sitting with colleagues on the bench when this happened. His wife and her sister glared from the public gallery – severe, stern, motionless and angry. As my colleague announced that the man would be sentenced to a month inside, I noticed that the man smiled – almost in relief that he would not be going home with those two ladies at the back of the court.

I did not see the man again after that and my enquiries failed to reveal what happened to him. I can only guess that his wife and her sister took him off somewhere well away from shops selling razor blades or perhaps he was confined to the house for ever after. Sadly, I will never know.

From time to time it was inevitable that folk we knew would appear in court. Magistrates are drawn from the local community for a purpose – so that people are judged by their peers, folk who live in the same area and face the same problems and opportunities.

One morning a young man sat at the back of the court with his grandmother. Both were clearly taken aback to see me on the bench. I knew them both by sight, but little more than that, although Yvonne was friendly with the grandmother for their paths had crossed when our children were young. The young man was charged with causing an affray on the top of a late night bus. Having heard an outline of the case, I was pleased when the young man opted for trail at the crown court, for there seemed to be room to drive a cart and horses through some of the so-called evidence.

A few days later I met the young man and his grandmother in the road outside my home – for grandmother lived nearby. As the case was no longer at the magistrates' court, I felt able to agree to the young man's request that he might tell me what had happened. It became clear that if what the young man was telling me was true – and I believed it to be so – he should plead not guilty and engage a good barrister to present his case. Suffice to say, he was found not guilty. I see the young man from time to time and his grandmother often. The young man has made something of his life and his grandmother does not stop talking, especially when making encouraging noises about my front garden and the begonias.

There were one or two occasions when I found it necessary to stand down from a case because I knew the defendant or one or the witnesses. There was the case of the retired police officer who was alleged to have leapt from his car to – allegedly – punch a young man delivering sandwiches outside Seven Kings Station. Martyn and I walked into Court Five, spotted who was in the dock, turned on our heels and walked quietly out again. Other justices took our place.

Then there was the lady who was in court on a charge of stealing from her employer – a shopkeeper whose premises were near where I lived. There was one charge only, when it was alleged that the lady had taken money from the till on a specific day. The notes had been marked by police and the lady was caught red-handed. The shopkeeper was certain that the thefts had been going on for some months, but they only came to light when his books were audited at the end of the financial year. The lady refused to have a string of offences taken into consideration, which would have meant a heavier sentence – for she was aware that proving the thefts would be nigh on impossible. I heard that the lady received a small fine – nothing near the punishment she deserved. I did not sit on the case, nor did I discuss this with colleagues – but I have the feeling to this day that when the lady sees me in the street she knows what I know.

One young man made the mistake of mitigating in his defence that the area where he was found with a bladed instrument was so rough that he and every resident would not go out at night unless they were *"tooled up".* He had been walking home with a mate late one Saturday evening when they stopped to sit on a front garden wall. What started as pleasant chat developed into a blazing row, so much so that a resident called the police. Arrested and charged with possessing a knife, he appeared before my colleagues and myself, and told us that he had been sitting on the garden wall of the home of Val-Across-The-Road, no less, when he was arrested, and this was the area which was so rough that residents would not venture forth unless they were *"tooled up".* When I pointed out that I had lived in a house almost opposite that garden wall for the past four decades and had never felt the need to get *"tooled up",* the young man realised he was on a loser with me!

When Tesco arrived

The courthouse at Redbridge was built in 1977 on the site of the first Dr Barnardo home for children. This fact is recorded inside the courthouse by a plaque on the wall in the first floor vestibule, erected by Mr Norman Gunby, a local historian and author – who had tried to find someone to cover the cost, but when his efforts met with the proverbial brick wall, he paid for it himself. Installed when I was Bench Chairman, we had a short ceremony with the Clerk to the Justices, a few lawyers, defendants and other miscreants watching. But Mr Gunby, a rotund, smiling gentleman, seemed pleased with his efforts, which is what mattered.

In fact the courthouse was built in the expectation that Redbridge Council would relocate its civic centre from Ilford High Road to the Barnardo Village Site at Barkingside. But having seen the courthouse built and opened in 1977, the worthy Councillors of Redbridge had second thoughts (with a few of them crossing the floor of the chamber to join the other side into the bargain) – and stayed at the Victorian Town Hall in the Town Centre. Thus the courthouse was the one civic building stuck out on a limb. Those same Councillors – and others who followed them – then spent the next thirty years pondering what to do about modernising the civic buildings in the centre of the town. As I write the debate continues in the Council Chamber and the corridors of power, although I have noted that more and more streets in town are being pedestrianised, presumably with a view to some major new civic centre springing up eventually. But I am unsure if I will live another thirty years to see it happen and if I do, I fear I may by that time be a grumpy old man (although some say I am that already, but perhaps things are best left there).

The Barkingside Barnardo Village stretched away to the East with the new head office building just down the road towards Barkingside Station. And talking of stations, there was often much confusion amongst barristers who had not previously ventured out from London to Redbridge Magistrates' Court. Not unnaturally, those travelling by Central Line from their London Chambers would alight at Redbridge Underground Station – which must have seemed both logical and sensible. Here they would ask a member of the station staff for directions to Redbridge Court – and having been sent across a road, found themselves in the foyer of a block of flats rejoicing under the name of Redbridge Court! I would guess that the station staff had many a chuckle as they watched frustrated barristers returning to take the next train to Barkingside Underground Station.

These flats were the scene of an early morning confrontation that was totally unexpected by all three magistrates who were involved. Shortly after retirement from the Bench at the age of 70, a male – and much revered – magistrate announced to some of his closest friends that he was to divorce his wife to live with one of our middle aged – and herself divorced – lady justices. For some time this was one of the best kept secrets at the courthouse. This event was not unexpected and they were married some two or so years later, living happily and moving away from the Borough to retire.

However, in the immediate weeks following the decision to co-habit – when it was top secret from the bulk of the magistrates on the bench – they rented a flat at Redbridge Court near Redbridge Station. It so happened at that time that one of our younger magistrates was himself going through a divorce and felt the need to undertake some part-time work to supplement the income from his full-time job. He took a post as an early morning cleaner at Redbridge Court – the flats not the courthouse.

Picture, if you will, the early morning scene. The young male magistrate is scrubbing the stairs at Redbridge Court when the now retired – and much revered – elderly magistrate steps out through the front door to one of the flats, closely followed by the younger lady magistrate. Both very nearly trip over the somewhat startled young male magistrate who is slopping the soap suds around on the staircase as he mutters an embarrassed *"Good morning, Sir – and Madam!"*

How do I know this? The young justice was so disturbed by what he had seen – and to some extent doubted what his own eyes had revealed – that he asked for a private and confidential appointment with me as Bench Chairman. I was able to put his mind at rest, but I fear that the experience stayed with him for some time to come.

Another event that occurred in the mid-1990s was the arrival of a brand new Tesco store next door to the courthouse. This, of course, produced considerable additional business for the courtrooms – with shoplifters busily working their way through the shelves and learning how to avoid the security guards, whilst the security guards started to realise that customers with long flowing overcoats that touched the ground and inside pockets big enough to hold goods to feed an army for a week were, in fact, not doing the monthly shop for large families.

A few days prior to the store opening, a gang of men arrived with some five hundred or so mature shrubs and proceeded to plant them in the prepared beds all in one day. The court superintendent at that time lived in the flat above the courthouse. At around ten that evening, he took a pleasant walk with his dog through Tesco's grounds, admiring the mature shrubs and enjoying the scent of newly turned soil. At seven next morning, the superintendent was out again – and discovered that every one of the five hundred shrubs had disappeared overnight!

The courthouse stands at a busy three-point junction, with Barkingside Police Station on one corner and a popular public house on another, with Sainsbury's very close by. Hardly, you might think, the best place to arrange for a consignment of illicit drugs to be transferred from the boot of one saloon car to another. But it happened one bright sunny afternoon, between the courthouse and Tesco's. Following a tip-off, plain-clothes police had tracked the two vehicles through the streets of London until they pulled up one behind the other at the kerbside in Cranbrook Road, about 50 metres from the front entrance to the courthouse and within sight of the police station. Leaping from their vehicles, the plain-clothes police went to arrest the four men, but one took flight over Tesco's car park with a bag of white powder slung over his shoulders. He was caught shortly afterwards. The gang came before the court on a day when I was sitting. The defendants looked suitably chastened when their choice of a spot to transfer the drugs came out in evidence.

One afternoon a particularly grisly scene was played out on the roadway immediately outside the courthouse entrance. A trial was proceeding in one of the courtrooms involving a fisticuff dispute between two families which had ended in a number of members of both families being charged with a range of offences of violence. When the lunchtime adjournment was announced members of both families left the public gallery at the same time. Members of one family grabbed a witness from the other family, frog-marched him out of the courthouse and into Cranbrook Road – where they laid him down in the middle of the roadway in readiness for another family member to bring his car round to drive over his prostrate body. A telephone call to Barkingside Police Station brought a squad of police officers down from the canteen (where they were tucking into roast beef and two veg) to intervene and prevent a blood bath.

The case of the seventeen cats

A three day trial in the late 90s was the exception rather than the rule at Redbridge Magistrates' Court and I appreciated beforehand that one involving alleged cruelty to seventeen cats would be far from a pleasant experience. But it had its lighter moments. The defendant was a lady in her late sixties who had been a cat-lover all her life, exhibiting maine coomes over many years. Retirement and divorce had left her with a house in one of the plusher parts of the Borough, but very little money – and some twenty-five or so cats to feed. Her son helped out with cash to buy food for the cats, but being unable to afford vets' fees, inbreeding soon meant that the cats were becoming feral and almost wild. They lived in the garden – and the gardens of neighbours – and all over the house. Inspectors from the Royal Society for the Prevention of Cruelty to Animals (RSPCA) tried their best to bring some order to the chaos that soon developed, but the lady spurned all offers of help. The house and garden degenerated, and the stench was said to be unbearable. Seventeen cats were removed from the house and garden – the rest avoided capture.

Prosecuting on behalf of the RSPCA was a well-known and respected local solicitor. He hailed from Wales and gave the impression that he had walked over many a mountain to reach his seat in Redbridge Magistrates' Court. Meanwhile, the defendant was represented by another equally well-known and respected local solicitor who was Jewish, whose rotund appearance made clear that he could not have clambered up a small grassy knoll, let alone a mountain.

In opening his case for the prosecution, the Welsh solicitor handed to the bench individual profiles and photographs for each of the seventeen cats that were the subject of the charges. Taking his time, the solicitor gave a detailed description of each cat and its condition when removed to a place of safety by the RSPCA.

I noted that the solicitor described some cats as *"whole cats"* – a phrase he did not use with them all. Mystified, I waited until the solicitor had completed his opening and then posed the question that had been nagging at my mind over recent minutes. But even as I started to speak, I realised that I was about to dig a very deep hole from which I might never crawl.

Looking the prosecuting solicitor squarely in the eye, I asked: *"You have mentioned that some of the cats were 'whole cats'. The bench would be grateful if you would please explain what you meant by this*?"

My heart was beating at a rate of knots and sinking fast towards my boots – for the truth had dawned upon me like a sudden revelation as the words were coming from my mouth, and there was nothing I could do to stop them.

Raising his eyes towards heaven and curling his tongue around his mouth to savour ever second of this moment-to-be-remembered, the solicitor said: *"Your worship – if I were to use the word castration, would that assist?"* It did!

Within an hour or so a fur ball the size of a tennis ball was lifted high within a sealed polythene bag by the prosecutor as Exhibit One. Passed to the defence for examination, Molly the Usher was invited to bring it onto the bench for the justices to peer at – and, if they were minded to do so, to feel. Now Molly was an Usher who was not to be trifled with, for prior to taking up her present appointment, Molly had been the custody officer with the specific duty of keeping an eye on lady prisoners down below in the court cells. Molly was feared by everyone within the courthouse – from the Bench Chairman and the Clerk to the Justices to the magistrates, staff and all court users – although, in truth, she had a soft spot for us all and this was reciprocated.

Sniffing haughtily and shaking her shoulders to make clear her displeasure at being asked to handle such a thing as a fur ball, Molly hastily conveyed the package to the bench, before retiring to the back of the court.

Later that morning I decided we all deserved a coffee break and indicated that the bench would retire for fifteen minutes for this purpose. Hardly had I risen from my chair when Molly dashed down the courtroom towards the bench.

"Sir," she cried, *"may I make a request."*

I nodded as Molly exclaimed: *"May I remove Exhibit One from the courtroom?"*

Not waiting for me to question the need for this, Molly stated: *"You see, Sir, since Exhibit One came into the courtroom, everyone has been scratching"* – adding in stentorian tones – *"including you, Sir!"*

After three gruelling days, we found the lady guilty of all charges. It was clear that she had not been intentionally cruel to the seventeen cats – each one of which she loved dearly – and so we imposed the minimum sentence of a conditional discharge, but ordered that she should not be permitted to keep cats for the next ten years.

The fact was, of course, that there were at least another dozen or so cats at her home – about which little could be done. I learned later that the lady appealed to the Crown Court against conviction. The same defence solicitor appeared before a judge and two justices from courts other than Redbridge – who disallowed the appeal and upheld our sentences.

The first time cats had featured in a case had been some years before when I sat with the formidable Nora in the chair in the Juvenile Court – the same Nora who had interviewed me prior to my appointment. Formidable – but kindly under all that glowering – tragically, Nora died in her early 60s – shortly after she had spent a year as International President of the Women's Co-operative Guild. Had she not died, I believe Nora would have been elected as Bench Chairman at some stage in her time as a justice.

Two lads of barely fourteen were before the court charged with causing unnecessary suffering to two cats. The allegation was that the lads had tied ropes to the tails of the cats and swung them against a wall until they died. Horrific.

After hearing the evidence and finding the boys guilty of the offence, we were presented with the harsh truth that our hands were tied and any punishment we might impose could not reflect the gravity of the despicable act committed by these youngsters.

Having announced our sentence – and I cannot recall what it was, but I know that everyone in the courtroom (except the two boys, perhaps) agreed that it was far too lenient, but it was what was permitted by law at the time for this offence – Nora and I rose to leave the bench and walked towards the magistrates' door.

As we reached the doorway, Nora suddenly turned and, looking the two boys in the eye, said words to the effect of wishing that she could bring back the birch for they both deserved a good hiding.

I guess Nora felt better having said that, but things came home to roost the following Thursday when the *Ilford Recorder* carried bold headlines on its front page declaring that a leading magistrate wished to bring back the birch. I heard that Nora was carpeted for allowing her feelings to reach the front page of the local press, but knowing Nora, I would guess that those who attempted to give her a wigging for this lapse got as good as they gave. And rightly so.

Elections and the like

Between 1980 and my retirement the means whereby we elected the Bench Chairman, Deputy Chairmen and Chairmen of Panels went through many changes. Some were for the better, others not. The Bench Election Meetings in the early 80s found the magistrates sitting in the well of Court Number One with the Bench Chairman and Deputy Chairmen arrayed high up on the Bench like a gang of prize-fighters. To a newly-appointed magistrate they looked menacing and appeared to be saying – without moving their lips – woe betide anyone who dares to vote against our reappointment. As a result, they were all re-elected year after year after year – often until they fell off their perch through death or retirement and sometimes both, although rarely at the same time.

An A4 sheet was handed out with the names of all the justices. Our task was to tick the name of the person we wished to elect as Bench Chairman and put a cross beside five other names to be elected as Deputy Chairmen. At our third or fourth Bench Election Meeting a young colleague and I decided to vote for each other as Bench Chairman. We were not elected, but I would guess that the Clerks who were counting the votes had a chuckle or two.

Things changed. Time limits on appointments were introduced. Nominations were required. Election took place at the Bench Election Meeting and if you were not there – for good reason or bad – you could not vote. Then the ballot was a postal one prior to the Bench Election Meeting at which the result would be announced. I was elected as a Deputy Chairman prior to the nomination procedure being introduced, but that system came into being during the year when I was elected Bench Chairman.

The Bench Election Meeting in the autumn of 1995 saw five candidates nominated for Bench Chairman – me amongst them. There was a strict rule that canvassing was frowned upon and certainly I kept a very low profile in the weeks prior to the election. Anita and Rosemary both confided to me prior to the election meeting that they were only standing to *"give you a run for your money"!*

Indeed, Anita went so far as to bring her daughter to court prior to the Election Meeting so that they both might sit in the public gallery to observe me chairing Court One. After the sitting, Anita sidled up to me and said: *"You'll do!"*

The evening of the Bench Election Meeting arrived and as the justices walked out of the retiring room into the corridor leading to Court Number One, the then Bench Chairman called me into his office. Standing side by side, looking over the grassy mound immediately below the window towards Sainsbury's, he told me that he expected me to be elected that evening. However, he did not think I would make a good Bench Chairman for a number of reasons, not the least of which was the fact that I would be too weak to stand up to the Clerk to the Justices and other professionals. It was his considered view and I respect him for having the guts to tell me to my face, for I do not think he intended to upset me. With that endorsement ringing in my ears, I trotted off to sit at the back of Court One, from where I learned later in the evening that I had been elected. The Clerk to the Justices, who was privy to the results of the secret ballot, told me that I had been elected by an overwhelming majority – which was encouraging for that gave me confidence in knowing that most of the justices supported me.

Did I stand up to the professionals? That is for others to comment upon. In fact, it was not a question of standing up to anyone for I aimed to work in partnership with those who worked professionally in the criminal justice service and in that I believe I succeeded. Confrontation between lay justices and professional court lawyers was not something in which I wished to be involved. Far better to work together to achieve change by consent – which is what I like to think I did.

Dress codes I have known

During my five years as Bench Chairman in the late 90s I had some experience of earrings and pony tails as accoutrements of male justices. In those days a minority of men sported such things – but they were the exception rather than the rule.

A new justice joined the Bench who was devoid of earrings at interview. On his first day, he arrived with a stud earring in his left ear. The effect was electric. Around the same time, a new lady magistrate of Indian origin came to sit in court in her national dress, which included silk trousers. To confound things even more, a male magistrate of some standing suddenly and without warning bedecked himself with a short pony tail.

Male magistrates took me into my office to demand that the earring be removed. Lady magistrates took me thither likewise, asking why they could not wear trouser suits – for the Indian lady was sporting trousers. And both male and lady magistrates demanded that I should sharpen a pair of scissors and slice the pony tail from the fellow who dared to appear in similar style to that of many of our defendants.

After a period of private prayer, a G & T, and a session with Chris De Burgh in the shed-with-the-overhang at the bottom of my garden, I devised yet another cunning plan. I drafted a Dress Code for Magistrates. It included a section on jewellery – that it should be unobtrusive. It covered suits – that these should be of appropriate and sober hue. And it was clearly multi-sex. I sent the Code to every justice, borrowed a tin helmet from Tom-next-door (who collected these artefacts of the war years) and awaited the storm.

I was lambasted from every side. In fact I was lambasted from above and below, too, for that matter.

One lady asked me: *"If I arrived in a red trouser suit, would you consider that an appropriate colour?" "Yes,"* I replied. *"And if a man came in a red suit, what would you say?"* I commented that this would be inappropriate. *"Sexist!"* she roared.

Lady justices brought their entire collection of jewellery for me to examine so that I might determine which of the dangly-type earrings were unobtrusive.

It went on for weeks – as I knew it would. And whilst they were arguing with each other in the retiring room, I would sit in my adjacent office devising all sorts of other cunning plans, many of them with the ready connivance of the Clerk to the Justices. These were issued to the Bench, but they were so busy debating the hue of their suits or the dangling potential of their earrings, that they did not appreciate what other cunning plans were being foisted upon them.

These included the first-ever Audit of Sentencing, which showed that if you came to Redbridge Court charged with driving whilst disqualified on a Thursday you would go to prison instantly – if not before – but if you were lucky enough to be bailed for the same offence to appear on a Friday you walked out of the courthouse with a probation or a community service order. And if beat your wife over her head with a frying pan and came to court on a Thursday, you might receive a pat on the back and a jam doughnut – for on Thursday's some of the ladies who dished out justice had little or no patience with their own sex – whereas on a Monday you would be sent hot-foot to prison for the maximum time possible.

The Audits of Sentencing went on over many months, causing some justices apoplexy whilst others saw the sense of the audits and applauded what we were trying to do. Sadly, we could not keep this up as the audit had to be carried out manually and we did not have the staff to do this laborious and tedious work. There was software that could have been used, but we did not have the funds to purchase this. All this took place at a time when computers were beginning to have a place in the court system, but we still had to telephone the DVLA in Swansea to check the history of a defendant's driving licence. Indeed, at one stage we were restricted to making four such telephone calls a day – after that we had to send a FAX in the sure knowledge that the reply would take two weeks (if we were lucky) and three weeks (more likely). How things have changed – for now the police can sit at the roadside and check a driver's details within seconds.

And the dress code? I issued a revised version when the rumbling had died down. By then my back was broad and my smile even wider. I survived – just.

The Big One(s)!

As I tuck into my breakfast each morning of toast (if it is warm) and porridge (on cold days), I am reminded of Friday 2nd August 1996 – the day that Charlie Kray, Ronald Field and Robert Gould appeared in the dock at Redbridge Magistrates' Court. For there hanging on the wall in my dining room is the original artist's impression by Priscilla, the ITN court artist, of the scene that day when I sat with colleagues Gerda and Colin in Court Number One.

The charge faced by the three defendants was one of plotting to supply and supplying £80M of cocaine – but I am leaping ahead of myself.

The day started like any other summer Friday morning, except that late on the previous afternoon the Clerk to the Justices telephoned to advise me that we would having a Big One in court next morning. On arrival at Barkingside, I noticed that there appeared to be rather a lot of police officers about. In fact there were forty or so – most armed. Some were in the grounds and on the roof of the courthouse; a few were on the roof of Sainsbury's and yet more were roaming the surrounding roadways.

Inside the courthouse there was a heavy police presence. Everyone – including the magistrates – entering the building was frisked by police. Briefed by the Clerk to the Justices, I was advised that police had received information to the effect that there would be an attempt to airlift one of the defendants from the courthouse by helicopter.

The public gallery in Court One was packed – with national press and TV reporters in the front row. Seated immediately behind was 70-year-old Charlie Kray's girlfriend, Judy – who appeared to be considerably younger than Charlie. Judy was hemmed in by three minders – brawny characters in dark suits and equally dark glasses, the kind of gentlemen I would be fearful of meeting on a summer's day let alone a dark night.

I remember little about the hearing, with the exception of one thing – the question of the length of adjournment. The prosecution had invited the Bench to remand all three defendants in custody whilst the formidable team of defence barristers had argued for a remand on bail. The defence team did their best, but they must have realised that they were on a hiding to nothing – for the chance of bail being granted in the face of the evidence before the court was about a million to one against. Before the Bench retired to consider its verdict on the question of bail and to formulate its reasons, the defence asked that should custody be the decision, that an adjournment of twenty-eight days be agreed. And the prosecutor rose to say that he would have no objection to this.

In the corridor behind Court One my colleagues and I decided to remand in custody. I made the point to my colleagues and to the Court Clerk that our powers were limited to a remand at first hearing of up to seven days. But the advice the Bench was given was that if prosecution and defence were agreed, we could remand for twenty-eight days.

Returning to court, I did just that – against, let it be said, my better judgement – and then retired for a well-earned cup of coffee for it had been a difficult hearing in view the fact that the air conditioning had broken down that morning so that the packed courtroom resembled a sauna at full heat!

But hardly had we started to sup our coffee, when Michael Faraway, Clerk to the Justices appeared somewhat red faced to inform us that we had been wrongly advised by both defence and prosecution together with the Court Clerk sitting with us – and that the remand in custody would have to be for six days. Back into court we went, up from the cells trotted the defendants and we made the change in the period of remand.

By this time all the modern technology stacked up in TV vans in the car parks at Tesco and beyond were sending the message to the world's media that the defendants were remanded in custody for twenty-eight days – so the Clerk to the Justices stood tall on the courthouse steps to inform all and sundry that an error had been made and that the remand was for six days and not twenty-eight.

I suppose the mistake over the length of the adjournment somewhat sullied the day for me, although I was assured that faced with the array of experienced barristers for both prosecution and defence, many magistrates would have done as I did – take the advice I was given and act upon it. But it still stuck in my throat that I had allowed myself to be misled when I knew the correct procedure.

I wandered into the kitchen attached to the retiring room to talk with Pat, the Senior Court Usher, and her colleagues – for I knew from long experience that they would be the best judge of what had gone on in court that morning. Pat told me that Priscilla, the ITN artist, had been at the court and that her artist's impression was to be beamed to the nation on the lunchtime news, adding, furthermore, that there was a very good likeness of me.

Arriving home in the early afternoon, I telephoned ITN's newsroom to inquire if I might purchase the original. Within minutes the artist's agent was on the phone and very chatty she was, too, asking me how I would like it framed and where I lived. Having recently refurbished our dining room in pine, I suggested that pine would be good. No problem, she said. How much will that be, I asked? That's £400 plus VAT, came the response. Some quick thinking followed and I agreed – for I guessed that a drawing with Charlie Kray might well be valuable one day.

The work of art was delivered some three weeks later to the courthouse. I was a little taken aback when I realized that the frame measured some three feet by two feet. It was much admired at court and when I took it home Yvonne agreed that it might hang in the dining room – provided it did not take up too prominent a position. Neighbours and passers by came in to admire – including Jim, which was fortuitous for Jim returned a few weeks later with some interesting news.

Jim was at that time a London taxi driver. One day shortly afterwards he happened to stop by the Old Bailey and took on board none other than Priscilla, the ITN artist. Jim guessed it might be her for the package she was carrying was roughly the size of the work of art which he had seen hanging in my dining room.

What, asked Jim, do you do with the originals when ITN have finished with them? That, said Priscilla, is where we make our money. How much do you charge, asked Jim, warming to his subject? That depends who is involved, said Priscilla. If it is a Queen's Counsel we start at £3,000. For a judge we would charge £2,000 and a barrister around the same. How about a magistrate, asked Jim? Ah, now that is tricky, said Priscilla. We would find out where the magistrate lived and keep them talking on the telephone to work out whether or not they have any money – and then fix a price. I guess I did well to settle for £400 plus VAT.

The other "big one" to come to Redbridge whilst I was Bench Chairman was the international fraudster Darius Guppy, friend of folk like Boris Johnson one-time MP, later Mayor of London, jovial guest chairman of *Have I got news for you?* on BBC1, and confidant of Earl Spencer, Princess Diana's brother. Convicted and jailed in 1993 for staging a faked jewel robbery and fraudulently claiming £1.8M from insurers, Darius Guppy emerged from prison having served half his five-year sentence, but apparently penniless.

He and his co-conspirator, Ben Marsh, were estimated to have made around £4M from crime (there was a spot of gold smuggling as well as the insurance scam) and both were ordered to pay a £533,000 fine at the time of their conviction.

Ben Marsh paid up the full amount, but Darius Guppy claimed his share of the money had been spent or given to a mysterious businessman who had vanished. His fine was reduced to £227,000 on appeal and turned into a criminal compensation order payable to Lloyd's. In 1994, he declared himself bankrupt in order – allegedly – to avoid paying the cash, but the judge, Mr Justice Holland, was unimpressed and ordered Darius Guppy to stay in prison until he came up with the money.

For a reason which I never fully understood, Darius Guppy appeared before Redbridge Magistrates' Court's Fine Enforcement Panel regarding payment of the compensation order. I can understand why he had to appear before a magistrates' court rather than the crown court where he was convicted because criminal compensation and fine orders were remitted to magistrates' courts for collection – but why Redbridge? As far as I could tell he had never lived in

Redbridge nor, I would guess, had he ever stepped into the Borough. Perhaps it was thought that Redbridge magistrates would know what to do – and we did.

As it happens, we had a very efficient Fine Enforcement Panel at that time, chaired by the assiduous magistrate, David. When Darius Guppy appeared at Redbridge, the bench sitting as a fine enforcement panel was chaired by Dr Geoffrey, an experienced justice, a deputy coroner and retired East End of London GP. Darius Guppy was brought from prison regularly over a period of some three months or so, and eventually, a deal was done and he paid £165,000 (borrowed from a benefactor) to get out of jail.

However, it has to be said that whilst the case attracted considerable interest in the press, it was the lady magistrates at Redbridge who became very excited – if not positively delirious with lust. Darius Guppy, for all his faults, was something of a playboy and good looker in the eyes of the ladies. A number of our lady magistrates would have given their eye teeth to be on the bench hearing the case but they had to make do with queuing in the corridor behind Court Number Two whilst Darius was in the dock and peering through the small glass panel in the door that led into the courtroom – sighing all the time with pleasure.

Cupboards and the like

After fifteen years on the Bench I found myself elected as a Deputy Bench Chairman in 1995 and then as Bench Chairman in 1996 – and was re-elected each year so that I served in that role for five years. In days of yore a Bench Chairman went on and on and on – but in the 90s all that changed and the maximum term was fixed at five years, later reduced to three. I believe five years is about right. It took one year to find out what was going on, another year to decide what needed to be done about it, two years to put things right – and the final year to bask in the glory of what had been achieved (or to hide away in the hope that no-one will find out what you have been up to!).

I soon realised that I had spent the past few years on the Bench in blissful ignorance of some of the goings-on. I learned that the bench in Court Number Two had been the scene of some debauchery or other out of court hours between a member of the legal profession and a lady whose blond hair I had often admired (but which was, I discovered, dyed to mask the grey).

Perhaps the most notorious part of the courthouse at Barkingside was a certain cupboard in which, it was widely rumoured, there had been goings-on between justices. I was reassured that during my time as Bench Chairman the said cupboard would henceforth be locked at all times – and I checked that this was so.

There were many things that were not spoken aloud. Visiting a local garden centre one Saturday morning, I bumped into a single-mother lady justice amongst the climbing roses. Suddenly – and without warning – the smiling face of an older bachelor male justice peered through the trellis. The lady introduced the male justice to me as her "rose adviser". When I mentioned this encounter to a lady justice who knew about these things, I was told that there had been a liaison between the two for many, many years.

Occasionally a justice would disappear – never to be seen again. One such was a young man who was something to do with the law. He – apparently –

fell out with a formidable Deputy Chairman – and was off and away before you could turn round.

During my time as Bench Chairman, two justices were found guilty of criminal offences – one involving the finances of a footballer whose accountant he purported to be and the other some sort of benefit fraud. Both denied that they had been involved in any wrong doing when first charged, but both agreed to stand down whilst their cases came to trial. Which was fortunate, for had they not agreed to do so, I would have found it necessary to prevail upon the Lord Chancellor to order them to stay away from sitting on the bench.

A councillor was interviewed by police alleging election fraud involving postal votes of residents in retirement homes. Whilst the investigations into these allegations were going on the councillor had to stand down as a justice which was highly embarrassing for him. The charges were dropped after some eighteen months but not before the allegations had been splashed in the press, which must have been highly embarrassing for the justice.

Granting justices short terms of leave of absence for a variety of reasons was part of my role as Bench Chairman. A justice would find that work or home commitments were so heavy that he or she had to stand down for a short period. From time to time a lady justice would inform me that she would be going into hospital and would need a few months to recuperate. In many cases this was for a hysterectomy operation, but – not unnaturally – ladies were somewhat reticent to say this to a male bench chairman in so many words. Here I found it best to introduce a measure of innocent humour into the conversation by asking upon which ear the operation would be carried out? That usually broke the ice.

I learned so much when sitting on the Family Proceedings Panel. My education in human biology had been almost non-existent (for I cannot stand the sight of blood and am unable to watch *Casualty* on TV), but the Family Court sorted that out. I said as much on one public occasion – which got me into hot water with my colleagues. We were attending a garden party at Snaresbrook Crown Court in company with colleagues, including Shirley, the redoubtable wife of a local farmer. In answer to a question as to whether or not I found the Family Court interesting, I announced in a loud voice that I did indeed, but that I had learned more about sex from the said Shirley than from anyone else. There were a few red faces – especially Shirley's, although it was an undisputed fact (in my mind at least).

Interviewing potential justices

For five years in the early 90s I was a member of the Lord Chancellor's Advisory Sub-committee for Redbridge and of the Advisory Committee for North East London – two bodies whose members interviewed and recommended – or not – to the Lord Chancellor members of the local community for appointment as justices of the peace. The process was vastly different ten years after my appointment and things have changed even more since that time. But in the 90s being on these committees was one of the more enjoyable aspects of being a magistrate.

The system we operated at that time in Redbridge was this. The Clerk would receive completed application forms and examine these with the chairman of the sub-committee – at one time a medical man of charm and tenacity and later a former air hostess. The sub-committee members comprised four justices from the Redbridge Bench, one lady justice from another court and a lay member. Two of us would be dispatched to visit the potential justices in their homes. We would be allocated two per evening – with the interviews starting at 7pm and 8pm, and finishing by 9pm.

As I do not drive, the lady justice from the other court would arrange to meet me outside the first home at five minutes to seven. With this interview over, the journey to the second home was exciting to say the very least. The London Borough of Redbridge is bisected from West to East by the A12, and this lady would only cross the A12 at the Green Gate traffic lights. Further, she would avoid at all costs having to turn right. Thus we journeyed by somewhat circuitous routes to the home of the second person to be interviewed that evening. On completion of the second interview, the lady justice would drop me at the most convenient – for her – bus stop and from there I would wend my weary way homewards.

I have always believed that if you are offered refreshment in someone's home, you should accept, but not that lady justice from the other court. I admit that there were times when I regretted my decision – such as the occasion when I was offered very, very, very hot somosas, but the Coca-Cola helped to cool them down.

On another occasion – and with a Redbridge member of the sub-committee – we entered a terrace house to find large glass tanks lining the hallway walls and even more tanks in the lounge. It took time for my eyes to become accustomed to the dim lighting, but my ears told me that the rustling in the straw meant that there were things lurking there that I would wish to meet. The tanks were home to lizards, alligators, snakes and the like of varying sizes and ferocity. The spinster lady we were interviewing lived in the house with her elderly parents and did not seem in the least concerned at our very obvious discomfort. In fact the reptiles were not mentioned.

An interview with a lady seated at her dining room table was going well when suddenly and without warning the door burst open to reveal a large, red-faced and clearly very annoyed man who asked what-we-were-a-doing-of-in-his-home-without-his-permission and-if-we-did-not-get-out-he-would-call-the-police – sharpish! Anita, my colleague, who had been an air hostess on flights from the sunny Caribbean to fog-bound London in the 1950s and knew how to handle a crisis, explained the point of our mission.

On hearing that his wife was applying to be appointed as a magistrate, he laughed and laughed and laughed – finally shouting as he left the room and banged the door behind him that such a thing would take place over his dead body.

Retaining absolute control and composure, the wife explained that the couple had fallen out a number of years ago and did not speak, although they continued to live in the same house. The interview proceeded, but was again interrupted on half-a-dozen occasions by the husband who was becoming more and more threatening and abusive towards Anita and me each time he barged into the room.

At one stage, he flung a pile of papers from the sideboard onto the table around which we were seated, but Anita was not be put off and, as she remarked later, I was sitting nearest to the door and the roaring bull of a man.

With the interview at an end, Anita and I withdrew to her car.

"May I have a cigarette," said Anita, who was normally a non-smoker, as she collapsed into the driving seat. I recall that we both had two soothing cigarettes before driving off into the misty night.

The second interviews for those who got through the first were held before the entire sub-committee in the courthouse. A member of the security team would meet the prospective justice and conduct them to one of the courtrooms, where they would be handed a court scenario to read.

These were invariably dreamed up by the Clerk to the Justices and consisted of cases for which there were no solutions known to man. We were not testing legal knowledge, but trying to adduce whether or not the candidate had what was called 'the judicial mind'.

Our recommendations had to take account of a number of issues. The bench had to be balanced between men and women. We needed a range of occupations – and not all school teachers or bank managers. Politics was taken into account, too, for the Lord Chancellor expected all shades of political opinion to be represented on the bench.

Every five years members of the bench were invited to declare in the strictest confidence how they had voted at the last general election. This information was sent to the Lord Chancellor's office where someone compared the make up of the bench with the votes cast at the last general election in the Borough. If there were a disproportionate number of magistrates of one political persuasion, things would be said and action expected.

In my time on the Advisory Committee the ethnic make-up of the London Borough of Redbridge changed dramatically. In the 70s and 80s, some 20 per cent of the population of the Borough was Jewish and this was reflected on the bench. By the late 90s, this had fallen to around 15 per cent, but the percentage of residents from the ethnic minorities had spiralled to some 30 per cent.

The bench had to take account of this and there was a spirited move by the Advisory Sub-committee, the Clerk to the Justices and my predecessor as Bench Chairman to engage the Black and Asian communities.

The members of a faith group would put forward their elders as the people with the most experience – but these were often over the retirement age of 70 and very rarely – if ever – women.

One of the first Asian women to be interviewed – and appointed – told the sub-committee that within her house her husband was in charge and she would do whatever he asked – but once she walked through the front door into the street outside, she made her own decisions. No, she said, she would not be fazed if she had to sit with two men and if she disagreed with them, she would have no hesitation in saying so.

Of course, it is all very different today – and probably just as well.

Some thoughts on Saturday courts

There was a tale that went the rounds about a Saturday morning at a nearby courthouse. Justices who were in danger of not meeting the minimum sitting requirement of twenty-six half-days a year – because their employers would not give them the time off from work – would turn up on Saturday mornings as the year end approached, anxious to get an extra tick recorded against their name. And so, from time to time, defendants coming up from the cells after a night of alcoholic jollification would find themselves face to face with not a single justice, but two or three or five or seven or even more. One such morning a defendant still the worse for wear made his weary way up the stairs from the cells. Peering over the dock, he spied not one but seven justices sitting in all their majesty behind the Bench.

"Good grief," cried the defendant, who was probably seeing double, *"it's the Last Supper!"*

How true that story is, I know not, but it is a good one nonetheless. And whilst Occasional Courts at Redbridge on Saturdays and Bank Holidays were presided over by a single justice they, too, had their own tales to tell ranging from the peccadillo to the so serious.

At one time in the distant past being a justice on the Occasional Court Rota was something of an arbitrary matter. If the Deputy Clerk to the Justices of the day deemed it right that you be on the rota, that is what happened. So there were the Great, those who thought they were Great and others who were clearly not. Some on the list were justices who found it difficult to meet the minimum number of sittings. Others were on the list for reasons that escaped understanding. All that changed in the mid-80s when the Bench Chairman and Deputy Chairmen decided that only experienced justices who were approved court chairmen should sit alone on a Saturday morning.

So how did it work on Saturdays? On the prescribed day – when other justices were considering driving to the courthouse for free parking whilst they shopped at Iceland or Boots – the justice listed waited anxiously at home for The Call.

Some justices were known to rise early, waiting for The Call all keen-eyed and dressed in their Saturday best. Others would lie in their beds, pulling the sheets tightly around their ears in the vain hope that The Call would not come.

At around 8.15am or so the telephone would ring. *"This is Security,"* said a dismembered voice, *"we have two."* Sometimes there were more – eleven was my top score. At other times there were none. In which case I contrived to find something to do of great urgency, for fear that Yvonne would have other ideas as to how I might while away the morning.

There were days when The Call did not come at all. And that was worrying. Had Security forgotten? Did they know who to call on that particular day? I would sit worrying, but then we were given the telephone number for Security and were able to ring them to check.

There was usually a very good reason why The Call did not come – such as that David forgot to tell 'em who was on duty. Although to be fair to David (and am I not always thus?), it could be because Mr A swapped with Mrs B who, in turn, swapped with Mr C – and forgot to tell David.

It was vital – and, indeed, a quality used in the selection process – that the Occasional Court Justice was relaxed and calm at all times. Excitable justices were in danger of falling at the first hurdle – the fact that there were no offenders in the precincts of the Courthouse at 10am when the Court was scheduled to sit.

Why was this, you may ask? Well, they remained in the comfort of Ilford Police Station because (a) the Van was at Havering, (b) the Van was in Lewisham or (c) no-one had the slightest idea where the Van was, nor could anyone care.

In the alternative, the police in Liverpool just happened to spot a driver late on Friday evening making a right turn where no right turn was permitted, stopped the driver, checked on the Police National Computer, found that there was an outstanding warrant for minor traffic offences in Redbridge – and were bringing him hot foot to Redbridge Magistrates' Court to face his just desserts with an estimated time of arrival of around 1pm – give or take an hour or three. I often wondered why the police in Liverpool – and other far off places – were keen to bring wayward defendants to Redbridge Court on a Saturday morning, defendants for whom warrants were outstanding for the most trivial traffic offences. Was it that they wanted a day or a weekend enjoying the delights that London offered? We will never know, but we had our suspicions and were not all born yesterday.

At this point the Occasional Court justice was well advised to consult with Roy or Clyde in the security office. They knew all things that were worth knowing. Yes, the duty solicitor was here. They had spotted someone who looked like a probation officer and the crown prosecutor had popped over to Tesco for breakfast.

At this stage the experienced Occasional Court Justice moved quickly to the kitchen to make the coffee. If Peter was the Clerk, chocolate biscuits had to be found and piled high on the plate beside a black coffee with one sugar.

Keeping the clerk happy was essential. Clerks were kindly folk, but even the kindliest had been known to outbursts in the most unexpected places. It was the wise Occasional Court Justice who checked to ascertain the last known date of outburst and was prepared.

Less experienced Occasional Court Justices might wander off to explore the delights of Barkingside High Street. Such incursions would bring an immediate response. Offenders would mysteriously appear in vans, whilst the prosecutor, solicitor and probation officer would surface from nowhere.

The bizarre one!

Endorsing a warrant to empower the police or other appropriate authority to search someone's home or business premises is one of the most serious responsibilities of a magistrate. Most applications for search warrants are made by the police and other authorised bodies during business hours at the courthouse and are heard in the courtroom before three magistrates. On occasion such applications will be heard by one magistrate and this is perfectly legal – it is just that where it is possible it is preferable for such applications to be made before three magistrates.

From time to time it will be necessary for an application to be made for a search warrant when the courthouse is closed. In some commission areas, it was practice for a court clerk to be present when such an application was made before a single magistrate at his or her home. Indeed, in some places the court clerk and magistrate travelled to the courthouse which then had to be opened out of hours for the hearing to take place.

In Redbridge during my time on the bench such applications were heard by a justice at his or her home. When I first came onto the bench, it appeared that police might call on any magistrate for this purpose. However, certain magistrates seemed to have all the applications coming their way. It was said that this was because those magistrates lived near the police station or their homes were on a particular police officer's route home for his tea. In one local court not far from Redbridge, most of the search warrants required by police appeared to be signed by a certain lady magistrate who could be found most evenings knocking back gins and tonics in a pub in the town centre. There was anecdotal evidence that this lady would sign anything for a gin and tonic, and having met the lady on one occasion at a training evening, I considered that there might have been an element of truth in that story. I learned later from the Clerk to the Justices that some warrants for searches in Redbridge were being signed by this particular lady justice – and at that point the Redbridge Clerk to the Justices decided that enough was enough.

The decision was made by the Bench Chairman and Deputy Chairmen of the time that a list of experienced justices should be drawn up who would be authorised to hear applications for search warrants at their homes. And that was how it was when I became Bench Chairman and remained so until I retired.

I was on the search warrant list for some fifteen or so years and had visits from police officers in the evenings, at weekends and in the middle of the night. Police officers would arrive and given their evidence on oath. If I was unsure of the legality of the application – and this did happen from time to time – I would telephone the Clerk or Deputy Clerk to the Justices. On occasion the application had been incorrectly filled in or was not within the law – in which case the officer returned to the police station empty handed. But generally the applications were correctly made, the evidence was clear and the responses to my questions convinced me that sufficient grounds had been made out and I signed the application. I would write up the evidence and send this in a letter to the Clerk to the Justices, who would file my notes with the copy of the application. The police were required to return the warrant to the court indicating whether or not this had been successfully executed. In my time as Bench Chairman, the Clerk and I would chase up the police to ensure that this was done. Only in this way could we monitor the effectiveness – or otherwise – of the evidence and questioning carried out in justices' homes.

Perhaps the most bizarre application I was involved in was when a detective constable rang me from Ilford Police Station at 2.45am – the middle of the night – on a Monday in May 2001.

The DC arrived at 3am with applications to search a flat in Redbridge and a car which was said to be parked outside. He told me that a female went to a police station in South London at 7pm on the previous day, stating that she had been raped.

The South London police contacted Ilford Police later in the evening requesting that they check an address in Redbridge and ascertain if a certain make and colour of car was parked in the vicinity. Voting register checks revealed that the flat was occupied by Mr A and that the car was registered in his name. Mr A was also known as Mr B, in which name he was said to have had a previous conviction. Police were outside the flat when the DC came to my home, keeping watch on the flat and the vehicle. If Mr A came out of the flat, police intended to arrest him.

The following information had been given to Ilford Police by the South London Police. The female had remained in a highly distressed state and as a result the information was somewhat confusing. The female, who lived in a coastal town and was the alleged victim, was an employee of a well-known publicist. She has been communicating with Mr A via the internet – to what purpose was unclear. She arranged to meet Mr A in Ilford on the Saturday, travelling to London by train and thence by bus. Mr A met her in the car which was the subject of the application and they went to an address which is believed to be the flat that was the subject of the application. The female did not know the address, but described it to the South London Police and Ilford Police believe this to be the correct flat – partly by the presence of the car but also by the description given. One other man and a woman were in the flat. The two men were said to have sexually assaulted the alleged victim on a number of occasions over the weekend. Late on Sunday afternoon they drove the victim around London and eventually dropped her in South London.

The warrants were sought under *Section 8(3) PACE 1984*. I was advised that police wish to search for evidence of clothing, body fluids and fibres in the flat and car. In addition, they wish to examine bedding and computer hardware and software in the flat. If arrests are made, the case would be handled by Ilford Police as the scene of the alleged crime was in Redbridge.

I signed the warrants at 3.20am. The DC advised me that the intention was to execute the warrants in an hour or two, when sufficient back-up arrived.

I took my letter and the copy warrants to the courthouse that morning, handing them to the Clerk to the Justices. In my notes I had included the names of the man who was alleged to live in the flat and of the well-known publicist. Both the Clerk and I were somewhat taken aback by the evidence I had been given, but we agreed that based on what I had been told on oath I had no reason not to sign the applications. The involvement of the well-known publicist and the suggestion that others had been in the flat at the time of the alleged rape indicated that this might end up at a higher court – and both the Clerk and I were anxious that my actions would stand testing. We were satisfied that they would.

Three weeks later on a Saturday afternoon another DC telephoned from Ilford Police Station at approximately 4pm and attended at my home at 5pm. This was the third application made for a search warrant in this case – the first had been made before me and the second at the courthouse before colleagues.

I was told that the warrant signed by me earlier had been executed that night. A number of items were seized for forensic examination. Mr A was interviewed by Ilford Police and bailed to return to the police station. Officers from Ilford travelled to the coastal town to interview the alleged victim as the interview at the South London Police Station had been carried out whilst the alleged victim was under considerable stress.

During the interview the alleged victim stated that the alleged rape had been carried out on a rug in the living room at the flat. A further warrant was applied for and granted (at the courthouse) and a rug and off-cuts of carpet were removed from the flat for examination.

The third warrant was now required because police wished to take fingerprint evidence to ascertain the identity of others who were said to have been at the flat during the alleged rape. The victim had now explained to police in more detail how she became involved with Mr A. She stated in interview that she was investigating a porn and prostitution ring involving well-known figures in public life. Having obtained some information, she went to the publicist, who expressed interest and told her that if she was able to obtain proof, he would pay her £100,000. Hence her visit to Ilford to meet the alleged suspect.

The alleged victim stated in interview that a former MP and his wife were present in the flat when the alleged rape took place, together with another unknown man. I asked the DC how seriously he took this allegation. He said that in view of the fact that the allegation concerned public figures, they were treading with extreme caution and that higher police authorities were being appraised of the progress of the investigations.

I asked the DC if any checks had been made as to the alleged victim's mental state and history. He confirmed that this had been done and there was no history of mental illness. I also questioned why finger prints had not been taken during the other two visits to the flat. The DC said that this required the attendance of a fingerprint expert and it was not deemed appropriate earlier. The new allegations made this now imperative.

I was advised that on each of the two previous occasions, Mr A had opened the door to police who had not had to use the warrants to effect entry. They wished to cover themselves on this occasion should the suspect refuse entry. Police intended to visit the flat during the daytime over the weekend just as soon as a fingerprint expert was available. I signed the warrant at 5.15pm.

I wrote up my notes and took them to the courthouse on the day following the Bank Holiday. I watched as the Clerk to the Justices read what I had written.

"If I did not know you as I do," said the Clerk, *"I would think you had made this up!"*

Some three months later the story hit the national TV evening news and the following day's newspapers. The former MP and his wife were seen on TV standing on the steps of a local police station as they were about to be taken inside to be interviewed. Suffice to say that the story rolled on over many weeks but eventually the former MP and his wife were completely cleared and totally exonerated of any wrong-doing. They had not been at the flat in Redbridge on the day in question.

The young lady involved had made up a tissue of lies and was convicted of a criminal offence resulting from this. And until now only the Clerk to the Justices and a couple of police officers knew that I had any involvement in the bizarre and very sad business.

Learned Clerks I have known

The lawyers who gave legal advice to the Bench at Redbridge were a truly remarkable group of people. Designated as Court Clerks in my day, we referred to them from the bench as Mr or Madam Clerk or as the Learned Clerk. It may sound a little twee to today's ear, but it seemed very right and proper then. The many hundreds of Clerks to the Justices have now been slashed to little more than a handful. In my day every courthouse had its own Clerk to the Justices, but now one such person operates over a dozen or so courthouses, whilst each court will have the less romantically named Bench Legal Manager.

The first Deputy Clerk to the Justices I knew was a cockney and former taxi driver. In those days you did not have to be a barrister or solicitor to be a court clerk, but he had studied the law whilst driving his cab around the East End of London and beyond. He called a spade a spade and took no nonsense from defendant, lawyer or magistrate. Everything was straight up and down to him. You were either guilty, in which case you got what was your due, or you were not guilty, when you might have got a clip round the ear had you been within reach for wasting the court's time.

He was not one for detailed justices' rotas. Rather he would peer into the retiring room at five to ten each morning with pen and the back of an envelope in hand – and decided who was sitting where as he propped the door open with his knee. He enjoyed his food and would cook up some delicacies in the justices' kitchen at lunchtime. The aroma drifted into the retiring room and down the corridors into the courtrooms.

Two Clerks from my early days were held in some awe by the justices. One was a short, stout lady whose husband was a magistrate at a court in another Borough. Dripping with jewels and doused with a heavy perfume which marched ahead of her presence, she would treat her justices with courtesy but with a firmness which bordered on the bully. Woe betides any justice who appeared to be about to step out of line for comeuppance would not be far away.

The second clerk was a youngish man, tall and well-dressed, who sported a moustache from time to time, and even – occasionally – a beard and spoke in what might best be described as Shakespearian tones. He had, I learned from an elderly justice, his dramatics – from which I gathered he was a thespian who strode the boards in local amateur dramatics. More experienced justices – mainly, let it be said, ladies of considerable years – bought tickets for his performances and in the weeks that followed spoke admiringly of his prowess, but always within his hearing, I noticed.

From time to time it would be necessary for a Family Proceedings Court to take place out of hours and in a justice's home – when a place of safety order needed to be taken out on a child, for example. If a certain lady clerk was on duty, I would often be the justice for not only did the lady clerk appear to take a shine to me, but also because the local authority's legal lady liked coming to my home for she was allowed to smoke whilst the clerk sat with me in another room as I wrote out my decision and reasons.

One tall, dark haired, handsome court clerk – who thought he was the cat's whiskers in the eyes of the ladies – irked me no end when he suggested that we might "pot" a defendant – meaning send him off into prison. I view sentencing anyone to custody as a serious matter – and "potting" was not a word I would have used in this regard.

Mention chocolate biscuits and Court Clerk Peter would be there like a flash. Born in Barking, Peter had the pleasure of being taught by a justice who chaired the Youth Panel and later became Chairman of the Bench, and another of his teachers became Chairman of a neighbouring court.

Peter studied hard, moving through the court offices at Redbridge to qualify as a barrister and be appointed as a court clerk. Married to a court clerk at Havering, Peter blushed easily – to the extent that a few ladies at the court would scheme to make it happen. Other lady justices, especially those of goodly proportions, would give Peter the occasional cuddle in the corridor – and Peter would disappear into their voluminous bosoms, but he always came up for air smiling.

For most of my time on the Bench the Clerk to the Justices was a tall, austere lawyer of considerable skill and highly knowledgeable in the law. Michael entered the courthouse each morning carrying nothing in his hands and left in the same manner at the end of the day. He attended meetings with the agenda and the minutes – and rarely any other papers. He had an almost photographic memory and did not need prompts. He wrote everything out in copperplate handwriting, eschewing typewriters, shorthand writers and dictating machines through to his retirement in the late 90s. In court he would allow things to proceed just so far without any intervention, but when – and if – he intervened, he did so with a vengeance. Woe betide the court chairman who got him or herself into the position when intervention was justified – for from that moment on the court belonged to the Clerk and not to the Justices. As a chairman you let it happen once – but never again. Michael was an innovator whose ideas were way ahead of his time. He retired to the West Country.

Michael was succeeded by the last Clerk to the Justices at Redbridge – a young man named Kevin, who hailed from the Midlands and was of the modern breed of lawyers who had fought their way up by hard work and tenacity. I like to think that Kevin and I made a good team in my time as Bench Chairman. We saw through a number of fairly revolutionary changes without rocking the boat, by taking magistrates and staff with us. Sadly, in the changes that came from on high at the beginning of the 21st Century, Kevin took early retirement from the court service. He now sits as a judge on immigration panels and handles appeals from some of the tickets for parking offences and the like that are now liberally dished out by all sorts of authorities. I have no doubt that Kevin does a good job, for he is a very capable lawyer, but I cannot help regretting that his skill as a Clerk to the Justices has been lost. I guess I retired at the right time.

Justices in all shapes and sizes

Drawn from a cross-section of the local community, it was inevitable that there were some characters amongst the justices.

There were three Joans. Two were Deputy Chairmen in the days when once you rose to be a Deputy you stayed there until you dropped off your perch; one a staunch member of the Labour Party who was kindness itself, the other the scourge of lady shoplifters. This was in the days when we had a rash of the middle aged ladies who – following the public humiliation of Lady Isobel Barnett of TV fame – were said to be offending to bring attention to themselves as they went through the menopause. But Joan would have none of it – and they were fined £100 irrespective of who they were – and bringing your Vicar to plead on your behalf cut no ice with her. The third Joan was always in the forefront when there was catering to be done – and she was not a happy bunny if you did not support every social event run by the Justices' Club where commitment was the byword. Later we had another lady justice who had a down on women offenders. Unlike the second Joan it was not merely shoplifters who incurred her wrath – but all women. Our nickname for her was the Rottweiler.

Former Tory Mayor Molly took no nonsense from anyone – especially the police. One young black guy was hauled up before Molly and me on some harassment charge. He would call Molly *"Your Majesty"* and after a couple of requests to him to desist, Molly gave up for he was clearly scared out of his wits. In his evidence he assured us that he had been laughing with a friend in Ilford High Road when a copper on the other side of the street thought he was laughing at him – and called the cavalry from the local nick to make the arrest and throw him unceremoniously into the back of a police van. Retiring to the corridor to consider our verdict, Molly plonked herself on the floor and looked me straight in the eye as she said: *"When it is a crime to laugh in Ilford High Road, I will resign"* and then, without a further word, strode into the court to announce a not guilty verdict.

Arriving home from court later that day, my teenage daughter asked me if I had had Micky in court. I had. It was the laughing lad. *"He is my boy friend,"* Heather told me. Up to that time I had not met him. He was indeed the boy friend for the next two or three years and a nicer lad you could not have wished to meet. I see him from time to time. He always stops his car to chat.

Linden had the kind of voice you would expect from a lady justice. Court Clerk Peter said that she sounded like the Queen – and she did.

Susie distinguished herself by arriving on her bicycle and changing into her court clothes in the small foyer in the magistrates' entrance at the rear of the building – on the assumption that as this was a Saturday no-one would see her. What Susie did not appreciate was that CCTV cameras had been installed recently around the courthouse – including the magistrates' entrance. Clyde, the security man, watched from his office enthralled and threatened to show the film at the Bench Election Meeting.

Dr Pat – a retired GP when I knew her – dispensed tablets in the retiring room and on the bench for every ailment suffered by her colleagues. You only had to sniffle and a tablet was produced from the generous caverns of her handbag. At court social functions Dr Pat would bring her own – and extra large – wine glass, strung around her neck by a cord.

Tacho Del was our motoring expert. What he did not know about tachographs was not worth knowing. Tacho Del was a staunch supporter of the Magistrates' Association, representing us at the higher echelons and beyond. He organised visits to police stations to view the alcohol testing machines and to try out the speed cameras. We even went to a weighbridge on the M11 with Tacho Del and great fun it was, too!

The best bench chairman we never had was outstanding in court, but he had some quirks. He would hand over the chair in Court One after coffee to a newly trained chairman – and spend the rest of the morning whispering in your ear, writing cryptic notes and passing these to you. Afterwards your performance was analysed in minute detail – long before the word 'appraisal' was heard within the hallowed walls of Redbridge Magistrates' Court. When a bail application was being made, he would pass a slip of paper with the words 'bail' or 'custody' and we were expected to tick whichever we thought appropriate. There was no retiring to consider our decision and the reasons, which he concocted alone and announced with impeccable precision.

In my early days he and I sat on a liaison committee of which he was chairman. One evening at around 9pm after a meeting of the committee that afternoon, my telephone rang at home. I had called the chairman by his first name on two occasions that day during the committee meeting and he was giving me a rap over the knuckles for doing so. I should call him Mr or Chairman – but never, ever by his first name during a formal meeting. Suitably admonished, I was allowed to put the telephone down. Later, much later, alcohol took control and as Bench Chairman it fell to my lot to invite him to retire, for the fumes were reaching the prosecution and defence lawyers at the front of the court.

Eileen was a divorcee and clearly finding it difficult to cope financially, but she was streetwise and down to earth, and knew every trick that there was in the East End. I enjoyed sitting with her, for Eileen could sort out the wheat from the chaff in seconds. Sadly, Eileen failed to buy a television licence, was summonsed and appeared at a nearby court where she was fined. She left the bench soon afterwards. Had I known before she departed what had been going on, I would have gladly paid for the licence myself – and there were others who felt the same, but in the 80s it was all kept under wraps until it was too late.

Anita, the former air hostess, still looked stunning as she threw her wrap around her shoulders and marched down the corridor to dispense justice with kindness most of the time, but with firmness when it was called for. Speaking with a slight plum in her mouth, Anita would refer to husband Barry as Bwawwy, but we forgave her.

Dennis sucked peppermints, calling the ushers in the black gowns his 'penguins'. We sat together one Friday afternoon when a defendant on some minor charge asked if his case could be heard first – as he had to get to the benefit office in Barking before they closed at 4pm. As he was about to leave the courtroom, he asked if he might borrow a pound for a mini-cab which he would need if he was to get to the office before they closed. I do not carry cash in my pockets, so I asked Dennis if he would lend me a pound. He did so and I still owe him that quid.

Open Days

The very idea of holding an Open Day at the Courthouse was viewed with something approaching horror when it was first mooted in the late 1980s. We were aware that such things were being tried in magistrates' courts in far distant places, but the prospect was most unwelcome amongst the majority of the magistrates at Redbridge. What would happen if hordes of defendants turned up, demanding that those who had sent them off into custody meet them in the foyer for fisticuffs – or worse? Would wives and girl friends of the men languishing in the prisons of the land march upon the open doors of the courthouse, armed to the teeth and ready to do battle with those who had sent their loved ones off to spend a month or two lounging around a prison cell whilst those left behind coped with the kids, the shopping, the washing and all the other tasks that fall to those who are, in effect, single parents for a time?

So concerned were the magistrates that the Clerk to the Justices was dispatched hot foot over the road to Barkingside Police Station. Here he met with the Chief Man who assured him that extra police would be on duty that day and kept on standby at the Police Station. At the slightest hint that trouble was abrewing, the coppers would be sent dashing across Cranbrook Road to quell the fracas – or worse. This came as something of a relief to those magistrates who had seriously considered booking a weekend break in Paris, Rome, West Hartlepool or wherever to provide a good reason to absent themselves from the courthouse on the dreaded day.

Invitations were sent out by the Bench Chairman to the good and the great of the Borough – MPs, Councillors and other worthies (well, at least those amongst them who had not appeared in the dock at some time in their eventful lives – and there were some, but it is best if I refrain from spilling the beans). Lists of local organisations were obtained and their members invited to join us for the Saturday at some time between 10am and 4pm. It was decided that it would be too bold a step into the unknown and the unchartered to invite youth groups or schools to participate, so the court did not do so.

Magistrates were asked to keep the day free. Folk involved with the criminal justice service were invited to set up stalls in the foyer to educate the public about what they got up to. And so we had the local police demonstrating how they caught those who exceeded the speed limit, the probation service explaining what they did with the felons committed by the court into their charge, the crown prosecution service telling folk how they amassed evidence to get defendants convicted – and the duty solicitor service showing how they worked to get those same defendants off the hook.

Meanwhile, the good ladies of the Women's Royal Voluntary Service (WRVS) made lots and lots and lots of cups of tea to sustain the people who stood goggle-eyed at what was being revealed to them for most (but, I suspect not all) had not been inside a courthouse before. The WRVS did a splendid job week in and week out in our courthouse, dispensing tea, coffee, soft drinks, cakes, sandwiches and whatever from the tea bar in one corner of the court foyer. It was good that they could be seen by those who came to the Open Day as a voluntary organisation providing a much valued service – at no cost whatever to the public.

For the rest, we relied on the excitement of being able to wander from Court One to Court Five unimpeded to keep the visitors happy. But perhaps the highlight for most was the chance to go down the stairs and into the custody suite, where they could sit in the cells as the doors were banged tight shut behind them.

We permitted the hoards to wander through the offices – but only when being tightly escorted in case they went where they should not. And places like the magistrates' retiring room were very strictly out of bounds.

All in all the day was voted a success, although the numbers of visitors petered out after lunchtime, so that future events ran from 9.30am to 1pm. We also discovered that nothing was stolen or filched that day, that magistrates, court clerks and staff were not molested and there was a total lack of violence (on the part of the visitors, for one or two magistrates took the opportunity to have a go at the crown prosecutor, raising their voices and waving their arms akimbo as they sought to discover why so many cases went down because the CPS did not have the papers or their witnesses ready at the right time in the right place and on the right day. Which was, after all, a little unfortunate for that was not the purpose of the event).

Over the next decade we held Open Days every two years or so. Having survived the first one, we introduced something new with each event. Mock courts were highly popular, with magistrates, court clerks, ushers and security staff playing their normal parts, but also acting as defendants and members of the public. One court usher became quite adept at playing the 'mother' of a 'defendant' sitting in the public galley and causing a disturbance when her 'son' was sentenced. Crown prosecutors, defence solicitors, probation offices and other court users all came into court on the Saturday Open Days to play their normal roles in the mock courts. As a means of explaining to the public why we did certain things, the mock courts were invaluable – for example, we were able to make clear how we were tackling the increased incidence of shoplifting by drug addicts who were stealing to feed their drug habit by introducing them to the Redbridge Court Drug Initiative.

Not only did we invite the Good and the Great, and adult community groups, but also schools and youth groups. We encouraged families, too, and if part of the fun for many youngsters was seeing the cells and sitting in the prison vans, there was an underlying lesson to be learned.

The spin-off from the Open Days came in the mid-1990s when we decided to do two things. Firstly, to encourage more magistrates to go out from the courthouse to community groups and schools as speakers to explain the role of the magistrates' court in the criminal justice service. Secondly, to encourage those community groups and schools to send parties to visit the court when it was in session.

We formed a panel of magistrates who were prepared to undertake speaking engagements on behalf of the court. A second panel was also enlisted of magistrates who would be prepared to host groups visiting the courthouse. Groups of twelve to fifteen visitors would arrive at the Courthouse at 9.30am. In Room Six they were briefed on the magistracy and how the court worked before being taken into Court One at 10am to observe the court in session. Two magistrates from the host panel did the briefing and accompanied the visitors in Court One, answering questions as they arose. Halfway through the morning the visitors were given tea, coffee and biscuits in Room Six before returning to the court for the rest of the morning. During the break and after the court had risen was the opportunity for questions and discussion.

Each year we circulated schools and community groups, inviting them to contact the court to arrange for hosted visits or speakers. And over the years we built up a large data base for this and for the Open Days. We invited the local press to our Open Days and almost invariably there would be a photograph in the next week's issue of a smiling child peering through the bars of a cell in the custody suite.

I am in no doubt that the Open Days, the speaking engagements and the hosted visits which took place from the early 1990s over the next ten years or so were valuable and valued. The Courthouse at Redbridge stands at one end of Barkingside High Street – a grey and forbidding looking building. For a few years the doors were flung open to folk who – in most cases – would never have entered the building otherwise. As public relations exercises they were invaluable. And never once did we have to call upon the police to come running across Cranbrook Road, batons akimbo, to quell a riot or tame a fracas during an Open Day. In fact, the only disturbances I can recall came from a magistrate or two who felt put out that they were not having the chance to bathe in the limelight of the bench at a mock court. As far as I am aware, the last Open Day at Redbridge Magistrates' Court took place shortly before I retired in 2003.

* * *

Occasionally in my latter days on the bench, when I had retired from full-time employment and had the hours to do so, I made notes of the day's proceedings on my return home. The following are some of those scribbles. They are but a snapshot of life on the bench over a couple of years, but they do – perhaps – demonstrate some of the frustrations and a few of the more satisfying aspects of being a lay justice at the turn of the century.

One of those mornings in 2001

I knew it would be one of those mornings when Court Clerk Peter appeared in the retiring room kitchen with that guilty look on his face that told me he had been at the chocolate biscuits again. With Glen leading and Judith taking up the rear, we entered Court Two for the Early First Hearings. The defendant stood glumly in the dock, but I noticed suppressed smiles on the faces of both prosecutor and defence solicitor – a sign that the morning was about to get better and better before it got any worse.

The defendant pleaded guilty to offences of driving whilst disqualified and no insurance. After the prosecutor outlined the facts, Peter informed the Bench that the defendant had one previous motoring matter on his licence dating back to last year when he was found guilty of an offence of assault and disqualified from driving for three months. Hardly had I opened my mouth to question, when the solicitor for the defence was on his feet offering to explain this unlikely combination of offence and sentence.

The law, said the smiling solicitor, is different in Scotland. No-one disagreed, so he launched into a tale of a day in Dundee when the defendant had a dispute with another driver. The defendant was alleged to have driven his car near the other driver, putting the other driver *"in fear of unlawful violence".* And this very act, said the solicitor, constitutes 'assault' under Scottish law – for which the defendant was fined and disqualified from driving for three months.

The offence of driving whilst disqualified with which we were dealing occurred just over a month later. And, here again, things are different in Scotland. The Scottish solicitor acting for the defendant in Dundee had told the defendant that whilst he had been disqualified for three months, in fact this only meant that he would be unable to drive for one month. The defendant was assured that this is how it works in Scotland – and, not unnaturally, believed the solicitor who, after all, dealt with these cases every day. So that was how he came to be driving in the second month of a three month ban. Not only that, but the defendant produced a letter from his boss at the mini-cab firm where he worked to confirm that this was what he had been told by the defendant when he reported for work.

The defence solicitor, anticipating that the Bench might expect this to be the only mitigation, smiled broadly as he indicated that there was more to come. By this time the prosecutor was also grinning from ear to ear, whilst Court Clerk Peter was moving about in his chair as if he had ants in his pants.

On the night in question the defendant had collected a lady from outside a well-known nightclub in Ilford. As the mini-cab moved along Ilford High Road, the driver realised that the lady was somewhat the worse for alcohol. Nothing unusual about that for driving drunks about is all in a night's work for mini-cab drivers, but the situation deteriorated as the lady began to racially abuse the defendant. There comes a point where enough is enough. Sensing that matters might get out of hand, the driver pulled over to the side of the road and telephoned the police for advice. Drive the lady to the nearest police station, he was told. So off he went.

On the A406, the driver realised that the lady was trying to get out of the car. As he was doing 40mph or so at the time, the driver decided that this might be dangerous so – again – he pulled over to the side of the road and once more telephoned the police. With the car at a standstill, the lady fell out of the now open car door onto the roadway. Sensing that the lady might have hurt herself, the driver got out of his cab to see what was what. On arriving on the other side of the car, the driver was somewhat taken aback when the lady sat up and punched him in the face.

At this point a motor cyclist happened to arrive on the scene. Spotting a lady sitting in the roadway with a man kneeling beside her, the motor cyclist assumed that the lady was being attacked, so he jumped off his bike and fetched the driver a second punch in the face. At that point the police arrived and arrested the lady. Then, as a matter of routine, the police did a check on the driver, only to discover that he had been disqualified from driving just over a month ago in Dundee – so, you've guessed, they arrested the driver too!

And that's not the end! The lady was charged and bailed to appear at Redbridge Court. The driver was bailed to return to the police station. The driver found a solicitor (but not him, the solicitor in court went to great pains to explain) and told him that he had a flight booked to go abroad a few days before he was due to return to the police station. That's fine, said the solicitor, I will let the police know. But he didn't. Nor, for that matter, did the solicitor let the police know that their witness to the lady's offence would be away at the date of her trial – with the result that the charge against her was withdrawn at court for lack of evidence.

The defendant appears in court today, the new solicitor informed us, because he wondered what had happened and went to the police station earlier in the week to find out – and he was bailed to appear with the rest of the Early First Hearings. And, you will have observed, said the solicitor (as the prosecutor smiled in agreement), that the prosecution have withdrawn the charge of failing to answer bail at the police station because the prosecutor believes his story.

My client, the solicitor assured us, is an honest man. Would he have called the police – twice – on the road if he had appreciated that he remained disqualified?

And would be have gone back to the police station on his return from abroad if he was anything but an honest man?

A defendant who is ill-advised by a Scottish solicitor and let down by an English one, deserves the understanding and sympathy of the court, said the third solicitor to get involved with the defendant who now looked glummer than glum.

The Bench took a lenient view, imposing a fine and penalty points. The glum look disappeared from the defendant's face. The prosecutor smiled approvingly. The defence solicitor nodded in agreement. And Peter looked up at the Bench with that expression on his face that indicated that another go at the chocolate biscuits would be much appreciated.

But – at that moment the Usher-who-must-be-obeyed appeared with the floating traffic list (an odd expression but one which was well understood by those within the criminal justice system at the time, so we will leave it there) and two appearances. The first was a tall lad who looked around him with fear from the top of his head to the tips of his toes. Peter put the charge. No English, said the defendant. I managed to elicit the fact that Russian was his only language, so we adjourned for three weeks for an interpreter to be present.

The next defendant entered the courtroom and smiled his way to the front. Peter put the charge. The smile remained, but no words came out. I asked the defendant if he understood what was being said. Still a smile and no words. Do you speak English, I asked. Smile and no words. His friend at the back of the court was smiling too. Do you speak English, I asked the friend? No, came the reply. What language do you speak, I asked the defendant? Still he smiled. I pointed to my mouth. Somalia, said the defendant. Again we adjourned for three weeks for an interpreter.

By this time I wanted more than a chocolate biscuit, so the Bench retired to look in our diaries to ensure that if Linda calls us for an extra sitting in three weeks time, we will all have other things to be doing.

Back in court, the rest of the morning passed comparatively quietly, whilst between times Peter consumed more chocolate biscuits than are good for him.

The final curtain

The Magistrates' Courts' Committee (MCC) at Redbridge was disbanded in 2001 – and the court came under the jurisdiction of the Greater London Magistrates' Courts Authority (GLMCA). Here are my personal reflections as a member of the former MCC, written at that time.

"And now the end is near
And so I face the final curtain"

Standing in the retiring room, reading the gold-painted names on the mahogany boards listing the Chairmen and Justices' Chief Executives of the Redbridge Magistrates' Courts Committee, future generations of justices might wonder just what that Committee achieved until it disappeared into the ether on 31st March 2001.

As a member of that Committee for a number of years prior to the night in late March 2001 when David popped a cork and invited us to toast the years gone by and to wish the new GLMCA well in its task ahead, I believe our MCC achieved a great deal and that the benefits accrued at our Courthouse will stand us in good stead as we move into a new era. Perhaps the time will come when some good soul will feel the urge to write a short history of the Redbridge MCC. The Minutes are there to be read, but for now I wish merely to place on record some brief personal reflections – whilst they are still fresh in my mind, as they say.

Over the years the Redbridge MCC was chaired by five quite different personalities. The gentle, but firm, Joyce was first in the chair, setting the tone and pace. Joyce was followed by John whose voice, it has been said, could be heard at the other end of Barkingside High Street if the wind was in the right direction – and sometimes if it wasn't.

It was in John's time that the writing was on the wall that Redbridge would lose its MCC, but John took up the cudgels through the Outer London Strategic Management Board (SMB), winning many a battle but having to accept – reluctantly – that the war raged on as he retired from the Bench at the magic age of seventy.

Both Joyce and John filled the joint roles of Bench Chairman and Chairman of the MCC, but with John's retirement the tasks were split and Colin took over the chair of the MCC and I was elected Bench Chairman. Colin faced the first visitation by Her Majesty's Inspectorate within weeks of taking over – and survived to tell the tale.

In John and Colin's time in the chair strategic plans were all the rage and when it seemed that the MCC might be overwhelmed with paperwork, the MCC took itself off just before Christmas 1996 to the wilds of Essex to an hotel for the Stifford Conference Weekend.

We learned a lot about ourselves and our task during that weekend, but my enduring memory is of watching Essex Man and Woman at dinner in the hotel's dining room on Saturday Night. Some fifteen of the Redbridge MCC sat, as you do, around an oblong table, with the sexes mixed on each side. Not so Essex Man and Woman elsewhere in the dining room. All the Men sat down one side of their tables and all the Women on the other. The Men talked to the Men, and the Women talked to the Women. It is an image that has haunted me ever since.

It was at Stifford where Colin announced that he would be standing down as MCC Chairman some months before his retirement from the Bench. Soon afterwards magistrate and head teacher Michael moved into the chair.

Clerk to the Justices Michael had guided the MCC throughout its gestation years and became its first Justices' Chief Executive (JCE). Michael had a remarkable ability to write complex papers to set the brains of the MCC whirling – all in longhand to be patiently typed by his Secretary.

MCC Chairman Michael was, in a word, thrown in at the deep end. Hardly had he settled into the chair when a few months later JCE Michael announced his retirement and the MCC set about what was delightfully called a 'restructuring process'. This involved much negotiation with the Lord Chancellor's Department in which MCC Chairman Michael was joined by me as Bench Chairman and David, Chairman of the MCC's Finance Sub-committee.

One day Michael, David and I travelled to the Lord Chancellor's London Office to discuss the progress of the restructuring. Here we were met – not unsurprisingly, I suppose – not by a be-wigged and be-gowned Lord Chancellor, but by two ladies of indeterminate age of the twin-set and pearls variety. We had – as you might expect – a series of questions. Each received a similar response, neither a clear, precise answer nor a blank "no", but something vaguely in between. Should we write a letter to seek clarification on some of the matters, we asked? You could do so, the ladies replied, for it would take at least a month for the letter to arrive at the desk of someone who might be able to answer, a month for the reply to be composed, a month for this to be circulated around the office for comment, and a further month for the letter to be typed, signed and posted. And in the meantime, the ladies smiled, you might have decided to take the bit between your teeth and take whatever action you considered best. Not unnaturally, we came away even more confused than when we set out , but determined to do what the twin-sets and pearls had suggested we might – whatever that was.

The new team emerged at Redbridge, with Deputy Clerk to the Justices Kevin promoted to Justices' Chief Executive and Clerk to the Justices. As it became clear that the clock was ticking for the demise of the Redbridge MCC as we knew it, the intention was signalled that the Committee's overwhelming task was to ensure that Redbridge Magistrates' Court was in prime position when the axe finally fell.

In Michael's time as Chairman – and that of David who assumed the role for the final two years after a most odd election process from which I was excluded and over which it is best that we draw a veil – the Committee poured over the performance statistics that came at it from all sides. We sharpened up on many things as a result – some on the administration side of the infamous 'Chinese Wall' (which Michael Faraway had erected on my appointment as Bench Chairman) for which the Chairman of the MCC was responsible and others in the judicial areas (which was my fiefdom and for which I took all the blame and little of the praise). We wrestled with budgets and should take pride in the fact that we did not sink into the red. The chances of that happening with David around were as likely as the sun rising in the West one morning only to set in the East that evening.

The Committee saw through a relentless programme of bringing the Courthouse up to speed for the 21st Century. We applied for capital funding from the Lord Chancellor's Department for a range of projects to improve the facilities for court users and staff (more of which later if you can bear to wait). In many we were successful; in others we were not. Some projects were funded from the Committee's own resources and others by trimming back where there was a bit of fat – although there was little enough of that to be sure.

Some of the improvements which made Redbridge Courthouse one of the best equipped locally included a refurbished custody suite; interview rooms for advocates and defendants in which the parties were separated by toughened glass – for the protection of both defendants and lawyers from each other; voice enhancement (microphones and loudspeakers, to you Henry) in Courts One and Two; provision for the Family Panel in Court Three; the reception desk suite; the witness and victims' room; refurbishment of the offices; the new counter area; CCTV and the security officers' room; a new kitchen for the retiring room (with a dish-washer to boot!) – just to mention a few.

How Room Six came about was interesting. The open foyer area outside the five courtrooms was vast and included a space between courts two and three which was a sort of no-man's land – one wall of which was shared with a wall in the magistrates' corridor. And so the Court Superintendent and his mate decided that they would partition off that bit of the open area and knock a door through to the magistrates' corridor. This they did – in their spare time – with much dust flying about during the hours of darkness and at weekends, only to settle everywhere and on everything by the time the magistrates and staff arrived in the morning.

Once completed the court had an extra room. We could not call it Court Six, for had we done so this would have thrown our performance statistics into chaos, and so it was referred to as Room Six. We used it for meetings and occasionally as a courtroom – but did not tell anyone. At one stage we thought it might make a very good Family Proceedings Panel Courtroom – nice and cosy and friendly and all that. But this would have meant we called it a courtroom – and that would never do. Instead, we fitted it out with shelving (or, rather, the Court Superintendent and his mate did so) and moved all the legal books from the justices' retiring room – which made a bit of space for the justices to move around, but not enough to hold a dance (which was fortunate, in my opinion, in view of some of the carryings-on which I was beginning to learn about).

Much later someone somewhere decided that the partitioning lovingly erected by the Court Superintendent and his mate was not of the right materials. There was talk of fire risk and such like, and so it was that the partitions lovingly erected were ripped down and a more solid structure put in its place – at considerable expense, I would guess.

And, at the last hour, a long-overdue revamping of the retiring room followed by re-carpeting of the corridors and offices behind the courtrooms with wall-painting in exciting (if psychedelic) colours. I was invited to choose the colour of the carpet and the paint to be used on the walls. I went for a sort of red and a kind of blue – the colours, I was to discover, of West Ham United, a fact of which I was totally unaware as I do not follow football. Someone had to take the rap for all this of course – and I did.

In the short – but vibrant – history of Redbridge MCC many justices and members of staff played their part. Some meetings were of reasonable length; occasionally they went on for an inordinate time; one evening we were still on 'any other business' after an hour-and-a-half, and one of the top guys walked out in a huff. A few cages may have been rattled over the years, but bring together twelve men and women, good and true, and this happens. Overall we did what we set out to do and if we did it our way, so be it.

"Hands off" as threat of closure looms

In the summer of 2001 – a few months after the demise of its MCC – Redbridge Magistrates' Court – now under the aegis of the GLMCA – was one of a number of courts in Greater London that were threatened with imminent closure, the work to be absorbed into courts in other Boroughs.

I was no longer Bench Chairman, but my successor Richard invited me to help with the publicity campaign to fight the closure. We called a series of press conferences, inviting a range of court users to join magistrates in presenting our case for keeping the courthouse open.

First I wrote a briefing paper which we distributed to the local press, MPs, Councillors and a range of opinion-formers. It was an historical snapshot of the developments that had taken place at Redbridge Magistrates' Court in the years leading up to 2001 to bring the court closer to the community it existed to serve. The paper made the point that a locally-based courthouse with magistrates living within the area is able to build and maintain a range of links with the community. Magistrates drawn from a cross-section of that community are able to expand those links to the benefit of both.

I listed some examples of how we had developed those links. Membership of the Redbridge Safer Communities Partnership meant that the Clerk to the Justices chaired the Racist Crime Steering Group and the court had observer status on the Racist Harassment Response Group – both groups linking with the Court Race Dimension Group, which monitored ethnicity and issues of race. The court had been proactive in setting up the Redbridge Domestic Violence Forum, which became an integral part of the Redbridge Safer Communities Partnership with magistrate representation.

The court was involved in a range of initiatives to make the Borough a safer place in which to live and work, including the Town Centre Steering Group which tackled violence in clubs and pubs, leading to the doorman licensing scheme. The group highlighted shoplifting in the main shopping areas. Police and the court co-operated in imposing bail conditions excluding persistent offenders from the town centre, where the installation of CCTV was a major outcome and the court was involved in a group concerned with violence on buses.

Under the Mentally Disordered Offenders' Diversion Scheme representatives of the mental health trust, social services, police, probation and the court monitored the work of the On-call Court-designated Community Psychiatric Nurse. Diversion at the police station where a mental disorder was diagnosed increased and the provision of psychiatric reports and placement under sections of the *Mental Health Act 1983* were fast-tracked to provide magistrates with appropriate sentencing options.

Six years earlier the court identified the growth of drug-related offending as a major concern. A group to progress the Redbridge Court Drug Initiative was formed comprising representatives of probation, police and the community drug and alcohol service. Probation orders with conditions of treatment and a deferred sentence scheme for those at risk of custodial sentences were introduced as sentencing options. Following the launch by government of borough-based Drug Action Teams and Drug Reference Groups, there was magistrate representation on both Redbridge bodies.

With funding from the Government Office for London via the Probation Service, the court was one of the first in London to appoint a full-time Court-based Drug Referral Worker. Protocols were written for sentencing (by magistrates) and treatment programmes (by the community drug and alcohol service, and probation). When the Metropolitan Police Arrest Referral Scheme was launched, the Clerk to the Justices and the Bench Chairman were invited to join the Arrest and Court Drug Referral Steering Group, which monitored and supported drug referral intervention at the police station and the court.

The paper highlighted the Court Open Days, the fact that magistrates spoke at meetings of community groups and that members of the Host Magistrates' Team spent mornings with groups observing courts. With a growing ethnic community, the court had forged links with minority groups, whose members had been encouraged to participate in Open Days and visits to the courthouse, and to put themselves forward as potential magistrates.

Work with secondary schools included Student Days and a Student Drug Awareness Event at the courthouse. Groups from secondary schools took part in hosted visits to the courthouse, geared to the national curriculum and the Duke of Edinburgh's Award Scheme.

The paper went on to refer to liaison with the local press, the positive response of the court to government's initiatives to speed up youth justice and the Court Users' Group which brought together practitioners at local level involved in the day to day working of the criminal justice service – police, crown prosecution service, probation service, duty solicitor scheme, victim and witness support, arrest and court drug referral workers.

Thundering to success with the local press

We launched the campaign to keep the court open with a press conference. Over the following two months we held a series of similar events, each with different participants joining the Bench Chairman to put across a different perspective. All four local newspapers – two paid and two free – gave the campaign their active support, sending reporters and photographers to the courthouse.

The *Ilford Recorder* published a cut-out coupon, encouraging readers to complete this and send the coupon into their offices showing support for the retention of the Borough's courthouse. Nearly a thousand coupons were returned to the *Recorder's* offices.

A senior colleague on the Board of the local mental health NHS trust was astounded at the support we engendered amongst the local community. The courthouse is, after all, he said, a place of punishment – and hundreds of people are springing to your support in keeping it open.

His point was that he could have understood such enthusiasm if it was a hospital or a school – but he was dumbfounded that people could become so keen to retain a building in which folk were fined or send to prison. And I guess he had a point.

Each press conference was preceded with the publication of a news release carrying headlines such as *Redbridge Magistrates' Court threatened with closure; Support pours in to keep Redbridge Magistrates' Court open; £1M of modernisation down the drain if Courthouse closes; Community and schools would lose out if Courthouse closes; Council Leaders weigh-in to support retention of Redbridge Magistrates' Court; Close the Courthouse and witness attendance will nose-dive, say Victim Support;* and *Youth Court Chairman – appalled at effect on delays and elderly vulnerable victims – slams Court closure threat.*

Barely six weeks after the launch of the campaign, Bench Chairman Richard was able to announce to the local press that the powers that be were listening and having second thoughts. A few days earlier, Richard had delivered a substantial dossier of documents – including cuttings of the extensive and supportive press coverage – to the GLMCA making it abundantly clear that any threatened Courthouse closure will be fought vigorously.

The dossier demonstrated that we had the unqualified support of our local MPs and Member of the Greater London Authority, the four leaders of the political groups on Redbridge Council, the North East London Mental Health Trust, Victim Support Redbridge, the Youth Offending Team, the Secretary of the Legal Aid Board in Redbridge, local solicitors, the Citizens' Advice Bureau, Redbridge Trades Union Council, Redbridge Pensioners' Action Association – to name a few. In addition many hundreds of members of the public had expressed concern – extending right across the spectrum and age range within the Borough. We had the welcome support of community groups representing the diverse cultures and backgrounds of Redbridge residents. A hundred youngsters at a local high school signed a petition, concerned that the Borough in which they were growing up stood to lose its Courthouse.

Bench Chairman Richard said: *"I sensed a tacit admission by the GLMCA that the statistics on which their court closure proposals were based are flawed. Part of the dossier from Redbridge Magistrates' Court proved beyond a shadow of doubt that the Barkingside Courthouse is both efficient and effective."*

Richard was confident that the GLMCA would take a deep breath before it issued any further consultation documents.

Speaking to the press, Richard said: *'The Authority is aware of the depth of feeling in Redbridge. We have fired a warning shot across its bows. The GLMCA will be well advised to heed that warning and continue listening to those who wish to see the preservation of local justice by local people."*

Two months later we were able to announce that the Borough's Courthouse at Barkingside was no longer under threat of imminent closure. Expressing his thanks for the support the court had received, Bench Chairman Richard told the local media: *"It is good news for Redbridge that the Borough will retain its own magistrates' court where local justice will continue to be dispensed by local people. However, the strategy document is a blow to other Boroughs in London who will lose their courthouses.*

"'There will now be a period of statutory consultation with Benches in courthouses scheduled to close. When that is completed, we will know for certain which courthouses local to Redbridge will close. At that time we expect work from those Boroughs to be transferred to Redbridge. If and when that happens, Redbridge Magistrates' Court will work to ensure that the contacts we have made with the local community in this Borough are replicated throughout the new area we will serve."

And that was that. The Barkingside Courthouse remains open and operational to this day.

Whether or not it is as efficient and as effective as it was at the time the GLMCA decided to give us a reprieve is for others to comment upon and not me. My lips are sealed and even if you were to twist my arms behind my back, stamp upon my bare toes and carve the insignia of West Ham United on my chest with a blunt penknife, I will say not a word.

Christmas Eve 2001

There is a hint of rain here in Aldborough Hatch, low clouds with sullen sky; a Christmas Day to remain in the warm.

We listed two courts, rather than five, to sit during the morning of Christmas Eve so that staff and magistrates could do their last minute shopping if they had the will to do so – and many had. The lists were kept purposefully short, with necessary remands in Court One and a short not guilty traffic trial in Court Two. The Courthouse would close around noon, enabling staff who were working to have a half-day. Six justices were on rota, all volunteers. Traditionally, the Ushers wear their dangly Christmas earrings and we try to bring a little of the spirit of the season into our doings, with Yvonne's mince pies replacing the chocolate biscuits so beloved of Peter and other court clerks..

I was chairing Court One and went down to the listings office just before nine to find the Listings Officer busily typing the overnights. There are eleven, she smiled, including a nine-hander alleged robbery. There was a hint of firearms. I walked upstairs with the printed lists and a heavy heart, for it was Christmas. The overnights would follow.

The Clerk to the Justices came off the telephone from Ilford Police. He had agreed security. Twenty police officers, including some from the TSG who would be armed, would be in and around the Courthouse. The Clerk had insisted – with my agreement – that only a necessary presence would be in the courtroom. Two uniformed officers would sit at the back of the court, with the officers in the case in plain clothes. Two uniformed officers would be in the magistrates' corridor outside Court One. A number would be in the foyer and the rest outside the building.

At ten only one prosecutor had arrived. No one knew where the Crown Prosecutor for Court One was, nor if he or she was on their way. We agreed to move most of the cases into Court Two, which started on time and worked steadily through the lists. The Pre-sentence Reports we had read for Court One were transferred. That court sat until gone 1pm.

The nine prisoners arrived in two batches from Ilford Police Station by 11am. All had solicitors or barristers, some of whom had been with them at the police station during interviews whilst others had not. Police were seemingly everywhere. The prosecutor for Court One arrived about 10.30, expecting a short trial. He had no idea what he had walked into and had he done so, might well have gone AWOL, disappearing in a cloud of dust amongst the Christmas lights and trees as the Great Day approached.

Messages arrived from time to time in the retiring room. The advocates wished to speak with their clients, but there was trouble in the cells. The prosecutor needed time to read the files. The Bench was warned that at least one defendant had made it known he would be jumping the dock and others had indicated that they would not be taking this quietly. Relatives and friends were arriving in the foyer, making their views known that they had Christmas shopping to complete and turkeys to pop into ovens.

We decided to take the defendants in two groups – one of four and one of five – for the dock was not big enough for nine together with custody staff. The ages ranged from 17 to 26, with four youths who would sit in the well of the court.

Just after 11.30am, the first four came up. The public gallery was packed. The Crown Prosecutor outlined the facts. The incident was alleged to have taken place mid-afternoon on Friday 21st, when all nine were said to have entered an upmarket shoe and trainer shop at Gants Hill. The shop owner and one assistant were present. The nine were alleged to have walked around the shop, shouting and swearing, taking expensive trainers from the shelves, jumping over the counter, looking behind a curtain where the £200 plus value trainers were kept. The owner locked the shop door. The owner and assistant were said to have been punched and kicked to the ground. The owner, fearing for his life, opened the shop door. More shouting and aggression were alleged. The nine were said to have run from the shop with two pairs of expensive trainers and the mobiles of the owner and his assistant.

Two cars were parked nearby. Police caught up with them in a nearby mews. An imitation firearm was alleged to have been found in one car. Both cars were said to have been stolen in the past few days, one at gunpoint. All were charged with robbery and with having a firearm with intent. Two were also charged with a robbery at a bookmaker's shop in North London earlier this month. There was said to be CCTV evidence.

All four made bail applications. The advocate for the defendant who was said to have indicated he would jump made much of the fact that there was a heavy police presence and that his client would not jump. His client then began shouting. Friends in the gallery joined in. The CPS asked for remand in custody for three who had previous convictions for similar offences, but not for one who had no previous. His advocate assumed we would agree. I made the point that the Bench made the decision. That seemed to surprise him. We retired. We returned and remanded all four into custody to appear at Snaresbrook on 3rd January. We had substantial grounds for believing that all four would not return to court if given bail for if found guilty of the offences they would receive long custodial sentences, they might commit further offences and would interfere with witnesses. Uproar broke loose in the dock and the public gallery. The mother of the defendant who had expected bail screamed. Relatives started to shout abuse. Defendants tried to jump the dock. The Bench retired. Calm was restored. Mayhem broke loose in the foyer.

The five remaining defendants came up at about 12.30. Two adults in the dock; three youths in the well of the court. One youth was chewing a long strand of liquorice. I decided to ignore this. The other two youths turned their backs on the Bench and were mouthing to their friends. The CPS again outlined the case afresh. We heard two bail applications.

There were constant murmurings from the gallery. One father in particular was loud and aggressive. I issued warnings. At some point, things became very heated. My impression on reflection was that this came mainly from the public gallery, but then the two defendants in the dock joined in. People stood up. I gave a final warning. The shouting continued. I ordered that the defendants be taken downstairs. Uproar broke loose. The Bench retired. It took a full five minutes for the custody staff and the Police to get the defendants downstairs and the court cleared. The father of one youth was, I understand, arrested by police. Another may also have been arrested.

Back in court the advocates for the five stated that they were not making an application for their clients to return to court and no further bail applications would be made. We remanded into custody in absence. One solicitor then launched into a statement to the effect that the police presence was intimidating to defendants, relatives and friends, and to the Bench, indicating that this had had an effect on the Bench, driving us to remand into custody. I stated that whilst the defendants, relatives and friends may well have felt intimidated, the Bench was not. We had made our decisions on the facts before us and were not – and never would be – intimidated by anyone.

The two police officers in the magistrates' corridor were chatty between the times we were in court. One had spent the past two days on a ship off the Isle of Wight suspected of carrying terrorist gear. He was lucky to be home for Christmas. Other officers from Ilford were going there for three days from Christmas Day. One of the officers had never been behind the scenes at a court before. I asked him for his impression of the morning. Well, he said, I had always imagined that magistrates were very tall, unworldly and stuffy, but you are very ordinary people. That made me feel a bit better.

Not a very Christmassy story. Nine young men, six of whom I was told afterwards had appeared regularly in our Youth Courts over the years, now face a grim future. Two men in a shoe shop – of all places – who must have been frightened beyond belief if the allegations are true. And nine families and countless friends whose Christmas was spent in sadness and, no doubt, recrimination – wondering where it had all gone so badly wrong. And not just at Christmas but over days, months, perhaps years in the past and ahead.

Boxing Day 2001

I was on duty at court this morning and had three overnight defendants. One was a young man I have known in the past for shoplifting and other drug-related offences. He is currently on a Drug Treatment and Testing Order from the Crown Court. Today he was up for domestic violence. He went to his former girl friend's home on Christmas Day by invitation to take his four-year-old son a present, but it all went badly wrong and police were called. There was no physical violence, just words. I bailed him with conditions which will keep him away from his former girl friend for a few days. Very sad.

Twas on a Saturday morning

Two characters were brought up from the cells on this Saturday morning – one a lady of some forty summers who failed to keep her probation appointments and the other a lad who failed to appear at court last September.

The first was well-known to me as one of our habitual drug-related offenders – a drug addict who tries to kick the habit. Her excuse was that she has moved to a Borough not far from here and lost track of time. I sympathise with her. Anyone who moves to that Borough would be in danger of losing track not only of time, but of everything they held dear. I gave her bail with a condition that she sleeps in her house every night. No dashing off to the South of France or the

Bahamas for her, poor soul. Come back next Thursday at 9.30, I called as she trotted off downstairs to have a cup of tea with custody staff in the cells before facing the harsh winds of Barkingside.

The next defendant was a young and sad looking fellow, who brightened up when he saw me sitting there. He was alleged to have stolen a car radio fascia in Tesco's car park at Goodmayes on the 7th of September last. Bailed by the police to appear at this courthouse on the 9th of September, he failed to do so. A warrant without bail was issued by the justices sitting that day and now he had his comeuppance. And facing an additional charge of failing to answer his bail, he pleaded guilty to both counts.

The duty solicitor told me her name, but uncertain if I had written it down correctly, the Court Clerk – who is a bright young man – said that I should pronounce it as Grand Prix without the Grand. Her client was sorry that he had not attended court back in September. At that time he was a drug addict and was to fly out to Bangladesh to a rehabilitation unit on the day he was due in court. Faced with the choice, he opted for the flight.

Returning before Christmas, his parents refused to have him back and he has been homeless, living in night shelters around the East End of London – but not, interestingly, the Redbridge Night Shelter, largely because he lives in Manor Park. He was of previous good character and decided yesterday to give himself up to the police as he guessed they might catch up with him one day.

Both charges were put and an anxious *"Guilty"* was entered. Sitting alone as I was, I could not deal with the sentencing and the question of bail had to be considered.

The Crown Prosecutor did not object to bail – but then she wouldn't would she? A charming, tall and erudite young lady, this Prosecutor appears rarely in our courts these days to prosecute, having been elevated to the Crown Court. But she knows me of old and as I was to chair Court One the following Monday, I bailed the young man to return that morning. He claimed he was drug free and wants to get on with his life.

Where did you sleep last night, I asked. In the police station, he replied! Where did you sleep the night before, I enquired. At the Newham Night Shelter. Which was more comfortable, I asked? The police station, he smiled. Resisting the temptation to invite him to the Redbridge Night Shelter, where comfort reigns supreme, I bailed him to Monday morning.

Make sure you are here by 9.30, I called, for I will be here. That seemed to encourage him. I'll be back, he said, smiling again. Have you any money for your bus fare, I asked.

The duty solicitor (but pronounced Grand Prix without the Grand) spoke with the defendant. He has his benefit paid into his bank account, she trilled, and he can go and draw some cash in the High Street. Satisfied on this score, I sent him on his way rejoicing.

Out in the High Street myself, the rain lashed, driven by a harsh and unrelenting wind. The defendant was nowhere in sight. Probably in the warmth of the bank, I would guess.

Saturday 26th January 2002

Letter to the GUARDIAN

Yesterday I sent a short, crisp letter to THE GUARDIAN by e.mail. It read as follows:

"Following Metropolitan Police Commissioner Sir John Stevens' comments on the Criminal Justice System, no-one has pointed out to him that a major part of the solution is in the hands of the police and the crown prosecution service (CPS).

"Magistrates despair at the constant need for adjournments because the police have not provided the CPS with the evidence to enable trials to proceed. Witnesses are not warned to attend and do not appear on the day of trial. Advance information and video evidence takes weeks to reach defence lawyers. Committal bundles for the crown court are not ready within agreed timescales. Memoranda from the CPS to the police are ignored. Any magistrate will tell you these are not isolated incidents but the daily norm."

Sadly, the letter did not appear in the morning's edition (but was published the following day). Promptly at 10am I walked into Court Five at Redbridge Magistrates' Court, preceded by my colleague Harmander, looking swish in his black turban, and followed by Alan in his best suit. Peter was our learned clerk and Tracey the Usher. It has to be said that we were all sharp as a cat's whiskers for a Monday morning, with two trials set down to take the full day.

The first mishap occurred quickly. Having bowed as is the done thing, Harmander and I were about to sit down when we realised that Alan was bereft of anywhere to sit. Pointing this out to our learned clerk, young Peter suggested we might retire whilst the seating arrangements were sorted. No, no, said I, insisting on waiting whilst Peter and Tracey extricated a chair from below us and hoisted it onto the bench.

Before entering the courtroom, Peter had advised us that Ms E was prosecuting for the Crown, indicating that the said Ms E was a bit of alright – as we say in these parts. And she was, indeed. Mr O, the first defendant, was up for careless driving, failing to report an accident and failing to stop – and Mr O was in a right panic. There were five prosecution witnesses without the courtroom and he had brought two witnesses to stand up for him, too, but he was missing his barrister, the redoubtable Ms F. I have been here since 9.15am, said Mr O, and have spoken to my solicitors who know not wither Ms F hath flown. Go and ring your solicitors again, I advised Mr O, speaking in my kindliest tones, for here was a man who had paid for his own representation and that representation was nowhere to be seen.

Out went Mr O and I suggested to Ms E, the prosecutor, that we might proceed with our second trail meanwhile. No, no, said Ms E. I came here to prosecute Mr O and have no file or instructions for Mr A, who had entered the court with a friend and stood looking lost and forlorn. Fortunately our learned clerk had a file on Mr A, which appeared to provide Mr A with some relief. The clerk explained that French and not English was Mr A's first language and he had brought his friend to help him. Why was an interpreter not ordered, I cried? Mr A has some English, said the clerk and Mr A and his friend nodded in agreement. But I do not have a file, said Ms E. Please go forth and find one, said I, and off went the bench for the first of many coffees and biscuits (both chocolate and fig rolls).

After reading the newspapers, studying the notice board, watching the shoppers entering and leaving Sainsbury's, we trooped back into the courtroom at about 10.30am. There was news of Mr O's barrister. She was at Reigate and Redhill – not Redbridge – Magistrates' Court, but would be here soonest. Calling the seven witnesses into the court, I apologised for what had happened and sent them off to discover the delights of Barkingside High Street until 11.30 when we would reassemble to consider our position. As two of them came from St Albans, I guessed they would enjoy exploring our High Street, but noted that they looked aghast at the very prospect.

Any news of the file for Mr A, I asked Ms E? No, but we are working on it, she smiled. More coffee and then a triumphant clerk appeared to tell us that the file had indeed been found, but the one prosecution witness, Police Constable E, was nowhere to be seen. But, said young Peter, Ms E is – again – working on it.

At 11.25 or so we walked – somewhat sluggishly, I felt – down the corridor to Court Five. Ms E had the file in her slim hands and the Police Liaison Officer (PLO) was at her side. I have the file, observed Ms E, but will have to apply for an adjournment as PC E is not here. Why not, I asked? It appeared that the case was first listed on 12th February and the defendant had appeared on that day to say that he was not guilty of having no insurance and a range of other motoring offences as he was pushing the car, which belonged to a lady and not to him, and he was not driving it.

To set the trial date the court had canvassed the crown for suitable days when the witnesses would be available. The crown produced a list – and we had it on the court file which I could see was before the learned clerk – of dates when PC E would be on leave, on a training course, having his teeth set, taking his mother-in-law to lunch, attending to the police station garden or be otherwise engaged on duties which would not permit him to come to our courthouse. With these dates in mind, the court fixed the trial for today.

Ms S had spoken to PC E on his mobile this morning, but the line was poor for he appeared to be standing beside a jumbo jet which was about to take off or land. Ms S could, therefore, not help us as to why PC E was not with us today. When was he warned of the date of trial, I asked? Last Thursday, said the PLO. How was he warned, I asked? He was on leave so the criminal justice unit left a message on his mobile. Did he respond, I asked? I do not know, said the PLO.

Not unnaturally, Mr A was miffed. He had been to court twice. PC E was somewhere noisy amongst aircraft. Mr A wanted the thing to go ahead today, for after all he had not been driving the car but helping a lady in distress.

In retirement the bench decided that the crown had not performed its duties with all due diligence and that the matter should, therefore, proceed in the absence of the witness. Ms E said she would present no evidence. We dismissed the case and the defendant walked from the court without a blemish on his character. There was no victim. And this would be another one for the Met's Chief Man to think about.

Just after 11.30am, in trooped Mr O, still barrister-less. Ms F, we were assured, is on her way, but had turned off her mobile. We will reassemble in an hour, we said – and off we went for more coffee and fewer chocolate biscuits, for

Peter, the learned clerk, had eaten them all. Hardly had the coffee started to slip down our parched throats when Molly, the reception usher, appeared to tell us the glad news that Ms F was but ten minutes away as she spoke.

Back in court at 12.15pm, Ms F explained that she had trooped all the way down South to Reigate and Redhill Magistrates' Court, rather than coming North to Redbridge, and had been travelling since 8am. But we were now ready to proceed and off we went. Inevitably, the case went part-heard at 5.15pm and we reassemble on Monday 22nd April at 2pm to conclude, so I will say no more on the matter.

But two further incidents that day are worthy of reporting. At about 1.30pm, I am standing in the queue at Sainsbury's to purchase my sandwich, a box of plums (which took my eye) and my week's supply of cigarettes, when I spot Ms E, the crown prosecutor, slip ahead of me into the queue. I let the matter pass, for I am a man who seeks a quiet life and I am not going to have a rumble with a crown prosecutor who queue jumps. As Ms E leaves, I smile at her and wish her a good lunch. She looks at me as if I might be about to snatch her sandwich and departs in a hurry, with a furtive glance or two as she glides through the sliding doors.

When the court adjourned at 5.15pm, the usher followed me out of court with a handwritten note from Ms E. It read: *"Dear Sir, My apologies for lunchtime – I did not recognise you in the queue. I hope you did not think me rude – otherwise I would have stopped to chat. I am so sorry."*

Feeling somewhat tired from the day's exertions, I telephoned for Radio Cars – the excellent mini-cab company in the centre of Ilford that I have used since time began. After a few minutes waiting in the retiring room, I walked across the road to the agreed pick up point outside Sainsbury's. Here I was approached by three schoolgirls in uniform who could have been thirteen at the most. Munching chips from rather large bags, one girl asked me for a cigarette. I refused, politely. All three then pressed me for cigarettes. I said no again. Have you got any, they asked? Enough for this evening, I lied. They walked on, but first offering me a chip, which I refused – again, politely.

Shortly afterwards, the three girls returned, but this time with a man in his twenties. Again they asked for cigarettes. At this point Ms E, the crown prosecutor, joined me having spotted what was happening from across the road as she walked towards Barkingside Station. Ms E made short shrift of the girls and the man, and off they trotted. Explaining that I was waiting for a minicab, Ms E told me that I should not wait about on street corners for *"this is not a very nice area".* Ms E again apologised for lunchtime, commenting that the members of the bench look quite different in the courtroom from the way they appear when queuing in Sainsbury's. We chatted about the dangers of old folk like me waiting about on corners for mini-cabs, as Ms E warned me that one of the girls might have stabbed me. At that point the cab arrived and I was whisked home, whilst Ms E walked under her brolly to the Central Line and her abode I know not where.

Arriving home, I presented Yvonne with the remainder of the box of plums I had purchased in Sainsbury's and – joy of joys – a present from Peter Scudder, our Learned Clerk. Peter had attached a note stating that on Saturday last he was in Woolworth's buying an Action Man Easter Egg for his son when he spotted a Will (Pop Idol) Young Easter Egg and immediately thought of Yvonne – so he bought it for her. Now wasn't that kind and thoughtful? Knowing that Yvonne preferred runner-up Gareth Gates, he was pleased that Gareth's picture appeared on the box, too. It was doubly kind of Peter, for following his clear infatuation that morning with Ms E, the crown prosecutor, he might well have presented the egg to her, but no – he stood by his intention of sending it home for Yvonne. He is a nice man, indeed.

Monday 11th March 2002

Not so!

My letter referred to above was published in THE GUARDIAN on Tuesday. Later in the week I bumped into Mike Gapes, MP for Ilford South.

"Saw your letter in THE GUARDIAN last Tuesday – what you called for is just what David Blunkett is trying to achieve," he said. I guess that's scored me a brownie point with the Home Office, which must be a first for me.

On Thursday I received the following e.mail message from a gentleman called Andrew:

"I am a serving police officer in Manchester," he wrote, *"currently attached to an Administration of Justice Unit that liaises directly with the CPS, providing them with the evidence, videos, witnesses and committal bundles that you refer to in your letter to today's 'Guardian'.*

"I have never previously responded to or written such a letter, but in this case I would like to offer you a different perspective.

"A defendant, say, is charged with an offence on the 10th March and bailed to appear at court on the 13th March. A simple 'expedited file' is all that can be sent in the time. He pleads not guilty, and the case is adjourned to the 10th April so that a full file can be prepared. On the afternoon of the 9th of April, whilst preparing work for the following days court, the CPS realise that they've failed to notify the police that further information was required. They request this information. The officer in the case is on a rest day. The next day a prosecutor (without a word of a lie) is able to tell the court that despite a CPS request for a full file the police have not sent anything. A member of the bench writes in disgust to the press. Apart from the last bit, I have witnessed just such a scenario.

"Whilst I am under no illusions as to the police's ability to cock things up with the best of them, we are often run a very close second by the CPS. In Manchester (at least), CPS admin. is in a permanent state of chaos. They have real problems with the retention and recruitment of clerical staff; their computer systems are incompatible with ours, and even more antiquated; their (hard-pressed) lawyers are based on the 5th floor of an office block, whilst all their clerical support is on the 8th. Therefore, files, upgrade requests, videos (and occasionally even staff!) are getting lost. I wouldn't suggest that you're being deliberately lied to in court. But the lawyer who addresses you will usually be repeating what they've been told by their support staff. And will at least be a paid advocate, with the opportunity to put the CPS case. An opportunity not afforded to the police."

In reply I told Andrew that I took his point about the CPS. In fact, I referred to both the CPS and the Police in the full text of my short letter which, sadly, was shortened even further by THE GUARDIAN – and in the process the point was lost.

(I sent him the full text, commenting that the first sentence had been truncated in publication.)

I then sent him a version of what had happened in court on Monday 11th March – which you will have read already, unless you are skimming through this book, stopping here, there and everywhere (in which case you may wish to skip back to get the full flavour of what is going on here. And yet you may prefer not to do so. The choice is yours).

I went on to tell Andrew that I had received a response to my letter from a magistrate in Inner London who told me that she was listed for an all day trial with five witnesses. None arrived and when she asked the CPS to find out when they were warned, the answer came back that letters had been sent the previous day – by second class post.

Thursday 14th March 2002

Both sides

Occasionally, very occasionally do we have a glimpse of both sides of a piece of criminal activity. Yesterday was such an occasion.

Chairing the Early First Hearing Court with my colleague Glen sitting beside me and David as the Court Clerk, we went through the usual list of drink drive, shoplifting and possession of drugs. Run-of-the-mill, but every case a personal tragedy somewhere along the line.

Late morning Miss C stepped into the dock, pleading guilty to a charge of assault occasioning actual bodily harm, an either-way offence which is triable in a magistrates' court or at the crown court. With a guilty plea, the bench had to decide whether or not the case should remain at the magistrates' court for sentence or go to the crown court if, from the facts of the case, it was so serious that our powers of six months' custody were insufficient.

The prosecutor told us that on Saturday 23rd February a private party was held after closing time at 11.30pm in a restaurant in the leafy lanes of Woodford. It was the manager's birthday and amongst the fifty guests were 18-year-old Miss C and her boyfriend, invited by the boyfriend's sister who worked behind the bar. Boyfriend sat at the back of the court and appeared to be about the same age as Miss C.

At around 1.30am it is alleged that an argument boiled up in which another guest, Miss B, was involved. It appeared to be about some issue in which Miss C's boyfriend had a part.

The crown's case was that Miss C had a wine glass in her hand and smashed it into Miss B's forehead. The attack, said the crown, was unprovoked. Miss B went to the ladies' room to mop up the blood before travelling to Whipps Cross Hospital. Miss C and her boyfriend left the party. Miss B required five stitches to her forehead, whilst two smaller cuts were glued. In addition there were slithers of glass embedded in her cheeks.

Subsequent identification of Miss C by party guests led to the arrest of Miss C on 11th March. Interviewed by police on tape, Miss C at first denied that she had assaulted Miss B. Later Miss C insisted she had been taunted and threatened by Miss B.

Prior to Miss C's barrister addressing the court, I pointed out to her barrister that the Bench would have to be mindful of the Court of Appeal Guidelines on Mode of Trial for offences of violence. Two criteria for sending such an offence to the crown court are that a weapon was used that was likely to cause serious injury and that serious injury had resulted from the assault.

Miss C's barrister put up a spirited case for keeping the matter at the magistrates' court. Miss B had, indeed, attended at Whipps Cross, but after a five hour wait for attention, departed for her home and, later on Sunday morning went to the Homerton Hospital where her wounds received attention. Furthermore, a wine glass is a household item and never, ever could it be described as a weapon. The crown had not produced medical evidence to back up their claim that the wounds were serious – merely a statement from the victim that five stitches and a bit of glue were needed. Hardly a serious injury in anyone's book.

The Bench invited the Clerk to offer legal advice prior to retiring. You have the Court of Appeal Guidelines before you, said David, and he was sure that we would reach the right judicial decision based on the criteria and the evidence we had heard. Previous convictions were before the Bench, including two convictions in a youth court for matters of violence and one at a Crown Court for common assault when a conditional discharge (CD) was imposed. The latter was interesting, for common assault is dealt with normally in the magistrates' courts; perhaps there was plea bargaining down to a guilty for a lesser charge when the case reached the crown court. No matter, but Miss C accepted that she is in breach of the CD in any case.

We retired. We returned. We sent Miss C to the crown court for sentence. With the agreement of my colleague, I stated our reasons for so doing. In our considered opinion a weapon – namely a wine glass – had been used and the fact that a wine glass is not a weapon in the normal sense was immaterial in our view, for it had been used as such in this case. It was also our view that a wine glass used as a weapon was likely to cause serious injury and that serious injury had resulted from the assault.

Sitting at the back of the courtroom throughout the proceedings, immediately behind Miss C's boyfriend, were three West Indians – two ladies and a man. They had remained composed and silent throughout. When Miss C left the dock, they stood and smiled, walking with dignity from the courtroom.

The prosecutor indicated that it would be helpful for the Bench to retire as she wished to speak to the family of the victim sitting at the back of the court. In particular, the prosecutor wished to arrange for a victim statement to be prepared and available for the crown court judge who would sentence.

I left the courthouse around 1pm, calling at Sainsbury's thence to the Woolwich for some cash, before moving to catch a bus to Goodmayes Hospital for yet another meeting. Standing in the bus shelter, I was joined after a few minutes by two of the West Indians – a man and a woman – who had been at the back of the courtroom. Guessing that they were relatives or friends of the victim, and with the case now on its way to the crown court, and in the knowledge that I would have no further part to play in the sentencing of Miss C, I felt able to greet the pair with a *"Good afternoon".*

The woman, in her late fifties I would guess, took my hand to shake it. *"Thank you for what you did this morning,"* she smiled. Her granddaughter was the victim, Miss B. The man was her son and Miss B's father. The other lady in court was Miss B's sister, who had now gone to her home elsewhere in Redbridge. The lady told me that Miss B was too distraught to attend court today.

"You may be interested to know," said the lady, *"that I saw the wounds on my granddaughter's face. The cuts to the forehead had exposed the bones. Her face was pitted with glass fragments."* Miss B went to Whipps Cross where immediate attention was given to the wounds by a nurse. The A & E was packed that night and Miss B left at about 7am to go home before travelling to Homerton Hospital where the stitches and glue were applied. *"The effect on my granddaughter,"* said the lady, *"has been devastating."*

At that point the bus arrived and we all boarded. Separated by seats and passengers, we could only smile. Perhaps, for once, the family of a victim felt that there is some justice around.

Saturday 16th March 2002

Second time in the ladies' toilet

The first half-hour in the Courthouse today was relatively quiet. Then it all began to happen. Marie roared from the lady justices' toilet to inform me that someone had thrown a heavy object through the window and shattered glass was everywhere.

My entry to the ladies' toilet this morning was the second I have made in my twenty-two years on the Bench. On each occasion I have been accompanied by a lady justice. The first was during my time as Bench Chairman some five years ago when a deputation of lady justices advised me that repairs to the door had not been carried out in spite of repeated requests that this should be accomplished. At least, I think it was repairs to a door. Certainly it was repairs to something or other.

The Clerk to the Justices was alerted – as he should be when a heavy object is thrown through the window of the lady justices' toilet. Clyde of Security attended – and went in search of the implement used for this dastardly crime. If it was a brick, he advised, it will be on the ground outside. If it was a piece is metal it would be in the toilet. No metal object was found, so we assume it was a brick, although Clyde did not return to confirm or otherwise. Roy of Security arrived to lock the door and post a notice forbidding entry.

Ladies who had need of the facility were sent to the foyer or the office downstairs. Aquida declined to go – adding that she only wanted to check her lipstick. I told her it was fine, although whether or not this was so I do not know, for I had left my glasses in the retiring room. But Aquida seemed happy with the reassurance. The window was repaired by 11.30am and ladies were able to check their lipstick thereafter uninterrupted.

Court Clerk Peter appeared clutching files from Saturday's court. Should he call the Community Psychiatric Nurse (CPN), he asked after outlining the history of the defendant who had mental health problems and had been remanded into custody over the weekend as there was nothing else that could be done on a Saturday morning. Yes, yes, I said when I had looked at the file. And he did, but Paddy was on annual leave and the lady at the 24/7 (which is not an all night shop, but a team which looks after mental health patients in the community for twenty-four hours a day, seven days a week) said she was too busy to come to court. I sent a brief – but curt – message via Peter. Ms B arrived from 24/7 and did a great job for us.

Then Stephen, our Court Clerk for the morning, hit me between the eyes metaphorically speaking with his request that I might act as a referee as he is now a Sunday School teacher. Had Stephen asked me to sign a shot gun licence or to act as a referee for an appointment as public hangman, I could have understood his request – for he often suggested to Benches that they should "bang 'em up" or "pot" them. But no. He wants to be a Sunday School teacher. Father of three girls, he now finds himself on Sundays teaching some twenty-two kiddies of five to eight-years. He told them the story of that fellow who climbed the tree yesterday – and sang them a song about it, too. Of course, I agreed to help the lad. What else could I do? Although in his defence he did say as a starter: *"You do go to church, don't you, Mr Jeffries?"*

Prior to court, in my role as stand-in for Shirley, Deputy Chairman and Her-in-Charge-on-Mondays, I read the list to an expectant throng of justices who all knew which courts they were in for they had dutifully telephoned the answerphone over the weekend to check. I also told them about the new answerphone number – although I realised that they knew it already or how else would they have telephoned over the weekend? But Shirley said I was to do so and do so I did. I told them about the new justices who had recently joined the Bench and Barrie, Head of Classics at a local school, went into a great diatribe about one of them who has a strange profession. No-one had heard of whatever it was but Barrie checked the word in the internet and explained it to us. As it would appear to have something to do with blood, I did not listen. I told them about stand-downs being available nationwide, and to watch out for late pre-sentence reports and late arriving custody vans. I have to say that the Monday lot stood there with their mouths agog whilst all this was going on. There was complete silence when I stopped, until Harmander (him with the turban) advised us that he is running in his 17th London Marathon, this time dressed as Bob the Builder, and he was seeking sponsors. That sent them all scuttling for coffee.

The morning passed peacefully. We did two Drug Treatment and Testing Order Reviews. The twenty-seven-year-old has a two-month-old baby girl, I discovered. Court Clerk Stephen said I almost had him (Stephen that is) in tears when I told the young man how lucky he was and that he owed it to his daughter to get off drugs. Yes, yes, the young man cried, I will, I will, Then the forty-two-year-old came in for his review and, lo, he has a seven-year-old daughter and, again, Stephen was close to wailing as I chatted away to this good fellow about his daughter. It was here when one of my magistrate colleagues lost her kindliness, for I told the forty-two-year-old that he had his life before him, unlike me who at sixty-nine realises that the clock is ticking away. Not on your life, said my colleague, I am not far behind you and no clock is ticking for me. And I believe her!

Later, much later, around 2pm I happened to pop down to Court Five to let the Clerk know that his Bench would be a few minutes late as they needed to snatch a sandwich after rising late from their morning sitting. The Clerk was none other than that Peter, who grabbed me and had me sitting on the Bench to hear two applications for Search Warrants before I could catch my breath. Have you had your lunch, I asked Peter? Yes, Sir, he quailed. More than I have, I said, trying to look pale and wan. But to no avail. The Usher swore the Officer in and we were away.

Monday 25th March 2002

Another Saturday

I had a good morning at court. Arriving at 9.45am, Roy of Security told me that the team on the prison van had all reported in sick. A new van was travelling from Charlton and the prisoners – two ladies – would be with us at around 11.30am. Standing in the foyer, Ms S, the CPS Prosecutor, told me she would dash home to Barking to put another load of washing in the machine. The duty solicitor said she would do some shopping in sunny Barkingside. Court Clerk Stephen rang home and received instructions to visit Sainsbury's. I trotted off to the garden centre round the corner, leaving my mobile number with Roy. At about 10.30am, Roy rang – just as I was in the midst of the rosemary bushes – to tell me that the prisoners had arrived and would I hop back up the road sharpish.

In the courtroom, the custodial man from downstairs explained that he was annoyed with the security company he worked for so he rang Ilford Police Station where he spoke to a nice duty sergeant who readily agreed that Ilford Police could shovel the prisoners up the road to Barkingside in their own police transport. That was kind. All was done and dusted by 11.15am.

Saturday 13th April 2002

A great evening

I went along to the Course for Alcohol Impaired Drivers (CAIDs) run by the Probation Service on Wednesday evening – filled with trepidation as to whom the second magistrate would be. Could it be Him, I asked myself? No, surely not. Even Court Clerk David would not do that to me! Or Mrs Her? Or the other Mrs Her? None of those, I trust, are on the list. Could it be the other Him, that well-known scourge of the courts?

Retired Probation Officer Malcolm greeted me. It was his final course. From now on the CAIDs jumps from eight to fourteen weeks in length. As Malcolm commented, they will have to speak more slowly in future to make it fill fourteen weeks. And he is not being allowed to carry on. The new breed of probation officer is required. Sad, really, for he runs the course so well.

Malcolm was pleased that I was on his last course. And he did not know who the other magistrate was. As it happened, no-one else turned up – and that did not worry Malcolm or me. Perhaps David had decided to be kind.

We had a great evening. A young, very attractive lady sat next to the other probation officer. I thought she must be a trainee probation officer, but no – she was an offender. Well spoken, she sorted the lads out well and truly. No-one got anything over her. If I had been fifty years younger, I would have invited her out for a G & T, for she was that kind of miss.

Almost without exception, the lads and the young lady told me that (a) they had learned so much about drink that in future they would have no drinks whatsoever when they are driving, (b) that this course should be run in all schools and (c) that Malcolm was a good guy.

I recognised one offender but just could not place where I had seen him. He looked at me very nervously, but said nothing. At coffee break, he spoke to Malcolm who suggested he speak with me. He is a trainee nurse at the local mental hospital where I am a non-executive director and I have seen him there many times.

He was dead scared for he feared I would tell the Trust. I reassured him that I would not do so. He was so relieved. He told me that he was so ashamed that he had not told anyone at the Trust. He was twice over the limit and a first time offender.

He was given the CAIDs course plus fifty hours community service – at Redbridge Magistrates' Court. He had completed the fifty hours within three weeks by taking time off as annual leave from the hospital. I told him he would have to declare his conviction if he applies for jobs immediately, but otherwise unless he was asked I did not see a problem with not telling his employer at this stage. He is not driving until the ban ends.

Wednesday 15th May 2002

Success

A letter to Samantha and Stephen, Barristers and Court Clerks at Redbridge Magistrates' Court,

"I write in the peace of this Bank Holiday Monday to wish you both every success in your future careers following you departure from the Courthouse at Barkingside on Friday next.

"Looking through my dairy for the coming week, I find that I have mental health appointments on Tuesday, Wednesday and Thursday which leaves Friday. Joy of joys, I thought. I will be able to join Sam and Stephen for their farewell bash on Friday afternoon with the Champagne flowing like water and strawberries in profusion (or even abundance). But there is a problem. Which is a pity, for I had intended to take up the offer indicated in the notice in the retiring room of revealing all to the assembled company. But it is not to be.

"Without boring you with the detail, I am committed to a day at the seaside with my daughter and grandsons this coming week – and Friday is my only free day. Over the summer holidays, Luke (now 10) and I have spent a day each week in London – on the London Eye, at the Science Museum, in Hyde Park, on the River and experiencing the bungijump-trampoline at County Hall (three times – but I resisted the temptation to take part, standing instead on the sidelines and taking photographs as Luke catapulted himself into the air). Luke took part in a sports' week at the Redbridge Sports' Club, following which he decided that his grandfather should participate in some healthy activities – and we have trekked to the swimming pool a few times.

"So it is with some sadness that I will be unable to regale the assembled company with my stories of the nights I spent at Barkingside with Sam. A pity in many respects, for there was the time when we sat together in the Chequers across the road, sipping a G & T, and supposedly discussing matters of a racial nature. The evening is something of a blur in my memory, but I believe violins played softly in the background. I thought that the young man behind the bar kept an unduly watchful eye on us throughout the time that Sam and I sat there – and it was only when I asked him if he would be good enough to call two separate mini-cabs to take us to our respective homes, that he confided to me that he was a friend of my youngest son. I thought he was going to say that he would not tell my son what I had been up to – but he did not.

"Then there was the night when Sam connived with Clyde to leave us alone and unattended in the Courthouse following an enlightening debate on waste disposal with colleagues and two men from the London Borough of Redbridge. What gave me cause for concern on this occasion was the speed with which Sam worked out which cell we should occupy should the man from the Town Hall not arrive in timely fashion to switch on (or was it off?) the alarm system. Even more disconcerting was the journey to my home as the dusk settled on Aldborough Hatch and Sam drove as only Sam can. Yvonne knew that something was up when on arrival home I went straight for the gin bottle. Happy days, indeed!

"As for Stephen, the tales I would have told were slightly more mundane. I recall his arrival at Barkingside and his constant concern that the justices should 'pot 'em'. But, like fine wine, Stephen matured with the keeping, finally accepting that he was often on a looser with me in this respect. Ever polite and respectful, Stephen always made me feel that my journey to the Courthouse had not been in vain. Stephen really came into his own in the Family Court, where his work will long be remembered with gratitude. My re-training as a Family justice following a five year break whilst I was Bench Chairman gave Stephen the opportunity to play-act as the belligerent father and give me hell – but I survived. I recall that Stephen always appeared pleased to have me as a member of the Family Panel, if only because I prefer to do the typing.

"I look forward to following your careers in future years. Stephen will charm the pants off the lady justices in Cambridge – in, I would hasten to add, a metaphorical sense – whilst Sam will be the scourge of all offenders East of the Tower of London. Indeed, Martin Narey would be well-advised to consider reopening the Tower as an overflow prison for once Sam gets going in the Crown Prosecution Service, the country's prisons will scarcely be able to hold the hoards of defendants who will be holding their hands up to offences rather than face the wrath of Sam.

"But hold on! My daughter has arrived. Luke is spending a second day at the Notting Hill Carnival with his father on board a float which is belching out music from Robert's sound system. The highlight of the day, I gather, was the fact that toilets are not provided on board and Luke had to pee into a Coca Cola bottle. Luke assured Heather that they each had their own bottle and that they went out of sight to perform the task – which was some comfort to Yvonne who has very fixed views about these things.

"Luke, it would appear, has been invited to the Play Station Exhibition this coming Friday and as the invite comes from Kendra, he may find the choice an easy one. In which case, we will go to the seaside on Saturday – which frees me up for Friday afternoon. But things change fast in the Barrow household where a week is an eternity.

"If I do not make it on Friday afternoon, good wishes to you both. On the other hand, if I do put in an appearance I promise to embarrass Sam, who blushes so easily and looks radiant when she does so."

26th August 2002

Not another Saturday!

We gave the two departing court clerks a good send-off on Friday. There was champagne and strawberries, together with a dish of chocolate buttons. The latter mystified me, but it all became clear when Stephen's children arrived. And I thought the chocolate buttons were for us.

I arrived home today after Saturday Court at 2.15pm. I caught a bus quickly from Barkingside to Gants Hill when the court rose at 12.15pm. And this is where the problems started. I could see that the traffic was slow moving down the A12 – but the only alternative would be to walk – so I boarded a 296 at 12.40pm. An hour later we approached the Green Gate traffic lights at Ley Street – we had moved barely a quarter of a mile in that time.

The road beyond the Green Gate was shut off by police so we took a diversion down Ley Street towards Ilford, then along Wards Road and up Aldborough Road South – where the A12 was open again. There had been an accident outside the William Torbitt School involving a motorcyclist and a car. The air ambulance had attended. I guess there was a fatality because the accident occurred around 10am and the police were still there at 2pm.

Had I know all this at the courthouse, I would have called a cab and taken the country route home – but never mind. I guess that leaving home after 9am and not going into court until 11.45am was interesting, but combining that with an hour on a bus in a slow moving queue really took the biscuit.

The prison van did not arrive until 11.30am, having travelled to Ilford Police Station via Havering Courthouse. Mr G for the CPS was grave. The duty solicitor was a Mr T, who I have not seen before. He appeared to be devoid of any sense of humour. The lady from probation read her gardening magazine. And Court Clerk David was David.

Sunday 1st September 2002

Oddly and even odder

The Bench Chairman had a problem this Saturday morning on learning that there were nine defendants. He had a meeting at 11.30am and, realising that he might not make it with nine custodies, suggested that I might like to take his place. Which was kind of him for otherwise I would only have sat at the desk sending e-mails to unsuspecting folk.

Court Clerk Peter and I coped and finished at 2.15pm. Crown Prosecutor Ms R was in fine form, telling me that former Court Clerk Sam is hard at it in the CPS with local solicitor Ms H joining the team at the end of October.

We had six male youths this morning. Three males aged 15 and 16 were arrested last evening with a 19-year-old in a stolen car. All had parents in court.

There were no objections to bail. The Youth Offending Team (YOT) lady was in court having been called in by Peter. Once more Ilford Police did not alert the YOT to the fact that they had these three youths in custody overnight. Oddly the 19-year-old who was driving was given bail by police as he had no relevant previous. The three youths who were passengers had a bit of previous – not much – and they were kept in custody. Perverse.

The other case was even odder. One 19-year-old male, two 15-year-old males and one 15-year-old female were arrested on 3rd September for a robbery alleged to have taken place a few days earlier at 11pm. They were all bailed back to Ilford Police Station for yesterday, Friday 20th September. They thought they were going to have an ID parade, but no – police charged all four with the robbery. The adult, one male and one female youth were kept in custody overnight to appear here this morning. The second male youth – with no previous – was given bail to appear here today. The female was also charged with a further robbery at the end of August.

CPS objected to bail, suggesting remand into the care of the local authority for the youths. The YOT lady could only offer possible foster homes, but admitted that in all probability they would go to their own homes as it was a Saturday and you know what the problems are on Saturdays!

I gave them conditional bail until Wednesday – with doorstep curfews, no association with each other, not to contact victims or witnesses and to report as directed by the YOT.

The adult was given similar bail conditions – but did not have to do what the YOT told him (but as most of the YOT were almost certainly away for the weekend, this need not have bothered him).

I have two questions. Firstly, why was the YOT not advised that there were six youths in the Police Station on Friday overnight? This is the second time this has happened to my knowledge in the past month.

Secondly, why bail youths back to a Friday at the police station if there is the possibility of charge and arrest – and the decision to hold in custody? Why not bail them back to the day before a Youth Court?

I had to raise both issues in open court. Ms R for the CPS concurred with my concern and asked if this might be raised with the Borough Commander, indicating to me that anyone lower down the pecking order would not be able to take the appropriate action. I agreed that the Clerk to the Justices would do just that.

Oh, yes, and by the way. We did not have any prisoners up from Ilford until 10.45am and even then there were no prosecution papers. Ms R had to telephone Ilford Police Station to have then sent up by fast car.

One good piece of news was that we had a Goodmayes patient in on a warrant. He is detained on Section 2 of the *Mental Health Act* and appears to have walked out of hospital and gone to Ilford Police Station to report his lost pension book. He was recognised as being wanted on warrant for harassment at the DSS, was arrested and brought here.

The Hospital Ward Manager must have got to hear of this for he sent a FAX offering to take him back if we made it a condition of his bail that he lives at the hospital. Wondering how we would have him conveyed back to Goodmayes and guessing that even the Ambulance Commander might not be too happy to have a call from us on a Saturday, the custody folk in court rang Goodmayes who sent two Staff Nurses in a taxi. That was a relief. From time to time there is real humanity out there.

Saturday 7th September 2002

Hosting the French

I have had a quiet sort of day. This morning I was part of a team hosting a group of French folk from a town near Lyon. It was an exchange visit involving churches in Barkingside, but as they brought their Mayor and Six Deputy Mayors (yes, six!), the Borough got involved. Councillor W was in evidence with Richard playing both Councillor and Bench Chairman.

They came to the Courthouse – all 25 of them with about that number of Redbridge folk. Our public galleries take about 25 so we put them in two courts. Two of us non-French-speakers made the coffee and tea – and organised the chocolate biscuits.

One Frenchman said he now understood why we call these placed "courts" – because we are "courteous" to the offenders!

Friday 4th October 2002

Revelation

Yesterday morning I read THE GUARDIAN as usual. Therein was a piece by the Assistant Metropolitan Police Commissioner responsible for illicit drugs which set me aboiling! He was expressing surprise that half of London's street crime is linked to drugs, commenting that *"this has been quite a revelation to us".*

But I have made THE GUARDIAN's letter's pages this morning. I have a short – and, if I may say so, pithy – response to the Met Assistant Commissioner's comment that half London's street crime is linked to cocaine use by asking a rhetorical question: *"Where has he been hiding?"* I guess I had best go into hiding myself now. If I drop a fag end in Ilford Town Centre, some copper will have me in a cell before I have time to light up another. Perhaps I should take to wearing my trilby hat and dark glasses now that winter is here.

Tuesday 12th November 2002

Mock trial

I chaired one of the mock courts at yesterday's Court Open Day. I think I was more nervous doing that than I have ever been in court – and that's saying something. When I made the pronouncement I found myself delivering a speech. I went way beyond my brief, but I felt I had to make the point for the benefit of the members of the public at the back of the court. I was impressed with the incisive questions from the Cub Scouts – but cannot for the life of me remember any of the things I was asked.

A colleague sitting with me had to provide a moment of drama when she tripped as we were leaving the bench. I could see the ambulance drawing up and

the press photographers taking shots of her limp hand drooping from beneath the blankets. Personally I was all for dragging her along the corridor by her legs and dumping her in the retiring room, but Clyde of Security rushed forward and sorted her out, gentleman that he is.
Sunday 24th November 2002

Red light emergency

I spent the day at the mercy of Luke, now 11. He took me out to lunch, followed by the latest James Bond movie. Luke told me that if I found the movie a bit much, I should close my eyes and cover my ears – which was some comfort, I suppose.

We had something of a red light emergency yesterday. Luke was here with Marlon (2) in the morning, but early afternoon decided he would like to go to his own home until his mother arrived back from work. This was all agreed, so Yvonne set off with Marlon and Luke. They boarded a 150 bus at Gants Hill. Yvonne alighted with Marlon at the bottom end of Barkingside High Road near the Courthouse, leaving Luke to complete the journey alone. At the top end of Barkingside High Street, the driver of the 150 announced that he was turning back and going to Ilford, and would not be travelling up to Luke's home area after all. Luke alighted and walked down the High Street searching for Nana, for he had no money having spent his last 40p on the bus fare.

After searching Nana's well-known and favourite haunts – Somerfield, Boots, The Woolwich, Sainsbury's – Luke finished up at Iceland. The realisation that he was an abandoned child hit him at this point. Off he went to a public telephone box to call Granddad who, fortunately, was at home. Reversing the charges, Luke told me that he had been left penniless in the High Street. Quick thinking on my part was clearly needed. Go to the Courthouse, I instructed, and ask for Clyde. A call to the Courthouse to alert Clyde of court security to his impending duties was followed by a request to Radio Cars to get a cab up here double quick.

On arrival at the Courthouse, I found Clyde and Luke in deep conversation about matters of national importance. Do you want to come home with me or do you wish to go to your own home, I asked Luke? My home, he said. Off we set in the cab and about twenty minutes later I was restored to 37 Spearpoint some fifteen quid the lighter. But that, I guess, is what Granddads are for.

Yvonne eventually arrived home at around five, having waited for two buses. At one bus stop a bus had gone by fully loaded, leaving Yvonne to freeze. At the second there was a thirty minute wait.

When I told Yvonne that Luke and I had toured the area in the warmth of a cab, I was advised that I am a soft touch and should have given Luke the 40p for his bus fare home and travelled by the same mode of transport myself, using my Freedom Pass at no cost to myself. I guess I cannot get it right all the time, can I?
Friday 20th December 2002

All-day trial

On Monday I have an all-day trial at the court. I saw one of the Court Clerks on Wednesday who warned me that I have a difficult case – so difficult that he has taken a day's leave so that he does not have to act as the clerk. He clerked the two earlier abortive trials.

The case is one of failing to provide a specimen of breath. It came to court a year ago and was stopped during the first trial when defence applied for judicial review of some aspect of the case. I recall this happening. Clerk to the Justices Kevin went to the hearing at the High Court. It was dismissed. It came back for a second trial, but was again stopped for judicial review. Again, it was thrown out by the High Court. When this sort of case is going through, the Justices are not told the details – so that we can sit on any renewed hearing, so I do not know the issues. I was told that Kevin had noted on the list for next week- "Requires experienced and firm chairman". I guess that's me. I gather that the defence barrister is – well, perhaps it's best unsaid. It could be a fun day on Monday.

Friday 7th February 2003

Retirement

What a week! On Monday I retired from the Bench – amidst much kindness – and brought a fine wooden bench home for the garden. Supplemental List magistrates appeared and the back of Court One resembled a chairmanship appraisal session. Linda Perham, our local MP and a former justice and now on the Supplemental List, defied the Prime Minister to come along, too. My final duty as a magistrate in court was to make an order for a drug addict that will – hopefully – help him to kick the habit. Ever the optimist to the bitter end.

Now that I am seventy the Lord Chancellor has decreed that I am no longer fit for purpose – as they say – but am consigned to the Supplemental List where I may sign passports but little else.

Saturday 21st March 2003

A cuddle to end all cuddles

It has taken time, but the tablets are beginning to have an effect. Walking in the garden has helped, for we do not have access to a darkened room.

Charlie from Number 39 finishing tiling the bathroom and toilet this morning did not help, especially when he used the electric saw to shave an inch off the bath panel. The more than occasional cigarette has soothed me somewhat. But the jitters return each time I recall the scene last evening.

It all started when we examined the seating plan on entering the Wanstead Golf Club. Working our way up from Table Ten, as one does, I discovered we were on Table One. It appeared an odd mix – the Aldborough Hatch Mafia with the MP, Clerk to the Justices, Bench Chairman, the erstwhile Father of the Bench, us – plus a Lady of Some Repute. I did not feel up to the challenge – not after Charlie had spent the day screwing 220 screws into the floor to secure the boarding on which he fixed the tiles. But it was a pleasant evening. Ms Bew gave me the cuddle to end all cuddles – and having thus exhausted herself, Court Clerk Peter could well find himself cuddle-less for a few days. Thomas expressed surprise that Caroline cuddled people (clearly he was not listening to a word I said). Yvonne's flowers were a joy and are on display in the porch for passers-by to see. The engraved tankard has pride of place beside the Waterford Glass gavel (presented to me to mark my five years as Bench Chairman) and the Silver Goblet (awarded when I organised the making and cooking of the World's Longest Sausage). What, I ask myself, will future historians make of all this?

And so darkness falls on the final chapter of my involvement with the judiciary. The light is fading but as I sit here typing at the keyboard I can see through the office window the bench down there in the garden as a constant reminder of it all.

Sunday 16th November 2003

There is life after court

Later in the year of my retirement after twenty-three years on the Bench, I wrote the following for the court magazine on life after court.

A pleasant letter from the Chairman of Council, the Magistrates' Association, around the time of my retirement wished me well (which was kind) and outlined the benefits of continued membership of the Association. Receiving *The Magistrate* and the *Annual Report*, and attending the Annual Meeting were three. In addition I might wish to *"call in at the office in Fitzroy Square to use the library and Members' Room, meet friends or simply have a cup of coffee and a chat".* There were other suggestions for spending my new found spare time, such as forming a local club for retired members of the Bench – for lunch and a chat.

I thought carefully. I doubted if I would have time – even with my Freedom Pass – to spend a day travelling to Fitzroy Square for a cup of coffee and a chat. Further, we have the Justices' Club at Redbridge where I can catch up with old friends and, equally importantly, new ones.

I dropped a discreet note to my bank to cancel my direct debit. Quick as a flash came another letter from the Association, signed by the Finance Manager, with the names of his two assistants who were standing by to *"assist me".* Had the bank or I made a terrible mistake, the letter appeared to say? If not, I was urged to indicate my reason for resignation. I must get around to composing a reply.

I have received so many messages, letters and cards from colleagues at the court, and have made up a book to contain them all for the edification of my grandchildren. And I have thought of my colleagues daily throughout the summer as I have sat with Yvonne on the bench so kindly given to me by my friends at the court – in the garden with our early morning cups of tea standing on the table beside the ash tray I removed from the court on my last day (I say 'removed' for I took it there in the first place).

There was a time, I am told, when the Lord Chancellor Himself wrote to retiring magistrates to give them a hefty pat on the back for their service. We have waited anxiously for the post each day, but no word from the current occupant of the post, whatever he is called these days. Never mind. I guess he is busily sitting on the Woolsack and has many things on his mind.

But I did receive a kindly letter from Thomas, in his role as Secretary of the Advisory Committee for North East London, thanking me for my services to the Commission Area and the Advisory Committee. Tom wrote in June and added an apology for overlooking my departure from the Bench. *"I guess I must have thought you were younger than you are,"* wrote Tom, adding: *"An easy mistake to make, I am sure."* Now there is a gentleman and a scholar, if ever I saw one.

Amongst my current interests is my role as a non-executive director of the North East London Mental Health Trust (NELMHT), which has found me buzzing around Waltham Forest, Redbridge, Barking & Dagenham, and Havering for the past four years.

Each of the six non-executive directors (or NEDs as we are known colloquially) on the Trust Board takes on a number of special interests. I resisted the request to be the 'Old People's Champion', considering that I might need such a person myself before long. Instead I asked that I might continue two of my interests at the court – mentally disordered offenders, and drugs and alcohol. As a result I am able to be part of developing services and to have occasional contact with colleagues at local courts.

Another special interest is the operation of the *Mental Health Act 1983,* where I chair the Trust Board's MHA Sub-committee. All NEDs sit as members of panels of three to hear appeals by patients against their Section under the *Mental Health Act* and to consider renewal of Sections. They are statutory hearings under the Act, with the patient present, represented by a solicitor or barrister, and written and oral evidence from a doctor, named nurse and social worker or community psychiatric nurse. And – shades of the Family Panel – we have to give written findings of fact and reasons for our decisions.

As there are some one hundred and fifty half-day panels scheduled across the Trust each year, plus a few extras thrown in for good measure, the Trust Board appoints a number of Associate Hospital Managers (AHMs) to sit on Panels and to join the NEDs in carrying out ward and unit Visits.

Part of my role when the new NELMHT was formed in April 2001 was to bring together the disparate groups of AHMs from the four Boroughs, to recruit new AHMs and to mould them into a team. In one Borough, sittings were scheduled ahead for the year – as we do at Redbridge Court. In others, NEDs and AHMs were called in at short notice when required. We now schedule across the Trust (which brings a bit of order to things) but, rather like the court, we cancel if there are no cases to be heard and ring up at the last minute when a Panel has to be convened at short notice. All very familiar.

The recruitment advertisements went into a wide range of publications, for we needed to ensure that the gender mix and ethnic make-up of the team was more representative of the local community. Again, as at the court, I believe this has now been achieved – for the present at least. Not unnaturally, a number of magistrates serving locally applied and were interviewed.

After short listing from over seventy or so applicants, the Director of Nursing and I carried out the interviews. On the day I had a fit of temporary deafness, which meant that colleagues who knew me were taken aback to find they had to shout to make themselves understood and folk who did not know me no doubt considered me to be somewhat eccentric. Perhaps they all thought I was eccentric but were too nice to say so. Three of our newly appointed AHMs are from Redbridge Bench and one from Barking – the latter joining two long-serving magistrates from that court. And so from time to time I find myself sitting with a justice I have known in another place. Further, one of our leading consultant psychiatrists, who gives evidence to panels from time to time and who sits in her own right on Mental Health Review Tribunals in other Trusts, is an established magistrate at Redbridge. Quite like old times.

Traditionally, chairman of Panels have been NEDs, but we are changing this and a number of experienced AHMs now take the chair. A bit like the court again, where in my early days it was Buggins' turn in the chair and long-service was the over-riding criteria for sitting in the middle, and where now training and appraisal determine these things.

Our next task is to – you've guessed! – introduce an appraisal process for AHMs; this is established for NEDs. That could well be a minefield I need to cross. I have, however, decided against attempting to introduce a panel dress code. Colleagues who are a bit long-in-the-tooth will remember my attempts to do so at Redbridge when I was Bench Chairman. The hilarious laughter still rings in my ears from the time I tried to legislate for earrings, ponytails, trouser suits and clothing of sober hue. Never, ever again. I bear the scars to this day.

When the time comes to depart from an organisation, it is so often the case that we promise to "keep in touch" but never do. The advent of the e.mail has changed all that. It is so easy to knock off a quick message, click the right button with the mouse and know that the recipient has caught your drift moments later. No more trundling off to buy stamps and put envelopes into post boxes.

I use e.mails to keep in touch with a number of colleagues at the court. Sometimes I hear about things before they do – which is quite amusing, but something between me and my computer. And on occasion a good friend will work off his or her angst through a message, and if it helps, so be it.

Kevin, our last Redbridge-only Clerk to the Justices, and I keep in contact in this way. Kevin is roaring around doing all sorts of interesting legal things and appears to be enjoying the new challenges these present. One warm day last summer we enjoyed lunch together out in the countryside. We chewed over past times, looked to the present and the future – for Kevin has his life ahead of him and whilst I may be seventy plus, I am not done for yet.

Heather, my daughter, is married to Robert, who hails from Barbados. They have two boys – Luke (11) and Marlon (3). Yvonne is daytime carer for the boys – and I help when I can and if Yvonne decides I am capable of the task.

Robert is a young man of bounding enthusiasm – as my colleagues who were sitting with me in Court Number Two on 25th July 1999 will recall. Heather had been admitted to King George Hospital Maternity Wards during the night and Marlon was born whilst I was in court. Just before noon, the rear door to Court Number Two burst open to reveal a grinning Robert, closely pursued by a harassed Usher. *"It's a boy!"* Robert cried to the amazement of my fellow justices, the court clerk, the prosecutor, the defence, the ushers and – no doubt – the defendant. *"The Bench will retire,"* I said. The Court Clerk looked up with a quizzical: *"Why?"* But I did not wait to reply for Robert was advancing towards the Bench and nothing – not even a Redbridge Usher – was going to stop him!

Robert and Luke were on board a float with Robert's sound system on Children's Day at the Notting Hill Carnival in 2002. Heather, Marlon and I moved slowly with the crowd from Notting Hill station, reaching a point from where we could see the procession over the head of thousands, but where Marlon was faced with a sea of legs. The crowd was good-natured and in carnival mood. When Marlon asked if he might have a whistle it was the only time throughout the day when he requested anything. He was content to enjoy, blow and observe.

Wending our way with the crowd – which is the only thing to do – we found ourselves at the southern end of Ladbroke Grove on an incline which swept down before us to the main procession route. We were, perhaps, a hundred yards or metres from where the procession turned into Ladbroke Grove from Arundel Gardens – the space between us and the procession being filled by the minute by more and more revellers.

It was now mid-afternoon and Heather rang Rob on his mobile. I will come to find you, said Rob. And Heather and I smiled at his optimism. Many calls later, Heather began to believe that he might succeed. There was a gap in the procession and Ladbroke Grove stretched before us to the railway bridge in the far distance.

"I am walking down the route towards you," said Robert – and he was doing just that, a lone figure on the now empty procession route.

We waved and he waved. Below us on the edge of the massed crowd and adjacent to the route of the parade was an area bounded by crash barriers in which some forty police officers were standing. We watched as Robert approached. Seeking out a young Woman Police Officer, we spotted Robert engaging her in conversation. Even from where we were standing, we could see that the WPC straightened up at what Rob was telling her.

"Stay where you are," said Rob on the mobile, *"the WPC is coming to get you."*

Transfixed, we watched as the WPC approached us, moving deftly and meaningfully, and signalling for us to join her at the barrier – which we did. Moving the barrier aside, the WPC ushered us with some deference towards the corner of Arundel Gardens and onto the pavement of that place. Here we were in splendid isolation with a perfect and uninterrupted view. Rob was on the other side of the barrier, grinning from ear to ear. Lorry after lorry went past, with children and their adult minders dancing and cavorting. Steel bands were a relief from the rib-shattering sound systems. As a couple of hours went by more revellers joined us from the distance – but not through the way we had come.

Later, I ventured to ask Heather what Rob had said to the WPC that made her lurch our way.

"He told her that you are a judge," said Heather.

Now it needs to be understood that, in spite of my efforts to persuade him otherwise, Robert has always referred to me as "the judge" rather than a magistrate. What remains uncertain is how the WPC interpreted Rob's comment that I am a judge. Did she assume that I was a high-ranking member of the criminal justice system? If so, she must have assumed that off duty judges wear floral shirts and trainers on these occasions. Or did she think I might have been a judge of the carnival? We shall never know.

(In 2007 and again the following year, Heather, Marlon and I had the opportunity to ride of one of the main floats at the Carnival. Robert had his sound system installed on the float and he and Luke were busy over the days before, during and after the Carnival weekend. I rode in the cab of one of the huge lorries, whilst Heather and Marlon sat high on the back. I hopped off from time to time to take photographs, which we downloaded onto the internet. One of the more amusing incidents occurred at the 2007 Carnival when I spotted a Consultant from Goodmayes Mental Hospital in the crowd. He could hardly believe his eyes at seeing a non-executive director of the Trust dressed in a floral shirt from M& S in the cab of a carnival float with music blaring out so loudly that your ribs shook!)

"A glimmer of hope"

If I am asked what was the most worthwhile thing I did in those twenty-three years I spent as a justice, it would have to be this. Standing in September 2003 – six months after my retirement from the Bench – at the counter of one of those exotic eating places in the Exchange in Ilford waiting to make our choice for lunch, my companion whispered in my ear: *"You know that I was banned from Ilford Town Centre, don't you? What do we do if a policeman recognises me?"*

I had to admit that the thought had occurred to me, but I consoled myself with the fact that the ban was imposed four years earlier in 1999, that my companion had served his time in Pentonville, had successfully completed a detox and rehab, is now settled in his own flat far from Ilford and is a trained drug, alcohol and bereavement counsellor. I guessed that few police officers on the beat that day would have recognised him – or me, for that matter.

But we have to go back to the early 1990s for the start of this story. Writing this more than a decade later, it seems almost impossible that at that time there were no drug tsars, that drug action teams had yet to be convened, drug treatment orders had not been invented and that drug-related crime was in its infancy in an outer London Borough such as Redbridge. It was around the mid-90s that we started to notice a changing pattern of shoplifting emerging. Gone were the middle-aged ladies going through the change in life and shoplifting to draw attention to their loneliness. The professional shoplifters were still operating – often in gangs, but using a single mother to do the lifting whilst they stashed the goods into a van around the corner.

But the new breed of shoplifters were taking packs of razor blades and batteries – with some branching out into half bottles of spirits and large jars of coffee. The blades and batteries were small items of comparatively high value, easily slipped into pockets. The spirits and coffee were more difficult to conceal, but a few could be placed in the copious pockets of a large overcoat – or the more daring would load up a trolley and walked nonchalantly out of the store to unload into a waiting car. And all these goods could be sold quickly in the pubs, on street corners or to order – for cash to feed an alcohol or illicit drug habit.

What is more the addicts who were doing the shoplifting were coming back into court time and time again. Fines, probation, community service and prison clearly did not work and had no impact on the offenders, who were caught up in a vicious circle – the revolving door syndrome. Nothing was being done and no-one seemed to care – and as a recently elected Deputy Chairman of the Bench that gave me cause for concern.

The final straw for me came on 10th March 1995 when a lady shoplifting drug addict appeared in court yet again, but this time something different was being offered. The probation officer in court told the Bench that the lady had been in Holloway prison for the past six weeks and was, therefore, thought to be drug free. He had secured a place for her at a detox centre in East London, but first she had to prove that she was in fact free of drugs. To do this she would have to travel from the courthouse in Barkingside to University College Hospital in the West End of London to be tested for drugs. The result would be telephoned through to the detox centre where she would be admitted at seven that evening if the tests proved that she was drug-free. It was eleven in the morning and I asked if the lady would be accompanied into London and out again. I was told she would not be and that she – vulnerable and without support – would have to travel alone by public transport. I could see that she had friends at the back of the court who would almost certainly offer her drugs or alcohol – or both – once she left the courthouse and that the chances of her lasting for eight hours without drugs were remote.

At home that evening I wrote to the Bench Chairman, copying my memo to the Clerk to the Justices. I expressed my frustration that nothing was being done to face up to what was clearly an escalating problem of drug-related crime. Both responded enthusiastically to my suggestion that the court should look into the issue of how we were dealing with drug-related offending.

Over the next four years Michael Faraway, Clerk to the Justices, his successor, Kevin Moore, and I worked with a number of professionals in the criminal justice system – court clerks, probation officers, social workers, solicitors, local authority staff. Our MP, Linda Perham, was very supportive, raising the issue in a debate in the House of Commons. Michael and Kevin were assiduous in their research, finding that a number of schemes to tackle the growing problem of drug-related crime were being set up in courts in other parts of the country. Hardly a week went by without some aspect to the problem being discussed at the courthouse and locally.

It would take a book in itself to catalogue the meetings, the frustration, the break-throughs, the disappointment, the ups and the downs of those four years as Michael and I became increasingly aware that something innovative was required, but that it would cost money which we would need to find, for at that time there was no government funding for working locally through the courts with those with drug or alcohol addictions.

And if that seems remarkable at the beginning of the 21st Century, it was a fact in the last decade of the 20th Century.

During the early 90s a young man emerged with his offending from the youth court into the adult court. He was one of a small group of teenagers living in Ilford who were persistently offending to feed their drug habit. In many ways Lee (not his real name) was a likeable lad. I had known him in the Juvenile Court and met up with him again now that he had graduated to the adult court. If I saw him in Ilford, he would smile and was invariably polite. But there was another, darker side to Lee, who could be violent and vicious – so much so that a number of solicitors refused to represent him in court. Lee had only to walk down Ilford High Road and police officers would follow him – for he was almost invariably out to commit a crime of some sort. Lee was in and out of prison, and looking more haggard, tired and unwell each time he appeared in court. Drugs and drink were taking their toll.

One Saturday morning Lee and a friend appeared at Redbridge Court, charged with stealing clothing from a store near Ilford Police Station. Both had been arrested the previous day on suspicion of committing a crime and taken to the Police Station where they were held overnight. Here their clothes had been taken for forensic study and they had been issued by the police with white paper suits – and turned out onto the street to make their way home. Neither Lee nor his pal were prepared to walk through Ilford Town Centre and face the ridicule of their friends and mates wearing white paper suits – and, in all honesty, who could blame them? – so they popped into a well-known chain store, took jeans and T-shirts off the shelf and went into the changing rooms. Walking out in their new gear, they were recognised by store detectives and arrested.

Appearing in court on Saturday morning – in the white paper suits – both decided that enough was enough and hopped over the dock and out into the open air of Barkingside.

Not surprisingly, they were caught making their way home and re-arrested, this time facing the far more serious charge of escaping from lawful custody – a charge which had to be heard at the Old Bailey. Some three months later Lee and his companion pleaded guilty, and on hearing their story of the white suits, the judge gave them a custodial sentence of such length that they would be released immediately.

Lee appeared at Redbridge Magistrates' Court for the last time a few days before Christmas 1998. He had been in custody for two months or so, and claimed that he was drug free. My colleagues on the bench decided to defer sentence for three months as Lee had an appointment to attend a day centre prior to going into detox and rehab.

Lee was in his mid-twenties by this time and appeared to genuinely want to move on with his life. Lee left the court. A day or so later on Christmas Eve he was found dead in the gutter in London's West End, having taken an overdose of a cocktail of illicit drugs. Lee's death stunned so many people who had known him – magistrates, court clerks, probation officers, solicitors. If it shocked the most hardened amongst us, it made me even more determined than ever to go ahead with what we now termed the Redbridge Magistrates' Court Drug Initiative.

Lee's mother wrote a letter to the court in early 1999 – a few months after his death. Not unnaturally, she was highly critical of the criminal justice system, feeling that it had let her son down badly. I wrote back – taking some time to word my letter carefully in the sure knowledge that here was a mother grieving for her son – a son who had not only committed crimes within the community but who had also burgled his mother's home on at least one occasion whilst the family were away on holiday.

I made the point that we had finally obtained funding and would shortly be appointing our first Court-based Drug Referral Worker – and not only our first, but the first such dedicated worker at any magistrates' court in London. I told Lee's mother that had that worker been in place earlier, Lee might well be alive now. I hoped this might be a comfort to her, but I heard nothing more.

At this point I need to go back a year or two when I first had contact with Mark who was to become one of the most persistent offenders Redbridge Magistrates' Court had known. Born in Liverpool, Mark became involved with drugs and alcohol, smoking cannabis and drinking to excess. Mark trained as a chef and took a job at a government establishment in Essex. Off duty, Mark would go into London and it was here where he became increasingly involved with drugs and alcohol. He lost his job and found himself living on the streets. His drug and alcohol use led to increased levels of dependence and offending to secure money to buy drugs. He received community and custodial sentences and always relapsed into drug taking on release from prison.

Whilst homeless, Mark used the Redbridge Night Shelter, run by the churches of Redbridge and at that time offering a bed and a meal in different church halls each night of the week over the winter months. It was around this time in 1998 that Yvonne and I had started to volunteer at the Shelter – working at Oaks Lane Methodist Church Hall on Sunday evenings and later on Saturdays. Yvonne cooked an evening meal for the eighteen or so homeless guests and I stayed overnight and served breakfast before clearing everything away until the next week.

I am unsure where I first met Mark – at the Shelter or in the dock at the court. At the Shelter he was often stoned out of his mind, but he was always polite to Yvonne and me. Offering shelter in church halls was a risky business. We were all volunteers and if our guests brought drugs onto the premises we were hard put to do anything about it. If it was done brazenly and openly we refused entry, but often amongst a group of smokers there would be some who were puffing cannabis – and I often suspected that Mark was one of them.

When he came up from the cells at the court, he would wave a cheery *"Good morning, Mr Jeffries".* In some ways it seemed to me that Mark was almost pleased to be in custody – at least he had a warm place to be in during the daytime and somewhere to sleep at night, with regular meals.

In the summer of 1999, Redbridge Magistrates' Court secured funding to appoint a Court-based Drug Referral Worker. The prime aim of this appointment was for the Drug Referral Worker to engage with drug-related offenders in an endeavour to break the cycle of re-offending. As I said before, Redbridge was the first Magistrates' Court in London to make such an appointment. I was involved in the interviews and we were fortunate in appointing Ashley, a young man who hailed from Liverpool with a background in criminology and in the treatment of those suffering addiction to illicit drugs.

The appointment was not without its problems. It was not only innovative, but to some minds revolutionary for here we were offering treatment programmes to men and women who – in the minds of some – should be locked up with the key thrown away. As illicit drug-taking came out into the open, waiting lists were building up for treatment from the statutory services and here we were offering queue jumping to those who had offended. We worked closely with the Probation Service and the Redbridge Drug and Alcohol Service (RDAS). Two professional members of those organisations were outstanding in their commitment to the Redbridge Magistrates' Court Drug Initiative – Nick of Probation and Tim of RDAS. Without their dedication I doubt if the initiative would have lasted more than a month or two.

We decided that only Ashley could convince the Bench that the initiative would work and to do so he would need to sell himself and what he could offer. Over two weeks early morning rota day meetings were held in the magistrates' retiring room from 9.15am to 9.45am in which Ashley outlined how the protocols on which we had all worked would be implemented. At the end of the two weeks it was Ashley's charismatic approach and his insistence that he would not be a pushover that won over the sceptics. Ashley made clear that he would only offer treatment as opposed to punishment where there was realistic commitment on the part of the defendant – and he staked his reputation on that.

One of the first cases I referred to the Ashley as the Court-based Drug Referral Worker was that of Mark. Ashley carried out a full drug and alcohol assessment – a first for Mark – from which it was clear that Mark's drug and alcohol use was such that he was in a life-threatening situation. At the age of thirty Mark was drinking in a day the safe alcohol intake for a week together with a cocktail of illicit drugs – heroin, cocaine, cannabis, the lot. Ashley pulled no punches with Mark – if he carried on like this his liver and kidneys would give out within five years and he would be dead. Mark realised he was losing control of his life and that if he didn't do something, he would never recover.

Mark was on remand at Pentonville Prison in the drug-free wing. Whilst there, Ashley obtained funding and a placement for a residential rehabilitation package. It was dependent on Mark remaining drug free and funding would not be available for a further three months. The bench which I chaired at Redbridge one Friday morning in May 1999 sentenced Mark to six months custody for a string of shoplifting offences – and Mark smiled and thanked me as he turned to go down to the cells.

The day before Mark was due to be released from Pentonville I asked Ashley if he would be meeting Mark to accompany him to the rehab centre in South London. Ashley said he would not for it was up to Mark to start taking responsibility for his own actions. I learned later that Mark was met at the prison gates by some of his old addict cronies from his days in Ilford who had drugs and alcohol for him – but Mark brushed them aside, walked the short distance to Caledonian Road underground station and took the tube to South London.

Ashley kept me in touch with how the placement was going. Over the next nine months Mark completed the course successfully. He was found a one bedroom flat in North London on a small estate of a dozen or so similar dwellings, mainly occupied by elderly folk and well away from his old drug and alcohol contacts in Redbridge.

On 10th April 2000 I wrote the following letter to Mark from my home address on my personal notepaper:

"Over the past few months I have received regular updates on your progress from Ashley. I have been pleased to hear how things have gone for you and to know that you are now in your own accommodation. It seems a long time ago when I last saw you in court at Redbridge. I knew at that time that you had a very difficult task ahead, but that you were the only person who could make it work for you. The fact that you stuck at it and persevered is to your considerable credit. It cannot have been easy and I understand that, but the fact is that you did so.

"I know that you are not living in the Ilford area, but neither Ashley nor I have your home address. Ashley will arrange for this letter to be forwarded to you.

"I wonder if you would be interested to meet with Ashley and me at some time? You may not wish to do so and if this is your wish, we would understand. If, however, you would like to meet with us, please let me know. My home address and telephone number are as above. We could meet in Central London if this is convenient to you – perhaps over coffee one morning.

"I will wait to hear from you. Meanwhile, I send my very best wishes."

I heard nothing more until almost three years later, on 22nd February 2003, when I received a letter at my home, written by Mark from his North London address. In the letter Mark told me that was in his own flat and had been drug and alcohol free since he entered prison in May 1999 and had now given up smoking cigarettes, too. Mark had completed the Certificate in Counselling at the Working Man's College and was studying for a Diploma in Humanistic Counselling. With this qualification as a counsellor, he would be able to work in his chosen field – drug and alcohol recovery. As part of this Diploma, Mark worked as a volunteer counsellor at the St. Luke's Aftercare Project in South London, facilitating men's groups and seeing clients on a one-to-one basis to assist in their ongoing development in recovery.

Mark gave me his mobile number and I rang him that evening. We agreed to meet in London with Ashley and did so on 21st March 2003, lunching at Pizza Express in Holborn. Mark told me that when we had last met in Court One at Redbridge in May 1999, I had said something to him as part of my sentencing that had remained with him every night and every day whilst he was recovering. I had said that the rehab we were offering was *"a glimmer of hope"* and one that he should grasp for it was the only way that he would live to enjoy life.

I wrote to Mark that evening as follows:

"It was good to meet with you and Ashley today. Thank you for making the time to do so. You looked very well. It must have been hard for you today and I realised this. I hope Ashley and I were able to put you at ease and that you felt the meeting was worthwhile.

"What is very clear to me from our meeting is that you have had a very hard road to walk in recent years. I guess I knew this, but it was not until you started to talk today that I realised the full implications of what you have been through. I have never underestimated the difficulties inherent in detox and rehab, although I appreciate that until you go through it personally you can never really understand. Your account today of the struggle to overcome and the need to focus on each step brought all this home vividly to me.

"I have nothing but admiration for what you have done and continue to achieve day by day. And I acknowledge that you have done this for yourself. Whilst Ashley and I, together with others, may have had a small part to play in acting as the trigger, no-one – and especially you – should doubt the simple fact that you have achieved all this for yourself. It is something of which you should – and must – be very proud. You have climbed a steep mountain and now you have the rest of your life ahead. If there are set-backs, I am certain you will find the inner strength to face them. If at anytime you want to talk or need help, please do not hesitate to pick

up the telephone or write to me. If nothing else, I will always try to be a good listener. I will be in touch about a visit to the Night Shelter. Meanwhile, take care."

Mark came back to the Redbridge Night Shelter to work over one winter with Yvonne and me at the new permanent building we were by then occupying in York Road in Ilford Town Centre. On his first night – a Saturday – at the conclusion of the shift at around 9.30pm I insisted on walking with him to Ilford Station, a matter of 300 yards away. I was very fearful that Mark might see some of his old cronies and be drawn back to them. Mark walked upright and purposefully, but as we approached the station a group of young men came past and one of them barged into me – probably accidentally for they were the worse for drink. But it was enough to make Mark rise up – and he would have had no hesitation in using his fists to protect me had it been necessary. Mark remained very vulnerable for some time.

I keep in touch with Mark, who told me that he started out mentoring people during his own rehab. After an introductory course in counselling, he aimed for a Diploma in Counselling. It was expensive and he had to save hard to meet the tuition payments every month. He heard about the Crisis Changing Lives award, created by the homeless charity Crisis to help people back into the workplace.

Three years of hard graft later – and with about £4,000 worth of Crisis Changing Lives grants – Mark had completed his Advanced Diploma in Counselling. During this time he worked for a London bereavement service – where he met Cate, his partner. They now have a beautiful daughter.

I have nothing but admiration for Mark who turned his life around – something that required considerable determination and effort on his part. I knew Mark when he was at his lowest and it is to his credit that he has taken control of his life in a very positive manner. When I decided to quit smoking in August 2004 after some forty years, Mark told me that giving up drugs had been hard and beating the craving for alcohol even harder, but the most difficult addiction of all to kick was the nicotine habit. He did all three – in that order – and won.

And so it was that Mark and I found ourselves side by side, without a dock separating us and not a probation officer or security guard in sight, in Ilford's Exchange supping coffee on that warm September morning in 2003. Who would have thought it possible in January 1980 or in May 1999 or in March 2003?

But that moment – that *"glimmer of hope"* – made the frustrations, the disappointments, the highs and the lows, the hopes and the fears of the past twenty-three years so very, very worthwhile.

Part Eight
Ramblings in retirement

I retired from full-time employment at the age of sixty-five at the end of March 1998 – having worked for some forty-nine years. The following observations were made contemporaneously in 1999 and then from the latter part of 2001 through to 2008. Each is date-lined. Some of the pieces were written for my own records; others were messages sent by email to friends and relatives.

During this time I was a non-executive director with Redbridge Healthcare NHS Trust and then the North East London Mental Health NHS Trust, a magistrate and Chairman of the Aldborough Hatch Defence Association. Yvonne and I volunteered at the Redbridge Night Shelter from 1998 onwards; we served as Trustees and Yvonne continues to do so. We have both been involved at St. Peter's Church, Aldborough Hatch, where Yvonne continues to sing in the choir and I wrote a history of St. Peter's which was published in 2007. We have enjoyed our garden. Our latest venture is involvement once a month for twenty-four hours as Duty Officers with Redbridge Voluntary Care.

In addition, we have tried to be the sort of parents and grandparents we would hope was acceptable, without being interfering, to our children, Graham, Heather and Richard, their partners, Polly, Robert, Stine, Danielle and our grandchildren, Annily, Luke and Marlon, and our step-grandchildren, Fraser, Finlay and Fergus.

The Great Fire of Aldborough Hatch

The Great Fire of Aldborough Hatch occurred in September, 1999. Little else has been talked about and mulled over in these parts since that fateful evening. And you, dear friend, knew little – or perhaps even nothing – of it.

I had turned off the computer at around 9.45pm on Friday, 10th September, tipped the contents of the ashtray into a screw of paper and placed it in the waste paper basket. I have done so for many a long year, for I always clear my own ashtrays. My practice has been to take the basket downstairs to the garden, whilst I washed the ashtray so that it would be fresh for the morning. But, that evening – creature of habit that I am – I did not do so. Rather, I took a shower. Standing under the warm water, thinking pleasant thoughts, I enjoyed the splashing until I sensed an odour strange to our bathroom – and to yours, too, I would suspect. I ran from the shower – unclothed as you will appreciate – but could not see the home study door across the landing for the black, acrid smoke.

Shouting to Yvonne to call the fire brigade, the police, the ambulance service, the Vicar and anyone else she might think of, I turned on the bath taps and carried water soaked towels into the home office, where a merry fire was by now licking up the front of my chair and sizzling away on top of my desk. I threw wet towels over the inferno, but on the third attempt recognised when I was beaten, retreated to the top of the stairs and closed the door. Which was the best thing I could have done.

What do I do now, I asked myself – as one would? I rushed into the roadway that is Aldborough Road North – wearing nothing but a bathrobe and barefooted to boot. Yvonne followed – also in a state of readiness for bed, I would add. Call Tom-next-door, I cried, and Val-Across-The-Road. Yvonne did so. And then the fire brigade arrived.

At this point Yvonne went all of a quiver. Eight young, tanned, broad-shouldered, lusty firemen of the sort she swoons over in *London's Burning* on TV dashed from two massive machines.

Up the stairs they went – but they turned back. Breathing apparatus was required. Hoses were run out. Shouts echoed in the darkened street. Folk we knew and folk we did not know, some who speak to us and some who nod, others we thought had been dead for years, all appeared from their houses and stood around in awe. The fire was, in fact, almost out. Closing the door had done this, for I had also shut the windows before turning off the computer. Water was not needed, just a good dousing with foam or whatever. But the smoke billowed from the front bedroom and the bathroom and roared down the stairs in a lazy hazy sort of way.

Where are the cats, cried Yvonne? One went out the front and the other out the back said a young fireman. Yvonne swooned visibly – as she would, for it is not every day that a handsome young fireman gives her his undivided attention.

At this point I sensed that my right hand and arm were a bit hot, having been persuaded by a paramedic accompanying the fire brigade that I should sit in his car for a moment. He put something over the hand and told me I would be off to the hospital in a jiff. No, no, I cried – for on Friday night the A & E at King George is like Paddington Station in the rush hour. Yes, yes, said the paramedic.

An ambulance arrived. My hand and arm were placed in a bag and I was given time to dress. Two police officers appeared. Hallo, hallo, what's been going on 'ere, they cried. And don't we know you from somewhere else, although you are normally wearing a suit and tie? Off we went to the hospital, where the staff were marvellous. Burns are dealt with within ten minutes, I was told, and they were. Another bag.

Next day we rang the children. Graham had moved house the same day, but wanted to come up immediately. He travelled from Christchurch in Dorset on Monday and spent the day sorting out the insurance claim. Heather was a great support. Luke just wanted to see granddad and Nana. Richard offered to come over from North London but we kept him at bay until the next day.

On Saturday morning Yvonne went out to buy stacks of cleaning stuff – as you would. On her way home, Yvonne tripped in the road a few yards from home, bruising her knee rather badly. A young man of our acquaintance, who was passing in his car, stopped to do the Good Samaritan bit. Just at that moment our milkman came round the corner on his milk float. Thinking that Yvonne was being mugged, he leapt from the float and started to drag the young man off by the scruff of the shirt. No, no, cried Yvonne – he is helping me!

Suffice to say that, three months on, we were back to normal. The insurance companies had been wonderful. Steve and his boys spent two weeks redecorating upstairs and the hall and staircase. Paul and his lads took all my books – bound volumes back to 1908 *et al* – and papers for cleaning and re-filing. They filled thirty-six boxes – and that was just from the office.

We have new carpets and those undamaged have been cleaned. I have a 'new for old' contents policy, so the computer is an all-singing-all-dancing state-of-the-art Pentium III job – a Dell Dimension XPS T500 no less – with combined photocopier/laser printer. Where once stood three assorted – and aged – filing cabinets we now have three pristine new sparkling ones. My thirty-two-year-old desk with leather top – how I loved it – and table are now replaced with a light oak two piece desk and corner unit. And the chair is fire-retardant.

Seven visits to the Broomfield Burns Unit at Chelmsford followed that evening at King George Hospital. Heather drove me first, then a number of friends took over. First I had a bag, then a glove and later a tubular bandage. The staff at the Unit were so patient and highly professional. On the Sunday I spent six hours there. They gave me morphine whilst a nurse removed all the blistered skin from my hand and arm. The skin has recovered; it's just a bit purple in places, but at my age it adds interest. The staff say it is because I am healthy and have a good diet. I have to return to see the consultant in February.

Meanwhile, the hand and arm are creamed three times a day and I continue to wear the tubular bandage – this applies just sufficient pressure to ensure that the skin continues to grow normally.

Our friends locally have been tremendous. We cannot thank them enough for their help in so many different ways. And the answer to the question which must be on the tip of your tongues is *"No, I have not given up smoking!"* But I have a new ashtray with water in the base!

The Tale of the Great Fire of Aldborough Hatch will go down in the history of this bit of London's suburbia as an event to be savoured and talked over. Ken next door is a man of few words. He has been our neighbours for all the thirty-nine years we have lived here. He did not appear on the Night of the Great Fire. Next afternoon, Ken called over the fence.

"Are you alright?" he asked. *"We did not get up, for we were tucked up in bed, but we could see you had it all under control."*

A bit like the time a year or two back when we had a new lounge suite delivered. The settee proved to be too big to manoeuvre through the door from the hall to the lounge. There was nothing for it but to carry the settee into the garden of the house on the corner and over two fences, including the fence separating Ken's garden from our own. Once in our garden, the settee was carried into the lounge through the patio doors. I knocked at Ken's front door, but there was no answer, so we went ahead and two men carried the settee across Ken's garden.

"I saw two men carrying a settee across my garden yesterday," Ken called over the fence next day, *"and guessed it was something to do with you, so I did not come out."* Trusting fellow that he is.

December 1999

The racecourse that was never going to be (not if I had anything to do with it!)

With my fellow members of the Aldborough Hatch Defence Association, I spent the best part of a decade fighting off the threat of the London City All-weather Racecourse being built on the Green Belt at the top of my road – at Fairlop Waters, on Fairlop Plain.

It would take a book in itself to tell the story, but here I will restrict myself to a summary of the evidence I presented – both in written form and verbally – to the Public Inquiry into the appeal by Wiggins PLC against the decision of Redbridge Borough Council to refuse panning permission.

Held in the Council Chamber at Ilford Town Hall during May and June 2001, my evidence as Chairman of the AHDA ran to some seventeen pages of A4 plus supporting papers. Here are extracts of what I said – in, I would add, my best speaking voice and wearing my sharpest suit, smart tie and well-pressed shirt (Yvonne – as ever – made sure I was well-turned out for the occasion).

Aldborough Hatch is a residential area, bordered on the North by the Green Belt of Fairlop Plain and to the South by the A12 Eastern Avenue.

There are some one thousand, five hundred homes with a population of around 6,000. Most houses were built in the thirties and forties. More recently, there has been some in-filling with low-level flats, houses and maisonettes.

It is an attractive part of Redbridge, on the edge of the countryside stretching uninterrupted into Essex.

My parents, like many others, moved from inner London to the then Borough of Ilford in the early thirties. I was born here and when I married, I decided to make Aldborough Hatch my home. It was then – and remains today – a pleasant and quiet place in which to live and bring up a family.

There is a strong spirit of local community, with an active social life based around the parish church of St. Peter. The halls at St. Peter's are used throughout the day and in the evenings by a wide range of community groups. The area has its own primary school and a secondary school is under construction.

Like many residents of Aldborough Hatch, I spent my working life in the City and West End of London. I returned in the evenings and at weekends from London to the comparative peace and tranquillity of Aldborough Hatch.

In his opening speech to this Inquiry, the Appellant's Counsel described Redbridge as an area of "glaring deficiency" in that it lacks buildings of outstanding architectural merit. We agree. Redbridge does not have a cathedral, a castle or a stately home of international repute. But all these are close at hand in London and in the nearby countryside. Referring to the design of the grandstand, Counsel stated that Redbridge is not well-endowed with buildings of this nature. We would agree – but where we would disagree is in his contention that there is a need for Redbridge to have a building of outstanding architectural design. Describing the building as "striking" and "an outstanding piece of architecture", Counsel claimed that this would enhance the area.

The Association would disagree. We do not live in Aldborough Hatch to gaze upon architectural treasures – although we would have to question whether a racecourse grandstand could possibly merit such a description. We live where we do because it has given us a congenial place to spend our non-working hours or in which to enjoy our retirement. In addition, it is the kind of open area we want our children and our grandchildren to enjoy.

Next I launched into a brief history of the AHDA which was formed over thirty-five years ago. It came about because local residents were concerned to protect and defend the Green Belt on the edge of the area in which they live.

Over the years the Association has built up a reputation as a responsible group of local people working closely – and largely harmoniously – with the Council to minimise the erosion of the availability of open countryside on our doorstep.

Extensive sand and gravel extractions have taken place on Fairlop Plain over those thirty-five years. Aldborough Hatch suffered from the effects of household waste infill, but in spite of the devastation caused when the extraction and infill were taking place, we have worked hard with the local Council to retain the essential countryside on our doorstep.

From time to time when fly-tipping occurred we have engaged in clean-up campaigns. We are proud of our bit of countryside and have worked hard to keep it that way.

I would describe the Aldborough Hatch Defence Association as a residents' community group working quietly in the background to preserve and enhance the area in which we live, but which galvanises into action when the need arises and the Green Belt is threatened.

We encourage family membership and currently have some one-hundred-and-twenty-six families and individuals who have paid the annual subscription. We do not actively campaign for new members and the income from subscriptions is sufficient to enable us to publish 'Open Space', the Association's newsletter, two or three times a year when there is a need to inform residents.

I mentioned that the Association galvanises into action when the need arises. It has done so when specific gravel extraction threatened. It has done so since August 1998 when residents first learned of the proposals which are the subject of this Inquiry.

In October 1999 the Association's Public Meeting at St. Peter's Church Halls – attended by Mr Geoff Lansbury of the Appellants – attracted over four hundred residents. Many stood in the cold and rain outside open windows to hear what was being said.

A similar meeting in October 2000 saw some two-hundred-and-fifty residents at the same venue.

It has to be recognised that many families have young children and only one partner could attend an evening meeting. Other residents are elderly. I would estimate that the four hundred residents at the October 1999 meeting represented some three hundred homes – about one fifth of those in Aldborough Hatch.

Both Public Meetings were open to all residents. It is interesting that at the first Public Meeting only two residents spoke in favour of the racecourse development. At the second Meeting just one resident spoke in favour.

I quoted the concerns of local residents. *George Searle, of Spearpoint Gardens, wrote to express his concern that "there would be insufficient car parking and that Aldborough Hatch will become an overspill car park and a target for car thieves."*

John Roberts, also of Spearpoint Gardens, wrote of his concern at traffic congestion and what he described as "the unwanted invasion of the residential area in Aldborough Hatch."

John Hale of Ramsgill Drive commented: "I have lived in the area for all my forty seven years, being born in Seven Kings and since a boy have enjoyed our rural aspect. Nothing could replace the tranquillity of a walk or cycle ride across the farms and plains of Fairlop. We do not need a racecourse, or more congestion or more pollution of both lungs and ears. I, like many others, sought to live in Aldborough Hatch for its location close to the Green Belt, not in the hope that one day we would replace this with a racecourse."

Miss Sugden and Mr Chauhan of Bawdsey Avenue wrote: "We have just moved into Bawdsey Avenue and cannot believe the proposal. We chose to move to Aldborough Hatch due to the quiet nature and surrounding countryside, which would be totally spoiled by the erection of a racecourse – not to mention the connecting roads and further traffic to add to the already busy A12."

Lynda and Daniel Bracken of Bawdsey Avenue wrote: "Like many others around us, we are very protective and proud of Aldborough Hatch. There is a very strong community spirit between residents. Please keep Aldborough Hatch a peaceful, rural and very special place to live."

I reminded the Inquiry that in May 2000 a petition with one thousand, two hundred and ninety-six signatures opposing the racecourse development was presented by Councillor Mrs Vanessa Cole to the Council's Planning Sub-committee.

I asked if there is a reasonable prospect that the development can be achieved? *Residents are fearful that if the development goes ahead and proves to be unviable, we will be left either with an unwanted and derelict white elephant eyesore in our midst or planning permission will be granted for a range of ancillary buildings that will further desecrate the openness of the Green Belt of Fairlop Plain.*

Having rattled on about the massive problems of traffic and transportation, I wound up with a slice of emotion, bringing tears to a few eyes:

Many Aldborough Hatch residents walk or cycle across Fairlop Plain. Some play golf, take part in bird watching and use the facilities of the lake. Others enjoy the openness from their homes and gardens.

In his opening speech, Counsel for the appellant's described Fairlop Plain as "a transition area between urban and open countryside."

Expert witness for the Appellants Sarah Reynolds from the Landscape Institute stated that Fairlop Plain is not an area of outstanding natural beauty, commenting that "it is unique because of its historical character, but I would have difficulty referring to the site as countryside at all."

The Association refutes that evidence and urges you to do the same. We invite you to accept the evidence of expert witness for Redbridge Council Moira Hankinson, Landscape Architect, who informed this Inquiry that the racecourse development "would make it harder for residents to reach the countryside, obstruct views across the plain and change the site from rural to urban."

We would contend that Fairlop Plain is countryside. There are four working arable farms on the Plain. One farm includes a popular pick-your-own facility and animal sanctuary. The Plain boasts a flock of Jacob's Sheep. The Plain leads directly without interruption into the open countryside of Essex.

It is the Association's submission that this development is not needed, nor is there a reasonable prospect that it can be achieved. It would desecrate valued Green Belt countryside on the edge of London's sprawl. It would have a devastating effect on the local road structure.

We urge you to give due weight to the views of local people whose quality of life would change beyond recognition were this development to go ahead.

June 2001

(Some eighteen months later we learned that the planning inspector had allowed the appeal but that his decision was overturned by the Rt Hon John Prescott MP, Deputy Prime Minister. And everyone, just everyone, said what a good chap Mr Prescott was after all! And so Fairlop Waters remains open and part of the Green Belt to this day.)

New spectacles

I have new reading glasses. The frames of my specs snapped on Wednesday. I patched them up with Superglue, but got more on my fingers than on the frames. My fingers stuck together. Nasty. Then I got some glue on the lenses. Even more nasty. I should have waited for Yvonne to come home to sort me out. Then the Superglue gave way.

I spent a happy hour or so in Ilford today with Vision Express, who offer a same day service. I now find that everything is much clearer and less fuzzy than before. The screen of the word processor is bright and alive. The pages of books are crystal sharp. It is a whole new world out there.

I have two sets of glasses. One makes me look like Mr Bean; the other tends to give me an intellectual appearance. The kind man at Vision Express suggested that at my age I should have robust spectacle cases in case I sat on them or dropped them or ate them for breakfast. The young lady who saw me first was about to charge me for the eye test. But I am a pensioner, I cried. Really, she said, all starry-eyed. That made my day if not my week.

I am only just getting over Ms A, Solicitor. You should know that Ms A has skin of pure porcelain, long black lashes and deep black – no, brown – eyes. I would guess Ms A is of Italian extraction. Ms A appeared for a patient on Wednesday at a Mental Health Act Appeal at Goodmayes Hospital. It is the second time Ms A has graced us with her presence. And what a presence. Ms A wears a black suit of the finest cut.

When I saw it was she who was appearing, I very nearly passed out. Had it not been for the fact that Derek and Omana were sitting closely at either side of me, I fear I may have slipped slowly onto the floor. But I got a grip – of myself, I would add. Professionalism took over. I conducted the Appeal with due diligence. Try as I might I could not find a good excuse to speak with Ms A afterwards.

I have decided that all appeals where Ms A is to appear should be chaired by me. It is only right and proper. I will talk to the Mental Health Act Administrator about this first thing on Monday morning. Where will it all end, I ask myself? And when Ms A sees my new specs, anything could happen – and probably will (but it did not – for I never saw the good lady again).

Friday 5th October 2001

Light up the Hatch!

The 'Light up the Hatch' Campaign got underway early on Saturday morning. I donned my warm duffle coat – the one Graham bequeathed to me when he had been at Oxford for two weeks and discovered that his peers wore dark grey overcoats of the kind you buy at Dunn's on Ilford Hill and the sort that I had long coveted for myself, but felt that I should not go in for such luxuries. I purchased a Dunn's coat for Graham and took over his duffle, which I continue to wear to this day when it is cold and bitter. But I digress.

Donning the duffle, I went into the plot we laughingly call the front garden, and set to work putting up one-hundred-and-forty white Christmas lights. Yvonne dreads this time of the year when she stretches high onto the tops of cupboards to bring down the Christmas decorations. When the children were younger, Yvonne would take them out for the day – anywhere – leaving me to the task in hand. Decorating the Christmas tree is something I carry out alone and unaided. Children around merely add to the confusion. I do it my way.

Without children these days, you would expect that the task would be somewhat easier. But it is not. Do the lights work is the first question? We test them in the boxes in which Yvonne packed them away last year. They all came on first time, including the new box of sixty white frosted lights I purchased in Woolworth's a week or two ago in a rash moment. But – and this is a big but – the new ones flash and they did not say that on the box. No sir! And I do not like flashers. Never have done. And now I am one myself. John-Over-The-Road comes across. I see your lights flash, he says, looking in the box. Yes, I say. But it does not say that on the box. John looks. You can adjust them to fast or slow flashing, he tells me. There are five settings. And so there are.

But I digress – again. It is 8am on a cold and frosty morning. I set to work with the flashers, having decided to put them on the Christmas tree which stands in the centre of the garden. My hands go numb after the first dozen lamps are fixed, using bits of garden wire which Yvonne saved from last year. Are you not pleased we saved the wire, Yvonne calls?

I go indoors to place my hands on the radiator in the hall. I thaw out. Back again. More lamps. More cold hands. More radiator and a coffee. Back again. All sixty are in place. I turn them on. Every other two flash but the thirds are dark. Nothing. No light. Where is the thingy that tests the wires, I call to Yvonne – who now wishes we had children again and she had taken them away for the day. Out comes the tester thingy. There is power. I look at the dark bulbs. I take one out and replace it with a spare. That one is broken. The lights all come on – flashing away.

It is your fault, I tell Yvonne. You must have broken that one when you helped me into the garden with the things. Yvonne looks resigned. If the lamps do not work it is her fault. If they do work, I have done it right again.

I move to the bush by the bird bath. Last year's set of forty go here. I give the bird bath to Yvonne to wash. The water goes a dark shade of brown over three weeks with dust from the Sahara Desert. It's a fact. It falls in my front garden but not on a similar bird bath in the back garden.

Yvonne uses one of her special cleaners and works a miracle. The birds will have a clean bath tub once more. The third set of forty lights go up around a shrub and onto the base of the Christmas Tree.

By now it is 10am and all is well in the Hatch. Men hurry by, take one look and are up ladders, searching out the lights in their homesteads. Wives quiver. Children rush by going – anywhere. It is all happening in the Hatch.

9th December 2001

Better than an orgasm!

It was the day before the day before Christmas Eve – Saturday evening, in fact. A light fall of snow covered the roof tops.

All was calm and still. And Yvonne and I were off for the evening shift at the Redbridge Night Shelter. Bags of food for cooking were standing in the hall. Fresh vegetables from the farm shop and homemade mince pies amongst them.

The minicab arrived on time. The young driver had little idea where York Road might be, even less how to get there. And to compound things, he was busy on his mobile.

I pointed out to him that the road was icy and he agreed. The crossing at Aldborough Road into the A12 was negotiated with one hand on the wheel. I could feel the tenseness behind me as Yvonne clutched the mince pies. Interspersing his conversations on his mobile with road directions, we finally arrived.

The evening went well. Yvonne's meal was a success and the warm beds upstairs in the newly decorated rooms were much welcomed.

The quote of the evening came from a Scotsman, who had been staying at the Shelter for a few weeks. A chronic alcoholic, I knew him from the court where he occasionally accompanied one or other of his friends who were up before the bench for some minor misdemeanour, although I had never seen him in the dock. I would guess that he had lost whatever accommodation he had due to his drink problem and was now finding refuge in the Shelter, where he was pleasant, polite and always grateful for the hot meal.

Downing his third mince pie, he turned to Yvonne.

"The pastry melts in your mouth," he said, *"it's better than an orgasm."*

Yvonne looked startled and returned to the washing up. I decided not to pursue the matter further. Yvonne's mince pies have something of a reputation hereabouts. Yvonne makes them for the carol singing and I take them to the court for Christmas sittings. That they are good cannot be questioned, but never ever have they be likened to or said to surpass an orgasm. I will never face a mince pie in the same way again.

Saturday 22nd December 2001

Hundreds and hundreds

I am off shortly to the Service of Nine Lessons and Hundreds of Carols, for it always seemed to be so when I was a young chorister. But I am taking a rest from the choir at present so will be in the back row with a couple of old flames – the Daft Old Bat and the Daft Old Bat's Friend, I call them. They love it – honest.

The politics of the choir got a bit too much last summer when some members of the choir and church complained that the organist played the hymns too fast. In the end the Archdeacon was called in, no less. Have a vote, he cried. We did. Some 30% said they were too fast, 60 % said they were at the right speed and 10% did not know. The organist, a young man in his 30s who teaches, was so upset by the 30% and the 10% that he resigned. I decided to stand by the Vicar, who was clearly distressed. I met with the two churchwardens. I very nearly threatened to return to the Parochial Church Council next year, but thought better of it. I decided to stand down from the choir as I would find it difficult to sit in the pews with some who sing so slow that there is a good chance that they will still be there when we have all gone home.

Of course, it goes without saying that hymns should be played at the speed indicated in the music, which was what our young organist was doing. Sadly some folk seem to have missed the point.

Following the resignation of our young organist, who was, in my view, brilliant as a musician, we now have a succession of stand-in organists. One or two, who join us on a few occasions, are highly competent, but amongst the others, some play slow, some play very slow and others play full stop.

Would you believe it – I am the longest serving member of St. Peter's, having joined the church choir in 1944. Only Old Mrs Chapman had been there longer – 1938, in fact – but she died last year, and she was ninety or so.

Sunday 23rd December 2001

A new mouse

We took eldest son Graham's advice. I have purchased a new mouse. A Logitech. Well, Yvonne bought it for me to be more precise. I spent a happy morning at the desk, whilst Yvonne went on one of her shopping forays to Ilford. Do you want anything, she cried as she tried to slip out the front door unnoticed? Yes, I said. Graham was concerned at the antics of my mouse yesterday when he spent some time sorting out my computer. It is sluggish and does not perform. Graham recommended a Logitech.

One computer chap in Ilford could not help. They sent Yvonne to a well-known store where a nice young man showed her the Logitech range – none of which were priced. On taking the first of two boxes to the till he announced that it would cost £49.99. No, no, said Yvonne. My son reckons it would cost less than £20. The second box was taken to the till. This one came up at £9.99. That's more like it, said Yvonne – at which point another assistant whisked both boxes off the counter before her very eyes, making a comment to the effect that if she could not make up her mind she should not handle the goods. This took Yvonne by surprise. Are you suggesting I am a thief, said Yvonne? The man looked dumfounded. The first assistant looked scared. Yvonne looked fierce. If you take these away, said Yvonne, I will go elsewhere and never enter your shop again. The second assistant now looked scared. This young man, said Yvonne, pointing to the first assistant, is being very helpful. Go away! With which the second assistant did just that. Yvonne thanked the young man – the first assistant – and paid cash and departed. Fascinating!

I gather from Yvonne that the first of the two boxes had a mouse that worked by radar. No wires. I believe Graham has one like that. Yvonne decided that for another £40 radar was not an option. Quite right, too, as it was my money she was spending. I installed the new mouse. There were two discs and I did all of that without mishap. Turned off the machine. Turned it on as instructed. It works. It scrolls. It moves at a good pace. It does not flit about like the old one. Great. No more fiddling.

Yvonne is in a lively mood today. Old Mr Clarke lived four houses away from here for all the years we can remember. His house has gone through two sets of owners since he died. The latest are rarely there, but have ripped the place to bits. They are building a house at the bottom of their garden, too. Not a shed-with-an-overhang but a breeze block edifice. We know not for what purpose, but I reckon it could be home to a few people when it is finished.

In their front garden they have dumped old Mr Clarke's bird bath by the dustbins. I have looked at it a number of times and it is clearly destined for the tip. I could not pluck up the courage to knock to ask if we might have the bird bath rather than see it disappear down the road on top of a skip, but Yvonne did so today. A workman answered. He promised to talk to the owner and if he is dumping it, he will let us know. It would be good to have old Mr Clarke's bird bath in our garden. He was a nice old boy who repaired our children's bicycles.

(A few days later the bird bath was moved to our back garden where it provides welcome facilities to the local bird population, complementing the similar arrangement in the front garden and outside the shed-with-the-overhang.)

Saturday 5th January 2002

Lively

Saturday night at the Redbridge Night Shelter was interesting. I sensed we were in for some lively business when we arrived just after six-thirty to find a crowd of guests in the backyard, sheltering from the cold in the wooden lean-to which serves both as a waiting area and a haven for those who smoke. Jostling to be near the door, the guests were keen to tell me who had arrived first and for some to let me know that they had not been in trouble with the law since we last met. I had brought an unopened packet of cigarettes with me, which was just as well for ten had gone within five minutes – and I had only smoked one.

Inside, Yvonne, Jan and Jenny worked in the kitchen. Home-made chicken casserole with potatoes and cabbage, followed by peach crumble and lashings of custard, the latter being the staple diet of drug addicts, I have learned. Margaret, the full-time worker, Sue and I prepared the reception area in the hallway, whilst Julie, the nurse, sorted out her kit. We now have a professional most nights of the week – a nurse, a GP or a drug worker. We topped up the urn and made ready the coffee, tea, soft drinks and snacks' table.

Part of the problem with the permanent building we now have for the Shelter as opposed to the church halls where we started is that the communal areas are small and cramped – just the hallway and the dining room. When we extend the building later this summer, we will have a sitting room and reception desk.

My duty when we opened the doors at 7.15pm was to let the guests in two at a time. Margaret booked them in – there are housing benefit forms to complete each evening which enable the Trustees to claim for those guests who are entitled to this – whilst Sue searched the guests and their baggage. We do the latter because we have had legal advice on the position which might arise if guests bring illicit drugs onto the premises. Inevitably the search is very much on the surface. Those with alcohol hand it in. Those with medication do likewise. Those with drugs either do not tell us or hide them before they enter the shelter.

Out in the lean-to, there was pressure to get to the front of the queue. We can only take eighteen sleeping guests. Others come for meals only. Generally the meals-only guests are in bed and breakfast, or flats, but miss their old companions on the streets and therefore return to have a meal and chat. R was keen to assure me that he has not been back to the court for a year or so now. I know, I told him. If you had I would have heard about it. R also wanted to tell me that J spelt trouble for us. J, said R, came out of drug rehab a week ago and was now high. He has a needle, said R. I warned Sue, but it was not found in the search. J has a history of dual diagnosis mental illness and has been an inpatient at Goodmayes Hospital.

Some guests went to their bedrooms to await the evening meal. We now have TV in all rooms, which is a brilliant idea as it takes the guests away from the restricted areas downstairs. But hunger brought many down to the dining room. We had booked in eighteen guests and two for meals only. One more remained outside. He told me that he had slept in a car the previous night. He was shaking. I could only offer a meal at this stage, with a promise of a bed if one became available. Little was I to know that this would happen in a way I had not expected.

A call from R to the dining room. I warned you, he said. And there was J, doing a sort of slippery slide down the wall in an 'S' shape. I called the nurse. At this point about six guests were keen to help J in his slide. It took time to get them to sit down, but they did. Julie, the nurse, moved J onto his side. He then started to move in spasms. Julie was on the telephone to the ambulance service and police. J continued to move spasmodically. Then he was still. Within five minutes two police officers arrived. Young in their early twenties, they were quiet and efficient, taking details from anyone who knew anything. Five minutes passed and the ambulance arrived, with two young lady paramedics who took notes and brought in a chair to take J to the ambulance.

Guests followed into the street. Four wanted to go with him to A & E. Finally one young girl agreed to be the sole friend accompanying him, but then she burst into uncontrollable tears. Margaret, the full-time worker, called to me to sort them out and bring back those who wanted to stay. Otherwise the doors would be locked. I gained the impression that I might be locked out, too, if I did not get a move on.

Off went the ambulance with J and the weeping lady guest. I encouraged others to return. One man held me back. I know you, he said. You are always wandering around Goodmayes Hospital. Are you a doctor? I explained that I was a non-executive director of the Trust. He looked confused. Hardly surprising really. He told me that he visits friends at Goodmayes.

Back indoors the meal was being served. Calm prevailed. M, the alcoholic who sits outside Fairheads all day, had three helpings of Yvonne's casserole. Custard flowed. Gradually the guests went to their rooms.

The male showers upstairs are out of order. When they are used, water cascades through the ceiling. The plumber has been alerted. Requests to use the female showers downstairs were agreed, provided each guest took no more than five minutes. I was put in charge of making sure they did. There is only one female shower. We had four females at first but one was now at A & E and J's bed was also available. The 19th guest was grateful that he would now have a bed for the night.

We needed a bed downstairs so that the three ladies would sleep in the two-bedded room. Margaret sent me to arrange it. I found that there was one bed without a bed – if you see what I mean – just a mattress. I decided I could manage that on my own.

Keep an eye upstairs, said Margaret. Make sure they are in their right beds. A young man took me on one side. I hear you are a magistrate he said. (The guests always seem to find this out – even the new ones and he is new to me. I do not tell them but the word gets around.) He told me that he came out of prison in Scotland a week ago and went to see his girl friend in Weston-Super-Mare, but she kicked him out so he came to London. He is banned from driving for ten years. Could he go to court to have the ban lifted after three years, he asked me? I said it might be worth a try but I could not give him advice. Try the Citizen's Advice Bureau, I suggested.

Yvonne called from the quiet of the kitchen. I ate a portion of peach crumble. Yvonne and I swabbed the dining room floor with mop and bucket. Then we filled up the urn and sorted out the drinks table again. It was a quarter to ten. The night worker and night volunteer arrived just after ten. We drove home with Jan and Jenny. It was about half-past ten, but if you had asked me how long we had been in York Road, I would have said a lifetime, although it was just over four hours.

Sunday 13th January 2002

Deaf

I am as deaf as a post at present. I caught a viral infection, according to the doctor, and this had upset things upstairs. I last went to see the doctor about three years ago. He looked at my notes this time, checked my age and carried out the kind of examination that indicated that he was looking to see if bits were dropping off or coming apart. Pour olive oil in your ears for the next few days, he told me, and fix an appointment with my nurse to have your ears syringed.

At that point I could hear a little. Since taking the antibiotics and suffering Yvonne's ministrations with the olive oil in my ears I have gone almost completely deaf. Tired of having to apologise to the neighbours for having the TV on so loud to hear the news, Yvonne has now found out how to bring the sub-titles on the screen.

Wednesday 16th January 2002

Relief

At just after one this afternoon I set out for the Health Centre. The going was hard, for there was a bitter wind blowing from the West. My goldfish bowl-like existence was telling on me. I was surrounded by almost total silence. Traffic whizzed by. Folk waved and I called back, trusting that my comment was appropriate.

A queue had formed outside the Health Centre when I arrived at twenty-past-one. Clearly there was clinic due for most of the people appeared to know each other. Ho, ho, I could sense them thinking to themselves, who have we got here – a new boy for the geriatric gentle exercises club, perhaps? I stood at a distance. How could I possibly converse with a gang of walking sticks and zimmer frames? A walking stick sidled up to me. I nodded in response to whatever he said to me. He seemed satisfied and went off to tell the rest.

Inside I explained to the receptionist that I was here to see the nurse and that as I was stone deaf could she please shout. I sat down as directed. Five minutes passed. A tap on the shoulder from the receptionist woke me from my slumbers. The nurse has been calling you, she shouted in my left ear.

Have you had your ears syringed before, the nurse asked? I think I did when I was a child. Do you have a perforated ear drum, the nurse bellowed at me? Not that I am aware, I shouted back. You do not need to shout at me, the nurse smiled, my hearing is fine. Hold this, the nurse instructed as she handed me what I believe may be referred to as a kidney bowl and draped me in a towel. It will be a strange sensation, the nurse confided. In fact, it was rather pleasant and I could have taken more. With one ear done and the water drained, I was aware of a humming sound. What is that, I heard myself shouting? It is the air-conditioning. Nothing to be alarmed at, said the nurse, as she prepared to give me fun in my second ear.

Out in the fresh air, I was aware that the world is a very noisy place. Down the pathway I skipped. I spoke – and realised that my voice had resonance and clarity. I sang a few bars. Waiting at the bus stop, I tried a full song, but I had to stop when a young man appeared from nowhere and ran off at speed. I telephoned Shirley with the good news. I had to tell someone.

Arriving at the mental health trust offices, I announced that the need to shout had receded. There was relief on many a face.

Yvonne sighed when I arrived home. No more will the TV be on full blast for the news. No more will Yvonne have to repeat everything twice.

So happy are we both, that I have booked a table for two at the Dick Turpin, our local restaurant, for this evening. Yvonne deserves a treat.

Friday 18th January 2002

Different place

It is clear that I have been partially deaf for some months for this morning the world is a different place. The word processor whirrs and buzzes. I have heard the creaking floorboard under the bedroom carpet. (I once tried to fix it by hammering in a couple of six inch nails, but a man who happened to be around at the time – why, I cannot recall – advised against. Pulling up the floorboard, he demonstrated that I could – and probably would – have punched the nail straight through an electric cable. The floorboard has creaked ever since, although I have not heard it for some time until today.)

Val-Across-The-Road fair bellowed at me when I delivered the discs for the BROADSHEET this morning. No need to shout, I cried. Yvonne took me to the lounge, turned on the television and demonstrated just how loud the sound has been over recent weeks to enable me to hear.

Richard is coming home for lunch today. We are taking the usual precautions – moving tinned and packet food from the kitchen and hiding the spare toilet rolls. He will be pleased that his elderly father is no longer the epitome of Mr Meldrew (well, in one respect at least).

Yvonne's treat of dinner at the Dick Turpin last evening went well all things considered. Having selected our dishes for starters and main courses from the big menu, we discovered that we could have these under the fixed price menu. The trouble started when the waitress returned to clear the plates. Do you wish to see the dessert menu, she trilled. No, said I. Coffee? No, said I. When the waitress had departed to sort out the bill, Yvonne suddenly and out of character cried: *"But I was looking forward to a pudding!"* Recognising that such extravagance might cost me a tenner, I railed on her to put such thoughts out of her mind. As ever, Yvonne agreed to pursue the matter no further.

I feel a bit guilty about that pudding in the cool light of day. But we did have a bottle of Chablis between us and I recall little of the walk home. Had we indulged in a pudding, anything might have happened. We watched some television and marvelled at the sound quality. I learned this morning that my eldest son was grieved somewhat that his mother had been denied her pudding and has promised to put the matter right at some time in the near future.

This morning I have asked Yvonne to fit a suppressor to the vacuum cleaner. I hope this can be done sooner rather than later.

Saturday 19th January 2002

Here and There with NELMHT

In 2002 and the following year or so, I wrote a series of short articles for *Mental Health Matters,* the occasional full-colour newsletter of the North East London Mental Health NHS Trust (NELMHT), where my role continued to be that of a non-executive director. Someone once asked what a non-executive director was? The answer was that it was a bit like a bidet; no-one knew what is was for, but it added a touch of class. In a way, I felt a bit like that. Here are the five short pieces I penned under the title *Here and There,* before *Mental Health Matters* was axed as part of the cuts to services that the NHS suffered from time to time – well, in truth, all the time.

I venture to Upton Park

When I set out one sunny Tuesday morning for West Ham Football Ground, I had two aims in mind. To find out just what the NHS Modernisation Agency was up to in North East London and to acquire two West Ham United pens for Stuart and his younger brother, Daniel. Why a football ground? Because this was the venue for the North East London Sector Non-executive Directors' Annual Conference, with the theme 'Modernising Health and Social Services in North East London'. What better reason?

Getting my priorities right, I sat on a plush seat, slipping into my briefcase the West Ham pen thoughtfully placed by the organisers on top of a notepad. That was for Stuart. A furtive glance to an unattended seat – and I had landed a pen for Stuart's younger brother.

With that vital task completed, I was free to concentrate on the modernisation bit. This was all good stuff. One speaker told us about an American *"who has done thinking at the leading edge".* It sounded a little painful to me. He went on to tell us that he had *"been invited to STRIP for North East London"* which made me wonder if this was the kind of event my wife would wish me to attend. But all was well, for STRIP was an acronym for The North East London Service Transformation and Redesign Innovation Project. Acronyms fluttered around – as they do. I learned that AWR is Assisted Wheel Reinvention and wrote down what TIDES stands for, but cannot now read my handwriting. I learned that 'bespoke' is not only used to describe a type of men's tailor, but also a programme.

The main thrust (I have caught the jargon) in North East London was an Out of Hours Service – a sort of 'Open all hours' without Ronnie Barker and Arkwright. When the 'Ideas Generation' session was called, my mental health colleagues and I scattered ourselves liberally amongst the tables – determined that mental health should get a look-in. This, again, was all high-powered stuff with phrases like 'multi-skilling', 'roving teams', 'critical mass' – not to mention 'centres similar to supermarkets and filling stations'. I tried to look intelligent and kept saying 'mental health'. I think my table caught the drift.

At question-time, one non-executive director told us about his mother, which was kind of him for I have not met the lady who, by all accounts, is not to be trifled with. We learned that, like many of the elderly, his mother is not concerned about modernisation – just as long as her GP is accessible and not based in a village miles away. I would hazard a guess that his mother does not live within North East London as villages are not in abundance in these parts.

But the best was yet to come in the late afternoon with the Presentations of the North East London Modernisation Awards 2003. When I spotted Jimmy, Geri and Charlie on the guest list, I knew that NELMHT had done it again. I caught up with them as Geri tucked into the cream cakes and we all delighted in the fresh strawberries and cream. Goodmayes Vocational Rehabilitation Service was Highly Commended in the User Involvement category and we now have another trophy to go in the long-awaited trophy cabinet at Trust Head Office.

(Sadly, a year or two later that Service was axed as part of yet another cost-cutting exercise – furtively disguised as a slice of modernisation. The Service ran the garden centre and a craft workshop at Goodmayes Hospital, where former inpatients who were being treated for their mental illness in the community, worked – some being paid but most volunteering. I like to think I put up a spirited case to retain the Service – all to no avail for I had little or no support from the professionals, some of whom I believe let down those who most needed their support by going along with the decision to close the service, very much against their better judgement. I still see some of those patients who found something constructive and worthwhile to do at the garden centre and in the workshop – now wandering aimlessly around Ilford Town Centre with nothing to occupy their waking hours. I guess that some – but not all – members of staff who used to buy their hanging baskets in the summer and holly wreaths at Christmas from the garden centre have taken their custom elsewhere and, sadly, do not give the service a thought as they direct their beady eyes at some other highly successful unit that is right for the axe of modernisation. What I found especially galling about this closure was that the decision was made some distance away from the garden centre and workshop and I doubt if many – or, indeed, any – of those who decided the service should be chopped had even taken the trouble to visit and see things for themselves.)

Walking home from the bus stop in the early evening, I went via Stuart and his younger brother's home. Stuart's mouth fell open in abject joy as I pulled two pens from my briefcase.

"This one is for you," I said.

"And the other one is for my Dad?" questioned Stuart.

I pointed out that the second pen was for Daniel. I should have realised that the whole family are mad keen on West Ham. Perhaps there will be another conference at Upton Park and, if so, I must book a place – if only for the pens. I arrived home with a goodly pack of reading on modernisation. It is in the summerhouse and will be read and absorbed – and you may ask me questions when the snow begins to fall.

Two fêtes and a barbecue

Trundling around NELMHT, my time is spent at Trust Board and Sub-committees, Hospital Managers' Appeals and Review Panels under the *Mental Health Act 1983*, Ward/Unit Visits, interviews, seminars, inquiries into serious untoward incidents (suicides in the main) – and occasionally something for Yvonne to enjoy with me.

One sunny summer Sunday afternoon, I threw soggy wet sponges at Leslie, Meadow Court's Manager. I paid a pound for five of the soggiest, but after two direct hits, I gave three back. With lots of folk enjoying the fête and stalls staffed by supporters from within Goodmayes and the community, over £1,000 was raised to spend on patients.

At the Woodbury Fête, Manager Marian smiled benignly, Chaplain Mike chatted with Associate Hospital Manager Malcolm (the latter bedecked smartly – as ever – in dark suit and tie, despite the searing heat) whilst Margaret (Her of the Nursing Directorate) spent a happy afternoon folding raffle tickets (as is her wont).

Keen to get moving with the new sensory garden, Activities Co-ordinator Mina jumped for joy as over £1,650 came rolling in. That should buy a few lavender and rosemary bushes.

Chief Executive Paul offered me a lift to the Friday afternoon Barbecue at Naseberry Court but, busy man that he is, did not tear himself away from his desk until late – by which time the cooks had retired and everyone had full tummies. Manager JJ and Project Manager Joanne took Paul, Annie, Margaret, Uncle Tom Cobley and all on a rip-roaring tour of the refurbishments – including the fine extension, the new showers and the special paint that came all the way from the U S of A (costing, so it was said, some £100 a gallon pot). One nameless lady tucked into chicken drumsticks with the best of us . . . and slunk away (as only she can slink) with a doggy bag for supper.

Where would I be without Google.com?

Assembled in the basement at the Falcon Banqueting Suite (Nan's Pantry before the make-over) for the Workshop on the Review of Rehabilitation Services in Redbridge, everyone else appeared perfectly at ease when the lady in charge told us that we would be using the *World Café Methodology.* Knowing nods and smiles abounded. Some sucked their lips, whilst others made cooing noises.

When faced with something I do not understand, I have learned that it is best to keep calm, to look intelligent – and never ever to raise my hand for an explanation. All is invariably revealed.

Glancing around, I spotted that Amy was clearly happy at the prospect – and if it's good enough for Amy, it's fine by me, but I sensed that Jean had positioned herself close enough to leap to my side should I bottle out.

Having listened to a lively resume of the draft report, white paper cloths were wafted onto the tables and the *World Café Methodology* was revealed. We would sit at tables of six, consider a question and write our answers on the tablecloth. After fifteen minutes or so, five would move on to another table, whilst one remained to tell his or her new found friends what the last lot had written on the tablecloth – in case they could not read, decipher the handwriting or understand what the previous gang were getting at.

And so it would continue until we had answered all the questions or were exhausted with trying. *World Café Methodology* was great fun and some serious business was done. The tablecloths were collected and, we were assured, the scribbles would be transcribed and noted.

A new facility I had not met before was the provision of 'mobile phone breaks', when we retired outside into the open air to pretend that we had received numerous messages of great urgency. Had I received prior warning, I would have asked Yvonne to leave me a few.

Back home, I went into Google.com. Here I learned that the *World Café Methodology "refers to both a vision and a method of dialogue. It evolved out of conversations and experimentation one evening at the home of consultants Juanita Brown and David Isaacs".*

I told my friend John. He, too, went into Google.com and informed me that he was *"slightly concerned to see that you have been to the sort of event that led to the French Revolution or the Birthing of the American Republic".* Perhaps John's Google.com is different from mine.

I must tell JJ, who delights in baffling me with science. Do ask him to show you his Ambient Indicator of Time when you are next in Waltham Forest.

Public transport

As a non-driver and the proud owner of a Freedom Pass, I travel around the Trust by public transport wherever possible. I am told it is good for the soul.

Twice since the Christmas festivities were underway I have been thrown off a train at Romford Station. On the first occasion a disembowelled voice told me that the electric cables were down at Chelmsford and on the second that something nasty had happened at Brentwood. Aware that a patient, consultant, solicitor, nurse, social worker and three colleagues would not take kindly to my arriving an hour or two late for a Hospital Managers' Panel under the *Mental Health Act 1983*, I hopped out of Romford Station to hail a cab.

"Mascalls Park!" I cried – and each time I noted that the cab driver had a blank, if not startled, look. *"Do you know Warley?"* I asked. That rang a bell and I spent each journey explaining that Warley (which had been a mental health site since the year dot) is no more and that Mascalls Park is now the place – and why, when and how. I think it is called public relations.

Making my way – when most sensible folk were eating lunch – from a meeting of the London Mental Health Act Network at St. Pancras Hospital to NELMHT's Naseberry Court in Waltham Forest would have taxed the most experienced explorer. Fearing I might be caught up in an earth-moving vehicle on the Channel Tunnel Terminus building site North from St. Pancras, I again called to a cab, whose driver took me through back streets and yards I did not know existed and hope never to visit again. But the train journey from Liverpool Street to Highams Park was the highlight of the day, with lots of back gardens to peer into.

Travel home from Naseberry Court is oft times by bus, but occasionally in Jackie's car – which is kind of Jackie for hers is a nice car and the conversation good. If it is the bus and I am at Thorpe Coombe, I stop by at Homebase to see what's new for the garden. When at Stonelea, I find the coffee at the Internet Café nearby makes the prospect of the bus journey home quite exciting.

I now take great care when waiting for the bus after visits to Woodbury and Tomswood. Last summer I sat sitting at the bus stop in James Lane when a motorcycle mounted the pavement, brushing past my legs and nearly taking me with it – trousers and all. A few seconds later a police car screamed past but – fortunately – stayed on the roadway.

Journeying home from Goodmayes finds me at the King George Hospital bus stop, where there is rarely a dull moment. I was once hugged by a lady acquaintance of many summers and was spotted in the process by another lady friend, who was so upset that someone else was at the receiving end of the cuddle that she took refuge behind the bus shelter and sent me an e.mail on the subject that evening.

I have learned more about people's operations at that bus stop than at any time in my long and interesting life. And as someone who cannot stand the sight of blood, that means that when I arrive home I have to seek solace with some light reading – a few Trust Board papers, for example.

And at this point "Mental Health Matters" hit the dust and "Here and There" went the same way!

Bent and frail

On Monday last I journeyed to Dorking. First the bus to Ilford, then British Rail (or whatever it is called these days) to Stratford. Why do the station announcers insist on referring to me as a 'customer'? I do not buy anything. I have a Freedom Pass which entitles me to go anywhere by public transport within Greater London. I am a passenger, not a customer. I do wish they would sort this out.

At Stratford, I moved to the Jubilee Line, which is a pleasure and a delight. Modern trains moving smoothly through Docklands and then into a tunnel, where the platforms are enclosed with Perspex screens. As the train comes to a halt in the stations, the carriage doors glide open simultaneously with doors in the screens. It is all very civilised and intended to deter would-be suicides from jumping in front of the trains.

At Dorking my brother was standing by his car. Now aged seventy-four, he is bent and frail. Arthritis has done its worst. Married, his main work was commercial antibiotic research for a major pharmaceutical company, whilst his passions in life were do-it-yourself, cacti and clinical bacteriology.

Moving in the 1950s from his first house in Chigwell (Essex) to Leatherhead (Surrey) required two removal vans – one for the furniture, the other for the cacti. A greenhouse across the bottom of his Leatherhead garden occupied him from 6am to 8am and then again each evening after seven.

He rang me one day in the 29th year of marriage. His wife had left him, he told me. Had you any warning, I asked? None whatsoever, he told me. His wife had been playing tennis at the Leatherhead Tennis Club for the past fifteen years or so. She goes there every evening and returns home between two and four in the morning, said my brother. Did that not raise any questions in your mind, I asked? None, said my brother. Not even when she came home at four in the morning. *"No – the tennis club is floodlit!"* he replied.

We are not a close family and time passed. The telephone rang early one morning. I am marrying my Spanish Secretary, my brother informed me. We attended the wedding. Time passed again and with another early morning call came the news that my brother was moving that day to retire in Spain. The cacti would travel – again – in a separate container van for planting in the grounds of the new villa.

From time to time we caught up – with telephone calls from Spain or London. My brother and his new wife travelled the world. Between times he planted out the garden at the villa with his precious cacti. All was well. Then he telephoned. Her mother had moved in and the locks had been changed on the doors. Back in England, with his cash sorely reduced, he rented a flat in Sussex. Always the epitome of a snob, he once told me that he could not understand why I continued to live in a terrace house. Nothing was ever good enough for him. One move followed another.

Then he met a cactus lady from his past, whose husband was seriously ill. When the husband died, my brother moved in within a month and romance blossomed once more. Builders were summoned to extend the bungalow and build three new greenhouses. Cacti were purchased from around the globe. They visited us one Christmas complete with pedigree spaniel who had special food and spent most of the day eating it. Flown in from America, the food not the dog.

Then disaster struck. The lady friend had a breakdown and was taken to hospital. Hardly surprising really, for the builders could do nothing right and the potting of the cacti took my brother most of the day and some of the night. Her solicitor sent a letter demanding my brother leave the lady's home. He did. Then began a protracted correspondence as my brother tried to recover some of the £30,000 he had spent on builders and cacti, not to mention the greenhouses.

Alone again, he set up home in a one bed roomed maisonette on the outskirts of Leatherhead. He moved last year – to the maisonette next door on the ground floor as his arthritis worsened. There he sits day by day with the eight-year-old spaniel and his books. I have visited twice in the past six months. He shows me his will and his investment documents. His two children and his grandchildren will have nothing to do with him for reasons that are in themselves both sad and bewildering, but the blame for the family split falls firmly at the feet of my brother. He is a sad and lonely old man. He promises to visit us in the spring and will, no doubt, question why we are still living in a terraced house.

He has a friend in Cornwall, who has two teenagers and lots and lots of animals and birds on a farm. He speaks with her each week – between visiting Sainsbury's and the special American dog food emporium, the library and the park, and calling to see his consultant, general practitioner, vet, dog hairdresser, chiropodist, dentist and anyone else who deals with ailments in dog or man. He has a full diary, indeed, interspersed with visits to learned lectures on genetics and cacti. His maisonette is immaculate.

He is worried that socks from M & S shrink after the sixth wash. He went back to confront M & S with this fact and they suggested he bought them a size larger. This works, he assures me.

He buys his fruit from Sainsbury's and places it on the window sill to ripen. It does so after seven days, but if he does not eat it within 48 hours it goes off. He is thinking of writing to *The Times* about this.

His private health insurance company has finally told him they have had enough and he is back to the NHS. I can hardly blame them. I have seen the file of correspondence. And the animal insurers have threatened to pull out too.

We had lunch at a pub near Reigate. We travelled in his car. On a stretch of road which was clearly marked 40mph he drove at seventy, assuring me that he kept within the speed limit for if he was stopped, he would lose his licence when the police found out how many ailments he has. When I ventured to suggest that the speed limit was forty on this stretch of road, he slammed the brakes on and we drifted by at fifty.

He drew my attention to all the points on the road where had had an accident or a near miss.

Saturday 26th January 2002

No major incident

The Aldborough Hatch Defence Association (AHDA) Committee Meeting passed without major incident. I arrived fifteen minutes early to find Councillor Vanessa sitting by the radiator. Councillor Vanessa holds her monthly surgery in the church halls on a Friday evening – and last night was her night.

The wind was hurtling around the churchyard at gale force as committee members started to arrive. Jean and John, neighbours in Applegarth Drive, were blown into the hall with an elderly man who wants to join the committee. He was very quiet throughout the proceedings, but I guess he enjoyed himself.

When there are two thousand copies of the AHDA's *Open Space* newsletter needing to be delivered Jean and John spring into action like a couple of field marshals, organising the house delivery teams as if war could break out at any moment.

As West Ham were not playing at home, we were expecting Ron. We knew the *Archers* were over, but realising that *Eastenders* started at eight made us fear that he might decide to stay home after all. To our amazement he came dashing through the churchyard at a minute to the hour. Joan told us that she had feared the sycamore tree in the churchyard might shed a bough or two, so walked via the road rather than take the shortcut through the gravestones. Graham made an entrance with his files of papers. He is a policeman in the Borough and is keen to raise the profile of the Metropolitan Police, assuring us that with himself and his colleagues guarding our streets we may sleep safely in our beds.

John from Barkingside 21 was with us to observe. He would have to leave by nine – I have the feeling, although no proof, that this is because he and some of his pals meet up for a pint or two on Friday evenings in a hostelry in Barkingside. (I later discovered that John, who is a year or two younger than me, had been a fellow pupil at Leyton County High School for Boys in the 1940s. We were able to share memories of our schooldays – which was pleasant.)

Councillor John appeared about twenty minutes after we started, hot foot from the surgery of Linda Perham MP. Linda sent her apologies as she was dealing with a queue of constituents with foot and mouth – at least, I think that is what John said.

The meeting was hardly earth shattering. As Chairman I wanted to involve the committee in making decisions about where we go next when the result of the public inquiry into the proposed London City All-Weather Racecourse at Fairlop Waters is announced. I had circulated papers for discussion, including two news releases – one if we lose the appeal and the other if we win.

Joan thought the releases were very nice. Ron wanted to know what was happening about the replacement of the tree in Ramsgill Approach.

Councillor John told us that as Vice-Chairman of Planning he could say nothing. He tells us this at every meeting, but then talks nineteen to the dozen, interspersing his revelations with a reminder that he cannot say anything as he is Vice-Chairman of Planning.

Councillor Vanessa played to the gallery as ever. Whatever happens, we can rely on Councillor Vanessa to support it. Councillor Vanessa is also on Planning and, therefore, legally debarred from saying anything. As a result most of her contributions last for ten minutes minimum – but, of course, do not refer to any matters pertaining to planning.

Fearing that we might be there all night and that Ron might wake up, I suggested we formed a working party. Graham volunteered – as I guessed he might. Linda, who had joined us silently at the back, offered to join him. Others looked at their boots and some counted the ceiling tiles. Suggestions as to what the working party might do came loud and clear. We will report back, said Graham – and I fear they will (although they never did!).

I agreed to prepare for the Open Meeting when the announcement is made. Everyone thought that was a good idea, but I was going to do this in any case. Jean and John wanted to know when the war will be declared so that they can assemble the troops to deliver *Open Space.* Ron asked who would issue the rifles and where the ammunition was stored. He also promised full support from the West Ham first team. Jan, sitting at my side and taking notes feverishly, admitted that her son supports West Ham and he would have a word when they were next playing at home.

Out in the air, I allowed the hurricane now blowing to waft me towards the warm lights of home. The man who turned up at last night's meeting went by this morning on his way to buy his newspaper. *"Good meeting last night,"* he called.

This morning I dashed up the road to see Shirley at the farm. Yvonne wanted some eggs and bird and squirrel feeding materials. Shirley was in good form. I took a daffodil I have grown in the porch, one of the half-hundredweight of bulbs sold to me by Farmer Peter last autumn and the first to burst into flower. I would have taken more but there are only six in flower and there is a limit. Shirley appeared touched. Spotting that I had noticed a length of plastic tied around her coffee table, Shirley explained that this is part of her physiotherapy for her healing foot. When she started to show me how it all worked, I beat a hasty retreat. Too much like *Casualty* for me.

Saturday 2nd February 2002

Dead – but alive

It is time to tell the story of the lady who was dead, but was in truth alive – and robustly so.

Part of my role as a non-executive director on NELMHT is to act as a shepherd to the team of Associate Hospital Managers. One Associate is eighty-two and a lady of considerable intellect and as astute as a button. A former director of social services in a local borough, Margery maintains all her marbles and a few more. I first experienced Margery's ability to sort out a young whipper-snapper such as me when I telephoned her home one evening. A man answered and promised to pass on my message. Meeting her a week or so later, I commented that I was grateful to her husband for taking the call.

"Young man," Margery rounded on me, *"do not jump to conclusions. He is not my husband, but my partner."*

Now I am generally very careful in this area. I never ever refer to wives or husbands, but invariably to partners. However, I thought I was on safe ground with an eighty-two-year-old – but obviously not.

A week or two back, Margery did not arrive at a business meeting for Associates. Jackie, the Administrator, was concerned for Margery always attends or sends her apologies. Arriving home, I received a call from a very worried Jackie. Telephoning Margery's home, her partner had informed Jackie that Margery was dead. Margery had a fall at home two weeks earlier, was taken to hospital, had a stroke and died. The funeral had taken place and her ashes had been scattered.

Jackie's gast was flabbered. Surely we would have heard of Margery's passing? As a former director of social services, the event would have been referred to in the local newspapers. I promised to make some enquiries and rang the present occupant of the post of director of social services in the appropriate Borough, a man known to me because he chairs the drug action team and plays 12th man for the court's cricket team. As luck would have it, he was out.

Minutes later Jackie was back on the telephone. A neighbour of Margery's had telephoned. Margery is not dead, but in hospital. Her partner was most confused.

Having the next afternoon free, I journeyed to hospital, by two buses and a Central Line train there and the same back again. Approaching Margery's bedside, I spotted the good lady sitting in a chair with zimmer frame close at hand.

Hailed with a wave, Margery called: *"I suppose you thought I was dead!"* Before I could confirm of deny, Margery explained that her partner is getting a little forgetful. She had indeed fallen and broken her hip, but a plate had been fitted and she was skidding around the ward on her zimmer, soon to be home and in full action again.

"You see," Margery confided, *"it was my brother who died. And he was only seventy-seven. I wanted to go to the funeral, but the hospital would not let me. I offered to pay for an ambulance, but they refused. The chaplain came to sit with me when the funeral took place, which was kind. My partner keeps telling everyone I am dead – and I am not."*

Is there anything I can get you, I asked?

"Yes," said Margery. *"I would like a copy of 'The Times' and some satsumas."*

I set off for the hospital shop. No '*Times*'. No satsumas. I purchased '*The Independent*' and some boxed jellies. Back on the ward, the jellies were well-received, but not so '*The Independent*'.

"I suppose that will have to do," said a disdainful Margery.

I telephoned Margery today. Home from hospital, Margery told me that she is making great progress with the zimmer frame, having guided it out of the house to the garage this morning. I guess Margery will be back to duties ere long.

Saturday 16th February 2002

Sunday morning

It is Sunday morning. I have a two day trial on Monday and Tuesday, following an alleged affray in an Ilford Club with a number of defendants and top barristers. Kevin, Clerk to the Justices, decided that he would use the Stipendiary for this one – on the basis that if top barristers see a Stip in the chair they will not mess about as they have been known to do with lay justices. The Stip had a stroke last week –

so Kevin was up a gum tree without a paddle. He rang me and asked if I would chair the trial. I agreed – but pointed out that if I had been Bench Chairman a lay magistrate would have been hearing the matter. We have no need for a Stip, no need at all. Kevin smiled. They will know they have got to behave when they see you up there, he told me.

This past week has been a bit fraught. The start button on my WP played up – and gave up completely on Thursday. Nick came over and took the front off the box thing. There is a bit of plastic that works the start button and this had snapped. Out came the Superglue and it all worked – for a day. Then it stopped working again. Nick has now taken the front away to try again and I am left with a tower with no front but easy access to the start button with a pencil. If Nick's Superglue does not work, I will ring the manufacturers to buy a new front. For a time I was like a man without arms, with e.mails that I could not access.

Half-term passed without incident. Luke (now ten) took me to see the latest Walt Disney movie, *Monsters Inc,* on Wednesday afternoon. I am unsure if I understood what it was all about. We had a medium popcorn, a medium diet coke and pick-your-own sweets. That little lot cost more than the cinema tickets.

Richard (approaching twenty-eight) came home on Friday for a day and a night. Luke took us both to the park on Saturday – he riding his skates and Richard carrying the skateboard. Richard took one look at the professional kids on the skate park and decided he would not try to emulate their expertise. I froze in the harsh wind. Back home, Yvonne had gone shopping with Marlon (now twenty months). I had left my keys indoors so we sat in the front garden for an hour waiting for Yvonne to return and I froze even more.

It is nearly lunchtime. I must prepare for the arrival of Heather, Luke and Marlon. Robert is working today. I will have a lie down at 2pm when the anti-virus programme automatically checks me for viruses. I have received the Magistrates' virus – yes, that's right, the Magistrates' virus – four times in the past year, but my anti-virus has quarantined it every time so no damage has been done.

Writing to a friend who messaged me earlier this week with a tale of a funeral in the north, I wrote to tell him that when I was elected as Bench Chairman, my predecessor told me that I would attend many such events. I purchased a dark overcoat from Dunn's specially. The funerals were fine and many, but the worst aspect was the fact that my predecessor insisted on sitting with me on each occasion. He is tone deaf and sings very loudly with no sense of tune or timing. These days I do the occasional funeral, but leave most to my successor as Bench Chairman. There are limits.

My friend complains that no-one speaks to him when he takes his dog walking. I suggest that he might try going out in his pyjamas and dressing gown with slippers – preferably the soft variety with a floral pattern. If he is arrested, I agree that he might give the police my telephone number. I will deny all knowledge.

Sunday 24th February 2002

Conmen

For some weeks past major building works have been taking place hereabouts. Immediately opposite our home, Steve sold his detached 1930s villa to a builder who had purchased a plot of land to the rear. There were mixed feelings that what had been a site for garages would now become a small housing estate. Not that there were objections to new housing; rather concern at the loss of garage space and the fact that yet another side road would now lead into Aldborough Road North. In particular, the position of the new road through Steve's old house would produce a dog-leg crossroads with our house in the firing line of one of the dog's legs – if you see what I mean (but do not fret if you do not).

The works have passed without major incident. Our early mornings are accompanied by the arrival of long low loaders whose drivers perform miracles at getting them in and out of the site along the newly built road where once Steve sat in his garden admiring his goldfish pond of splendid proportions beneath his Eucalyptus tree. Yellow brick walls are presently going up along the side gardens of Ruth and Michael's homes adjoining the new road. Fourteen houses are now roofed.

On Monday morning I received a message at court from Yvonne on my mobile's answerphone. Yvonne told me that a carpet fitter from the new estate had called that morning to apologise for the inconvenience we have been caused by the building works opposite our home. To alleviate any suffering and as a gesture of goodwill, he wished to make us an offer.

The builders had over-ordered on the carpets, not appreciating that many of the new owners would prefer to have wood block floors rather than wall-to-wall luxury. Holding a pattern book in his hand, he showed Yvonne four or five plain carpets – two greens, a terra-cotta, and a couple of light fawns. We can offer this carpet for £3 a square metre, he said, and we can fit today. Yvonne warmed to one of the greens for our dining room, but said that she would have to discuss this with me first, and as I was not as home, Yvonne would have to await my return before reaching a decision. Clearly expecting to clinch the deal there and then, the man expressed surprise that Yvonne could not make the decision without reference to me. Yvonne suggested that the man return later in the day. When he attempted to push Yvonne into a decision without me, Yvonne let slip that I would be returning from court that afternoon. The man looked surprised and Yvonne, not wishing the man to think I was before the bench as a defendant, explained that I was sitting in court as a magistrate. Taking his leave, the man said he would be back.

With that Yvonne left the message on my mobile. Later that morning I rang Yvonne, but by now the scene had shifted. A friend from down the road was with Yvonne. Two men in a plain white van had called at our friend's home earlier in the morning. Much the same story had been given and our friend, who recently celebrated her eightieth birthday, saw the opportunity to have her lounge, hall and staircase carpeted at the same time.

The white van stood outside, with some carpet rolls protruding from the rear doors. Indicating that they would fit the carpet that very day, the two men said that they would need a cash payment of £870 to supply and fit. When our friend explained that she did not have that amount of cash in the house, the two men offered to take her to the building society in Ilford Town Centre. Into the van jumped our friend. Returning home, four rolls of carpet were unloaded into the house, as our friend handed over the cash and the men went off to collect their tools.

That was the last our friend saw of the men and their van. An hour or so passed and she contacted Yvonne. Alert by now that something was amiss, Yvonne and our friend went over the road to the builders' site office. Their worst fears were confirmed when the site manager told them that there are no carpet fitters on site.

Our friend now has four rolls of un-inspected carpet of unknown – but somewhat suspect – quality and no-one to fit the stuff.

I telephoned the police at Barkingside from my home and two officers arrived within the hour. Inevitably, they recognised me as a magistrate at Barkingside and former Bench Chairman. I sensed that they knew this before they set out from the police station, in spite of the fact that I had not divulged this when speaking on the telephone.

Our friend came to our home as she did not want to upset her husband, who would be confused at the arrival of the police. After describing the men and outlining the facts, our friend admitted that she had been a fool. But the police officers would have none of it and reassured her in what I can only describe as a caring manner. It is their profession, said one officer. Our friend took the officers to her home to inspect the carpet. The officers then called at all the houses between our home and our friend's house to check if others had been offered a similar deal. None had.

Stories of conmen appear regularly in the local newspapers. Yvonne and our friend's experience – and mine, albeit from a distance – highlights the fact that conmen are professionals skilled in their art. How easy it is for intelligent, worldly wise people to be taken in by them.

Tuesday 26th February 2002

Ticket tout

Returning to Ilford from London late this evening after having a meal with Graham and Richard, I had to wait for a bus at Ilford Station for some time and was able to observe a ticket tout in action. A young man in his twenties, he stood on the pavement outside the station, asking passengers for their one day travel cards. Those who were not catching buses, but walking or driving home, seemed happy in the main to hand him their tickets. He then proceeded down the road a safe distance and asked passers-by walking towards the station if they would like to buy a travel card? About one in five bought a card from him for coins – I would guess one pound a time for it was after 9pm and they were probably only making one journey into town. Two of his pals sat on the pavement nearby, drinking from cans.

There were no Railway Police about – and had they been, they could only operate within the station forecourt. And there were no police anywhere to be seen. I gained the impression that the people purchasing the tickets were perhaps 'regulars'. The tout certainly had the situation under control.

Monday 4th March 2002

Top the poll!

I received the following message today from a Councillor friend at Redbridge: "*At the adjourned council tonight I was congratulated on getting you to stand as a Lib*

Dem candidate for Aldborough. He will top the poll, I am told from all sides. Well now it's £8k a year and a delightful role in the public's affections."

I have replied today as follows:

"Sadly, you are too late in inviting me to stand for the Lib Dems in Aldborough in the May Council elections. I have already decided to stand as the Stop-The-Racecourse-No-More-Gravel-Extraction-Sing-Hymns-Faster-Bring-Back-Hanging-For-Conmen-Candidate. Or STRNMGESHFBBHFC for short – and just try getting your tongue round that!

"I have a full team of supporters waiting for my signal to hit the doorsteps. Yvonne will be in charge of releasing the balloons and fixing banners from trunk to trunk in the tree-lined avenues around the Hatch – Yvonne is good up ladders. Luke will hand-deliver leaflets, equipped with skates for speed – Luke is a whiz on skates, but will avoid knocking old ladies off their feet. Marlon will address street-corner meetings, dressed in his Bob-the-Builder T-shirt and socks – his repertoire of words extends from Mummy and Daddy to Digger, but mainly the latter. Guests from the Redbridge Night Shelter – which closes at the end of March for the summer months – will sleep in the garden shed of any resident displaying a rival's election poster in their window.

"I will remain at my desk throughout the campaign, writing news releases daily for e.mailing to the local press. I am working up the slogan for my campaign. Initial thoughts include: *'I may have a Freedom Pass, but I can still walk to the bus stop – just'* or *'A free tomato plant with every vote'.*

"I guess the news will send a shiver or three up the spines of a few councillors, and would guess that your lot will infiltrate the Hatch with bows and arrows to burst the balloons as they fly majestically overhead and pen knives to cut the banners loose. But let's keep the fight clean.

"I have decided to continue sitting in court throughout the campaign. The ushers will distribute my campaign literature at the reception desk. Defendants who pin the 'Vote for Ron' badges on their chests will receive a 50% discount on all sentences. Those carrying balloons will be given an absolute discharge without having to plead.

"Sir, the fight is on. May the best man win!"

Wednesday 6th March 2002

Sixty-nine

My 69th birthday on Monday last came and went as 69th birthdays should. The Redbridge Night Shelter Open Afternoon the previous day found Yvonne serving tea and homemade cakes to the visitors, whilst I acted as one of the tour guides.

Linda Perham, MP for Ilford North, confided in me about the long-awaited decision from Lord Falconer on whether or not the London City All-Weather Racecourse planning inquiry result goes our way or the way of Wiggins PLC.

Showing Linda around the bedrooms for the homeless guests, Linda suggested that the moment was right for a photograph for her constituency newsletter. Calling up a volunteer to take the picture on her digital camera, Linda took my hand and led me towards one of the beds. Do you want me to get under the covers to give the impression of an anonymous homeless guest, I asked? No, no, said Linda, taking my hand and pulling me down onto the bed beside her. And then we were captured, side by side sitting on the bed. It is the first time I have been anywhere near a bed with an MP, and a lady MP at that – let alone on a bed (but, let it be clearly understood, not in it) – and is a moment I will treasure.

My birthday evening was unusual. At about 5.45pm I rang Una Paul to thank her for her birthday card and box of begonia corms, to find that she had collapsed half-an-hour or so earlier. Yvonne and I went to her home. Auntie Una (eighty-four and rejoicing locally as Auntie Una to everyone since the day some thirty or more years ago when my daughter, Heather, started to call her that) was on the settee, unable to move.

We rang her GP and Una's son and daughter. The GP arrived at about 8.15pm. He diagnosed vertigo and rang King George Hospital to warn them of Una's impending admission. He rang the ambulance service. Una's son and daughter-in-law arrived about 8.30pm from Chelmsford. We stayed with them until 10pm when they were still waiting for the ambulance. Before leaving I checked that an ambulance was on its way – and it was.

The next evening Heather dropped us off at the hospital. Auntie Una was on a trolley in A & E, waiting for a bed. And not a very happy Auntie Una at that. A young man in porter's uniform arrived to take her off to a Ward, but appeared to think that any time would do.

After an hour of watching him drink tea and chat up the nurses, I enquired if we might proceed to the Ward. Not without a nurse, the young man told me. Then, suddenly, we were off, complete with nurse.

Inside the Ward we waited whilst Auntie Una settled. Another porter passed by. *"Hello,"* he said, *"you must like it here. I either see you here or in Goodmayes or smiling at me from the ILFORD RECORDER."* And with a *"Have a good evening,"* he trundled off with an empty trolley.

Wednesday 20th March 2002

SIM cards and the like

My eldest son suggested that I meet him in London for lunch, for he would have my birthday present with him. We found a sandwich bar round the back from the Houses of Parliament. Over the coffee, Graham handed me a brightly packaged parcel.

Inside was a Nokia mobile 'phone. Before I could mention that I already have one, Graham asked me to produce it from my briefcase. Placed side by side and compared with the new model, my old mobile resembled a manual lawnmower rather than an electric job. It was like a hand-pumped organ compared to an electric keyboard that does everything except make the tea.

Opening my old mobile before my eyes, Graham extracted the SIM card, inserted it in the new all-singing-all-dancing Nokia – and to prove it worked we rang Yvonne. The old machine was six inches long and resembled a brick. This is less than a quarter the size.

At home, ten-year-old Luke was thrilled. You have a thirty-three-ten, he chuckled in delight. Thirty-three-tens are the latest, he told me. Taking the mobile in his chubby hand, Luke showed me how to insert numbers, play tunes, enjoy games

– all, it seems, at no cost to me whatsoever. Luke played happily for half-an-hour, before handing the mobile back.

Left alone, I have inserted a few telephone numbers of folk I often ring – including Yvonne, who enjoys my calls when I tell her I am on the bus on the way home. I think I have mastered how to call the numbers up. Graham sorted out the ringing tone – loud – and the vibrator. If it rings and vibrates at least I will know it is my mobile that is jumping into action and not the mobile of others on the bus.

Graham travelled to London by train from Southampton. There was one mobile-free carriage. It also happened to be the only smoking carriage on the train. Graham put up with the other mobiles.

Wednesday 20th March 2002

Joseph – thirty-three years on

"Earlier in the evening we listened to a 'pop cantata'. Under one baton a symphony orchestra, a 'pop' group complete with electric guitars, organ and singers, a boys' choir and the organ of St. Paul's performed 'Joseph and the Amazing Technicolour Dreamcoat'. It is impossible to describe it but if you have the opportunity to attend a performance or to hear the new LP recording do so."

Last evening Yvonne and I watched the 1999 film of *Joseph* on DVD. Filmed at Pinewood with Donny Osmond, Richard Attenborough and Joan Collins, it runs to an hour-and-a-half or so. The DVD includes a sequence on the filming, with Tim Rice and Andrew Lloyd Webber recalling that the original *Joseph* was written for an end of term performance at Collet College in West London. It ran for twenty minutes.

I wrote the piece above in January 1969. As Editor of THE SCOUTER as it then was, I attended the second public performance in November 1968 at St. Paul's Cathedral. Andrew Lloyd Webber played the piano, leading the 'pop' group. The boys' choir was from Collet College.

Fresh as I was to writing and editing – and reviewing, for that matter – my text was short, but to the point. Little did I know that I was watching the birth pangs of what was to be a musical played throughout the world and to become the most popular musical ever written for schools to perform. In my collection, I have LPs and CDs bought over the years as the show progressed and grew in length.

Thursday 21st March 2002

Tadpoles

A friend sent me an e.mail this evening asking if I knew where he might find some tadpoles for his young son. I replied as follows.

"As for tadpoles, we may be able to oblige. We have two small ponds – well, more like large bowls really – in our garden. One is for goldfish (of which we have but one as he ate the others) and the other for frogs.

"There is a lot of spawn is in the frog pond, although the frogs tend to wander between the two. Yvonne spends many an hour in the summer moving frogs from the goldfish pond to the frog pond, but they do not seem to take the hint – and hop back again.

"I would be delighted to supply you with some spawn for our original spawn came from frogs in the garden of a Chief Inspector of Police. He bought it round in a jam jar, making the point that where the tadpoles spawn is where the frogs will live. So there was no point in bringing frogs to us – you have to have the spawn. Just let me know when you would like some – it might be a good idea to make it soon for it turns into tadpoles as quick as it arrives.

"I should tell you that one day in the spring a couple of years ago Yvonne was walking down the garden when a frog attached itself to her ankle. Try as she might, Yvonne could not shake the thing off. It clung to her and started to do weird things the like of which Yvonne had not experienced before, let alone from a frog. Eventually with my aid, the frog let go and grunted as it hopped on its way.

"I mentioned this to Shirley at the Farm, who is something of an expert around here on animals of all varieties. Frogs, said Shirley, make love at this time of the year and if there are not enough partners to go around, they will attach themselves to anything that moves. Hence the frog going at it with Yvonne's ankle. On hearing this, Yvonne stayed indoors for weeks on end, only venturing into the garden when I was around to ward off sex-crazed frogs. It had quite an effect on her, I can tell you.

"Don't let this put you off tadpoles, will you? But just make sure Laura wears knee high boots when going down the garden in the springtime."

Thursday 28th March 2002

Easter at Church

Easter is a time for trotting up the road to church. I have been five times since Maundy Thursday evening, although I will have to admit that it was in reality four-and-a-half times. We went at 8am on Easter Day. When I stayed with Yvonne in her Suffolk home at Easter, her Mum had us up at 6am for the 7am service.

Heather, Luke and Marlon came at 10.30am – but Marlon – at twenty months – is not over keen on church. He wants to visit Nana in the choir stalls. Heather and Luke went in at 10.30 and I took Marlon for a walk to the farm by the Dick Turpin. We saw the geese, rabbits, pot-bellied pigs, donkeys and chickens.

We arrived in church for the Eucharistic Prayer. Marlon managed to stay put at first, went with Heather and Luke to be blessed – and then he was off. No, he would not stay in the pew. Off he went to see Nana and gave her a big wet kiss in the midst of the communion hymn. Back he came – then off again, this time into the pulpit where he played peep with the children in the front row. Most folk smiled. The Vicar was highly amused – but then he goes at the end of April, so what does he care? A couple of ladies huffed and puffed.

I worked in the garden this afternoon whilst Yvonne washed gravel in a large colander we have for that purpose. I think Yvonne enjoyed the experience.

Monday 1st April 2002

Lady of the Bed Chamber

Each time I switch on the TV there is yet another Lady of the Bed Chamber ranting on about the Queen Mum. I do not have a problem with the Queen Mum, but when all is said and done she was 101. Where all these Ladies of the Bed Chamber come from beats me – and I am equally uncertain what they did whenever it was they did it. Yvonne assures me that they looked after the Queen Mum's clothes, but I have my doubts. They were up to something in that Bed Chamber for sure. We know – for we have been told many times – that the Queen Mum liked a Gin and Dubonnet anytime after 11am each day. Perhaps they were in charge of washing the glasses and taking the bottles to the bottle bank.

And, I ask myself, what are they all going to do now that the Queen Mum is with St. Peter? Perhaps we will see advertisements in the press as they offer their services to anyone looking for someone to do things in their Bed Chamber. I could do with one here, I can tell you. Not that I drink Gin and Dubonnet – yet.

Sunday 7th April 2002

Not printed!

First thing this morning I went straight to the front door to pick up the newspapers. Last Sunday morning I wrote a letter to the *Church Times*. I was not surprised to note this morning that it had not been printed. Here is the text:

"Dear Sir,

"I sit in the pews on Sunday mornings for Morning Prayer or Holy Communion – this morning the former. We have two readings from the Bible – Old Testament, New Testament, Gospel, Epistle. This morning we were back with Moses and the Egyptians, and then with Thomas. The Vicar preached well on the latter.

"Two Centuries have passed since contemporary writing was included in the Bible. I have no problem with that nor should I have. However, during those two Centuries spiritual writing has continued. This occupies acres and acres of bookshelf space but, sadly, only a minute selection is readily available to me in a busy life.

"As I sat in church this morning, I mused on the possibility of a third reading. With two Centuries of spiritual writing to draw upon, would we not benefit immensely from a short extract read as part of our liturgy from the billions of words that have been written across those years? Is it not time for a second Bible to be written as a compilation of that writing? After all, the word "Bible" has a variety of definitions, including – colloquially – 'any authoritative book'.

"It would need a committee, certainly a working party. It might well take a few years for agreement to be reached, for what to include and what to leave out would occupy minds. But surely something worth the effort for a living church committed to reaching out in the 21st Century.

"Amongst the congregation this morning were members of a family new to the parish and a group in their twenties mourning the death of their mother. I guess they appreciated our pre-occupation with Thomas and may even have understood our concerns for the Egyptians. However, a reading from one of the great spiritual writers of the more recent past might have demonstrated that the church moves on and continues to have something relevant to say in a world that has changed beyond recognition in the last fifty years, let alone twenty Centuries."

Friday 12th April 2002

Water feature

We have a new water feature. I knew that Yvonne would like one and I saw this advertised in last Sunday's OBSERVER. In a rash moment I rang the order line – and it arrived on Wednesday.

It consists of a large ceramic bowl with three smaller bowls above and a jug on top – all glazed on the inside. There is a pump – which I gather is essential to the operation. It all connects up with black metal – if you get the picture. There is also a solar panel, but I have put that away for the time being. Sun is not in strong supply hereabouts. It therefore works off the electricity – of which we have a lot.

It came without water or pebbles. Yvonne bought the distilled water (not essential, but it saves furring up the works so the leaflet tells me) and carried it home from Hainault Station where she happened to be collecting Luke. Now that Luke is ten – and starting this week – he is allowed to travel from Coppice School to Hainault Station on the bus with Samantha, his current girl friend, provided they sit near the driver, hold hands and do not talk to anyone.

Yvonne met Luke at Hainault on Tuesday and Wednesday, and I did so today. It is all working out well and I get a big wave and smile from Samantha, who travels on to the next bus stop.

But back to the water feature or, rather, the water. There were five litres in the plastic can. It was very heavy. I had difficulty carrying it down the garden let alone from Hainault Station.

We set it up with a few pebbles we had hereabouts and it works like a dream. The man at Hainault Station – in a shop, not the station itself – is getting pebbles in stock this weekend and Yvonne will bring them home next week. I guess they could be heavy, but Yvonne is a strong lass, born and bred in the Suffolk countryside, so a few pebbles will not deter her.

We have it for the moment in the summerhouse, but there is a problem. Tom next door is painting his summerhouse and tells me that the sound of running water makes him want to go to the toilet – so he keeps rushing indoors and is not getting the job done.

When we have the pebbles we may move it to the patio with the seat, the Japanese Willow tree and milk churns (the latter sorted out by the Good David at car boot sales, for he knows I had something to do with milk).

Mention of Tom reminds me that he had built a rather fine shed at the bottom of his garden a year or two prior to my deciding to purchase and erect my summerhouse in a similar spot at the bottom of my garden. Calling over the fence as Martyn and Patrick put the summerhouse together, Tom said that he would not have put his shed there had he realised this would be a built up area.

Thursday 18th April 2002

Buttercup yellow

We have covered the walls of the dining room in Buttercup Yellow. Two coats. It looks faintly bilious, but Yvonne seems pleased with the result. I fear I may need dark glasses as I take my vitamin pills at breakfast. We completed the decorating just before lunch today and started the task of bringing back the books and pictures and things. I fear this may take a day or so for Yvonne insists that each book is dusted, glasses are washed and pictures are given both a wash (of the glass) and a polish (of the frame). But I am excused most of this.

Yvonne fell off the stool yesterday whilst painting a high bit. It was, of course, her fault for climbing on the stool in the first place. I told her to leave the high bits to me, but during one of my breaks for a cigarette, my orders were disobeyed and wham! She caught her wrist at an awkward angle. It appears that nothing is broken but badly strained. One aspect of the fall was that she managed to get Buttercup Yellow right across the back of her hair. I thought it looked rather good – as though she had suddenly gone blonde. But Yvonne insisted it be removed. I tried to strain it back into the paint pot, but it would not work, so we lost a bit of paint.

When Shirley heard of the incident she was quite short with me on the telephone. It's about time, said Shirley – in her magistrate's voice – it's about time that you realised you are getting old and gave up climbing up ladders and onto stools, she said. Get a man in to do the painting in future, she ordered.

I fear that the next time we decorate we will have to hang black curtains at the windows so that Shirley cannot see what we are about. Or we will have to get a man to do it.

Sunday 25th April 2002

Murder in the Hatch

We had a murder yesterday, on Aldborough Hatch Farm beside the footpath that runs from St. Peter's Church to the bridge leading to Barkingside Station and beyond – on the edge of the golf course at Fairlop Waters.

A young lad was cycling from The Chequers where he works when he spotted the half naked body of a young woman on the grass verge. Soon the place was swarming with police with the helicopter above. The farm is still roped off with a heavy police presence. Amanda and Peter are the tenant farmers – they have to book in and out with the police even now. Peter was harvesting on his tractor about fifty yards from the spot. It's the path I use to cycle to court and Yvonne walks most days to Barkingside. But I guess it was between two people who know each other as with most murders.

(In fact, it was not. It was a murder committed by a young man with mental health problems – the victim just happened to be walking from her parent's home in Aldborough Hatch to Barkingside. Tragic.)

26th June 2002

Blended

Geoff Platt, Editor of MILK INDUSTRY, sent me this story today from a Zimbabwean newspaper:

"*While transporting mental patients from Harare to Bulawayo, the bus driver stopped at a roadside shebeen (beer hall) for a few beers. When he got back to his vehicle, he found it empty, with the twenty patients nowhere to be seen. Realising the trouble he was in if the truth were uncovered, he halted his bus at the next bus stop and offered lifts to those in the queue. Letting people board, he then shut the doors and drove straight to the Bulawayo mental hospital, where he hastily handed over his 'charges', warning the nurses that they were particularly excitable. Staff removed the furious passengers; it was three days later that suspicions were aroused by the consistency of stories from the twenty. As for the real patients: nothing more has been heard of them and they have apparently blended comfortably back into Zimbabwean society."*

1st July 2002

On travelling by bus with a Freedom Pass

On learning that Freedom Pass holder Shirley travelled on a bus on 17th September 2002, having only ventured onto an omnibus once since she was in her early teens (and that was in Israel, so it hardly counts), I decided that Shirley needed some helpful tips on the how, the where and the why of bus travel in the 21st Century. In compiling the following notes, I took into account the fact that Shirley's last bus ride could have been when conductors rode on buses, wearing uniforms and carrying blocks of brightly coloured tickets with a contraption slung around their shoulders to enable them to clip the tickets – hence the nickname Clippies.

"On arrival at the bus stop: these are clearly marked with long grey poles with a sign on top reading 'Bus Stop'. They will be found at intervals along the road on bus routes. At some bus stops you will find a three-sided shelter with a red shelf – this is for sitting. If on arrival other folk are occupying the red shelf, squeeze yourself onto one end and push gently until the person at the far end drops off. They will enjoy this. Smile at those who are waiting and if the wait is extended, sing a song or two. This will be appreciated by the other travellers, who may join in.

"When a bus approaches: step forward and raise your right arm in a nonchalant fashion, waving it about in the air. When the bus comes to a halt, stand back and allow the other passengers to embark first. If it appears that the bus may not have room for all those waiting, step forward and give one or two of the older folk a sharp knock on the ankle, preferably of sufficient power to fell them to the ground. Step over – or on them if they appear to be getting up – to climb aboard.

"On entering the bus: greet the person sitting inside the glass box and holding a large wheel with a comment such as 'Hi yer mate!' or 'How-are-a-you-doin'?' He or she is the driver. Never – ever – have your Freedom Pass readily available. Spend a few minutes ferreting around the innermost parts of your handbag looking for the pass. The man in the glass box will enjoy watching you. Walk down the bus, smiling and greeting all the other passengers. If there are children under the age of five, tell the adult accompanying them to keep the brat under control.

"On the journey: if the bus is in a long queue of traffic, it behoves us all to entertain one another. Community singing is much welcomed these days. If any passengers refuse to join in, tip them off at the next stop. Always occupy a seat near the centre aisle and sit on the very edge. Thus when the bus jerks to an unexpected halt or swerves around a sharp corner, you will be catapulted onto the floor and along the aisle. This will cause much merriment amongst the passengers, especially if you can contrive to empty the contents of your handbag as you glide

along. When a passenger walks past to alight from the bus, stick your foot out to trip them up. It is best to target a passenger with four or five Sainsbury's or Tesco carrier bags. If you are near the exit, suggest that they alight and you will pass their shopping to them. Throw each item out of the doors, aiming to hit as many people on the pavement as possible. Repeat the exercise at each bus stop and you will find that your fellow passengers will keep score for you. Or not.

"Should the journey be a long one: it is a good idea to take a flask of freshly made tea, some home-made cakes, a bottle of window cleaner and half-a-dozen yellow dusters. Serve the tea to those sitting nearby and offer the cakes around. Suggest to those sitting nearby that the windows could do with cleaning. Spray the window cleaner liberally on the windows – making sure you spray the heads of all bald persons at the same time – and hand out the yellow dusters. Keep a few home-made cakes to offer as prizes for the cleanest windows. Watch out for passengers wearing wigs. You will spot them if you are observant for they are the folk whose hands go automatically to their heads should the bus stop suddenly. Make a mental note of the wig-wearers and as they pass you to alight, give their wigs a sharp tug. They will enjoy this. Not a lot.

"On reaching the end of your journey: walk back along the bus to the driver. Tell him or her how much you have enjoyed the journey, referring to any places of interest passed along the way. Wish him or her a good day, and assure the driver that you look forward to travelling with them again very soon. If you have any home-made cakes left, offer them to the driver. If the driver rejects your kindness, stuff them up his or her jumper. Wave goodbye to everyone on the bus and go merrily on your way."

Wednesday 18th September 2002

It's the earthquake!

Last evening Yvonne and I were watching *BBC TV London News* – as we do. Suddenly and without warning, there was a roar in the kitchen. More a roar followed by sliding noise, then a shudder and finally a smashing sound with glass and metal setting up a delightfully out of tune cacophony.

Yvonne was quick off the mark. I followed. I have learned to do that in these situations. We were greeted with a sight of smashed glass, saucepans and the like, with one wooden shelf (pine, as a matter of interest) stuck in the sink. Two lower shelves remained affixed to the wall, but the top one was a goner.

Yvonne set to with dustpan and brush. I fetched a black sack.

"It's the earthquake," declared Yvonne. *"The one in Dudley. I knew it would affect us."*

Dudley is somewhere in the Midlands, but I decided not to mention this. Yvonne has decided not to replace the shelf. Two are sufficient for us. I agree. Saucepans have been relocated. All is now well.

I met Nancy of Ramsgill Drive on the bus today. Nancy woke up when the earthquake struck in Dudley. Yvonne tells me that one of her friends told her last night that the box she has fitted in her chest sprang out when the earthquake struck. Nasty.

Reading THE GUARDIAN today, I spotted the following true story of the earthquake:

"Emma from West Bromwich contacted the BBC to report that she and her husband, having returned home at midnight and not feeling tired, decided to make love. They went to bed but the earth moved earlier than they had intended.

"We were just about to get down to it when a jug of water fell off the side table and spilled on the cat," she said. "The cat leapt on the bed and on her husband's naked back where he sank his claws leaving several scratches."

I guess Emma's story is better than mine.

I bought two new suits today. I was wandering back from a Drug Action Team Meeting in the Town Hall and saw a SALE sign so I meandered into the shop where a man found a suit that fitted – dark grey and lightweight, for I cannot carry heavy material around anymore. Before I could thank him, he rushed up with another one of the same size but of lighter hue.

"You can have the first one for £99," he called. *"It was £179 until last week. And,"* he grinned, *"you can have a second one for £50."*

That's what the sign in the shop window said, so I knew it was true. Buy one and get one for £50 it said. Well, I could not resist that. Shirts and ties, said the man – but at this I put up massive resistance. That's where these chappies catch you with their £50 shirts and ties that cost a fortune. No, no, I cried – as I paid up and ran out of the shop. Into M & S I went – and bought two shirts and two ties and three pairs of socks. The madness of it all.

Tuesday 24th September 2002

"This is a major emergency"

Our gas central heating system is with the gas company's Three Star Service. It gives me comfort to know this. Earlier this year an engineer called for the annual service. A few weeks later Yvonne mentioned that the gas fire in the lounge appeared to be slightly out of line. Perhaps the engineer did not put it back properly, Yvonne said. And I agreed. Ring British Gas, said Yvonne, for I cannot get it to move back. As it was about a quarter of an inch out of line, I did not consider it to be an urgent matter so I put a note on my pad to do so – but did not get around to it.

A few weeks back Yvonne said that she could smell gas in the early morning. But she wasn't sure. I could not detect it, but said I would ring the service engineer to come out to realign the fire and sort out the mystery of the gas smell. And I put this on my pad for later, too.

Yesterday morning Yvonne again smelt gas in the lounge and was worried about the unaligned gas fire. I rang the service engineers. Can you please do this winter's service early, I asked? Why is this, said the voice at the other end of the line? I explained that the engineer had not replaced the gas fire in correct alignment. When was this, the voice asked? Last January, I replied. There was a sort of pregnant silence, so I dropped as an aside the fact that Yvonne thinks she can smell gas.

At that point a dramatic change took place. This, said the voice, is a major emergency. I then gained the impression that the voice was in overdrive and reading from a script. Do you live in a house or flat, asked the voice? Open all windows and doors, said the voice. Do not smoke in or near the house. Are there any senior citizens or young children present? Yes, I replied, my wife and I are senior citizens and we have a two-year-old child. Again there was a silence. Are you sure that you are senior citizens and have a two-year-old child, said the voice. Of course I am, I replied. Again silence. Can we get this right, said the voice – and then I cottoned on. It's our grandchild, I explained. That seemed to satisfy the voice.

Where is the main gas entry point, asked the voice? I assume it is the cupboard under the stairs, I replied. Go there, said the voice. I did so, followed by Yvonne with a torch. Turn off the main supply, said the voice. How do I do that, I asked? This is a major emergency, intoned the voice, as it told me to pull the lever. It will not move, said I. Pull it harder, said the voice. I did. It worked.

Open all doors and windows. Do not smoke. This is a major emergency. The voice droned on and on. Transco will be with you within two hours, said the voice. When they have attended, we will send a service engineer within four hours. And rang off.

With doors and windows open, I went off to Ilford to the bank. On my return I could see the Transco man's backside sticking out of the cupboard under the stairs. You have a leak, he said. Ring the service engineer and he will fix it. I did so. Another voice told us the service engineer will be with us within four hours. I went off to a meeting. I knew Yvonne could cope best without me.

A call within 20 minutes from the service engineer assured Yvonne that he would be with us within minutes. He was as good as his word. He found a small slow leak behind the fire. Why did we not blow up, asked Yvonne, for my husband has smoked in this room for months? I guess it went up the chimney, said the engineer as he fixed it and realigned the gas fire. He had moved the gas cooker at one stage. I will leave this for Him to put back, the service engineer told Yvonne, for it is too heavy for me to manage on my own. Oh no you won't, said Yvonne, I will help you. We do not leave anything to Him in this house. And together they returned the cooker to its rightful place.

From now on I promise to listen to Yvonne. When Yvonne says there is a gas leak, I will action this immediately. If Yvonne says that there is a drip, I will call the men instantly. I will write this on my pad.

I had a nightmare last night. I was on my bike in Barkingside when there was a terrible storm. As I rode across the fields, Aldborough Hatch Farm was flooded. Thick black mud was oozing across the church path. The churchyard was a lake of water with all the gravestones covered in thick black slimy mud. As I came round Oaks Lane, Tim was sweeping mud from the vicarage doorway, and Sue and Roger were in the church doing likewise. I rode through the mud to the church door – and woke up! I aroused Yvonne from her slumbers to tell her about it and she was not all that happy at my doing so – for it was the middle of the night.

Tuesday 8th October 2002

Diversified

I believe you ought you know that I have now been diversified. Dr Annie, the good Medical Director, achieved this reasonably painlessly between 9am and 12noon yesterday.

Four members of the NELMHT Board were required to lie on the floor, but I was not called upon to do so. They will remain nameless.

The last hour was spent in twos during which we unburdened our souls – going back in time to infancy. John and I unburdened ourselves to each other.

I am unsure if I will recover after stripping away the veneer that is my public persona.

Even more unnerving was the fact that the good doctor occasionally listened in. But I guess she has heard worse in her time.

Wednesday 20th November 2002

Candle wax

It is Boxing Day and Yvonne and I have spent a happy hour removing candle wax from the gas fire in the lounge. It came about in this wise.

Richard, who is vegetarian and in favour of all things organic, bought his mother a large, white candle for her birthday. Impressive is how I would describe it. So much so, that the candle formed the centrepiece for our Festivities. We even took it with us to Heather and Robert's homestead on Christmas Day where it sat at the heart of the lunch table, whilst we tucked into turkey and Richard enjoyed a nut roast made lovingly by his mother.

On returning home that evening, Yvonne, Richard and I settled down to endure *Eastenders.* Jamie died, a wedding nearly did not happen (but did), that Beale lad kicked his wife out whilst the turkey was still in the oven and one or two other disasters occurred which I cannot recall.

We missed The Queen's Speech and the repeat, which has left Yvonne distraught.

At some stage in the late evening, Richard announced – calmly, I thought, considering the implications of what he was about to say – that the candle was doing things one does not expect a candle to do. The fine glass bowl in which it stood was filled with melted wax which was gently flowing down the gas fire, leaving lumps of the molten stuff which glowed in the warmth and settled in a pool in the hearth.

It was a pretty sight, but caused Yvonne to leap into panic mode. Richard took control, proposing that all attempts to remove the wax should wait until the morning. I noted that the brass candlesticks on the mantelpiece were charmingly covered in red candle wax, for the two candles had burned down to their base.

At about this time the Lights started to flash. Not the Lights in the front garden – which have attracted much comment in these parts – but the Lights on the potted Christmas tree that stands in the garden outside the patio doors, sending a warm glow into the lounge. Now you should know that these Lights are not supposed to flash – but they did. They went out for a second, flashed on, went out, flashed on – and then died.

It is the connection, said Richard, who clearly knows about all sorts of things since he took up with Stine, who comes from Norway. Into the kitchen strode Richard – and by touching the plug, he sorted it. But again the Lights flashed. More plug touching. And again – and more plug touching.

There was nothing for it. We all retired to our beds, too exhausted by the goings on in Albert Square and the movements of the molten wax, not to mention the flashing, to sing a couple of verses of *Silent Night.*

On rising this morning and taking my vitamin C tablet, I set forth to sort out the Lights. The fuse was a little loose. All is now well. But the candle grease took much longer. An hour, I would guess. I tackled the candlesticks, being rather a dab hand with the Brasso.

When Yvonne was reaching exhaustion point with the candle grease on the gas fire, I took over. All is now well there, too.

Thursday 26th December 2002

Seventy!

What a week! On Monday I retired from the Bench. On Tuesday – my birthday – I attended an all day Trust Board, with a special buffet lunch attended by staff from around the Trust.

Here I was presented with a card signed by one and all – with photographs of lamp posts at Goodmayes Hospital – to mark the fact that I led the campaign for adequate lighting in the hospital grounds, which ran for over thirty-one months before the street lamps were restored, during which time nurses were encouraged to bring torches and I sent enough emails that should they have been printed, a large forest would have been required to provide the paper, but I doubt if anyone read them let alone saw the need to print them off.

A splendid cake was devoured – and I took the balance to Martha Ward where the patients were having their evening meal. They sang *Happy Birthday* through mouthfuls of meat, potatoes and two veg. Yvonne and I had a quiet dinner in the evening at Umbertos in Ilford.

Wednesday and Thursday I chaired a panel to interview sixteen international psychiatrists for NELMHT from 8am to 6pm. That was an experience and a half.

On Friday I stopped off at the bank in Ilford. The newspaper seller from outside Ilford Station came in, rushed up to shake my hand and commented that my picture appears every week in the ILFORD RECORDER. Whilst this is something of an exaggeration, I am not sure what the other customers made of it all, but he seemed pleased to have found me alive and walking around.

And this morning I am going into the garden to plant yet more seeds in the greenhouse.

Saturday 21st March 2003

We have the seaweed!

We have the seaweed – a necessary part of Yvonne interpretation of David Copperfield at next weekend's St. Peter's Flower Festival, as I am sure you will appreciate. We were up at crack of dawn on Saturday, bound for New Milton in Hampshire.

Our eldest son was waiting in his brand new grey Aldi (complete with airbags and others safety precautions), revved up and eager to go. Stopping only for lunch (freshly caught Lemon Sole á la Jamie Oliver, cooked to perfection by Graham, who must take after his mother in his culinary expertise) and to meet the two kittens, rekindle our friendship with the rabbit and two guinea pigs, and to have a cuddle with Annily, our granddaughter – and we were off in the Aldi for the beach at Friar's Cove.

Tossing caution to the wind, Yvonne stripped up to her knees and was soon wading in the water. Annily joined her in a smart little bikini, Graham stood as lifeguard, holding the carrier bag, and I took up my supervisory position on a groin. Soon the carrier bag was bursting with long lengths of seaweed and even something which Yvonne described as a dead cuttle fish. Within ten minutes the task was complete – and we all retired somewhat exhausted (well, I was anyway) to a nearby kiosk for refreshing ice creams. Our return journey brought us to the homestead around 9.30pm when we tipped the seaweed into a bucket of water and retired – eventually – to our beds.

This morning the garden has a strong whiff of seaside about it. Yvonne tipped up the bucket and I supervised as she selected the best bits, which are now hanging out to dry. We have a fine selection, to be sure. The rest – which, I have to say, is rather unpleasant – is now safely in the dustbin ready for collection by the Borough first thing tomorrow morning – and not too soon, in my opinion. On completion of the task, I insisted that Yvonne wash her hands.

Yvonne has decreed that we are now ready for the Flower Festival – which is a great weight off my mind, I can tell you. Dried grasses are on standby. Items collected by Richard, our youngest, when he kitten-sat for Graham a week or so ago with his Norwegian girl friend (Richard's girl friend, not Graham's) – three chunks of chalk cliff, a bag of pebbles, another of stones, some shells and a buoy (complete with rope) – are all lined up. What joy!

Sunday 22nd June 2003

Didn't we have a luverly time the day we went to Gatwick?

The Good Sir Ian put my name in the ring to appear on a Panel of three so-called Experienced Non-executive Directors (NEDs) at a two-day Induction Course for new Chairmen and NEDs organised by the NHS Appointments Commission. It happened yesterday six miles from Gatwick.

I set out at around 11am, all eager and willing. The journey was uneventful, except that somewhere before Tower Hill the District Line carriage filled up with twenty schoolgirls aged eleven or so – dressed in black traditional gear – and one boy, plus two teachers. The noise level was high as they screamed at each other and ate crisps, apples and an assortment of fast food. The single boy looked bemused, bothered and bewildered. The teachers were harassed. I closed my eyes.

The Gatwick Express from Victoria was air-conditioned coolness. Resisting the chance of a flight to some exotic part of the world, I hailed a taxi to the Effingham Park Hotel. Here was a stately pile if ever I saw one. Perhaps £500 a night would be about right, but a man called Chris – who appeared from nowhere at the end of the event to send the delegates on their way rejoicing – assured us that the NHS had negotiated a good deal at £150 per delegate for two days. Perhaps he was right, but I sensed a few folk were suggesting he might pull the other one.

I sat through a session entitled "Reality Check" in which two lady social workers told us what it was like in the real world of an acute hospital. That was good stuff. Then the Assistant Director of Clinical Governance Reviews at CHI told us about Old Chi and New Chi. After a few minutes it became clear to me that these are not holiday resorts in the Far East, but an existing body and a new one about to be born. The Assistant Director said that delegates could ask questions as he went along. They did. His forty minute slot was seriously over-running – but he went through his last three slides in a way that made clear that a taxi was standing by for a quick burst to Redhill – and he was gone at dead on 3pm.

On arrival I was told to sit by Karen. Are you from the Leeds Office, I asked Karen. No, I am from the London Office, she told me, dealing with Southern appointments – but not London. There is another lot who deal with London, said Karen, indicating by the tone of her voice that I should not get her muddled up with them. Is the Good Sir Ian here, I asked? No, said Karen, he came first thing to open the day (as I had noted on the programme), but left after his lunch. He is a man who knows which side his bread (or lunch) is buttered. Is Tom here, I asked? Yes, said Karen, he is the one who stands by the door and goes out when the speakers start. It was Tom who had telephoned me, you see, but I decided he had better things to do, so I did not seek him out whither he had gone. Is Gail here, I asked, for Gail had sent me the programme? No, said Karen, Gail is in Leeds – which must be nice for her, I thought.

Whilst I sat listening to the fun and games, another man appeared and was told to sit by Karen. Lucky Karen! He turned out to be John, a NED and Vice-Chairman of a primary care trust in the West of London. We conversed across Karen, who did not seem to mind, and wondered where the third member of the Panel could be. Ah, said Karen, he is not coming. He was from an acute trust. Just as three struck, the man who appeared to be chairing the afternoon approached John and me. He had gathered who we were, which was nice. Perhaps he was psychic. If so, he looked good on it.

John and I were told that we should introduce ourselves and then wait to be pelted with questions by these newly-appointed Chairmen and NEDs. John went first. He was a banker, having worked all over the world, but mainly in Hong Kong, before he was appointed as a NED three years ago. I decided that the delegates needed cheering up and told them the story about the NED and the bidet – which had them rolling in the aisles. I said I had worked as an editor – when a lady of ample proportions called out from the back of the room that she was a journalist and could we get together sometime? I made a note to watch out for her afterwards for my Mum had told me about ladies like that. I also mentioned that I retired five years ago and am now seventy – which was a mistake, because afterwards – whilst I waited for the taxi – a number of delegates walked past, thanked me for the session and said that if they look like I do when they are seventy, they would be pleased. Those who asked me how I did it got the usual response – I have a good wife and diet and I smoke.

The questions came thick and fast. John and I did a double act – a bit like the two Ronnies, except that his name was John. Is it right that you need only spend three to five days a week? How do you cope with all the reading? What sort of relationship should you develop with the executive directors? (I told them that as the Mental Heath Act NED, I related to a lady – and lots of them made *"Ooh!"* and *"Ah!"* noises.) How do you hold the executive to account? (John really got his teeth into this one, so I told the story of the Goodmayes street lamps – which took the heat off a little.) Do you have to understand the accounts? (Again, John got carried away – but then he would, having been a banker in Hong Kong. I smiled and we moved on to the next question.) Finally the man who was chairing the afternoon hove down upon us – and it was all over. This was when Chris appeared from nowhere.

The taxi driver to Gatwick told me that he knew it was an NHS do as he had taken the CHI man back to Redhill, en route for Folkestone. I assumed he lived there, but for all I know he might have been making his escape across the Channel at the thought of New CHI. The Gatwick Express was relaxing. I tried to look as if I had returned from foreign parts, but do not think I succeeded. The walk up Aldborough Road North from the bus stop was exhilarating. Home! Six-and-a-half hours for thirty minutes on the platform. But it was something different and it kept me off the streets for a day.

In case you are wondering who paid my travelling expenses, I had a word with Tom before I departed homewards. Ah, he said. You need an expenses claim form. Yes, I said, I think I do. But I do not have one, he replied. Shall I e.mail Gail, I asked? What a good idea, he smiled – before he wandered off to do whatever he did when he wandered off. So I sent Gail an e.mail. This morning. And Gail replied. She is asking someone to put a form in the post. I suppose that might be Chris or Tom – or Dick or Harry? It was the first time I have rubbed shoulders in person with the Gang at the Appointments Commission. Very interesting – as a man used to say on the wireless (which was television without the pictures).

Wednesday 9th July 2003

Bloomin' wonderful!

An e.mail to Aldborough Hall Farm:

"We – my Good Wife and Me, that is – would wish you all to know that we consider that you have played a vital part in our having been awarded Third Place in the *'Best Front Garden Category of Redbridge in Bloom 2003'*. For, it has to be said, where would we be without the bags of Ericaceous and Potting Compost, and Forest Bark that you have supplied so liberally from your Emporium at Aldborough Hall Farm? Where, indeed!

"The service we have received has been exemplary. All I have needed to do is mention that I required a delivery, and the White Van has been loaded up and sent speedily down Aldborough Road North. The rear doors have been thrown open and the bags carried to our very doorstep by that fine Farmer and his delightful daughter.

"And not only that, for the occasional word of Wisdom from the Worthy Shirley has not fallen on deaf ears. A few weeks back, the said Shirley hinted: *"You need more colour"*.

We took the point. And colour we went for. We propagated like we have never propagated before. Indeed, we propagated to such an extent that I had to have a lie down afterwards. Seedlings and cuttings were nurtured. Liquid feed was brought from far and wide, and poured into the pots and containers. My Good Wife was heard to comment that if she stood still long enough, she might have have had a watering with the feed as well.

"Such is the debt that we owe to you in assisting us to reach these dizzy heights, that we have decided that you should be empowered – if you so desire – to erect a sign above the door of your Farm Shop which reads: *"Purveyors of the Finest Ericaceous and Potting Compost, and Forest Bark to the Third Prize Winners in the Front Garden Category, Redbridge in Bloom 2003"*. That, if we may say so, will hit 'em between the eyes!

"We have been invited to the Redbridge in Bloom Ceremony in the Council Chamber on 17th October when the Worshipful The Mayor of Redbridge and fellow Councillors will dish out the prizes.

"Sadly, we have not been invited to bring along guests. Had we been permitted so to do, we would have put your names forward. We will, however, make a point of advising the Worshipful of your part in the achievement and, for that matter, anyone else who happens to be passing by. You bet your sweet life we will.

"Whilst I am writing, may I request the Farmer to please assist us with our Spring Showing? Delivery as before of half-a-tonne of Daffodil of the Yellow variety would be much appreciated at the right time of the year. An order for further compost and bark will also follow. And come next Spring when we prepare for the Summer Showing, we will be seeking advice and assistance from the Worthy Shirley.

"Happiness and joy to you all as we consider the erection of a suitable statement for all to see. This is presenting us with something of a problem, but we are encouraged to do so by the fact that a Lady of Some Repute residing not far from here and within gun-shot fire distance remarked to us that She had not personally entered the Competition.

"The same Lady also announced at a meeting of the Redbridge Night Shelter that we should not advertise yesterday's Coffee Morning too widely as we only have a small house."

Sunday 20th July 2003

Funerals and fêtes

It has been funeral time here in Aldborough Hatch. First, Tommy next door died tragically aged sixty-one. He is the sign writer and antique collector who has a shed next door to mine at the bottom of the garden. He was also a postman in Bethnal Green and having recently taken up jogging, he made it to the riding school and back a couple of weeks ago – and collapsed in his garden. Yvonne went in to revive him whilst I gave Marlon his tea – but to no avail. Very sad. His funeral was last Tuesday. Tom and Cathy have been good friends over many years.

Then a lad who was in the Scouts locally rang me to tell me his Mum had died in Oaks Lane. Her funeral was last Thursday.

And on Tuesday last Tommy Fletcher, a good friend for fifty years, died. His funeral is tomorrow. He has been in KGH and was eighty-nine. I am speaking the appreciation, which I wrote on Saturday. Another very real loss.

Yvonne and I made it to Mascalls' Park Fete on Saturday – but only just! This event celebrated one hundred and fifty years of care for the mentally ill at Warley. We set out, all cool, calm and collected, at around 1.45pm – as the temperature soared ever higher for it was mighty hot.

On arrival at Ilford Station, we discovered that trains were running ninety minutes late. We waited for forty-five minutes – when three trains going East arrived in convoy. We boarded the first, whilst the other two heaved away in the intense heat on the bridge leading down into the station. Five minutes later, we were turfed off as the train had a mechanical fault. After ten minutes we were off on the second train. The driver kept us informed of progress. The overhead cables between Stratford and Liverpool Street were melting in the scorching heat and had come down. Similarly the cables between Shenfield and Colchester. Fortunately, Yvonne had the foresight to bring cold drinks – Winnie the Pooh cartons, destined for Marlon but gratefully guzzled by Yvonne and me.

On arrival at Mascalls around 3.30pm, we found the Medical Director in great form. I had the impression that she would look cool and still be talking if the temperature touched a hundred – as it did yesterday. Steve, the Operations Director, was welcoming as ever and clearly cock-a-hoop at the event's success – three Mayors and an MP had arrived and had their ears bent over Mascalls reprovision in the exhibition of memorabilia. In-patient and community teams manned stalls.

A group of Belly Dancers performed contortions in the arena with the heat blazing down to which they appeared oblivious. All were ladies of ample proportions, so Yvonne did not allow me to linger for fear that my blood pressure might go through the top of my head, and we took refuge under the trees with cool drinks and homemade cakes.

Our arrival at the tombola stall was at just the right moment. Six prizes left and only a dozen tickets. We bought six tickets and won two candles and a set of cake forks. I purchased the remaining tickets and gave them to the staff on the stall – who scooped the rest, including a bottle of Harvey's Bristol Cream.

The journey home was uneventful. After a cold shower and a salad, I spent an hour watering the garden in a vain attempt to rescue everything from the unbending heat. Will it ever end, I ask myself?

Monday 11th August 2003

A Strip-O-Gram in the Town Hall

This evening Yvonne and I attended the fiftieth Birthday Celebrations of Omana at a Town Hall in East London. Omana is an Associate Hospital Manager with the Trust, a Non-executive Director with her Primary Care Trust, a Councillor, in full-time employment in the caring profession and a mother. And an author of some repute, whose first book I read in proof form whilst on overnight duty at the Redbridge Night

Shelter – in one sitting lasting seven hours, simply because I would have to speak at the book launch the next day – but that is another story.

The invitation stated that the event would run from 6.30pm to 11pm. With the temperature in the 90s, we decided that four and a half hours would be more than body and soul could cope with – and therefore we set out at 7.30pm by mini-cab, arriving some fifteen minutes later.

The room was packed to the walls with family and friends, whilst in a clearing in the centre stood a redoubtable lady, the Master of Ceremonies for the evening. This good soul was hovering around a tall, greying, man who was in full flow. I recognised him as a Professor of English at a Scottish University, who had acted as literary adviser to Omana. The Professor had been talking for about five minutes when the MC decided that he had said enough – and started to hover with menaces. Taking the hint, the Professor came to a halt.

A number of speakers followed – the Chief Executive of the PCT, the Civic Ambassador of a London Borough, an elderly lady who appeared to think she was Omana's mother (but I know this not to be so for her mother died two years ago – but I did not feel it would be polite to say so). Then the MC called on me – as Omana had warned me six months earlier that she might – and I spoke, but only briefly, for the MC was a-hovering. I told the assembly that Omana calls me the Romeo of Redbridge – which went down rather well with the ladies, but I would guess not so well with the men folk, some of whom looked distinctly hurt on learning that Omana has a toy-boy of seventy summers and winters.

We were told that other speakers might arrive – one local MP was on holiday and another was in Liverpool, but could drop in at any minute. Meanwhile, Omana addressed the sweltering throng. Starting with her birth in India, Omana regaled us with her life story in every possible detail. But Omana had not reckoned with the redoubtable MC – who started to hover after ten minutes. Five minutes later she hovered in earnest as the signals came from the kitchen that things were about to erupt unless something was done mighty quickly. Finally, grabbing the microphone, the redoubtable informed Omana that her time was up and dinner was served.

Here Yvonne and I found ourselves right at the front of the queue, which was just as well, for the throng lining up to eat soon stretched round the room and back again and we were both starving. The Chief Executive of the PCT was nearby and told me that the MC was a barrister and even a QC, he thought. It appeared that she was Chairman of an NHS community trust before becoming Chairman of a mental health trust at some stage in her career. I bet her Trust Board meetings were fun – and how.

At this point the heat was starting to get at me, so we made for a fire exit and stood outside to eat the delicious Indian food, near some huge dustbins that reeked of stale fish. A lady of some vintage joined us, telling us that she lived near the docks and letting slip the fact that she had made the birthday cake, which was now melting slowly in the heat. The Civic Ambassador also tagged along, with her Deputy. I had to ask what a Civic Ambassador is – and learned that as the Borough elects its Mayor, they do not have a Mayor to go around patting folk on the head, but a Civic Ambassador and Deputy are appointed to do this kind of work. Both clearly enjoyed the job and explained that the most difficult part was remembering that you do not open the door of the Civic car, but wait until it is opened for you.

Leaving the stench of the dustbins behind and drifting back indoors for a bowl of refreshing fruit, we were just in time to witness the main event. Now what, you must be asking, would that be? And you would never guess in a thousand Sundays. A Male Strip-O-Gram! Yes, it was so. Tall and rather dashing, dressed in black, he advanced upon Omana, by now seated in the centre of the clearing. Ripping off his jacket and shirt, he poured liquid down his chest, before another rip – and his trousers had gone, leaving a pair of black briefs. At this point I decided that Yvonne should visit the dustbins again, but she would have none of it. I believe the male retained his modesty, but cannot be certain for by this stage perspiration was pouring down my forehead, into my eyes and my glasses steamed up.

I have to say that Omana retained her cool throughout the proceedings. Looking petrified when the stripper appeared, I take my hat off to her in that she entered into the spirit of the evening and hardly batted an eyelid. I fear that had it been Yvonne she would have died on the spot.

With the cake cut – or, rather, spooned, for it was made of pure cream we were told – the disco took over from the MC – who told us that she would not be speaking again that evening which, I would guess, came as a great relief to many. Being cowards, Yvonne and I bade our farewells and went into the night, like two roly-poly puddings that had been rather well-done in the oven.

Monday 11th August 2003

Relax

Questionnaires for completion arrive on my desk. Filling in some is mandatory – for there will be a warning that the sender has given me a number, to protect confidentiality, but also to come down on me like a ton of bricks if I fail to tick the boxes and pop the form into the post box. Others may be discarded with impunity, for there is no-one waiting anxiously in some distant office to check my ticks and crosses – indeed, there may be someone who will be relieved that I have not sent the form back for it's less work for them on a Monday morning.

Occasionally, very occasionally, a form will be accompanied by the kind of offer you cannot resist for something you do not need but cannot live without. This happened a month ago. The form was long and the questions torturous. I nearly cast the questionnaire forth into the waste bin but as it started to flutter from my fingers, I spotted the *free gift*. So I ticked and crossed away for ten minutes, and popped it in the post next day.

This week my free gift arrived in the post – a three CD box set entitled *Relax with the Classics.*

"This collection," I was informed, *"has been specially chosen with peace and relaxation in mind."* Well, I can do with a dollop of that.

"Close your eyes and feel the stress fade away" (it gets better) *"to the hypnotic sounds of the world's favourite classics."*

There are three discs – as there would be in a three CD box set – entitled *Tranquillity* (Aaah!), *Relaxation* (Wow!) and *Nostalgia* (and as someone once said that *"nostalgia is not what it used to be"*, I guess that will be exciting).

Tearing myself away from the keyboard, I hurried to the shed-with-the-overhang, turned on the machine purchased from Dixon's for just such an occasion, sank into my favourite chair and wafted away to the sound of Pachelbel's *Canon in D Major*, before moving on to Schumann's *Piano Concerto in A Minor.* That was just *Tranquillity* (with Brahms, Chopin, Schubert and Vivaldi skipped for the moment), so what *Relaxation* and *Nostalgia* will do beggars thought.

The three discs are now in the kitchen. Yvonne has a similar machine-from-Dixon's placed strategically behind the bread-maker. Yvonne plays her music whilst ironing, filling (or emptying) the washing machine, hanging out (or taking in) the washing in the garden, making cakes, buttering toast, peeling potatoes, rearranging things in the freezer, flushing out flower pots or just day-dreaming (but the latter only if there is time). I guess Yvonne will enjoy a bit of *Tranquillity* and *Relaxation*, but I am unsure as to whether or not *Nostalgia* would be a good thing for she might grow to like it.

Saturday 20th September 2003

Guest at Goodmayes

There is a thing called patient confidentiality and unless the patient and/or his nearest relative agree, an NHS Trust that is treating a patient is unable to confirm or otherwise to the press, TV or anyone else that he or she is in residence. The fact that we have had a media circus in Barley Lane, with a helicopter zooming over the grounds of Goodmayes Hospital complete with a photographer hanging out with his telephoto lens, trying to get a photograph of our guest – a famous boxer – on the ward, is neither here nor there.

Alfie, one of our dear long-term patients, who sleeps on the floor all day at reception, was discovered by a manager being interviewed by *The Times* last week. It was all a bit pointless for all Alfie wants is a cigarette – and most days he gets at least one from me. As a non-executive director, I am due to carry out the annual visit to the unit in question this Wednesday. Our high profile guest – who is, of course, not here – is appealing against his Section, with the hearing set for Thursday week. I will be chairing so I should get to know him quite well over the next two weeks.

It is all sad for he is very unwell by all accounts and needs some peace. The unit at Goodmayes is highly regarded in the profession as being one of the best low secure psychiatric intensive care units in the country. The doctors and staff have won a number of awards over the past two years, so he is in good hands. We have a helpline being manned eighteen hours a day to take get well messages and enquiries from his friends and members of the public. We are unable to confirm or otherwise that he is here – but take the messages which are all being passed to him daily. We also have an unused ward open to receive the flowers, chocolates and food which are arriving – all have to be searched of course. And security guards are patrolling, trying to keep the media out.

But some good is coming out of it for mental health which tends to get a poor press or no press at all. There have been some supportive editorials in the local press about the fact that people should leave him alone to get better and that one in four of us suffer from MH at some time in our lives. One of the national

tabloids that carried a front page banner headline in very poor taste had to apologise. And rightly so.
(I chaired the Panel hearing the boxer's appeal against detention under the *Mental Health Act 1983* a few days later. The boxer was calm, pleasant and polite to everyone at the hearing. He took a particular shine to Julie, who administered the appeal. Julie, who is a very attractive young lady in her twenties, sat behind the boxer, who turned to wink at her from time to time. Poor Julie blushes very easily and did so that morning – and how! All went well until the patient leaned across the table separating us to ask if I had been a brigadier? I said I had not, but he insisted that I had. My protestations were not accepted as the boxer kept insisting that I must have been a brigadier because I looked like one. It was all very good humoured. The appeal was unsuccessful, but there were no hard feelings on the boxer's part and we parted good friends. Walking back to Trust Head Office from the unit a few minutes later, I was amused when a social worker spotted me from across the grass, calling: *"Hi Brigadier!"* That story soon got around the hospital.)
Monday 29th September 2003

A Rector cometh

I see from this morning's *Church Times* gazette section that: *"The Rev Clare Nicholson, Priest-in-Charge of Springfield, to be Rector of Aldborough Hatch".* Good news indeed – but we do not have a Rector nor a Rectory. We have a Vicarage and a Vicar. What are we to do?

I went straight to the Oxford Dictionary. A Rector in the Church of England is *"the incumbent of a parish where all the tithes formerly passed to the incumbent".* A Vicar is *"the incumbent of a parish where tithes formerly passed to a chapter or religious house or layman".* Which helps me no end, for although I have been a member of St. Peter's since 1944, even at my great age I cannot recall tithes being passed to anyone.

If, indeed, we are to have a Rector – and it appears that we are – what changes should be made to the Vicarage to turn it into a Rectory, I ask myself? Should we paint the front door purple?
(In fact, a Vicar was inducted, not a Rector after all. I am unsure if anyone else locally spotted the error made by those who compile the *Church Times* gazette section. If they did, they kept very quiet about it.)
Friday 3rd October 2003

Calypsos in the evening

We were guests at the 70th birthday party at Fairlop Waters of a lady friend who hails from Sierra Leone. You may not know the lady, who lives in Barkingside and has attended every Open Day at the Court since they were launched. I have spoken at her women's group twice. At one time I helped her when her neighbours were racially harassing her by putting her in touch with the Council who sorted things.

Then the lady met the security man at the courthouse in Barkingside. He, too, was invited to the party, but is unwell with gout – although I have the feeling that he was being a bit circumspect in these matters.

Amongst the one hundred and twenty guests Yvonne and I were two of only three white faces. There was a calypso band, a few speeches, a hymn and very long prayers before we ate. But we were made very welcome and lots of folk wanted to cuddle us. Tessa Sanderson was there, too, but sadly did not seem to want to cuddle me.

Saturday 4th October 2003

New glasses – again

A month or so ago I was sitting on a Mental Health Act Panel in Waltham Forest. I took my glasses off to look across the table – when the right-hand earpiece dropped off onto the hard surface – making a noise similar to that of a bomb exploding. The patient thought this highly amusing and even more so when I had to spend the rest of the hearing holding the one earpiece in my hand in order to balance the glasses on the end of my nose to read the papers. Indeed, the patient spent most of the remaining time smiling and laughing – which was great for it took the tension out of things. Even the solicitor and doctor joined in.

Realising that I had to sort this out, I caught the bus to Ilford and went to the optician where I had purchased the glasses a few months ago. At that time I had two pairs – but I lost one pair during a photo-shoot for the *Ilford Recorder* on Fairlop Plain when I was being interviewed for yet another piece on the racecourse saga.

The young lady took one look at the broken glasses and assured me these could be fixed within the hour. But I would have to have different frames for they would need to cut the glass pieces to fit the frames – and clearly something smaller was called for as you cannot make the glass pieces larger. I would add that the lady took her time to explain this fact to me and used very simple language that I would have little difficulty in understanding. Clearly she is well trained in dealing with pensioners who arrive with their bus passes in their hands. As always in these situations, I threw myself at her mercy and asked her to choose something that would be suitable.

I realised my error when she gave me the bill for she must have gone to the top of the range – and how. But I do not like creating a fuss in public places and accepted the inevitable.

I wandered around the Exchange in Ilford for an hour, idly working out who were the shoplifters and who were the store detectives. Just after two I reappeared complete with new glasses.

Yvonne noticed immediately I arrived home. Others have not been so observant. Some have asked if I have had to have glasses – implying that they had not noticed that I have worn them for about twenty years or more.

One or two have stared – and said nothing. Another friend wanted to know if I had gone for the Far Eastern Look, which – he assured me – is fashionable these days.

All this reminds me of a somewhat unnerving occurrence a few weeks ago at a Mental Health Act Panel in Waltham Forest – a panel of the kind that I had been sitting on when the right-hand earpiece of my spectacles dropped off. The patient was represented by a young solicitor who had little if any experience of mental health, mental health law in general or of mental health panels in particular. He drew the panel's attention to a sentence in the consultant's report which stated that the patient was inclined to inappropriate sexual behaviour. Turning to the consultant, the solicitor asked precisely what he meant by this statement – but before the consultant could answer, the patient stood up and said that she would demonstrate for us – promptly removing her tights and starting to strip off her skirt!

A brief adjournment followed.

Wednesday 29th October 2003

Foot washing in Aldborough Hatch

After 18 months of Interregnum, the Rev Clare Nicholson was Inducted and Installed at Vicar of Aldborough Hatch last evening. It was my seventh Induction Service at St. Peter's and unique in many ways.

The Good and the Great were assembled, with Her Majesty the Queen represented by the Patron's Man from Downing Street as her Majesty was rather busy with preparations for her operation on Friday next. All very understandable, for no doubt Her Majesty was sorting out her Tupperware boxes to be certain that the right cereals are in place for breakfast.

The Mayor of Redbridge, her Consort, a smattering of Councillors, an array of clergy, the local Rabbi – they were all there. Late arrivals found themselves standing at the back until chairs could be found. I was tucked up in the back pew with Daphne and Owen, who sang with great gusto.

All went well. As the sermon ground to an end, the Bishop of Barking told us that he had been shopping that morning at Walthamstow Market. There he had purchased a white plastic washing-up bowl for £1.25 and a white towel for an undisclosed sum (but I would guess for under a quid). Moving swiftly towards the new Vicar, the Bishop filled the bowl with warm water and proceeded to wash the new Vicar's feet. I sensed an air of terror amongst the ranks of the clergy that the Bishop might move in their direction with his plastic bowl. No doubt they were regretting the fact that they had not changed their socks, but they need not have been fearsome, for the Bishop stopped at the Vicar.

Yvonne sat demurely in the choir stalls and appeared relieved when the Bishop put the washing-up bowl aside – for Yvonne was wearing tights and the very thought of having to remove them would have been more than the Good Woman could cope with after a day of baking cakes for the celebration party that was to follow.

In the church halls it was every man and woman for themselves at the buffet. Standing by I watched as the food was devoured with relish. Senior citizens were in the forefront, closely followed by the clergy who appeared not to have eaten for days. This group clung to the tables and showed reluctance to allow anyone near the mountains of sandwiches and cakes.

An interesting and uplifting evening, following which I have winged off an e.mail to the Vicar to advise her – in my capacity as Editor – that I need her article for the January St. Peter's BROADSHEET yesterday.

A footnote. I do find that whenever a group of clergy of the Church of England is assembled – as they were today – that they appear to be a very odd bunch. I am aware that appearance does not count for everything, but I would have hoped that the clergy might take a little trouble with their appearance. Long, unkempt hair needing a wash, baggy jeans, grubby sweaters and muddy trainers – and that's just the lady clergy! Had they not been wearing clerical collars, they might have been taken for – well, for anything *except* the clergy! Do try a little harder, ladies and gentleman of the cloth, and if you are so hard up that you cannot afford a haircut or some washing powder, please let me know and I will proffer a few quid for the purpose.

Wednesday 10th December 2003

Arrested

Last Sunday was one I will remember for ever and a day. Robert, Heather's husband, works for a large supermarket chain. In the late afternoon a well-known shoplifter and local drug dealer entered the store and was seen on CCTV stuffing goods into his jeans and pockets. Robert approached him, asking him to put things back – which is the practice, rather than call the police as this happen half-a-dozen times a day in this East London supermarket. The shoplifter hit Robert, so Rob and two other staff members got him on the ground and sat upon him whilst awaiting the arrival of the police.

It took the constabulary some twenty minutes to arrive during which time Rob and the other two were abused and punched by the shoplifter they were attempting to restrain. The shoplifter had a nose bleed and when the police arrived – in force, complete with white van, squad cars, the lot – the shoplifter calmed down. He admitted he was shoplifting, but accused Robert and the other two staff members of assault. The police walked the shoplifter out to their car, placing him in the comfort of the rear seats. Returning to Robert and his two colleagues, the police arrested all three, handcuffing them roughly and marching them unceremoniously to the police van.

Perhaps I should have mentioned that the shoplifter was white and the three staff – including Rob – are black.

Robert telephoned from the police station, where I arranged for a local solicitor known to me to join Heather and me. The incident occurred around 4pm, but four hours later the CID had yet to start interviewing so Heather and I drove home, leaving our solicitor with Rob.

At midnight Robert was released on bail. Heather and I drove to the police station to collect him, whilst Yvonne sat with Luke and Marlon at their home. Rob and his colleagues were bailed to Wednesday evening next week on charges of grievous bodily harm. They were not charged on Sunday – as the shoplifter was taken to A & E at Whipps Cross Hospital – from where he did a runner (and if the police appeared surprised at that, I most certainly was not).

Yvonne and I arrived home at 1.30pm – although I thought for one moment we might have to sleep in the porch – for Richard had put the latch down on the inside door. Richard had been out to a gig, arrived home at midnight, saw our note on his bed – but had already dropped the latch. He sleeps with ear plugs as I shout out in the night if I am having one of my nightmares and wake him up. We telephoned, but the answerphone was on. We rang the door bell – and eventually he heard us.

This week's local newspaper had the story on the front page – naming the shop but not the individuals. I guess the police placed the story for who else could have done so? Robert told me that customers have been calling all week to ask if it is him? Heather is a PA in the local authority offices near the shop when Rob works. Again, her colleagues know Rob – and are asking questions.

We hope that on Wednesday the police will drop the charges as I doubt if the shoplifter will give himself up. If the police find him and he presses charges, we will defend to the hilt. If the police drop the charges, my solicitor is advising us to go to the police complaints authority. We shall see.

(As it happened, the charges were not dropped. All three reported at the police station at 5pm on Wednesday. Interviewed separately, the police offered Robert and his two colleagues cautions. The two accepted, but Robert did not, holding out until late evening after three interviews with his solicitor present. At around 9pm the charges against Robert were dropped.

Robert decided not to proceed with a complaint – fearing that he would be a marked man in the eyes of the local police were he to do so. I can hardly blame him, but the incident confirms my very deep concerns about the police in whom, I regret to say, I have had little confidence for some time.

Two young men without previous convictions now have criminal records. After what I can only describe as an attempt to bully and harass by the police, Robert emerged without a stain on his character. One of Robert's colleagues had a solicitor; the other did not. Robert was represented by a solicitor known to me. I wonder what might have happened had Robert and I not insisted that a solicitor be present throughout the interviews?)

Sunday 25th April 2004

We are the judges!

We have battled with the elements this week as we waited for the *Redbridge in Bloom* Judges to drop in on us. The rain accompanied by unseasonable gale force winds took its toll on Tuesday and Wednesday. Sycamore leaves blew around the corner from Ramsgill Approach, bypassed the first two gardens and filled our front pathway. Yvonne and Marlon did their best each afternoon, and I joined in on returning home. Lots of nice leaf mould, but some devastation to the gentle boughs of fuscia and geranium. I could have cried over the hanging basket, which we had taken in a couple of weeks before to give it some respite in the greenhouse after the winds did their worst. Then this week we had to take it indoors at night to stop it blowing off to Fords Sports Ground or Seven Kings Station or the River Thames beyond.

Over the past eight weeks or so, I have gone into the garden morning and night to de-head, usually in my pyjamas and summer dressing gown in the morning and more properly attired at night. Yvonne and I have taken turns at the watering – with the hose and with the watering can, the latter when feed was called for. Passers-by have often stopped. One lady told me that she pauses each morning on her way to collect the newspaper and spends a few minutes just standing and staring. One or two have asked me if I take on gardening assignments and I have had to decline, for Heather's and Stella's fronts occupy me too – and also, now, Cathy's where I have one or two pots on display so that Cathy does not feel left out of things.

Yvonne has carried home the odd plant or three from Romford or Ilford, and Ruth has contributed as ever. We have begonias out there given to me by Una and Ruth now in their third summer as a result of drying off the bulbs in the greenhouse over winter. There are pots we bought when we were away on holiday, a mixing bowl given to us by Ivy and a colander of massive proportions which Tom next door bought at a car boot sale.

Around noon on Thursday I was walking down the pathway, bound for Goodmayes on the bus, when two ladies entered the gate. You could have knocked me down with a couple of petunias for they were Judges, no less, for *Redbridge in Bloom*. They stood there looking around themselves whilst I moved towards the gate, making pleasant sounds and trying to look very old and 'umble – which is not very difficult. I explained that in the autumn the greenhouse becomes home to those plants that will not take kindly to the frost and bulbs are planted for the spring. One of the ladies handed me a card to tell us that they had visited.

I did not hang about, for the ladies were clearly enthused by what they saw. I wished them a happy day and made some comment to the effect of hoping that they enjoyed their job. *"We would if all the gardens were as good as yours,"* one of the ladies replied. And with those words ringing in my ears I hopped off round the corner to Goodmayes.

I rang Yvonne when I was on the bus. Yvonne told me that the ladies stayed for a good ten minutes, taking photographs and picking up the heads of fuscias to examined them, standing here, there and everywhere to take in the view. But I guess they do that with all the gardens. We should hear in about two weeks' time. Meanwhile, we continue to de-head and nurture, and will water when it dries up again.

Saturday 9th July 2004

London in Bloom

Yvonne was sitting quietly in the dining room when she spied what she described as a *huge* white van with the words *Redbridge Leisure Services* emblazoned on the side.

It came up the road, slowed outside our house, rumbled along to Val-Across-The-Road, did a big U-turn and came back to rest outside Number 37 – no less. Three men in suits alighted. Two stood at the gate making notes on clipboards, whilst the third rang the door bell. Yvonne answered the door.

The man introduced himself as Patrick Buttress, Parks and Countryside Manager, London Borough of Redbridge.

"We have come to judge your garden," he smiled.

"But the judges came last week," Yvonne smiled back.

"Ah, yes," said Mr Buttress, *"that was Redbridge in Bloom, but we are from London in Bloom."*

Well, you could have knocked Yvonne down with a couple of dahlias.

Mr Buttress stood on the doorstep and sighed.

"It is," he said, *"a little oasis."* And the men in suits at the gate appeared to agree.

"Now this is Ron Jeffries' garden, isn't it," said Mr Buttress and Yvonne admitted that it was – being a bit bashful she did not mention that the entry is in our joint names. Mr Buttress asked Yvonne if she helped and the good lady admitted that she did.

Then looking up, Mr Buttress asked: *"It is* the *Ron Jeffries, is it not?"*

Yvonne looked a bit stunned.

"Is it?" he pressed. And then Mr Buttress told his colleagues that they were standing in the garden of the former Chairman of Redbridge Magistrates' Court. And they all look suitably impressed, confused, astounded – or just bored.

But Mr Buttress was clearly impressed to be in *the* Ron Jeffries' garden and made lots of notes and noises about it being a *"little oasis".*

Yvonne came indoors to recover from all this. The three stayed a while and then drove off.

We have checked the rules. The finalists for the *Redbridge in Bloom* Competition are entered in the *London in Bloom* Competition. We await all agog for a white envelope through the door. It is all getting too much for hardly do we put our heads outside the front door and a passer by knobbles us to ask if we have won.
(In fact we came second, having come third last year, in the front garden category. We attended the Town Hall for the presentations later in the year – the M & S voucher was much appreciated.)
Saturday 16th July 2004

Day Sixteen of No Smoking

It is Day Sixteen today of No Smoking. I am sitting here sucking my dummy – a Boots the Chemist Inhalator with a nicotine capsule. I am permitted twelve capsules a day – this is my second today. I need to get the nicotine levels up in the blood stream.

Next I have my second cup of coffee – and possibly a third before I go off at ten this morning to smile at the local photographers and growl to the reporters about the potential invasion of the nearby Green Belt of Fairlop Plain by the London City All-weather Racecourse.

Yvonne is downstairs – building the wooden railway track with Marlon (4), which is the early morning ritual hereabouts. It takes about half-an-hour and has to be a different layout each day, with Marlon giving the instructions. Nursery started yesterday – so that gives Yvonne the morning off. Today Yvonne is painting the summerhouse with preservative.

I had to replace a few pieces of wood last week on the roof of the summerhouse – Yvonne helped me to carry the timber from B & Q as it was too long to get on the bus.

We made a fine pair, two pensioners carrying timber along the A12 – with Marlon marching in front to make sure we did not bump into any old folk with zimmer frames.
Tuesday 6th September 2004

Day Twenty-one

Today is Day Twenty-one of the No Smoking Regime. I continue with the dummy. I have it in my mouth all the time I am at the desk and often when I am walking outside home. I get weird looks, but folk in these parts seem to be getting used to the sight and no longer comment – well, not aloud or in my presence.

Richard is home for a long weekend from Oslo. The main purpose appears to be to purchase goods which are either unobtainable in Norway or are cheaper here. He has a long list of medications – some cold cures, for example, are only available on prescription in Norway, whilst a whole range of headache pills are so expensive as to rule them out of most people's purchase. So Richard is acting as a sort of drug courier, which worries me somewhat. He did some work for his previous employers on Friday – they paid him in cash so off he went to HMV to buy DVDs. These, he told me, will keep him going till Christmas. He finds Norwegian TV a problem. I suppose the main difficulty is that he speaks little Norwegian and is finding it a hard language to learn.

Meanwhile, Heather appears to be spending more time at A & E than is good for her. Her neighbour's daughter – 19 – was bitten in Hainault Forest. Her leg swelled up, so Heather took her to A & E – and has been back twice this week to see the GP in A & E as the swelling got bigger and bigger. Then Marlon fell off his bike yesterday, so Heather took them both. Marlon has a large black eye. Gemma has an even bigger swelling.

It is now just after 8am on Sunday. Richard did not come home last evening from a visit to friends in London. I have told his mother that he has probably been arrested as a drug runner.

Richard – now thirty and living with his girl friend in Norway – has a six month contract at an art gallery in Oslo. His task is to assist in taking digital photographs of all the pictures in the gallery.

It is the gallery where *The Scream* by Edvard Munch was stolen in July and it was in all the papers. Richard had been working there just a week when the burglary happened. No-one has interviewed him to date – which is a bit strange, but perhaps he does not look like a burglar.

Sunday 12th September 2004

The Lights – again!

I decided to check the Christmas lights a little early this year. Now that I have not smoked for some three months, the stress levels tend to be a little on the high side. Fearing that if I left it until a couple of weeks before Christmas, only to find that they were not working, I moved early – and, should there be a failure, I have time to sort things out.

Last Sunday afternoon at around 3pm I advised Yvonne that I wished to check the Christmas lights. Yvonne went pale, but got a grip of the situation in a matter of seconds. Upstairs we went. Down came the Christmas boxes from the wardrobe. Out came the lights – and we were off.

These days Christmas Lights are more sophisticated than when the children were young. Few sets had transformers, which meant that there was a massive – or so it seemed – surge of electricity every time they were switched on and off. Hence the number of bulbs that blew up. Well, at least, that is my understanding of the situation.

Three sets lit first time. Two sets had half the lights unlit. I tried the tester thingy – but this did not help. So I started the painstaking business of taking out each bulb and putting in another. This worked on both sets – and all was light.

I noticed that Yvonne was visibly relieved that the Lights had come on without too much trouble. I have given notice that the Lights will go up on 11th December. Yvonne thought this was a little premature, but on checking her diary discovered that she would be out that morning – and, therefore, readily agreed that the 11th is a good day for this purpose.

3rd December 2004

Grumpy old man

I am now five months and five days without smoking. I no longer cough or wheeze. I am told that I look healthier and my skin is a rosy red.

I have opened a monthly savings account with the Woolwich, putting in the money I would have spent on cigarettes. I keep an account of this on the computer in Excel and pull up the programme each week to gloat. I have become a miser and a grumpy old man all at the same time. Heather says I have always been a grumpy old man. Be that as it may, I feel stressed and chewing Orbit Professional Gum does not begin to make up for a good cigarette.

Wednesday 26th January 2005

On a flatbed truck

I have today ordered a Slate Water Feature for the front garden. We are going all out to win first prize this year in the *Redbridge in Bloom Competition Front Garden Category.* The general consensus around these parts is that a water feature should tip the balance in our favour.

It is expensive. However, I have convinced myself that I can afford it – simply because I have given up smoking. We have gone for the Mountain Quarry Water Feature with a thirty inch stack at £229 – I said it was expensive. We have chosen this model because the water tank is underground – which means that the sum will not shine on the water which will not turn green. I have taken advice from Shirley, who has a similar edifice – except that it does not have a stack but the water bubbles over slates. Shirley has had hers for a year – and all that has happened is that the slate has gone a bit green – but this can be washed off. Yvonne will enjoy washing the slates – so I have no worry here. I have decided to place it in front of the Christmas tree rather than on the left-hand side under the bird feeder. I think that is too near the pavement and may attract some lout to tamper with it. John parks his car outside the home of John-Across-The-Road. On Wednesday night he had all four wheels stolen. Yvonne spotted this on Thursday morning and knocked on Margaret's door to tell them.

I may need to install a light in the front garden to deter thieves. They would not find it easy to remove the water feature for they would have to take each piece of slate off the central pole and then empty the water tank. However, we had a model pagoda stolen from the Japanese garden at Goodmayes Hospital last summer. It was about five feet high, was cemented in and valued at £1,000. They brought a digger in to shift it. Somehow I do not think they would bring a digger into the front garden at 37 – but you never know.

(The water feature arrived a week or so later – on the back of a flatbed truck, having travelled from somewhere North of Newcastle. It was packed on a pallet and had to be unloaded onto the pavement by crane. Yvonne was nowhere to be seen at this point, so I unpacked and carried it through the house, bit by bit. Realising I had bitten off far more than I could chew, I am pleased to record that Clive came to the rescue and installed the thing over a period of a couple of weeks. It is magnificent. And is much admired by those who pass by, although Ken next door believes that it would be better in the rear garden and will not impress the judges in the front garden competition. And he may well have been right – for we have not won a thing in *Redbridge in Bloom* since the water feature started to gurgle.)

Friday 25th February 2005

Water cascading up the stairs!

For some weeks we have battled with a garden hose that has seen better days. The nozzle end shoots off when you least expect it to do so. Far worse is the fact that the connection from the garden tap on the wall outside the kitchen to the hose reel is such that more water runs away down the drain than goes into the hose pipe. This is because the plastic thingy has worn so that the brass wotnot does not fit. Robert came over a few weeks back and looked at it for us. He did something which stopped the leak for some days – then it all started up again. I got some wire and bound it very tightly to hold it in position – but that lasted only a day or so and we were off again.

Today we purchased a new hose, reel and accessories. This one has wheels, which is rather good if you want to wheel it anywhere. But I do not. Be that as it may, Heather drove Yvonne and me to B & Q this morning. Well, to Toys R Us actually, where they went to purchase our birthday present for Marlon whilst I went to B & Q. The hose is thirty metres in length. Back home I fitted it out and this evening Yvonne watered the back garden whilst I watered the front. Not at the same time, of course.

All went swimmingly, as they say, until I started to bring the hose back through the hall into the rear garden. I reached the foot of the stairs when without warning the nozzle flew off the hose and water started to cascade all around. For a few seconds I was transfixed, for I had not seen such a thing before. Water was spurting along the carpet, cascading up the stairs and even onto the shelf above the hall table where much of Yvonne's best glass is displayed. It was a very pretty sight, I can tell you. A shimmering sparkling display amongst the glassware.

But suddenly it dawned on me that this should not be happening. I called to Yvonne to turn the water off at the garden tap. Running down the stairs – for Yvonne was up there at the time – and sloshing through the sodden carpet, Yvonne did as I requested.

I am now upstairs writing. Yvonne is downstairs, mopping up the water. And it has started to rain outside. I will now have a shower and try to keep the water inside the cubicle.

Monday 18th July 2005

"Two poached eggs, lightly mind"

He was a familiar figure around Ilford and was well-known to many volunteers at the Redbridge Night Shelter. When the Shelter met in church halls and in the first months at York Road, Mickey (a chronic alcoholic) rarely ate the evening meal, but would ask for *"two poached eggs, lightly mind"*. When Val-Across-The-Road or Yvonne gave them to him he would say: *"You're a diamond!"*

Rehoused a year or so ago in a specially adapted ground floor flat in Clayhall after he lost the use of his legs, Mickey would travel by bus from Barkingside to Ilford to sit in his wheelchair under the awning at Blockbusters in Cranbrook Road – or when the sun was shining, outside Fairheads – supping from his favourite can.

Despite the tireless efforts of Terry, Susan and Karen over many months, Mickey refused to take full advantage of the help offered by social services. He was a proud and independent man, but his generosity of spirit and inherent kindliness led him to allow others into his home. Eviction loomed, but his so-called friends beat the eviction order by turning Mickey onto the street.

For over a week in early August, Mickey slept in his wheelchair off Cranbrook Road. The efforts of Terry and others to get him back into his flat failed. He collapsed in the early hours of a Monday morning and died later that day at King George Hospital.

Friends from the Night Shelter travelled to Frinton on the Essex coast for the funeral at ten fifteen on a warm Monday morning. There were thirteen in the congregation – fifteen if you count the Minister and the Organist. The Minister was Vicar of St. Andrew's in the Drive in Ilford in the 70s and 80s – now retired and living in Walton. There were five floral tributes – including one from Mickey's friends at the Shelter.

Mickey's father – in his late 70s and a former London taxi driver – was present. Mickey's grandmother aged 99 was lively and sprightly in spite of being wheelchair bound. She lives in a nursing home nearby. Mickey's elder brother was also there, with his son and daughter. The family were clearly pleased to see us.

Two of Mickey's male friends were present. Both knew Mickey when he was young – and one had photographs of Mickey as a smiling, good-looking young man. We learned that Mickey worked in an advertising agency when he left school and was an accomplished and talented artist. Drink took hold and Mickey became a hardened alcoholic. Later he worked on market stalls. Both friends had tried to keep in touch with Mickey – one had helped him in recent months with furnishings, bedding and so on for the flat.

Approaching his fiftieth birthday, Mickey's body was wasting away; he could have passed for a man in his eighties when he died.

It was a bright, warm, sunny, fresh morning as we drove through the sparkling green Essex countryside back to Mickey's old haunts in Ilford, but dark,

brooding clouds were bearing down over the horizon and soon the streets would be awash as the pavements were lashed with heavy rain. Rather like Mickey's life, I guess.
August 2005

All is safely gathered in – well almost

It is that time of the year when the greenhouse is cleared for winter storage of fuscia and the drying of dahlias and begonias. It would be an exaggeration to state that all is safely gathered in, but we have made a start – Yvonne and me, that is. I do the sorting and storing; Yvonne does the carrying and the washing of the pots – and very well she does it, too.

There has been a change of somewhat dramatic proportions in the front garden (Third Prize *Redbridge in Bloom Front Garden Category* – 2003, Second Prize 2004, No Prize 2005). The ivy-covered tree stump with the bird box on top is no more. The stump was once a tree, which grew from a six inch sapling, brought home from Sweden in the early 1980s when I visited that country as Editor of MILK INDUSTRY. The time came some ten years ago when I decided it had to come down, but I decided to leave the tree stump and fixed a bird box on top. Yvonne spotted a root of ivy near the house. Plant that at the foot of the stump, Yvonne suggested. And I did. That small piece of ivy multiplied as only ivy can multiply. It soon covered the tree stump and started to attack the bird box. Each year I hacked the ivy back – but it continued to attack. Last summer its growth shattered the roof of the bird box and it was clear that a new one was required.

Yesterday I set about removing the bird box, but as I did so, the stump collapsed. It had rotted completely at the foot. Just sawdust! Now the stump rests behind the shed-with-the-overhang where it will attract wildlife galore – beetles, woodlice and other creepy-crawlies in abundance.

At the nursery in Whalebone Lane yesterday afternoon I purchased a fine, freestanding bird table with nesting box. Having placed it in Heather's car – with the front seat down – we drove home.

The heavens opened. Carrying the splendid bird table into the house, we were soaked to the skin. Here I affixed the bird feeders – the ceramic one which replaced the two stolen from our front garden a few years back (by bird feeder thieves, of which there are a few hereabouts), the apple shaped feeder and the upright one.

When the rain had subsided, I carried the bird table into the front garden and placed it in position on four pieces of crazy paving amidst the shrubs. And very smart it looks, too. I sprinkled some birdseed on the table, hung the fat balls and waited for the sparrows to return for their supper.Looking out in early evening, there were no birds, but a very happy squirrel, resting under the rooftop out of the rain and gorging himself on the birdseed. But the sparrows are back this morning.

We are unbowed by our failure to be amongst the winners in *Redbridge in Bloom*. We will enter again next year when the judges will have their minds blown away – if only by the bird table.

(We did – enter, that is – but we did not – win, that is. We gave up finally after the debacle of 2008, when the judges came three weeks after the beginning of the

week when the competition was due to be judged. They spent all of a minute-and-a-half giving our entry a cursory glance, observing things from the pavement, taking only one step into the garden and not examining a single fuscia. Things are not the same since that nice Mr Buttress retired. We will not enter again, but continue to tend the garden to bring pleasure to those who pass by and to ourselves.)
Sunday 2nd October 2005

One year on – and counting

It was Sunday 22nd August 2004 at 1.30pm when I lit my last cigarette – one year, eight weeks and three hours ago (and counting) as I write. And so at the age of seventy-one and after some forty-eight years of the nicotine habit, it all came to an abrupt, sudden and dramatic end.

Why? I looked around the lunch table that Sunday at my wife, daughter, son-in-law and two grandsons. Their faces, as I coughed yet again, made clear what I had to do.

I got through the rest of the day – just. Monday morning found me in Boots the Chemist in Ilford Town Centre shortly after they opened. Here I purchased a pack of nicotine inhalators – a kind of short cigarette holder into which you insert a capsule of nicotine. For the next month I could be seen puffing on the inhalator, until I tired of the white thing sticking out from the side of my mouth like some gangster in a 1920s silent movie.

The lady in Boots the Chemist was mightily impressed when I told her I had been off the cigarettes for four weeks. At one point I thought she might give me a hug and a kiss, but instead she offered me some nicotine chewing gum – as she told everyone within sight in a very loud voice what a virtuous fellow I am.

I preferred the chewing gum to the inhalator – much less conspicuous. Whilst the gum was not as expensive as smoking, it was costly all the same. Just as I was weighing up how this was hitting my pocket, I learned that the gum is available on prescription. Off to Dr Clark, my GP – and gum was free on prescription as I am a pensioner.

At a very early stage I had decided to tell my relatives, friends, acquaintances, enemies and those I meet at the bus stop that I had quit the weed. This I did and, of course, it made it impossible for me to go back to smoking again. The shame of having to admit failure would have been too much to bear. My fate was well and truly sealed at the NELMHT Annual Meeting at the end of September 2004. Here before assembled colleagues I was presented with a framed certificate congratulating me on successfully completing thirty days without a cigarette.

I also telephoned the local NHS helpline which claimed to offer support to those who had ditched their crutch. Expecting to hear a sympathetic and supportive voice, I was disappointed to find an answerphone. I left my number and said I had quit. A month or so later a lady called on the telephone. You are doing well, she cried – with a cheery *"keep going"* as she rang off. I suppose I am now just another statistic helping a PCT to gain a star.

My GP, the kindly Dr Clark, sent me to King George Hospital for tests. After run-of-the-mill X-rays and blood tests, I was despatched for some in-depth scanning involving men in white coats, computers and a tunnel. The consultant was considerate, especially when he discovered that I was on the nearby Trust Board. He suggested I might have a puffer inhaler to relax my tubes and so nowadays I puff night and morning. It clearly pleases Yvonne to see me doing so.

After two months of the nicotine substitutes, I now chew ordinary gum. On learning that I did so, my eldest son suggested that I should indulge in Orbit Professional as being more in keeping with my status in society. When I discovered that they cost 45p as opposed to the 30p charged by others, I declined to follow his advice.

I continue to save the money I would otherwise have spent on cigarettes. At the end of each month, I may be found transferring money into the new account with a Scrooge-like curl on my lips. And I am determined not to spend it on fripperies, but to save it for my *real* old age.

Am I stressed? You bet your sweet life I am. In addition to the multivitamin tablets, my wife has put me on a course of some herbal remedy or other. I am unsure if they are doing me any good, but I will not give them up for fear that I might discover that they are – if you see what I mean.

One unopened packet and a packet with twelve cigarettes nestle next to the envelopes in my desk drawer in my home office. They are a sort of comfort, for should breaking point be reached, they are there – waiting. But the Scrooge within me allows me to resist. Meanwhile, if you see me taking deep breaths, please look the other way.

(Some two years later, Marlon – my grandson, then seven – took his mother on one side and with a grave face told her that he did not know how he could break the news to Nana that Granddad had started smoking again. Heather assured Marlon that this was not so, but Marlon insisted. You see, he said, I was not looking, but the drawer in Granddad's desk was open this morning and he has two packets of cigarettes in there.)

Friday 21st October 2005

Heavy frosts

We have had very heavy and thick frosts yesterday and today. The garden and rooftops are snow white.

Our boy cat brothers – Sooty and Socks – went out as usual in the middle of the night – and seemed very pleased to come in again when I went down to make the tea around 7am. Lady cat Tabby stayed in all night. I think she has more sense than to venture outside these cold nights.

We had the tree-fellers in last Saturday to trim off some twenty-five feet from the top of the fir tree at the bottom of the garden. We bought the tree in Romford Market when we moved here on the early 1960s. Actually, we bought two but fortunately one died. They cost one shilling and sixpence each – but today I had to shell out £300 to have the top lopped off the one remaining.

Yvonne was at the church Bazaar on the cake stall that morning, so I was in charge of making tea and coffee for the two men up the tree. They had ropes and pulleys, chain saws and a huge shredder machine parked out the front. As they cut branches, they carried them through the house and fed them into the shredder. Yvonne had moved the glassware from the shelf in the hall and ornaments from the top of the bookcase. They spent about three hours here and when they had gone, I started to clear up – and could not work out how to turn on the vacuum cleaner. It is a new one which Yvonne has had for about six months. I put my spectacles on and realised I was pushing the label with the name of the manufacturer. I worked it out in the end. A man up the road asked me if the men working in my garden would call to fell a tree for him – which they did after leaving me. They will also be trimming the trees in the churchyard as a result of doing our tree. I think I deserve some commission.

Off to Goodmayes Hospital this morning for a briefing on the Trust's smoke-free policy which comes into effect on 1st January. All NHS sites will be smoke free – no smoking will be permitted even in the grounds. Patients will be the exception – they will be permitted to smoke in designated areas, but there will be no smoking rooms on the wards as in the past and they will have to go outside into gardens to smoke. This is a hospital for the mentally ill, many of whom find a cigarette is a great reliever of stress. I fear it will result in patients and staff smoking in toilets and bedrooms – with the consequent fire risk – but no-one listens to a reformed smoker like me.

Friday 18th November 2005

Excitement

We had a bit if excitement last evening and early this morning. We returned from volunteering at the Redbridge Night Shelter at around 10pm. Yvonne and Cathy, our neighbour, had been cooking.

Cathy went into her house and a few minutes later Cathy rang our doorbell – her house had been broken into.

One of her front windows had been forced from outside and the kitchen window had been opened with the key. Nothing was disturbed downstairs, although they had taken her mobile phone from the hall to her bedroom – and left it there. Drawers and cupboards in her bedroom had been opened with stuff spread all over the floor and bed.

But the only thing Cathy could establish that had been stolen were some Christmas present M & S vouchers, a collection of coins and four hundred American dollars from her son's bedroom which have been there since he moved away a year or two back.

I dialled 999. Asked how old the owner was, I said she was elderly and lived alone. Cathy – who is in her late fifties – was not best pleased with me for saying this until I told her it could mean that she would get a better service from the police – which she did.

Two lady officers attended at about 10.45pm. Just after midnight two scene of crime officers – again ladies – arrived to fingerprint. All the police officers were helpful and understanding.

We 'secured' the front window with tape – all we could do really – and Cathy came into our home to sleep in our spare room for the night. Cathy has had a cup of tea and has now gone home – to contact insurers and someone to secure the front window.

Sunday 8th January 2006

"Not after dark – at your age!"

My elder brother is now seventy-eight and continues to be housebound in a ground floor flat in Dorking, Surrey. His arthritis has become severe. He is bent double and walks with great difficulty with two sticks.

I visit him every three weeks to take him cash and to do a few jobs for him around the flat. We speak on the telephone at least once every day. He has social services help with shopping and housework – and two ladies who walk his dog, Shadow, but he is fiercely independent and not the easiest of people to get on with. I visited him on Monday last.

Yesterday following two falls he was admitted to Dorking Hospital, a cottage hospital with just one ward for rehabilitation. I spoke during the day to the district nurse who arranged admission and also rang one or two of my brother's contacts to advise them what had happened and to arrange for Shadow to be boarded out with one of the dog walkers.

I rang the hospital in the evening to say that I would visit on Friday and asked for the visiting hours. I explained that I live in Essex and would travel by train.

"I imagine you are quite elderly," said the nurse to whom I was speaking.

"I am seventy-three," I replied.

"I guessed so," said the nurse. *"You will not want to be out late in the evening so I suggest you come at about 1pm – then you can be home before it is dark."*

I said I did not worry about the dark.

"You must not be out alone in London in the dark," said the nurse. *"Not at your age. There are lots of wicked people about."*

I asked how far the hospital is from the station.

"It is a long walk," she said. *"But there is a bus – although when you get off the bus there is a hill to climb."*

"I will get a taxi," I said.

"They are expensive," the nurse told me, *"at least £3.50."*

I said I thought I might be able to manage that.

"You can walk back," she said, *"it is downhill."*

On Friday I will rush home before darkness falls, bouncing downhill from the hospital to the station like a roly-poly pudding!

16th March 2006

The man in the bicycle shed

Yvonne found a man in the bicycle shed yesterday and it happened like this. Around two in the afternoon, there was an almighty bang outside the old homestead. Yvonne thought it was a gas explosion. Logical, in that the gas men have been in these parts laying new main pipes. Rushing to the front of the house, Yvonne spotted police cars and policemen all over the place. In fact, the street was littered with them, so much so that you could have formed a football team, but it would have to be a mixed one for there were both male and female officers rushing hither and thither. Guessing that the police would not arrive so quickly if it was a gas explosion, Yvonne ventured further into Aldborough Road North – to discover that a car had crashed into Charlie and Margaret's garden wall in Ramsgill Approach, which is two houses away from us.

Three young men had been driving a car along the A12, pursued by the constabulary in a number of cars. A sting was said to have been thrown down to puncture the tyres – which made the car veer off and skid down Ramsgill Approach and into Charlie and Margaret's wall – which, incidentally, has a nasty dent in its brickwork. Nick and Simon from over the road were quickly on the scene and pronounced that the car smelt of cannabis. Yvonne did not ask how they knew what cannabis smelt like, and I must take this up with them later.

Yvonne learned that two young men had decamped over Charlie and Margaret's wall and into the garden – two away from us. Is your back door locked, Yvonne was asked? I think so, she replied – at which two police officers accompanied Yvonne into the house to check. The back door was locked so the officers departed.

One young man was caught three or four gardens down from us and carted away in handcuffs. We learned later that he had knocked at Vic's back door. Opening the door and asking him what he wanted, the young man said he needed to get to the front of the house – so Vic led him through without further question. The lad belted up the front garden path – into the arms of waiting police.

Yvonne stood in the kitchen, ironing and looking into the garden, when she spotted that the step ladders were on the ground. That's odd, thought Yvonne, and then noticed that the door to the bicycle shed was moving slightly – and inside was a young man in a hood kneeling down.

At this point Yvonne moved at the speed of sound through the house and into Aldborough Road North. Summoning a police officer, Yvonne explained what she had seen in the bicycle shed. A woman and man police officer called for a dog handler and dog – and into the house they went, leaving Yvonne in the front garden to admire the water feature and the daffodil, which are coming into flower at this time – and a fine display they will become in a few days' time. Here Nicholas and Simon, Jean and Val-Across-The-Road intervened and took Yvonne off to their home for a stiff cup of sweet tea. They were kindness itself.

Suffice to say that the police dog ate the cats' food in our kitchen and then sorted out the young man in the bicycle shed and he, too, was carted off.

As things were calming down, I came round the corner from Goodmayes Hospital. The policemen in Ramsgill Approach were stood there with Simon, who advised me to go home as Yvonne could not stop shaking. I did so – and they were right. Poor girl, she was affrighted and there's no mistake. But another cup of tea and a cuddle and Yvonne was right as rain.

I gather that Charlie and Margaret's wall is now a hazard and is taped off. The bicycle shed is undamaged and Yvonne had a large whiskey last evening and a good night's sleep.

(Later that day two men were sent by the Council to demolish the wall that ran down the side of Charlie and Margaret's garden. They erected wire caging – which is still in position nearly three years later. I gather there was a mix up with Charlie's house buildings insurance a couple of weeks prior to the incident so that he was uninsured on the day in question. Efforts to encourage the Metropolitan Police to pay for a

new fence have completely failed. Councillors and MPs have tried – but the Met will not pay up. I am appalled – for putting down a sting in a built up area was foolhardy in the extreme on the part of the police when there is open countryside a hundred yards up the road. Apart from the damage to the wall, someone might have been walking on that bit of pavement when the car careered round the corner. The lack of at least some sort of fencing means that Charlie, Margaret and their family have no privacy in their garden and – to some extent – our privacy is not what it was either.)
21st March 2006

Homeless problem

We are back from the rough sleepers' count – a national survey organised by the Government every so often to show that there is not a homeless problem – well, that appears to be the purpose. The team found thirteen men sleeping out in the open in the Borough – which is good news of a sort, for I gather that if there are more than ten rough sleepers discovered in a Borough, the Government considers that there is a homeless problem after all and the probability of funding support becomes a possibility.

Phil and Mark from the Welcome Centre (a church-based unit in Ilford catering as a day centre for the vulnerable, the homeless and refugees) picked Yvonne and me up from our home at 4am. Phil and I covered Seven Kings, Goodmayes and Chadwell Heath north of the railway line; Yvonne and Mark did the bit south of that same railway line. Phil and I found no one sleeping rough. Mark and Yvonne found two – but as one of those was sleeping on a bench in Tesco's at Goodmayes, Phil and I consider he was ours – as Tesco's is north of the railway line. But as Phil and I visited Tesco's but failed to spot him, we thought it best to keep quiet.

One was found on the steps of an office in the Seven Kings end of Ilford High Road. Six were found in the town centre. Three were found in tents near the A406. One was found in a churchyard in Wanstead – the man mentioned in this week's *Wanstead and Woodford GUARDIAN* (the Rev John found him). One man was found walking near York Road – he was drunk, so I gather this hardly counted for he was moving (albeit erratically) and not standing still (you have to be motionless to count as homeless).

Redbridge Night Shelter was represented by the Rev John, two former guests, a man and a lady (whose names I did not catch), Yvonne and me. Phil and Mark were accompanied by a young lady volunteer at the Welcome Centre. Two staff members at the Centre were cooking breakfast. Peter from the Borough's Housing Department was co-ordinator – there were a couple of ladies with him who I assume were from Housing.

There were about ten police officers – who had concentrated on the parks and the town centre. Two of the men found in the town centre were fighting – and were arrested.

It was an interesting night. There was a wet drizzle but it was not too cold. Yvonne and I went to some places we did not know existed. We both visited Seven Kings, Goodmayes and Chadwell Heath Railway Stations. The booking halls were locked, but there was easy access to the platforms and the waiting rooms were not locked (I gather that this is to prevent these places being broken into with the consequent damage and the need for costly repairs).

If Yvonne chucks me out, I would go to Goodmayes Station – far superior accommodation, with a nice, warm waiting room with glass all the way round affording a good view of the passing freight trains.

We went to the Welcome Centre for the debrief – but Yvonne would not let me stay for breakfast as we had to get home for Master Marlon. Mark kindly drove us. The smell of bacon stayed with me all the way home – but when I asked Yvonne if I could have some, she told me that she had run out of bacon. I ask you. I had to make do with toast and marmalade.

Yvonne is busy getting Marlon off to school and is then going to Romford Market to buy the vegetables for Saturday at the Night Shelter. I feel like a lie down – for I am older than Yvonne as she is always telling me (even if it is only by nine months).

6th May 2006

Check-up

Yvonne sent me to see Dr Clark, our GP, yesterday. Not that I am unwell, but Yvonne likes to have me checked over from time to time to be certain that no bits have dropped off, and finds some excuse or other to ring the surgery to make an appointment.

This time it is because I have about four or five quite violent coughing fits each day. This is in spite of the fact that I gave up smoking two years, one month and twelve days ago (and still counting).

Dr Clark smiled as he tapped away at his keyboard and read my history on his screen. I explained why Yvonne had sent me – I would much prefer that he knew it was Yvonne rather than me who was insisting that he take a look at me. He sounded my chest back and front, declaring that I was fine, fine, fine. The antibiotics he prescribed earlier in the year had helped the cough – so we will try these again – but this time I will put you on a five day course of steroids, he told me. Now that shook me to the very roots, I can tell you. Not that I said anything, of course, because my Mum had always said that you should not question a doctor. But steroids? Those things they give to athletes who are subsequently banned from taking part in the Olympics?

I collected the prescriptions and boarded the bus home. As the chances of my being selected for the Olympics are somewhat remote (until they introduce dominoes as an Olympic sport), I had best take the course of steroids.

Yvonne was delighted with the tablets, I can tell you. I now take sixteen tablets and a couple of puffs each day – as follows: Breakfast – one garlic tablet, two herbal tablets to calm me down, one antibiotic, one puff at the puffer; Mid-morning – six (yes, six!) steroids; Lunch – one antibiotic, two herbals; Supper – two more herbals, one antibiotic, one puff at the puffer.

Ah well. It is a bright sunny morning so I am off into the garden shortly. Until the Mid-morning coffee when I take the six steroids. I will have a sit down after that – you never know with steroids, do you? By the way, Yvonne is very pleased

with things so far as I have not coughed all night – which is not really so surprising as I was asleep – but do not tell Yvonne. It's best she does not know.
Saturday 7th October 2006

Poppy collector

It is just before eleven and I am home, having had a warming cup of coffee. All went well this morning at Gants Hill Central Line Station where I was the poppy collector for the British Legion's annual appeal. We had a very heavy frost over night – it was the coldest day so far this winter. I wore my vest. I have taken to vests again – having ceased wearing them some twenty-five years ago when my teenage daughter told me that vests were for old men. In fact my daughter now approves because I do not wear a vest but a T-shirt, which I am told is cool – whatever that is.

On arrival I had to sign in at the station master's office. He told me that if there was a fire I should escape along the subway and assemble on the A12. I made a mental note to go home in the unlikely event of the station bursting into flames.

I stood in the booking hall from 7.40am to 10am. It was very windy down there – gusts suddenly blowing up the escalators and whistling around the subways. The worst bit was my knees – which appeared at one stage to be stuck firmly in the upright position. I would hazard a guess that I collected about £200. One man gave me a £10 note – another a penny.

Two men congratulated me on winning the fight to stop the all-weather racecourse being built on Fairlop Plain – I did not know either of them, but one was the man who gave me the £10 note. Two magistrates of my acquaintance rushed by – neither bought a poppy – one said that she would be out collecting herself at the weekend, the other already had a poppy.

Young Asian ladies – aged sixteen to twenty-five – seemed my best customers, all good lookers, of course. Perhaps there is something about the older man that they like – either that or they wanted poppies. I also offered pins. Some folk said they would not take a pin as they wanted the poppy for their desk. A few men – mainly in their twenties – gave me money but would not take a poppy. I smiled at everyone. Some smiled back.

Now to have a lie down before I go out on my bicycle to deliver some copies of OPEN SPACE to Aldborough Hatch Defence Association committee members. Then there is a Table Top Sale at church tomorrow morning, Night Shelter in the evening and visiting my elderly brother on Monday. Where do the days go now that I am retired, I ask myself?
Friday 3rd November 2006

Something new

I decided a week or so ago that I need something more to keep me ticking over. I am busy at St. Peter's, editing the weekly NOTICESHEET and monthly BROADSHEET, and keeping up with Yvonne's social and fund-raising activities. Also with the Night Shelter – Yvonne and I volunteer every other Saturday evening with Yvonne cooking a meal for the eighteen homeless guests and up to twenty meals-only clients – and I peel the potatoes and then generally swan around

(Yvonne says I get under her feet in the kitchen). Things are quiet on the racecourse front now that the developers have gone bust and the council has bought the lease back from the administrators. We are waiting for the council to consult on what the future might hold for Fairlop Waters.

So – I wrote to the Council's electoral registration department about helping out at a polling station or with the count. They have put me on their database. Also I wrote to three local secondary schools to see if they wanted invigilators at examinations. One has written back to say they will contact me nearer the examination time in the summer. I wait to hear from the others.

The garden is uninviting at present – although I did spend an afternoon in the greenhouse last week, planting the tomato seeds and potting up six oak saplings. Marlon (grandson now six and with us every weekday before and after school) picked up six acorns on his way home from school last October. At his suggestion we planted them in potting compost – and now have four oak saplings about six inches in height and two with roots and short sprouts. When they are bigger we will plant them – one, perhaps, in the churchyard and the rest in Hainault Forest.

I continue to visit my elderly brother every three weeks – seventy-nine today and eaten up with arthritis so that he can hardly walk. I ring him every day. He has always been a difficult person and miserable to boot. I have to say that he is a right know-all. I do not blame his former wives and children for wanting nothing to do with him. When I visit I defrost the fridge, clean the insides of the windows and sort out his bedding and washing. When I am there he shouts at me most of the time – great fun.

A week or two back, I allowed the de-frosting of the fridge to get out of hand – in my brother's eyes, at least – for some of the de-frosted water crept across the kitchen floor.

"You are useless," he cried, *"and I will not allow you to defrost my fridge again. I will ask one of my dog-walkers to do it for me."* As if I mind!

(My brother's health deteriorated over the next few months. I visited every week and spoke on the telephone each day – often more than once. A care package provided help with shopping and cleaning, whilst his two dog walkers continued to take Shadow out every day. Spells in hospital, constant falling in the flat with paramedics being called out on too many occasions finally led to a care package with carers attending three times a day. But all to no avail as he slipped into a painful and debilitating illness from which he died in December 2007. He was a lonely and bitter man to the end. And, sadly, I am unsure if there was much that anyone could have done about it for he would not permit of anything.)

Tuesday 16th January 2007

Bargain hunters

Since retirement caught up with us, Yvonne and I have become bargain hunters extraordinaire. Not only am I to be seen lurking in the Pound – and the 99p – Shops in Ilford for mint imperials (for Heather and me), Toblerone (for Luke), plastic gloves (for gardening) and moth balls and strong curry powder (to scare off the squirrels from my pots of bulbs in the garden). But – we are now on the track of reduced price printer supplies.

Double-sided sellotape at £3.45 is reduced to £2.75 in Owen Clark. The fine photo paper I use with my colour printer which retails in most places at £14 for twenty A4 sheets, has been selling for £10.40 in our local supermarket for some weeks – and Yvonne had bought my supplies there. Today in Ilford's shopping precinct the packs were '"buy one – get one free' at £14 – so £7 a pack. But just as I was about to purchase, Yvonne rang from the supermarket (how did we cope before mobiles?) where they were selling the packs at £2.99. Yvonne bought me four packs – but went back this afternoon to purchase another five.

And why, I hear you say, do I need all these photographic supplies? I have started a cottage industry – making Christmas Cards and Notelets to sell at the St. Peter's Flower Festival and Christmas Bazaar. I took photographs of St. Peter's Church in the snow – and these are the Christmas Cards. Then I have lots of photographs of flowers in my garden – and they are the notelets. I have purchased a card trimmer and am beavering away as though Christmas was around the corner. The digital camera and ability to crop and enhance photographs makes this so much more professional.

And then I have another job. I am to be an Examination Invigilator at Oaks Park High School starting with SATS, O, AS and A levels in May and June. I have been police checked and have my CRB Certificate to prove it. I had thought of posting it in the window, but Yvonne said she would take it down. No sense of adventure.

With the aid of Graham and Richard, I have downloaded SKYPE. We can now ring Graham and Richard at no cost whatsoever. This must be magic. No longer will Yvonne have to buy those £5 phone cards that give you £9 of time – or the £3 ones which give you £5 – from the little man on Ilford Hill – who always looks as though the police are about to raid him. Not only can we hear each other, but I can see Richard as he has a web cam thingy. Graham has a web cam thingy – but we cannot see him. I do not have a web cam thingy – and with all this techno-stuff, I am unsure if I want one.

(Later my family bought me one – so now we can all see each other, although I have to admit that the novelty has worn off and we tend now to just chat.)

I went out on my bicycle yesterday – to B & Q. We old folk have a special card which gives us a ten-per-cent discount on Wednesdays. The pensioners flock there and the rattle of walking sticks and zimmer frames is music to the ear. Soon an ambulance will be stationed outside B & Q on Wednesdays – on standby!

Thursday 8th March 2007

Nightmare

I had a nightmare last night. I dreamed that I was back at Redbridge Magistrates' Court as Bench Chairman. Clerk to the Justices Michael called me into his office, where there were a number of tall men in black suits and ties, with white shirts and dark glasses. Michael told me that they were from the Lord Chancellor's Office and the Crown Prosecution Service. A very big trial was to take place at Redbridge which would attract national media attention and would run for some weeks. It had been decided that I should chair and that Peter would be the Court Clerk. I asked what the charges were. Michael looked very grave – as only Michael could. He called Peter into the office, who was grinning from ear to ear – as only Peter can.

"The charges," said Michael, *"are of a sexual nature. That is why Peter is the Clerk, for he understands these things."*

"What is more," continued Michael, *"all the magistrates sitting with you will come from the Neighbouring Bench"* (here I will refrain from naming the Bench, for fear of upsetting local sensibilities and refer to it as the Neighbouring Bench) *"because their justices are experts in sexual matters and our Redbridge magistrates are not."*

I wanted to correct Michael and remind him of cupboards and court two and the like, but the men in the dark glasses were moving ominously towards me – so I did not say a word.

"Further," said Michael, *"as there are many different charges and the Neighbouring Bench has magistrates who are expert in different types of sexual crimes, you will have forty magistrates sitting with you. We have had to adapt Court One to accommodate all the magistrates, who will be arrayed on both sides of the Bench and at the ends. Those sitting at the front will have specially adapted chairs on stilts. Peter will be in the middle and you will sit at the end."*

And with that Michael, Peter and the men in dark glasses led me into the courtroom. There, sure enough, were the forty justices from the Neighbouring Bench.

All were sitting round the Bench – some on chairs on stilts and talking to each other in very loud and rather posh voices, as one might expect from magistrates from the Neighbouring Bench.

I tried to bring some order to the chaos – but the justices from the Neighbouring Bench continued talking and laughing and shouting. And Peter? He sat in the chairman's chair, smiling like a Cheshire cat that had got the cream and was not going to let anyone else have it.

And then I woke up. It was about 3am. So I aroused Yvonne from her deep slumber to tell her about it, but she was not best pleased.

I drifted off to sleep – and then I had another nightmare. It was the same scene. Michael came onto the bench to tell me that the case would run for months – but that the main evidence would be given next morning – so we were all to adjourn across the road to the pub on the corner for an evening meal.

We boarded luxury coaches in the car park as the justices from the Neighbouring Bench refused to walk the hundred yards or so – for they are a bit like that.

Waiters buzzed around taking orders. Michael chose the wine and told me that it would cost us about £50 each – as the justices from the Neighbouring Bench did a lot of drinking. I had a tenner on me and started to panic – and woke up.

It was about 5am. I decided not to go back to sleep. And Yvonne agreed that it would be best to stay awake. You never know what these justices from the Neighbouring Bench – who were experts in sex – might get up to. And as for Peter, well . . .

Sunday 11th March 2007

The night of the stolen mini-cab

It was just after ten last evening when there came a ring at the doorbell. I had watched the headlines on *News at Ten* and had settled to drink my glass of cold – but nourishing – semi-skimmed milk and to munch those small, round, slightly salty biscuits which Yvonne buys for me with a piece of the finest mature Cheddar.

Yvonne went to open the door. Yvonne always opens the door in our house and as I was in my dressing gown, having recently showered, I thought that right and proper. Then it occurred to me that it was, perhaps, rather late for callers, so I leapt from my chair and made my way towards the front door – just as Yvonne called out to tell me that there was a man outside.

We had locked the outer porch door earlier as I like to leave the inner door open on these cold evenings to keep the plants warm and cosy. The lights were on in the porch, making it something of a bright beacon on this dark, frosty evening.

As I unlocked the outer door, the man stood back and asked me in a very quiet and nervous voice if I would please call the police, for his car had been stolen. Are you a mini-cab driver, I asked? He said he was. I invited the man into the porch as Yvonne went to fetch the telephone and, somewhat reluctantly, the man moved onto the doormat. I dialled 999 and within about ten seconds the call was answered and, after another ten seconds or so, I was passed through to an operator who took down the details. I could hear a keyboard being used in the background and assumed that what I was saying was being input to a computer. (This was confirmed when the police arrived for they had a printout of the facts as I had relayed them.)

The man told me that he was from Bangladesh and had bought the car a month ago. He had difficulty in remembering the last three letters of the registration – but the police operator tried a number of variations involving V and C – and came up with the correct registration, make of car, owner and address as given by the man. His home was a mile or so away in Seven Kings.

The driver told me the name of the cab company for whom he worked. I obtained their number via directory enquiries and rang them so that the driver could tell them what had happened.

About fifteen minutes after I made the 999 call, two police officers arrived in an unmarked car. They took down further information and also inspected the area in the roadway where he driver told them the car had stopped. Here they found coins on the road which the driver said had fallen from his money bag as it was stolen.

The driver had been called to a Chinese restaurant in the Barking Road. Two young men and two girls – all aged in their early twenties – asked to be taken to Aldborough Road North. On arriving here, they asked the driver to pull into Ramsgill Approach, a small side road without houses, leading to Ramsgill Drive. The driver told them that the fare was £8 – but at this point the man in the passenger seat punched the driver on the forehead. They all got out of the car and the driver did the same – the other young man then punched the driver in the mouth, and grabbed his money and mobile phone. All four got back into the car and drove off.

As one police officer took down more details, I noted that the other was looking around our dining room. He examined closely the family photographs on one wall and then turned to look at the painting by Priscilla, the ITV artist, of the scene at Redbridge Magistrates' Court on 2nd August 1996 when I had chaired the Charlie Kray appearance. The officer was clearly interested, so I told him the story.

"I think I may have seen you in court," I said to the officer, whose face was vaguely familiar.

"I have only been in the force since 2003," the officer told me. *"I was 16 and still at school in 1996 when Charlie Kray was at Redbridge Court!"*

It is said that you are growing very old when police officers look very young. I guess you must be very, very, very old when police officers were still at school when you chaired the court at Redbridge. I will keep taking the tablets.

The two police officers asked the driver to accompany them to the police station for forensics, promising to take him home after the formalities were completed. We wished them a good night, I supped what remained of my cold milk and we went to bed.

Wednesday 21st March 2007

Tainted

An email to Court Clerk Peter:

First, congratulations to Master Matthew on being accepted for the local public school. Well done. Yes, I guess it is a better option than other schools I might mention. I would, however, suggest that at least once a month Peter takes Master Matthew for a ride on a 150 bus to Ilford and back – just to keep the lad's feet on the ground. At his school he will be mixing with Very High Class People and the Better Class of Gangsters' sons – and needs to see how the plebs live from time to time. The 150 bus is an education in itself.

Yes, indeed, I do remember the lady magistrate at Havering with whom I share a surname. We caught up from time to time at training and other events, but I always felt that our relationship was somewhat tainted by the experience we had at Danbury when we first met. We were not mistaken as husband and wife – but it went something like this.

I arrived early for the magistrates' training weekend – with a colleague I would guess. We booked in and off I went to my room which was in one of a number of blocks. I settled in, had a shower and prepared for the evening meal and bash.

Suddenly there was a knock at the door. Opening the door – in my dressing gown – I found an ashen-faced receptionist with the said lady magistrate behind her – glaring angrily and accusingly at me. You are in my room, called Mrs J. And you should know better, she continued, for this is the ladies' block and you should be in the men's block. I tried to protest my innocence – but Mrs J clearly was under the impression that I had gone into her room in the women's block with an ulterior motive in mind – one which, on reflection, I should not enlarge upon in case it sullies Peter's mind in some way.

So, you see, Mrs J and I started off on the wrong foot – and never recovered. I was assured that she was a very kindly lady – but I fear she thought I was some sort of sex maniac who made a habit of going into ladies' blocks on training weekends.

Performance related pay for court clerks? Whatever next, I ask myself? How will 'performance' be measured? I recall that Steven was always keen on magistrates 'potting' defendants – I guess he would have been at the top of the ratings.

26th March 2007

I am a Veteran – Official!

It all started when I met George-Up-The-Road as I paused on my bicycle to catch my breath before carrying on to the farm to buy nuts for the birds, our front garden being a veritable haven for sparrows who, we are told by those who know, are in short supply these days.

You did National Service, did you not, called George? Yes, I did, I replied. Well, did you know that you are entitled to a Veteran's Badge, said George. All I would need would be my national insurance number, dates of service and my armed services number. I do not know my services number, I told George. You must remember that, said George as he rattled off his number. And I can remember my Mother's Co-op Dividend Number, too, said George – as he intoned this with a grin on his face that stretched from ear to ear.

I told George that I had indeed served in both the Essex Regiment (for three weeks) and the Royal Electrical and Mechanical Engineers (for two years less three weeks). George appeared impressed.

I looked up the Veterans Agency on line (noting that they have dropped the apostrophe – what is the world coming to?). Sure enough, all the information was there – so I completed the form and apologised that at my great age I could not recall my Armed Service Number. I decided not to let on that I could not recall my Mother's Co-op Dividend Number, either, for that seemed pointless.

Yesterday a package arrived. Inside was a very smart blue box with gold trim. Opening the box, I was stunned to find a Veteran's Badge nestling on blue velvet, with a Pure Gold Crown at the Top. And as if that was not enough, inside the lid the following words were printed in Pure Gold on White Damask: *"By Appointment to Her Majesty The Queen"* (yes, The Queen!) *"Suppliers of Gold and Silver Laces"* (yes, Laces – we got the magnifying glass out to check) *"Insignia and Embroidery – Toye, Kenning and Spencer Ltd, London, FOUNDED 1685".*

This is really thrilling. If I need Gold or Silver Laces I now know just the boys to supply me. I have tended to use leather or cord laces up until now, but if I decide to move to Silver or even Gold at some time in the future, I will contact Toye, Kenning and Spencer and that's for sure.

And there was a Very Fine Printed Card, too. The following words (in purple, naturally) told me that the Badge came with the *"Compliments of the Under Secretary of State for Defence and Minister for Veterans".* I had no idea that I have My Very Own Minister. I must write to him. Perhaps I might call to see him, for I note that he is in Whitehall and my Freedom Pass would mean that the journey would be free and gratis – if I leave after 9am that is, unless it is a Saturday or a Sunday when I may leave at any time of the day or night. My Minister might allow me to go out onto his balcony – he is sure to have one in Whitehall – so that I could wave to the crowds below. That would be an awful lot of fun, especially if I am wearing my Veteran's Badge. The joy of it all.

My Minister goes on to tell me that the Armed Forces Veteran's Badge (with apostrophe, which is a relief) is presented to me *"in recognition of your service to your country".* So all that battling in the NAAFI queues in Warley, Blandford Forum, Gosport, Arborfield and Aldershot had been worthwhile. All that saving up my sweet coupons to bring home bars of Aero chocolate for Yvonne on my weekend leave had not been in vain. All that learning to type and running with a bayonet on the end of a rifle and ramming it into a sack stuffed with straw had been worth every minute.

My Minister also tells me that I may "*wish to wear it"* (the Badge, of course) *"on suitable occasions when dressed in civilian attire".* My Minister does not, however, enlarge on these *"suitable occasions".* I am off to Ilford to the Woolwich and to the Pound and 99p Shops shortly. Is this a *"suitable occasion"* I ask myself? I will be in *"civilian attire"* for sure, but is it a *"suitable occasion"?* Perhaps I should ask George-Up-The-Road. He would be sure to know. A man who can remember his Armed Service Number *and* His Mother's Co-op Dividend Number must know when it is a *"suitable occasion".* How exciting!

Tuesday 27th March 2007

Two envelopes

Yesterday morning the postman (who is quite small in stature, wears shorts even on the coldest of days and runs from house to house) called here with some envelopes.

Amongst the offers of £50 off a case of wine and free soap powder for a year, were two envelopes, each addressed to me as a JP and both emanating from Redbridge Magistrates' Court.

The first was a circular from that nice man, Mr David, regarding the Redbridge Justices' Club Dinner on Saturday 8th March. Yvonne and I intend to be there. I note that the dress is black tie optional, but I guess I will wear a bit more than that. It can be quite cool in March and at my age you cannot be too careful.

The second letter came as something of a shock and a surprise. Written on notepaper of Her Majesty's Court Service (HMCS) and purporting to come from North East London Area Redbridge Magistrates' Court, it was headed *TO ALL COURT USERS* and addressed: Dear Sir/Madam. This was the first surprise for surely, I said to myself, they know that I am a Sir and not a Madam?

The subject matter was highlighted in bold type and read: *Overnight Cases for Saturday 10th & 24th November 2007.* Now, I asked myself, what is going on here?

Firstly, I was unaware that I was a Court User. For what purpose do I use the Court? When did I use it thus? And why? And what for? Secondly, the text of the letter did not help, for it merely stated that Waltham Forest Magistrates Court (without the apostrophe – when will people learn?) is to take overnight cases on these two days as a Youth Training Day will be held at Redbridge. The letter ends with an apology for any inconvenience caused. But – and you will not be surprised to learn this – I remain at a loss as to why the letter had been sent to me in the first place and, in any case, I had not been inconvenienced so why the apology?

Noting that the letter was signed by someone called B. Gilbert, who says that he or she is Bench Legal Manager, I ran my eyes through the list of folk shown at the bottom of the letter to whom it had been copied. I see that a Ms C Ripper is something to do with the CPS and I would guess that with a name like that she is not to be trifled with. Then there is Ms M Jolley at Ilford Probation Centre. I'll bet she is a bit of a laugh. Lastly there is a Ms Curry, PA to Tom Ring, and I am sure that she is hot stuff.

I also note that Mr P Scudder is included and that he is referred to as a Legal Adviser. Can this be the Peter Scudder I once knew as a Learned Clerk? I doubt it, somehow, for someone who was once a Learned Clerk cannot have sunk to the depths of being a Legal Adviser. No, no, no, no, no, no, yes!

But to return to the subject matter of the letter. Who are these Youths who need two days to be trained? Have their mothers and fathers fallen down in their duty as parents and failed to train them?

I see that the Redbridge Bench Chairman has been copied in on this correspondence. Be that as it may, there can be little doubt that this would not have happened in Guy's time as Chairman of the Bench. No Sir, indeed. Any untrained Youths would have been horse-whipped along Barkingside High Street. Mind you, that nice Phoebe would have been waiting for them at the top end of the High Street with a Best Butter Bagel and a cuddle.

How I am expected to respond to this letter? Should I attend at Redbridge on the days in question armed with a banner sending miscreants off on the 150 and 179 bus to Waltham Forest Magistrates' Court? Or perhaps I should attend at Waltham Forest, standing outside the Courthouse to welcome Redbridge felons with a steaming mug of hot chocolate?

Sunday 4th November 2007

Redbridge – unhygienic, rude, concrete jungle

I fear I have become the epitome of Mr Meldrew, him of the BBC TV sitcom *One foot in the grave* or, perhaps, of *Disgusted of Tonbridge Wells,* for my letters appear with some regularity in the *Ilford Recorder* and occasionally in the *Wanstead and Woodford Guardian.* Here is but one example, published yesterday in the *Recorder:*

"I write in sadness as a life-long resident of the Borough. Why is it that those purchasing homes in the area where I live find it necessary to rip out the insides of the houses immediately they take up residence, building into the roof and going outwards and upwards?

"In addition, when they do so why do they have to bring heavy vehicles and concrete mixers onto the pavement, breaking up the paving stones, and leaving sand and rubble behind? A walk on the pavements of Aldborough Road North and roads nearby now resembles a ramble on a rough unmade country lane.

"These new residents concrete over the entire front garden so that they can park their cars off-street. Whilst I regret the passing of the cultivated front garden, I accept – with some reluctance – the need for off-street parking, but why do they not leave any open ground through which the rain may drain and on which some greenery may grow? When it rains, the road drains are totally unable to cope with the quantity of water which runs off the concreted front gardens. To cross the road, you have to pick your way through puddles, which lie around sometimes for days. I fear that if there is a heavy deluge, floodwater will enter my home.

"Even more amazing is the fact that a number of new residents are now not only concreting their front gardens, but their entire rear gardens as well – and building bungalows and massive extensions in the gardens, too. Aldborough Hatch will soon no longer be a green and pleasant place in which to live.

"Spitting in the streets was a thing of the past. Not any more. Foul language is to be heard wherever you go, especially on public transport. Litter and used chewing gum are thrown down throughout the Borough. The Council has adequate litter bins and chewing gum boards in the town centre, but these are ignored. The last straw for me came recently when a mature lady spent the journey into Ilford on a 296 bus carrying out unmentionable personal ablutions and then wiping her hands on the bus seat cushion. Later that morning I spotted a used condom at the bus stop outside Ilford Station.

"The time has come to take a stand against the lowering of standards. National legislation is needed to make it a criminal offence to concrete over entire gardens. Locally planners should refuse permission to make a driveway across a public pavement unless the homeowner makes adequate allowance in their front garden for water drainage and some green space. Planning permission for bungalows in back gardens should be refused.

"Police Officers and Police Community Support Officers should be given the powers (if they do not already exist) to impose instant fines on those who spit, use foul language, and drop litter or chewing gum. Bus drivers should be instructed to call the police when foul language is used and other unmentionable carryings on take place on their vehicles. And those who do not pay their fines within the required time should be given community service orders by the courts during which they would clear up some of the mess that they and others like them have caused.

"Enough is enough! Let the silent majority stand up and be counted."

(My point about concreting over front gardens was tackled with legislation and changes to local planning laws a year or so after this letter was written – perhaps someone was listening?)

23rd November 2007

Hands off our newspapers, fruit and veg!

Yet another letter to the ILFORD RECORDER today and this, too, was published – in the first edition of the New Year:

"Hard on the heels of the news that Redbridge Council is revoking the licence for the newspaper stand outside Ilford Station, I hear that the landlords have refused to renew the lease for the fruiterer, greengrocer and florist on the opposite side of the road near the entrance to the Exchange.

"I understand that the decision on the newspaper stand is not final. There is still time for residents to sign the petition and for Redbridge Councillors to act decisively in their constituents' interests to stop this from happening. But the fruit and veg shop opposite was given a month's notice and closes this Friday 4th January.

"Both businesses provide a much valued quality service to residents and visitors. Sweeping them away would be disastrous to the town centre and send more people off to other boroughs, their shops and markets.

"It is nonsense to claim that the newspaper stand is some sort of health and safety risk for pedestrians by cluttering the pavement. If this is so the adjacent bus stops and shelters, and clusters of passengers standing all over the pathway should be removed for the same reason, and people wanting a bus – including me – should be made to queue elsewhere. What a farce!

"As for the landlords of the fruit and veg shop, I join the many customers who are appealing to them to revoke their decision at the last minute. Good quality fresh fruit and vegetables at reasonable prices, available near bus stops, are essential for the health and well-being of young and old alike. If closure goes ahead, many of us will go elsewhere, and the shops and stores in Ilford Town Centre will be the losers."

(The newspaper stand was saved, although a year later the lady who ran the stand decided to call it a day when she injured her foot. It all happened suddenly and I was sad not to have the opportunity to chat to her before she retired – but I met her in the Town Centre a few weeks later in her wheelchair; we talked and I was able to wish her well. But the lease on the fruit and veg shop was not renewed and the shop closed. There were rumours that a coffee chain would be opening in place of the fruit and veg shop, but nothing came of that and over the next few months it remained empty and boarded up. I wrote to the landlords – three times over the coming months before finally receiving a somewhat non-committal reply twelve months later. Shortly before Christmas 2008, the shutters on the shop front went up, revealing a bargain-basement jewellery emporium. I can only assume it is a temporary business to catch the Christmas trade – but how sad that the fruit and vegetable purveyors were not given the chance to stay put to provide a much needed and appreciated service?)

30th December 2007

Too expensive!

Yvonne and I spent this morning in Ilford. I am unsure if I will be doing so again in the near future. Some months will have to elapse before we set forth in similar fashion, for it is all far too expensive. You see, some three years ago, shortly after I gave up smoking, Yvonne and I went to Ilford to buy a suit. But instead of buying one, I purchased two suits – one black (for funerals and solemn occasions) and one light green (for happy days). But shortly after this I retired from the board of the mental health trust and the number of times when I would need to wear a suit dropped dramatically. In fact, I would guess that I have worn both suits on less than ten occasions each – at funerals (of which there seem to be a glut at the moment) and our Golden Wedding (of which there was one).

The suits were both thirty-two inches at the waist and thirty-one inches inside leg, which had been a little worrying at the time as I had been a thirty inch waist for more years than I care to remember.

Last year I attended a funeral. It was not a happy occasion for I felt like a trussed chicken in trousers that were clearly too small for me. Martyn knew a man who would add a couple of inches to the waist. He did so. With both suits.

Earlier this week I attended yet another funeral – this time of a former court colleague. Pulling on the black suit trousers – now, let it be said, thirty-four inches at the waist – I had to call for urgent assistance from Yvonne. The Good Woman pulled whilst I inhaled very, very deeply – but to no avail. There was a gaping gap in the front where there should not be a gaping gap. We tried again. This time I breathed in so hard that I thought something might fall off. It did not, but when Yvonne brought the clip into the metal bit at the front, I was relieved – but found myself almost incapable of breathing either in or out. It was most unpleasant – but as the funeral was but minutes away, I had to put up with things. My friends were kindness itself, commenting on how well I looked. Little did they know that my ruddy complexion was the result of restricted breathing around the middle regions.

I am off to another funeral on Monday, hence the urgency today to purchase a suit with a thirty-six inch waist and thirty-one inside leg. I am horrified! How can I possibly measure more around the waist than I do from the top of my leg to my ankle?

Now you may find this difficult to believe, but whilst I am trying on the dark grey suit that I thought would double up for both funerals and weddings, the man in Moss Bros was persuading Yvonne that I also needed a light grey number.

"These have just come in," he told Yvonne, *"and I am so taken with them that I am having one for myself,"* he confided to Yvonne – who, of course, believed him.

Before you could say *"where is your credit card",* I had bought two suits and a new black leather belt – specially made, the man assured me, for men of ample proportions. Me – a man of ample proportions? Whatever next?

In a day or so Yvonne will be taking two suits to one of the charity shops in Barkingside. So if you know of a man who is a thirty-four inch waist and thirty-one inch inside leg, send him off to Barkingside. He will have a bargain for a tenner.
1st February 2008

Tailing and folding

A leaflet dropped through my letterbox is headed: *"Quality Serving Your Commercial and Domestic Need Throughout The" (sic) "London".* It goes on to tell me that *"We are happy to offer the following"* and lists amongst a range of services – such as Paving and Plumbing – *"External and Internal Tailing"* and also *"Folding Furniture".* Sadly I do not have the need for tailing, neither internally nor externally. I am, however, intrigued to know how they (whoever they are) will fold my furniture. But, there again, as I have no requirement for such a service I will never know.

I have also received a similar offering from someone who informs me that he carries out *"all kinds of building works with guarantee",* including *"cellar and dumping"* together with *"new designing, partition and fitting".* It is fortunate that I have no need of these – whatever they are.
Saturday 9th February 2008

Free TV!

I have this morning received through the post my free Over 75 TV Licence. How about that? And what is more the licence is accompanied by a letter from a gentleman who rejoices under the name of Paul Stanfield. In this he writes: *"You may notice"* (from which I would hazard a guess that he may think that because I am seventy-five I may not notice anything unless it is written in letters two feet high and painted in brilliant red), *"You may notice that your new licence shows dates as far ahead as 28 February 2011."* The reason for this, he explains, is because they will only send me paperwork every three years.

Mr Stanfield goes on to say that I *"don't need to do anything except put your licence away in a safe place".*

It is kind of Mr Stanfield to tell me that I don't need to do anything, but I fear that inertia may result in my starving to death or being run over by a speeding motorist. I have no doubt that I should also continue to take the tablets, walk slowly with my eyes wide open, eat five portions of fruit and vegetables and drink five litres of water every day. Sadly, he does not tell me to do so, but then I guess he is a busy man for he signs himself CUSTOMER SERVICES.

His letter also informs me that I should *"Remember – you need take no action."* Which is interesting, because I was not going to do so anyway.

Finally, Mr Stanfield says that I should *"Just continue to watch TV with your free Over 75 TV Licence".* But he does not tell me how I should do this. Do I have to sit with the licence in my hand whilst watching TV? Perhaps not, for Mr Stanfield told me to put the licence away in a safe place – and my hands are anything but safe these days. Should I frame the licence and hang it on the wall? Would this be a safe place?

I also note that the licence covers me and *"anyone living with you for the use of TV at the address shown on your licence."* This could make me a mint of money. I might advertise for people to come to live with me between 7pm and 10.30pm on weekdays (they could not stay later as that is my bedtime now that I am nearly seventy-five – Jeremy Paxman eat your heart out, for watching *Newsnight* will soon be a thing of the past).

They would need to bring a suitcase and a change of clothing to meet the legal requirement of being domiciled with me. Everyone would be welcome – except others who are seventy-five or over for they should stay in their own homes and continue to watch TV with their free licences as I am sure Mr Stanfield has instructed them to do.

Life gets very exciting the longer you live. In another five years I will be eighty and who knows what delights await me then? I believe I may receive an increased heating allowance – which would mean that Yvonne and I could run around the house throughout the winter with the heating turned up full blast so that we would not need to wear clothes – and thus save on both washing powder, electricity for the washing machine and the cost of new clothing. I can hardly wait.

It is now mid-afternoon, so I will have a lie down before it is time for me to watch TV with my free Over 75 Licence.

What joy! What bliss! Who let the dogs out, I say?

Monday 25th February 2008

Our bicycle and wheelbarrow are standing by

It all began for us as we were galloping at a very fast rate towards our seventy-fifth birthdays. Married for some fifty summers and an equal number of winters, we have both been involved actively in many voluntary organisations locally, but had managed to avoid becoming embroiled in Redbridge Voluntary Care.

Part of our secret in this is that we do not drive – cars that is, for we drive bicycles, wheelbarrows and the like, but not those big things with seats inside that race up and down the roads, scaring the living daylights out of cats and squirrels. And if you cannot drive a car it is pointless offering to help take the elderly to and from hospital appointments – for few would relish being pushed along the A12 towards King George Hospital in a wheelbarrow and even less sitting astride the basket of our bicycle.

We thought we had got away with it when some very nice ladies of our acquaintance started to target us in that very gentle – and, indeed, gentile – way that very nice ladies have when they want to encourage you to do something for them.

"Have you ever thought about being a Duty Officer?" said the first one, who went on to explain that it was all very simple really.

"All you have to do," she said, metaphorically twisting our arms behind our backs in the way that nice ladies have of turning the screws, *"all you have to do is sit by the telephone for a day, taking telephone calls and arranging for our volunteers to help those who are unable to help themselves."*

How very worthy, we thought – and so simple. All we have to do is sit by our telephone for a day. It could not be easier.

Two other equally nice – and, let it be said, both gentle and gentile – ladies said very much the same when we happened to meet them on the bus or over a cup of coffee. And gradually we warmed to the idea. After all, we could tell our family, our friends – and one or two selected enemies – that we are now Duty Officers and enjoy the look on their faces as the importance of all this began to sink in.

And so it was that we were given our training by one of the very nice ladies. We were handed a Big Red Book and asked to read, mark and inwardly digest it with care. We considered placing the Big Red Book under our pillows at night so that we might better absorb its contents, but we could not decide whose pillow and had to abandon the idea.

We observed the nice lady at work as a Duty Officer and, with her words of encouragement ringing in our ears, waited in eager anticipation for our first stint as Duty Officers.

We have now had four sessions. Bright eyed and bushy tailed, we awaited the arrival of The Boxes that first afternoon. We have learned that everything revolves around The Boxes for without The Boxes all would be lost. These arrive at the start of the Duty Officer session and are carried into our house with all due ceremony – to remain in a place of honour for the next twenty-four hours. And the passing on of them to the next DO (as we are called by those who know) is a matter that needs to be taken seriously – for a DO without the boxes is a bit like fish without the chips or salt bereft of pepper.

The first task when we are DOs is to transfer the Redbridge Voluntary Care telephone number to our phone, which requires lots of tapping in of numbers, something Yvonne has proved to be a past master at carrying out.

Our sessions have passed without major mishap – at least as far as we are aware. We have not sent anyone to the wrong address or on the wrong day, nor have we despatched a wheelchair where one was not required. Although it has to be said that if we did so the good folk who were sent hither rather than thither have been kind enough not to mention it.

What sort of tasks, I hear you cry, are we required to match with volunteers who are standing by just waiting to spring into action when the call cometh? It has to be said that a lot of the work involves taking vulnerable folk to and from hospital appointments – and clearly there is a real need for this kind of support and one which Redbridge Voluntary Care is uniquely geared up to provide.

But there are other things that we have been asked to sort out. We are not surprised at the number of beds that need to be moved downstairs, but we are concerned that we are never asked to take them upstairs again. We can only assume that throughout Redbridge there are many, many beds that once were upstairs that are now downstairs.

One lady told us that the light switch to her flat was inside a cupboard and she could not open the door to reach it to turn the lights on. A man had been given a DVD for Christmas, but needed someone to show him how to work it. During one conversation with a lady, we could hear the TV blaring away in the background, making it difficult to understand what the lady wanted. When we asked her to please turn the TV down, she said she would prefer not to do so as she was watching the programme and was stone deaf.

Perhaps the one unusual call that gave us pleasure to be able to sort out came from a social worker. A Chinese gentleman of her acquaintance could only speak Cantonese and desperately needed someone to befriend him who could speak his language. Now it so happens that there is a Chinese Christian Church not far from where we live and we were able to pass on the contact telephone number.

Working as a team of two is a help – for one is able to deal with the telephone whilst the other writes up the day book, and the client and volunteer cards. So far there has been no necessity for us to take the bicycle from the shed or to trundle the wheelbarrow through the house, but both are standing ready should the need arise.

Thursday 13th March 2008

The Phantom Compost Thief of Aldborough Hatch

It is 3.30pm – or thereabouts – on a Thursday afternoon in late May here in Aldborough Hatch. The weather is warm, but there has been a steady drizzle of rain for the past one-and-a-half-hours – the period of time that Yvonne and I have spent in St. Peter's Churchyard, exposed to the elements, so much so that we returned home soaked to the very skin with our hair hanging in sodden dampness and our socks squelching in our boots (or trainers, in my case).

Why, I hear you cry? And, furthermore, what is all this about a Phantom Potting Compost Thief? Well, if you are sitting comfortably, I will begin.

The story has its roots a long, long time ago – and may well take a long, long, time to tell as a result. In fact, it goes right back to 1951 – a period in history of great austerity when sweets were on ration, the sun shone brightly and warmly each day in summer, and the water pipes in the rooftops of every homestead froze up in the winter. It was in this year that my father died and was buried in the churchyard at St. Peter's. Hurrying forward (which I am sure will come as a relief) to 1975, this was the year in which my mother died and joined my father in the churchyard.

Now I have to admit that I am not a great one for graves and graveyards. There are some – and I take my hat off to them and would be the last to criticise – who take great pride in keeping the graves of loved ones tidy and replenished with fresh flowers, bedding plants, holly wreaths at Christmas and the like. As for me, I respect the fact that my parents have a plot in the churchyard at St. Peter's in which their earthy bodies were placed. I like to see it tidy and I put a daffodil or two there on Mothering Sunday. The grave is in the shade of a flowering cherry tree and I enjoy standing beneath its bows in the springtime when the pink blossom bursts forth and the petals drift idly to the grass beneath. But that is about it.

When there is a workday in the churchyard, I do my bit. Some years ago I spent a happy morning with my good friend Les Goodman, clipping the hedge onto Aldborough Road North – and the next two months covered in lumps and bumps and bites! We had to call out the Council to de-fumigate or debug or whatever – for the hedge was alive with a virulent strain of insect which took a distinct liking to Les and me. In fact, it had Les and me for breakfast, lunch and supper. On that occasion I was strutting about with my hedge clippers in a pair of fashionable shorts. These days when I am in the churchyard I wear long trousers with everything buttoned up. But I digress.

We now move to more recent times and the sad fact that my elderly brother slipped quietly away in hospital in Reigate. His immediate family, and friends and colleagues from the worlds of pathology, bacteriology and cacti, gathered at Leatherhead Crematorium in January to pay their last respects.

The question arose as to how we should dispose of my brother's ashes. I made the suggestion that it might be fitting for the interment of the ashes to be at my parent's grave here at St. Peter's. It would be a sort of homecoming, for my brother and I played in the fields and meadows hereabouts in our youth, scrumping for apples in the orchard at the Dick Turpin. We also pulled the odd stick or two of rhubarb from Farmer Edwards' field next to the church to take home to our mother – who asked no questions as she baked a rhubarb pie the like of which only Yvonne can surpass.

And so it was agreed with Linda and Martin, my brother's children, that Martin would keep the ashes safely in his greenhouse until the interment could be arranged at St. Peter's. We considered that Martin's greenhouse was a highly suitable spot for the ashes to rest – for when my brother was not taking blood samples and doing other things that pathologists and bacteriologists do, he was in one of his many greenhouses, tending his world-famous cacti collection.

The interment of ashes is scheduled for July this summer. It will be a family affair on a Sunday morning. Yvonne will prepare a buffet lunch and if the weather is fine, folk will be able to sit in the shed-with-the-overhang, on one of two benches in the garden or on a large flowerpot in the greenhouse.

Now knowing that the family would be assembling at the graveside for the interment of ashes, I decided that I needed to do something to enliven and enhance my parents' grave. It consists of a freestanding headstone, with an area of ground in front and a large bush behind, over which tower the branches of the flowering cherry. A year or so ago I planted some fresh daffodil bulbs which flowered in early March, but I decided new thinking was required – I believe it is called Blue Sky Thinking or something.

I decided that I would plant lavender bushes, which are good ground covers. More than that, my mother loved lavender. When we were on the top deck of a bus going into London in my childhood, my mother went out of her way to point out to me the statue of a lady standing on a plinth outside Yardley's scent factory in Stratford, who held in her arms a wicker basket filled to the brim with cut lavender. It became somewhat boring after the first half-dozen journeys, rather as my family tell me I am boring when we pass the Blind Beggar public house on the Mile End Road and I draw their attention – yet again – to the fact that the Kray Twins committed one of their most dastardly crimes within its walls.

With the decision made, I planned to do the planting in the spring. First, however, I needed some good quality compost for the soil in the ground around the gravestone was of doubtful quality.

In March I prevailed upon a local purveyor of high quality compost to drop off four of his forty litre bags at the gate to St. Peter's Church when he delivered a number of bags to my home. Later the same day, I tried to carry the forty litre bags from the gate to the grave – but gave up, for they were mighty heavy. In fact, forty litres heavy! Soon I was trundling the bags through the churchyard in a wheelbarrow where I dropped them off beside the headstone.

From time to time during April and May, I looked across to the grave on Sunday mornings and could see that the four bags were still there. And, of course, they were, for they were hardly likely to walk off. I waited until mid-May – for the late Farmer Rudge told me that you could expect a frost up to the 19th of May – and then I went hot foot to B & Q on Pensioners' Day. Six fine lavender plants were purchased together with some white Busy Lizzies. I watered them all well over the coming days so that they would be ready for planting. Everything was in place for the work to begin.

At lunchtime today, Yvonne and I assembled the tools and plants, and with the assistance of Marlon (age seven and strong with it), we set forth for the churchyard. And it was here where the full horror of what had happened hit us – like a chunk of Portland Stone hurled from the top of the church tower.

Would you believe it? No longer were there four forty litre bags of best quality potting compost piled high – but just two. And what is more, the two empty compost bags were neatly folded on top. The Phantom Potting Compost Thief of St. Peter's Aldborough Hatch had pounced!

Whilst I stood standing still, thunderstruck by the audacity of what had happened, Yvonne took matters into her own hands. Striding off purposefully, the good lady scoured the churchyard from end to end, but nowhere could she find eighty litres of freshly debagged compost. It had, as they say, disappeared into thin air.

At this point the rain started to settle in for the afternoon. I might well have turned on my heels and returned home, to sit and ponder in the shed-with-the-overhang – but Yvonne and Marlon are made of sterner stuff. And so we set to.

We removed the top soil and weeds, placing it neatly in the hedgerow. We then stretched out a sheet of that black porous stuff that gardeners use to stop the weeds coming through. We bedded down six lavender bushes in a liberal sprinkling of compost and placed the black porous sheet over the top, cutting holes for the bushes to come through. The remaining compost was then spread on top and the Busy Lizzies planted. We had just enough compost – but only just. Four bags would have been perfect – two were barely enough.

With the work done, Yvonne, Marlon and I wandered home, bedraggled and damp, with the rain running down our cheeks. Yvonne insisted that she would wash the muddy tools whilst I had a shower. But Yvonne is like that.

And now we are left to ponder. Who is the Phantom Potting Compost Thief of St. Peter's Aldborough Hatch? What did he do with the compost? Why did he take it out of the bags in which it was delivered? How did he carry it forth? Did he bring his own bags? Where is it now? Why did he bring the bags back from whence they came? And, even more poignantly perhaps, why did he fold the empty compost bags so neatly and place them on top of the two filled bags? And was he coming back for the other two? For if he was, he will be disappointed – and that's a fact.

Thursday 29th May 2008

Unmasked – The Phantom Compost Thief!

I am advised on Very Good Authority – Yvonne – that at the St. Peter's Parochial Church Council Meeting last evening the person responsible for the theft of two forty litre bags of potting compost was unmasked.

I would appear that early last month one of the two gardeners who cut the grass in the churchyard was using the strimmer between two graves when his feet slipped into a gaping hole. Realising that this could cause considerable damage to the foot of anyone casually walking between the graves, he looked around for something with which to fill in the hole. He spied my four forty litre bags of best potting compost – and in a trice he had solved his problem. Being a tidy soul, he returned the two empty bags from whence they came, folding them neatly as he did so. My only comment is that I am just grateful that the hole was not bigger and only two of the four bags were required. I would have been in real trouble with no compost and six lavender bushes and Busy Lizzies to plant.

12th June 2008

Shouting at squirrels

Sitting this morning in the front window eating our toast and marmalade at around 8.30am, we spotted a squirrel squatting on one of the troughs hanging on the front garden ranch fence. He had removed the netting, ignored the moth balls and black pepper (washed away by the rain, I would guess) and was munching away at my crocus bulbs. Infuriated, I ran out from the front door into the garden shouting at the squirrel, who made a hasty retreat up the road.

Just at that moment a young lady in her twenties was walking by. Poor girl must have been frightened out of her life – to see this old man in his dressing gown and slippers suddenly emerge from the house, shouting at the top of his voice. Sadly she did not stop long enough for me to apologise, but probably ran home to her mother for comfort.

I have had to place seed trays over the tops of all the pots containing spring bulbs in the front garden – but did not do so with the troughs. I will take these into the greenhouse and replenish the crocus bulbs, and keep them there until the bulbs start to shoot. When Yvonne went out into the back garden to clear the slug traps (we have beer in them so that the slugs are attracted by the alcohol, get drunk and die a happy death by drowning) she found that the cats had brought her a present of two – yes two – field mice. Both dead, fortunately.

Sunday 5th October 2008

Fairheads closing – never!

I have been to Ilford this afternoon for I had heard that Fairheads is closing. And it is true, in spite of the fact that the emporium (for it can hardly be described as a shop as it is much more than that) celebrated its 100th Anniversary earlier this year.

As I explained to Joan and her friend who were in Fairheads when I dropped by, I have been calling into Fairheads once a year just before Christmas for the past fifty years. Some years my visits have been in early December, but more usually I dashed through the doors on Christmas Eve. And why, you may ask?

Fairheads has a splendid selection of ladies' handkerchiefs, made of the very finest linen and embroidered in plain or multi-coloured silks. For under a fiver, I could purchase a box that I knew would bring a smile to Yvonne's face on Christmas morning.

Yvonne always expresses surprise when she discovers that the package contains handkerchiefs – which is very kind of her for she must spend Christmas Eve wondering what colour the embroidery will be this year and whether or not the flowers will be the same ones as last year.

But now Fairheads is to close in early December. Hence my visit in October. I selected five packs of their finest and told the lady at the till my story. She was kind enough to suggest that I must have been very young when I bought the first box of Irish linen and went all of a dither when I explained that I was seventy-five going on seventy-six. Never, she cried – and I feared she might ask me for my birth certificate, but she merely gave me my change and smiled at the customers standing behind me who – as far as I could tell – were buying up most of the towels and bed linen in the shop.

Why five boxes? I need a box at Christmas for at least the next five years and I now have them in store. I may dash back before they bring down the shutters and buy a few more, for I expect to see at least another ten Christmas Days, if not more. And Christmas morning without Yvonne opening her box of handkerchiefs would be too much to bear.

Fairheads – like Moultons and Wests (both of which have gone long ago) – had a system of cash collection that held me spellbound as a boy. At each counter a lady shop assistant in black – they were always in black and were, very obviously, ladies and definitely not women – would take the cash (for my mother only ever paid in real money) and wrap it up inside the bill which she had written out by hand. The bill and the cash would then be placed inside a brass canister with a screw top lid. This would be fixed in some way to a wire and when the assistant pulled on a contraption – that resembled the chain and handle we pulled at home to flush the toilet – the canister would whiz across the ceiling on a wire to the cashier's glass box. Here the cashier would remove the bill and money, and send the canister whizzing back with a receipt and any change. And brass canisters were whizzing all the time – back and forth on many wires strung across the ceiling. I was entranced and I still am at the very thought.

Sadly, the whizzing cash system disappeared long ago. Moultons is now Boots the Chemist and Wests – well, it just went and was gutted to be replaced by a row of small shops. And soon Fairheads will go, too. We will miss the row of flags that fly throughout the year over the top of the three shop fronts to be replaced at Christmas with trees and winking lights.

On the other side of Cranbrook Road, Saville's (selling gramophone records), Hanmers (the upmarket grocers) and Prentices (the greengrocer and fruiterer) went long ago.

Ilford sported two bookshops – Wilsons in Clements Road and Ruggs Library in the Cranbrook – the former also stocking stationery, whilst the latter sold new books and ran a small lending library. W H Smith and Waterstone's had yet to appear – although there was a small branch of Smith's in Gants Hill.

The family stationary and artists' supplies business of Owen Clark stood on the bend of the Cranbrook Road and is there today – one of the few remaining retail businesses in the town. I bought my first bottle of Quink washable blue ink at Owen Clark in the early 1940s and I continue to do so. I have purchased my Parker fountain pens there and received courteous and excellent service when repairs were necessary.

We still have Harrison Gibson in the High Road, but it is not quite what it was in days of yore. But it has to be said that there are some splendid concessions occupying the floors, one of which supplied our lounge suite in recent times (and very comfortable it is too, I can tell you). We were there when the second fire destroyed Harrison Gibson in the late 1950s. Living off the Drive, we heard the fire engines and joined the mighty throng that stood transfixed as the flames tore through Harrison Gibson and jumped over the roof tops to wreak devastation on Moultons a few doors along.

What a night – and some character with an eye for a quick buck took a photograph and went hot foot to Fleet Street, where it appeared on the front pages of the tabloids next morning.

More recently the Ilford Pioneer Market has been raised to the ground – to be replaced, so we are promised, by a skyscraper with flats and offices and shops. How I loved the fresh aroma that wafted over the open counters of Radfords selling bacon, butter and eggs. I did not like the butchers with their blood soaked sawdust floors and I was not much taken with the haberdashers and the purveyors of wool for knitting. My mother was a great knitter and would linger over the trays of patterns and the racks of wool, often with me in tow.

Best of all was Holmes – who had a row of shops stretching across the back of the market selling fruit, vegetables and the most magnificent fresh flowers you ever did see. I can smell the scent of the flowers and the earthiness of the vegetables. All long, long gone.

Tuesday 14th October 2008

I am worried about my milkman

This morning – with sixty-nine days to go before we put the turkey in the oven for Christmas Dinner – our milkman delivered a leaflet purporting to offer 'Great Gifts for Christmas', and very exciting it looks, too, with Christmas cards and lots of jolly festive things to buy.

But it is the section of the leaflet headed 'Gifts for Him' that gives me grave concern, for I can only assume that our milkman and those who send him out each day – come rain or shine, in all weathers – must think I am some sort of nutcase who would be as happy as Father Christmas himself if I were to unwrap one or two of the suggested 'Gifts for Him' in the bosom of my family on the Great Day itself.

Why, I have to ask myself, would I want a Hand Warmer? Priced at £2.99, the leaflet tells me that full instructions are included – which is just as well because the Hand Warmer consists of 'Magic gel'. It is said to be good for golf, fishing and all outdoor activities – and muscular pain and sports' injuries.

I do not play golf and would find sitting on a bank with a fishing rod in my hand too boring for words. Furthermore, I am fortunate in being a non-sufferer of muscular pain and I am wise enough not to play any sports so that I do not have any injuries to worry about.

But wait! How about a Remote Control Infra Red Helicopter? How could they have known that this is something I have long craved for – and not just remote control but infra red, too. But that costs £14.99 so perhaps I should ask instead for a Remote Control Mini which is priced more reasonably at £4.99. It goes forward, reverse, turn left, turn right and stop. What more could one ask apart from going straight up in the air? I see that it is recommended for folk aged six plus – so I would guess I may well have one of these in my stocking on Christmas morning and not the Remote Control Infra Red Helicopter which is only for children of eight plus.

And then there is the Wind-up Torch. Surely a must-have if ever I saw one for it is a Tritronic LED Dynamo Wind-up Torch – no less. One minute of winding gives thirty minutes of light, which means that if I spent sixteen minutes winding, the torch would stay alight throughout my eight hours of sleep and scare away any intruders who would might otherwise think I am awake and playing with my Remote Control Mini whilst keeping my tiny frozen hands cosy with the Hand Warmer.

I trust that no-one will order for me the Drywash Car Cleaning Kit. Surely they will realise that I do not drive, nor do I have a car, and if I had one I would wish to have a wet wash rather than a dry one. How in the name of all that is true and honest and kind and gentle – how can you have a *dry* wash? We use wet water where I come from.

Finally, there is the Steel Tool Box with a recessed ergonomic handle and padlock eyehole. I think not. The box might well be a good idea, but the handle and the padlock are both highly suspect.

I see that the 'Gifts for Her' section includes a set of Embroidered Sentiments Cushions – *"three great cushions to choose from to give to your dearest".* At £2.99 each they are a snip, but which one to choose, that is the question?

One is embroidered with the message: *"Grandmas are like priceless antiques*". I am not kidding. I can think of a few Grandmas who would give me a swipe with their zimmer frames if I dared to give them a cushion that likened them to an antique.

"My Mum is my best friend" reads another, whilst the third brings tears to the eye with its statement: *"Friendship isn't a big thing, it's a million little things".* Hand me the smelling salts, Mabel.

Friday 17th October 2008

Off to the markets of London Town

Last summer Yvonne and I made a bold decision. We have been retired now for some ten years and rarely – if ever – spend a day together doing what we want to do. Now do not get me wrong, we are often together, but doing all the things that have to be done in the home, in the garden and in the local community in which we live and breath and have our being (as they say).

But we do not set off to spend a day wandering around London, for example, and as the Greatest Capital City in the World is on our very doorsteps, this seems a great pity. So we determined to put it right and we have done just that.

We decided that we would visit some of the places in London where my parents were born or lived. So off we went to Essex Road Station in Islington, walking down Almorah Road where my father must have played with his spinning top (for I am sure he had one). Sadly I do not have the number of the house and the sweet shop that I refer to earlier in this book was demolished a couple of years ago; today flats stand on the spot. We rode on a bus from Essex Road to Holborn – the route I must have taken in reverse when travelling from the Lyceum to my father's old home that Christmas in the 1930s.

Over to the South of the River, we dropped off in Tooting to find 68 Undine Street. Sadly the occupier was out but I sent a letter to the house with a copy of my parent's wedding photograph taken on 26th December 1926. The gentleman who has lived there for the past ten years, rang me. He could not be certain that the back of the house in the photograph is the same one – for new windows have been fitted and the outside toilet (with bricks holding down the felt roof) has long since gone. The bus journey from Tooting into London took over an hour, but sitting on the top deck clutching our Freedom Passes, we enjoyed peering into back gardens and through windows where there were no net curtains to impede the view. I felt guilty for I doubt if my Mum would have liked me doing that.

We also called in at Clapham Junction to seek out the house where my mother was born, but it must have been bombed in the war for there are flats where her home once stood.

We decided that our next adventures would be visits to London's many markets. First we were off to Spitalfields Market – an indoor affair in the old Spitalfields building, all cleaned brickwork and exotic foods. From there we trotted to nearby Columbia Road Flower Market, for it was a Sunday morning and we were playing truant from church. This was a blaze of colour with the overpowering scent of flowers mixing with freshly-made coffee and bread. I bought some spring bulbs, cut flowers and cyclamen.

Our visit to Crisp Street Market was something of a disappointment. Advertised on the Docklands Railway at All Saints' Station, we had often been intrigued as we passed through to find out what it was like. The present market dates from the post-war era when new flats were built and provision made for a market with some permanent buildings. Ivy's (established 1951) offered Pease Pudding, Faggots and Savaloys, but we popped into the Pound Shop and bought some Christmas candles at a very reasonable price.

Walthamstow Market runs for seemingly a very long way. Here they were selling fruit a *"pound a bowl"*, lots of exotic vegetables and Tubby Isaacs offered his world famous seafood. Yvonne bought three T-shirts for a tenner which were said to be ex-M & S stock. On arrival home only one was the size it stated on the hanger (for all the labels were cut out) and the other two do not fit.

Our final visit was a return one for us both for at various times when we worked in the City of London, Yvonne and I would dash along to Leather Lane during our lunch hour. It is little changed. Yvonne bought a leather purse and we stocked up on fruit for the family. We travelled there and back on the Number 25 Bendy Bus from Ilford – and watched as so many passengers hopped on at the back doors and did not pay their fares or check off their Oyster Cards.

I fear it may now be too cold for wandering around market stalls, but we will be off again come the springtime for there are many more to be explored and enjoyed. I have taken photographs at all the markets we have visited, but Yvonne worries that I am a target for a mugger with the digital Nikon my family gave me for Christmas a year or two back hanging around my neck. I guess they would have to garrotte me first to snatch it.

Tuesday 21st October 2009

Down at the station

I have now completed three sessions selling poppies for the British Legion at Newbury Park Underground Station – from 4pm to 6pm on Thursday and Friday last week, and again last evening, and now I am off for my final stint this year.

On Thursday I had been selling for about fifteen minutes when a dozen police officers, two drugs dogs and a knife arch appeared. One young lady was sorted out by the dog – but after a strip search (out of sight, I would add) nowt was found. The lady looked very relieved. The children loved the dogs, but a number of people were clearly petrified. I gather from today's *Ilford Recorder* that some cannabis was found – and people were given warnings. A number of people had been at or near a place where drugs had been used – but no drugs were found on them. It is all a bit worrying, for how are we to know if we have been at or near a place where drugs have been used? Best to stay indoors.

On Friday evening two young ladies arrived who, I would guess, were off to the West End for a night out. I could hardly believe my eyes for they were wearing what I can only describe as their knickers with tops that hardly covered anything. And it was *freezing!* My eyes were out on stalks for a few seconds.

Last evening two things happened. A Year Eleven Oaks Park High School boy came up to me. You are an invigilator, aren't you, he asked? I said I was. I've got a maths GCSE tomorrow, he said. Will you be there? I had forgotten – but at home I checked the dairy – and sure enough, I was due at Oaks Park this morning. I went – and towards the end of the exam the same lad put his hand up. He asked if he might go to the toilet? I accompanied him to the door and waited outside, but he did not need the toilet – he just wanted to ask me if I was the man he saw at the station giving out poppies!

Then a man in his late 20s came into the foyer at the station carrying some twelve flat trays of chocolates. He put them down on a shelf, walked over to me and bought a poppy.

"You were at Redbridge Magistrates' Court," he said, *"but you are doing a much better job here selling poppies than at the court – although you were a very fair judge."*

I replied saying that I am now retired from the court.

"Yes, I know you are," he said, *"I read about it in the local paper."*

I asked him why he had all those trays of chocolates and he told me that they were selling them off cheap at Sainsbury's so he bought a few boxes and will flog them to his friends at Christmas. And with a cheery wave of his hand, he was gone.

Thursday 6th November 2008

Fascinating – and yet boring!

Back in March 2007 I was appointed as an examination invigilator at Oaks Park High School, which opened its doors a mile or so from where I live as a brand new secondary school at the turn of this Century. I started in May 2007 and it is without doubt, one of the most fascinating tasks I have undertaken during my life, but at the same time it can be one of the most boring jobs I have ever had.

Why do I do it? One reason – and not the only one, I would hasten to add – is because I have reached that time of life when it would be very easy to believe that you are no longer valued. I am involved as a volunteer in a number of activities within the community (at St. Peter's Church, in the Aldborough Hatch Defence Association, at the Redbridge Night Shelter, helping out at the British Legion's Poppy Appeal, Redbridge Voluntary Care) and that is fine, but from time to time it is a nice feeling to note that you have earned a small sum of money for your labours – a sum that might be saved or spent on something that will bring pleasure to family and, occasionally, to Yvonne or myself.

The second reason is because I do not want to vegetate by sitting around the house and garden all day. I may be three-quarters of the way towards my Century, but I am not in my dotage and still have something to give to the local community – even if it is only walking up and down the aisles of examination desks giving out and collecting papers, sharpening pencils, loaning calculators, rulers, compasses, set squares, mirrors (yes, mirrors, in the maths exams!) and such like, and conducting students to the toilets (where I stand on guard outside just in case another student comes along and they compare notes about the examination they are sitting. Not that it happens, but just in case it does).

Thirdly, I have met a number of people with whom my path through life might well not have crossed but for GCSEs, AS and A Levels and SATS – the Head, Deputy Heads, Assistant Heads, Year Heads, Subject Heads, teachers, support staff and those concerned with curriculum access. The latter are folk that I did not know existed. They assist students – the term schoolchildren is no longer in vogue – who have learning difficulties or a disability, both in the classroom and when they sit examinations. If a student breaks an arm shortly before the examination period, for example, he or she is able to take the papers with a member of the curriculum access staff writing to the student's dictation. A much valued – and valuable – service which was not around when I was at school. Had it been, my fight with a debilitating stammer would have been resolved much earlier.

And I have started to learn something about today's young people and to respect them for what they achieve. At some point during each examination I find the opportunity to glance at the questions the students are tackling around me with such gusto. From time to time I am able to make a reasonable stab at an answer, but more often than not I am all at sea without a lifejacket. Please do not tell me that examinations are getting easier or that today's students are lazy or impolite.

Within the school over ninety-nine per cent of the youngsters are well-behaved and respectful. Outside – on the bus, at a bus stop, at the station, in the town or on the pavement outside my home – they acknowledge me with a smile, a wave and a cheery *"Hallo, Sir"*.

I have not been jostled getting on or off a bus by students, but I have been shoved, poked, knocked and kicked by pensioners who are past masters at queue jumping and are not averse to using the occasional swear word as they flash their freedom passes at the bus driver.

Finally, I am working with a team of invigilators who I am getting to know and whose company I enjoy. Sue, who is in charge, is taking a rest from full-time teaching and was persuaded by the Head to take on this role. Quietly spoken, but firm when there is a need, Sue has a daughter and a son at University. Sue sorts out the rotas and keeps order – amongst both students and invigilators. It has to be said that both students and invigilators are well-behaved, although I was very nearly sent to the Head by Sue when I left my mobile in my rucksack and failed to turn it off. My mobile rang out and vibrated during an examination, much to the amusement of the students who are not permitted under the rules to bring mobiles, Ipods or other such things into the examination hall. Fortunately it was a mock exam. My colleagues are ladies in the main, a few former teachers, others parents who became involved in the invigilating business.

Ann flashes an infectious grin as I walk by, whilst Pam spots a label on a drinks bottle from a hundred metres and homes down with the scissors to slice it off with her scissors (labels are not allowed as students could write formulae or dates on these). Angela, who hails from North Wales, was interested to know that I had visited Hawarden Castle to interview Sir William Gladstone, for her home was nearby. One retired man has recently joined us. At the height of the examination season our numbers are boosted by former students who are at university or college. All are very friendly and great fun.

The short examinations (twenty minutes or so, often multiple choice, where the students have to pencil in a circle against what they believe to be the correct answer – and we dash up and down with pencil sharpeners and rubbers) are no problem, but the longer ones (two hours or so) require great determination and grit (from both students and invigilators).

We have high stools on which to perch, but are expected to walk up and down from time to time. I pass the seconds, minutes and hours by working out the percentages of girls to boys, left to right handers, blondes to dark hair. I plan what I am going to do for the rest of the day and the week – and then a student raises his hand and wants a piece of tracing paper or her biro has dried up and I return from my reverie.

In the summer months I cycle to and from Oaks Park; if my duty starts at 8am in the winter Heather takes me there by car on her way to work. Allison greets me from behind the reception glass, Debbie waves, staff members call out cheerfully as they pass by and another days starts with lots of smiles. Often the first examination starts at around 8.30am and the majority of students are there in good time, waiting to be called into the examination hall.

20th November 2008

Winter fuel payment up!

That the nice man Gordon Brown has increased the Winter Fuel Payment to us old folk from £100 to £125 – each.

Today Yvonne received notification of this from the National Pensions Centre in Newcastle – which is a long way away, but the letter arrived safely. Isn't the post office wonderful?

Yvonne always receives her letters from the Pension folk before me, which is odd for not only am I older than Yvonne (by nine months) but also my first name is ahead of hers in the alphabet.

Be that as it may, we will not have to sit here with hot water bottles and woolly socks, sheep skin liberty bodices and chunky sweaters. No Sir! And I gather that when we are eighty – only four years and four months away for me – all this goes up to something over £400. What joy! What bliss!

We have a winter fuel allowance, a free TV licence and we had our flu jabs, too – for the NHS sent us letters telling us to get along to our GP sharpish and, of course we did just that. In fact, we were on the telephone to the health centre hardly had the postman departed down the front garden path.

What will they offer us next? Free warm hats and gloves, perhaps? Hot cocoa piped into the homestead each night at bedtime? Attractive young nurses to tuck us up in our beds every evening? Where will it all end, I ask myself?

We have switched from our current gas supplier to the gang that has brought electricity to our home – and it all happens from Tuesday next, 25th November. For the past nigh on fifty years we have had our gas from same supplier, but no more.

It seemed sensible for all those years, for how could a company that supplies electricity possibly deliver gas to this house? Gas goes down gas pipes. Electricity flows along wires. How can gas come down a wire?

But things got desperate a month or two ago when our gas supplier told me that prices had gone up and that my monthly direct debit would not just double, but almost treble.

I rang them. One of those know-all bright young men (the sort who will have his stag night in Dubai) told me that I would have to grin and bear it. But I am in credit to the tune of nearly £100, I cried. So what, said the bright young man? Pay up or we will cut you off. Do you worst I said – and he agreed to cancel the direct debit there and then.

I rang the electricity folk. I gave them all the information they required from my gas bills. They did some sums and told me that they would not increase my direct debit – but reduce it by £8 per month. Great, said I. Go ahead. And they have done just that.

The old gas company rang me. It was a nice kindly lady this time (no doubt wearing a twin set and pearls). You have been so loyal, the lady said, that we would like you to reconsider things. No way, said I. If you can treble my direct debit one minute and offer to reduce it the next, you can go and take a running jump off a very long gas pipe. But you are so loyal, said the lady. No I am not, said I. I am being sensible at long last. And I felt a bit sad, for the lady was kindness itself.

I must now walk down the road to pay the newspaper bill and then Yvonne and I are to place the winter covers in the two benches in the rear garden, for snow is forecast for the coming night. Later I may do some work in the greenhouse. It is nice and cosy in there, for I can turn up the heater so that it blows warm air up my trouser legs. I need to check the geranium cuttings and prepare for planting the tomato seeds ere Christmas is upon us.

Saturday 22nd November 2008

He's busy!

When Jenny is on duty in the kitchen at the Redbridge Night Shelter with Yvonne, John takes us and brings us back in his car if he is not working. Otherwise we use the ever faithful Radio Cars in Ilford Town Centre.

Jenny and John's daughter, Clare, who teaches in a junior school in Kent, recently asked the children to discuss what their grandparents did.

One little girl piped up with: *"My granddad is busy – getting ready to die."*

This reminded me of a joke Pat told me some years ago. I cannot retain jokes in my brain – all except this one. A man rang his friend. The telephone was answered by the friend's three-year-old son.

"May I speak to your father?" said the man.

"No," whispered the boy, *"he's busy."*

"May I speak to your mother?" said the man.

"No," said the boy, again in a whisper, *"she's busy."*

"Who else is there with you?" asked the man.

"There's a policeman," said the boy.

"May I speak to him?" said the man.

"No," said the boy, *"he's busy."*

"Is anyone else there?" asked the man.

"Yes," said the boy, *"there's a fireman here".*

"May I speak to the fireman?" asked the man.

"No," said the boy, still whispering, *"he's busy."*

"Who else is there?" said the man.

"There's an ambulance driver," said the boy.

"May I speak to him?" said the man.

"No," said the boy, *"he's busy."*

Frustrated, the man asked the boy why everyone was busy?

"They are all looking for me," said the boy.

November 2008

Fruit stall axe may be the last straw

Twelve months after the closure of the fruiterers opposite Ilford Station came news of another market stall being closed down in the town centre. My letter – under the above heading – appeared in the *Ilford Recorder* today. I am on a mission!

"The news that the fruit market stall outside The Mall has been shut down by Redbridge Council deals yet another hammer blow to Ilford Town Centre as a viable place to go shopping *(Fruit stall axe has traders in a pickle, Recorder, December 11).*

"Surely the Council could have transferred the lease to those running the business, who are well-known and highly respected by those of us who value the service they have provided over many years.

"At this time last year the highly popular fruit and greengrocery business opposite Ilford Station was forced to close because the landlord refused to renew the lease.

"There were rumours that the landlord wanted a more upmarket business in its place, but the premises stood empty and derelict until recently, when a few market stalls selling cheap jewellery and toys moved in.

"With Fairheads gone, Woolworth's closing any day, a number of shops nearby holding closing down sales, huge sale notices that hit you between the eyes wherever you look and two shops leased to cheap jewellery and toy stalls, the impression created for visitors coming to Ilford for the first time via the train station is that they have arrived at a town that is run-down and on its last legs. Closing down one of only two fruit stalls in the Town Centre is just one more nail in the coffin of Ilford Town Centre as a place to go shopping.

"I want to buy good quality fruit from established businesses that I can trust, where the staff are friendly.

"I call on our elected Councillors to take up this issue with the faceless bureaucrats who have made this decision without any consultation whatsoever with the many hundreds of residents who use and value the market stall that stood outside the Mall for so long.

"Unless the Council has second thoughts, I will have no alternative but to shop in Romford."

Thursday 18th December 2008

From YUPPIE to TWERLY

Now that I have my Freedom Pass I am what is known as a Twerly – a name derived from the fact that if a Freedom Pass holder attempts to board a bus before nine in the morning, the driver will slam the door in your face with the comment that you are *"too early"*.

All of which reminds me that back in the 1970s we had the YUPPIE (a Young Upwardly Mobile Person) and the DINKs (Double Income No Kids) or the DINKYs (Double Income No Kids – Yet). Then along came the TWINKIES (Twin Income, Nannie and Kids), the SINKs (Single Income, Numerous Kids), the SMELLY (Single Male Earning Lots of Lolly) and the YUMMY (Young Upwardly Mobile Mistress). I have to pause here to comment that some of these do not fit the letters, but according to my notes made at the time, this is how they were expressed and written. Next came a BOBO (Burnt Out But Opulent) and a LOMBARD (Lots of Money But A Real Dick) and after the stock market crash in the mid-80s we had the DCM Awards (Don't Come in on Monday), the recipient of which was often a PUPPY (Previously Upwardly Mobile Person) – but surely that should be a PUMPY, or perhaps not.

Friday 19th December 2008

"Whatever you did unto one of the least . . ."

One evening in August two youngsters dossed down in the porch at St. Peter's Church up the road from here. Gavin said he was nineteen, Tracey seventeen (although those are not their real names). Gavin said his home was on the Essex coast; Tracey said she was from Norfolk. Yvonne dug out a single duvet which we kept as a spare for although the nights were not cold, sleeping on the stone floor of the porch was coldness itself. We found them some food and John-Across-The-Road took tinned soup to warm them.

We encouraged the pair to go to the Redbridge Night Shelter, but they knew that if they did so, the staff would be obliged to call social services as the girl was under age – and they wanted to stay together. The Vicar talked with them. Why not go home, we asked? But they told different people different stories of being thrown out or leaving home because they did not get along with parents. They used the facilities in the church halls in the morning before wandering off, only to return in the evening. The Police Community Support Officers spoke to the youngsters. Things turned nasty when they started begging for money from parents who brought their toddlers to the pre-school nursery which meets in the church halls. And then as suddenly as they arrived, they disappeared. A week or two later the Vicar learned that they were staying in a hostel for the homeless in Tower Hamlets.

Two Sunday afternoons ago Gavin and Tracey appeared again. My telephone rang at around three in the afternoon. They found a St. Peter's BROADSHEET where my name and telephone number are published as editor.

"We recognised your name," said the young man over the telephone. *"We are in the church porch, but the wind is blowing the rain onto us and we are bitterly cold."* They had slept there on Saturday night, but at around two in the morning they dialled 999 on their mobile for an ambulance as Gavin was so cold that he was

having difficulty breathing. Discharged from A & E mid-morning, they returned to the church porch in the early afternoon.

Over the next twenty minutes or so Yvonne rustled up a mouth-watering shepherd's pie and we took this – piping hot with two spoons – to the porch, together with yet another duvet. Fresh fruit, packets of biscuits and Yvonne's homemade cakes also found their way up the road.

We rang the Vicar, suggesting that they might come into the warmth of the church for evening service. John-Across-The-Road again took soup and sustenance when he learned they were back. The Vicar decided they should sleep in the vestry room attached to the church halls overnight for they said that they were being housed on Monday by a neighbouring council. They had spoken to the housing department on Friday and had been assured that they would be found accommodation on Monday. I met the Vicar later on Monday morning, who told me that she had had to clear up some rubbish that the young couple had left behind.

A knock at our front door on Tuesday afternoon and there were Gavin and Tracey – fresh, clean and smiling broadly. The Council had found them a one bedroom flat in the next borough. They had called to thank Yvonne and me for what we and others had done to help them. We would like you to visit us and have a meal when we are settled in, they said. Hurrying off to the church porch to collect their few belongings, they left their address on a scrap of paper. Perhaps we might see them again, but on the other hand we might not.

From time to time someone crosses your path not once, but a number of times. And one such was a young man who must now be in his late thirties. I will call him Jay, although this is not his name. I first met Jay when I was adjudicating in the Family Panel Proceedings Court some fifteen years ago. He and his partner were serious drug addicts, living in a council house not far from here with one or two very small children. I sat on a preliminary hearing and recall that he was tall – well over six feet – with dark features that were already carrying the tell-tale signs of serious drug and alcohol addiction.

I next met Jay some six or seven years later at the Redbridge Night Shelter when it was operating out of a different church hall each night of the week over the winter. Jay was alone and, much as I would have liked to enquire, I could not ask him what had happened to his partner and their children. Jay, still on drugs and drinking heavily, recognised me from the court – for he had appeared over the intervening years for minor offences of shoplifting to feed his drug and alcohol habits. He was always pleasant and courteous to me, and on one occasion when a guest at the night shelter moved to attack me, Jay stepped in, lifted the man by the shoulders, carried him outside and dropped him on the pavement until he had calmed down.

One evening Jay arrived very much the worse for alcohol. The Chairman of the Shelter Trustees was on duty with us that night. After dinner Jay would not calm down, shouting and abusing the other guests. After several warnings, the Chairman finally decided enough was enough and told Jay he would have to leave. I understood what the Chairman was doing, for there comes a point where the well-being of the other guests and the volunteers has to take precedence. It was pelting with rain and a raw wind was blowing as Jay asked me if he might take a couple of blankets and some black plastic sacks so that he could bed down in the porch outside. Throughout that night I went outside to Jay every hour or so with a hot drink. He warmed his hands on the mug, grinning his thanks as he sobered up through the long hours of the night. Next morning he was off and away.

A year or so went by and Jay returned to the Shelter, now in its permanent premises in the centre of Ilford. Jay teamed up with a girl of his age who was from Eastern Europe. After a few weeks they left the Shelter.

We heard of Jay from time to time, and learned that his girl friend was pregnant. I met Jay one morning outside Ilford Station. He told me that he had hitched a lift from Colchester – where he and his girl friend were living – to try to find work in Ilford – and he needed his fare back, which I gave him.

Again a year or so later I met Jay in Ilford. He was running a gardening business, he told me, living with his girl friend and baby in a one bedroomed flat in Woodford. On two or three occasions our paths crossed again – and each time he told me that he was gardening and providing for his young family.

And every time I met Jay over the years, he was polite and almost invariably mentioned how grateful he had been on that cold, dark, wet, windy night at the church hall when I had taken hot drinks to him outside on the hour every hour.

It has to be said that there were those who did not support the help some were giving to Gavin and Tracey as they shivered and crouched out of the wind and the rain in the porch at St. Peter's. And there are some who are highly critical of the work that is being done for the homeless at the Redbridge Night Shelter, believing that those who come to the shelter should take control of their lives themselves – overlooking the harsh reality that many are mentally unwell, highly vulnerable, addicted and inadequate without help and support. Some have become institutionalised through time spent in the armed services, in prison or in mental hospitals where everything was done for them and they had lost the ability to care for themselves. Others have been the victims of crime or domestic violence, or been thrown out from their home by parents, wives or husbands. Each has his or her own story to tell and often they make bitter and sad listening.

I am unashamedly proud of the fact that it was the churches in Redbridge that saw the need and launched the Redbridge Night Shelter in the early 1990s. These days the Shelter not only offers a warm bed for the night, a hot meal and shower, but practical help to enable guests to get back in work, into a home of their own and the chance to learn the skills that will enable them to make a success of independent living, together with the ongoing support of a team of volunteers. Over the centuries many of our caring institutions owe their beginning to like-minded people, sometimes working independently, often in groups, invariably (but not always) springing from a church or faith-base – hospitals, hospices, probation, sheltered housing, supporting victims, protecting children, visiting prisoners.

I guess that Jay, Gavin and Tracey will not be the last who cry out for support when it is cold and wet, and the nights are dark, and they are shivering with hunger. My prayer is that someone, somewhere will not turn a deaf ear, look away or walk on the other side of the street, but listen and do something about it.

Sunday 21st December 2008

(Above left) My great grandparents Joseph (1809-1874) and Ann Jeffries were married in 1833. Joseph was a chimney sweep – on his death Ann took over the business. (Above right) My grandparents Charles (1850-1905) and Annie Jeffries (1856-) on their Silver Wedding 1904.

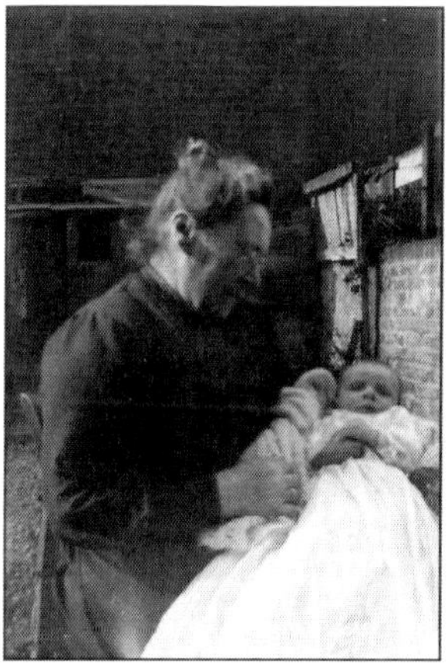

(Above left) Rose Eleanor Stanley – nee Jeffries (1887-) – Tall Auntie Rose. (Centre) My grandmother, Annie Jeffries nee Bonsor with my brother Len at Almorah Road circa 1928. (Right) My father, Leslie Jeffries, and his sister, Tall Auntie Rose, in the yard at the rear of Almorah Road, the family home.

(Above left) Cousin Lily Stanley, Annie Jeffries (grandmother), Vi Jeffries, Auntie Annie, Tall Auntie Rose with Len at 19 Church Road in 1931. (Above right) Me, Lorna and Len at Church Road 1938.

Wedding of Leslie Thomas Jeffries and Florence Violet Raine – 26th December 1926
(Back row) Rose Stanley (1887) – nee Jeffries *(second from left),* Richard (Dick) Raine (1902) *(third from left),* Ernest Stanley (1888) – formerly Seberg *(far right);*
(Middle row) Annie Jeffries (1885) *(second from left),* Rose Jeffries – nee Pavitt (1891) *(far right);*
(Front row) Ernest Edward Jeffries (Eddie) (1918) *(far left),* Annie Jeffries (1857) – nee Bonsor *(second from left),* Lillian Stanley (1915) *(third from left),* Leslie Thomas Jeffries (1898) *(fourth from left),* Florence Violet Jeffries (1899) – nee Raine *(fifth from left),* Florence Raine (1876) – nee Labdon *(seventh from left),* William Raine (1875) *(eighth from left),* Rose K Jeffries (Rosie) (1917) *(far right)*

Me in the garden at 19 Church Road (above left) with my mother in 1933 and (above right) in 1934 on the black rug from the best room.

(Above left) William Raine, my grandfather, and (centre) in the garden at Undine Street, Tooting, with canary show trophies. (Above right) Dick Raine, one of my Mother's two younger brothers.

(Above left) With sister, Lorna – 1949. (Centre) National Service – 1953. (Right) Yvonne – 1955.

(Above left) With Yvonne and Roy, on the haystack at the junction of Painters Road and Hainault Road – early 1950s. (Centre) Thorpeness Halt Station, near Yvonne's Suffolk home. (Right) Ted Friend, Yvonne's father – early 1950s.

The Dick Turpin prior to bomb damage in 1944.

This 1906 photograph of the cottage, halls and church at St. Peter's Aldborough Hatch – little changed when I joined the church choir 28 years later in 1944.

St. Peter's Aldborough Hatch Choir 1950 – (Back row) Tony Mathews (Server), 'Mr T' (Lay Reader), Mr Cornish, Ron Jeffries (Server), Mr Bretton (Choirmaster), Mr Smith, Mr Webb, Mr Vernon, Colin Brett, Mr Fairey (Organist), Brian Brett (Server); (Middle row) Ted Vernon, Geoff Griffiths (Server), Bob Smith, Raymond Woolmore, Adrian Lankaster, Brenda Harmer; (Front row) Lawrence Tasker, John Bretton, Revd Joseph Palanque Byng (Vicar), Barry Priest, Brian Heaton.

(Above) The Vicarage Meadow at St. Peter's Aldborough Hatch, circa 1950, during a Vicarage Garden Party – the 1st Aldborough Hatch (St. Peter's) Scout Group are much in evidence running sideshows.

(Above left) Scout Leader, 1st Aldborough Hatch (St. Peter's) Scout Group – circa 1963.
(Above right) On appointment as Editor of THE SCOUTER and General Editor, The Scout Association, 1968.

(Above left) Interviewing Sir William Gladstone at Hawarden Castle prior to his appointment as Chief Scout in 1972. (Above right) My family in my home office at Spearpoint Gardens in 1975.

(Above left) Geoff and Charlotte Platt's wedding in 1976 – my daughter, Heather, is the bridesmaid second from the right. (Above right) Lord Maclean on the night I retired as editor of SCOUTING.

(Left) The first few yards of the two mile sausage are brought from the refrigerated vehicle and onto the frying pan in the early morning in London's Hyde Park at the Great Children's Party in May 1979. The Garnett family – Norman, David and Joyce – are there supporting the sausage, together with Charlotte Platt, Paul Moynihan and Scouts and leaders from Greater London North East County. Eight years later the event was repeated in Hyde Park with a 9.89 mile sausage at the St. John Ambulance Centenary Party.

(Above) With the TV artist's impression of Charlie Kray's appearance at Redbridge Magistrates' Court, August 1996 which now hangs in my dining room.

(Above) With Yvonne and granddaughter, Annily, December 2008.

(Above) Stine, Richard, Annily, Marlon, Heather, Luke and Yvonne at Bransgore, July 2008, on Graham and Danielle's wedding day.

(Above left) Graham, Danielle and Yvonne at the wedding in Bransgore, July 2008.
(Above right) The boys – Luke, Fraser, Finlay, Marlon and Fergus.